Deeper Insight Into The Illuminati Formula

ISBN 1451502699
EAN-13 9781451502695

Deeper Insight into the Illuminati Formula
by Fritz Springmeier & Cisco Wheeler

Book in chapters

Important Explanation of Contents
DEDICATION
WARNING, READ THIS FIRST BEFORE READING THE BOOK
INTRODUCTION by Fritz
GLOSSARY OF HOW BASIC TERMS ARE USED IN THIS BOOK
INTRODUCTION

CHAPTER 1. SCIENCE NO. 1 - SELECTION & PREPARATION OF THE VICTIM
BREEDING GOOD SUBJECTS for HYPNOSIS-hypnosis as it relates to selection & preparation of the victim.
GENETICS
TRAINING THE UNBORN CHILD
COMMON ILLUMINATI WORK WITH TWINS
SELECTION OF ADULT CANDIDATES FOR MIND-CONTROL
U.S. GOVT. MIND-CONTROL LEVEL 1.   U.S. GOVT. MIND-CONTROL LEVEL 2
U.S. GOVT. MIND-CONTROL LEVEL 3.   GOVT. MIND-CONTROL LEVEL 4   U.S. GOVT. MIND-CONTROL LEVEL 5
TESTING YOUNG CHILDREN TO PLAN THE PROGRAMMING.

CHAPTER 2. SCIENCE NO. 2--THE TRAUMATIZATION & TORTURE OF THE VICTIM
DAILY ABUSE WORKS BEST FOR PROGRAMMING
ANGER-MANAGEMENT-PROGRAMMING TRAUMAS
SILENCE PROGRAMMING TRAUMAS to TEACH SILENCE
TORTURE FOR NO-WRITE PAY ATTENTION TORTURE A COMPLIANCE TORTURE -- The Black Slave Chair.
A TRAUMA TO DEVELOP ANIMAL ALTERS TRAUMA TO ISOLATE THE VICTIM

CHAPTER 3. SCIENCE NO. 3 The USE OF DRUGS
ADMINISTRATION OF DRUGS FOR PROGRAMMING
MORE PROGRAMMING DRUGS (these were not listed in the Vol.2 Formula book)
STABILIZING THE PROGRAMMING
EXTENSIVE RESEARCH DONE TO INFLUENCE HUMAN MEMORY BY DRUGS
The BASIC PHASES of MEMORY
WHAT the MIND-CONTROL PROGRAMMERS USE to MANIPULATE memory.
HIDING THE CODES
PROGRAMMING WITH LSD-25 (Lysergic Acid Diethylamide)
CHEMICALLY TRIGGERING NATURAL INSTINCTUAL DRIVES
SEXUAL STIMULATION-PROGRAMMING
THEIR ABILITY TO MANUFACTURE (SYNTHESIZE) BRAIN CHEMICALS TO MAKE MIND-CONTROL DRUGS

CHAPTER 4. SCIENCE NO. 4 - HYPNOSIS
HYPNOSIS & the OCCULT
UNDERSTANDING THE BASICS ABOUT HYPNOSIS
THE POWER OF HYPNOSIS
UNDERSTANDING THE DEEPER MECHANICS of HYPNOSIS   Intention System cognitive demon processes
PROGRAMMING AIDS Fasting

USING HOLOGRAMS as an ACCESS AID
KEEPING THE MIND IN ALPHA STATE
PREPARING THE BRAIN
EARLY TRAINING FOR SLAVES
MAGICAL TRAINING ON THE STARLIGHT LEVEL
FINETUNING
THE MONARCH PROGRAMMING SCRIPT FOR OVER THE RAINBOW
DEEP TRANCE PROGRAMMING
COLOR PROGRAMMING
THE ASSOCIATION OF COLORFUL SIGHTS, SOUNDS, RHYTHM & DANCE.
LIGHT & COLOR Elizabeth Clare Prophet
SPECIAL COLORS
HEALING BY CORRECT VIBRATIONS & RAYS
USING HYPNOSIS TO HEAL THE SLAVE AFTER ABUSE
REINFORCING THE PROGRAMMING WITH A DECOGNITION PROCESS
HYPNOTIC CODES, CUES AND TRIGGERS cipher color-alpha-numeric code
MONARCH MIND-CONTROL CODES A-T
Program Codes During 1972-1976 for Dr. Green
The Illuminati.
The Network
The establishment, the System.

CHAPTER 5: SCIENCE NO. 5 - THE SKILL OF LYING, THE ART OF DECEIT
DECEPTION DIMINISHES POWER
PROGRAMMING DECEPTIONS
BE WISE AS SERPENTS
DISINFORMATION TO MAKE THEIR DOUBLE-AGENTS LOOK GOOD
SLEEPER AGENTS
NAMES of TYPES of DISINFORMATION AGENTS
TRICKING SUSPECTS
THE NAMES OF DECEPTION TRICKS
STANDARD DECEPTION DEVICES
MASKS
COVERS
ONE OF THE GREATEST DECEPTIONS OF ALL TIME: DISNEY
INTRODUCTION
Observations about HOW THE ILLUMINATI LIKE TO HIDE BEHIND PERFECT FRONTS.
CONTENTS IN THE DISNEY DECEPTION SECTION OF CHAPTER 5.
a. an introduction
b. an overview
c. Who was Walt Disney?
   PERSONAL DETAILS
   MICKEY MOUSE
   OCCULT PORN KING
   A possible CHRONOLOGY OF EVENTS surrounding WALT DISNEY'S ILLEGITIMATE BIRTH
   WALT DISNEY'S CHARACTER
d. Who was Roy O. Disney?
e. Who is Roy E. Disney?
   The battle between the two Disney factions
f. What do we know about them in general?
g. A history of Disney Harry Cohn Bank of America Bank of Italy Claude Debussy EPCOT center

SOME DISNEY people of interest. Warren Beatty Shirley Maclaine Shirley Temple Black Stephen Bollenbach Warren Buffett The Tommy Dorsey Band Michael Dammann Eisner Rich H. Frank The Osmond Brothers Michael Ovitz Frank G. Wells

h. Disney and its mob connections Some MOB HISTORY.
   How the Disney Executives have figured out how to steal land all across the U.S.
i. Disney and its government connections
j. Disney and mind-control
   DISNEY VACATIONS FOR THE ELITE
   MELODYLAND
   DISNEYANA FOR THE PROGRAMMED & OBSESSED.
   Mind-control features in Disney movies. Bette Midler
k. Detailed Script of how one Disney movie is used for programming.
   SUMMARY
l. Partial List of Sources

CHAPTER 6: SCIENCE NO. 6-THE USE OF ELECTRONICS & ELECTRICITY
Section A. An Overview of the subject
  A1. Where this article is headed
     GLOSSARY OF TERMS FOR UNDERSTANDING ELECTRONIC MIND CONTROL
        Bio-medical telemetry
        EMF weapons
        Psychotronics
        Remote Viewing (RV for short)
        Syntel
  A2. Where the NWO is headed Pyramider

Section B. An intro to implants
  B1. Three typical implant victims
  B2. Documentation of implants
     REFERENCE PAGE FOR UNDERSTANDING ELECTROMAGNETIC WAVES & MIND-CONTROL
  B3. GWEN Towers
  B4. Body suits
Section C. Specific Implants
  C1. Audio implants (a. public. b. secret)
     BACKGROUND INFORMATION
     BRIEF CHRONOLOGY OF AUDIO IMPLANTS
     BASICS OF HOW THE IMPLANTS CAN FUNCTION
     USES OF THE IMPLANTS
     TYPES OF AUDIO IMPLANTS:
        Part A. Publicly admitted audio implants
        Part. B. Secretly implanted audio implants COCHLEAR DENTAL AUDITORY RIDGE
  C2. Body manipulation implants
  C3. Visual holographic implants
     HOW THEY WORK
     TYPES: FIBER OPTICS ARTIFICIAL LENSES BIO-CHIPS HOLOGRAPHIC OR H-INSERT
     HOLOGRAPHIC IMPLANTS VIA NANOTECHNOLOGY & NANOBOTS
  C4. Memex/Brain Link implants
     INTERFACE DEVICES
ORGANIC BIOPROCESSORS LINKED TO VIRUSES
 PSYCHICS
  C5. Torture/Nerve & Muscle Stimulation Implants
  C6. Tracking & I.D. Implants

Section D. Direct monitoring & manipulation of the brain/mind
D1. Direct monitoring
TESLA WAVES USED TO READ MINDS & IMPLANT VOICES
D2. Direct manipulation
SUMMARY OF ELF WAVE MIND CONTROL CAPABILITIES

Section E. Auxiliary uses of electronics & electromagnetic waves
E1. hypnotic induction
E2. polygraphs
E3. attacks against people & objects
LIQUID CRYSTALS
"ALIEN" implants
BED COILS STANDARDIZED FOR MIND-CONTROL POTENTIAL
E4. virtual reality

CHAPTER 7: THE SCIENCE OF STRUCTURING
A. STRUCTURING OF MPD WORLDS
WORKING WITH PARTS OF THE MIND
CONTROL ALTERS called PROCESSORS
BASIC DESIGNS of an ALTER SYSTEM
RINGS The Ferris-wheel subsystem MULTIPLEX
DATA ENTRY POINTS
TESTING ALTERS TO SEE IF THEY CAN BE USED.
THE SCRIPTS.
Assassination Models (Delta Models).
  AUTHORITY FACTORS ARE MAXIMIZED
  ACCOUNTABILITY & ANONYMITY
Monkey Alters.
Plant alters.
Presidential Models
Prostitute Models.
Psychic models.
Reporting Alters.
Repunzel alter.
Transformation alters.
Internal Wall alters
Structuring Internal Programmer Alters.
STRUCTURING WITH THE GRAND DRUID COUNCIL.
STRUCTURING THE SHADOW ALTERS
STRUCTURING IN THE MIRRORS
STRUCTURING THE TAPESTRY
STRUCTURING THE ALTER FAMILIES BY SPINNING

CHAPTER 8: THE SCIENCE OF BODY MANIPULATION & PROGRAMMING
A. CRANIAL MANIPULATION
INTRODUCTION
CRANIAL BLOOD PRESSURE has been kept a SECRET
CEREBRAL SPINAL FLUID kept SECRET
THE CHINESE SECRET OCCULT SOCIETY CONNECTION
The ancient EGYPTIAN CONNECTION
THE TIBETAN CONNECTION
ANOTHER EXAMPLE

THE JAPANESE CONNECTION
THE EARLY EUROPEAN OCCULT CONNECTION
NINETEENTH CENTURY OCCULT CONNECTION
THE WITCHCRAFT CONNECTION Phrenology
THE MODERN AMERICAN OCCULT CONNECTION Osteopathy and chiropractic Anne L. Wales
BONE & SKULL STRUCTURE
CEREBROSPINAL FLUID
TRANSCENDENTAL MEDITATION (TM) & the HINDU CONNECTION
The 3-in-One school Connection. Applied Kinesiology
B. GENETIC MANIPULATION
Transgenic humans Chimeras
USING RADIATION & CHEMICALS TO CHANGE GENETICS associated WITH THINKING
WHAT WE'VE COVERED

CHAPTER 9: THE SCIENCE OF MIND MANIPULATION BY PSYCHOLOGICAL PROGRAMMING METHODS:
BEHAVIOR MODIFICATION, PSYCHOLOGICAL MOTIVATION & NLP
"STRIPPED" OF FEELINGS
PROGRAMMING TO HIDE REVEALING DREAMS
PROGRAMMING LANGUAGE
EFFECTS OF PROGRAMMING
FALSE IMPLANTED MEMORIES
PERCEPTION CLOUDS MEMORY

CHAPTER 10: THE 10th SCIENCE — USING SPIRITUAL THINGS TO CONTROL A PERSON.
PART A. Intro on the importance of spiritual programming tactics.
PART B. The history of Programmed Golem
  KABBALISTIC BLACK MAGIC
PART C. The 3 foundations: Loss of identity, Fear, and Demons
  UNDERSTANDING THE RELATIONSHIP BETWEEN FEAR & DEMONS
  DEMON POSSESSION & SPIRIT GUARDS
  The Use of Giving Demonic Assistance to entrap.
  The Use of Occult Focal Points.
  DOES IT GLORIFY DEMONS TO CAST THEM OUT?
PART D. A complete Chronology of how the victim experiences the early spiritual programming. Steps a through o. (by Cisco)
  FINE-TUNED
  HIDING THE INTERNAL SELF-HELPER
  INTERJECT DISKS
PART E. Specific spiritual programming maneuvers
  WHITE GOLD, other information

CHAPTER 11: SCIENCE No. 11- INTERNAL CONTROLS
A. TEACHING OCCULT PHILOSOPHIES
B. INTERNAL COMPUTERS
  Installation of the Standard Programming
  Front Programs of Front Computer.
  Misinformation Computers.
  Beast Computer.
  Programmer Access to the Computer Areas.
C. INTERNAL HIERARCHIES
  THE INTERNAL HIERARCHIES form RATIONALES

CHAPTER 12 SCIENCE No. 12-EXTERNAL CONTROLS
Advertising & Trauma-based programming.
ASSET CONTROL
SURVEILLANCE.
HARASSMENT
CAR COLORS
TELEVISION
BUILDING FAMILIES AND COMMUNITIES THAT HAVE INTERWOVEN PROGRAMMING
ISOLATION
BOARDING SCHOOLS & BODY PROGRAMMING.
When controls fail, THE FINAL SOLUTION.
The Programmers

APPENDIX 1 - PROGRAMMERS/RESEARCHERS
DIRTY PSYCHIATRISTS involved with MIND CONTROL
DIRTY RESEARCHERS
DIRTY TAVISTOCK CONTROLLERS
SOME OF FREEMASONRY'S MIND-CONTROL PEOPLE
REMOTE VIEWING MIND-RESEARCH
ODDS & ENDS
LIST of PROGRAMMERS (continuation from the list given in Vol. 2)
A FEW random CIA/INTELLIGENCE MEN involved WITH MIND-CONTROL
Anton LaVey--Profile of a trauma-based mind-control programmer
WHAT TO LOOK FOR.
MICHAEL AQUINO, a military/cult mind-control programmer
  HIS CAREER
  PERSONAL HISTORY.
  UNDERSTANDING The CHURCH OF SET
  UNDERSTANDING SOME OF AQUINO'S PROGRAMMING.
  BACKGROUND
  SEQUELAE OF ABUSE

APPENDIX 2. THE PROGRAMMING SITES

APPENDIX 3. CLONES, SYNTHETICS, ORGANIC ROBOTOIDS AND DOUBLES
PUBLICLY ANNOUNCED GENETIC EVENTS
Section A. The "Future Shock" that this topic subjects the common person to
Section B. Instructions on how to clone a person
  A TECHNIQUE--INSTRUCTIONS HOW TO CLONE A HUMAN
Section C. The four types of "clones" that are used by the Illuminati,
  1. actual clones,
  2. synthetic people,
  3. organic robotoids,
  4. doubles (look alikes)   How the memory of a person is transferred for the organic robotoids
Section D. Secret cloning sites (See also Appendix B, where D.U.M. bases are listed.)   Simon Wiesenthal
  OREGON'S UNDERGROUND SECRET CLONING FACILITY
  FURTHER INVESTIGATIONS AT DULCE'S UNDERGROUND CLONING FACILITY
SUMMARY OF THE FOUR METHODS.
FINAL NOTES.   Clintons

Important Explanation of Contents

A successful treasure hunter of the sea said, "You have to convince others of what you are looking for, and be incredibly persistent in looking for it." I, Fritz, could really identify with what he was saying. I have searched for truth like a treasure hunter, I have sifted the dusty pages of documents, like a patient miner panning for gold. How far & deep are you willing to search for truth? Cisco and I feel we are accountable to tell you the whole truth as far as we know it, what you do with that is up to you. This book will explain many occult ideas and beliefs, many of them never before publicly revealed. There is an important reason why these occult ideas and beliefs are introduced, we need to study our enemy and know how he thinks. The U.S. Army used indian scouts to track the indians. Gen. MacArthur learned everything he could about the Japanese so that he could defeat them. Christ was extremely savvy as to Satan's tricks. The Apostle said, "We are not ignorant of Satan's devices." Time and time again, this author has seen powerful Masonic clergyman do their handshakes, their codewords, etc. in front of the common people and the Christians do not catch on. On the one hand the Christians want proof of what is happening, but on the other hand, they are not willing to learn how to identify what the opposition is doing. Such doublemindedness has contributed to the churches becoming, sad-to-say, fronts for the Illuminati. I have included the Illuminati's understanding of things and other occult beliefs, because I have witnessed that knowing these things can be helpful in defeating the mind-control. If I were trying to help a refugee who was trying to escape the Yakuza, I would study the tactics of the Yakuza. If I were trying to free a witch of JuJuism, then I would learn about JuJuism. I strongly recommend that readers always stand on the foundation of the Word of God, and that they use the Word of God as a refreshing bath to cleanse their minds. This author has found tapes with scriptures to be an encouragement.

Some Christians have criticized this author for the content of the books, because it doesn't portray the lighter side of Christianity (whatever that is). It seems some people only want enough of God to to make them cozy, but not so much that their sleep would be disturbed. Some have even gone so far as to claim this author is not a Christian because the content of the books is so heavy. It is sad that many Christians do not know their own Scriptures nor where hope comes from. True hope is given by the Spirit of God, because hope is the vantage point that the Spirit of God has for the situation. A therapist may be optimistic about a victim of mind-control, but the therapist's optimism only turns to sincere hope when they become involved personally with the tragedies of the victim through caring and prayer. The Biblical hope is not a warm fuzzy that has its head in the sand pretending that everything is "rosy and peachy". Quite to the contrary, if we look at the following portion of scripture, we will see the Word of God portraying trauma after trauma with a light still at the end of the tunnel! Such is the power of our hope, that we have hope in spite of how fierce evil manifests.

Lamentations chapter 1

1 I am the man that hath seen affliction by the rod of his wrath.

2 He hath led me, and brought me into darkness, but not into light.

3 Surely against me is he turned; he turneth his hand against me all the day.

4 My flesh and my skin hath he made old; he hath broken my bones.

5 He hath builded against me, and compassed me with gall and travail.

6 He hath set me in dark places, as they that be dead of old.

7 He hath hedged me about, that I cannot get out: he hath made my chain heavy.

8 Also when I cry and shout, he shutteth out my prayer.

9 He hath inclosed my ways with hewn stone, he hath made my paths crooked.

10 He was unto me as a bear lying in wait, and as a lion in secret places.

11 He hath turned aside my ways, and pulled me in pieces: he hath made me desolate.

12 He hath bent his bow, and set me as a mark for the arrow.

13 He hath caused the arrows of his quiver to enter into my reins.

14 I was a derision to all my people; and their song all the day.

15 He hath filled me with bitterness, he hath made me drunken with wormwood.

16 He hath also broken my teeth with gravel stones, he hath covered me with ashes.

17 And thou hast removed my soul far off from peace: I forgat prosperity.

18 And I said, My strength and my hope is perished from the LORD:

19 Remembering mine affliction and my misery, the wormwood and the gall.

20 My soul hath them still in remembrance, and is bowed down within me.

21 This I recall to my mind, therefore have I hope.

22 (It is of) Jehovah's lovingkindnesss that we are not consumed, because his compassions fail not.

23 They are new every morning; great is thy faithfulness.

24 The LORD is my portion, saith my soul; therefore will I hope in Him.

25 The LORD is good unto them that wait for Him, to the soul that seeketh him.

26 It is good that a man should both hope and quietly wait for the salvation of the LORD.

We are in a battle for our minds, are we willing to seize the hope that is before us, or will we resign and say "all is lost"? Discouragement is not of faith. Do you think Almighty God is a discouraged person? He is calling people to serve others, because God knows that you will never find happiness in selfishness. God is calling people to bind up the broken shattered multiples and to let their deeper parts know that they are loved and worthwhile. To adopt an attitude of defeat before freedom loving men and women have exhausted all potential remedies for this mind-control is inexcusable.

DEDICATION

This book is dedicated to the two million Americans and counting who have been programmed with Monarch-type trauma-based mind control. This book is written to destroy trauma-based mind control before it destroys the human race. It's time for this horrendous secret to end. It is also written as part of God's end time work to propel people of faith to the high calling that is prophecied of the Body, but cannot be attained without men of faith understanding these things. Humanity's great prophet said he came to heal those whose hearts had been broken--literally split and crushed, and to free those who are captive. That work needs to go forward. Blood, sweat and tears are associated with this book. The blood of the innocent victims of this mind-control cries out in a single unison, along with the pungent sweat of those who have tried to minister help to the shattered humanity left by the sadistic programmers, and the pools of tears shed as this book was written, "How long, O Lord, holy and true, do you not judge and avenge our blood on earth?"

HOPE

.... Thou shalt know that I am Lord: For they shall not be ashamed that wait on Me. Shall the prey be taken from the mighty, or the lawful captive delivered? But thus saith Yahweh, even the captives of the mighty shall be taken away, and the prey of the terrible shall be delivered: for I will contend with him that contendeth with thee, and I will save thy children. Isaiah 49:23b-25

WARNING, READ THIS FIRST BEFORE READING THE BOOK.

IF THERE IS ANY CHANCE you the reader have had mind-control done to you, you must consider the following book to be DANGEROUS. If you are consulting a therapist for DID (also known as MPD), it is recommended that you consult your therapist before reading this book. The complications that could result for those under mind control learning the truth--could be fatal. The co-authors take no responsibility for those who read or misuse this information. The reader's mind is like a garden. It may not be time to plant the truth in your mind. Perhaps you need some weeding or ground preparation, before the garden of your mind is ready. Perhaps the weather is too stormy to plant the truth. Pray to the Lord of the Harvest. The blessings that flow from planting the information of this book in your mind, will require the presence of living waters of love. If you do not have love in your heart, this book is not for you. The information contained in this book is the biggest news-story of the 20th century, and still the biggest secret. It will challenge you, shock you, horrify you and hopefully motivate you to redouble your efforts to humble yourself and seek strength from God Almighty.

The programming procedures which are described in this book are based on research and consultation with deprogrammers, ex-programmers, therapists, counselors and pertinent literature. To the best of our knowledge the statements made in this book are factual, although they may not reflect the latest or currently accepted methodology among each and every faction of the New World Order which carries out Monarch-type programming. This book tends to devote more emphasis to Illuminati programming, which is the highest level of programming. For individual application in understanding a survivor of Monarch programming, therapists are admonished to use this material with consideration for the Monarch victim's personal case and situation. The authors disclaim any responsibility for therapeutic work based upon this material.

Fritz Springmeier and Cisco Wheeler have co-authored They Know Not What They Do, An Illustrated Guidebook To Monarch Mind Control. Both Fritz and Cisco bring years of experience in dealing with Monarch programming to bear on the writing of this book. Fritz has researched the Illuminati, while he has worked with victims of its programming. He has authored The Top 13 Illuminati Families, and several other books.

INTRODUCTION by Fritz

There are many dangers to the human race, some real and some imagined. I believe that the trauma-based mind control which this book exposes is the greatest danger to the human race. It gives evil men the power to carry out any evil deed totally undetected. By the time the astute reader finishes this book, they will be as familiar with how to carry out trauma-based mind-control as some of the programmers. Ancient and more recent secrets will no longer be secrets. Over the years, I have spent thousands of hours studying the Illuminati, the Intelligence agencies of the world, and the occult world in general. The centerpiece of these organizations is the trauma-based mind control that they carry out. Without the ability to carry out this sophisticated type of mind-control using MPD, drugs, hypnosis and electronics and other control methodologies, these organizations would fail to keep their dark evil deeds secret. When one of the mind-control programmers of the Church of Scientology, who has left Scientology, was asked about MPD, he said, "It's the name of the game of mind control." Research into this subject will never be complete. This book has tried to give a comprehensive view of how the programming is done. The basic techniques were developed in German, Scottish, Italian, and English Illuminati families and have been done for centuries. Some report that some of the techniques go back to ancient Egypt and ancient Babylon to the ancient mystery religions. The Nazis are known to have studied ancient Egyptian texts in their mind control research. The records and secrets of the generational Illuminati bloodlines are very-well guarded secrets.

Even when I've learned about the location of secret depositories of some of the Illuminati's secrets in Europe, America, and Asia, their records and secrets are too well-guarded to be examined. The intelligence agencies, such as MI-6 began investigating these mind-control techniques early this century, but their records have been routinely destroyed and tampered with. There are some survivors and professionals who know that the British used programmed trauma-based MPD (DID) agents in W.W. I. In Jan., 1987, Richard Kluft submitted an article to the American Journal of Clinical Hypnosis about 8 MPD patients who were between 60 and 72 years of age. Traugott Konstantin Oesterreich (1880-1949), who was professor of philosophy at Tubingen University, Germany studied MPD and demonic possession and wrote a classic study of it in 1921 entitled Possession Demonical & Other, which was translated into english in 1930. His classic work on this subject provides documented cases which reveal that the basic trauma-based mind-control was going on in Germany, France & Belgium long before the 20th century. Although he is unable to put together all the pieces and the clues for what they are, the reader of this book might enjoy reading the 1930 English translation of his classic work after they finish this book. Oesterreich's research in early 1900s was the type of research that the Nazi mind-control programmers were very aware of. In 1921, the Germans such as Oesterreich would describe personality switches, by the term "somnambuliform [hypnotic states] possession" or "demonical somnambulism" or what might be called

"Besessenheit von Hypnotismus und bösen Geistern."

The ability to study both the spiritual & psychological aspects of mind-control phenomena, is often lacking today. There are exceptions such as Dr. Loreda Fox's book The Spiritual Dimensions of MPD. In the 1920s, the Germans also were aware that the human mind has a variety of ego-psycho-psysiological states rather than one unified mind, which they termed "Sub jecklose Psychologie" or the psychology of having correlated psychological states rather than the concept of a single ego. The Germans and Italians under the Nazi and Fascist governments began to do serious scientific research into trauma-based mind control. Under the auspices of the Kaiser Wilhelm Medical Institute in Berlin, Joseph Mengele conducted mind-control research on thousands of twins, and thousands of other hapless victims. Himmler supervised genetic research. The Nazi research records were confiscated by the Allies and are still classified. A trip can be made from downtown Washington D.C. on a gray-government van which serves as a shuttle to the Suitland Annex where the government's secrets are buried including research papers captured from the Nazi Mind-Control research. Most of Mengele's concentration camp research is still classified. Much of it dealt with mind control. A researcher can visit the top floor, but underground below the top floor are the real secrets. The real secrets are lying in millions of sheets of classified documents hidden behind blast proof doors. There they have vault after vault, and row after row of top-secret files that only a few privileged persons with security clearances above COSMIC--such as with a "C3" or "MJ" security clearance can visit. Everyone with these high security clearances which I have identified is connected to the Illuminati. Each underground area at Suitland Annex has its own subset of secret access words, known only to the initiated. Most of the OSS records have been destroyed, a few have been left, the important ones have been misfiled or remade. (This is according to a reliable British intelligent agent.) Also according to reliable inside sources the CIA is working night and day to remake old records, to expunge all the real dirty secrets from their records. The basement of CIA HQ is known as "the Pit," In the Pit documents are being shredded and burned on a round the clock basis. The large remains of these secrets are sold for landfill. The Illuminati have developed secrecy to a fine art. They train their people in the art of secrecy from the time they are born. Most everything they do, is done orally. They are trained not to write rituals and other things down. There is very little paper trail left by the Illuminati.

The creation of slaves with photographic memories facilitates this secrecy. But this book is not about how they have managed to keep their trauma-based Monarch Mind-Control a secret. They have managed only to keep it a secret to the general public. They have not been able to completely cover-up the millions of wasted lives that their programming has ruined. For many years, they were able to shut-up and quietly discard their programmed multiples by labelling them Paranoid Schizophrenics. But therapists are now correctly identifying these people as programmed multiples and are not only diagnosing them better but giving them better treatment. After Candy Jones's husband deprogrammed her enough that she could participate in writing a book exposing some of what had been done to her, the secret was out. (See The Control of Candy Jones Hypnotism and the CIA by Donald Bain.) Ever since then, the intelligence agencies and the Illuminati have been carrying out damage control. Their biggest damage control campaign has enlisted the power of Hollywood and the controlled Media. This campaign is known as the False Memory Syndrome campaign, or as those of us who know the facts like to call it ""the false memory spin-drome." The headquarters of the False Memory Spin-drom Foundation is located at 3401 Market St., Suite 130, Philadelphia, PA 19104. Some of the original founders were doctors of the University of Pennslyvannia. The inside story about these early FMS doctors of the University of Pennslyvannia is that they practiced Satanic Rituals during their work days. What is unusual about this--is that generally satanic rituals are performed at night, but these doctors did their coven work during the day. I know about these men. Now you can see why these men started the FMS! They started it to cover their own sins, because many of them were abusers themselves. In other words many of the EMS people are abusers of trauma-based mind-controlled slaves, or the victims of abuse who are in denial about their own abuse from trauma-based mind-control. Martin T. Orn (the person credited with founding the FMS) had ties to the CIA. Two members of the EMS advisory board, Ralph Underwager, Ph.D. and theologian, along with Hollida Wakefield, M.A. let the cat out of the bag when they publicly supported pedophilia (that is adults having sex with children). Their support of pedophilia came in an interview with a Dutch magazine Paidika, The Journal of Paedophilia (Winter, 1993).

Although the False Memory Syndrome Foundation gets upset at any mention that there might be a conspiracy by the perpetrators of mind-control, because conspiracies supposedly don't and can't happen, they want us to believe that all therapists are conspiring together to implant false memories of abuse into their clients, which could not be further from the truth. Monarch slaves typically run into a great deal of denial by their therapists that anything like this could be happening. The bottom line is that Multiple Personality Disorder (now refered to as Dissociative Identity Disorder) is a recognized bona fide diagnosis. False Memory Syndrome is not a recognized medical or psychological diagnosis and does not appear in the American Psychiatric Association's Diagnostic and Statistical Manual III-R nor the recently released DSM-IV. Those who followed Fritz's writings have learned about the close working relationship between the Mondavi's and the Rothschilds (see his article about the Mondavi/Rothschild Napa Valley winery). Guess who got the court precedence which gives the EMS some legal ground to attack therapists? The precidence was supposedly a wife who went to a doctor who told her she had syphilis. The wife assumes she got it from her husband and divorces him. Then she learns she doesn't have syphilis. The husband then sues the doctor. Upon this bizarre case rests the legal precedence for a third party to sue a person who gives advice, such as family members suing a therapist.

Upon this weak precidence, an abusive father who worked for Monday in a winery in California successfully destroyed a legitimate therapist who was trying to save his daughter who was a programmed Monarch victim. Supposedly the therapist had implanted false memories of rape in his daughter, when the record shows that the daughter's mother told the therapist the girl had been raped by the father. When a valid case of SRA and repressed memories went to trial in Washington state involving a police officer whose family was MPD, Dr. Richard Ofshe of the False Memory Spindrom showed up to cause mischief. And mischief he did work. The case involved the children of a ""Christian"" police officer named Ingram who had satanically ritually abused his family for years. The daughter won in court, but Ofshe of the EMS was not above writing a book full of lies and distortions about the case. Lynn Crook, who was the abused daughter in the case wrote up a paper exposing what EMS person Richard Ofshe did to her, The controlled media is giving full license and great coverage to the EMS people. Rather than fighting the government for scraps of declassified documents which have had their secrets marked out, and which may even be fake documents manufactured by the CIA, I have decided that there is a much better approach to expose the Monarch Mind Control to the world. If a person could never go to Nepal, he can see pictures of it and believe it exists. If a person can not get into the top secret records of the CIA and Office of Naval Intelligence and MI6, they can be given the exact RECIPE for creating a Monarch slave. I believe that by giving the step by step recipe, people will see that A. all the ingredients are available, B. it is possible to combine the ingredients, C. all it takes is the motive to do it, and that motive is self-evident. We'll even provide some of the names and places as we go along. This book will provide the step-by-step recipe for making a Monarch Mind-Controlled slave, It is a trauma-based mind control which programs multiple personalities using every known technique of mind-control. Every type of mind-control technique has been combined into a group package which makes the total package almost impossible to break. It is this ability to synthesize all these methods into a group package which is so powerful.

Edward Hunter, author of Brainwashing In Red China, testified in 1958 before a U.S. Congressional House Committee on Un-American Activities: "Since man began, he has tried to influence other men or women to his way of thinking. There have always been these forms of pressure to change attitudes. We discovered in the past thirty years, a technique to influence, by clinical, hospital procedures, the thinking processes of human beings. Brainwashing is formed out of a set of different elements ... hunger, fatigue, tenseness, threats, violence, and in more intense cases...drugs and hypnotism. No one of these elements alone can be regarded as brain washing, any more than an apple can be called apple pie. Other ingredients have to be added, and a cooking process gone through. So it is with brainwashing..." Hunter said brainwashing was a Red Chinese threat. He said that the chinese were the ones using these tactics. In reality, this mind control was being done in the U.S. and Hunter was a pawn to help justify the criminal activities of the programmers should they ever be found out behind their cover of "National security." The handlers of mind-controlled slaves carry around a black or grey 3 ring notebook or a lap top computer with the access codes and triggers. Some of the programmers and handlers have this all memorized. The deepest parts, core/gems/executive committee, false trinity etc. are charted in esoteric language such as Enochian, Hebrew (which is considered magical), and Druid symbols. I have never gotten the opportunity to look at one of these, although a number of the slaves who I've talked with have while they were being programmed. These notebooks have color-coded graphs showing the arrangement of alters, the structure of the system, the training of the alters, the history of the alters and other details. All the primary tortures carried out on a slave are coded using dates/no.s so that the memories can be pulled up by the programmers. There is a standard set of hand signals, gestures, and codes that allow a handler to work with someone else's slave, but the accepted code among the handlers is to leave another man's slave alone. As one leading psychiatrist put it, "Different ideologies use the same methodologies of mind control."

The Illuminati have secretly put in base programming that allows them ultimate control over many of the other groups' slaves. This will be described within this book.

For both the ease of reading and the ease of writing, I have dispensed with most footnotes. To provide my sources would double the size of the book, and many of them are confidential. (In the past, when I have attempted crediting information, some people have gotten bruised feelings for having been passed over or for being named. When information comes in from several sources, it becomes difficult to pass out credit.) I have made conservative judgement calls about what material I could use. Most of this information has been verified by several reliable sources. Confidential eyewitnesses are often the only source, when there is such a powerful conspiracy to keep this vast NWO mind control secret. Paper trails were not left or are not available. Programmed slaves who have worked for the military as mind-controlled slaves have witnessed their files expunged and sanitized. The New World Order in 1981 made training films for their novice programmers. Monarch slave Cathy O'Brien was used to make both the film "How to Divide a Personality" and "How To Create a Sex Slave." Two Huntsville porn photographers were used to help NASA and the NWO create these training films. Undoubtedly, other porn training films exist too. In others words, there is film evidence of the Monarch Total Mind-control but these porn films are kept in very secure sites. During the last few years, I have visited with ex-programmers, I have visited with hundreds of victims of the Monarch type programming. I have gone to programming sites, I have visited with therapists who work with the victims of this mind-control, and I have met several of the programmers of the CIA/Illuminati face to face in the adventures of trying to save people from their programming.

I hope that God gives me the strength and the opportunity to get the information I have learned out to the world in general. When this information gets out, hopefully it will help lift some of the secrecy of the Monarch Programming. The Monarch Programming is a foundation rock of the New World Order that when pulled up, will reveal the most evil two-legged bugs and slimy critters. When their rock is lifted, they will have to scurry to hide. Because the authors know what the programmers do, they must honestly record several areas of programming that will be controversial. The programmers are very much into demonology. Before therapists close their minds to this subject, the authors would like to point out, that they personally know of cases where Monarch slaves whose Christian personalities & other alters didn't believe in demonology were talked into participating in real deliverance, and the slaves discovered much to their surprise that work they had unsuccessfully tried to do for years with their therapist was accomplished in a day or two.

Some prestigious researchers have decided the subconscious doesn't exist because they can't find it--its mysterious. To the man in the street the concept "subconscious" is as mysterious as the concept "demon". Both have been the objects of intense research by U.S./Brit./Ger. Intelligence groups. In fact, many of the concepts in this book have been purposely obscured by the Illuminati's control over the media and universities. These obscured concepts include M.P.D. (DID), recovered memories, hypnosis, demonic possession, aliens, mind-control, the subconscious, a conspiracy to bring in a NWO, truth, etc. The smokescreens of controversy will continue; but those who love the truth, if they seek it, will realize the importance of this book. It's on public record that MK ULTRA, the mind control research which CIA director Admiral Stansfield Turner admitted to in 1977 spent millions of dollars studing Voodoo, witchcraft, and psychics. On August 3, 1977, at a Senate hearing the then CIA director Admiral Stansfield Turner disclosed that the CIA had been conducting mind control on countless numbers of unsuspecting victims for years, without their knowledge or consent. These CIA mind-control operations were carried out with the participation of a least 185 scientists and at least 80 American institutions, including prisons, pharmaceutical companies, hospitals, and 44 medical colleges & universities. Many of America's most prestigious institutes of medical research, had cooperated with the CIA. as well as numerous big name corporations. Casey admitted that day that the CIA did mind-control consisting of drugs, hypnosis & electro-shock. A few of the victims of the Monarch Project were even awarded financial compensation for their misery. But what was admitted was admitted in the spirit of covering up the extent of the full truth. The compensation was actually hush money, because victims were given "gag orders" by judges not to talk about what had happened to them. It's been a disaster for Monarch victims that so many ministers have ignored those words of their Scripture, "For we are not ignorant of the devil's devices." 2 COR 2:11 This book is a must for those ministers who seriously believe "Having therefore these promises, dearly beloved, let us cleanse ourselves from all filthiness of the flesh and spirit, perfecting holiness in the fear of God." 2 COR 7:1. In 2 TIM 2: 19-21, believers who "nameth the name of Christ" are asked to purge themselves of their uncleanliness (unclean spirits). There are many top notch Christians in the churches today who are under mind-control, incl. many of the Christian leadership. I would like to remind Christian ministers that Isaiah the great prophet said, "The Lord GOD hath given me the tongue of the learned that I should know how to speak a word in season to him that is weary: he wakeneth morning by morning; he wakeneth mine ear to hear as the learned." Ignorance is not godliness. Isaiah learned to speak with the great learned men of his day, just as Paul the great apostle could speak to the learned men of his time. One of the character traits of God is that He is all-knowing. WHO says it is godly to be ignorant? The prophet Daniel said Yahweh God "reveals the deep and secret things." (Dan. 2:22a) God's instruments will do this revealing. Jesus' advice to his disciples was in effect to "Be wise as serpents, and gentle as a lamb". This advice certainly applies in helping the victims of trauma-based mind-control. Paul in his letter to the Thessalonians (1 Thes 5:14) says that in effect that different people need different counseling, but they all need to be treated with patience. The first step in suggesting a cure is to find out what happened. That is what this book is about. This book is about how the Occult Network creates the problem that therapists and a few ministers try to deal with. But the keys to open doors to healthy solutions for the victims of trauma-based total mind control will reveal themselves in this book for the reader as this book reveals the nitty-gritty of how the total mind-control happens. Christ came to free the captives (Isaiah 61:1). Satanic ritual abuse has a history that is almost as old as history itself. Good King Hezekiah was a victim as a child of SRA. (2 Chr. 29) who got free. Moses confronted the satanic magic of Pharoah's magicians who could create live snakes from sticks. The Apostle Paul had to deal with Simon Magus, a leader of what is now known as Satanism. Solomon, one of the greatest men of faith, backslide and became one of the greatest satanists of all history. We have "no fellowship with unfruitful works of darkness, but rather reprove them" (as per EPH 5:11). While we have no fellowship with evil, the mind-control programmers are counting on us being so ignorant of their devices that they can hide their control devices behind perversion & filth that many people shy away from. We must be strong enough to face evil and not shy away from it. The victims of mind-control must look evil in the face & not look away to gain their freedom. We, who want to help them, must be courageous & strong enough to do this too. This book is written for that divine goal "till we all come in the unity of the faith, and of the knowledge of the Son of God, unto a perfect man, unto the measure of the stature of the fulness of Christ." Eph. 4:13 If the body of Christ is to attain fullness, we need this book to weed out the hidden terrible cancer that is consuming the body from within. This book is written for ministers, secular and Christian therapists, and truth lovers of all kinds. If you love the truth this book is for you. If you see something good in the human race so that our species should be preserved as well as the spotted owl and the sand flea, then this book is for you. IF YOU LOVE THE TRUTH, this BOOK is for YOU.

GLOSSARY OF HOW BASIC TERMS ARE USED IN THIS BOOK

For those readers who are not familiar with these basic terms let us introduce you to the definitions under which this book uses them.

Alter-Our usage is trying to follow the programmers usage of this word. A dissociated part of the mind which has a seperate identity and is given cue codes by the mind-control programmers to trigger that dissociated part of the mind to come to the front of the mind. The alter's identity may be a gem, rock, a tape recorder, a poodle, a white kitten, a dove, a horse, or even think of itself as a person or a demon. It all depends on its programming. An alter is different from an alter fragment in that the alter fragment is a dissociated part of the mind which serves only a single purpose. The programmers will give an alter a history, and insure that shadow alters will provide a full range of accessible emotions. Sometimes the distinctions between alters and alter fragments is vague, but examples from the two ends of the spectrum are easy to tell apart. We use the word alter in this book to conform to what the programmers' charts are encoding as alters. A typical main Mengele-created grid would be a grid of 13x13 principal A-coded alters, which is 169 principle alter personalities. In Illuminati systems, ceremonial "alters will consist of 3 alters placed on a spinning pedistal together into triad goddesses or gods. That means that an A-coded alter on some levels is actually 3 alters spinning together, which must be locked in place to communicate with, and then rotated to communicate to the other two.

Beta--This is the second Greek letter, and it represents the sexual models and sexual alters that the Programmers are creating. The primitive part of the brain is involved in this type of programming. An early sexual abuse event will be used to anchor this programming. These sexual slaves will develop sexual abilities that are far beyond what the public is aware is even possible. They also receive the worst kind of abuse far beyond what most people's imagination can picture. Beta alters generally see themselves as cats.

Councils (Illuminati)--The Illuminati has frequent meetings. Some of these meetings are organized to appear "acephalous" and "accidental" in their meetings, when in reality they are structured and planned. One group, MJ-12 has gone by the following names: the Group, the Special Study Group, the Wise Men, the Operations Coordinating Board (OCB), 5412 Committee, 303 Committee, 40 Committee, PI-40 Committee, and Policy Planning Group (PCG). Some of the formal policy and ritual groups have names that all Illuminati members who have gotten high enough to learn, will recognize:

The Council of 3, Council of 5, Council of 7, Council of 9, The Grand Druid Council, The Committee of 300, and the Committee of 500 (known as Fortune 500). Many of the meetings are conclaves without formal names. The Grand Druid Council is not something fictional, but an actual body of people who formally meet and whose membership, we have been trying to keep track of. The groups which make decisions to control this planet are networked together. Each decision has its own origin and route that it takes.

Delta--This is a Greek letter shaped like a triangle which symbolizes change in calculus. It has become a favorite word to use in naming things for the occult elite. Delta teams are 4 person assassination teams which usually are secret teams. Delta Forces is an elite unit that operates under the Joint chiefs of staff that is made up of highly trained total mind-controlled slaves. Delta models are slaves whose sole purpose is assassination. Delta alters are alters within an Illuminati alter system which are programmed to be assassins. These alters are often some of the deepest in a system and in a Genie bottle or with Umbrella programming.

Deliverance ministry-(This book is about HOW the mind-control is done, it is not a textbook on solutions.) The use of the term deliverance ministry in this book connotates any person(s) who via faith in God is able to pray for divine help in a fashion that a victim is helped from demonic activity. A deliverance ministry is a natural outgrowth of a life in harmony and fellowship with Yahweh God. However, this is not to be confused with Exorcism of the traditional Catholic or witchcraft nature in which certain spells and incantations are used in a prescribed method. "Deliverance" connotates divinely inspired faith, exorcism involves ritual. A deliverance ministry might perhaps teach a person about forgiveness, or how they can renounce an oath, or how to apply Jesus Christ's atoning blood to their life. In this fashion, the person finds deliverance through biblical spiritual principles rather than the efficacy of some ritual or hocus pocus spell. This book is in no way meant as a blanket endorsement of every spiritual warfare tactic. If anything, this book suggests that ministers learn more about mind-control, as well as grow stronger in their walk with Almighty God.

Illuminati--The Illuminati are 13 elite bloodlines which have manuevered themselves into control over this planet. They lead double lives, one for society and a hidden one which is based on a gnostic luciferian philosophy which consists of lots of blood rituals.

Monarch Programming--This was a specific Project carried out by secret elements of the U.S. government and intelligence groups. There were, according to someone a few years ago who had access to the computer(s) which contains all the names of active monitored human slaves, 40,000 actively monitored Monarch slaves. However, this book uses the term generically to include all victims who have suffered this type of trauma-based mind-control. In the same way, that a brand name like "Hyster" is used to describe all lifts--when we use the term we use it in its broadest sense. This is the only way it can be used and technically correct, because as of this date, the authors have not seen who is on the active Monarch Program list of slaves.

System-- This term is used in several ways. It is frequently used to refer to a victim of total mind control because the victim consists of alters, programming, implant(s), internal computers, and numerous dissociative states which function together as a system. The word is also used in this book to refer to the body's functional physiological units, such as the respiratory system. The word is also infrequently used to denote the established social-economic-political system controlling the world, also known insiders as the Network. Other standard meaning may also occasionally be used for the word.

Multiple Personality (DID)--Multiple personalities or MPD or Dissociative Identity Disorder is the situation where different dissociative parts of a single brain view themselves as separate persons. The DSM-IIIR definition of MPD is the guideline for determining MPD for this book.

New World Order-- The New World Order is the global design for a One-World-Government One-World-Dictator and its constituents. Insiders call themselves the "network" and "the neighborhood".

Satanic Ritual Abuse (SRA)--This is used to represent all categories of ritual abuse which would be inspired by the desire to rob, kill, or destroy something worthwhile in a person, especially their freedom of thought. Many groups carrying out SRA do not mention Satan by that name. They may make Pacts to Baphomet, and call upon Rex Mundi, or Belair, or Lucifer, or the Father of Light, God, or Kali or even "Jesus" or "Jesus Christ" (there are demons which call themselves "Jesus", who are not to be confused with Yeshua or Yehoshua ben Joseph who is known as Jesus Christ of Nazareth.) SRA is not a value judgement by the authors against some group, the victims themselves on some level know that he or she is being abused.

Switching--This is when one part (fragment) of the mind takes over from another, or in simple terms, this is when one alter personality (or alter fragment) takes the body from the alter which is holding the body. Switching can occur via the Programmers' codes for calling up alters, or by external or internal stimuli that trigger an alter to come out. Switching will usually cause at least a flicker of the eyes, and for outside observers, who know the different personalities, they will observe another personality take the body.

The BASIC Theoretical Concepts of the RELATIONSHIP BETWEEN PHYSICAL FEATURES OF THE SKULL & FACE & PERSONALITY which are used for purposes of mind-control.
(See Cranial Manipulation, Chapter 8)

HIGHER THINKING AREA

The Frontal Lobes are crucial for higher thinking, and conscious thinking, and conscious choices. The proportion of brain cells in this area indicates how much brain matter is available for higher thinking.

FACIAL EXPRESSION AREA

Our minds use this facial area to communicate what we are thinking. This communication is both conscious and unconscious. People watch this area of the face to determine what we are thinking, which is why the poker face developed.

MOTION AREA

What causes the body to move? The body combines info from its senses & compares these to its emotions. The emotions then give final review as to what motion the body will make. The cortex has a series of motor areas, & the parietal lobes process sensory info. K-lines have been built into various areas of the mind that are activated to produce the desired sequence of muscle contractions & body activity to get the desired action. The brain size of the motion area shows how much brain is available for motions and actions.

AREA FOR FEELING & EMOTIONAL TRAITS

In the back of the skull contains memory. The secondary and primary visual areas lay in the back part of skull. The basal part of the frontal lobes contain primary speech & fear/identity centers. The eyes are an extremely valuable sense organ that the body uses for much of its new information.

drawings & text by Fritz Springmeier

Pic p_cranial2.jpg

pic p_basic-structure1.jpg

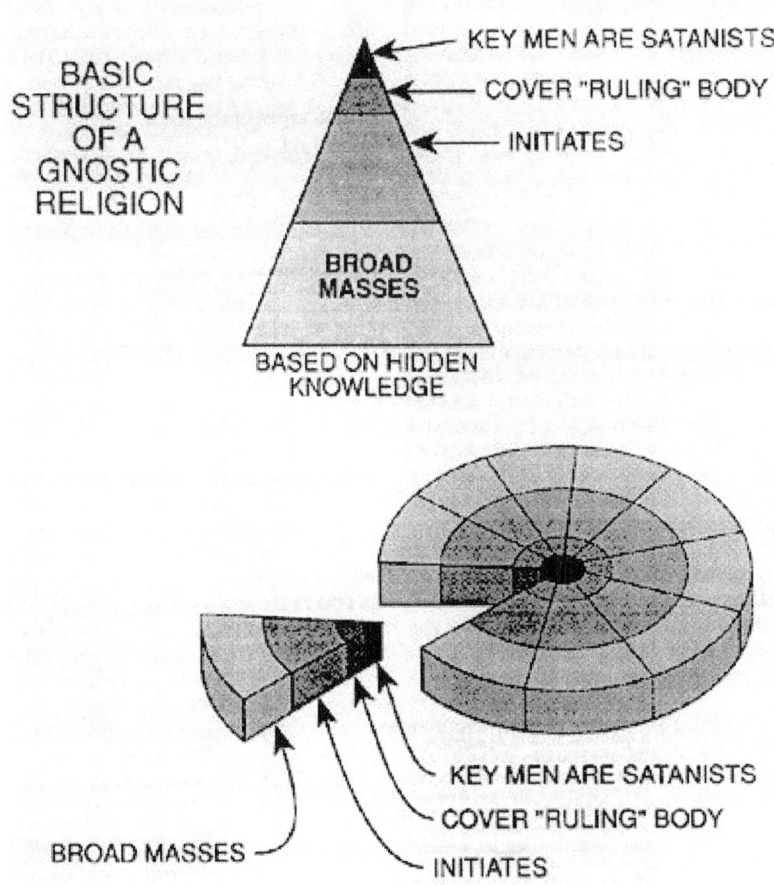

Pic p_records2.jpg

20 OCT 1975

MEMORANDUM FOR: Director of Central Intelligence

FROM : Inspector General

SUBJECT : Destruction of Records on Drugs and Toxins

Action Requested:

1. None. This memorandum is for your information.

Background:

2. At your request, we looked into the destruction of Agency records related to drugs and toxins. We limited our investigation to avoid interfering with other ongoing investigations of this matter, including that of the FBI. We held discussions with several people in the DD/S&T, Records Center, and Archives and reviewed a number of OTS files. Our findings and conclusions follow.

Summary Conclusions:

3. MKULTRA Records: This was an umbrella project for funding sensitive TSD activities including research into methods for controlling human behavior:

-- No drug-related MKULTRA files were turned up during our investigation.

-- A number of documents concerning the destruction of MKULTRA drug records are attached at Tab A. In general, they show that the records were destroyed on the instruction of Dr. Sidney Gottlieb, then Chief, TSD, on 31 January 1973. Both Branch files and records retrieved from Archives were destroyed.

-- Tab A also contains statements by Messrs. _____ of OTS. These statements indicate that the destruction of MKULTRA drug files was ordered by Mr. Helms.

INTRODUCTION

In Jan. '96, I bound the first copies of The Illuminati Formula Used to Create Undetectable Total Mind-Controlled Slave. Hundreds of people in the United States and other countries were reading this book, and were expressing their appreciation and praise for the work. Some also contributed more details about the Illuminati's mind-control. It was also gratifying that the illustrated Guidebook to Monarch Mind-control, which contains my co-author's art work done under programming, was translated and sold this year ('96) as a paperback in Japan. The word is getting out, and people with ears to hear are grateful. The original goal was to write the Vol. 2 book to be about 300 pages long, but it spilled into 500 pages. At 500 pages, it was brought to a grinding halt. In this DEEPER INSIGHTS book, I bring you more profounder mysteries of the Illuminati's mind-control abilities. These deeper insights were some items left out of the Vol. 2 due to space, as well as some things that have been found out since the Vol.2 book was written. Those who were intrigued by the Vol. 2, and cut their teeth on the subject of mind-control via my writings over the past 5 years, will enjoy this further expose of the deeper secrets of Illuminati mind-control. For instance, scattered in several sections including Chapter 3 is a great deal about the base programs which are laid in using controlled LSD trips in sensory deprivation tanks. Another exciting set of new revelations are Cisco's information on the core, and her revelations giving the chronology of layering in the mind-control programming. I have also done a great deal of research into Cranial manipulation (see Chapter 8), which has been an extremely well-hidden mind-control secret known only to a few select people worldwide. Another area of intense research has been to expose the role Disney played in mind-control. Although other writers have superficially touched on implants, nanobots, thought-transfer, soul entrapment and other secret technologies, I decided to provide many details to expose these new technologies that are being used in conjunction with the dissociative programmed multiplicity. Beside learning countless programming secrets, the reader will take another quantum leap into understanding what has been going on in this mixed-up world. If life is a riddle, then this book contains many answers to the riddle of life. During the summer of 1996, I had the privilege to speak on mind-control to audiences in 12 major American cities, as well talk on over 50 radio stations. The response was encouraging. People are beginning to wake up, and are hungry to learn the truth about how the movers and shakers of this world have developed sophisticated methods to make children into undetectable Illuminati robots (from the cradle to the satanic throne), as well as their extensive abilities to control the common person's thinking from the cradle to the grave. When Christ asked the question, will I find faith when I return? it was a serious question. We no longer live in a situation where we can depend upon our mind and our thoughts actually being our own. Our minds are under a constant assault and manipulation by those who control things. No one is exempt. Fortunately, there are still some rational thinking humans, who can challenge and expose their plans for total control over the minds of the entire human race. I, as a minister & researcher, along with the victims represented by Cisco Wheeler and others, can't expose this mind control on our own. We need the help of others. Will you help us get the message out about the New World Order's/the Illuminati's mind control? Cisco has consulted with me, and we decided to make two continuations. The continuation of the Illustrated guidebook would be authored by her, and the continuation of the Vol. 2 book would be carried out by yours truly, Fritz Springmeier. We have combined these two continuations into this book called for short DEEPER INSIGHTS into the Illuminati Mind Control Formula. This volume is meant to be an extension of the previous volumes. IF YOU HAVE NOT READ the previous book entitled Vol. 2 The Illuminati Formula used to create an Undetectable Total Mind Controlled Slave, THEN you are not really prepared to understand this material. In my previous books, I have shown how the intelligence agencies are simply prostitutes and fronts of the Illuminati. The Illuminati always "sterilize" their activities, so their actions can't be identified in the flurry of secret intelligence activities. Recently, at one conference on mind-control, victims of government mind-control were told that their stories were not welcome because the conference was on "cult" mind-control. Dear reader, the intelligence agencies are cults, and not only that, but they have a dark satanic side to them, which not only brands them as cults, but "occult cults." Witchcraft and Freemasonry refer to themselves as "the Craft"; how appropriate it was for Allen Dulles, DCI-head of the CIA, to entitle his book "The Craft of Intelligence". How appropriate it was that people within the CIA referred to their top management as the Knights Templars. As the Vol. 2 Formula book indicated, the intelligence agencies which work for the Illuminati have kept only the minimum of records, and the records they do keep are out of reach of people like you and I. But that doesn't mean that the researcher like myself can't work backwards. One of the side effects of the traumas that create multiple-personalities (DID) is that sadistic or criminal alters are often formed, and with careful research the historical record of criminals with multiple personalities can be traced back into history. The Illuminati have created trained-multiples for centuries, but insiders say that programmed DID (MPD) was developed in the Nazi concentration camps. The worldwide Illuminati planned the camps with the goal to determine what programs would work on children, and used the cover story of Nazi racial hatred to hide the real purpose of the camps--mind-control experiments which used large numbers of children traumatized by their separation from their parents.

With today's sophisticated programming and structuring of MPD worlds, these evil alters can be controlled better than in the past, and yet we still have serial killers like Wayne Cox, and serial rapists like William Stanley Milligan, who were programmed multiples stalking our streets. Kenneth Biani, the LA Hillside strangler who killed 9 people was diagnosed as a multiple, but claimed he had faked the disorder. Thomas W. Piper in Boston in the 1870s, and Paul Miskamen, one hundred years later in California, are examples of multiples who had an alter capable of murder and another alter who was a good Christian. One of the best disinformation campaigns of the Illuminati, is to make people think programmed-multiples are just for espionage, prostitution and assassination. They have taken over our pulpits, like the Illuminati programmed multiple Jimmy Swaggart, and they have taken over our political offices, like Al Gore, and our universities. Even with the elite's secrecy intact via their control of libraries, publishing houses, and newspapers, the record still shows the traces of the Illuminati's history of creating controlled multiple personalities. The historical record of criminals with multiple personalities includes the Illuminati coke multimillionaire Harry K. Thaw. He was one of the elite of society, who had charming sophisticated front alters, and sadistic deeper alters. His position prevented him from being convicted of a murder he committed in public on June 25, 1906. However, another multiple Henry Spencer, who didn't have such clout was hanged after killing Allison Rexroat in 1914. Another multiple William Heirens, who murdered two women in the '40's, had one of his front alters write in the mirror after a murder, "For heaven's sake, catch me before I kill more, I cannot control myself." He had an alter George who was doing the murders. The story doesn't stop with evidence of physical murders, but includes the vast numbers of spiritual deaths that have resulted from the spiritual manipulation of the masses via programmed multiples. Programmed multiples have been great for carrying out religious deceptions. Many of the great spiritist mediums were multiples. In the 1920's, Patience Worth was a famous name of an author. Patience was an alter of Mrs. John Curran. As a child Mrs. Curran had played the piano in her uncle's Missouri Ozark church when young and then she later grew up to be a famous medium and writer. A Dr. Charles E. Cory investigated her multiple-personality disorder. He discovered that her author alter was much more intelligent than the front alter who did the housekeeping & normally held the body. The occult world has manipulated MPD to manufacture validation for their theories of reincarnation, spiritism etc. Where once the Word of God was accepted as truth by society as a whole, now society questions whether there is such a thing as truth. When it has come to finding out about mind control from the first level of perpetrators, the government, there have been a number of manufactured (bogus), sanitized and original CIA documents released to the public under the nearly worthless Freedom of Information act. The Freedom of Information Act has been manipulated to lead people to think that the public has access to secrets.

A letter of inquiry in 1995 requesting declassified documents on Mind Control, Monarch, MK Ultra, Artichoke and Blue Bird got the following response from the CIA, "...as you might expect, we have already conducted broad-ranging and exhaustive searches and reviews on every conceivable aspect of human behavior, including mind control and brainwashing, and have located and released 11, 336 pages of material on the general subject of human behavior studies under MKULTRA. Most of the 11,336 pages of this previously released material are very limited in scope and consist primarily of financial records." (quote from a CIA letter of response in answer to a request for declassified mind-control information.) Yes, and long-story-short even those 11,336 pages only got released due to a mistake.

In one CIA document pertaining to mind control released under the Freedom of Information act, which is a memorandum dated 20 Oct. 1975 to the Director of Central Intelligence from the Inspector General Donald F. Chamberlain, the Inspector General states, "From his investigation of the project [MKNAOMI], Dr. Stevens has concluded that gaps in the files are the result of a conscious policy on the part of those involved to keep very little paper on the project from its inception in 1952 to its demise in 1970. People formerly connected with the project interviewed by Dr. Stevens asserted that the practice of keeping little or no record of the activity was standard MKNAOMI procedure." Philip Agee, who wrote an expose of the CIA entitled Inside The Company: CIA Diary (Toronto, Can.: Bantam Books, 1975), said that as an employee of the CIA "You get so used to lying that after a while it's hard to remember what the truth is." Philip Agee writes, "The life of a CIA operations officer ... There is not much time to think about the results of your actions and, if you try to do it well, the job of operations officer calls for dedication to the point of obsession. But it's a schizophrenic sort of situation. You have too many secrets, you can't relax with outsiders. Sometimes an operative uses several identities at once. If somebody asks you a simple question, "What did you do over the weekend?" your mind goes Click! Who does he think I am? What would the guy he thinks I am be doing over the weekend? You get so used to lying that after a while it's hard to remember what the truth is. When I [Philip] joined the CIA I signed the secrecy agreement... [now] I may have violated that agreement. I believe it is worse to stay silent, that the [security] agreement itself was immoral." [bold added to quote] On Nov. 15, 1996, DCI Deutsch of the CIA paraded himself and some politicians before a public meeting in south L.A. (broadcast on C-Span) and told the people the CIA would investigate allegations that the CIA had run drugs. One man asked CIA Director Deutsch, "Everyone knows that the CIA was running drugs in Vietnam from the Golden Triangle, and that they have continued doing it to today, and you want to come here to south L.A. and pretend to us that this hasn't happened when everyone knows it did. Are you crazy?" Deutsch couldn't help but show a revealing smile. (The above quoted question was taken from C-Span's broadcast & is a closely paraphrased version.) One of my questions to Deutsch would be, "When a drug addict's life gets out of control, he'll go into denial, and he'll steal from everyone in his life, including his own mother, and live a life of lies, and when an intelligence agency gets out of control, they are like an addicted person, they stay in total denial and keep secretly hurting everyone in sight, WHAT can and should the people do to get an out-of-control intelligence agency to stop its power addiction? Unfortunately, the problem with power addiction, addiction to lying & deception, and drug addiction began centuries before the CIA within the Illuminati families that started the CIA. The CIA is simply reflecting the problems of its parent. Their addiction to lying keeps the common gullible man in public ignorant. Their total mind-controlled slaves are used extensively for disinformation campaigns, and are helpful to disseminate WHITE, GREY, & BLACK propaganda for the New World Order's Network. To coordinate their lies requires a special intelligence group that keeps meticulous records of the disinformation that has been disseminated, so that they don't get mixed up in their lies. It is extremely rare to get the truth out of the perpetrators, the mind-control programmers. Recently, on television a movie portrayed a victim of trauma-based mind control trying to get one of her programmers, who she'd taken prisoner, to confess to what he'd done. He defied her, and did all he could to make her think her memory was her imagination. It was an excellent portrayal of how hard it is to get the truth out of the perpetrators. The sadistic programmers have exercised their power for decades in secrecy. They have understood the implications of their power for decades. However, the implications of this undetectable mind-control are staggering, actually overwhelming and beyond the man in the street's ability to comprehend. It means every organization can be infiltrated ("penetrated" as they say), and used as a front or controlled. It means nothing is as it appears. It means that Russia can hate America on the surface, and be working hand in glove on the secret level. It means every one of the millions of new immigrants from Russia, China and Eastern Europe into the U.S. is a potential time bomb. It means much of what has been blamed on Christians has had its origin in Satan. Satanic programming has seriously damaged the reputation of Christians. The programmers are major players in how the world's events unfold, while they receive absolutely no attention. These men are illegitimate rulers of the world. They have never gained from the common man the right to rule. Therefore they rule through puppets who owe their total allegiance to their mind-control masters. They are rapidly trying to establish legitimacy for themselves, and plan to culminate their plans to gain legitimacy with the rule of the AntiChrist, who will rule based on mass-produced myths and fantasies that the Illuminati will articulate to the imaginations of millions of slaves worldwide. They have already begun to market the AntiChrist and his reign to the world. The campaign for the acceptance of homosexuality is just one part of this marketing effort. They are also skillfully justifying their AntiChrist's rule, by creating problems that only his superior management abilities and leadership skills will be able to deal with. The strength of New World Order and the AntiChrist's rule is the total and undetectable mind-control that is being carried out on a mass scale to little children and people who fit specific profiles. According to a reliable deprogrammed source: Adults, who have the following profile are subjected to mind-control. This profile is:

· alone without a support system of family or friends.

· an I.Q. above 120.

· good hypnotic candidate

· has other attributes worthwhile to exploit

More about this will be discussed in chapter 1, where an entire overview of how the intelligence agencies take adults and program them will be given. Adults who are used by the intelligence agencies for WET OPS or one-time one way missions are programmed in stages. These stages are designated levels 1-5. Level 4 is where these slaves begin to resemble the total mind-controlled slaves of the Illuminati who have been subjected to mind-control since they were defenseless babies. The men involved in the programming of little defenseless children are skilled. They have been earned their jobs on the basis of a dog-eat-dog environment. They are ruthless. They operate out a hidden zone, which I will call the twilight zone of believability. Anyone who tries to expose what they are doing, must write about things that are outside of that box of things commonly believed in. It is as they intentionally gauge what is believable and then step outside of that zone in which to operate. These ruthless programmers have egos which think they are god-men. Somewhere deep in their minds, they inwardly know they are worms. There is a part of themselves deep down that knows the truth, but Satan has buried that so deep, that they cannot face the reality of who they are. They seek eternal life by stealing the life force of innocent victims. They know that their father is Satan. They are victims of Satan. Where does one draw the line between who is a victim and who is an abuser? There is no line. The word of God indicates that God has turned many of these men over to Satan due to their wicked minds. It's sad to think that some of these men are dependant on Satan for spiritual life. Many of the slaves still have a spark of reality and a spirit that cries for freedom.

They have ears to hear the truth, should it come their way. This book is written for those who love the truth and love the liberty that Almighty God has given us to seek and to love the truth for ourselves. Although only a minority of the people today have Total Mind-Control, the Illuminati are attempting to confuse and manipulate everyone. One of their favorite tactics to scare people with is the ambiguous bogeyman of national security. They constantly use their spin-doctors to whip up fear, so that the public will gladly surrender their freedom to protect "national security". Unfortunately, or ironically, the very concept of "national security" is being used as a cover for the Illuminati to steal every last vestige of freedom left to the American people. American tax-dollars support secret conferences such as the classified conference sponsored by Los Alamos on Nov. 16-17, 1993 where the Applied Physics Lab of John Hopkins University taught our military about "non-lethal" weapons. The satanist/ ex-Green Beret Dr. John Alexander, now head of the Los Alamos National Lab, gave one of the opening talks on 11/16/93. The next day, the military men gave talks on the technology involved in controlling people's minds electronically via both implants and energy beamed at them. Dr. Dave Morgan, of Lockhead Sanders also gave a specific talk on their "syntel--synthetic voices they place in the heads of victims with telemetry to auditory implants. You will read more on their implants in chapter 5. The battle for the freedom of the human mind must be fought now. The battle gets increasingly difficult, but we must fight it whether we win or lose, for the human spirit and the human mind was not created by God for slavery to Satan and his AntiChrist. Over and over, the truth of Jesus' words still shine forth, "And you shall know the truth and the truth shall set you free." Let us realize that the man who said those eternally powerful words also said, "I am the way, the truth, and the life." For His light shone in darkness, "and the darkness has not overcome it." If those of us who still have free minds must die--then let us die for the TRUTH, that the Truth in Christ Jesus shall live.

The hidden World Order government that increasingly controls our lives operates through many clandestine operations and groups. What you see is not what you get. In order to maintain total secrecy of such a vast scale of operations, they use millions of mind-controlled slaves world-wide as well as numerous willing servants who out of raw terror will not buck the system. On the surface, EPIC is just another secret military unit. The patch below belongs to the EPIC unit, a clandestine unit which is doing the real banking for part of Mexico, much of the U.S. and part of Canada. This agency (El Paso Intelligence Center--EPIC) is obviously not a U.S. jurisdictional agency, but operates under FINCEN (Financial Crimes Enforcement Network- as in crimes against Big Brother). This unit is stationed at Ft. Bliss, which contains Army & Air Force units. American elections are rigged, and there is no longer a government of the people, for the people and by the people (if there ever was one). The American people are kept in place because they think they elected the government that rules them. Mind-control is pervasive and is being used not just to create sexual slaves, or banking employees, but to control society at all levels. Will we continue to allow a shadow government to rule us? Will we continue to let them tell us that these things have to be secret in the interest of "national security", when in reality they are only in the interest of NATIONAL SLAVERY?

EPIC is also involved with the NAFTA machinations, many of which were done with the help of mind-controlled slaves. Within the NAFTA agreement was the U.S./Mexico Border XXI Framework Document, (based on the La Paz Agreement signed in '83) which in effect ends American & Mexican sovereignity over all land within 52.5 miles of the border. Special international agencies have been created to regulate the various environmental and legal needs of the Border XXI region, as the border is dissolved into a border region. The U.S./Mex. Border XXI document created the Border Cooperation Project & the North American Development Bank. The World Bank will also provide financing, and some funds will come from Mexico. EPIC is well situated in the approx. geographic center of this border region.

CHAPTER 1. SCIENCE NO. 1 - SELECTION & PREPARATION OF THE VICTIM

The average person who has been spoon-fed what he knows from the controlled establishment (the establishment's news, churches, and schools) is overwhelmed and in denial that mind-control can be happening. Who would want to carry out mind-control? One category are those groups who use the Cabala. Hasidic Judaism, Freemasonry, and Witchcraft are all based on the Cabala. Llewellyn's magazine New Worlds of Mind and Spirit (a prominent witchcraft magazine) in their June/July '94 issue state on page 56, "The golem of Prague is perhaps the most famous example of 'practical cabala'- the use of cabala for magical cabala." Golem are mind-controlled beings. There are several cabalistic and witchcraft written references that point out that the creation of mind-controlled zombies (golem) was the highest goal of the cabala. Albert Pike, perhaps the most important Freemason of all times, clearly stated as the head of Freemasons worldwide that Freemasonry is based on the Cabala. A cabalistic psychiatrist in Psychoanalysis Review, '44, issue 31, p. 180 wrote, "Victory over the world would be secured by any man who possessed the Shem...[We shall control the world (words to this effect)]...when we shall attain the consciousness of the Shem within us and will control the power of the Golem to regenerate the world." [The Golem are energized by the magic Tetragrammaton, which the Jehovah's W.s emphasize so much.] In The Worldwide Weekly, Defense News of 3/20-26/95, the Defense News an official military paper indicated that the navy was attempting to produce an "Army of Zombies". The Defense News stated:

"The research, called Hippocampal Neuron Patterning, grows live neurons on computer chips, William Tolles, the recently retired associate director of research at the Naval Research Lab, said March 15. This technology that alters neurons could potentially be used on people to create zombie armies, Lawrence Korb, a senior fellow at the Brookings Institution, said March 16 .... The research has captured the attention of the U.S. Intelligence community."

I have taken the space to give you the reader a paper trail that shows that YES INDEED, there are groups of people that desire human zombies. So where do they select their candidates for their zombie creating programs? That's what this chapter will deal with. You'll have to go to some of my other books to learn how these mind-control groups all interconnect.

The previous book by this author The Top 13 Illuminati Bloodlines was intended to help people begin to understand the major role bloodlines play within the Illuminati. When this author was on speaking circuit, he ran into a number of researchers who had researched the New World Order and the Illuminati for years and not realized the significance of the bloodlines. In tracking the bloodlines, it became apparent that the European Illuminati bloodlines were trying to integrate some of the American Indian bloodlines into their own bloodlines. Why? They wanted the occult power that these bloodlines contributed. And it seems that not only do generational spirits help in many ways, but there are reasons to believe that the Aborigines of Australia, the Bushmen of the Kalahari, and some of the American Indian tribes such as the Cherokee have high paranormal abilities in addition to their demonic spiritual abilities. Some believe that the psi-gene was valuable for the survival of primitive hunter tribes, while tribes who went into agriculture lost some of the power of the primary and secondary psi-genes since natural selection would not have encouraged psi-genes in agricultural based societies. The primary psi-genes are thought by some to be some genetic coding which enhances proteins to be better biophysical batteries, storage units, and other roles. The secondary genetic psi-coding are thought to be codes for creating richer and higher-functioning neural pathways, and neural capabilities. Whether this was true, if the Illuminati believed it was true, it could account for their penchant for mixing in American Indian blood with their elite "blue blood."

BREEDING GOOD SUBJECTS for HYPNOSIS-hypnosis as it relates to selection & preparation of the victim.

Hypnosis and programming work well in the alpha state of the mind. This is why the child is traumatized even in the womb, so that it will naturally be in that alpha state even before birth. The man in the street may think that the hypnotist looks for weak-willed subjects, however the mind-control programmers and professional stage hypnotists say that a "fighter", "a determined forceful personality" are the types they search for to have a successful hypnotic session. Weak-willed persons are usually incapable of seriously concentrating for the successful pursuance of any idea, and usually are the worst subjects. Intelligence is often helpful, and (as stated in the first volume) the ability to be creative is extremely important to the programmers. An extremely important factor for the subject of mind-control to have is the "emotional drive to pursue to its successful completion a given objective." (McGill, Ormond. Professional Stage Hypnotism. pp. 87-88.) One reason the programmers like to work with children who were preemies is that they are fighters. Another reason the programmers like to work with intelligent children, and not waste time trying to program lower-than-average intelligent children, is that they are easier to hypnotize.

This does not mean that only people who appear intelligent are programmed. During the programming process, many of the victims are programmed to appear stupid to others and to themselves. Only the master (and those who work with him) are to use the full potential of the victim. The victims' talents are stolen from them. An intelligent child, who comes from an intelligent family, and who is programmed with total mind-control may grow up into adulthood thinking he or she is of average or below average intelligence.

GENETICS

Pres. Theodore Roosevelt, who was blood related to both President Martin Van Buren and to Franklin Delano Roosevelt, is on record, "Some day we will realize that the prime duty, the inescapable duty of the good citizens of the right type is to leave his or her blood behind him in the world; and that we have no business to permit the perpetuation of citizens of the wrong type .... The problem cannot be met unless we give full consideration to the immense influence of heredity .... I wish very much that the wrong people could be prevented entirely from breeding; and when the evil nature of these people is sufficiently flagrant, this should be done .... The emphasis should be laid on getting desirable people to breed." Many of the people within the Illuminati bloodlines have made statements like this, and have done all they could to leave many secret offspring behind, because these elite bloodlines have felt they were the chosen to lead humanity. Your ancient aristocratic families such as the Cabots, Lodges & Delanos have been in favor of placing the blame on society's problems on the "bad blood" of the common man. They forget all the evils that have been perpetrated on these common people by the blue blooded aristocratic families that think they are so superior. For instance, Illuminati kingpin Harriman's wife purchased land at Cold Springs, NY to promote a eugenics program. She said that being raised around good race horses helped her appreciate good breeding in man. Eugenics is the philosophy that some humans are genetically superior to others, & that inferior genetic races/individuals should be destroyed. The first eugenics program started in the United States was by John Humphrey Noyes, the cult leader of communist Oneida communities. John Humphrey Noyes' father was a Vermont Congressman, and his mother was a relative of Rutherford B. Hayes, the 19th U.S. President. His family was from the burned out district, from Putney, Vermont. In 1833, Yale granted him a license to preach. Noyes began creating his communist communities around 1836, and he dictated all their major decisions, including their group sex and eugenics policies. In 1869, John H. Noyes selected 53 women and 38 men to be the only ones in his communities allowed to produce children. The goal was to perfect the genetics of the community by only allowing well bred children. This is believed to be the first eugenics program. All members of the community were encouraged to have sex with everyone else & not to form emotional attachments around it. However, they were not to have procreative sex. The Oneida group can clearly be tied in with European occult groups that tie in with the illuminati. The Oneida group used central committees and social control through mutual criticism to keep their members in line. Their social control methods were extremely effective. Years later, Chinese communism began using these innovations of Noyes'. Charles Guiteau, who assassinated Pres. Garfield, was a member of Noyes' Oneida community. He became a member because his father, a disciple of Noyes, took him there as a boy. Charles stated that at the Noyes' community, he came under the influence of Noyes and "I was unable to get away from that influence ... A man was just as isolated from the world as if he were confined in state's prison or lunatic asylum. I suffered greatly in mind and body and spirits during incarceration in that community." He claimed he had never gotten free of the control that began when he entered the Oneida community. In 1880, he began hanging around the Republican Party's NY HQ. This was a very strange thing, because Charles Guiteau had never had any interest in politics his entire life. He bought a pistol from a "gentleman", and then shot President Garfield. Knowing that Illuminati mind-control was already taking place at this time, certainly makes this assassination an area for further study. John Noyes had his groups conducting seances and carrying out initiation rites. He personally sexually initiated the girl children of his communities at these rites. In June, 1879, when the authorities came to arrest him for mass rape of little girls, he fled to British Canada, where the British government gave him asylum. After Noyes skipped the country, the community was incorporated as a joint-stock corporation called Oneida Ltd., which later burned a large amount of the personal records and the diaries of the members to keep their sexual activities forever secret. It's interesting to note, that long before 1879, in June, 1847, Noyes' had treated a woman Harriet Hall for tuberculosis & dropsy by holding a seance ritual and sexually sealing the spiritual cure with intercourse with the woman. After the woman's husband reported this, a grand jury indicted Noyes. He skipped bail and an almost sure conviction by fleeing to New York. People have wondered how he managed to practice his odd sexual behaviors for years and never get into trouble with authorities.

Margaret Sanger, an early feminist, was also an advocate of eugenics. In their zeal to make her a hero, modern feminists have neglected to notice this side of her. Sanger advocated sterilization of the feeble-minded by he government. This all sounded good at the turn of the century before legitimate research showed that genetics played only a partial role in how people turned out, and that environment and choices by individuals also played just as big of a role in how people turned out. Many of the people who were sterilized under eugenic laws were realized to have been victims of pseudo-science and hysteria. The Great Depression leveled many proud and haughty people down to the same level as the common people they had sneered down upon. Rich and poor found themselves in bread lines. The financial elite and the academic elite were humbled and the eugenics racial theories in the U.S. largely disappeared. Finally, H.J. Muller, a famous and respected geneticist, gave an outstanding and courageous speech to the Eugenics Society in NY in 1932 where he lambasted the eugenicists for using false better-breeding theories to rationalize the criminal behavior of the elite. The Illuminati had suffered a temporary setback in legitimizing their criminal rule over humanity. In recent years, the Illuminati's evil ideas about superior and inferior blood lines are being given more credence again. The National Institute of Health funded a $1.7 million study at the University of Hawaii's Behavioral Biology Lab to get solid information on how genetics relates to intelligence so that "informed decisions" about population control can be made in the future. Almost every state has now adopted genetic screening of new-born babies in the U.S. While the Illuminati may not be able to fully implement their superior blood theories in society in general, they have been secretly working feverishly in labs and in secret rituals around the world to redesign mankind to their preferences. Many Illum. members are the end result of carefully monitored genetic engineering. They want to manufacture the future via control over human genetics. Many years ago, the first step in the Illuminati genetic program was the creation of specifications. When these specs, these criteria, were set as goals, they then worked to realize them. They have been working at them, and refining the results as they continue to work toward specific goals. They have sought the perfect assassin. They have sought the perfect slave. They have sought the perfect baseball player and golf player. They have sought the perfect soldier. The borders between these manufactured Illuminati total mind-control slaves and an industrial robot are fast becoming blurred. The end of the human race as we know it, and civilization as we know it, is rapidly approaching. Via molecular biology and genetics, humanoids that are vastly different from normal humans have been created in secret underground installations. They have been modifying humans to design para-humans, and then applying mind-control to them. The Illuminati is not only controlling humanity, but under their control redesigning it. Lest anyone forget, the descendants of John Noyes' Oneida Colony, and the genetic model wonder children born in Nazi Germany are still around. According to one source, the Nazi's produced numerous offspring of Hitler which were secretly taken to many countries and then later reassembled in certain special towns. These children received mind-control as well as being specially endowed with as many special traits as the Nazi's could give them. If this is true, it could have some significance in the future. Illuminati kingpins are also able to store their semen via cryogenics for all kinds of scenarios. Frozen sperm can be used to create a son after the father had died. Should an Illuminati kingpin want to impregnate his grand-daughter 10 years after his death, it would be possible. On the flip side, single women can choose semen from sperm banks. Another twist that the Illuminati have taken advantage of is taking the fertilized egg of one set of parents and implanting it into a brooder slave to raise the child as a surrogate mother.

It should also be mentioned that ex-Illuminati members have explained how planned births are coincided to have the child be born on particular special occult dates. (The Illuminati have a intense lifestyle of secrecy, so most of their members do not carry the last name of the bloodline they belong to. Some members are given significant occult names for their legal name, and others use legal names which have no significance. Having a legal occult-significant name is not essential, because the alter system will receive a secret Illuminati occult name.)

The bottom line is that bloodlines, genetics and genetic engineering is playing a role in the selection process of who is programmed a certain way. Also the Illuminati has particular research goals that have been structured into their 20 year, 30 year and 50 year plans. Case histories show that a child will receive education and programming in order to participate in secret research projects years down the road. Some of today's marked children are invariably being quietly educated to help with future research goals. As might be suspected the inbreeding within the secret Illuminati bloodlines and their secret satanic lifestyles take their genetic toll..

How do the Illuminati get rid of their leftovers, the children their bloodlines have that aren't going to amount to a great deal? In terms of mind-control, the male children that are the programming leftovers, the ones that are not really fit to make into politicians, doctors and lawyers, will be made into stalkers, according to an ex-Illuminati programmer, who worked in this area of programming, the ratio of men to women that are programmed for stalking is about 90% to 10%. Why discuss how the Illuminati makes stalkers? First, many people doubt that there is a controlled conspiracy by the Illuminati to control the world, because in their limited understanding they think that there are too many uncontrollable people around for the world to be controlled. They don't realize that a large share of those crazy people were intentionally created by the Illuminati. The Illuminati programmers and handlers during the 40's through the 60's, according to insiders, had specific quotas on how many people to have go crazy so that the mental institutions (which were used for programming) could maintain their government financing.

Readers, who have followed this author's lectures, have heard him explain how a. the Illuminati make a decision to "solve" a problem they have created, then b. get the government and private groups to study the problem for years so that eventually it looks like their (secretly preplanned) decision is the best course of action for the country, and then c. their lackey's in the political process implement the decision supposedly for the "good of the people". After 30 years of good financing for the mental institutions so they could do their assigned task of programming hundreds of thousands of people with tasks for the NWO, the Illuminati then set things up so that the mental institutions dumped their populations out onto the streets, where they can carry out the missions they had been programmed to carry out.

They next step was to privatize the prisons, which are being used for mind-control (not to mention hard-core porn of women victims in prisons). The Illuminati's long range plans for mind-control included that they would turn over the prisons to people like the Illuminati's Order of the Skull & Bone's Wackenhut Services, Inc., Coral Gables, FL, (ph. no. 305-666-5656), and the Illuminati's GE Government Operations, Cherry Hill, NJ under James Becker at 609-486-5042. In the 18 page Heritage Foundation's study of prison needs entitled "A Guide To Prison Privatization" (done on May 28, 1988, Wash. D.C.), the Heritage Foundations gives all the correct Illuminati answers to the question of privatization of prisons, including listing the following "corporations that provide prison services ... Behavioral Systems SW, Inc.,... Eckerd Family Youth Alternatives, Inc., ... GE Government Operations, Cherry Hill, NJ.. .Wackenhut." All groups that this author's research indicates are Illuminati and involved with mind-control. An example of several studies that this author has obtained that were done to show us that privatization of prisons is the best answer to our problems is The Development, Present Status, and Future Potential of Correctional Privatization in America by Charles W. Thomas, Prof. of Criminology & Dir, of Private Corrections Project; Charles H. Logan, Prof. of Sociology, Univ. of Conn., & Visiting Fellow, Fed. Bureau of Prisons. This paper was done May 1991. Our government also got into the act and the GAO wrote up a govt. report in Feb. 1991 stating that the government could save money by privatizing prisons. The Illuminati need their people seeded at all levels of society, at the gutter level as well as in palaces. This is where the stalkers, their leftover children used for programming are handy. Many of these stalkers had secret Illuminati lineages that are hidden via adoption. As one ex-Illuminati member said, "They are the weak links." The Illuminati must have dependable people everywhere, even in the gutter and prisons.

Why create stalkers? There are a long list of reasons. It is somewhat difficult to explain unless readers are already familiar with the bigger picture. People, who have sat in on Illuminati meetings where their 20, 30, and 50 year plans were discussed, will explain how the Illuminati wanted to break down the family structures and bring violence into the schools. This is Ordo ab chaos. However, the schools had rules to protect themselves from dangerous violent activity done by children, so they had to create violence in the streets, to get violence into the schools by the backdoor. Stalkers were part of the program to create violence. Another purpose stalkers serve for the Illuminati is that they make excellent spies if they get attached to someone. They will find out everything they can about that person. Their minds will creatively invent all kinds of ways to get information about their fixation.

How does the Illuminati program a child to become a stalker? They have the programming techniques to create a stalker down to a fine science. In short, it consists of 1. they bond the child extremely close to its mother or a woman as it grows up. This creates a side-effect of homosexuality. The mental mechanics of this side-effect are that the male has an unmet need for men. The Illuminati will manipulate this latent homosexuality but not allow its expression. They want to continue to strengthen the apron strings that attach the child to the mother image. Meanwhile they utterly destroy all self-respect and self-image of the child. It is totally disgraced so that its only identity is its identity with its mother figure. The child can not stand on its own two feet without the support of the mother-figure. When the boy approaches puberty, they are watched very closely by the Illuminati, be that in a military school or tightly controlled cult family setting, etc. They do not want the apron strings to ever be cut. They want them to remain dependent when they would naturally become independent. They want to insure that the young boy doesn't develop a sense of who they are. The victim of stalker programming will never emotionally grow out of that age of about 11-13 when boys would sever the ties to their mother. They stop growing emotionally at about age 12. This is all carefully crafted by the Illuminati. These young men never understand themselves or their programming. They don't understand the impulses and uncontrollable drives that hit them. They can't get off their programming merry-go-round, because it is rooted in the first brain, their maternal instincts, the "reptilian brain" which has no conscience. Their stalking of their mother figure is a survival instinct that they don't understand. They make good spies. They will persist in tracking and stalking a victim, until they break down the victim's walls of privacy by their sheer tenacity, persistence, and force of will.

This is because it is a survival instinct that has been harnessed by the Illuminati programmer. Because this programming is laid in at the reptilian first brain level, these stalkers can be violent without a higher brain conscience, and their minds will manufacture some justification to protect this survival need to stalk. The mind protects itself, so they have a strong denial system. Every time someone "rejects" them, it triggers their programming. Because they are driven by their reptilian first brain (the various brains are explained later in this book) they only think in the here-and-now, long-term projects bore them, they don't have the stick-to-itiveness needed for many jobs, except their eternal quest for an identity with the mother-figure they stalk.

TRAINING THE UNBORN CHILD

The Illuminati in its typical schizophrenic way, has not neglected the opportunities to begin the programming process in the womb. The scientific research in this area has been kept quiet, but from an ex-Illuminati programmer it is clear that they are aware of much more about the unborn child in the womb and its thinking processes than the public knows about. I was privileged to read the excellent book The Secret Life of the Unborn Child by Thomas Veiny, M.D. with John Kelly. This book is written from a loving Christian viewpoint and incorporates scientific research about the thinking of unborn children. Interestingly, Veiny studied research into the mind of the fetus from researchers at the Max Plank Institute, Munich, Germany, from the Esalen Institute, Big Sur, CA., from the Center for Research on Birth and Human Development, Berkeley, CA which are all institutions involved in mind-control and mind-control research. Just one example of the learning abilities of the unborn child, an autistic child remembered the english her French speaking mother was around during work while the child was in the womb. Veiny writes, "The fetus can see, hear, experience, taste and, on a primitive level, even learn in utero (that is, in the uterus--before birth). Most importantly, he can feel--not with an adult's sophistication, but feel nonetheless." (p. 12) Research has clearly showed that the fetus can think and is shaping its (his or her) personality while in the womb. Maternal thoughts, feelings, actions, and fears all reach the child in the womb and affect the child. The maternal bonding with the child while in the womb is also critical.

Researchers have been unable to pinpoint when a baby in the womb begins to think, and have a consciousness, but some theorize that it goes back clear to the beginning of conception. One study taught fetus babies to kick on the cue of a vibration. The researchers have determined that the unborn child hears what is being said around it, and is beginning to associate its language skills around the voices it hears. The unborn child hears and reacts differently to different music played. Soothing words and soothing music will calm a fetus. One conductor remembered into his adult years, the cello music that had only been played while he was an unborn child. According to excellent research, the start of awareness is clearly evidenced between the 28th and 32nd week. At that point, the brain's neural circuits are just as advanced as a newborns. This is why the Illuminati can get away with causing so many preemie births to enhance dissociative abilities. From the 32nd week on the child shows that it carries out REM sleep. It is also interesting the children, teenagers and adults have widely divergent sleep patterns but the time spent in REM sleep stays constant. Researchers have been able to trace memories going back to the sixth month of pregnancy. In other words, from the sixth month of pregnancy onward, some of what the unborn child learns will be remembered. (See pg. 23 of Varny's The Secret Life of the Unborn Child.) This is why the Illuminati has made a point of having the unborn child hear the voices of people who will play a role in the trauma and programming of the child. The child may already know the hypnotic voice of one of its cult programmers at birth. Researchers found that by playing a tape of a mother's heartbeat to new-born babies that the babies felt dramatically more secure, and were much healthier and did much better. A child who has been trained to its father's soothing voice in the womb, has been proven to remember it and hear it after birth and to respond to it in a positive way. In fact, the emotionally healthiest children have been found by researchers to have had their father's voice in their life prior to birth. Unborn children do not like to be poked at. In the eighth week of life, the unborn child is already using his physical abilities to show that he dislikes intensely to be poked. One of the early fetus traumas, that the Illuminati like to carry out is to poke the fetus with a sharp object to make it dissociative in the womb. By the fourth month, the unborn baby is making facial expressions. Four to eight weeks later they are sensitive to touch, and don't like to be tickled while in the womb. Sometimes children are tickled during medical exams. If cold water is injected into the mother's stomach, the baby intensely dislikes it. The child can be overwhelmed while in the womb with horrible sounds, bad tastes caused by what the mother eats, being touched in ways that it dislikes, etc. Rock music drives unborn children crazy. Programming drugs that cause particular thinking in the fetus can also be administered. Can one see that the traumatization to cause MPD can easily start in the womb? In fact, with many Illuminati babies, they do create womb splits, and have even started trying to teach Christ to the child while in the womb, to speed up the process of when they will purposefully make the child feel rejected by God and to experience the black communion with Satan. The foundation of trauma-based total mind-control is fear. A deep spirit of fear cripples a person spiritually & emotionally. The foundation of fear can begin to be layered in while the child is still unborn. The unborn child has near-sighted seeing. He can detect light shined on his mother's stomach. In fact, the fetus's eyes, which are living in a dark world, will hurt when light is shined onto the mom's stomach. A long-term unresolved personal stress on the mother will be one of the worst stresses her unborn child has to deal with. Short term stresses don't seem to have the long term side effects that long term stress has. Short term stresses are soon forgotten by the child. Somehow, the love that the mother has for the child is transmitted to the child, and forms a protective shield so to speak for the child to resist traumas and stresses. When the mother is ambivalent (even though outwardly happy) or cool in their emotions, the babies have been proven by researchers to consistently have more physical and emotional problems.

If the Illuminati want to create an effeminate gay man, they can administer progesterone and estrogen to the mother during her pregnancy, and this will influence the development of male children to be effeminate. Certain researchers have been warning about the hormones that are in our daily food because modern techniques of raising cattle and producing milk include giving hormones to the animals.

It is also known that the child's concept of "I" the self starts in the womb. Those children who have had a secure womb feeling have been shown to be more confident with their sexual lives later on in life. While those who were terrified in the womb had a tendency to have sexual problems. The traumas that are induced into some of the babies for programming purposes may have a destabilizing effect on the sexual stability later on in life, and it may be that the programmers take advantage of the unsure destabilized feelings that are a consequence of terror in the womb. Children born from induced labor have a statistically high relationship to sexual sadism, and males typically have masochistic personalities. (See pg. 19 of The Secret Life of the Unborn Child). Since certain Illuminati children have their birth's induced to match certain dates of the year, this is one contributing factor as to why Illuminati males, born into bloodlines that have for centuries considered certain birthdates important, have such a high incidence of sadistic tendencies. Verny believes that C-section babies, due to what happens to babies during the birthing process in contrast to a normal birth, have certain emotional needs that later as adults are expressed as promiscuous lives. Women due to their C-section birth, develop a deep seated desire to be held, and intercourse later becomes the price they have to pay to satisfy this deepseated need.

COMMON ILLUMINATI WORK WITH TWINS

The Illuminati mask the removal of babies from pregnant mothers with "alien abduction of fetus" cover stories. When twins are in the uterus, it is common for the Illuminati to skillfully take one of them. This is part of why the disappearance rate for a twin baby is 75%. It is so prevalent that it has been given the name "the Vanishing Twin Phenomenon". The Vanishing Twin Phenomenon is well established by statistics. Establishment doctors generally claim that one twin has absorbed the other twin. Some researchers claim that this can not be the real explanation for any part of the birthing process. Elizabeth Noble in her book Having Twins, (Houghton Mifflin, 1990) states, "With increasing use of ultrasound, it has been observed that more multiples are lost in the uterus than previously thought--some studies say as high as 80 percent of twin pregnancies. Considering that there are still 2 in 75 people born as twins, what a great number of twins would be born if the disappearance rate were not so high. There are many cases of two heartbeats being detected only hours before the delivery, and yet only one baby being born. Many mothers have been suspicious, but the doctors tell them that the second heartbeat "was only a mistake." The explanations that doctors give for disappearing babies who are never born often do not seem satisfactory. There are different kinds of twins:

a. There are dizygotic, also called fraternal twins. Two variations of this is when eggs from two consecutive ovarian cycles are separately fertilized, or a single egg divides and each of its halves gets fertilized.

b. There are monozygotic, which are identical, or clones so to speak of each other. Identical twins are always of the same sex. They share the same genes, the same fingerprints, dental characteristics, etc.

c. There are monozygotic mirror twins, which have identical characteristics on opposite sides of their body.

When one twin disappears, the surviving twin will often develop psychological problems around the disappearance, even if the child is never told that they had a twin disappear. The Illuminati believe that the soul of a dead twin goes into the live twin. They consider twins which have two souls very powerful individuals. One doctor, William Baldwin, has written in his book Spirit Releasement Therapy: A Technique Manual that he believes that the dead twin astrally attaches its soul to the surviving twin. Dr. Alice Rose believes that some eating disorders are the result of a twin dying in the womb due to competition for food.

To further complicate things, the Illuminati program their slaves to believe that they have a twin somewhere. Elvis Presley, a Monarch mind-controlled slave, believed he had a twin that communicated with him spiritually. In the Angel Times magazine, (Oct. issue), a childhood friend of Elvis states that Elvis communicated with beings as a child. These being had showed Elvis a vision of dancing, and of people "dressed in white with colors all around." While it is popular to dismiss the vanishing twin phenomena with superficial medical explanations, or with alien theories, at least of some of the phenomena is the result of the Illuminati's massive system of abuse, where they need babies for sacrifice, experiments and programming.

SELECTION OF ADULT CANDIDATES FOR MIND-CONTROL

There is an ongoing operation within the intelligence agencies to identify adults who would make good candidates for mind-control. For this reason, the CIA set up many years ago chains of weight-loss centers (as well as stop-smoking centers and stop-drinking centers) that help people with weight loss, & breaking drinking & smoking addictions. At these centers, people trained to identify clients with high levels of suggestibility have been identifying for the intelligence agencies, (esp. the CIA) potential mind-control victims. Intelligence assets are located around the country and even outside of the United States. The perpetrators try to look for individuals that come through immigration, who come into county clinics and hospitals, government hospitals, etc. who have the following initial attributes:

a. they are over 120 I.Q.

b. they are alone without a support team of family and friends

c. they do well on their first session where hypnosis is clandestinely perpetrated on the individual

d. they have other attributes that can be exploited to the advantage of the intelligence groups.

If a person is identified at a weight-reduction center (which is a CIA front) as having a weight problem that needs to receive hospital treatment AND they are also highly suggestive, they will be subjected to mind-control while hospitalized. According to one source, IF the individual, who has been a. spotted, b. singled out and c. placed under hypnosis without their consent, d. looks likes a useful candidate for mind-control to the psychologists and intelligence field officers, THEN a file will be started and they will be placed in a CALL FILE. The initial hypnotic session may be in a dirty doctor's office, or in some cases in emergency rooms. Dirty doctors working in emergency room settings are careful to work undetected by clean hospital workers. The hypnotic suggestion is implanted that the victim return at a particular date to a location where more detailed work can be done.

U.S. GOVT. MIND-CONTROL LEVEL 1.

A proper candidate, that is one with an I.Q. above 120 and proper hypnotic abilities, will be given a code cue, that is an alpha-numeric code, or a number or a word code that identifies them. This is embedded hypnotically. If the person has no relatives that are important, they will be instructed and secretly helped to move to a location chosen by the intelligence agencies. The programmers will cover their tracks so that what has happened at this level is deeply embedded in the subconscious mind & can't be retrieved.

U.S. GOVT. MIND-CONTROL LEVEL 2.

At this level the person is used operationally at very easy and unimportant tasks. He is also assigned someone. The hypnotist programmer is beginning to soften the victim up and make them more pliable to suggestions. If he successfully performs these small jobs that have been hypnotically written into the mind, then he will be given a RECALL SERVICE

NOTICE by the person who is in contact with the victim. Now the person moves on to level 3, which is a fully operational level.

U.S. GOVT. MIND-CONTROL LEVEL 3.

When the victim is instructed to come in, they do not realize what is in store for them. Now their own personality will be re-written according to what script the programmers want it to have. The person will be set to carry out his instructions as needed. The slave will now be given specific trigger codes to carry out assignments. All field agents of the intelligence agencies get level 3 control.

GOVT. MIND-CONTROL LEVEL 4

This level is reserved for candidates who are very intelligent and very loyal to hypnotic commands. Victims of this level of mind-control will follow out any command they are given, whether it be suicidal or harmful. Because these victims of mind-control are now under total mind-control, just as many members of the Illuminati grow up under, the intelligence agencies want to protect their level 4 slaves. They will be given a new life along with a total new identity. All the credentials and paperwork that the new identity needs will be created. The slave has now received a totally new life, and whatever SCRIPT (agenda) the intelligence agencies want. The programming that was placed in up to level 3 is erased in a sense and an entire new life script is placed in. This is done with the use of drugs, deception, and other sophisticated mind-control techniques described in Vol. 2 and this book. Complete areas of memory are erased at this stage and then a new history is written into the pre-puberty area of memory. This takes some time, and is accomplished using a number of techniques our books have described. The old memory is erased and OVERWRIITEN with the new history and script. The brain assimilates this new knowledge as if it's always been there, because it feels comfortable putting something into a void spot. The programmers prefer to find a period in the original person's life when nothing happened. It is easy to erase a memory block when nothing significant is in original memory, i.e. it is basically blank anyway. As a sleeper the level 5 slave may marry and lead a relatively normal life. One clue that the person is going to be used on a mission is if he suddenly leaves his wife & goes somewhere. This may be a clue that the handlers are positioning the person for a mission. They may also have nullified the slave's external life, so there isn't the purpose of life to prevent a suicide mission.

U.S. GOVT. MIND-CONTROL LEVEL 5

This level is reserved for people with an I.Q. of at least 130. This level will require taking the slave to a special programming center, where they are taken down to the comatose level of subconscious awareness to place the programming in at the deepest levels of the mind. The victim may be comatose for days or months, and this requires a catheter in the neck, urinary and digestive tracts to keep the body properly functioning. Because the person will be hospitalized for quite a while, a popular cover story is that they had an automobile accident. Remember, in Vol. 2, it was discussed how Roseanne Barr (now an actress with MPD/DID) had as a teenager an "automobile accident" during which she received significant programming. Many of these level 5 slaves are placed as sleepers into organizations of all kinds, where they lead "normal lives." The level 5 triggers activate programs deeply embedded and NESTED into the memory of a person. A team of programmers work on level 5 slaves. They must make sure that the victim has a support system so that they do not self-destruct. They may have psychologists in normal life set up to serve as a support person for the slave. It was interesting to see that AFTER learning from people in the know about how memory is erased and a new identity given, that the show "No Where Man" portrayed this happening to a black man. Whoever wrote the scripts for No Where Man had an excellent understanding of what is going on in mind-control.

TESTING YOUNG CHILDREN TO PLAN THE PROGRAMMING.

In Vol. 2, chap.] it was explained how the programmers can test the preverbal child to determine & plan how they will program them. EEG's & Gittinger's Tests were discussed. Here is more information. Researchers have been able to study the personalities of unborn children and to watch how these personality traits stay with the children through their lives. In the Vol. 2 book it was explained how the Illuminati has used EEGs to determine the personalities of pre-verbal children so that they know what type of programming is best suited for that personality. Interestingly, on Mon., April 12, '96, 11 p.m. after the Vol. 2 book was out on the market, 20/20 did a show where they showed researchers using EEG electrodes to monitor childrens' brainwaves for their happiness potential. It is known that brain potentials associated with voluntary movements have been identified, thereby giving big brother the potential to predict when a person is going to make a particular movement. The brain is dynamically looking at patterns and continously generating hypnotheses about its environment which are then validated or invalidated by information picked up by the senses. The P300 wave (known as the P3 wave for short) allows neuroscientists to track decision making in a brain's cortex. The P300 wave shows when the mind's thought processes have been internally surprised. In this way, detection of the P300 gives a method of lie-detection superior to the polygraph. When surprised the brain creates P300 wave by internal brain functions--such as what chapt. 4 will call "cognitive demon processes". Initially, EEGs are taken of child victims, with an analysis of the different wave forms. Next, will come tests of VERs (visually evoked responses). This is valuable for instance, because bright children will show asymmetric (high amplitude) responses during VERs from the right hemisphere. Children with low I.Q. show the same evoked response from both hemispheres. This is just one window on the mind that the Illuminati programmers have of the preverbal children. There are other evoked-potential tests that are being used to determine personality traits too. Evoked-responses can also be used to show whether the person is conscious, or how deep they are in a coma. The early components of the evoked-response, which occur 10-20 milliseconds after a stimulus, are believed to come from the brain stem and can be used to determine a level of a coma. Evoked-responses are also used to determine particular learning disabilities within a child. Right-handed children will show even prior to birth, an anatomical specialization that favors language acquisition in the left hemisphere. So they can even determine what handed-ness the child has very early on.

Image2.gif

Baron Guy de Rothschild, of France, has been the leading light of his bloodline. The Baron is an Illuminati Kingpin and slave programmer. For those who have bought the cover story that the Catholic Church is not part of the Illuminati's NWO, I would point out that the Baron has worked with the Pope in programming slaves. This photo was picked for the trauma chapter because the Baron has a droopy left eye. Many of the deeper Illuminati alters show droopy left eyes due to the trauma they have received. The authors are not aware of what the official explanation for his droopy left eye would be.

CHAPTER 2.

SCIENCE NO. 2--THE TRAUMATIZATION & TORTURE OF THE VICTIM

The basis for the success of the Monarch mind-control programming is that different personalities or personality parts called alters can be created who do not know each other, but who can take the body at different times. Let's review some important points that were mentioned in the Vol.2 book, 'The amnesia walls that are built by traumas, form a protective shield of secrecy that protects the abusers from being found out, and prevents the front personalities who hold the body much of the time to know how their System of alters is being used. The shield of secrecy allows cult members to live and work around other people and remain totally undetected. The front alters can be wonderful Christians, and the deeper alters can be the worst type of Satanic monster imaginable--a Dr. Jekyll/Mr. Hyde effect."

A great deal is at stake in maintaining the secrecy of the intelligence agency or the occult group which is controlling the slave. The success rate of this type of programming is high but when it fails, the failures are discarded through death." Each trauma and torture serves a purpose." To create alters (dissociative parts of the mind) the worse the trauma, the better the amnesia walls, so programmers have been spending years trying to outdo each other in creating the world's worst traumas that humans can survive, so they can program people. Readers may at first wonder why cover this gruesome part of the programming? There are a number of reasons. People who pretend to be helpful people--such as some ministers, and some professional therapists--are unwilling to look at the facts of what have been done to the victims they claim to want to help. How can the victim ever come out of denial and face the issues around their dissociation--IF the people helping them who didn't experience these traumas first hand can't even face the existence and nature of these traumas? Many therapists encourage the victim to maintain their amnesia walls, "let the past be the past". They say, "You can't change the past." No matter how appealing this advice sounds, this advice for victims of trauma-based mind-control this is defective, idiotic simple advice. This type of advice only continues the mind-control and the abuse of the victim. No wonder Christian ministers who are under their mind-control are used to spout off this type of defective advice. It is important to cover programming traumas because it validates the memories of recovering victims, and because there are standard types of trauma that are used for certain types of programming. For instance, traumas that desensitize a person to killing--i.e. traumas where the victim is forced to kill innocent people--are used to program assassination alters. The base of the programming is FEAR layered via trauma. Hopefully, the readers will be inspired and motivated like this author to try to stop this horrendous mind-control.

DAILY ABUSE WORKS BEST FOR PROGRAMMING

To insure that the programming and abuse stays hidden from even the slave, the slave is given daily traumas as a child to keep them dissociative. The Illuminati's programmers get the cooperation of a vast network of abusers who traumatize the children who are being programmed. One of the Illuminati's fronts is the Catholic church, which the Jesuits manage for the Illuminati. Under the cover of religious retreats and their religious image, many Catholic clergymen have been participants in the vast trauma network actively creating trauma-based mind controlled slaves. The problem in exposing this is that first the people who are being traumatized have trust in the clergymen who are doing the traumas. Second, if the victims or parents of the victims suspect anything, they usually go to church officials rather than the police in order to clear up the problem, yet protect the church. Additionally, in most cases both the corrupt religious system, working behind the corrupt police and judicial system manoeuver to protect the abuser and to further victimize the mind-control victim and anyone coming to the person's rescue. The following are but a few examples of a widespread network of secret abuse, that will not be uncovered because the system to catch abusers has long ago been corrupted and infiltrated and controlled by mind-controlled slaves, as well as by blackmailed or bribed dirty persons of authority.

Roger Trott, a Catholic Priest in Delmont, PA convicted of molesting 12 boys, got a suspended sentence by the judge. Can you believe such unbelievable leniency?

Father John Engbers (b. 1922, in Holland), catholic pastor at Leroy outside of Lafayette, LA. He baby-sat for a family, in which he sexually molested their children, their five daughters. He was treated as a member of this family and the mother, who was of Amer. Indian descent, was very close ("worshipped"-according to one daughter) to Father John. She spent long hours alone with him. He would tell his victims that they were his "puppet, like Pinocchio." He molested some of the girls almost every day, and had them under his control enough that they returned even when they were living at a distance from him. He had what appeared to be a hypnotic type spell over them. Father John Engbers molested many children during his years as a Louisiana priest, until he fled in 1985. He had lots of money to spend. The Catholic church had known he was molesting children clear back in 1952, when some parents complained. The Catholic hierarchy helped him escape back to Holland in mid-1985, when reports and law suits over how he sexually molested children came out. The case of Father John Engbers has all the earmarks of a participant in the daily Monarch mind-control abuse given to children.

Dennis Dellamalva, a Pennslyvannia Catholic Priest, who molested boys, and the judicial system protected him from prosecution. The judge, a catholic order the records of this paedophilia priest sealed, and the catholic church which knew of his deviant behavior continued to give him a position of authority.

Michael Peterson, a child molesting priest, who was a drug addict and a homosexual, was one of the catholic hierarchy's main men involved with investigations of pedophilia, who died of AIDS, and his rich sidekick Stephen B.C. Johnson II, who administered a catholic facility near Boston, Mass. Michael Peterson lived a rich lifestyle in Marsalin, and later Suitland, next to St. Luke and told people that he was not worried about anyone, because he had the goods on them to force them to comply. Michael Peterson's St. Lukes was used by the Catholic church to receive many priests that were caught doing paedophilia. In the first six years, St. Lukes claimed to have cured 55 child molesting priests.

Monsignor William A. Kraft, (b. Rochester, NY), Knight of the Holy Sepulcher, was pastor of St. Therese during the '60's, and by 1978 the rich pastor of St. Charles Borromeo, San Diego. His father was a chief executive with Eastman Kodak. Kraft's sexual molestations of children have all the earmarks of being a Monarch mind-control abuser. He was protected by the Catholic hierarchy and the system from prosecution for molestation of children. When children are being tortured and traumatized by persons who are respected in society, and when these children see the police and judges protect these people, do you see why this further traumatizes them, and convinces them that there is no hope? Once they lose hope of outside help, their minds are further propelled to obey the commands of (continue with the picture below. The text continues under the girl in the left upper corner. Editor's note)

p_little_girl2

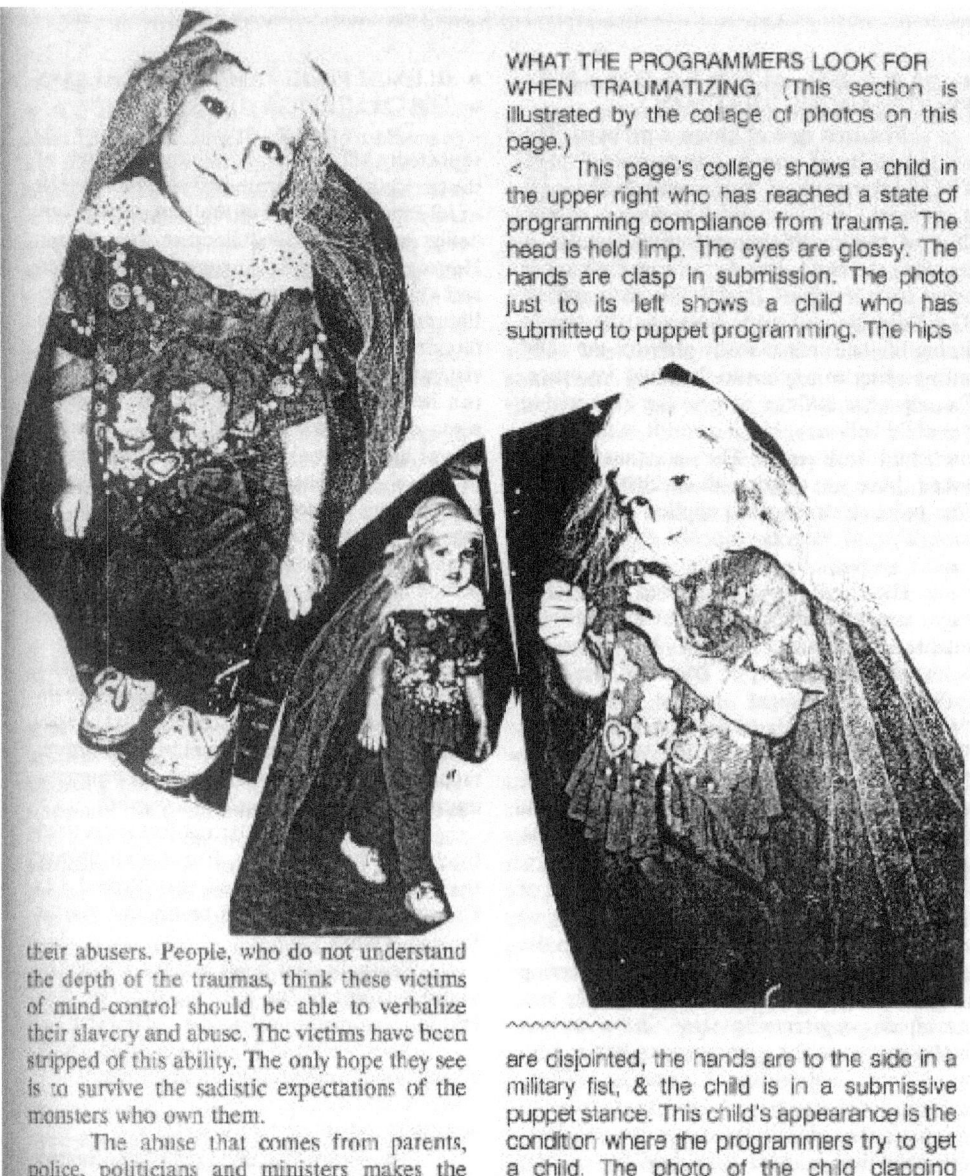

WHAT THE PROGRAMMERS LOOK FOR WHEN TRAUMATIZING (This section is illustrated by the collage of photos on this page.)

< This page's collage shows a child in the upper right who has reached a state of programming compliance from trauma. The head is held limp. The eyes are glossy. The hands are clasp in submission. The photo just to its left shows a child who has submitted to puppet programming. The hips are disjointed, the hands are to the side in a military fist, & the child is in a submissive puppet stance. This child's appearance is the condition where the programmers try to get a child. The photo of the child clapping shows a slow robotic clap due to the puppet training. The child in these photos has in fact, showed every indication of having received total mind-control, and has been under the care of Roman Catholics.

their abusers. People, who do not understand the depth of the traumas, think these victims of mind-control should be able to verbalize their slavery and abuse. The victims have been stripped of this ability. The only hope they see is to survive the sadistic expectations of the monsters who own them.

The abuse that comes from parents, police, politicians and ministers makes the victim feel like there is no one safe to run to. The ongoing secret abuse keeps the child very dissociative. We are discussing general abuse, later this chapter will cover some specific programming traumas.

ANGER-MANAGEMENT-PROGRAMMING TRAUMAS

The first type of abuse is prenatal. The second series of abuses occurs from 2 to 4. The third round of programming abuse, is given to the child around 5 to 6 years of age. One of the specific programming abuses is teaching the child slave to redirect their anger away from Papa or Daddy the slave owner. The Papa Bear, Daddy figure in the slave's young life will intentionally provoke the child with teasing to aggravate the child into rage. Exactly what is done to provoke rage within the child will vary, but the result is the same, the child feels rage. The question is then asked, "Are you angry with daddy?" "Yes!" at that point electroshock is applied to the head, toes, tips of fingers, nipples & inside the vagina, or penis by electrodes attached to the child. The child will be brought to the level of rage, and then allowed to cool down for 30 minutes. The child's alters are then via behavior modification & hypnosis taught to redirect their anger toward themselves. "WHEN YOU ARE ANGRY WITH YOUR FATHER, YOU WILL HURT YOURSELF. DO YOU UNDERSTAND? The message will be played over & over & the question "Do you understand?" will be played over & over. The child is shocked until they are compliant. The suicide programming will be layered in. Part of layering in the suicide programming, is to create pain in the right ear via a needle to the ear, with the creation of horrible disorienting sounds, while pulsing lights drive the brain into its alpha programming state. At a certain brainwave state the programming begins with repetitious self-destruct messages. These messages debase the value of the person to reinforce the suicidal destruct messages. After the child has learned that they are to hurt themselves, then they will learn specifically to cut themselves if they get angry at Papa or anyone in the Illuminati family they belong to. After this training, the child will attach subconsciously a fear of pain to the concept of anger toward its Illuminati controllers.

SILENCE PROGRAMMING TRAUMAS to TEACH SILENCE

One way to teach silence is to repeatedly kill persons of all ages in front of the person being programmed while telling the mind-control victim that the people who are being sadistically killed because they talked. However, the "no-talk" lesson will be repeated and embedded in many different fashions for Illuminati mind-controlled slaves. Perhaps a favorite Illuminati method is to expose the victim to watching dental tortures. The viewing can be reinforced by subjecting the victim to some dental tortures themselves. A common dental torture would be to extract the tongue of a live and conscious victim. Then dental tortures are done to the victim, and the intense jaw pain of the torture is linked to tripping the no-talk programming. If the person talks--their jaw hurts and they may pull up the dissociated feelings of seeing a person lose their tongue. This then will be further backed up by training an alter to carry out Russian Roulette if the system talks, and training numerous other alters other types of suicide if the system talks. In other words many back up programs mutually support each other in overkill. Considering that dental torture is used for no-talk programming, it was with dismay that this author discovered that Virtual I-O Co. is now making virtual reality eye glasses for dental work. Seashells and other images are linked to the concept of "no-talk" via programming laid in using methods described elsewhere.

Another "no-talk" program is the "Don't tel me" telephone no talk programming.

TORTURE FOR NO-WRITE

The victim has their right hand bound behind their back and then is made to walk on their knees like a dog.

PAY ATTENTION TORTURE

There are a host of these, one example is a needle inserted up the nostril behind the eyeball.

A COMPLIANCE TORTURE -- The Black Slave Chair.

The Black Slave was invented by a Syrian doctor who helped supervise torture, hence its arabic name al-Abd as-Aswad. The victim is strapped to this metal chair. What is unique about this chair is its design & its hole so that a hot skewer can be shoved up the anus. Another device for programming is a harness used as a suspension device. Yet another is an electrofied water bed for turning one in an electric eel." Compliance is also taught by taking an eyeball out of the victim (later replaced), and by dislocating an arm at the shoulder. After this the victim can be wrapped as if in a cacoon within bandages. The supposed treatment for the dislocation, places the victim in sensory deprivation, another trauma.

A TRAUMA TO DEVELOP ANIMAL ALTERS

Helpless humans will be displayed to child victim of mind-control. These helpless humans will be visciously killed by some animal, a lion, a tiger, a snake, a wild dog or whatever. The programming lie emphasized at this point is that it is better to be that particular type of animal than it is to be human. Then the animal is sacrificed and its spirit is ritually joined to the child's alters. Other programming is added to insure the dehuminization process to make certain child alters into particular animals. When finished, the child will contain viscious protector animal alters within their system. The prior example of a programming trauma actually pertains to structuring. The mind-control science of structuring MPD (DID) is discussed in chapter 7. It may be of significance to stress to the reader that traumas come in many shapes. The traumas are not done without some thought. Specific traumas are given for specific desired outcomes. The power and horror of a trauma is hard to gauage. It often results in a type of subconscious adrenlin-rush addiction. The traumas involving sensory deprivation and betrayals of trust can be just as devastating as painful tortures. Sad to say, sometimes for programming purposes all three types may be skillfully combined into one horrendous experience that overwhelms the mind.

TRAUMA TO ISOLATE THE VICTIM

A birthday party will be given for the victim. The birthday cake will contain a bean somewhere. It is announced that whoever gets the bean will get a surprise. When someone gets the bean, the mind-control victim finds out that the surprise is that they must take the life of the child who has found the bean. This programming trauma is part of a series of traumas designed to make deeper alters afraid of accepting any gifts from outsiders. The deeper alters are programmed that gifts always come with a sacrifice. Gifts always cost something. Nothing comes free. "SEVER ALL TIES, HAVE NO FRIENDS" are the programming messages. In reality, what Satan is doing with this trauma on a spiritual level is what the British Empire did with small countries. The British would warn small countries, "you are in danger, we will protect you. (The Spirit of Fear says, gifts are dangerous, let me the Spirit of Fear protect you.) When the British moved into small countries like this, they called them protectorates, & then they took over. (The Spirit of Fear, pretending to protect the victim, takes over and the victim develops a deep-seated free-floating phobias towards gifts from anyone. What pretends to protect, actually ends up controlling & enslaving.) As the reader treks through this book, he or she will encounter places where other traumas are discussed, such as tortures via implants, & traumas via rides in amusement parks, & spinning traumas during the structuring for creating alter families from an alter. Finally, the waves of fear created by repeated traumas layer in Spirits of Fear, which form a dark spiritual foundation.

Deeper Insight Into the Illuminati Formula

A Democrat in beast's clothing

Vice President Al Gore and his wife, Tipper, pose for a Halloween photo in costume on the front steps of their residence in Washington, D.C. Halloween is Tuesday.

Associated Press Photo

above. Photographic evidence of mind-control dehumanization. This female called "Queen S___" who has managed professional wrestlers on a team called "the New World Order" gives visible proof that professional wrestling is tied to mind-control. One of her wrestlers Macho King Savage claims his favorite thing to say is "You'll bow before the Kingdom of Madness." Compare her photo with programmer Al Gore dressed as a Beast in a recent news article.

p_clothing2.jpg

p_adrenalchrome2

CHAPTER 3.

SCIENCE NO. 3 The USE OF DRUGS

IN REVIEW

The science of Pharmacology (drugs) has given the Programmers a vast array of mind-altering and body-altering drugs. Some of the drugs are not used to directly alter the mind, but to change the body (make the skin burn), or make the person vomit, or some other reaction that can be harnessed to further their nefarious programming goals.

DRUG RESEARCH

One of the sites which has done research/programming into MPD and drug action on the brain has been Bethesda, MD where Dr. Irwin J. Kopin was Chief of the Laboratory of Clinical Science, at the National Institute of Mental Health. He was active in research into how drugs can affect the mind.

CLASSIFYING MIND-DRUGS

When this author studied differential equations, and higher mathematical it became clear that everything can be reduced to a mathematical explanation. Sometimes a mathematical notation is easier and clearer, than other explanations. This author suggests that drugs that affect the mind could be classified on three scales:

Scale X: the wakefulness or arousal scale, which runs from a coma, to asleep, to alert, to hyperalert

Scale Y: the attitude, or affect scale, that is one's manner of feelings, responses etc., running on a scale from suicidal and depressed to euphoric, blissful and elated.

Scale Z: the integration of reality scale, which runs from confusion, delusions, and psychotic thoughts to integrated, clear, lucid thinking.

Many (if not all) of the drugs that were listed in Vol. 2 and this chapter can be plotted along one of these scales, and sometimes 2 or 3 of these scales, which means an x,y, z axis configuration can be used to compare such drugs. In terms of naturally occurring brain substances which are manufactured synthetically and injected according to the programmers' needs, it could be stated that the original purpose of the substance can be malevolently tampered with.

p_mind-drugs.jpg

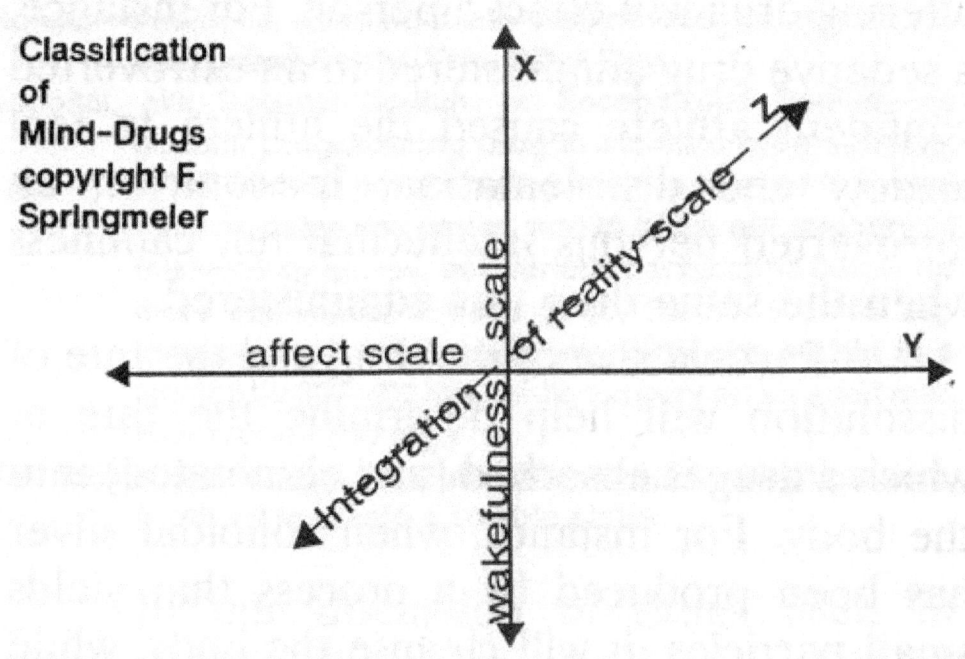

ADMINISTRATION OF DRUGS FOR PROGRAMMING

The distribution into the brain of a drug is dependent upon many factors. Under microscopic-level inspection, one discovers a person's brain is physically constructed to allow certain molecules to enter into the brain in certain complex ways. Just because a substance is put into the blood doesn't mean it gets into brain tissue. Researchers have discovered such drug properties such as lipid solubility, the ionization, its tissue-protein bonding abilities, and its molecular size all play a role in how well drugs get into the brain. Further, the Cerebrospinal Fluid (CSF) which will be discussed indepth in Chapter 8 can play a role in drug absorption. Several studies during the 1960's showed that the removal of drugs or substances from the CSF, can reduce the effective concentration of a drug in the extracellular spaces which make up perhaps 12% of the brain's volume. These physical factors are not the only factors involved.

Researchers have repeatedly discovered that different people respond to mind-changing drugs in many different ways-- including two different people having opposite responses to the same drug. There have been a number of studies about this phenomena, including: (SarwerFoner, 1957), (Henninger, et. al., 1965), (Rickels & Downing, 1966), (McNair et al., 1966). Over the years, it has been discovered that a person's mental abilities, expectations, prior drug experience, age, sex, race, personality traits, and personality types can all potentially influence how a mind-altering drug will effect a person. For instance, a sedative drug administered to an extroverted confident athlete caused the athlete to feel anxiety and disorientation. In contrast, an introverted nervous intellectual felt calmness when the same drug was administered. Particle size of the drug and the rate of dissolution will help determine the rate at which a drug is absorbed (and eliminated) into the body. For instance, when colloidal silver has been produced by a process that yields small particles, it will cleanse the body, while larger particles of colloidal silver will kill a person. Different companies and different preparations of the same drug may have different outcomes upon the body. The persistence of a drug in the body is calculated by programmers using half-lives of a drug. This means that at one half-life, one half of a drug is left in the body. At two half lives, one-half of one-half is left or (1/4). At three half-lives there will be 1/8 left of original drug. In other words, the rate of elimination decreases with time. When heroin is processed into morphine, its characteristics change. The heroin takes affect quicker, but doesn't last as long as morphine. This is because of enzyme mechanisms in the liver and how they react to the morphine in contrast to the heroin. Different drugs react differently with the complex enzyme mechanisms of the liver. Phenobarbital amazingly increases the enzyme content of the endoplasmic reticulum with habitual use of the drug. Phenobarbital will then enhance a particular type of toxicity. Low doses do not hurt the body, but there is a threshold where damage from phenobarbital will begin occurring to the liver and kidneys. This is a sampling of why it is important that the Illuminati use extremely skilled medical personnel in the application of programming drugs. The programmers are far more skilled than most legitimate therapists in understanding how much of what drug to give to which alter personality. The mental makeup of an alter will influence how that alter will respond to drugs. Some deeper alters can resist drug influence due to training. Some deeper alters are so fine-tuned that they only need small doses. With their superior knowledge of how a System of Multiple Personalities has been created within a victim's mind, the programmers have a distinct edge over deprogrammers in how to administer drugs. On top of that the programmers, place in all types of programming to prevent anyone but the programmers (or approved people) from administering drugs. An example of how strong the mind can be over drugs--is when the programmers "SET THE STAGE", "PRESENT THE SCRIPT' and then use Seconal to obtain deeply embedded programming commands. Setting the stage is a programming term for talking to the victim in such a way that the mind is receptive for what the programmer wants the victim's mind to do. Presenting the script is the actual set of commands that the programmer gives to the victim. For instance, the programmer functioning as a hypnotist tells the victim that a powerful sedative will be given but that part of the mind will be strong enough to overcome the sedative effect of seconal. The victim is instructed "WHEN YOU HEAR THE WORD [trigger power code word, for instance: ZEBRA COME FORTH]...YOU WILL RESPOND TO WHAT I AM SAYING." The seconal is given and the person is placed in an isolation chamber. A good programmer skilled in hypnotism can actually get a victim's mind to respond under the influence of seconal in an isolation chamber. Then the programmer will lay in deeply embedded commands while the person is in a sleep deeper than a twilight sleep. When the human body receives several different kinds of drugs, sometimes drugs compete with each other during the excretion/elimination phase. This may create a buildup or a retention of one of the drugs. As discussed in Vol. 2, the programmers don't like to use combinations of several drugs because it complicates things. There is still a great deal of unknowns concerning adverse drug reactions. Some people do not show an allergic response to a drug until it is administered several times. Because of the potential for allergic reactions or side effects, the Programmers are helped because the programming centers, according to ex-programmers are extremely well stocked with different drugs, & the Programmer can if need be shift to an alternative programming drug. Most slaves are programmed to stay away from the use of drugs, except those drugs that the programmer/handler approves. By reducing the use of drugs of all kinds, the problem of adverse drug reactions, and other complications is reduced for the programmers. Some people who are health freaks who stay away from drugs are actually carrying out a front program for their programmers.

MORE PROGRAMMING DRUGS (these were not listed in the Vol.2 Formula book)

Acetophenzine aka Tindal--(this anti-psychotic has been used on multiples, it mutes anxiety, suspiciousness and delusions. it would fall more into the control category of uses rather than for actual programming.)

Amines--(this is a general term for many types of the brain's own chemicals used to produce moods, and feelings)

Damiana--(aka Mex. Witching Herb, the extract is used w/ other herbs during progamming for a relaxed pleasure state.) »An example is Damiana-Biack Kava Kava-Valerian-Skullcap-Wild Lettuce Opium, which makes a "it's-nothing-but-a-dream" state.

Chloral hydrate--(which is a hypnotic put in pill form such as chioral betaine, Beta-Chlor, and given with something like a glass of milk. About 500 mg. of Chloral hydrate are given for a hypnotic for an adult.)

Cyciohexamide--(produces retroactive amnesia)

Cylert--a type of speed

Datura aka Jimsonweed, or thorn apple--(sometimes used to help a child conjure up their personal spirit.)

Iminodibenzyis-- (used for sedation)

Lettuce Opium--(tradition Hopi shaman trance drug)

Mandrake--(from the Mandragora plant, an ancient occult drug, a traditionai witchcraft drug for causing people to sleep)

Methaqualone--(a rapid hypnotic drug that produces a dissociative high, it can be used to put someone into a coma)

Pemoline-magnesium hydroxide (aka PMH, helps enhance conditioned avoidance training by acting as a stimulant, is helpful for repetitive learning situations by a general alerting effect on the mind)

Phenothiazines--(used to raise the threshold of electrical stimulation tolerance, to tranquilize or induce sleep)

Rowan--traditional sleeping/death herb of witches; May Day is also called Rowan Tree Witch Day.

Seconal, aka Seconal Sodium or Secobarbital Sodium--(a popular programming drug to stabilize programming, to set in deep programming into the base of the mind such as dates and codes, and to block out memory of missions by slaves, see various paragraphs below for more explanations. Used in 10, 20, 30, 50, 100 mg. increments. A tubal pregnancy/birth can be hid in a woman by 300-400 mg., while surgery on an adult man may require 500 mg.)

Tetradoxyn (made from the Puffer Blowfish, used by Voudoun, & others to create a zombie state)

In our discussion of drugs used in programming, this chapter will expand upon the previous book by discussing the application of drugs to:

a. to stabilize the programming after torture b. hiding the codes

c. building in deeply embedded structures and beliefs, and the creation of false identities

b. to influence the memory by drugs c. to stimulate instinctual behaviors

d. to create moods and attitudes by synthetically manufacturing and injecting the brain's own natural amines.

STABILIZING THE PROGRAMMING

The total mind-control of the Illuminati is called "trauma-based mind-control" because repeated traumas are inflicted upon the victim is a very systematic calculated inhumane way. The tortures and stress are all parts of a programming package. After a particular harsh session of programming the victim's mind will be in a high state of terror, shock, dissociativeness and splintering. The victim's mind can't take much more, and the potential of having uncontrolled splintering of the victim's mind and thereby having the destruction of the mind and programming threatens the programmers' control. The programmer wants the mind and body to rest so that the programming can set in, without destabilizing events occurring. For instance, after severe water torture (drowning) the programmer will want the programming (hypnotic script) to set in, and he will give seconal (aka seconal sodium or secobarbital sodium) to induce a deep sleep. Sleep occurs within 10 to 15 minutes. Sometimes a victim's heart has been pushed to its limits during a trauma and they must shut the body down to let the victim rest. Seconal is a drug of choice for this. Seconal is administered in hospitals or programming sites where trained personnel know how to give the drug. Dirty psychiatrists, who understand the relationship between drugs and human behavior and who are either programmers themselves or assistants to programmers often are the ones who give the victims drugs like seconal.

EXTENSIVE RESEARCH DONE TO INFLUENCE HUMAN MEMORY BY DRUGS

The complete list of researchers who have studied the effect drugs have on memory would require a massive book. However, we will just mention a few that pertain to this book briefly. One of the places the effect of drugs on memory was researched was at the Univ. of California at Irvine, CA. Another was at institutions in the Boston, Mass. area such as the Massachusetts General Hosp., in Boston. Dr. Talland in Boston tested the effects of PMH on human memory. He discovered PMH could help people relearn material that had been partially forgotten. The Illuminati programmer Cameron (aka Dr. White) also tried out various approaches including the administration of RNA and RNA-synthesis stimulants. John C. Lilly, who admits being a member of an Esoteric Mystery School, was a government researcher on the use of LSD to program people. He did part of his work on LSD programming at the Maryland Psychiatric Research Center under admitted government financing. His book Programming and Metaprogramming in the Human Biocomputer (NY: Julian Press, 1967, & revised format 1972) is an excellent paper trail of how the Illuminati has used LSD to program total mind-controlled slaves. Originally, the book was given out only to a few select people. The book attempts to hide what it talks about behind a long intro, long sentences, big words and arcane psychological terms, but it does spell out how they do the mind-control programming with LSD. A section later in this chapter will lay out for the reader how they do this.

ONE TYPE OF EXPERIENCE OF VICTIM HYPNOTIC DRUG A MIND-CONTROL

The drugged victim feels like he is looking through a keyhole and the hypnotic voice of the programmer is the key hole. The world may be very shadowy and drawn in on itself. The mind has its attention on the hypnotist/programmer.

The BASIC PHASES of MEMORY

The human memory process can be basically broken down into 3 phases, the registration phase, the retention phase and the retrieval phase. Great amount of research has gone into how to use drugs to manipulate each of those phases. Great amount of research also went into how to measure people's abilities to a. learn, b. remember, c. and to do non-learned behavior such as arm-hand steadiness and visual time reaction.

WHAT the MIND-CONTROL PROGRAMMERS USE to MANIPULATE memory.

Scopolamine was found to impair short-term memory. It was discovered that retrograde amnesia could be created by electroshock several hours after the brain had learned something. This lesson caused the Illuminati and those working in mind control with them to use cattle prods and stun guns.

If a person performed something they were to forget they can be stunned or given scopolamine to deaden their memory. A quick anesthetic applied immediately after something has been done might also impair the retention of what had happened. Yet another way is seconal, which will be discussed soon. Low doses of analeptic drugs given about 10 to 20 min. before training were found to help learning. Analeptic drugs include bemegride, diazadamantanol, pentylenetetrazol, picotoxin, and strychnine. It was discovered that strychnine helps enhance classical conditioning. It can be administered either before or after the learning has taken place. It is believed that memory storage is enhanced by strychnine and strychnine sulfate. Strychnine was also found to help protect the mind's memory against the effect of electroshock. Abusers out on the street have been turning to GHB and Rohypnol to decrease inhibitions and to cause memory loss in their victims. Rohypnol (which sells for up to $10 a tablet) is dependable but more expensive than the GHB. A number of women who have been raped by adding these drugs to their alcoholic drinks at the Club Boca, Palm Beach, FL made the paper after they were drugged and raped after partying at the club. (The Palm Beach Post, Mar., 1996 pp. 1B, 10B.) GHB (Gamma Hydroxy Butyrate) is a compound essential to the body. It acts similar to a neurotransmitter. It helps release the Human Growth Hormone and removes inhibitions around intimacy, as well as some other beneficial effects. GHB crosses the blood-brain barrier and metabolizes into GABA. GHB's high degree of safety was proved over 25 years of research, and was basically an established fact before the FDA and the media demonized GHB. Several sources seem to indicate that the FDA banned GHB --not because it has dangerous side effects, which it doesn't have inspite of the established media's disinformation campaign with half truths--but because it is not patented by the drug companies and would cut into their profits.

GHB also has a great aphrodisia effect. It reduces inhibitions to have sex, but because the woman clitoris is more sensitive it interferes with female orgasms. However, when the women do achieve it, it is longer and more intense, according to GHB researchers. (This author got much information on GHB from the Centurion Aging Research Lab.) GHB is described here because it is a drug that is known by the type of people who use sexual slaves and other people, and its use and misuse pertain to mind control. Like so many things involved with mind-control, GHB and many other items could be put to positive uses if used in the proper way. Sometimes the programmers use drugs rather than ECS (Electroconvulsive shock) to destroy the memory in slaves after they have done some mission for the Illuminati, the Syndicates, or Cult they belong to. The decision to use drugs rather than ECS is largely personal tastes. The very sadistic programmers enjoy using ECS, while the less sadistic ones often use the drugs, which in some instances actually perform better, but are not as violent to the victim of mind control. Retroactive amnesia can be caused by an intracerebral or a subcutaneous (under the skin) shot of Acetoxycycloheximide, cyclohexamide, or puromyxcin. A more sophisticated technique incorporates the drug seconal (aka Seconal sodium), the victim's dissociativeness (the MPD), and hypnosis. Seconal is a strong sedative that puts people into sleep. The programmers have considered it "wonderful". The victim's mind is conditioned hypnotically to be able to remember the drugged-seconal state. Then the hypnotic command is given that if anything about a particular mission is remembered, the person will immediately trigger (pull-up to the front of the mind) the seconal memory. This is why many therapists discover their clients getting sleepy when they get close to certain thoughts, or when they try to do therapeutic work.

HIDING THE CODES

Chapter 4 provides some of the programming codes, some of which are standard and some of which are unique to a particular slave. Seconal was the standard drug used during the 1950's and 1960's to hide the programming codes in the mind's memory. The procedure is to give a small child under 50 lbs. perhaps 10 mg. of seconal. The programmer has already "SET THE STAGE" and presented the script. After the child goes into its deep sleep, the programmer pulls the child's mind awake hypnotically (actually to be technically correct, the programmer pulls up those alters/parts of the mind that the programmer wants to work with). The child may awake on an satanic altar or other programming setting. The child is then programmed. After the programming, which may include satanic rituals, the child slave is given 20 mg. more of seconal and allowed to go into a sleep again. A cover program (a cover story--that is a false code will be planted hypnotically in front of the real code. "IF YOU SHOULD REMEMBER THIS..." If a slave starts to remember any code, in spite of the hypnotic commands not to, and all the threats and alters trained to protect the codes, etc. then the programming to sleep kicks in. Also remember that the codes are placed in when the victim is groggy, so to pull up the memory will cause the slave to abreact the drugged-state. Not all the alters are drugged. In setting the stage, the programmer orders some alters to back off from feeling or associating the experience. They are hypnotically commanded not to experience the drug's effects, or to only experience it in a partial manner. This can be done with small amounts of seconal. Larger amounts of seconal will override the mind's ability to block the drug's effects. The programming experience where the codes are put in, will likely be remembered by the slave as something similar to the following, a sleepy blurry picture of a nurse, then a doctor and a table, and then an IV, then the memory fades, and the slave gets sleepy thinking about it.

It should be pointed out that the mind has strong natural abilities to dissociate painful memories. Not only must the victim try to retrieve memories by fighting the mind's natural dissociative abilities, the victim must fight the hypnotic suggestions, the irrationality of conflicting ideas due to the false cover memories laid in, the DRUG memories attached to induce sleep if the victim remembers, the memory shattering from the shock of the stun guns, and the fear of countless other threats internal and external if the memory is recovered. It is no surprise that most victims of this horrendously abusive mind-control have front alters who are totally unaware of the mind-control and abuse.

PROGRAMMING WITH LSD-25 (Lysergic Acid Diethylamide)

The Programmers use controlled and manipulated LSD trips for mind-control purposes when layering in the programming for the Illuminati slaves. The victim's mind is trained and mentally prepared before actually being subjected to the drug. The programmers understand how the mind unleashes its fears, including its fear of LSD itself, while under the drug, so that small doses are given at first and then increased. This is so the victim of mind-control can learn to face and manage the effects of the drug.

When the Illuminati want to set the foundations for a system, they will use LSD in a sensory deprivation tank on a child to program in such things as: the hell-pit (a dungeon in a castle), the images of evil guardians, worlds & stars & galaxies which contain alters, the outer space in a system, and the protective program where the mind spreads out like molecules and loses the ability to think. The sensory deprivation tank will be set at 92.0 to 95.0 F. isothermal skin, saltwater suspension, zero light, near zero-sound levels. The victim will be naked without contact with the side of the tank and in remote isolation for several hours. Electrodes can be hooked up to shock the victim if they move to prevent the victim from wanting to move. Victims usually are conditioned to like the sensory deprivation tank before they are programmed inside it with LSD. After having listened to two ex-programmers describe LSD sensory deprivation programming, this author was amazed to discover that the LSD programmer John Lilly had actually written a book about how to do the programming! (John Lilly was also into witchcraft & aliens.) The government wasn't quite as thrilled with his book as I was, they withdrew research funds from him in 1968 when only a few copies of his book came out. And now finally almost twenty years later, the human LSD programming that John Lilly described is finally being put into its larger context--that of trauma-based total mind-control. On page 126-127, Lilly explains that implanted programs in the child can be placed in below the level of the mind's awareness, but which will affect their entire outlook on life, and which will control their thinking and behavior far into adulthood. The programs can even be done to control the most basic functions of life. Lilly says that the programming possible with the use of LSD is "...not achievable outside the use of LSD-25. This amount of control can be said to resemble other ways of achieving control and visual projection but in actual intensity I know of no other way to achieve it. Hypnosis is a possible exception." (Programming and Metaprogramming in the Human Biocomputer, p. 20) On page 19, Lilly states that LSD can be used to change an experience to have a negative or a positive charge on it. Sometimes people who work with the mind refer to negative experiences as "negative charges on an experience", and good experiences as "experiences with a positive charge". Apparently, according to Lilly, the brain can switch chemical charges on an experience and shift its attitude from viewing as either positive or negative. In fact, this very thing is done during Illuminati programming. For instance, it may be done if a memory surfaces that the programmer doesn't want the alter being programmed to understand. This last paragraph is interesting when one realizes that under LSD the subconscious mind is allowed to release its thinking into the conscious. If a person has been traumatized, the subconscious mind under LSD will release the trauma memories and flood the person with horrible thoughts. So before one can get to the transcendental wonderful creative thoughts, a person has to deal with this garbage. The sub-conscious erupts like molten magma. Before the child is given the LSD, the child is going to have to be mentally prepped. Just as Seconal could only be used after the hypnotist programmer had SET THE STAGE, so also with the LSD. The LSD programmer if he is experienced will have an idea how the victim will react to the drug. Each person reacts in his or her own way, but there are patterns of reaction. The programmer will hypnotically warn the victim, YOU'RE NOT TO FEAR such and such thought. They may tell the victim that it is just their imagination, when it is repressed memories of trauma surfacing. The programmer will let one alter carry the true feelings (such as fear) of the surfacing traumas, and another to carry the story line being programmed in with LSD. The programmer may have to calm the victim down while they are in the tank. The Illuminati use hypnosis in conjunction with the LSD programming trips. They also use some other mind-control items too. Further, LSD is not the only programming hallucinogenic that they have used for some of this type of programming, they have tried Peyote, but LSD seems to be the drug of choice. On page 20, Lilly describes the use of mirrors along with LSD to create visually projected images. The Illuminati programmer will play a movie, a script over and over so that it is constantly in the forefront of the victim's mind. Then the stage is set and the script (such as TAKE WHAT YOU SEE INTO THE MIRROR) is hypnotically given. The victim goes under LSD and in about 15 minutes reaches their LSD high. Most people can be talked to by the programmer during the programming, and the programmer can get some feedback from what is happening in the victim's mind. The victim will be placed in front of a mirror. Then the victim will project the image that was repeatedly shown him or her (say for instance, Alice In Wonderland, or Tinkerbell, or Mickey Mouse) onto their own image in the mirror. A special state of consciousness is induced where the person's perception is altered and they see the projected image as their own reflection. While watching the projected image on the mirror, the mind under LD will also project its own feelings and facial features into the mirror. If the victim is angry, happy, in pain, admiring themselves, etc. then projected image (for instance, Mickey Mouse) will also been seen this way. Using this type of programming, the programmers can create twinning parts. That is if two people are to be twinned, parts that see themselves as the other person are created using the LSD mirror programming. Ceremonies and demons will also be added to strengthen the twinning, and this may be done to a 13 year old teenager within the Illuminati. These projections can be maintained and worked with for about 30-40 min. during the drug's high. After this length of time fatigue sets in and the person must rest before being brought to another high. A clean slate alter can be prepared by the script and then will actually believe that it saw itself as the projected image. By the time, the session is through the clean slate alter believes it is Alice in Wonderland or whatever character the programmer(s) wants it to be. During the trauma of an LSD programming trip, the mind may see flickering images, melting, mosaics and other things. These distortions can form a cover memory if the programmers wants them too. During the sensory deprivation tank experience under LSD, the victim can be asked to open their eyes, or close them. If asked to form a mental screen, the victim under LSD will see a blank screen differently if their eyes are open as compared to closed. If the victim is allowed to look while in a dark tank out into the darkness under LSD, they will visualize themselves as merging with the infinite universe and not even having a body. This memory is used to build in the outer space of a system. On page 32, Lilly describes the type of programming used to create an Infinity, a Rubicon, or Outer Space within a system. He says, "The self is still centered at one place but its boundaries have disappeared and it moves out in all directions and extends to fill the limits of the universe as far as one knows them. A person taking LSD may experience, whether being programmed or not, that they are in touch with all the stars of the universe.

LSD distortions in reality can also be used to protect the programming. If the mind gets too close to remembering something, then the mind triggers automatically a memory of its molecules expanding into the universe and losing their ability to think. This is simply a controlled LSD memory. When external stimuli is ceased, the brain takes over the spaces that were formerly occupied in the thinking process by external reality, and replaces it with feelings and thoughts from the internal mind. Lilly states on pg. 24 that when programming people under LSD, "The blank screen is the most difficult one to work with but is the least 'driving' of the group. The blank screen interferes least with one's creative efforts;..." In other words, if the victim is closed off to external stimuli, the mind can focus all its energy into free associative creativity. Once the victim is in isolation, religious music can cause the brain to free associate religious visions, cartoon voices can cause the brain to free associate the cartoon figures, etc. The Illuminati/Intelligence agencies must wait 3 to 6 months between LSD programming sessions. If they do it more often, they run the risk of hooking the person's mind on the drug state. Then the person will lose interest in reality, and simply try to escape reality into the LSD world as a drug addict. From recollections from ex-programmers and victims, its clear that as the child victim is traumatized during the [SD sensory deprivation (including being shocked) experiences it goes through a sequence or chronology of changes which are noted in detail by the programmers. Certain splits occur at certain points in time which will be used for special tasks. For instance, at a particular extreme moment the victim may go into a "nothingness state" which is between life and death, where the mind quits perceiving that it has a body. This is not an out-of-body experience, it is a nothingness experience due to an extreme near-death experience. This clean slate can be used for the Cabalistic programming of the Ain Soph Aur. The Ain Soph Aur is the cosmic egg from which the universe supposedly began, ain = vacuum, soph limitless, and aur = limitless light. For Satanists they interpret this to the light at the top of the pyramid, Lucifer. Alters created in such a fashion may be placed in a succession of realms. If true Caballism is followed this will consist of 4 realms (worlds) of 10 clean slates. These four worlds are Atziluth = boundless world of divine names, Briah the Archangelic World of Creations Yetzirah = the Hierarchal World of Formations Assiah = the Elemental World of Substances

The child victim in the sensory deprivation tank is not allowed to move without being shocked. Gradually the will of the victim is broken by the total control the programmer maintains over the child in the tank. But the will of the child continues to be broken until the will of the child to live is broken. At this point, when the mind has given up the will to live, the programmer (or assistant programmer) will tell the child in the tank, "If you create such and such types of persons and such and such no. of them (perhaps 10 or 20 are asked for) then you can come out and we'll stop hurting you. Give me a signal that you've done your job and I'll stop hurting you when the job is done. Move a finger or blink your eyes three times if you've done your job."

Blinking three times generally feels the safest for the child, and is generally the limit of what the mind and body can muster to save themselves. The alters, which are made when the mind & body have lost the will to live, are the dissociated parts that will be made into suicide alters. Their breathing is very shallow, they are in pain in the tank. When these parts take the body, they still function in that state. Years later, if the adult body has these suicide alters take the body, there is a good chance they will commit suicide, if not simply die from the shallow breathing. Lilly states on page 31, "One experiences [under LSD programming] an immediate internal reality which is postulated by the self. It is apparent to me that one's own assumptions about this experience generates the whole experience. The experienced affects, the apparent appearance of other persons, the appearance of other beings not human, one's own past phantasies, one's own self-analysis, each can be programmed to happen in interaction with those parts of one's self beyond one's conscious awareness."

While the victim is in the sensory deprivation tank, the programmer can ask the victim to create guard alters within the castle images they create. These are equivalent to the imagery that is done in witchcraft. These image alters are not the same as a trauma-created dissociative alter. The following are the type of beliefs that can be programmed into a person in the sensory deprivation tank under LSD no matter what their prior beliefs (this is substantiated by Lilly, pages 4 1-49 and ex-programmers).

a. The person could successfully park the body and leave the body somewhere, astral project and explore new universes. The victim can be brought during an LSD trip to this thinking and experience the astral projection from around 20 mm. to 2 hours.

b. The victim can be made to feel as if they are a tiny mote, a tiny dot, a single microflash of energy in their own view of time, a mere particle. Time can become infinity and the victim a mere microflash. The victim during this experience seeks a god who is a great being to control him. This is used in the Illuminati alien programming to program in the evil and good aliens, or evil or good gods. The gods or the aliens on such a programming trip will not be so strange that the victim as a mote can't understand their purposes and activities. In other words, the aliens on programming trips like this turn out humanoid. The victim experiences being nurtured by these beings or the god(s) that he sees. The victim may perceive these aliens on the trip experimenting with us. One UFO researcher and author about the aliens has used his LSD trips to research aliens. Sad to report, this researcher is a programmed multiple. It is easy to see how the mind could think that it was learning about aliens, because this is a common easy-to-create LSD programming script. Again in summary, this second set of beliefs is that the person is a mere mote, a small flash in infinite time. When an alter of a slave thinks or goes internally where it shouldn't, this programming is attached to the mind so that the victim loses sight of who they are and feels very insignificant and only a dot.

c. The next program that LSD naturally lends itself to, is that the victim is only part of a vast computer, only part of a vast mind. For some reason, the LSD is able to hit a part of the mind that regulates the perception of free-will. In this type of programming, the victim under LSD is convinced that he or she has no free will and must participate each second with some larger mind or computer.

d. Personalities that have been seen externally by the victim will be incorporated within the person's internal world.

e. LSD changes the victim's perception of time, and can be used to go back or forward in time in the mind. Under guidance, the programmer can manipulate this ability to build into the mind false memories and images.

f. If "white noise", that is random background noise is placed into an isolation tank trauma, the programmers have found that under LSD the brain tries to make sense of the random sounds and projects the voice of God into the random noise as a method to turn chaos into something comprehendible. With the right dose, and under the right conditions, the programmers can get the voice of "God" to say about anything they want. Because the sense of hearing in the sensory deprivation tank is not feeding the mind anything, the human brain under LSD can easily substitute in the voice of God.

g. For girls, who have been determined to have personalities with low sexual appetites, the sexual desires of certain alter personalities can be manipulated during an LSD trip by having these alters hold the body and the body go through exaggerated pelvic movements and other experiences. This is an example of the type of training that Gittinger (see Vol. 2) discovered was necessary in order to change thinking patterns within a person--in this case with the MPD (DID), some alters can be radically changed from the original personality.

The overall effect of such LSD programming on anyone, whether child or adult, is that the mind at a deep level begins to doubt its ability to grasp the real from the imaginary. Therapists sometimes wonder why alters are not more anxious to determine reality. Part of this may be the side-effect at a profound level of the brain beginning to doubt its abilities to separate reality from fiction. If the LSD trips were not controlled by the programmers, insanity could result for the victim. Further, the LSD trips pose a danger that they could clutter the internal world of the victim and splinter their mind uncontrollably. This is why the trips must be carefully guided, controlled and monitored.

CHEMICALLY TRIGGERING NATURAL INSTINCTUAL DRIVES

The brain when a child is born is like a computer which is ready to go, and just needs the software loaded on. In other words, the brain is already a functioning complicated programmed piece of hardware, it is not a blank sheet. The mind is preprogrammed to carry out important instinctual functions, such as drinking water, eating food and sleeping. Likewise, the adult mother instinctively has maternal instincts. Selectively applied chemical or electrical stimulations to the brain will elicit the instinctual behaviors that are pre-programmed into the brain. A microinjection of a soluble sex steroid into the anteromedial hypothalamus would likely trigger the maternal instinct in a person. The various instinctual behaviors that are triggered by microchemical injections or small select electrical shocks will last for up to an hour. (A.E. Fisher was one of the principal researchers in this line of research during the 50's and 60's.) For instance, A.E. Fisher and E. Vaughan, discovered that the male instinct for sex could be stimulated by a small shock to a specific part of the brain. (See "Male sexual behavior induced by intracranial electrical stimulation", Science magazine, 1962, 137, pp. 758-760.) Steroids are one of the chemicals that are used as well as selective minute electrical shocks to trigger instinctual behaviors. Reliable responses can be obtained from a victim, if the correct chemical is placed at a place in the brain where the chemical will cause the brain to send an electrical signal to trigger an instinctual behavior. A searching reaction can be created so that a person or animal searches for something in his surroundings by electrical stimulation of the hippocampus. Eating can be reliably induced electronically or by drugs. Perfusate taken from ventricles or neural tissue of a person who was starved before death, and placed into the lateral hypothalamic area will cause the person to eat whether they are hungry or full.

SEXUAL STIMULATION-PROGRAMMING

The users of slaves need some of the parts to be nymphomaniacs. In order to program this type of behavior, the programmers not only use the reversal effect when pain becomes pleasure (see Vol. 2), but they also use hormones and drugs to make certain parts nymphomaniacs. If they were not artificially stimulated they could not endure the over-use they are subjected to at times.

THEIR ABILITY TO MANUFACTURE (SYNTHESIZE) BRAIN CHEMICALS TO MAKE MIND-CONTROL DRUGS

Part of the ability to do mind-control has to do with their ability to synthesize the actual specific chemicals that the brain produces to alter itself. When the brain wants to relax, or excite itself it uses certain compounds. A large number of the brain's chemicals have been cataloged and can be reproduced in the lab. The messages the brain sends have to jump from one neuron to another via transmitters. The rate that the brain releases these transmitters can be both directly and indirectly changed by drugs. In other words, one can tailor make moods and emotions in the brain chemically.

Page 36 ...

The term "Amines" (which are compounds that have a nitrogen atom that can accept a proton) came to have a specific meaning for brain researchers. The transmitters between neurons in the brain are Amines such as dopamine, epinephrine, histamine, norepinephrine, octopamine, serotonin, and tyramine. The principle method to synthesize these transmitter amines is "decarboxylation of the parent amino acid." In other words, the chemist takes Tyrosine and applies Tyrosine Hydroxylase (an enzyme) and produces Dopa another similar compound; and then the enzyme Dopa Decarboxylase is applied and from that the similar Dopamine amine is created. Then Dopamine-Beta-oxidase (another enzyme) is applied in the final step of the three enzyme steps to create Norepinephrine. Both Dopamine and Norepinephrine are neural transmitters. If norepinephrine is diminished in the brain, sedation occurs. Alpha-methyl-p-tyrosine (as well as other compounds) was found to be one of the things that would prevent the brain from creating (synthesizing for itself) norepinephrine. Serotonin (5-hydroxytryptamine) is created in a fashion similar to dopamine, in that tryptophan is taken and acted upon by the enzyme Tryptophan hydroxylase to get 5-hydroxytryptophan, and then a decarboxylase converts this compound to serotonin. To reverse things, and prevent the brain from having serotonin, they can prevent selective parts of the brain from creating it with p-chlorphenylalanine.

ADRENALCHROME (Adrenal Chromaffin)

This naturally occurring yellowish brown drug was not mentioned in the Vol. 2 book, although it was mentioned in this author's newsletters in '93 and May '95 The drug is obtained by sacrificing a terrified person, perhaps by plunging the athame into them, and then taking a hypodermic needle and extracting the adrenalchrome from the base of the neck in the pineal gland. A sacrificed person only yields about 10 c.c. so the drug is not only very secret on the black market but very expensive. A Scientific American article by Carmichael and Winkler is the best thing that I have discovered on the adrenalchrome. The Max Planck Institute in Germany did research into Adrenalchrome. Dirty law-enforcement officials and others have worked to keep the existence of adrenalchrome a secret. It is not known if Adrenalchrome has ever been used for programming, but it is a popular secret drug of the elite Illuminati kingpins. For many years, they were not able to synthetically produce the drug, and had to rely on human sacrifices as their source. It is possible that in the last year or so, that some method to synthesize the drug may have been found. Chromaffin cells secrete adrenaline, noradrenaline and other substances into the bloodstream which exert a great deal of control over tissue, and organs.

HERBS

Another place that programmed DID Satanic Ritual Survivors may encounter herbs is the use of herbal charms to enhance magic spells.

OILS

The Illuminati have also used oils for their powerful properties. Recently, a doctor who was trained by the Freemasons has been helping people discover the powerful properties of these oils. Christians also have been rediscovering the powerful healing powers in pure Fennel, Frankincense, Juniper, Lavender, Peppermint, Pane and other cold pressed Oils and combinations of oils.

Summary of Major Point.

The guided LSD trips in the sensory deprivation tanks are crucial for laying in the foundational programming. Readers will learn more about guided LSD trips & programming drugs throughout this book.

Page 37 ...

CHAPTER 4. SCIENCE NO. 4 - HYPNOSIS

HYPNOSIS & the OCCULT

From the Egyptian Sleep Temples to ancient shamans, the occult world has been putting hypnosis (including self-hypnosis) to work for centuries, even millennia. During the 18th and 19th century, the Masonic lodges put hypnotism to use. In 1882 Jean-Martin Charcot, considered the world's greatest neurologist at the time, gave hypnotism respectability by publishing his own studies, which included recovering A. trauma memories blocked by amnesia, and B. memories presumed permanently lost by organic amnesia. At that time, a group of french medical doctors located at Nancy just a 100 kilometers southeast of the Mothers-of-Darkness castle, had a school of hypnosis that influenced doctors all over the world including Freud. These french doctors had caught on to the power of suggestion to the subconscious.

In the 1780's, Marquis de Puysegur was putting people into deep hypnotic trances and then commanding them to forget the hypnotic session. James Esdaile in his book Mesmerism in India & its Practical Application in Surgery and Medicine. (pub. Longman, Brown, Green, Longmans, 1846) pp. xxiii-xxiv, describes and lists hundreds of surgeries (some quite serious) which he did in India using hypnosis as his anesthesia. He found his patients could heal quickly and experienced no pain under hypnosis.

In modern medical history, every type of surgery has been successfully carried out without drugs and "without pain" by using hypnosis. In the VoL 2 book, it was brought out that perceptive researchers have figured out that the pain under hypnosis is placed by the mind into a dissociated piece of the mind, which is essentially what MPD (DID) is all about. Tests have shown that hypnosis to reduce pain does not work by the brain releasing endorphins (see Hilgard, 1975 & Spiegel and Leonard, 1986). The mind simply diverts the pain into a "mental floppy disk" that it doesn't look at. In the early 1880's, occult researcher Edmund Gurney found he could give post-hypnotic commands that would be successfully carried out in the future.

What amazed him was that subjects would fulfill commands exactly as commanded at a particular time on a particular day without even looking at the clock. Various European doctors, too numerous to mention, discovered in the 1880's that they could cure various diseases via hypnosis. The cure rate was not 100%, but significant enough to make hypnosis an option in some treatments.

This author (Fritz) has reported that programmed multiples are able to increase the temperature of one body part, or one side of their body. Cisco, the co-author of this book, when she hits certain programs, turns ice-cold on the right of her body and burns on the left side. It was with great interest then when this author located the 1920 work of hypnotist J.A. Hadfield who published his work in Lancet, 2: pp. 68-69, under the title "The influence of suggestion on body temperature.

"Using hypnosis, Hadfield could get a subject to drop his temperature in one hand to 68.0 while the other hand stayed at 94°. Here is the paper trail to what they have been doing to programmed multiples for half a century. Today, the occult world uses sophisticated hypnotic techniques as one of their programming tools to create mind-controlled slaves. The slave's mind is structured into a robotic-computer controlled by a master. Parts (alters) of the slave will learn how to trance (self-hypnosis) on cue. The better conditioned a subject is to hypnosis, the easier they fall into trance. The victims of mind-control are all very conditioned for hypnosis, even though their programmers then hide that under post-hypnotic suggestions that no-one else is to be allowed to hypnotize the slave. The ancient saying is that a picture is worth a thousand words. In conveying suggestions to the subconscious mind, the occult world of black magic and the programmers are very aware of the power that picture images convey. The good programmer will be able to utilize images to give him tremendous leverage in hypnotic techniques. An alter which needs to create something in the mind can be prepped with images, and can be asked to borrow images, such as borrow such and such quality from this person or animal. The child alter who becomes a Lion after eating a dead lion's parts can imagine the qualities (speed, agility, fierceness) of the lion easily. The image of the lion is worth a thousand words to the hypnotic programmer. If the programmer wants an alter that is trained in karate to be agile, quick and fierce, they don't mind dehumanizing that alter to become a lion or tiger. One element of why this is done is the power of the image for hypnotic commands. The deeper Illuminati alters will be highly skilled in self-hypnosis & the ability to change at will into various states of consciousness. This is part of their witchcraft training in order to practice witchcraft.

UNDERSTANDING THE BASICS ABOUT HYPNOSIS

The Programmer is attempting to produce suggestions that the unconscious mind will accept. If the subconscious mind accepts the programmer's suggestions then the suggestion becomes reality to the victim, just as if the victim had experienced it as reality over a period of time. The programmer, if he is good, will be able to get the subjects imagination involved. He will also build rapport with his victim. For instance, the master might hypnotically stroke the forehead of kitten sexual alters before giving them their code to go back into the mind. The good handler/programmer is not simply working off of fear, but he wants to have the trust and cooperation of the victim. This is similar to how Hitler was both feared and trusted by the German masses. In fact, hypnosis was an element in Hitler's control of the masses. Nazi propaganda films showing Hitler and other Nazi leaders giving directives always have the Hitler Youth's actions slightly speeded up so that subconsciously the viewer is taught obedience to their commands.

The programmer will not tell the slave something is hypnotically happening until it has already happened. He will use the art of timing his words at the correct time, of using repetition, of combining several mutually supporting suggestions, and of having total confidence in his words to add strength to his hypnotic commands. Muscular rigidity and deep breathing are one way to increase suggestibility within the victim being programmed via hypnosis. The programmer will also use other hypnotic tricks, such using his own body language to suggest something, and to use what is called a "voice roll". When the programmer moves his voice into a monotonous patterned style he is using the roll voice. Words are delivered at the rate of 45 to 60 beats a minute. To empower the suggestions, the programming hypnotist uses the victim's five senses. The victim visualizes something using his five senses, such as the imagery of the holy spirit (done in mockery of God) and then breathes this imagery in. For instance, the victim breathes in the message of the programming and roots it deep deep down into the oak tree. (In VoL 2, it was explained that the oak tree is the structure that the programs are attached to.)

THE POWER OF HYPNOSIS

During the hypnotic trance, the human mind is at the pinnacle of its ability to quickly learn. What might take years to learn and weighing the evidence, will be accepted quickly by the victim's subconscious. The mind strings together a series of "cognitive mental demons?? that is a series of mental processes--similar to how a computer programmer writes a program. These strings have been called K-lines. Much of what the mind does is simply activations of various K-lines (a habitual ways of doing things), so that the mind can focus its limited conscious thinking. The mind also takes micronemes (such things as a particular aroma, or a particular intonation for which it has no word, but for which it has a series of sensory clues) and builds these into K-lines too. Once a K-line works, the mind in order to prevent itself from making reckless changes, gives priority to those K-lines. Under hypnosis, the mind willingly allows the hypnotist to change K-lines without the normal unconscious conservative restraints. Under behavior modification techniques, abnormal K-lines (that is K-lines that wouldn't normally develop) can be forced into the mind.

A hypnotic suggestion given to normal subjects lasts about a week, so reinforcement is helpful. The programming suggestions are layered in using methods far more powerful than mere hypnosis, and are locked up in dissociated subconscious states, so that these programming scripts which are layered in are almost impossible for the victim to be aware of to challenge them. The emotions of women have been found to slightly detract from the hypnotic trance, while male victims take the hypnotic words in an unemotional matter-of-fact way. The male victims will simply accept the programming and directly comply. That is one reason why the suicide programs that are layered into the men are so deadly. The female victims of programming may emotionally play the suicide out and survive; the male slaves when they trigger suicide programs, comply with the programming in an unemotional direct way.

How deep is the slave's trance? There are tests for trance depths, but from what this author can ascertain, sometimes it can be difficult to determine exactly where the mind is at. If a memory is laid in at a particular trance level, the slave may be able to avoid an abreaction later on by going above or below the memory's trance level. A deep level, where for instance, the person can't move a body part due to hypnotic suggestion, would be called the "cataleptic stage" or level.

UNDERSTANDING THE DEEPER MECHANICS of HYPNOSIS

Let us suppose for the sake of discussion that as you are reading this, it is supper time. You are hungry. You've starved yourself all day, and even though you are on a strict diet, you are trying to think of a good restaurant to go to. Now let's see, as your mind scans the different possibilities, it thinks of some that are close, some that are quick. some that have lots of easy parking and others that have good looking waitresses. Mechanically, your thought processes went like this:

a. Particular sensations and chemicals cause the mind to feel what it mentally describes as a pang of hunger. This is perceived as an important need.

b. The mind has a process that we can call an Intention System that creates specific intention messages that are sent throughout the brain. It stores these Intentions temporarily. If an intention is not freshly created and restacked at the top of the clutter of intentions in the intention store, then it gets buried underneath the "mind cluttered desk of things to do" and forgotten. In our example, the mind is searching its memory banks for options on how to satisfy its hunger.

c. The mind must decide upon one particular course of action. The mind quits focusing on other matters, and concentrates upon deciding which course of action to take. The mind has now activated all kinds of what some researchers call "demons". Because we are not talking about spiritual demons, but rather we are referring to units of cognitive processes--which are very similar to UNIX computer demons--we will refer to these demons by the name "cognitive demon processes." Some of these cognitive demon processes are action demons and some are word demons, and some are recognition demons.

Recognition Cognitive Demon Processes go running through the mind, "shouting" the wishes of the Intention store. A number of lower level cognitive demon processes wake up and make themselves known if they identify with what the recognition demon is shouting about. Many may think they match the request, but other demon processes check them out to see how close they match. Now the checkers come up with a list of cognitive demon processes who are concerned with eating at restaurants, who have woken up and are all scrambling for attention. Cognitive demon processes establish themselves in families, and develop relationships that are automatic. (Cognitive Demons do not die, but some go to sleep and others can get somewhat rusty in their relationships.) The "demons" that respond to the shouting of our recognition demon go through a series of "interviews" with a hierarchy of other demon processes, and soon the messenger demon can rush back to the Intention Store with the name of the choices available.

All this happens extremely quick. If the mind did not set up a series of automatic cognitive demon processes that become habits, (called K-lines) it would find itself involved in the conscious relearning of trivial matters that would make it impossible to get much accomplished. Every skill would have to be constantly relearned. A person might easily end up spending all day dressing. As long as the mind remains in a static environment, where habits work, it's great. But life is such a changing environment, that our entrenched habits can cause the mind to pull up a cognitive demonic process out of habit, when it is neither wanted nor appropriate.

Emotions and needs (which are tied to our emotions) will trigger the mind to search out cognitive demon processes. For instance, if our emotional need for someone we are looking for is great, let's say a wife waiting for a long expected war-husband, it may send a need down the brain for the cognitive demons that are attached to the identification of the long-awaited person, and the mind triggers itself to see his face in the crowd at the busy railway station before its owner arrives.

Cognitive Demon Processes live in close proximity to other demons, and when one gets excited, others in the area do too, although their excitement may be much less. If a cognitive demon is being used a great deal, it will be on its toes, but little used demons can go to sleep, and somehow need to be hollowed at very loud to wake up.

The Intention System after a while will set itself on autopilot for certain mental functions, which frees the conscious mind for other problems. The conscious mind can only focus on a small amount of material--it is like a computer which has limited memory. It is constantly in a state of redeployment, and the Intentions system has only a small sway over how the Attention part of the mind decides to focus. The Attention part constantly asks itself, which tasks can be relegated to habit. Then when the Intention system sends out cognitive search demons, they do not have to involve the conscious mind, because everything that is habitual is set up like a script, with families of "cognitive demon processes" already knowing the roles/relationships they are to play. (Again, Behavior modification is used to strengthen the relationships of demonic processes, and to make some well used and awake, so that certain behaviors become habits.) When our minds meditate or go into a hypnotic trance, what is occurring is that our conscious mind is delegating its limited computing memory for the focus of its attention upon one object. What happens to the cognitive demon processes that would normally take instructions from the conscious mind?

During meditation the untrained cognitive demon processes bubble up to the top of the conscious mind. However, the opposite happens during hypnosis. During hypnosis, the mind has made the decision (for whatever reasons) to accept control statements from the hypnotist. The mind has surrendered or at least temporarily or partially abdicated his or her position as the master of his or her Intention System. Some of this power is given away. The hypnotist now has access and control over many or all the cognitive demonic processes, including some that the person would not normally activate. Cognitive demon processes that are asleep or deeply buried can be accessed by the hypnotist, in a much quicker direct way than the Intention System would. By suggesting that the subject has a cat on his lap, the hypnotist is actually causing the recognition cognitive demon processes to wake up and act out their jobs to such an extent that the subject sees a cat. By suggesting that the subject's body stiffen, the hypnotist has gained control over those cognitive action demons that cause the body to stiffen. Age-regression brings up demons that are associated with the subject's childhood.

Although it is unpopular to admit publicly that the hypnotist has power over the subject, a close look at the process of how hypnosis works at the neuronal "cognitive demon process" level shows that the hypnotist has indeed been given power. In fact, the hypnotist has been given power to activate cognitive units of demon processes that the mind itself would allow to remain inactive or asleep. The mind would not normally use its ability to activate them. Today, it is politically incorrect to admit that the hypnotist has power to make an individual do what they wouldn't normally want to do, but unfortunately hypnosis does give this power.

PROGRAMMING AIDS

Because the programmers control the slave's life to such a high degree they can add other elements that move the brain into programmable states.

Fasting along with a high sugar intake will make the brain more suggestive. (The military also used this in basic training. This was done to this author at West Point during Beast Barracks, where during the first two weeks he ate all-total enough food for one regular meal; however, New Cadets were allowed to go to chapel and eat all the brownies, cookies and kool-aid they wanted.)

Physical discomforts and the chanting of rituals in witchcraft ceremonies are also ways to move the mind into programming states.

Lights, sounds (for instance repetitive beats such as with any rock music), and smells are all used to encourage the brain to go into a programmable state.

In the chapter on electronics, it discusses how the functions of the mind-body such as breathing and the heartbeat can be regulated by external stimuli ---that is lights and sounds which are electronically produced. If the repetitive beat is ranged between 45 to 72 beats per minute, many people will go into a programmable state with their eyes open. This is because this beat is close to the beat of the heart in a relaxed state.

Some secret Illum. programming centers have areas that are constructed for the greatest hypnotic sound and lighting effect. The child/ or adult victim is cut off from the world at these programming centers. The victims' freedom to walk outside into normal life depends upon their cooperation with the programmer(s).

Lullaby music is used as a cue for some alters of slaves to induce trance when their systems are older because the child alters still respond to the cue. Anything can be a cue, but it appears the programmers often pick cues that are naturally reinforced by the mind. The lullaby or carousel music is a good cue, because the lullaby is taking advantage of the natural desire of the brain to retreat from reality to the nostalgia of childhood fun. The retreat of the mind to childhood naturally evokes the helplessness and dependence that a child feels.

The programmers are powerful enough to place in cues that don't need natural reinforcement, but from observation it is apparent that they will often skillfully strengthen the hypnotic power by the choice of a cue which carries its own natural reinforcement. One supporting element in programming is that the programmer sets himself up as "god the creator" of the victim, or an alien of a far-advanced race.

In hypnotism, this fulfills the need that all hypnotic subjects must have faith and trust in their hypnotist. Hypnosis is subjective in nature. If the programmer is the creator of the alter being programmed, and the alter is additionally under a hypnotic drug that makes it willing to obey, it is easy to see how the victim lets go of all inhibitions, because "god" or this "superior alien" knows what is best. The better and stronger the relationship between the victim and his master programmer, the better the hypnotic commands work. If the slave sees the master as a religious guru prophet (or a great doctor) it enhances his willingness to accept hypnotic commands. Bear in mind that the slave is conditioned to love their master without reservation. Yes, the benevolent dictator has historically received the devotion of the masses, (and many of the Illuminati programmers are actually simply egotistical sadists).

USING HOLOGRAMS as an ACCESS AID

The Illuminati is now even resorting to creating talking hologram images to access their slaves with their hypnotic cues.

KEEPING THE MIND IN ALPHA STATE

The entire alter system of a Monarch slave has their sleep patterns controlled. Many alters are programmed not to get real sleep. They actually sleep in a hypnotic alpha-state sleep, or what may be called trance sleep.

Hypnotists (and brain researchers) will tell you that true sleep and a hypnotic sleep are not the same thing for the brain. Some alters (but not many) must stay awake 24 hours a day internally and carefully watch all that happens in the system of alters. Someone has to take the body and sleep--but whichever alters are set up to do it, they are hypnotically commanded to only sleep about three hours to insure that the mind stays in an alpha state easy to program. Because alters which do not hold the body "rest" mentally in a sense--when they take the body they are fresh. The mind dissociates when it is given unpleasant things to hear which it doesn't want to hear.

The electronic implants that send voices to victims are used to create dissociation within the slaves, plus certain implants and devices send specific electro-magnetic wave patterns to the mind to put the slave's mind into the alpha state. See chapter six for more on the mind-control implants.

PREPARING THE BRAIN

The programmer places the victim in an acute state of anxiety and guilt. The tension reduces the power of the judgement part of the mind. One of the tortures for slaves is to keep them from going to the bathroom and relieving themselves. This is part of the hypnotic programming package. The anxiety that this creates increases the power of the programming in the brain, because the anxiety causes slight malfunctions with the brain's judgment abilities. Mental and physical fatigue are also sought in the victim. For instance, water deprivation is common. (This was also done to the author at West Point, where one of this author's classmates was hospitalized for dehydration during Beast Barracks.) Offensive language also helps drive the mind into tension and encourages it into an alpha state.

EARLY TRAINING FOR SLAVES

The children who are being programmed are taught 4 IMPORTANT HYPNOTIC ABILITIES. These four abilities are a. relaxation, b. visualization, c. concentration, and d. projection, which work in handling the slave along with the alpha state.

Relaxation and visualization go hand in hand each enhancing each other. When given a good pleasant image to visualize, the victim relaxes, which leads to the hypnotic concentration, which then produces good projection. Initially, the child victim is given drugs that induce euphoria and deep relaxation. They are then taught to work toward that drug euphoria by going to it mentally. They develop the ability to go into that euphoria mentally as a trained behavior. Many of the children will have their training in visualization and concentration reinforced when they go to public schools, many of which are now involved in the programming process. To teach the child concentration and visualization, the child is given an apple and trained to visualize it. The first time, the child will be given drugs which will enhance the experience and perception greatly to around 100 times the perception without the drugs. There is no pain involved in this early programming at around the age of 3 or 4. After the child has gone through the visualization of the apple in the drugged state he or she will work toward the mental ability to visualize it intensely without the drugs. The visualization script used with the apple (in both the drugged and undrugged exercises) will vary slightly from programmer to programmer, yet will be close to the following:

"VISUALIZE AN APPLE. HOLD IT IN YOUR HANDS; TURN IT AROUND; FEEL IT. FEEL THE SHAPE, THE SIZE, THE WEIGHT, THE TEXTURE. NOTICE THE COLOR, THE REFLECTION OF LIGHT ON ITS SKIN. BRING IT TO YOUR NOSE AND SMELL IT. BITE INTO IT, TASTE IT; HEAR THE CRUNCH AS YOUR TEETH SINK IN. EAT THE APPLE; FEEL IT SLIDE DOWN YOUR THROAT. SEE IT GROW SMALLER. WHEN YOU HAVE EATEN IT DOWN TO THE CORE, LET IT DISAPPEAR."

By the way, an apple training incident very similar to this (which is given by the Illuminati to child slaves from the ages 2 to 4), strangely turned up occurring in a setting that the author, who never was a slave nor never in the occult, found himself in when this author was a 4-H counselor at a 4-H camp as a 16 year old. The first thing all the counselors were given was an apple exercise so that we could appreciate each camper for what he or she was. The person who led the exercise was a psychologist. Where had he learned it? The apple visualization must be done to a standard of excellence by the child victim. The victim's life depends upon learning to visualize vividly, so that the internal structures (internal mental images) it builds within the mind will stay strong and firm.

The programmers want the child to have good visualization so they will work with the child to have the most successful experience. For instance, the child will be offered a variety of apples to look at, yellow, green, red etc. The child can choose the apple that it likes so that its visualization exercises will be the most successful. The entire imagery of an internal system will be built upon the foundation of the child's ability to visualize an apple. The child will be taken through a succession of exercises where the child learns to visualize the apple in greater and greater detail using all the senses. Eventually, the child is able to visualize his or her apple to the point that the child can dissect or chop the apple up in any way and reconstruct it mentally. The internal seeds of the apple can be seen brilliantly by the child. Upon this ability to visualize, the programmer will then teach the child that the apple can become anything the child wants, a river, a couch, a book etc. The five seeds of the apple will be turned into 5 castles. This is why essentially all Illuminati Mind-controlled slaves have 5 major castles in their system of programming. One approach by therapists has been to cast out/remove the castles. However, the castle imagery is based upon the apple seeds which is based on the apple. The real thing to deal with for therapists is the apple. If the castle is returned to its original image of being an apple seed, and the rest of the apple-and its tree imagery dealt with, then some progress can be made. Unfortunately, not being aware of the original imagery, the therapists have been frustrating themselves with the superficial imagery rather than the foundational imagery.

Another script for teaching the young 2 to 4 year old slaves simple visualization is to have the child close his or her eyes and imagine that they are looking at a white wall or blank screen. Then they practice visualizing simple geometric shapes, and then visualize the screen in different colors, and then finally visualize the objects changing colors.

MAGICAL TRAINING ON THE STARLIGHT LEVEL

The Illuminati begin training the child victim to work at the starlight level. This is called magical training. The child's abilities to relax, visualize, concentrate and project are then harnessed in the alpha state by "MAGICKAL TRAINING" which opens up the STARLIGHT CONSCIOUSNESS. Starlight consciousness is the other way of knowing that which belongs to the right hemisphere, and it allows the victim to make contact with the "DIVINE WITHIN". The Divine within the victim is actually the generational spirits, which are placed in during the Moon Child ceremonies described in detail in Vol. 2.

The generational spirits are laid in to help build the programming and to guard it. However, as in so much spiritual work, the victim's (technically speaking, the alter's) will & thoughts work hand in hand with the spirits. The child must learn to visualize and participate in the mental building of the internal worlds, structures, etc. However, the demons will be strategically placed to protect the structures once the programming is built into the mind. (For more understanding of this see Cisco's section on "Programming, foundational, destruction of".)

FINETUNING

The child victim's mind is FINETUNED. This means that the child can function excellently at visualization, relaxation, concentration, projection, while in the alpha state and can work with their subconscious mind. The mental work done in the subconscious can not be retrieved easily. Only through outside assistance or special training can most people access what is done at the starlight level of the mind. The programmers are using the child's abilities with its 5 acute senses to develop the 6th sense (which is its ability to work in the Starlight consciousness, which includes such mental activity such as psychic abilities--which will be discussed in other locations in this book.) Enhancing the mind so that it can work in the subconscious area called the starlight consciousness is referred to by many insiders as astral.

THE MONARCH PROGRAMMING SCRIPT FOR OVER THE RAINBOW

One of the most important concepts of the programmers is having slaves "go over the rainbow." Although in recent years other methods have been substituted for this, there are many hundreds of thousands of slaves for whom "going over the rainbow" is part of their programming. What is the script for programming this?

The PROGRAMMING SCRIPT FOR GOING OVER THE RAINBOW

(Three dots in this script do not indicate missing parts, but rather pauses. In other words, pauses are indicated by three dots.)

INDUCTION TRAINING SCRIPT

"BREATHE DEEP --- YOU ARE FLOATING DOWN ... DOWN ... ON A BEAUTIFUL RED CLOUD, AND YOUR WHOLE BODY IS RED -- AS YOU GO DRIFTING AND FLOATING .... ROCKING GENTLY ... DEEPER ... AND DEEPER ... DOWN ... [this repeated, one time, for each color of cloud-orange, yellow, green, blue, and violet clouds.] "LAND VERY GENTLY ... VERY SOFTLY ... IN THE CENTER OF A ROUND, BLACK PEARL. SEE IT GLOWING, SOFTLY, GENTLY ... NOW TURN AND FACE THE EAST ... AND THEN THE SOUTH ... AND THEN THE WEST ... AND THEN THE NORTH OPEN ALL OF YOUR INNER SENSES." [The rainbow gives the much abused victim of mind-control and trauma, a safe mental place to travel to; and this serves as a "home base" for the mind to return to when things get difficult. If the programming begins to be destroyed and a deeper alter experiences real life--its coping mechanism to face the harsher realities of life will be a knee-jerk reaction to go to safety over the rainbow.]

BRINGING THE SLAVE OUT OF TRANCE (Switching to the FRONT PERSONALITIES after programming)

After the slave has been switched to deeper personalities who are in trance in order to have the slave a. be programmed b. be programmed & carry out a mission, c. go to a ritual, then it is important that the programmer takes time to get the slave to emerge slowly and gently from their altered state. The induction process is reversed. The repetition of trances will reinforce the depth of the trance state, and keep the undetectable slavery operating smoothly:

"IN THE PEARL, PREPARE TO AWAKEN. WHEN YOU AWAKE, YOU WILL FEEL REFRESHED, ALERT, RENEWED, AND FILLED WITH ENERGY. YOU WILL REMEMBER ALL THAT YOU HAVE EXPERIENCED. NOW TURN AND FACE THE EAST ... THEN THE SOUTH ... THEN THE WEST ... THEN THE NORTH. [this helps the slave orient themselves internally]

TAKE A DEEP BREATH ... INHALE ... EXHALE ...

"YOU ARE FLOATING UP ... UP ... ON A BEAUTIFUL VIOLET CLOUD, AND YOUR WHOLE BODY IS VIOLET AS YOU DRIFT GENTLY UPWARD ... "ON A BEAUTIFUL BLUE

CLOUD ... UP ... UP ... AND YOUR WHOLE BODY IS BLUE AND YOU ARE BEGINNING TO AWAKEN GENTLY AND YOU DRIFT GENTLY UP ... ON A BEAUTIFUL GREEN CLOUD ... AND YOUR WHOLE BODY IS GREEN ... AS YOU DRIFT GENTLY ... UP ... UP ... "ON A BEAUTIFUL YELLOW CLOUD ... GETTING MORE AND MORE AWAKE ... AND YOUR WHOLE BODY IS YELLOW ... AS YOU DRIFT GENTLY ... UP ... UP ...

"ON A BEAUTIFUL ORANGE CLOUD ... FILLED WITH ENERGY AND VITALITY ... YOUR WHOLE BODY IS ORANGE ... AS YOU FLOAT UP GENTLY ... "ON A BEAUTIFUL RED

CLOUD ... ALMOST FULLY AWAKE NOW ... AND YOUR WHOLE BODY IS RED AS YOU FLOAT GENTLY ...

"STAY ON THE RAINBOW ... [at this point the script for the slave's programming or mission or ritual will be placed into the mind].

After the programming session, the mission, or the ritual the handler/or programmer finishes...

"LEAVING THE MEMORY IN THE BLACK PEARL AND CLOSING AND SEALING THE BLACK PEARL. YOU WILL REMEMBER ONLY THOSE DETAILS THAT I TELL YOU TO REMEMBER. AND IN A MOMENT YOU WILL COUNT TO TEN AND GO BACK INTO YOUR SPACE, AND RED 2001-A [whatever the code is for the alter] WILL RETURN."

DEEP TRANCE PROGRAMMING

If we rate trance depths on a scale of 1 to 13, then the deep trance that is being described here is 7-10. At this 7-10 depth, the person must be constantly watched. The victim is turned on his side so that the victim will continue to breathe. If the person monitoring has doubts whether the slave is alive, the programming staff will poke the lungs and neck. The person's breathing will be encouraged by the programmer breathing along with the person being programmed as he says "BREATHE ... BREATHE ... BREATHE". This is important because at this level the slave is so tranced their body can forget to breathe.

COLOR PROGRAMMING

While we are still on the subject of the rainbow and its colors, and before we continue onto other parts of the hypnotic programming process, let's deal with color programming.

When Illuminati slaves are being programmed as little children, they usually will get music and color programming. Most readers are like this author, in that they are not interested in learning magic. However, because this author (Fritz Springmeier) was interested in helping victims understand what's been done to them, it was important to dive into trying to understand the thinking of the occult world in regards to colors.

If I write that the occult world views yellow as a healing color, and blue as a relaxing color, and purple (violet) as a spiritually enlightened color, that is not because I want to teach that as a doctrine, but so that therapists can begin to understand the hidden mannerisms & thought patterns of these powerful generational occult families, who believe in such odd practices as child sacrifice.

In the 1940's, as the Illuminati were applying scientific investigation to their ancient skills in mind-control, a number of researchers investigated color psychology. Cecil Stokes' color research on the influence of colors on the mind led to the Auratone films, which were used to treat the "mentally ill".

Walt Disney Studios produced one of the best occult attempts to free associate color, light and music in their movie Fantasia, especially Fantasia's opening selection of Stokowski's adaption of Bach's "Toccata and Fugue in D minor". Walt Disney also used selections of music from the Satanist composer Igor Stravinsky in Fantasia. Igor Stravinsky is an anarchy-espousing Satanist. Fantasia was a long labor of occult devotion for Walt Disney and his studios. It took many years to create the film, and when it was finished, it was used as a programming foundation for alter systems. (Chapter 5 will have more on Disney. Chapter 5 will also give a very detailed script for HOW Fantasia has been used as the primary foundation programming tool.) Disney's Dick Tracy movie is also a classic example of how color is employed in a movie which is used covertly for mind-control programming.

The five primary areas of occult thinking that were investigated by this author in terms of color programming were:
1. witchcraft books such as Raymond Buckland's Practical Color Magick,
2. an extensive study of several New Age Groups such as the I AM Movement, and Church Universal & Triumphant (CUT) using hundreds of documents that ex-insiders of these groups provided,
3. masonic & rosicrucian sources, such as Manly P. Hall's book The Secret Teachings of All Ages, and
4. Metaphysical books in general such as the excellent The Rainbow Book being a collection of essays & illustrations devoted to Rainbows in particular & Spectral Sequences in general focusing on the meaning of color (physical & metaphysically) from Ancient to Modem Times. The Rainbow Book was done by the Fine Arts Museums of San Francisco in assoc. with Shambhala of Berkeley & London, 1975.

And finally, the last primary source -but not least- was interviews with an ex-programmer. What did I find out? After lots of weeding, I have some siftings from these sources to share. In Buckland's Practical Color Magick, we learn about a type of Voodoo called Poppet dolls. These dolls are made according to the color that is appropriate for the person's problem. For instance, they make a green poppet doll if the person needs help with finances. The name of the person is written on the doll according to the color that corresponds to their astrological birthdate. For instance, Leo is orange, and Pisces is Indigo. Those who need success are advised by Buckland to make a "Color Treasure Map" which is simply a collage of the things they want, making sure that the pictures are bright colors.

This is another example of color magic. Buckland provides a Color-Number Code as follows:

1 = Red; 2 = Orange; 3= Yellow; 4 = Green; 5=Blue; 6=Indigo; 7=Violet; 8=Rose; 9 = Gold

The letters of the alphabet then are corresponded to these 9 numbers and by adding up the numbers in someone's name (numerology), Buckland tells us we can get the name's Color from such a process.

What did I learn of value from Buckland? some tips on how occultists assign colors to numbers and objects. For the average person these witchcraft teachings are simply trite imaginations. Even so, the fact remains for those of us confronting Occult mind-control, colors are important to total-mind-control programmers of the Illuminati. Colors are important to their world-view. A programmer who knew color magic would likely use color magic in their programming, programming scripts and codes. Now, both you and I know some more about how to second guess the programmer's mind. (By the way, Color programming was dealt with in a major way in Vol. 2, but the tips in this chapter may also be useful.)

THE ASSOCIATION OF COLORFUL SIGHTS, SOUNDS, RHYTHM & DANCE.

Dance has been associated with color from ancient times, to greek and medieval courts up to modern times with the use of colored floodlights. Keys in music have been associated with colors by many famous musicians. Beethoven referred to B minor as the black key. Schubert compared E minor to a "girl robed in white with a rose-red bow on her breast". Rimsley-Korsakov interpreted the keys of C, D, A, F, & F# major as white, yellow, rosy, green, and grayish-green. Handel had his own idea of how the keys related to the colors. The brighter hues of a color have been associated by some with the major scale, and the more subdued hues of a color with the minor. Goethe stated that a painting of powerful effect was like a piece of music with a sharp key, while a painting with a muted effect was like music in a flat key.

Certain colors have been associated with violin music. In Wassily Kandinsky's book The Art of Spiritual Harmony, we learn a great deal about color and music. The following comes from Kandinsky's observations, and may relate to Mengele's programming. The ringing notes of a violin have been associated with a cool red. The largo of an old violin is associated with orange. The placid middle tones of the violin are associated with absolute green. A dark blue is like a cello. White is like the pauses in music that temporarily break the melody. Black represents "the final pauses, after which any continuation of melody see the dawn of another world."

The Rainbow Book is definitely the most comprehensive book this author has seen on the significance of color both physically and metaphysically. An interesting chart is given on page 125, which examines the relationship of the frequencies of electromagnetic waves in the visible light spectrum with an octave of music just above middle C. In order to make the comparison (which is charted below) the light frequencies which are 1012 are written without the powers of ten and taken down 40 to match the note octaves. This gives us a chart which we will arrange by:

COLOR/ORIG. FREK - 40 // OCTAVE FREK/NOTE

Using this arrangement we get:

Very dark red/391 .3 = 392/G NOTE darkish red/418 = 415/G# note

Orangish red/445 440/A note light orange/464 = 466/A # note yellow green/495 = 494/B note green/ 523 = 523/ C note

Bluish green/555 = 553/ C# note Indigo/573-600 = 587/D note

Indigo violet-light violet/618-627 = D# note

Dark violet/655-673 = 659/E note

Very dark violet/682 = 698/F note

Although there is no single one-to-one correspondence between music and color, because there are different patterns to consider and the role of association is such a complex issue, there are several things that naturally suggest themselves: an increase in pitch does seem to suggest an increase in brightness. An increase in brightness also is suggested by an increase in tempo. Colors also fit the mood of a piece of music. A mass of color can suggest the musical ground.

Musical intervals have also been related by the ancients to the orbits of the planets. This began with the spherical theory of the cosmos by Pythagoras, where the different astrological bodies made different sounds. Another correspondence with merit is to associate colors with "properties", & then associate with music intervals, then assoc. with related cords, and related planets, and then associate with other things.

For instance, Orange would be associated with the Sun, Energy, Glory, and Power. In turn, it would be associated with

Re (pronounced "Ray" in music, the whole tone, D). Its related cord would be minor, and its related planet would be the Sun "Apollo." Violet would be death, separation, advanced spirituality. It would be associated with Ti ("Tee") in music, the Maj. 7th, B, and its related planet would be the moon "Diana". There is no way all the different associations can be reviewed here. The chinese have had a number of music-color association schemes, as well as the Hindis, the Tibetans, and others. Is this section on color going somewhere with these associations? Yes, Joseph Mengele, the original Dr. Green (the name Green got passed on to a least one of his proteges), played the violin and piano while doing the color programming to slaves. He was the original master at associating both a tone or chord with a particular color or color scheme. He loved using Fantasia for programming.

LIGHT & COLOR

According to Hilton Hotema's book Ancient Sun God (Mokelumne Hill, CA: Health Research, 1956), light & fire are associated with Sun worship. "Pyra" is Greek for fire, and "Midos" means measure. Pyramid is a combination of the greek words pyra and midos, which together meant "light-measures". In other words, the pyramid was the eternal ascending flame, the spark returning to its maker. The eternal flame of Prometheus is a recurrent theme within all the modern revolutions (which by the way were all created secretly by the occult hierarchy).

The Tower of Babel most likely followed the pattern which the ancient babylonian cylinders say was used by the Babylonians in building their temples. Each level was dedicated to one of the 7 planets, and was built in that color. In other words the Tower of Babel looked like a rainbow. The lowest was to Saturn and was black. The next was to Jupiter and was orange. The next was to Mars and was red. The fourth was the sun and was yellow. The fifth was Venus and was green. The sixth was Mercury and was blue, and the top or seventh level would be white.

A good example of color programming and a New Age group which is involved with Illuminati/government mind-control is Church Universal & Triumphant. In the Covert Action Information Bulletin, No. 30, Summer, 1988, Church Universal & Triumphant was exposed as a conduit of CIA funds. Another clue as to how CUT connects in is that Elizabeth Clare Prophet, CUT's prophetess, speaks in Masonic emples.

E.C. Prophet claims she is Marie Antoinette. (One of the first Illuminati programs that this author ran into when working with programmed multiples was Marie Antoinette programming.) Another obvious CIA asset (who is not part of CUT) has been directing implant victims to go to CUT and solve their implant problem by seeking the "I AM force" within them. (The I AM is a system programmed into slaves.) Initiates into CUT have received a letter, "Keeper of the Flame: the need for harmony and love between all the master's servants united in a common effort cannot be overemphasized. Working and serving together, we form a mandala of light through which the masters of the Great White Brotherhood will awaken humanity." (Quote from a letter by CUT Chairman of the Outreach Committee Michael Veys to CUT's Fraternity of the Keepers of the Flame, c. 1980.) Elizabeth Claire Prophet's "Fraternity of Keepers of the Flame" as she calls her initiates learn such things as astrology, crystals, white magic, color magic, Hinduism (reincarnation, karma, meditation, chakra points), how to decree, how to dress (for instance what color to where at what time), and how to become divine at Summit University.

Elizabeth Clare Prophet (that's the name she wanted) established Summit University, and CUT's headquarters in Colorado Springs, a house in Santa Barbara, and an underground fortress for the end times in a valley in Montana. Details about Elizabeth Clare Prophet and her organization are hard to come by. If a person gets serious about being part of her organization, they are expected to make a once in a life-time gift of everything they have to the CUT and its head Elizabeth Clare Prophet. (Sources: Notes, Summit University Student and Confidential Interview.) After that they are expected to tithe (one-tenth). Church Universal and Triumphant Tenets, Colorado Springs, CO: 1975, p.12 under Art. XII Law of the Tithe. In return, they are initiated into what I call "the supreme Grand Flattery", "You shall become an enlightened God."

One of the programming tricks by the Mind-control programmers is to have some of the alters, incl. front alters believe that they are divine gods. Although members are told they are divine, when people on E.C. Prophet's staff got revelations from the Ascended Masters that she channels, she threatened to expel them if they talked about their revelations. E.C. Prophet does not want any one else to prophecy in her organization. CUT makes their mind-controlled slaves think that they are too smart and intuitive to ever be deceived. In this way, they use New Age ideas and the person's pride to blind them to the fact the person is a mind-controlled slave who is fooled much of the time. When students are invited onto staff it is a commitment. They are told, "Your life will never be your own again, but was it ever your own?" They have already been taught "Ascension Keys".

Elizabeth Clare Prophet tells her students that to Ascend to Godhead is their birthright, the divine right of every person. (see Pearls of Wisdom, Vol. X, No. 23, June 4, 1967, The Summit Lighthouse, p. 41 -"...has robbed men of the birthright of their Ascension...") This matches what the Illuminati teach their people. See also Pearls of Wisdom, Vol. X, No. 19, (May 7, 1967), The Summit Lighthouse, p. 24 - "The Divine Right is the Immortal Plan...Inherent pattern of unique Christ manifestation..." In the Ascension Dossier of Serapis Bey initiates are told "The capacity of the externalized self must be given in toto." Also-"You must abandon your past to God." In Lanello's Message(a channeled message), 4/20/73 the students are told, "You do not have to wait for the carnal mind to evolve, for the carnal mind will never evolve. It must be put off and cast into the Flame." (See Lanello 4/20/73 in the Pearls of Wisdom, Vol. 16, #32, 8/12/1973.)

After emptying themselves of all their past and of what they knew, the initiates are then restructured by CUT. In Serapis, Ascension Class they are told, "The Ascension Flame is the Flame of Mother."

SPECIAL COLORS

It can't be overemphasized that Green is the highest color in Satanism--it is Satan's color. It is not by accident that green has been used in uniforms, although the decision also was dictated by its advantage in camouflage. In the Omega computer programming a CODE GREEN for many victims means "self-destruct", the ultimate sacrifice for one's satanic programming.

Interviews with witches, as well as a person in witchcraft who the Masons tried to recruit, and an ex-member of CUT, and an ex-member of similar New Age group called the I AM movement reveals that they all wear special colors of clothes on certain days. Due to the large influx of new converts, it has been difficult for CUT to keep up the teachings on wearing different colored clothing during different times of the day, and for different days. Newer converts may be unaware of this teaching. The colors of purple and white are especially esteemed. The magical properties that Masons & New Agers believe are intrinsic to purple is why the 33rd degree has written books using purple, and several New Agers have published books on purple paper. The programmers also manipulate such things so that child alters believe that color "magic" has accomplished things.

HEALING BY CORRECT VIBRATIONS & RAYS

Masonic Sources match CUT teachings-

· "The second method of healing was by vibration. The inharmonies of the bodies were neutralized by chanting spells and intoning the sacred names or by playing upon musical instruments and singing. Sometimes articles of various colors were exposed to the sight of the sick, for the ancients recognized, at least in part, the principle of color therapeutics, now in the process of rediscovery." Masonic Hermetic Qabbalistic & Rosicrucian Symbolical Philosophy, p. CXI

· "50. "The force of the obligation is therefore in the obligation and not in the reason. As a matter of fact, the real reason is scientific to the last analysis; scientific to a degree beyond the penetration, up to the present time, of the 'radiant matter' of the Roentgen Ray of Modern Science. The Word concerns the science of rhythmic vibrations, and is the key to the equilibrium of all forces and to the harmony of Eternal Nature." Ancient Mystic Oriental Masonry, p.48.

USING HYPNOSIS TO HEAL THE SLAVE AFTER ABUSE.

Sometimes the handlers "TRADE DOWN" the symptoms that result from abuse so that the slave will heal quicker, others attempt to remove the symptoms immediately. For burns, the hypnotist can suggest cooling. For other injuries, suggestions for warmth are applied. For bleeding suggestions for stopping blood flow are used.

REINFORCING THE PROGRAMMING WITH A DECOGNITION PROCESS

The programmer has gotten the results that he wants via drugs, torture, hypnosis, and deception. Now he must build in back-ups to insure the programming holds up.

The decognition process has 3 steps.

Step 1 is to program the slave to get inadequate sleep, eat poorly, and work hard. It is called REDUCTION OF ALERTNESS.

Step 2 is to create confusion in the mind via programmed confusion using a series of alters. The person may go into revolving from one alter to another, or may have alters coming and going with conflicting messages so that the person remains in a PROGRAMMED CONFUSED STATE. In military "training" conflicting orders would be rapidly issued to confuse the mind.

Step 3 is to cause the mind to have something simple to focus on so that it goes into a FLAT STATE. In the military, this author became aware that the beat of the drum and marching would shift the mind to a flat state. For centuries the military have known that they could shut off the critical thinking of the mind and put their soldiers into a flat, non-thinking state by training them to the beat of the drum and the sound of marching feet. Now you know why those British Red-coats marched so non-thinking into the barrels of American guns in battles such as New Orleans and Bunker Hill. The mind feels good to shift into this simple flat state. The brain quits thinking and withdraws into a state that it quits thinking except for what the controllers want it to think. This is why marching has been so important in military training. Chanting and singing will also move the mind into this flat state, which is why the French Foreign Legion requires its men -to sing sing sing. When this author lived in the Indian subcontinent, I saw Hindu holy men who had meditated in a flat alpha state so long their brains no longer functioned in anything but a flat state. This non-thinking flat state is believed by Hindus to be nirvana, but God didn't give us minds to throw away and waste, but to use. He gave us independent thoughts so that we could show our love for Him by choosing to love Him. God didn't want brainwashed followers, which is what some of the churches think God is calling for. The programmers can induce a mood or state of mind hypnotically which will make retrieval of something learned dependent upon going into that particular mood or state.

And THE BEAT GOES ON...

It is clear that some of the psychologists have NOT got wind that the mind-control is being exposed. The American Journal of Clinical Hypnosis had a recent article (10/1996, p. 105-114) promoting the use of the Wizard of Oz metaphor in hypnosis with "treatment-resistant" children. For a therapist/hypnotist to hypnotically use Wizard of Oz material on child victims of mind-control will get a response from them! The authors of the article say that they use the authoritarian approach to hypnosis (p. 107) for "treatment-resistant" children. The Wizard of Oz metaphor is given on page 108 of the article, which boils down to: the Straw Man, Tin Man, Lion, Dorothy and Toto were surprised at their success- and that they already had brains, a heart, & courage.

HYPNOTIC CODES, CUES AND TRIGGERS

This chapter will provide some more of the hypnotic codes, cues, triggers or whatever one wants to call these words, noises, and sensory inputs that manipulate these poor victims turned into Monarch robots. The reader is encouraged to refer to Vol. 2 for the principle list of codes. Other chapters will explain about the structures these codes go to, and also the spiritual dimensions of these codes and structures.

Another way to see things is to recognize that the programmers have created "power words" to which they have attached memory and programming. If a de-programmer observes closely the word usage of the victim, you will begin to spot power words of the abuser, for instance, "follow the yellow brick road".

Unfortunately, people who are not initiated into the arcane world of handshakes, grips, codes, signals and cues allow the appearance of these things to be interpreted from their own frame of reference. Usually, because these events are not perceived as being significant, outsiders forget them immediately and therefore remain oblivious to some of the most overt clues.

Once the reader is aware of the types of programming themes used: the Wizard of Oz, Alice In Wonderland, and Star Wars and Star Trek, etc., he will begin to realize our entire American culture has been transformed into one big mind-control programming center during the second half of the twentieth century!

Unfortunately for the victim, apparently harmless little things, for instance, the arrival of flowers to their hospital bedside, a dead bird on their doorstep, or the words "NEW BEGINNINGS" and "NEW LIFE" may signify programming commands. One Illuminati slave in this area has started a large church called NEW BEGINNINGS. The name was not by accident.

A cipher is when symbols are used to represent letters. One can use letter frequencies to break ciphers. There are charts for letter frequencies for the chief languages. Likewise, there are frequencies to codewords. The Illuminati's intelligence agencies have programmed thousands upon thousands of slaves. There are only so many code words to pick from and some of these code words are favorites. In the previous book many of their favorite code words were listed, but words starting with A's, B's, T's, U's, V's, 'W's, X's, and Y's, were not given and will be now. (A plus sign indicates other words are attached to the root word.) From the co-author Fritz Springmeier's experience, the following is a continuation of favorite code words that have been used to program slaves with:

AARON, ABBY, ABIGAIL, ABLE, ABNER, ABRAHAM, ACACIA. ACE, ADAM, ADELPHI, AGATE, AIR +, ALABASTER, ALADIN, ALBERT, ALFA or ALPHA. ALICE, ALLEY CAT, ALLIGATOR, AMOS, AMY, ANGEL, ANNA, ANTHONY, APACHE, APOLLO, APOSTLE, APPLE +, ARCHER, ARGUS, ARK, ARROW, ASK +, ASTER, ATHANTIS, ATLAS, AUDREY, AURORA. AUTUMN +, AZTEC, B +, BABE, BABY, BACK ROOM, BACK BONE, BAD, BAKER, BALD, BAMBI, BANANA, BANJO, BANKNOTE, BARBARA. BARK, BARON, BEACH +, BEAST, BECKY, BEE HIVE, BEETHOVEN, BELSHAZZER, BERMUDA, BERTHA, BETA, BETSY, BETTY, BEULAH, BEWITCH, BICYCLE, BIG BROTHER, BINGO, BIRD DOG, BIRTHDAY, BLACK, BLACK +, BLACK

SHEEP, BLACK WIDOW, BLANCA, BLONDIE, BLOODHOUND, BLOODY +, BLUE +, BOA. BOB CAT, BOMBAY, BONANZA. BOODLE, BORAX, BOXCAR, BRASS +, BRIDGET, BROOMSTICK, BUCCANEER, BUICK, BULL, BULLDOG, BULLFROG, BUMBLEBEE, BUNNY, BUTTERCUP, BUZZARD, BYRON, T-BIRD, TADPOLE, TALISMAN, TAN, TANGO, TANYA, TARA, TARZAN, TEACUP, TEARDROP, TEEPEE, TERRIER, TERRY, TESTAMENT, THOR, THREE SISTERS, THUNDER, THUNDERBOLT, THUNDERCLAP, THUNDERFLASH, THUNDERSTORM, TIAMET, TIGER, TILLIE, TITAN, TOM CAT, TONI or TONY, TOPAZE, TOPSOIL, TORNADO, TOTENKOPF, TRINITY, TURTLE, UGLY, ULYSSES, UMBRELLA, UNCLE +, UNDERDOG, UNICORN, UNIFORM, URSULA, VAGABOND, VAMPIRE, VANCOUVER, VARSITY, VELVET, VENUS, VERONICA, VICKY, VICTOR, VIKING, VIOLA, VIOLET, VIPER, VIRGINIA VOODOO, VULCAN, VULTURE, WAGON WHEEL, WALDORF,

WALLFLOWER, WANDA. WARRIOR, WASP, WATCHDOG, WEASEL, WHISKEY, WHITE +, WIDOW, WILD CAT, WILLOW, WINNIE, WINTER +, WIZARD, WOLF,

WOLF +, WYOMING, X-FORCE, X-RAY, XYZ, YANKEE, YANKEE DOODLE, YELLOW, YOGI, & YO YO.

The intelligence organizations prefer to code a single project with a single word, and an ongoing operation with two words. A nickname of something will consist of two words. The reader needs to bear several things in mind. First, the programmers generally have intelligent, well sounding codes, that do form patterns. For instance, a woman's name from the Bible will be used as a code, with subparts or subcodes having other female names from the Bible. Deeper Illuminati parts will have goddess & god names, and king & queen names for cult alters. These are the names the handler or cult uses--NOT their access codes.

The codes for slaves follow patterns. There are standard and unique codes. During the 1940's through the 1960's there were only perhaps a dozen American master programmers travelling around. (After that the number of programmers appears to get quite large.) The master programmers would lay in the foundational programs and codes. They developed the scripts. The codes and systems used from system to system do follow patterns. The child's creativity & their purpose in life would contribute to the uniqueness of the programming. Each child visualizes differently and the programmer works with the child's mind.

The master Illuminati programmer would allow the handler--the "Daddy" figure in life to have the day-to-day ownership. The Daddy figure, often the actual pedophile father of the child victim, would be allowed to put in his own codes in the sexual part of the system. Some Daddy figures used their own songs, their own poetry and their own interests in this area of the coding. In other words, most of the system's codes will reflect the master programmer (such as Dr. Mengele), and the sexual part of the system will reflect the "Daddy" figure's programming.

The standard method for many of the memory and alter codes is to use a combination of the date of the child's birth along with the date of the trauma for part of the code. A color will then be attached to this, to produce a color-alpha-numeric code combination. These are placed into the internal computers. The standard computer codes were given in Vol. 2. They can be used to temporarily stop programming to give a victim some respite and a chance to regroup. The programmers did not especially care if the front part of a system is discovered and although they hide the anarchy (coven level) witchcraft alters, they don't hide them like they do the hierarchy alters. The coven alters have simplistic codes. The hierarchy alters which are placed in another area of the system and much deeper, receive a great deal of cabalistic codes and mathematical codes. You will not find the mathematical codes in the front part of a system. The internal programming alters have the power to change codes if they need to protect the programming. They will have to hypnotically work with alters when they trance out at night.

In other words, most of their programming of front alters will be done when a system lies down for "sleep"--more accurately described as lies down "for trance." If the internal alters change many codes, in their efforts to protect the system, they will even make it difficult for the handler/programmer to get into the system. The science of Ciphers developed rotors that require lines to line up. Some simple schemes using this principle appear in some Monarch systems. This is part of the science of structuring. Intelligence codes often come from the Bible or popular fiction books. The deeper codes are occult words, often in foreign languages such as Arabic, which is an important language in the upper occult world. Slaves will be given COVER NAMES for ops, and often males receive female names and vice versa.

The patterns used in programming slaves will represent the world view of the programmer. If the interests of the programmer are known, that will be a major clue to the codes they like to install. For this reason, it would be worthwhile to review the access clearance codes that are used for external security of some agencies, because these same types of clearance codes may be found in mind-controlled slaves.

A BIGOT list is a list of names of those who have clearance to a particular set of information. Within a slave there would be numerous BIGOT lists, because persons (personalities) are compartmentalized somewhat like the CIA and the Puzzle Palace (NSA). Agency Codes for clearances include B, C3, K, L, M, N, 0, T, COSMIC, MAJIC (MJ), SI, SCI, and Staff D. (As this author has only examined these secret societies from the outside, some insiders may know of other clearances. In other words, it would be foolish to think that this clearance code list is comprehensive, but it has hit upon the major clearances.)

The exercise in judging whether a person can have access to compartmentalized information is called ADJUDICATION. A group of persons (agents) working under one handler is called a NET. The FBI which also uses mind-controlled slaves likes to call its groups NETS.

FUNNY NAME is intelligence slang for a pseudonym. GRANNY is a CIA asset used in the US which is not under their direct funding. The American military-intelligence groups publish a periodical called JANAP 299 which lists the cover names (code names) for many of the ongoing projects, groups, or installations.

There are other code books too. C can stand for Controller or Control, which means the person(s) handling a mind-controlled slave. A person, who is neither a controller, nor a slave, nor asset, but who consciously advances the desires of the controller is called a TRUSTED CONTACT. Sexual slaves would not be expected to respond to such a term, but a middle level slave/agent of an intelligence agency might be familiar with this type of intelligence jargon.

The BIRD was a name for Fort Holabird, MD where intelligence operatives were trained as well as subjected to mind-control. DIA used the code name EMERALD for drug-trafficking. Boy, does this code word have a double meaning. Since the DIA, which is playing both sides, also is involved with drug smuggling & using Monarch slaves heavily coded with EMERALD type coding. Very shortly, we will provide more of the Monarch hypnotic cues (codes) for the multitude of functions that a Monarch's mind must carry out. These cues are reinforced as a conditioned response by the programmer. In other words the response becomes so well trained that it becomes automatic.

The type of programming which is placed in a slave varies. Remember, for intelligence operations the slave will have to have BONA FIDES, which are codes to allow two people to meet. All slaves are given CONTROL SIGNS which allow them to indicate via a code that they are in trouble. A RECOGNITION signal allows two people to make contact. For instance, the handler might fly his distinctive sounding plane over a slave's house in a pre-arranged signal. It might also be a particular colored scarf, and a particular set of phrases. A GO-AWAY code is a prearranged signal that means it is unwise to make contact. The go-away signal may be simply placing one's hands in one's pocket or turning the porch lights off. A "GO TO GROUND" signal means to go into hiding. A BLACK ENVELOPE, which is in actuality a black-colored envelope, has been used by intelligence to hold the real name of an agent being used. In the case of multiples, a chief of a station might have a BLACK ENVELOPE with the actual name of a mind-controlled agent being used in his field of operations. A MAYDAY BOOK exists for Illuminati and Intelligence slaves which allows them to call if they are about to be arrested. A telephone number is left open for just this purpose.

Also common universal Illuminati codes can be used by the slave to get set free from police and judges. BACKSTOPPING is an intelligence term for setting up proof to support the cover stories the intelligence agencies give their agents and assets. Some of the programmed multiples they use, need BACKSTOPPING.

Within the Jehovah's Witnesses, especially their headquarters, the Illuminati uses Enochian language to program with. With Druidic branches Druidic symbols are used. With the Jewish groups, Hebrew is used. Other languages are also used. An Illuminati System can easily have 6 different languages used as programming codes. The foreign language codes will be for small parts of a system only. Special artificial languages are also employed, as well as sign language. The Illuminati employs signs which they teach some of their slaves with pick-up sticks. This system of secret symbols is a series of crosses and horizontal & vertical marks. These marks can be drawn on anything, and consist of up to 7 lines. They are believed to be used in regards to ritual dates/ceremonies. These secret signs resemble similar secret symbols used by the Romany tribe of Gypsies. T

he masters of mind-controlled slaves also use a technique where one signal or code will carry several messages simultaneously. This is called MULTIPLEXING. We are all aware of the phenomena of how the brain can selectively hear. The brain can select certain sounds to pay attention to, such as when a person is in a noisy room listening to someone, or a football player is trying to hear the quarterback's calls, likewise certain alters hear certain codes/cues/triggers while others don't. The internal programmers and reporting alters may internally hypnotically make telephone noises that are fake, so that host alters loose the ability to discern what is real and not real, so that they don't pay close attention to access calls. This ability of the brain is manipulated in MULTIPLEXING.

MONARCH MIND-CONTROL CODES
A. ALPHA (basic)
B. BETA (sexual)
C. CHI (return to cult)
D. DELTA (assassination)
E. EPSILON (animal alters)
F. OMEGA (internal computers)
G. GAMMA (demonology)
H. HYPNOTIC INDUCTIONS
I. JANUS-ALEX CALL BACKS (end-times)
J. OMICRON
K. TWINNING (teams)
L. THETA (psychic warfare)
M. RHYMES, SONGS, TONES
a. NURSERY RHYMES
b. SONGS
c. TONES & CORDS
d. RINGS, CREDIT CARDS, TOKENS etc.

N. ZETA (snuff films)
O. Sample codes
P. Catholic programming
Q. MENSA programming
R. HAND SIGNALS
S. Scriptures in programming
T. Alien Programming

A. ALPHA (basic)

· Basic Commands. (These basic commands are also found used in many slaves, although there will be exceptions to everything.) Many of the basic structures/codes will be put in using a sensory deprivation tank and LSD. For the most foundational levels of a system, the programmers may use the Hebrew letters associated with the attributes of God and the angel names. This can also be worked into English, as there is a cabalistic equivalent in the letters B through K for the Hebrew letters associated with God's names used in magic to conjure angels. In the basic Alpha structuring, Illuminati slaves will have stars as power sources, and the ditty Twinkle, Twinkle Little Star will pertain to this programming. The Hansel & Gretal story is used for obedience programming.

Another story line that is used in programming is the Cassandra and Apollo myth. Common access triggers are "HELLO PRINCESS', 3 knocks, flashes of light, tones, and sequences of blank phone calls.

If the slave leaves their answering machine on, a recording may be left "IF YOU WOULD LIKE TO MAKE A PHONE CALL PLEASE HANG UP & TRY YOUR 911" accompanied by a beep-beep-beep. This activates a program within the slave to call a prearranged phone number for further instructions.

B. BETA (sexual)

· SEXUAL ALTERS---most of the following codes are for deep sexual alters. In Illuminati Systems these are called Beta alters, in CIA systems they create Beta models whose primary function is to provide sex, usually perverted sex and S&M for the perverts who run our secret government and visible government. BETA models are those who are primary job is sexual, such as service as a Presidential Model (sex slave for a President). These System models may be numbered BETA 1, BETA 2...BETA 601, etc. Sexual programming for espionage and seduction, such as is done at Disneyland, may well involve the use of hundreds of dolls, such as Wonderwoman, Genie, Barbie type dolls. The names/codes would tie in with these dolls.

TIME CLOCK programming is placed in to cover the time that the sexual alters were on a mission, so that they can switch back to the - front and nothing be remembered.

Colors attached to sequences of numbers have been used for some of the Beta programming. For other sexual operatives, the intelligence agencies trigger them via specific sequences of chess moves.

Betty Boop programming is used sexually. Betty Boop was a 1930's cartoon character who was an attractive "vivacious vamp". She was described in one cartoon as the "kitty from Kansas City." She had cartoons about Gigolos, Bimbos, Little Red Riding Hood, Mother Goose rhymes which were used as programming themes. Plays on words such as "CHESS-NUT" were used in the cartoons.

C. CHI (return to cult)

Chi programming uses a lot of idiosyncratic phrases, and little ditties. Some of the nursery rhymes listed in the song section will be Chi programming. Some of the Chi programming has been listed in the Alpha programming section of Vol. 2.

p_solemetric.jpg

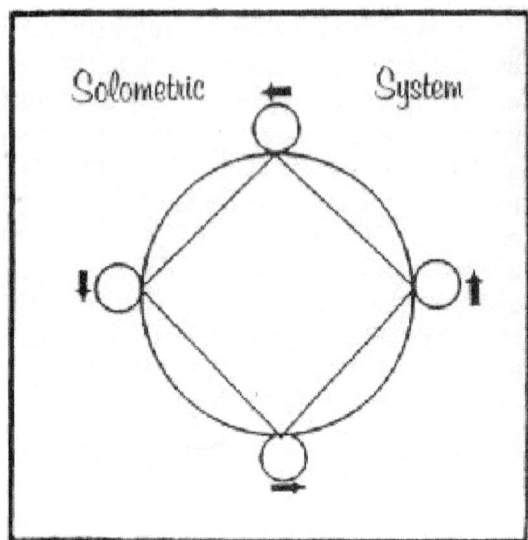

The number of hang-up calls may serve as a code, incl. when the hang-up calls happen.

D. DELTA (assassination)

· Delta alters --are activated to kill by the following three things: seeing specific clothing, items held in a persons hand, and particular words. Since these items would specific for a particular murder there is no particular specifics that can be given.

It is thought by some people that the following TV ad may have been used to trigger Hinkley when it was time for Hinkley to attack President Ronald Reagan.

p_hero.jpg

One man who was programmed as an Delta-type assassin by the NSA in the NJ region, was programmed to be activated for assassination mission via the David Letterman program, Clinton's speeches such as his speech touching on the baseball strike with "little kid" wording, and by several movie stars (Arnold Schwartzenegger, Slyvester Stallone, etc.). I Dream of Jeannie programming is used for assassination, as well as at the CIA's Farm the song Old McDonald's Farm is used with programming done to CIA assassins. Distinctive jewelry & clothes. Emerald ear rings used as a signal to others that a message was being carried. Emeralds mean drugs, rubies mean prostitution, diamonds (rhinestones) presidential model work. Red, White & Blue worn sometimes by presidential models.

E. EPSILON (animal alters)

F. OMEGA (internal computers)

The Omega programming works along with an Executive Control Board (or Grand Druid Council) and Internal programmers. The Executive Control Board is associated with both numbers of the clock, and precious gems and metals such as "9 O'CLOCK GOLD".

For G. Gamma programming see Cisco's section on "Programming, Foundations's

H. HYPNOTIC INDUCTIONS

NICRO NECTRUM NECTO--take one back to one's "true time period". When the child victim is hypnotically inducted by counting numbers during programming by a Doctor and a Mother-of-Darkness, these two will reassuring they child that things are O.K. and sweet talking to the child as it is inducted.

I. JANUS-ALEX CALL BACKS (end-times)

END-TIME ACTIVATION CODES

Most slaves have end-time programming. The programming to activate a slave's end-time programming often runs pages upon pages of coded messages. A number of Monarch slaves have been de-programmed enough that they began accessing and spewing out pages and pages of these activation codes. In the end times, there appears to be a great deal of color coding for operations. Many of the people who are taking part in the end times events are not American. For instance, the different lists of people to round up are categorized by color. The Red list in America are anti-NWO opposition leaders to be executed approx. 2 weeks before martial law. The blue list are anti-NWO order people who will be programmed or killed in the process. The yellow list is people to be rounded up for reeducation camps after martial law. Other countries apparently have different color codes. The red & blue lists have been distributed, & are periodically updated. The blue routes have already been marked by blue patches of color to guide those transporting prisoners when martial law is declared in the U.S. Within Monarch slaves, some of them apparently have an internal crystal/and or rocks that are programmed to explode at a certain point in time--thus releasing the victim's end time programming. The internal crystal (mental image) contains at least the four basic colors, red, green, blue, purple. One sample of part of end time programming was given in the previous Vol. 2 book. Still another example is as follows:

BB 243-ABCD-XXZ^2 (blue ray)

CC-458 ABCD-42T (red ray)

CD-379 ABCD-H1^2 (yellow ray)

CE-211 -ABCD-JKL (green ray)

CF-531-ABCD-ZZU (purple ray)

TMFT.47 ZONES 7-12

17876747270 OCEAN SIDE

PORT 18,22,34,41 CONTACT

YELLOW RAY SHOVE 79230 A2

TO RIGHT SIDE DAGGER HANGS

LOW ON PART SIDE FISH

SCHOOL CLOSED ROOM 37-56

RAILS EXIT END

17876747270 COL. BLACK PATCH

TO MALL 76747270 THIEF

AZT FMT BZT CET

11,4,6,9,32,101, 70

YELLOW FLAGS AT HALF MAST

YELLOW DOG ON RUN

BLUE FISH AT HOME

[This program is related to a slave contacting other slaves in some end time operation.]

A team leader will have a down line of around 4 people--which are coded red ray, yellow ray, green ray, blue ray. When the activation code hits a slave team leader during the end times, they will in turn activate their people, who in turn will have people who are team leaders and have a down line. At least two false callback alarms will be sounded (tested) before the real one.

J.>> Omicron programming—relates to programming of slaves for the Combination (between Intelligence- the Mafia and Government.)

K. TWINNING (teams)

L. THETA (Psychic warfare)

The following is only speculatory, but worth taking note of. This author believes that some of the Theta models got chess programming. Within the system of Enochian magic is the magical system of Enochian Chess. The Golden Dawn has been identified as one of the groups carrying out mind-control. Some Golden Dawn leaders have recently put out a reference book Enochian Chess of the Golden Dawn by Chris Zalewski (St. Paul: Llewellyn Pub, 1994). Enochian chess is played with four players, on a chess board that is divided up into four squares, one for each of the magical watchtowers of air, water, earth, and fire. It has only been since 1992 that researchers within the Golden Dawn (specifically the New Zealand branch which is called the Emerald of the Sea) reinvented a set of rules to play enochian chess. The moves for Enochian chess may have been used in recent years as a programming script. Since only a few people have mastered the game, and since the game is more than a game, it is magic, it would stand to reason that the temptation would be there to use it as a programming script if the programmer knew the game.

M. SONGS & NURSERY RHYMES

a. NURSERY RHYMES
b. SONGS
c. TONES & CORDS
d. RINGS, CREDIT CARDS, TOKENS etc.

· What follow is a list of Nursery Rhymes Used As Triggers, & Songs which have Monarch programming meanings &, such as access parts, or soliciting a behavior or thinking.

a. NURSERY RHYMES

The Illuminati create imaginary worlds for many of the deeper alters to live in. They keep these alters living in such unreality and nonsense that deeper alters have a difficult time separating their subjective programmed reality from the objective reality of the outside world, which doesn't understand them. Nursery rhymes function well for programming in messages. Often these nursery rhymes are distorted slightly to serve their programming purpose. Some of the programming distortions and uses of these nursery rhymes are provided below. Major corporations and advertising groups working for the Network place nursery rhymes into their television ads. These nursery rhymes are constructed in the ad to activate on certain slaves which usually are sleepers. Some were given in Vol. 2, here are some additional nursery rhymes beyond those listed in Vol. 2:

A Tisket A Tasket
Baa, Baa, Black Sheep (used for money laundering scripts, and drug money, drug carrying scripts)
Bye, Baby Bunting (used with actual rituals where the slave child is placed within a skin, cocoon programming with a butterfly coming forth etc.)
Diddle, Diddle Dumpling
Ding, Dong Bell (Dr. Mengele liked to use this--message: don't disturb the mouse that runs the internal   system clock.)
Fa Fe Fi Fo Fum (Movement within the system's bean sprouts in the system, and also a death threat.)
Farmer in the Dell, The (Used by the CIA for a serious program)
Georgy Porgy
Gingerbread Man
Hey! Diddle Diddle! (used for astral projection programming)
Hot-Cross Buns!
Humpty Dumpty (used for shattering the mind programming)
I'm a Gold Lock (used to instill cover programming to hide the truth)
I Love Little Pussy (kitten programming)
Jack, Be Nimble

Jack and Jill
Jack Sprat (possibly cannibalism programming)
Little BO-Beep (come home to Papa programming)
London Bridge (This was used at the Presideo and other sites for learning the chants, and the spells. At the Presideo it was used with barber pole programming. They all fall into a stupor at the end.)
North Wind, The
Queen of Hearts, The (swearing an obedience oath programming)
Rub-a-Dub-Dub (refers to the 3 internal programmers)
There was an Owl
Three Blind Mice
Three Little Kittens

It should be pointed out that the mind-control programmers have long ago discovered the power of a rhyme in the mind. Rhymes have a hypnotic quality to them. An example of how rhyming was used by internal programming alters to reprogram an alter wanting free is given in Daniel M. Traver's book (Phd dissertation) Dissociative Disorders and Mind Control. Wichita, KS: Daniel Traver, 1996, p. 52,

"What the hell man/ you can't stand! a winter worse yet/ you'll cry and you'll die/ as we place the mind-set/ you won't know what to do now/ you'll hear every rhyme/ and you're cravings will be as an addict in crime...." This rhymed program would accomplish its goal of wearing down the alter and bringing that alter into line.

b. SONGS

Yankee Doodle (used for sexual obedience programming "mind the step" and the word "girls" was changed to "boys" to make "and with the boys be handy". "Yankee Doodle keep it up" was ref ramed to mean "slave yank yankee doodle (the penis) sexually up." MTV is blatantly using programming rock-and-roll songs. Aleister Crowley is featured in some of these. Maiden (a satanic rock and roll band) blatantly places the words "POWER SLAVE" on one of their CD covers along with snakes and an enlightening pyramid. Anton LaVey has had an MTV song video shown, where he sings in detail how he is going to make the listener into a sex-slave, etc. etc. Some of this is blatantly mind-control in the open, it is so open it is dismissed by many of the public.

c. TONES & CORDS

In the Vol. 2 book, it was written about how telephone tones are used for codes. These type of codes tie in with the computer and the lower levels, such as the dungeon. You will find that access to items has been encoded by using the telephone tones to spell them backwards. For instance, if we were to take castle, find the numbers that correspond to C=1, A=1, S=8, etc. on the telephone, and then put those tones out backward. But to make this code unbreakable the programmers will add something like some piano cords--something that can still be played out via the tones. To make it further unbreakable the programmers will have a code (such as a combination of cards) assigned to that level which also must be toned in. An example of this in its totality would be 14 tones + 3 cords to open up a person's dungeon (hell pit the lowest level). In other words, such an access would take the programmer from a distance about 1 1/2 mm. to open up the dungeon, whatever time he needed to work in it and 1 1/2 mm. to close it down. A 5 mm. phone call might be sufficient. This gives the programmers the ability to internationally use telephone tones to access deeper items within the victim's mind. And as standard practice the reversal of the code closes down that part of the mind, and gets the programmer out.

d. RINGS, CREDIT CARDS, TOKENS etc.

A ring with a snake swallowing its tail called Ouraboros signifies rank in the Illuminati. Rings, credit cards, business cards, tokens and keys are all used as codes, triggers and signals. For instance, one slave had an old distinctive skeleton key. In another instance, a slave was given a token from a particular business as a BONA FIDE. In another instance, the BONA FIDE was a programmer's business card from his notional job. In another instance, a particular credit card would get the user into particular parts of the slave's system.

Zeta is the sixth letter, and it's ancient meaning was a sacrifice. (These codes are not known by the author.)

O. SAMPLE CODES FOR ALTERS.

As an example of the type of code names (called operational cryptonyms) used for an intelligence asset one intelligence asset had the following cryptonyms: AECHALK, ARINIKA, CHICKADEE, HERO, IRONBARK, RUPEE, & YOGA.

Monarch I.D. code reviewed:

These codes are purely a representative model-not any particular real system. The overall system code at times consists of [birthdate + programming site codes + birth order + number of generations family was in the Illuminati.]

For our hypothetical system Mary we have the hypothetical overall system code of: 6-13- 51- 14 - 02 - 12. In order to give the codes for a hypothetical alter system we will have to explain some things as we go. The Programmers have for each slave both medical programming files, and a grey or black binder with the programmed access, trigger, codes & cues, & structure.

A typical Illuminati system will be a cube (although spheres and pyramids are also used). The principle alters will be the "a" alters. A typical section of alters will consist of a 13 x 13 grid of alters. These are alters who live in a world together and must function together. A 13 x 13 section will have 13 families of "a" through "in" alters. The "a" alters will be the primary alters that the Programmers will interact with. The Programmer may call up an "a" alter and ask it to go get the "c" alter in its family, rather than directly asking for it. This initial page of alter codes will be the primary or "a" alters.

If we are dealing with a 13 x 13 x 13 cube of alters, then the initial page has 13 "a" alters of each section. Each of these alters will have an access code which will often include the following components: AN ASSIGNED COLOR + AN ALPHA NUMERIC CODE + A PERSONALIZED MAGICAL NAME.

This will equal 1/3 their access code. These code words must be repeated three times to pull the alter up. However, if an alter is trained well, and hears his master's voice, an alpha-numeric code can pull the alter up. For many of the alters, the reversal of their access code puts them back to sleep. This is an important point, because some alters would be dangerous to leave in control of the body.

The "a" alters are regular alters. Many of them have been hypnotically age advanced to see themselves as teenagers or adults. Sometimes "b" and "c" alters are also aged. The "d" through "in" alters are generally left as they were split and most of them are infantile, with little concept of how old they are. The little ones will be the ones who often remember the programming very well, and know things about the system. The top alters will also sometimes receive personal names from their handler. This is in addition to all their codes. If the alter is responsive to its master, the personal name might pull the alter up too. Do all of the alters get charted? There are several groups of alters which get charted separate from the rest or don't get charted at all. Because of the competition and distrust between the different programmers, they often place in secret back doors into the person's mind that only they know about. Worlds of secret alters loyal and devoted to the programmer may be built into the system and not appear on the regular charts. The core, and some of the primal splits from the core will not appear on the regular grids. They will be placed on a separate sheet, and their codes will be in some magical language.

The Illuminati commonly employs 20 magical languages, and Hebrew, Latin and Greek are also often used for charting the core and its primal splits. Enochian is a good example of a magical language used by the Illuminati. Some alters will be created solely by the slave in order to cope with life. Hour glass alters have entire sentence access codes. Deaf & blind alters need their access code signed on their hands by moving their fingers up and down, etc. End time alters may have access codes that may entail reading an entire page. Reporting alters are often small children, that are hidden in each section, and may require slaps to the face or jabs with a needle to pull them up. Spinner kittens will be accessed via their mama cat, who acts like a Madam in a "cat house". The codes for this was given in the Beta section codes of Vol.2.

Telephone tones are frequently used to be able to key in (that is access or trigger) parts of the computer program matrix. Dominoes also are used for the computer programming. The dominoes are put in so that the programmers can get a domino effect, if they want to set off a series of programs. Dominoes and flashing sequences of lights were used to train the child to automatically respond to a certain pattern of dots.

P. Catholic Programming (by Jesuits etc.)

KEYS TO THE KINGDOM = world domination by mind control

In the 1940's, the Jesuit branch of the Illuminati placed tatoos onto their mind-controlled slaves. These tatoos consisted of the sacred heart with a rose & a dagger, & were generally placed upon the left hand. The Jesuits have discontinued the practice of tattooing their slaves. Now all types of people are using this sacred heart tatoo.

The Rite to Remain Silent is a programming trauma which is a satanic reversal of the Catholic Mass. The VOW OF SILENCE is a keep quiet program activated by "THE WALLS HAVE EARS & THE PLANTS HAVE EYES SO YOUR SILENCE IS TANTAMOUNT TO SUCCESS." It is explained to the victim that the sea shells & the plants have the ability to hear, and that a sensitive occultist (programmer) can psychically pick up what the plants and sea shells hear. "MAINTAIN IT" --is a command to maintain the Vow of Silence. "MAINTAIN IT & LISTEN."-- a command to keep silent & listen to a command.

"ENTER INTER INNER DIMENSION TWO" is a standard Jesuit infinity program (2 is a sacred voodoo no.) Pontifax is a demon &/or alter placed in Jesuit systems.

BABY BREATH, BLACK ROSE, and WHITE ROSE are codes/triggers that are all used in Jesuit mind control. The Baby Breath and the black rose relate to programming having to do with death. The WHITE ROSE is a trigger to cue a person to release programming. The black rose is also used by the Mafia. The black rose was also used by George Bush, drug kingpin for the Illuminati, on his no. 1 helicopter for the upholstery pattern.

When the Catholic Priests do the handsignal genuflection across their chest, this has the second meaning which is a programming meaning of north, south, east and west.

Q. Mensa Programming (by MENSA)

The MENSA codes are sequences of numbers.

R. HAND SIGNALS

Masons and monastic orders who program are very keen on hand signals. A very skilled handler can do morse code with winks and eye rolls.

Rotating the hands around each other and then gesturing with the hands toward the person with both hands means--"did you get the signal?"

Sign of distress. Arms raised over the head with palms forward. Then lowing the arms to a bent position with the hands at head level, and then lowing the hand to chin level, and then dropping them to the side.

Drawing the right hand across the throat with the thumb of the hand pointing to the throat. (used in connection with oaths, such as fidelity to death.)

· Sign of faith. Hand on the heart.

· Sign of plucking out the heart.

· Sign of Reverence.

· Sign of Satan made over solar plexus.

· Sign of touching the crown of the head.

· Sign of two hands pointing to the solar plexus.

· Sign of Preservation. Consists of placing one hand over the heart, and raising the other to form a right angle at the elbow, with the hand pointing to heaven.

The movie "Dune" showed male & female Ilium, hierarchy hand greetings, as well as showing signet rings, which are indeed often worn on pinky fingers. (The movie also shows the Karat goddess, how a man becomes a Grand Master by learning control of the demons, astral projection through the spheres which are conquered by the Grand Master, &

control of the int. weather, etc.)

S. SCRIPTURES USED IN PROGRAMMING (cont. from Vol. 2. chap. 10)

· 1 KGS 7:21 --talks about 2 pillars on the outside of the Temple. The pillars of Joachin and Boaz are important to Freemasonry and are built in the slaves mind at an intermediate level. Joachin is a white pillar of light associated with fire. It is easy to see how this association could be built by certain traumas. Boaz is the shadowy pillar of darkness and is also associated with water. A dark water torture would make this association. The two pillars represent the two sides of the Illuminati's "the Force". Between them is the door to the Illuminati's House of God.

· 1 KGS 10:18--description of Solomon's Temple used to build the imagery and the lion guards to the internal Temple programmed into victims.

· 23rd Psalm--used as a cue to signal a ritual time.

· Song of Solomon--Used in the ritual of the Great Rite, a ritual pertaining to the Middle Earth, where the High Priest & Priestess join in sexual union as the God & Goddess creating fertility for the land.

· Ezekiel chap. 1 and chapter 12 are being used for endtime callback codes.

T. ALIEN PROGRAMMING

· Blue beams of light are used as a hypnotic induction for slaves who are given the cover story of being abducted by aliens.

· The All-Seeing Eye is used to represent the planet Sirius. Sirius is important to the Hermetic magicians, and some of the programmers are deeply into hermetic magic. Satan is said to come from Draco or Sirius, esp. the dog star Canis major. Masonic programming may well have the "blazing star" portrayed in the programming as a pentagram, with the name Sirius. Sirius may represent the Master, the creator of the system in some systems where the programmer is steeped in Masonic philosophy. A sickle may be involved with the Garden of Eden story for some victims of this type of programming, because supposedly the Golden Age ended with a sickle splitting heaven from earth. The ability of the handlers signals to the slave in so many mediums makes it difficult to communication and accessing, to send different prevent communication and accessing.

Program Codes During 1972-1976 for Dr. Green

One mind-controlled slave, using her photographic memory, managed to sneak into the programming files of her programmer, who went by the code name Dr. Green. Her information was included in the book U.S. Government Mind Control Experiments On Children which was compiled by Jon Rappoport and presented before a congressional committee & put on public record. The co-authors recognize some of the programs.

In the late 60's and early 70's, all the programming was revamped. The best programs were identified and then used. The continual revamping, editing and modernizing of programs has continued to strengthen the mind-control. The recovering victim's name is Chris De Nicola, b. 7/62. She worked full-time at Disneyland for 7 years (from '83-'90). Her father Donald Richard Ebner worked with her major programmer who was Dr. Green. She received standard Illuminati trauma-based mind-control.

In 1970, she received Radiation Experiments on her neck, throat, & chest. In 1972, the experiments concentrated on her chest, and in 1975 the radiation tests concentrated on her uterus. She was programmed in Kansas City Univ., Tucson, AZ, & in the desert in AZ. During her programming, the assistants were careless and she was able to sneak into the Programmer's office and look at the files with her photographic memory. She was caught twice in the files, and tortured, but simply used her ability to nest memories to their disadvantage.

Chris was such a poor programming subject, so much so that finally the programmer tried to trigger her suicide programs to activate, but they failed and she managed to survive. Suicide alters repeatedly tried to kill her body, and they came very close to killing her. On 3 occasions she had to have her stomach pumped, and one occasion when the paramedics found her she'd stopped breathing. She has survived her suicide programming countless times, praise the Lord, and provided what she saw with her photographic memory. The following codes were remembered by Chris without the aid of hypnosis. Cisco and this author recognize some of these programs. What Chris saw were the files. Each program (script) is given a name and then its file has a standard access code assigned to it. Chris saw the standard access codes.

The standard method for coding a program is to use the DAY OF BIRTH CODE, THEN THE DAY OF THE TRAUMA that puts in the program into the slave's mind, and then the STANDARD ACCESS CODE. Evidently, Chris got into the file with level D programs, which means she was looking at programs 4 levels deep. Comments about the programs are this author's and reflect his understanding, and may be subject to correction. [Spellings are exactly as program names were spelled.]

Program Name Standard Code

Relevance D-1000

Kick-It-Back D-1010

Cross Fire D-1011

Sophis. Electromagnetic Fields D-1012

(D-1012 makes the slave think they have an electrical field on them. In order to cover their electrical field tests, that they actually do place on slaves, they have the ability to confuse the slave, and prevent detection by activating a programmed abreaction that makes the field seem real, when it doesn't exist. This prevents detection.)

Gorilla Warfare D-1013

Retreat D-1 014

Nautical Science D-1015

River Runs Deep D-1016 (D-1016 is a powerful program which tells the slave that there is no escape, because the programming runs deep through every fiber of the person.)

Educated Mentality D-1017 (D-1017 is a program to allow the slave to look intelligent when needed.)

Glass House D-1018

Corporate Extrapulation D-1019

Closing In D-1 020

Frog Man D-2000

Catastrophic Indifferences D-2020

Quality Control D-2030

Protocol Virus D-2040

Operation 2000 D-2050 (This relates to Project 2000, which is end time programming.)

Pro-Life-Go D-2060

Conspiracy Action D-2070

Verified Suggestion D-2080

Finish Line Protocol D-2080

Fraternity Leads D-2090

Rotten Egg D-3000

Kaiser Confrontation D-3010

Co-Op Protocol D-4701

Forensic Criterion D-4702

Mediator Response D-4703

Mentor Divisible D-4704

Biopsy Synchroization D-4705 [This is a very harsh program.]

OSH-AMP-RIE D-5000

D.O.A. D-6000

Laser Documentation D-7000

Freak Out [just what it sounds like] D-7010

-[From here on I will select specific programs, and will not review the entire list of programs that she saw the files for.]

Foolish Games D-7060

Periodic Mind Lapse [a forget code] D-7080

Creepy Crawlers D-8040

Shock Permanence [to shock oneself] D-9000

One-For-All D-95452

[punish all for 1 alter's misbehavior]

Counter-Transference DIA-5001

Border-Line-Schizophrenic DIA-5009

[If the slave misbehaves, they can be triggered to act schizophrenic & get themselves incarcerated into a mental hospital for prgrmmg.]

Lens-Reverse-Angle DIA-5011

Canary-Sings DIA-5015

[reporting alters tattle-tale or an alter sings a script.]

Suicidal Mission [just as it sounds] DIA-5017

Mission Completed [go to "sleep" prgm] DIA-5018

Train-Wreck-Perception DIA-5021

Starvation Tactics [starvation prgm] DIA-5022

Bare-Metric Pressure Process DIA-5023

Fundamental Theology [rel. cover prgm] DIA-5025

Project 2000 412-2000

[This is end-time programming. The word project followed by a number usually refers to the date the project must be completed. Standard methodology for coding then would be that on 4/12/2000 this end-time programming must be completed.] -codes not remembered for these programs which she saw in files-

Candy [candyland programming]

False Memory Syndrome [even in c. 1973 they were setting up the False Memory Syndrome campaign to take down their opposition.]

Forced Brain Wave Activity

Frenzied State [just as it sounds]

Call-Of-Wild [survival techniques]

Hocus Pocus [magic programming]

Mass [cath. mass programming]

Phoe-net-ical Difficulties [obvious]

Self Mutilation [obvious]

Van-der-built [related to Vanderbilts III. family]

Warped-Speed-9 [Star Trek programming]

-(Her med. file no.s of radiation lab experiments are given chptr. 8)-

p_levels.jpg

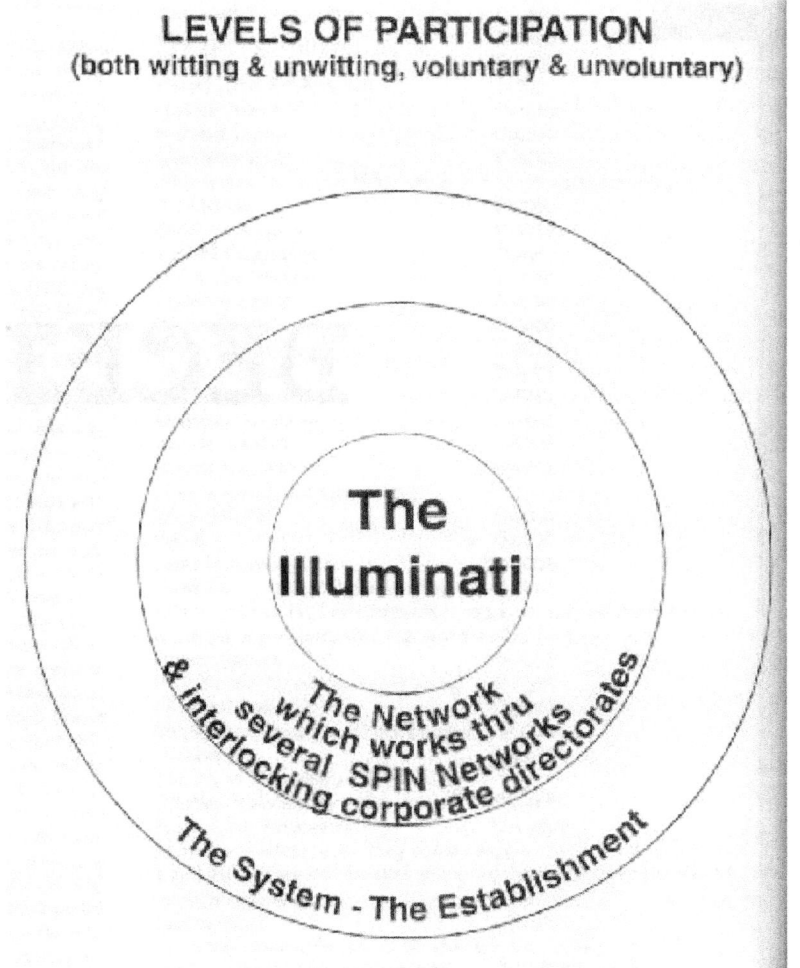

A programmed multiple can work at several different levels of participation.

The Illuminati.

This is the secret hierarchy level. It is secret by virtue of almost all (if not all) its members being programmed multiples from elite powerful bloodlines- This is hardcore generational Satanism that believes in a Gnostic Lucifer/an doctrine, hence, they may be called your elite Luciferians.

The Network.

This level of activity is secret by virtue of its secret ties. It includes the anarchy level of the Illuminati, the various criminal syndicates, the music industry, the various fraternities, new age institutions and people in power all over the globe. It is held together by fear, blackmail, and common bonds of lust and greed. The network includes atheists, self-made satanists, opportunists, and many mind-control slaves. It is far more cohesive and controlled than meets the eye. It is very eclectic. It doesn't matter at this level what you believe, what matters is whose control are you under. This is the hidden seamy power side of the World System.

The establishment, the System.

This level is open for the common people to participate in. This level remains stably operating in their control because of secret election fraud across the board in U.S. elections, extensive blackmail, extensive control of the masses through the establishment media (TV, radio, newspapers), interlocking corporations and government agencies that control the economic life, and many mass mind-control techniques that these groups use. Most people are unaware of how powerful the establishment is. As long as they drift in its current, they will never see the control. It is only when one tries to swim upstream against the current that you find out how powerful the establishment is. The Illuminati sets up controlled opposition to the System, such as the Hip pie movement, militant environmentalists, Hell's Mgels, Neo-nazis, John Birch Society, the Communist Party, etc. Controlled opposition gives people a chance to vent their anger without threatening their control. It also gives them dialectic conflicts which they can control to their advantage.

CHAPTER 5: SCIENCE NO. 5 - THE SKILL OF LYING, THE ART OF DECEIT

The Illuminati have refined the art of deception far beyond what the common man has imagined. The very life & liberty of humanity requires the unmasking of their deceptions. That is what this book is about. Honesty is a necessary ingredient for any society to function successfully. Deception has become a national pastime, starting with our business and political leaders and cascading down to the grass roots.

The deceptions of the Illuminati's mind-control may be hidden, but in their wake they are leaving tidal waves of distrust that are destroying America. While the CIA pretend to have our nations best interest at heart, anyone who has seriously studied the consequences of deception on a society will tell you that deception will seriously damage any society until it collapses.

Lies seriously damage a community, because trust and honesty are essential to communication and productivity. Trust in some form is a foundation upon which humans build relationships. When trust is shattered human institutions collapse. If a person distrusts the words of another person, he will have difficulty also trusting that the person will treat him fairly, have his best interests at heart, and refrain from harming him. With such fears, an atmosphere of death is created that will eventually work to destroy or wear down the cooperation that people need. The millions of victims of total mind-control are stripped of all trust, and they quietly spread their fears and distrust on a subconscious level throughout society.

One problem about lies is that one lie will call for another and then another. It's hard to keep lies single. They seem to want to breed more of their kind to protect themselves. Soon the liar becomes a victim of his own lies, trapped in a dishonest web that demands lots of energy to protect his false fronts. This is the sad fate that the intelligence agencies have painted themselves into. They must maintain groups that oversee their double-agents' lies to insure that the lies that they have disseminated don't contradict themselves. Finally, they have put out so much disinformation, they lose track of reality themselves.

Far from saving this nation, the intelligence agencies have spread the cancer of deception into all walks of life, so that this cancer is contaminating and killing anything of value in the United States. The soon-to-come death of this nation's sovereignty, as well as the destruction of this nation's morals are the results of this cancer. People who have attended high level Illuminati meetings were instructed in how the Illuminati plan to bring in the NWO AntiChrist reign by making everything appear as if it has happened naturally. The Illuminati have decided to camouflage their actions with the creation of normalcy to avert any suspicions.

An example of something which appears to have happened naturally is the O.J. Simpson case, which was planned based on previous murder scenarios which had been successfully covered up. O.J. Simpson was a CIA mind-controlled slave, and the entire Simpson case was concocted as an elaborate effort to cause racial tensions. The Mishpucka, the CIA, the Mob and the Illuminati have all had their dirty hands involved in the entire affair. The entire affair reeks of manipulation and planning. It is not the goal of this paragraph to go into the case, but just to drop a couple details. Joey Ippolito, Jr. is both CIA & Mob. Ippolito at one time lived in Hallendale, FL, a mob housing subdivision which was protected by a police force run by the mob. He has helped run drugs and wet ops for "the Combination" which interconnects with the Illuminati. O.J. Simpson's friend Cowlings worked for Joey Ippolito, as well as O.J. Simpson. Simpson distributed cocaine for Joey Ippolito & the Combination. Simpson's lawyer also is tied to the Illuminati, the CIA, and the mob. One of his lawyers on TV said the trial reeked of government corruption. Nicole Simpson lived next door to Carl Colby (former CIA director Bill Colbys son). Colby's wife and kids have been subjected to mind-control. Colby's wife testified in O.J. Simpson's trial, but was addressed as "Miss Boe" rather than by her name. O.J. Simpson's mother worked for a California State Mental Hospital in San Francisco for 30 years. Many State Mental Hospital workers have children who have been programmed. When one of the jurors in Simpson's case, Tracy Hampton, had her mind-control programming go haywire, she began staring for long periods at a blank TV and hearing voices. She had to be dismissed.

During the Simpson trial, Judge Ito gave Joe McGinniss the best front-row seat that a journalist could have. Joe McGinniss was the coverup author who wrote a book covering up about the McDonald-Fort Bragg Drug Smuggling Case. The McDonald-Fort Bragg Drug Smuggling Case involved the Illuminati drug smuggling operation within the U.S. military during the Vietnam War. On and on the stink goes.

The manipulation of history by those in power has been well-covered over. An example of how mind-control and its role in manipulation of events has been covered up by the perpetrators is an article written in the Journal of the American Medical Association (JAMA) in the Sept. 11, 1967, Vol. 201, No. 11 issue. The article, which was submitted to the magazine from three CIA doctors (Mark, Sweet, and Ervin), claims that riots are caused by brain disease. While the article is correct in the subpoint that only a small percentage of underprivileged urban dwellers participate in many of the riots, the article's thesis is obviously a slide to prevent people from catching on that the small number of deviants who create riots might be under mind-control or might have some other motivation beyond simply being brain-diseased. Any deception, whether it is an exaggeration or an understatement of the NWO's capabilities is considered a useful deception for the Illuminati's double-agents to spread. The german battleship the Bismarck was sunk due to a little lie sent to Germany by a double-agent which underestimated the range of British radar. The Germans, thinking they were out of British radar range, made some bad decisions that cost them the battleship.

DECEPTION DIMINISHES POWER

Knowledge is power, and lies diminish the knowledge of deceived dupes, and therefore diminishes the power of the deceived. Deception obscures the alternatives that people have. It also clouds up various objectives people would work toward. Some people give up certain objectives due to their mis-perceptions that the objective is undesirable or unattainable.

PROGRAMMING DECEPTIONS

In the programming, colors and directions are used. Be prepared to find out that sometime programmers use their creative imaginations such as using the color "octarine," or the direction "TURNWISE" or perhaps "WIDDERSHINS". During the most fundament programming which is done via LSD trips in sensory deprivation tank to lay in foundations of the Alpha, Beta, Delta, Ome and Theta programs, each programming memory will be given a code. Where one popular programming deception takes place that the programmer knows ahead of time h to sequence his memory codes so that instance, the fifth memory is coded as trip, and strenuous methods are used to cover up the memories of the first four trips. The victim's s mind will be told to forget the first four trips. The memory codes are deceptively designed to fool the deprogrammer and the victim alike. Part of the reason the programmer does this, is that they know that IF a therapist should stumble onto these first memories, the backup programming to protect these memories is so severe that the therapist will shatter the victim's mind. Backup programs such as Atom bombs and vegetable programming are locked into place to protect the fundamental programs.

BE WISE AS SERPENTS

The Holy Spirit moved an apostle to write, "We are not ignorant of Satan's devices." Christ warned his disciples to "be wise as serpents and harmless as doves." The Israelites sent out spies before entering the promised land. Within the text of The Art of War by Sun-Tzu (a book studied today by men in intelligence), he discusses "hidden provocation agents" in Book 13.

Sun-Tzu was born in 534 B.C. and lived most likely until after the year 453 B.C. In 500 B.C., some men were farmers, and some were agent provocateurs. Today, both occupations still exist. The modern American farmer is vastly superior to the ancient farmer of 500 B.C., so how does the modern agent provocateur compare? He is vastly superior also. It appears the Word of God is accurate, for it warns that God's people will be destroyed for lack of knowledge.

The difficulty in obtaining honest information in today's Big Brother world is aptly described by an intelligence asset over the Internet, "If you are lucky and work hard, you will find some of the truth. If you are lucky and work REALLY hard, you might find the WHOLE truth...as someone wants you to know it. If you are PHENOMENALLY lucky and really work your tail off, you might even go on to find the REAL truth. But no outsiders...and in fact, very few insiders ever ... EVER ... learn the WHOLE REAL truth."

This book & our two previous books on mind-control) are the result of extremely hard work and numerous miracles of God, and what non-Christians would call lots of luck". The story behind the books is amazing. This book's two authors have had to "swim upstream" for years in search for the real truth. One thing is very clear to this author, during the last seven years of exposing the NWO almost every person who is believed to be a leader against the NWO has tried to impede the work this author has been doing. People need to be aware that the New World Order created their own opposition long before some of us began sincerely trying to expose it. This author's informed opinion is that essentially all (about 98% of the people leading the opposition to the NWO are double agents), and no less than 50% of the therapists are double-agents. In this state, this author knows as a fact that 50% of the licensed therapists working with programmed DID patients are programmed DID (MPD) slaves themselves. Recently, one of the therapists in this area, who the False Memory "Spin"-drome & the Illuminati took down, was a therapist who had also been on a local T.V. talk show revealing that she was a multiple & a SRA victim.

DISINFORMATION TO MAKE THEIR DOUBLE-AGENTS LOOK GOOD

"A Force" was MI-6's group that carried out deception. They would have their double agents pass out CHICKEN FEED (which is what they call classified information that can be thrown out to the public) to establish their double-agents' credentials (BONA FIDES) as agents against the British. Today, there are numerous anti-NWO people who are actually double agents. They are distributing chicken feed to make people think they are legitimate. By the way, it is interesting to note for those who realize how important carousels are to programming that MI-6 (HO in Vauxhall Cross, Eng., with a training ctr. at Ft. Monckton, near Gosport, so. Eng.) is nicknamed (actually its cryptonym) "Carousel" by its daughter organization Mossad (officially aka Central Intelligence Collection Agency). An example of a double-agent who is popular among Christians is an Illuminati witch named Gretchen Passantino, who tours around to Christian conferences belittling the idea of mind-control. Dr. Loreda Fox reports in The Spiritual and Clinical Dimensions of MPD that 74% of women abused by SRA come from "Christian homes." The Christian churches are heavily infiltrated.

SLEEPER AGENTS

In the Vol. 2 book a number of references were made to sleeper agents. The idea of placing someone somewhere in society and letting them lead a normal life for years without ever being used is designed to provide a legitimate smokescreen about what they are all about. Mind-controlled slaves make excellent sleepers. The concept of making sleeper agents in not a secret. The CIA has publicly admitted that they tried to discover long-range sleeper agents in the Los Niñios children of Republican Spain who were the descendants of communist Spaniards who returned to Spain in the 1950's. They also have admitted to having tried to weed out long range sleepers in the Trebizond Greeks who lived near the USSR in Turkey and returned in the 1950's to Greece. As the CIA and KGB mirror-imaged each other in their manufactured Hegelian Dialectic mock dual (which was very real for the "little" person) you can well imagine that the CIA sent sleeper agents against the KGB.

NAMES of TYPES of DISINFORMATION AGENTS

The intelligence agencies have their own lingo for the types of disinformation agents they send against everyone else. So far, we have named only double & sleeper agents. Here are some of their disinformation agents:

AGENT OF INFLUENCE--These agents can be unwitting, under mind-control, or ideologically motivated to use their positions of influence to sway the minds of others. Examples of Agents of Influence are anchor men on T.V., journalists, labor leaders, TV commentators, academics quoted by the media, & some politicians.

CONFUSION AGENT--An agent whose job is to produce confusion by disseminating confounding information.

CONTRACT AGENT--These are the rogue agents, such as the mob, who the CIA get to do particular jobs on contract. Their connections can be denied.

DEEP COVER AGENT--A sleeper agent (often a programmed multiple or person with mind-control programming) who has been a long term sleeper agent.

DISINFORMATION AGENT--This is a highly placed agent who passes disinformation to other governments.

NOTIONAL AGENT--A fictitious non-existent "agent" which is created with a real-looking identity to mislead.

PROVOCATION AGENT--An agent sent in to provoke & destabilize the target group to do foolish things.

SPOON-FEEDER AGENT--Someone who dribbles out legitimate information, this is often done to build up a person's credentials (bona fides). Lots of the people who are pretending to expose the NWO are spoon-feeder agents who provide a little new information, tons of already known secrets, and sprinkle in a measure of disinformation for added fun. Generally spoon-feeders increase their percentage of disinformation once they gain respectability. There are very few people really exposing anything of consequence about the NWO. This author has endured the loss of several of the really legitimate whistle blowers who were friends being assassinated since he began writing exposes.

What this means is that agents for groups that do mind-control may: have been sleepers for many years and look very legitimately innocent, they may give good correct information to our side, they may say all the right things and try to get us motivated to do more than we would want, they may talk about other friends who are giving them information who do not even exist. It takes discernment to spot people who are not on our side. Unfortunately, such discernment seems to be fundamentally lacking within the public at large. For instance, I have seen people choose obvious NWO agents over this author as a source of "information" (which is in reality disinformation). Most people have bought so much disinformation during their lifetime, perhaps it's unrealistic to expect them to purge out all the junk they've accepted. Just as people in the world need to toss out their worldly thinking, people in the church need to toss out all the indoctrination they've gotten from the numerous kinds of harlot churches.

At the moment, the system is set up so that the perpetrators of the mind-control are in control of the credentialing process, so that they can provide their stooges/and agents with the best credentials. As the reader can see, the roots of power behind the mind-control go deep.

TRICKING SUSPECTS

One trick (or variations of it) that has been used with suspects is to arrest them, place the suspect in a situation where the police are in two groups--one group looks like police, the other group looks like the group the suspect has come from. After the suspect arrives, the group pretending to be arrested group members, overpowers the police contingent and escapes to another setting where another police group pretending to be even more of the suspect's group ask him who he is and to explain his credentials. Letting his guard down, the original suspect explains what he is all about, thereby giving them the information they needed in the first place. Variations of this script can be run. English intelligence calls this basic script CACKLEBLADDER because chicken blood is used on the police actors that are overpowered to make them look injured.

THE NAMES OF DECEPTION TRICKS

FOUR FACES refers to pretexts used by agents to get interviews. DANGLE is the craft word for luring a victim into a provocation. A dangle operation would be an operation to provoke a group or individual into a particular action. This was done with Elohim City and many other groups that the NWO is trying to set up as patsies.

STANDARD DECEPTION DEVICES

Agents use BLEEP-BOXES to tap telephones and in other instances to make free-of-cost telephone calls. A CABMAN is a device to remotely activate a telephone with a radio beam. It can be used without entering the building where the telephone is located.

MASKS

The use of masks in the occult world is ancient. For centuries, the gypsies have used them for their hypnotic powers. Special healing masks for their people are kept secret and never shown to the public. Masks have a shock value & fascination value. Gypsy and other occult groups have special rituals to create the masks, including using hair clippings from the person who will wear the mask. Gypsy healing masks are destroyed after the patient gets well. Illuminati programming masks may or may not be destroyed after their use. The Illuminati's mask-making abilities (according to deprogrammed victims of their mind-control) are very high quality. Sometimes the programmers simply wear halloween cartoon character masks that anyone can obtain, to fulfill their role in the programming script that they are involved in during the time.

COVERS

Some beginners who have just started into studying the World Order question why the Illuminati would use legitimate religious covers. Why would the Illuminati want to create a slave who is an evangelist? Why? Because those new converts will go to some establishment church where other programmed multiples in leadership positions will demand obedience (and then support those demands by quoting scriptures that make them seem like they are God's authority over that new convert. Because the evangelist or missionary and the bishop or pastor are controlled puppets, the convert will never get the full truth, just enough truth to keep him working hard for their organization. Even though the convert "got God in my life", the Illuminati never lose control over him.

The Christians have as much vested interest in preventing the exposure of the Illuminati programmed multiples who are big name Christian ministers running Christendom, as the Illuminati has. Imagine what would happen if the world found out that most of Christianity was run by the human-sacrificing, slave-making Illuminati? This is one of the sad effects of the infiltration.

Perhaps the subject of covers can be explained from another angle. The reader knows that the elite like monopolies. They play monopoly for real--for us it's only a board game! To establish a monopoly, you find a good product that everyone wants or needs, and then you eliminate all the competition by either destroying them, or owning the competition yourself.

In the U.S., the Illuminati can't have a one-religion monopoly. In Russia, they had communism with Marx, and Lenin as the Father God and Gon the son figure. Communism had a monopoly on worship. In the U.S., they have established a monopoly by controlling all the various religious groups. (This author wrote an 800 page heavily documented book Be Wise As Serpents to show the details of how this is done.)

It's not a matter of what they teach, it's a matter of control, so that the elite have a monopoly. And when you, as a mover & shaker in the world, control all these various religions via money, blackmail, & programmed multiples under your leadership, etc. which religion would you pick to emphasize the most? You will pick the one that sells the best, i.e. the best product. And which brand of Christianity will sell the best? The televised charismatic brand will sell the best.

Covers that slaves use to explain what they do in life are almost always "legitimate". A missionary, a military officer, a salesperson, etc. will usually actually do their cover job most of the time. Their cover is their occupation, their service as a mind-controlled slave is almost an unwitting avocation. Organizations are used as covers. The Illuminati use military, social, intelligence, education, banking and other organizations as covers. (See my Be Wise As Serpents book for many of these.) Moriah's front organizations, such as the CIA, in turn use other organizations. Here is just a sampling of CIA fronts, to show the variety of fronts used:

· Asia Foundation was an academic organization created by the CIA.

· Castle Bank & Trust Co. has been a bank in the Caribbean that is a CIA front.

· Forum World Features has been a front created for CIA propaganda purposes and based in London, UK.

· Geschicter Foundation for Medical Research (as well as the Josiah Macy Foundation) was used as an intelligence front to launder money used for mind-control.

· Air-Sea Forwarders, Inc. was the legal corporation name of a CIA front in North Hollywood, CA. The company was involved in moving freight. In the last few years, this corporation sued E-Systems, the company which builds the CIA and the NWO's electronic systems such as their communications satellites. In court, the company proved that it was a CIA front, in spite of CIA denials.

As this chapter provides information about some of the Illuminati/ intelligence connections to Hollywood, bear in mind that this CIA front was proven in court to be a CIA front in Hollywood. A feat that rarely occurs

---

ONE OF THE GREATEST DECEPTIONS OF ALL TIME: DISNEY

INTRODUCTION

For years, I have heard many Americans say that something is terribly wrong in this country & that things are "going to pot", and yet Americans can't put their finger on what exactly is wrong. When I first began to receive reports from victims of Illuminati mind-control about Disney's involvement in their mind-control, I kept an open ear, but I wanted some tangible proof. After investigating for myself, there is now no doubt in my mind that Disney (the man, the movies & the entertainment parks) has been a major contributor to the demise of America, while maintaining a very well constructed front of wholesomeness.

In this chapter, you will learn why Disney is one of the best deceptions of the Illuminati. This author has read a good portion of what is available to the public concerning Disney. This exposé is undoubtedly the deepest on Disney that has ever been done. Perhaps part of my motivation is that I've tired of Christians talking and acting like Disney stands for sainthood.

Christians, who should have known better, are some of the ones who have swallowed "hook, line and sinker" the enormous deception that entails Disney. They feed their children a steady diet of occultism and witchcraft because they have been programmed to think of Disney as wholesomeness and everything that is good about America. Many writers over the years have tried to expose Disney, most have been stopped before they could get their books published. The few authors who have managed have faced vicious attacks on their character & integrity, and have faced enormous struggles against public relations campaigns paid for by the Disneys. The Disney's power, and the power behind them, has frightened most people away from challenging them. But someone needs to speak on behalf of the victims. Whether anyone listens or not, the victims will know that somebody cared enough to stand up & write the truth. Disney has not only left mind-control victims in its wake, but they have harassed land-owners, stolen employee idea's and left all kinds of hurting victims in their path. Disney has risen to become the unquestionable largest media-entertainment conglomerate in the world, & was ranked company no. 48 in the top 500 companies by Forbes 500.

Observations about HOW THE ILLUMINATI LIKE TO HIDE BEHIND PERFECT FRONTS.

There are numerous Illuminati homes, restaurants, wineries and other institutions that are today carrying out the same type of strict standards upon their employees that Walt Disney Studios maintained. While Hollywood was immersed in moral filth from the start, Walt Disney Studios had strict standards. In the 1930's, Disney had a dress code that required men in ties, and women in sober-colored skirts. If a man looked lecherously at a woman at Walt Disney Studios he risked being instantly fired. Walt was a shining example of the strictest legalism. Even during the '50's, if an employee were caught saying anything considered a cussword such as "hell" they were instantly fired no matter who they were. Walt would not allow his male employees to have any facial hair, even though he himself sported a moustache.

He never allowed employees to have alcohol at the studios, (which might not be a noteworthy standard except that Walt himself drank heavy amounts of alcohol in his private office at work for decades). Initially, Walt was very reluctant to have his young artists, who were being trained by Don Graham, draw live nude models, but reluctantly gave approval. Again the motive was not to serve God, but to make sure the Disney reputation remained untarnished. With the power of the establishment media behind Disney, Walt had nothing to worry about, news about the nude drawing classes and their detailed drawings never reached the light of day. Behind such strict fronts of legalistic morals, cleanliness & soberness, you will often find lots of guilt and high level satanic ritual.

For instance, Hitler (who was by the way also a failed artist & who liked mechanical things more than people) obsessively washed his hands many times a day (out of guilt), and so did Walt Disney. Walt obsessively washed his hands several times an hour, every hour. Walt liked animals & his trains more than people. This author has seen some alters who were forced to take another human's life, and when they relived the memory, the alters then tried to physically wash the blood guilt off of their hands.

Another example is that over the years this author has discovered that many of the exclusive restaurants that are meticulous in every detail are tied in with the mind-control and criminal activities of the elite. Dirty money is keeping the places looking sparkling clean. Walt Disney worked very hard at maintaining a great image for himself and his company.

An example of this, is how he exploded in rage and wrote an angry memo when a Disney character was placed in a beer ad. (Memo mentioned in Thomas, Bob. Walt Disney An American Original. Hyperion, 1994, p. 7.) He had a personal image builder, Joe Reddy, who worked full time to build Walt's image. Joe Reddy was a cigar-smoking Irishman who loved the catholic college Notre Dame's football team. He also was a publicity agent for Shirley Temple. But the Disney deception entails far more than Joe Reddy's decades of image making, and Walt's own abilities to create good images of himself. Just as with Billy Graham (see Vol. 2 about Billy Graham), the entire Illuminati threw their weight behind promoting Walt Disney.

Ronald Reagan and Walt Disney were good friends and both cut from the same die in many ways. Both men were high ranking Freemasons, both came from socialist backgrounds (Ronald's mother was Eleanor Roosevelt's best friend, & Walt's Dad was a socialist leader), both were paid FBI informants, and both were involved heavily in the abuse of mind-controlled slaves. Walt always generously supported Reagan's political campaigns, and in turn Reagan did political favors for Walt as Gov. of California.

For instance, Disney's Mineral King mountain resort needed an access route through the Sequoia Nat. Park at a time when there was lots of congressional pressure to preserve the last stands of redwoods. Gov. Reagan got his friend Disney his road through the park. Reagan served as the emcee for the opening day of Disneyland on July 17, 1990. He returned with Illuminati TV host Art Linkletter for the 35th anniversary. Ronald Reagan & Art Linkletter both pumped Disney publicly.

Another slave abuser that spent time with Disney was Bob Hope, who would spend time on the golf course with Walt. On the opening day's telecast, cameras showed Sammy Davis, Jr. (a member of the Church of Satan) and Frank Sinatra (a mind-control slave handler) driving the pint-sized Disney ears at the Autopia ride. When Disney celebrated its fifty yr-anniversary with a two hour special on May 20, 1991, the program included people like occultist Bill Campbell and was named "Best of Disney, 50 Years of Magic." For the silver anniversary of Disney World in Oct. '96, the Clinton's were invited to help open 15 months of celebrations. The theme of the anniversary celebrations was "Remember the Magic". A Boy's & Girl's Club sang 'When you wish upon a star' (a popular programming song). Hillary Rodham Clinton (herself an Illuminati Grand Dame and a mind-control programmer) shared with the audience that she and Bill "first brought daughter Chelsea to the Magic Kingdom when she was four." Roy E. Disney, nephew of Walt, told the public that Disney World "is the story of men and women who took hold of a dream and never let go." There is a double meaning to that. Many victims of trauma-based mind-control have taken hold of the illusions that were programmed into their mind secretly at Disney, and never let go.

Among the visitors to Disneyland have been all the American Presidents from Eisenhower to Clinton, over a dozen kings & queens, as well as Emperor Akihito of Japan, Anwar Sadat, and Robert Kennedy (who rode the Matterhorn with astronaut John Glenn.) Both Denmark's & Belgium's kings who are in the Illuminati visited, as well as the dictators of Indonesia, the Shah of Iran and Ceausescu of Romania. (As a side-note Roy E. Disney was forewarned by Arab leader that the Shah was to be deposed.)

Organizations that have been actively working for a New World Order for many years gave big awards to Walt in his early years such as the B'nai B'rith (Man of the Year Award to Walt) and the Chamber of Commerce. In 1936, Walt was given the Chamber of Commerce's annual "Outstanding Young Man" award. The establishment's Yale & Harvard Universities gave him honorary degrees.

Walt Disney biographer Leonard Mosley, who researched Walt Disney for years (as well as writing books on the duPonts, the Dulles brothers, and Hirohito) wrote in his book on Walt Disney, "The studio publicity machines in the film colony had, as usual, gone out of their way to try to persuade me, as a writer for a powerfully influential British newspaper, that this was a city of lawless gods and goddesses, full of clean-living, sanitized stars. "It was even more of a deodorized world at the Walt Disney Studio where the publicity men insisted their boss was faultless--never drank too much, never used a swearword, never lost his temper, never quarrelled with his wife or family, never let down a friend. And woe betide anyone who tried to suggest otherwise. Members of the resident foreign and local press risked their jobs if they dared to write stories inferring that Walt Disney could be domineering, implacable, and unforgiving (as was the case, for instance, before, during, and after the 1941 studio strike). The Disney flacks were capable of exerting heavy pressure on editors and proprietors or, through the advertising pages, against anyone who inferred Walt Disney was not the epitome of well-scrubbed and benevolent perfection." (Mosley, Leonard. Disney's World. New York: Stein & Day, p. 10.)

Disney is perhaps the epitome of Illuminati abilities to create images. They have created great images for things Disney, incl. Walt Disney, Disney movies, and Disney's Amusement parks. In some cases these things have been overrated, in other instances the sinister side to them has been carefully hidden. In order to make movies that contain the typical smut of Hollywood, sex and violence, Disney did a slight of hand and created subsidiaries which Disney runs, which has allowed them to keep their good image. They also never showed the public the hard core porn that was made for years in secrecy for the elite.

Behind Disney's good front lies hard porn, snuff films, white slavery, Illuminati mind-control, and the seduction of several generations into witchcraft. Disney's involvement in these kind of things will be explained in this chapter. Nobody has sold America witchcraft as well as the Disney brothers. Movie after movie has cleverly brought the occult into the warp & woof of American thought, all under the disguise of entertainment. For instance, it was Disney that brought us cannibalism and told us that it was a "triumph of the human spirit" (a direct quote from Disney's Touchtone Producer Robert Watts concerning Disney's movie "Alive" featuring survivors of an airplane crash who turned to cannibalism).

Under the disguise of entertainment & showing us how "triumphant" the human spirit was, they subtly promoted cannibalism. Mickey Mouse plays a leading role in "The Sorcerer's Apprentice." And yet when this author has suggested that Disney movies aren't wholesome, many Christian parents come unglued and have gotten angry with this author. The deceptive image that Disney movies are wholesome is a triumph in Illuminati deception. Parents would be surprised what is slipped into cartoons. In Disney's "The Little Mermaid" the castles are male sexual organs. In one cartoon Mighty Mouse is shown without comment clearly snorting cocaine. Walt Disney Studios Chairman Joe Roth is in charge of Walt Disney as well as subsidiaries Touchtone, Miramax, and Hollywood Pictures, which were all created to camouflage the Disney production of adult films. Disney operates in a clandestine manner regarding the promotion, distribution and p_mermaid.gif DISNEY MAKES MALE PHALLUSES INTO CASTLES.

rating of the films produced by their subsidiaries. Roth oversaw Disney's subsidiary Hollywood Pictures' Evita film. Evita has as its main start "Material Girl" Madonna. Madonna is in reality a mind-controlled slave who has appeared in numerous underground porn/& ritual porn movies. (This author has an underground catalog from a porn business, that has recently changed its location of business. The catalog offered a film of Madonna performing an actual blood sacrifice.) She also was the main actress in Disney's Dick Tracy film which is reported to be used for mind-control. During an Arsenio Hall show, Madonna, who as a guest acted dissociative, was picked up by the cameras during the show kissing her Baphomet ring.

Disney controls the products that are associated with the movies of their subsidiaries. In Evita's case they are marketing hats and other items, as just one more of Disney's countless artificially generated consumerism campaigns. In Ruth Stein's interview of Madonna, Madonna appeared bored with plugging Disney's consumer products. When asked about the tango dresses and hats inspired by Evita that popped up in stores after the film, Madonna said, "Believe me, I have nothing to do with it. Disney is pushing the whole thing." (San Francisco Chronicle, 12/29/96, Datebook section). In one interview Madonna states she wants her daughter to grow up knowing Catholicism, but she doesn't believe that it would be good for her daughter if Madonna married the father of her child from Lourdes, Carlos Leon.

In another interview, Madonna says, "Actually, I'm a very good role model, because I say, 'Look, these are my standards'..." She then goes on to plug homosexuality, same sex marriage, and single families in the interview. Walt Disney stated that it plans to release an album by DANZIG, a heavy metal band whose songs contain "dark themes". The Disney press release announces on its by-line "Mickey Mouse is going heavy metal." Disney's album ,,BLACK ACID DEVIL" was due to hit the music stores Oct. 30, 1996 during Halloween time. According to Disney this music has no satanic references, but does have "dark, Gothic and sexual" overtones. Glenn Danzig denies that he is a satanist.

CONTENTS IN THE DISNEY DECEPTION SECTION OF CHAPTER 5.

a. an introduction
b. an overview
c. Who was Walt Disney?
   PERSONAL DETAILS
   MICKEY MOUSE
   OCCULT PORN KING
   A possible CHRONOLOGY OF EVENTS surrounding WALT DISNEY'S ILLEGITIMATE BIRTH
   WALT DISNEY'S CHARACTER
d. Who was Roy O. Disney?
e. Who is Roy E. Disney?
   The battle between the two Disney factions
f. What do we know about them in general?
g. A history of Disney Harry Cohn Bank of America Bank of Italy Claude Debussy EPCOT center
   SOME DISNEY people of interest. Warren Beatty Shirley Maclaine Shirley Temple Black Stephen Bollenbach Warren Buffett The Tommy Dorsey Band Michael Dammann Eisner Rich H. Frank The Osmond Brothers Michael Ovitz Frank G. Wells
h. Disney and its mob connections Some MOB HISTORY.
   How the Disney Executives have figured out how to steal land all across the U.S.
i. Disney and its government connections
j. Disney and mind-control
   DISNEY VACATIONS FOR THE ELITE
   MELODYLAND
   DISNEYANA FOR THE PROGRAMMED & OBSESSED.
   Mind-control features in Disney movies. Bette Midler
k. Detailed Script of how one Disney movie is used for programming.
   SUMMARY

Deeper Insight Into the Illuminati Formula

1. Partial List of Sources

B. AN OVERVIEW

Disneyland and Disneyworld are world famous and the pride of America. They are also extremely important programming centers for the Illuminati to create total mind-controlled slaves. Disneyland is also involved with providing a place for rituals, porn and other satanic activities. In terms of deception, Disney movies and Disney Amusement Parks rate as one of the best deceptions. According to deprogrammed ex-Illuminati slaves, the Illuminati in the 1960's needed to shift their programming away from the military bases, because too much publicity (heat) was shined on the military bases. Their goal was to have someplace that people from all over the world could come to without raising any suspicions, and a place which would be the perfect cover for many of their criminal activities.

According to a witness, the Illuminati Programmers got a big laugh out of using Disneyland as a major Illuminati base for criminal activity. Under the disguise of entertaining the world, they carried out money laundering, child slavery laundering, and mind-control. They nick-named Disneyland "the little syndicate of mind-control." When a child of 3 or 4 was kidnapped, they could torture the child and then put him on a ride such as a ferris wheel or carousel that: a. created dissociation from the pain, while also b. going along with some fairy tale programming script.

An abducted child while waiting to be picked up from one Illuminati non-parent caretaker by another, could be kept happy and distracted while waiting for the pickup. For years, Disneyland was an Illuminati center for many of their world-wide activities. Now Disney has created other sites around the world such as EuroDisneyland 20 miles east of Paris and Tokyo Disneyland.

Tokyo Disneyland in 1991 had 16 million people attend. With such huge crowds, it doesn't take much imagination how the Illuminati have been able to do sneaky criminal activities right in front of people, and the public never sees it, in the middle of all the activity. EuroDisney has been a money losing affair, but the Saudis who benefit from its mind-control, gave Disney the money to keep it financially in business. Walt Disney Records is the largest children's record label in the world. Disney through their movies, books, toys, records, etc. has made a tremendous impact on the children of the world. Their movie Return from Witches Mountain was one of the most powerful witchcraft promotions ever made. Ducktails, which has deliberate Monarch mind-control triggers written into the script, is also broadcast in Poland and the former USSR. From the time of the Roman Empire (at least, if not before) the oligarchical leadership, who have been in control of both the Mystery Religions and European aristocracy, have known about BREAD & CIRCUS.

Bread and Circus refers to the concept that IF the masses of people are given entertainment and food staples, THEN they are easy to control. Walt Disney movies have played a key role in providing entertainment for the masses to insure Illuminati control. Walt Disney's friend the Masonic prophet H.G. Wells in his book A Modem Utopia that there would be lots of shows in the New World Order. The World Future Society in a book review in their publication Future Survey Annual, 1993, (ed. Michael Marien, Bethesda, MD: World Future Soc., p. 91) describes Disney: "Control of commodities [such as entertainment] and access to commodities translates into control over people. 'The postmodern US is a massive rush of disconnected commodities, each seeking a moment of our attention." The world of commodities is our soma, and entertainment is the current form of public discourse. Walt Disney World, spread over 27,400 acres of central Florida swamp and scrub forest, 'is the most ideologically important piece of land in the U.S.' What goes on here is the quintessence of the American way. It is visited by over 30 million people a year--not only the major middle-class pilgrimage center in the US, but by far the most important entertainment center in the world. It is clearly Oz, utopia as a marketing device."

Two Disney brothers Walt (Walter Elias) and Roy O. Disney have been at the center of the creation of amusement parks and popular Disney films. In more recent times, two other men, Eisner and Katzenberg have been notable at Disney. Eisner & Katzenberg, as well as others will be discussed later. One of Disney's directors, Victor Salva, was convicted of molesting a boy and filming one of the sexual molestations. Recently Disney Director Salva produced the Disney movie "Powder". (Victor Salva's sexual molestation conviction was covered by newspaper articles such as Robert W. Welkos of the LA Times, in newspapers such as The Oregonian, Weds. Oct. 25, 1995, A sect.)

The impact of the Disney brothers is monumental. Mickey Mouse teeshirts can be seen being worn by natives all over the world. Disney World and Disneyland are the quest for a large segment of humanity, who often esteem these amusement parks as the highlight of their life. What is highly esteemed among men, is an abomination to God according to the Word of God. The Bible arbitrarily makes this claim, but sadly, research by this author over the years proves that a close examination of Disney & mankind's esteem for "Disney" things does vindicate the Biblical expectation. In other words, as readers of this article will find out, behind the appearance of wholesomeness of the Disney brothers and their creations lays abominations-- some of the most grotesque aspects of generational occultism the world has ever seen. Disney's Magic Kingdom has become an American Institution that impacts people all over the world from the cradle to the grave.

C. WHO WAS WALT DISNEY?

In the large book The Art of Walt Disney from Mickey Mouse to the Magic Kingdom by Christopher Finch (N.Y.: Harry N. Abrams, 1975) on page 11 an interesting and revealing statement is made: "By definition, public figures are known to everyone; yet, even after talking with some of Disney's closest associates, it is impossible to escape the conclusion that nobody really knew him. Always there was some aspect of his personality that was just out of reach." Those who got to know Walt too closely make complaints such as he was "self-satisfied, intractable, and arrogant." He could bring his artists to tears or anger in a matter of seconds. Finch is not the only author who has tried to warn his readers that the public's image of Walt Disney was just that--only a false image. Mosley also writes in his biography of Walt Disney, "Since Disney is regarded by millions of people, particularly in the United States, as perhaps this century's most brilliantly successful creator of screen animation, I think I should make one thing clear right away. I share the general admiration of a man whose cinematic achievements were always so happily inspired and inspiriting. But--and this is where I differ from uncritical idolaters--I have to know all the facts, no matter how unpalatable, as well as the romantic myths about any great man or woman I admire. Many of the myths that have been created by his publicists about Walt Disney are unpalatable, unbelievable, and unsatisfactory because so much of the real Walt Disney has been deliberately concealed...Walt Disney...had grave flaws in his character." (Mosley. Disney's World, pg. 9)

Years ago, an Illuminati Grand Master and programmer stated, "If the world only had the eyes to see the fibers which lay under the surface of Walt Disney's image, they'd tar and feather him, and drag him through the streets. If only they knew what Disney's primary goals."

PERSONAL DETAILS

Walt had black hair with a black mustache, and bright quick eyes and was about 6' tall. He used his own facial features to clue artists on how to draw Mickey Mouse's features. He liked specially rolled brown cigarettes which he smoked up to 70 a day. He picked up the smoking habit in the army. He loved expensive Scotch Whiskey, red sunsets, and horses. He had a vacation home in Palm Springs, CA called the Smoke Tree Ranch. He often wore the Ranch's letter STR emblazoned on his necktie. He played lots of golf with Bob Hope and Ed Sullivan at the ST Ranch. His main home was an estate in Holmby Hills. The Holmby Hills estate was located in a plush area where lots of rich show-business families lived. It was located between Bel-Air (an occult word for Satan) & Beverly Hills.

Walt spent many of his nights at the Disney Studios and later he had his own private quarters at the center of Disneyland. He had reoccurring bouts of insomnia. (For his nerves and insomnia he'd take alcohol and tranquilizers.) He'd go weeks on end without stepping foot on the Holmby Hills estate and seeing his family. The main topic at the studio by the staff during different time periods was Walt's bizarre behavior-- he would not be available until late afternoon, when he would emerge from the studio's subterranean maze of tunnels, where supposedly he was "chatting with the maintenance engineers" everyday. The value of his estate when he died was 35 million dollars of which Lillian his wife inherited half.

In his later years, when Disney took a vacation he went to Paris for 3 weeks, and 3 weeks at the Hotel du Cap, in Antibes, and then cruised on Fritz Loew's yacht with Ron and Diane Disney. In England, Walt spent time with the British Royal family and met privately with masonic prophet H.G. Wells. In Rome, Walt visited privately with the Pope and the dictator Mussolini. In 1966, Walt Disney died. Prior to his death he had investigated cryogenesis--being frozen, and it is believed by some that his body is frozen somewhere in California, while others claim he was cremated.

MICKEY MOUSE

According to one source, the inspiration for Walt to create Mickey Mouse came when he was unemployed and saw a mouse in the gutter. There are quite a few stories in circulation as to where the idea came from. Ub Iwerks claimed he thought Mickey up at an animator's meeting in Hollywood. Walt once said, "There is a lot of the Mouse in me." (biographical article written by Elting E. Morison, p. 131) In fact, Ub Iwerks told Walt that Mickey Mouse "looks exactly like you--same nose, same face, same whiskers, same gestures and expressions. All he needs now is your voice." Walt often did serve as Mickey's voice. A book put out by Walt Disney Co. in 1988 reveals that Walt Disney told Ward Kimball "Quite frankly, I prefer animals to people."

Walt usually was the voice behind Mickey Mouse, (even though he wasn't the artist.) His mother was chilly for years about the work Walt did. Around 1940, after much pleading, he finally got her to watch Mickey Mouse. His unsupportive mother (which he would within a few years learn was not actually his biological mother) told him she didn't like Mickey Mouse's voice, to which he told her it was his, and then she responded by saying he had a horrible voice. The "cold towel" she threw on Mickey Mouse helped convince Walt to quit making Mickey Mouse cartoons. Very few came out of Disney after that, and the very next Mickey Mouse full-length feature cartoon, Fantasia, had Mickey mostly silent. Walt's idea for The Sorcerer's Apprentice was based on some of his own ideas. Walt had had the dream which was used for Mickey Mouse in The Sorcerer's Apprentice of having "complete control of the earth and the elements." Disneyland and Disneyworld were partial fulfilments of that dream for control.

Walt's final pet project just prior to his death was the meticulously restored version of the witchcraft film "Bedknobs and Broomsticks." (Disney Magazine, Winter 96-97, pub. by Disney, p. 96 mentions this.) As a programming device, Mickey Mouse works well because it plays on the subconscious genetically transmitted fear of mice that women have. Mickey's image can help create a love-hate relationship, which is so valued during the traumatization & programming of mind-controlled slaves. Some sources state that Walt's love for animals came from the time his family had a farm near Marceline, Missouri. Walt began his schooling at Marceline, but continued it after the age of eight at Benton School in Kansas City, MO. Walt's Dad had a serious gambling problem and passed the spirit of gambling to his son Walt. Walt never graduated from high school. He had a natural love and a flair for art work, although (contrary to his public image) he never became proficient at it. He joined the army in W.W. I as an ambulance driver by lying about his age. During the war, he also chauffeured dignitaries.

He also did some other things that are very revealing. He enjoyed drinking & gambling while in the service, and he ran a scam where he doctored German artifacts picked up on the battlefield to sell to people. War relics were tampered with to get them in shape to get the most money from them possible. Walt took the battle souvenirs - and dressed them up, for instance, coating the insides of helmets with grease, hair & blood and putting holes in them to make them into expensive souvenirs. This shows that Walt was willing to build illusions if it paid. He could be deceptive if he saw an advantage to it.

From gleanings from things Walt said to people, it appears that as a child, he'd seen the darker side of life (for instance, his father had a habit of beating him in the basement) and had had some interest or exposure to magic as a child. Bob Thomas writes, "Walt took a boyish delight in playing tricks on his parents. He was fascinated with magic tricks..." (Walt Disney, An American Original, p. 35.)

After the military, Walt hoped to have a career as an artist. He applied to the advertising agency of Pesman-Rubin. Roy, his brother, claimed that Pesman-Rubin hired Walt as a personal favor to Roy who handled the agency's account at the bank Roy worked at. Walter lasted a month until the advertising agency let him go due to Walt's "singular lack of drawing ability." According to Current Biography 1952, in 1923, Walt and Roy had together $290. They borrowed $500 from another Disney, one of their uncles named Robert Disney and began to try to make cartoons. Robert Disney had retired in the L.A. area in Edendale, CA after a successful mining career. Robert had always been close to Walt's father Elias, and helped Walt and Roy out when they came to California. Walt loved to study Charlie Chaplin (a member of the Collins family). He scrawled notes about his body language, facial features, and his gag methods. He also read everything he could about animation and cartooning. They worked out of their uncle's garage in Hollywood, CA. They were finally able to make a good cartoon Steamboat Willie in 1928, which became an instant hit. As with many things in life, the cartoon was not only good, but Walt finally had the right "connections." On Nov. 18, '28, Steamboat Willie was shown in a small, independent theater without any advance promotion or advertising. But amazingly(!) the New York

Times, Variety, and Exhibitor's Herald all ran rave reviews of the cartoon the next day. Was this an accident? did journalists from all these prestigious periodicals just happen to go to this tiny independent theater? no it was connections.

The reason the elite decided to promote Walt Disney after Steamboat Willie came out as Hollywood's newest "boy wonder" was to deflect enormous bitterness that had been generated by the Stock Market collapse toward Jewish financiers. Hollywood, even in its first two decades, was known as "Babylon" and "Sin City". The movie industry was well-known to be run by Jews, and many people blamed the Stock Market Crash on the moral degradation that Hollywood had introduced to this nation. There were calls for government regulatory groups to stop the smutty Hollywood films. Edgar Magnin, the spiritual leader of the major movie makers who were part of the Los Angeles B'nai B'rith reportedly encouraged those in the Mishpucka and others who were B'nai B'rith movie makers that Hollywood needed to protect itself by putting Walt Disney in the limelight as a Christian "white knight with family values". (By the way, Edgar Magnin was nicknamed "Rabbi to the Stars", because he was "the Hollywood rabbi".) E. Magnin's grandfather's department store chain was one of the first major accounts of the Bank of Italy, and Edgar Magnin had continued his family's close association with the Bank of Italy. The closeness also came from the Bank of Italy's close ties to the B'nai B'rith and ADL.

In 1930, the movie industry made a production code which stated that the industry must make a special effort to make movies appropriate for children. Hollywood directly praised Disney in that code as an exemplary model of what the movie industry wanted to do. With the power of the B'nai B'rith and ADL behind him, Walt began sailing to fame. Movie studios that had been turning out smut, with lots of sex and violence all jumped on the bandwagon to show Walt's clean wholesome cartoons. Walt was the facelift Hollywood needed after the Depression caused Americans to think about America's morals. Many of the regular movie makers were so corrupt they were out of touch with moral issues, but Walt Disney knew black from white. The Jewish movie makers "pushed the man [Walt] they considered their best hope to the front of the pack" who was billed as a fundamentalist Christian (albeit a masonic "Christian" who rarely stepped foot in a church). (quote from Walt Disney Hollywood's Prince of Darkness, p. 50.)

Strangely, the biographies indicate that Walt quit doing the actual drawing in 1927, and Walt devoted himself entirely to the development of the cartoon business, such as raising money. In other words, the image of Walt Disney being the artist who has created the Disney cartoon's is inaccurate. The Disney brothers actually hired many other artists to do the art work. If Walt quit drawing in 1927, and their first marketable cartoon was in 1928, that clearly shows that Walt did not do the actual cartooning. He continued to oversee the work, walking in and rigidly inspecting what was being done to suit his own intuitive tastes. Actually the genius cartoon artist (animator) who made Walt Disney a success was Ub Iwerks, about whom Walt on a number of occasions said was "the best animator in the world". Without Ub Iwerks to take Walt's ideas and turn them into reality, Walt would never have become famous. Ub was an incredible genius who had a sense of line, a sense of humor, patience, organization and a great sense of what Walt wanted. Walt treated him cruelly at times, interrupting him, playing tricks on him, and not being totally honest with paying him, but he stayed with Walt over the years and made Walt the success Walt became. (The books Disney's World and Disney Animation: The Illusion of Life have information on the unheralded genius Ub Iwerks.)

Another unknown great artist was Floyd Gottfredson. Floyd Gottfredson drew all the Mickey Mouse cartoons from 1932 until October, 1975--which is a period of 45 1/2 years. Floyd Gottfredson was a Mormon born in a railway station in 1905, and raised in a tiny Mormon town, Siggurd, 180 miles so. of Salt Lake City. In 1931, before Floyd totally took over the Mickey Mouse drawings, he would take suggestions from Walt on what to draw. For instance, Walt puzzled him by insisting he do a cartoon series of Mickey Mouse committing suicide. Floyd had said, "Walt, You're kidding!" But Walt thought that a series on suicide would be funny. Over the years the Walt Disney products never mentioned Floyd's name. The bulk of the fans were led to believe Walt did the cartooning of Mickey Mouse himself. (See the book Walt Disney's Mickey Mouse in Color. Ed. Bruce Hamilton, pub. The Walt Disney Co., 1988.)

Fred Moore was involved in the creation of Pluto and some other cartoon characters. The idea for Pluto was Walt's and it was Norm Ferguson's genius at drawing that took the idea and created the actual images. Walt Disney was awarded 32 personal academy awards for the work that was done by his studios. Walt Disney's famous signature was actually designed by someone else, and was taught to Walt. (Schickel, Richard. The Disney Version: The Life, Time, Art and Commerce of Walt Disney. NY, 1968, p. 34.) Walt could only make a crude Disney signature, so he delegated the writing of the signature to several artists including Bob Moore, Disney's publicity artist. Later, after much practice he learned to make it well enough to do for publicity. Many people who wrote letters asking for his actual signature, and who actually did his signature, thought that they had received forgeries by his staff, because the famous Disney signature was so crude. The nicer looking ones were the forgeries. One cartoon animator who joined Disney in 1940 recalled that Walt told him the first day, "You're new here, and I want you to understand just one thing. What we're selling here is the name Walt Disney. If you can swallow that and always remember it, you'll be happy here. But if you've got any ideas about seeing the name Ken Anderson [his name] up there, its best for you to leave right away."

OCCULT PORN KING

Walt grew up fascinated with the occult and in an abusive home situation. He was fascinated with cartoons, nature and children. He had an intuitive sense for quality cartoons that would appeal to children. At some point, the syndicate got him indebted to them. At that point he was their man. He owed them a debt that they held over him. In secret, Walt became a porn king. A victim remembers that he was sadistic and enjoyed snuff porn films. His interest in children was far from altruistic.

The Hapsburgs of the 13th Illuminati bloodline had a sex salon in Vienna, where a porn photographer named Felix Salten worked. Felix Salten wrote a book Bambi, which was then translated into English by the infamous communist Whittaker Chambers. The elite were just beginning to form the roots for today's environmental movement. The book appealed to Disney, because Disney liked animals better than people. In the book, tame animals view humans as gods, while the wild and free animals see humans as demons who they simply called "Him." The book begins with both free and tame animal viewing humans as rightly having dominion over them. In the end, the animals view all humans as simply being on the same level as animals, a vicious animal only fit to be killed. Disney instructed his animators to make the animals "to be human. I want people to forget they are watching animals." Bambi was to receive a Christ-like manger birth, with the animals hailing him as a "prince." Due to his sexual problems, Walt at one point permitted himself to be subjected to the packing of his genitals in ice for hours at a time. (Elliot, Walt Disney Hollywood's Dark Prince, p. 83.)

Children were instructed to call Walt "Uncle Walt." An example of this were the Mouseketeers. For those who know how mind-control programmers have traditionally liked to be called "uncle" by their child victims, the insistence by Walt to be known as "uncle" is distasteful. From what this author has learned from some sources about Walt's non-public life as a hidden sadistic porn king, it raises questions about other parts of his life. For instance, Kenneth Anger in his book Hollywood Babylon II, p. 192, "Some animators stated that the boss [Walt Disney] seemed to have fallen in love with the boy. There may be some truth in this..." The boy, who Walt fell in love with, was a small young attractive boy actor named Bobby Driscoll who signed up in 1946 with Disney. He acted in Song of the South, Treasure Island and Bobby's voice was used in Peter Pan. Bobby Driscoll was very intelligent and attractive. Did Disney help or abuse him? If Disney was such an upbuilding wholesome atmosphere, & this child actor had everything going for him, why did Bobby become a methamphetamine addict at 17 & die within just a few years? Why didn't his talent & early career lead to something positive in his life?

From those who knew Walt personally one learns that he had an obsession with the buttock part of anatomy. He enjoyed jokes about this part of the anatomy, which he told to his staff quite frequently. The staff edited out many of his crude posterior jokes from cartoon scripts. Two examples that got by the editors are a Christmas special where a little boy is unable to button the drop seat of his pajamas. The little boy's problem in maintaining his modesty is the running gag of the cartoon. In the end, Santa gives him a champer pot. The 2nd example is the paddling machine used on the wolf in The Three Little Pigs. Numerous Disney cartoons feature buttocks of characters provocatively twitching.

AS A WITNESS BEFORE CONGRESS

After W.W. II, Walt Disney was called upon by Hollywood to testify in their defense at the Un-American hearings which were being carried out by congressmen who were concerned about the heavy communist influence within Hollywood. Walt downplayed any communist influence in Hollywood to Congress. Interestingly, Walt's father was an outspoken Socialist Party leader in the United States who advocated a socialist New World Order. He regularly voted for socialist presidential candidate Eugene Debs. One of the first drawings Walt did as a boy was to duplicate the socialist political cartoons he found in a socialist periodical Appeal to Reason that his father subscribed to. When Walt asked in the 1930's how his father felt about socialism's successes, his father Elias said, "Today, everything I fought for in those early days has been absorbed into the platforms of both the major parties. Now I feel pretty good about that." (Thomas, Bob. Walt Disney, An American Original, pg. 147-148)

Walt's movie Alice's Egg Plant (1925) was pure communist doctrine where the red hen (communist) leads the working chickens on a strike against Julius the farm manager (representing capitalists.) The strike at Disney and unionization of Disney in 1940, soured Walt toward communism. The workers at Disney publicly made personal verbal attacks on Walt & he never forgave the humiliation. In spite of his public distaste for communism, his Magic Empire (his castle where he was king) was run like a socialist dictatorship, similar to what the NWO plans. Employees at Disney did not have titles; it was faceless egalitarianism with an all powerful dictator Disney at the top. It was racially elitist too. The only full-time African-American during Walt's lifetime at Disney was a black shoe shine man.

Was Walt a socialist of the National Socialist (Nazi) variety? Arthur Babbitt claims, "On more than one occasion I observed Walt Disney and Gunther Lessing there [at Nazi meetings], along with a lot of other prominent Nazi-afflicted Hollywood personalities. Disney was going to meetings all the time." Lessing was mobster Willie Bioff's crony. Bioff had spent his earlier days running a whorehouse, before coming to Hollywood for the mob.

In the final panel of the Mickey Mouse comic strip of 6/19/40 a swastika appeared. Some people have wondered what this & other "secret signals" in Disney's work meant. Disney was not Illuminati. The powerful elite are very skilled at controlling people that rub shoulders with them, those who are beginning to become independently wealthy. For instance, they destroyed Robert Morris, the great financier of the American Revolution. They simply used Hegelian Dialectics on Walt Disney. Their Unions and the Mob made Disney's studio one of their prime targets. In order for Walt to protect himself from the unions, which he perceived as communist, Walt got help from the FBI and the mob. Walt was vulnerable to the unions, because he treated his workers terrible, with long hours, low pay, in addition to repeated abuses to their dignity. Walt's large number of employees essentially never received any credit or recognition for their years of creativity and hard work, which was all essentially stolen and credited to Walt by the establishment to build his image. (I write "essentially", because someone might find some obscure exception, but across the board, Walt got all the credit for what his creative workers produced.)

Perhaps Walt needed the ego boost from all the purloined public praise which he stole from his staff to be seen as a great animator, because he had wanted to be an artist/cartoonist and failed. The praise helped sooth the wounds. One worker recalls that Walt "had no knowledge of draftsmanship, no knowledge of music, no knowledge of literature, no knowledge of anything really, except he was a great editor." This may not be much of an exaggeration, because Walt was a high school drop-out, who grew up in poverty on a Missouri farm. Walt's first official attempt to direct a film (and last) was the film The Golden Touch in 1935. The film was an embarrassment. Walt had to pull it from distribution. If Walt lacked abilities to animate, and direct, what was Walt's talent? Walt was the driving force, the spirit so-to-speak behind Disney. He was the dictator who was feared enough to demand more from his workers than they knew they could give-- and he could get it. He was the driving force that took a mob of artists, and gag creators, etc. and shaped them into a powerful force to make cartoons and later movies. He was the hard-driving genius who knew what he wanted and got others to create it for him. He was the driving force that kept an army of costumed sanitation men meticulously cleaning Disneyland. In normal year, Walt would have 800,000 plants replaced at Disneyland, & Walt refused to put up signs asking the "guests" (visitors) not to trample them. How powerful was Walt? Here is a man who during his lifetime and even up into the 1990's had a rule in the studio & Disneyland that no male employees could have any facial hair, yet he himself wore a mustache for most of his life.

A possible CHRONOLOGY OF EVENTS surrounding WALT DISNEY'S ILLEGITIMATE BIRTH

It is beyond doubt that Walt Disney was an illegitimate child, but that fact resulted in a long list of mysterious happenings. It also gave power hungry men, something to blackmail Walt Disney with. Because this chapter 5 on Deception is focusing on Disney, and the big boys used blackmail to keep Disney in line, this information is pertinent. The following chronology of events is what this author's believes most likely happened. Without any genetic tests, it is difficult to determine beyond a shadow of a doubt who Walt's biological parents were, and what the actual history of Walt Disney was. Several people have spent many years investigating the real facts surrounding his birth. Many interesting and tantalizing clues have been found. This author believes that the following chronology issuggested by the evidence. (This author's chronology is offered without hundreds of pages of evidence, because the mysteries around Walt Disney's birth are here to stay, no matter what excuses people come up with, and this author doesn't want to stray from the intended purpose of the chapter. This is to show that Walt Disney had a secret bastard birth which gave J. Edgar Hoover --and his superiors-- blackmail leverage over Walt Disney. Walt may also have had gambling debts and an abnormal sexual appetite which also helped entrap him. For those who want more evidence and facts, the following are recommended: Almendros, Mojacar, Corner of Enchantment, p. 83; Interview magazine, no. 242, ""Walt Disney Was from Almeria"", and last but not least Eliot, Marc. Walt Disney, Hollywood's Dark Prince, chapter 11.)

1890--An attractive spanish woman Isabelle Zamora Ascenslo of Mojacar leaves Spain and travels to California to a Franciscan monastery. In the same year, but later on In 1890-Walt's future father Elias, who fancies himself a ladies man, leaves his family to seek his fortune in the gold fields. In California, he meets another newcomer to the state, Isabella Ascensio, and the two newcomers in California have much in common, have a sexual affair and fall in love.

1891--Elias fails to make a fortune and returns to Chicago, but he doesn't forget Isabelle.

1893--Isabelle and Elias have a son, and Elias convinces his wife to accept the baby as theirs rather than have the family's reputation, their marriage, and their family ruined. The son doesn't look like the first two boys at all.

1901--Isabelle and Elias have another bastard son, who Elias brings home and names Walter after the minister of the church he attends. The two bastard sons do not look like the older sons of Elias, and they never have much to do with them, but cling to each other as brothers.

1903--The minister of the church Elias attends finds out about the bastard children and Elias quickly moves out of state so that the scandal will remain secret. Elias has also run up gambling debts.

1905--After moving to Marceline, Missouri, Isabelle is hired as the Disney's maid, so that she has an excuse to move in with them without creating suspicions. She probably does much of the raising and care of the two boys.

1918--J. Edgar Hoover is busy involved with the prosecution of draft dodgers in WW I, and it crosses his desk about the case of Walt Disney committing the crime of forging his parents signature to join the army. Cases like Walt's were watched because people who could be blackmailed could be resources in the future for Hoover. That year, Walt discovered that he had no birth certificate. Waft observes his parents strange reactions concerning his birth certificate & other questions, & begins to deeply distrust his father.

1938, Nov. --Walt's mother dies by gas, and the Disney's maid pulls Elias to safety from the fumes, but Walt's mother dies.

1939-40--Hoover offers Walt Disney to help Walt locate his real parents if Walt will work for the FBI. Either Hoover already knows that he is a bastard child, or he soon learns the truth from an investigation. This gives Hoover blackmail power over Walt Disney, and assures Hoover that Waft will be loyal. Hoover informs Walt Disney of the truth, and then moves to generously protect Disney & his father's reputation. Two FBI men plant baptismal information of a child born to Isabelle in 1890 named Jose Guirao in Mojacar, Spain. This date is 10 years off of Walt's birthdate, and is intended to throw people off track. They can't plant a fake birth certificate for Waft in the records for 1901, because everyone knows from WW I that none exists. Therefore, they plant a fake birth certificate for Walt in the Illinois State records in the year 1890. They hope people will think that somehow a filing error occurred. This way if anything leaks, and worst came to worst, Waft could at least pretend he was adopted and is not an illegitimate bastard. They pay off townspeople in Mojacar to tell a particular story. Townspeople probably receive ongoing payments.

1941--Walt confronts his father with the truth, and his father commits suicide, and his real mother comes to live with him as his maid.

1954--In order to reinforce the myth that Walt was born in Spain, a group of Franciscan monks goes to Mojacar and visibly inquires about the birth records of Jose Guirao and/or Walt Disney. They spend time with the mayor and make sure that everyone connects Waft Disney with Jose, who is a fictitious (nominal) character that the FBI has created records of.

1967--A year after Walt's death, a large group of Americans (a large group was needed because they are not skilled like the 2 FBI men in 1940) pretend to be on "official" business for the American government. They go to Majacar Spain to destroy all the records of Jose Guirao to insure that there will be no spanish claimants to Walt Disney's fortune.

Later to insure that the fictitious story is solidly in place to mislead the few who might get by the cloud of secrecy over Walt Disney, the Spanish government does a favor to certain powerful people and pays an investigator to investigate the spanish origins of Walt Disney. People of the village willingly tell people without any fear or without any fanfare that Walt Disney was born at their village. Unless they have recently done so, the village has never done anything--no monuments, no markers, or anything about the birth site of Disney. They probably didn't do this for years, because some of the village probably knew it was a lie. With the older people gone, the lie has probably become well entrenched as truth and there is most likely some type of memorial to Walt Disney.

WALT DISNEY'S CHARACTER

Because the Disney deception is such a major Illuminati deception worldwide, and because Walt Disney was the major catalyst behind all the Disney theme parks, movies, trinkets etc. it is of importance to examine his character. In studying historical figures, this author has tried to get to the rock bottom truth. One may ask, how can this be done? -especially since there have been decades of myths spread by the establishment and their media? The following procedure which has worked with other historical figures was also done by this author with Walt Disney.

The first part of this author's own procedure is to study everything that one can find on the man, paying special attention to what bias and vantage point another author comes from. Special attention is also paid to biographers who try to give the whole truth as they have found it, rather than approved biographies that repeat myths, platitudes, and flattery. The investigator has to be careful because there are authors who deceptively say in their introductions that they are "detached investigators" who are "going to be painfully honest in their reporting" when they actually are skillful coverup artists for the person they write about.

When your author, Fritz Springmeier, finished investigating written material about Walt Disney, then I mentally placed what I knew on the shelf temporarily, and did a handwriting analysis based on the scientific principles of Graphoanalysis as well as the broader field of Graphology. This author is a Certified Graphoanalyst who has done handwriting analysis professionally. Using Graphoanalysis/graphology is an excellent way to get an unbiased very deep look at a historical figure. It is a way to by-pass all the propaganda and myths. However, a close historical look and the handwriting analysis (of various historical figures) have always matched each other, as they did in this case too.

Here is what was found. The following paragraphs are how Walt was in the 1920's. The personality profile you will read did not endure. Under the pressure of micromanaging Disney Productions as well as living with financial stresses, by the 1940's, Walt could be found in rages giving rough treatment to his wife, and rough spankings to his two children. He went to psychiatric counselling to cope with the stress. And unfortunately with the progression of time, by the 1960's Walt had become a sadistic egotistical alcoholic. One biographer described him as "...a bully and a know-it-all" (Disney's World, p. 220) Even then Walt had men working for him, such as Bill Walsh (who had been a orphan as a child) who worshipped Walt.

But here is how he was in the 1920's: Walt was a self-motivated individual with lots of energy which was constantly seeking some outlet. (People have written much about this trait of his.) He was more the giver than the taker in relationships. (In the first few years, when he was responsible for making business contracts he often gave away his work without setting prices for profits. He even wrote letters to his boss to the effect that his first priority was good cartoons not profits, and that he'd work without profits, but he did want some appreciation for his work. That was his sensitive nature showing.) Walt wouldn't wait for others to come up with an idea or someone else to make a move--he was there first.

He could communicate his ideas with clarity and ease and move easily from idea to another. (He would storm into Disney Productions and spew one idea after another into his workers' ears.) He enjoyed competition. He had a quick mind and keen perception. He frequently acted on intuition and impulse, taking chances and endangering his own security. (He frequently gambled all his life savings and everything he could scrape together on a project.) Long projects bored him. (Fortunately the real tedious work of cartooning was done by a large staff of artists.) House chores and repetitive chores bored him and he avoided them. (He was absolutely a total slob around the house as a bachelor.) He was impatient with vague philosophies, he liked concrete realities.

He was difficult to get along with because he had both a playful side (even to the point of cruel practical jokes) to his personality and an aggressive intolerant impatient side that wanted to achieve. Naturally, people around him were disconcerted because on a subconscious level they never knew which side of him they would deal with. (The reference series Current Biography "Disney" article p. 248 gives the following Walt Disney quote, "We don't even let the word 'art' be used around the studio. If anyone begins to get arty, we knock them down.")

He was geared for action. He was always inventing ways to get what he needed. He could be explosive when provoked. (The old time associates of Walt remember his explosive temper.) He was a person of dynamic energy, sensuality and keen thinking, and a disciple of the pleasure principle. Because his father was so abusive and misused his position of authority, Walt came to be deeply ingrained with defiance toward authority. (The themes of his films repeatedly sympathize with those who rebel against authority, and the police and other authority figures are consistently shown as absurd. One way he expressed irresponsibility was with lively dance scenes, which has been a hall-mark of teenage rebellion during the 20th century. "Comic anarchy reaches its fullest expression in Alice Rattled by Rats, which shows what the rats do when the cats goes away!) He felt that rules were for others to follow. (That is one reason he would step outside of the law and commit illegal acts. This is one trait that may be responsible for some of the criminal activities Walt ended up participating in.)

Walt also didn't like to be closely supervised. (He wanted to manage his Disney Magic Kingdom as if it were his own kingdom. He wanted to be an authority figure, and indeed became the dictator of his Magic Kingdom. When his workers differed with his own views he felt that they were infringing upon his own inalienable rights as an individual.) He was somewhat of a melancholic temperament, that type of perfectionist who still enjoys life. He felt a need to protect himself against intimacy with others. He was most home in a setting which he made for himself. Walt had the traits of an executive. He was slow to reveal his innermost feelings, and definitely set his own goals. Walt was one of those persons that when the going got tough, he hung in there. Likewise he would cling to his ideas, plans, and possessions. (His stubborn refusal to allow his brother Roy to stop the creation of Disneyland led to events that split the brothers. His determination to succeed was taken advantage of by the crime syndicates to blackmail him with some debt. In order to get his dreams, he was willing to give them what they wanted.)

A clue to Walt's macabre sense of humor, at times almost a graveyard sense of humor, and his high tolerance of seeing pain in others, is that Walt was seriously thinking of volunteering again as a medic after the W.W. I fighting in France was over, when volunteers were needed for the Balkan fighting. Walt loved animals more than people. The only human being that he had rapport with while growing up on the farm was his Uncle Ed (who he called Uncle Elf), who looked like a cross between a leprechaun and a prune. Uncle Elf could make animals sounds and bird whistles to Walts delight. Walt loved the charm of the farm and nature and he loved royalty, pageantry and a strict social hierarchy such as Freemasonry provides. He often wove a combination of the barnyard in with royal parades and other trappings of royalty.

For instance, in Alice the Piper, the King Hamlin is a farmer who sleeps in a farmhouse. In Puss in Boots the local king lives in an authentic palace incongruously placed in a village. His early film Alice's Day at Sea includes both the features of a royal court and an American circus. In typical Disney disdain for authority, he pokes fun at criminal fraternal groups with their rituals and passwords in Alice & the Dog Catcher, Alice Foils the Pirates, and Alice's Mysterious Mystery. And while he was a secret FBI agent, he went against Hoover's wishes and poked fun at the FBI's authority. Walt was loyal to what he believed and could be loyal to those individuals who he deemed worthy of his loyalty, but he didn't want anyone to have authority over him. (Walt was a 320 Freemason & an occultist, he was loyal to that philosophy and loyal in his early years to his older brother Roy O. Disney, who was a father figure to him.) If anyone at the studios agreed with him when he was angry at his brother Roy, he or she risked losing their job. Both brothers were protective of each other, and felt they were the only ones who could criticize the other one.

D. WHO WAS ROY O. DISNEY?

Roy O. Disney was born in 1893, and his brother Walt in 1901. They had three other brothers, but Roy and Walt (1901-1966) were only close to each other and not to their other brothers, who didn't resemble them. Walt was named Walter Elias, his middle name derived from his father's first name. The Disney family had immigrated from Ireland to Canada and then to the U.S. The father of the brothers as stated was Elias, and their mother of scottish descent, who may not have been the biological mother, had the maiden name Flora Call. Roy died in 1971, shortly after the opening ceremonies for Walt Disney World. He kept his promises to his brother to build Walt Disney World. He reneged on his promises concerning the city of Epcot (which was derailed into becoming EPCOT).

Roy O. during the 1930's lived in North Hollywood. Roy's family later located in Napa Valley, CA, and was associated with the Illuminati kingpins in the area. Napa Valley has been nicknamed the Valley of Kings. This "Valley of Kings" plays a major role in the dirty activities revealed in this chapter. Roy 0. Disney played a bigger role at Disney Studios than people realize. For example, it was Roy O. who made the decision to cut 45 min. out of Fantasia, so that Walt's pet project could be distributed to movie theaters. Roy O., considered by some insiders as the more evil of the two brothers, kept the financial books for the Disney's down through the years. It is known that Disney kept two books during the 1950's, so it is hard to believe anything except that Roy 0. was fully aware of how Disney brought in their money. The big boys always kept the financial screws to Walt and Roy. The big boys often figured out scams to take their money. When the Disney brothers had an arrangement with Columbia Studio (run by Harry Cohn) they were advanced $7,500 for each cartoon which cost them an unprofitable $13,500 to make. Further, Cohn liked to cheat them by not sending them their money, and taking a ridiculous amount of time to pay them what he owed them. The cash flow problems of the Disney brothers also came from Walt's desire to keep improving and upgrading the technology they used. When Walt went to color over Roy's objections, Disney's profit margin was damaged and the studio was left with shortages of cash. In 1937, Walt's repeated gambles with cartoon production ideas caused Roy O. to say, "We've bought the whole damned sweepstakes."

From 1940 through 1946, Disney lost money every year. In '46, he lost $23,000. Finally in 1947, things turned around and the Disney studio made a profit of $265,000. Cartoons and movies were not really big money-makers for the Disney brothers, until it was realized that old films could be replayed on television. Overall, from the 20's through the 50's, the Disneys may have broke even with animation. This is why Disney Studios at Christmas, 1931 was unable to pay its payroll.

Pinocchio cost $2.6 million to make in the late '30's, an amount hard to retrieve at that time from the box office, and Fantasia's original release in the '40's was a dismal financial failure. When Sleeping Beauty was released in 1960, it was a loser, movie goers were apathetic towards it. The real money made by the Disney brothers in the 1930-1950's came from the merchandising of Disney products, the production of underground hard porn, and the kickbacks from various groups which used Disney for mind-control programming, and money laundering.

When Walt died, his shares in Disney were worth $18 million. His family all in all held 34% of the stock in Walt Disney Productions. Roy O. Disney's daughter Dorothy Disney Puder & husband Episcopalian Rev. Glen Puder purchased property at 1677 Sage Canyon Rd., Napa Valley east of Rutherford. (This is close to the Rothschild's Opus One Temple mentioned in VoL 1.) O.J. Simpson's lawyer Johnnie Cochran Jr. was in the Rothschild's hard-to-enter Opus 1 when the jury arrived at a decision in O.J. Simpson's case.)

It is very typical for Mafia families in south Boston to have one family member in the clergy & one full time in organized crime. (See author's Be Wise As Serpents for an expose on the Episcopalian Church, which is simply a branch of Freemasonry.) All kinds of interesting Mafia figures, Illuminati, and Bohemian Grovers live up the Sage Canyon Rd. This is an area that has a large well-kept cemetery for pets. Frank Well's sister and Rich Frank, who will all be discussed later in this chapter, also live on Sage Canyon Rd.

E. WHO WAS ROY B. DISNEY?

Roy Edward Disney (nephew of Walt) is the son of Roy Oliver Disney (brother of Walt). Sometimes he has been called Junior. The 9/5/94 Newsweek story on Disney's Magic Kingdom called him "Keeper of the Flame." Roy is an executive with Walt Disney Co. at 500 5. Buena Vista St., Burbank, CA 91521. He has worked as an asst. producer at Walt Disney Co. from 1954 to 1977. He has also been the vice-pres. of Walt Disney Co. He is president of Roy E. Disney Prodns. in

Burbank. He is chairman of the board for Shamrock Broadcasting Co. As if that weren't enough, he is on the board of directors for St. Joseph Med. Ctr., fellow U. Ky. Recipient of the Academy award nomination for Mysteries of the Deep. He is a director of the Guild American West, the Writers Guild, which is important. He belongs to the 100 Club, the Confrerie des Chevaliers du Tastevin, and St. Francis Yacht Club. He likes speed boat racing.

Roy E. Disney was the cocky son of Roy O. He married a gal named Patricia. He was merely tolerated by his uncle Walt, especially after Roy E. made some snide remarks about Walt's plans for Disneyland, which he and his father opposed until Walt Disney personally got the project going. Walt's son-in-law Ronald Miller is one of the Disney clan who can't stand Roy E. The two never liked each other, and in the power struggle between them after Walt's death, Roy E. won and ended up with Disney. Although people called Roy E. "Walt's idiot nephew", he eventually (with the help of his father & outsiders) won the various power struggles at Disney after Walt died, and is now a powerful figure. Roy E. Disney and Stanley P. Gold work together in various ways, and are both on the present Disney Bd. of Dir. They are friends and worked to prevent hostile takeovers of Disney in 1984. Gold is in charge of Shamrock Holdings, Inc.

(Chapter 5 page 2)

The battle between the two Disney factions

In 1953, the two brothers and their respective sides of the family split when Walt created RETHAW corporation. The two sides have fought ever since. When Walt Disney created RETLAW (his name Walter spelled backwards), this alienated his brother Roy O. & Roy's side of the family. Without going into all the details, what RETLAW did was cut Roy O.'s side out of the money that was to be made. But Roy's side didn't stand by and idly let their share of the pie be lost, they fought back and held their own.

Their big break came when Michael Milken and his band of junk bond artists carried out a "greenmail" on the Disney Corp. Only a few insiders know how greenmail works. It is a legal form of blackmail. Milken would work with his friends Saul Steinberg, Sir James Goldsmith, and Carl Icahn. Milken would provide them the financial clout, to make them look financially capable of financially purchasing a corporation that they had selected as a target. According to insiders, Milken got 40% of the upside of any "greenmail" that went right. The targeted corporation would learn that someone like Saul Steinberg was going to buy them out. In order to prevent the buyout, and to keep their jobs, the officers of the targeted corporation would get frantic, and either do suicidal refinancings, or buy the stock of the potential acquirer for much greater prices than the Milken group paid for them. The "greenmail" artists would then take their loot and go on their way. The stockholders of the targeted company are the real losers of "greenmail", because the management of the corporation in order to finance their protection spends the stockholder's money, takes on new debts, and deprives the stockholders of some profit-making potential of their shares.

Michael Milken's group made feints to take over a large number of corporations, including Walt Disney, Phillips Petroleum and Avco. Saul Steinberg made what looked like the beginnings of a sincere hostile takeover of Walt Disney through Reliance. At one point Reliance became Disney's largest stockholder. Steinberg filed an amended 13D saying he intended to acquire 25% of the corporation. The CEO of Walt Disney, was Walt Disney's son-in-law Ron Miller. Saul Steinberg is a dear business partner with London's Jacob de Rothschild. Originally, Ron Miller (Stanford Univ. grad.) and Ray Watson (a Bohemian Grove member from Stanford Unive.) of Walt Disney's management brought in the Bass brothers to help them deal with Saul Steinberg's takeover and to buy and develop land (esp. in Florida). Ray Watson was Ron Miller's key right hand man to run things. The Bass brothers are mafia. Disney acquired the Bass Brother's Arvida, and brought the Bass brothers into Disney's management. The Basses sold their stake in Texaco back to the oil co. & then used this money to bolster Disney. Sid Bass & Chuck Cobb (chief exec. Arvida) worked out a deal with Disney. Arvida (sold to Disney for $200 mil.) would profit from developing Disney land in FL & Disney would profit from the new financial strength that getting Arvida would provide. Arvida owned oil fields, theme parks, and had helped create planned communities.

For Ron Miller, on the one side was the Illuminati and the other side of things was the mafia. He didn't trust either, but

Steinberg's takeover could eliminate Disney's management and both he (and Roy E. Disney) wanted to save Disney from a takeover by Steinberg. At first, Roy E. wrote a letter to Ron Miller & the other board members stating his concerns about the acquisition of Arvida For Disney management, at least the Bass brothers would let Walt Disney continue to make their family movies. After the Bass brothers joined the Disney management (and became one of Disney's major stockholders), they soon joined sides with Roy E. in a management fallout over whether Disney should buy Gibson Greeting Card Company. With enough votes on the board, they sent Ron Miller packing. With Ron Miller, and those management men aligned with Walt's side of the family gone, then CEO Michael Eisner, Frank Wells, Rich Frank, and Jeffrey Katzenberg and some others made the modern Walt Disney Corporation.

Disney's Touchtone studio which was mentioned above in connection to the movie Alive was created in 1984 by Walt Disney's son-in-law Ronald L. Miller. Ron Miller's management style was lackluster. The new management has really gone gang busters. Although Walt's side of the family is out of the management end of Disney, they still receive financial rewards from various Disney enterprises. The Bass brothers acquired more land for Disney in Florida. But under their tutelage, Disney now has a management team that is skilled in land grabbing techniques. The Bass fortune began with Perry Bass, who created a company called Bass Enterprises. In 1969, Perry retired and turned things over to his eldest son, Sid Richardson Bass. Sid has three younger brothers Ed, Robert and Lee. The Basses owned 27% in Prime Computer, as well as sizable real estate and oil holdings. The Bass brothers founded a local prep school in Ft. Worth, TX. Their HQs in Ft. Worth is full of modern art.

The Bass brothers were very clever in their deal with Disney. In exchange for their $14 investment in Arvida, they had gotten (over a period of time) $950 million dollars worth of Disney stock. In 1985, they liquidated Bass Brothers Enterprises and divided the assets between the four brothers. Sid Bass was able to shift his interests from finances to culture and high society.

One of the Bass brothers is involved with wineries in Napa Valley. The Bass Brother's financial strategist was Alfred Checchi, now of Beverly Hills, who has been a supporter of Mishpucka member Sen. Dianne Feinstein (D-Calif.). Roy is involved in criminal activities, and several people investigating him have been bluntly warned that if they continue, they will see their children murdered. Napa Valley's Illuminati activity also connects in with CIA activities as well. The Napa Valley Illuminati families all have CIA connections. For instance, British millionaire Kenneth Armitage, who had to flee from England to avoid arrest on numerous charges of theft, deception and false accounting, had some of his good friends in the Napa Valley, such as Dr. John Duff, Johnny Beck, & others. Armitage has since mysteriously died in prison in England. Armitage had intelligence connections which tie in with twilight world of the criminal activities of the numerous intelligence acronym monsters. Also his company was authorized to provide people with Central American government documents.

There is more-- much more to sordid affairs which swirl around Roy Disney. Napa Valley, where many members of the Disney family live, has the Illuminati's Opus One temple owned by Rothschilds, as well as two roads lined with meticulously kept wineries owned by Illuminati kingpins and connected via secret underground tunnels. To top off this incredible collection of Illuminati wineries (Rothschild's, Mondavi's, Rutherford's, Christian Brother's, Sattui's etc), on the north end of a series of wineries on highway 29 lays the CIA's medieval-looking Culinary Institute of America Greystone (at 2555 Main St., St. Helena, CA 94574), where numerous people have suffered torture. The Greystone Culinary Institute of America recently had the person who runs their campus store mentioned in House & Garden, Sept. '96.

F. WHAT DO WE KNOW ABOUT THE DISNEY FAMILY IN GENERAL?

Several members of the Disney family came to England with William the Conqueror. They were not known as Disney then, but because they came from the French Norman town of Isigny, they took the name d 'Isigny, and anglicized it into Disney. Walt had two daughters, Diane Marie (bn. 12/18/33) and Sharon Mae. Diane made some revealing comments when she said, he didn't spoil us. Like a lot of adolescent girls, I was crazy about horses, and I got quite good at riding. I yearned for my own horse, but Dad wouldn't buy one. And we didn't have a lot of clothes and other things." For being one of the richest men in the nation, Walt can't be accused of having spoiled his children. He was also famous for his ten cent tips at restaurants, which became the talk of the town.

Sharon Mae was adopted and arrived at the Disney home 12/31/36. (She died in '93.) The adoption was kept very secret. The newspapers around the country announced that Lillian had given birth to Sharon, and the Disney family kept up this lie for years. The reason given for Sharon's adoption was that Diane needed a playmate. For years, Walt Disney didn't care much for Sharon and seldom acted like he even knew her name. Walt had wanted a son, but his wife wanted to adopt a girl, so it was a beautiful girl that Lillian picked out to be a companion for her first daughter. When Sharon was kindergarten age, Walt would take her to the carousels in Griffith Park on Sunday afternoons. Sharon was sent to private schools. She went to Westlake School for Girls, and later was shipped off to Switzerland to a girls' boarding school. She had soft blond locks and was attractive. In June of 1948, Walt took Sharon, who was then an attractive 12 yr. old to Alaska with him for about 2 months. For most of this trip Walt and Sharon were alone together.

For a father, who had ignored Sharon for years, now Walt was totally obsessed with Sharon. He bathed Sharon every night, combed her hair, washed her underwear, and carefully dressed her each night from head to toe before taking her to nice restaurants. He even followed her when she sleep walked. Why was Sharon a dissociative person? That summer in Alaska, Walt and his personal pilot took a trip in August to Mt. McKinley, AK. Both were drinking scotch whiskey and they barely missed hitting a mountain, and almost ran out of fuel before finding a runway. Sharon first married a presbyterian Robert Borgfeldt Brown. Later, Sharon went on to marry William Lund. Years later, Walt's wife Lilly even prevented a biographer from revealing that Sharon was adopted. Sharon died relatively young.

It is important to look at the Disney family rather than just Walt Disney in trying to understand the Disney phenomena. For instance in 1958, the Wall Street Journal mentioned that Lillian B. Disney was beneficial owner of over 10% of common Disney stock. Lillian, Walt's widow, quietly purchased property in Napa Valley and moved there in the late 60's. She bought the property through Walt's Retlaw Enterprises and the Lillian Disney Trust. Lillian and her 2 daughters ran Retlaw for years. Diane Miller, her daughter, also bought land and moved to the Napa area. The Lillian Disney Trust bought the Silverado Vineyards, which Diane & her husband manage as "gentlemen growers" as they call it.

This side of the Disney family is shunned by the Illuminati insiders in the Napa Valley, as well as by the Roy O. side of the family. Although very private, there are occasional moments of publicity from Diane Disney Miller, when she donated wine for a fund raiser for the Planned Parenthood Shasta Diablo held at the estate Niebaum-Coppola, owned by director/producer Francis Ford Coppola. Francis F. Coppola comes from an old mafia family. He owns a big winery & directed Disney's Caption EO film. Locals in the Napa area do not trust any of the Disneys, especially the Roy O. side of the family. There are other Disney's who tie in with the occult world. Wesley Ernest Disney, a 32° Mason & Shriner, who was a U.S. Congressman, a state official & lawyer in Kansas who had a brother Richard Lester Disney-- who is a Rhodes Scholar and a Mason too. Wesley Ernest Disney, by the way began as a lawyer in Muskogee County (a Satanic controlled county), and was a Christian Scientist. He lived in Tulsa, a powerful city of the Illuminati hierarchy. Doris Miles Disney has been a writer of occult fiction, such as The Magic Grandfather the Chandler Policy (1972) and Trick or Treat (1972) as well as many other occult novels.

G. A HISTORY OF DISNEY

"The story of Disney's silent film career is not so much a struggle for artistic expression as it is a fight for commercial stability." During the 1920's, Walt stayed safely within the confines of comic animation as defined by others, such as the producers of Felix the Cat, Koko the Clown, and Krazy Kat. In other words, when many of the ideas were coming from just himself, Disney's movies were not any better than others. In the 1930's, Disney got some of the best talent available and he began to settle for only the best results from that talent. With the mob, and the Illuminati behind him, and driven by an indebtedness to them, Disney began to achieve outstanding results in animation. Between 1924 and 1927, Walt Disney made a series of 56 silent Alice Comedies which used three different girls (6-year-old Virginia Davis, Margie Gay and Lois Hardwick) to act as Alice who romps around in a make-believe cartoon world. These cartoons combined live action and animation. By the time the series was done, Walt Disney wanted to try working solely with animation.

Margaret Winkler in NY (who married Charles Mintz) distributed Walt Disney's Alice Comedies. From the beginning, children were the center of everything Walt did. The occult world that backed Walt, as well as Walt himself, believed that if they could bring out "the child" (that part of a person called "the child" by various psychologists), then they could appeal to the curiosity and feelings of the "child" part of adults. If it worked with adults, they could do the same with the child part in children. They knew even in the 20's & '30's what had to be accomplished in the secret Great Plan for a New World Order. The Illuminati Great Plan called for family life to be destroyed, for children to rebel against their parents, and for the world to become more violent. Children needed to immerse in images of violence so that a violent society could be created.

For instance, the 1925 film Alice Stage Struck shows little girl Alice strapped to a log leading to a buzz saw. They also wanted to make occultism--witchcraft the common belief of the American people. The Illuminati felt they could bring in witchcraft if they appealed to the curiosity of the child in every adult. For instance, the Donald Duck cartoon Corn Chips (1951) shows Donald harassing Chip and Dale who then get back at him by stealing a box of popcorn and spreading it all over the front yard. Now what does a cartoon like this teach kids? It teaches that stealing to repay a grudge is O.K. and that doing pranks is funny.

In Disney's 1920 films, he shows kids cutting school, shoplifting and playing hookey. He shows Alice running away from responsibility to have adventure. He shows prisoners escaping and hobos escaping work. His films are expression of misbehaviour being successful. What does this teach children? In the 1951 cartoon, Get Rich Quick Goofy wins money at poker and his initially angry wife who doesn't like gambling forgives him when she sees how much he's won. Goofy indicates that they can have a spending spree by telling his wife, "Easy come, easy go!" The gambling spirit is a very powerful spirit that the Illuminati want to instill in this nation. How can a cartoon that promotes gambling be wholesome for children?

Lt. Col. Dave Grossman is a military expert on how to condition people so that they will kill. He writes in his superb book On Killing (Boston, MS: Little Brown & Co., 1996) that the same process that the government has used to condition soldiers to kill, is being used by the entertainment industry. The only major difference is that in the military, men are taught to kill only on command, while our children are being taught to kill whenever they want to via TV's "entertainment." Grossman states on page 308, that the conditioning to kill begins with cartoons. "It begins innocently with cartoons and then goes on to the countless acts of violence depicted on TV as the child grows up... .Then the parents, through neglect or conscious decision, begin to permit the child to watch movies rated R due to vivid depictions of knives penetrating and protruding from bodies, long shots of blood spurting from severed limbs, and bullets ripping into bodies and exploding out the back in showers of blood and brains." While children see horrible deaths on T.V., they learn to associate this suffering with entertainment, pleasure and their favorite soft drink, their favorite candybar, and close intimate contact with their date. (See On Killing, p. 302)

Disney has the appearance of Wholesomeness; this appearance is quite deceptive. A close study of Disney cartoons will reveal lots of violence that could not be depicted if the violence was actually real life & not animation. It's the wholesome front which is one of the deceptions that makes Disney cartoons & films so dangerous. Yes, the image of Disney has been that its cartoons are wholesome. No wonder Illuminati mind-control programmers have laughed at how naive the American public is toward Disney. The Disney Gargoyles cartoons are a television series that is pure demonology. The story line is that a race of demons protects New York City. One of the Gargoyles is even named Demona. The Illuminati programmers are amazed at how stupid the masses of people are, and how easily deceived.

How the Disney movies are used as programming scripts is very involved so only one detailed example is given at the end of this chapter. The Illuminati and Mafia knew that Walt had the ability to get the job done that the Great Plans called for. (Source: confidential interview.) They knew they had the "carrots and the sticks" to get him to cooperate. There is no doubt that Walt was a hard worker who in turn expected high standards from his employees. One co-worker of Walt wrote, "Walt made a simple statement, that you can lick them with 'product' if you make your product good enough, they cannot deny it.. . .In Walt's estimation, everything that was done had to be executed with a great deal of thought and finesse." Neelands, Barbara, compiler. About Ben Sharpsteen, article by David R. Smith (2nd Impress.) Calistoga, CA: A Sharpsteen Museum Reprint, pg. 2-3.

One big turn in Walt's outlook toward quality came in April, 1927 when the head of Universal Studios wrote a scathing report on the quality of Disney studio work. It forced Walt to realize that up to then he had been slipshod and sloppy. He resolved to never take the easy way, but to work with dedication toward making his drawings come to life with character and interesting situations. In 1922, Walt made a film Cinderella. This is not to be confused with the later animated film also of the same title released in 1950. The 1950 feature was re-released numerous times. The Alice cartoons were made with a 6- year-old girl playing Alice. The first six Alice comedies had extensive live-action beginnings, and then went into cartoon. A few of the 1920's Alice silent cartoon titles include:

Alice's Wonderland (1923)
Alice Hunting in Africa (1924)
Alice's Spooky Adventure (1924)
Alice Plays Cupid (1925)
Alice Cans the Cannibals (1925)
Alice Rattled by Rats (1925)
Alice Chops the Suey (1925)
Alice Charms the Fish (1926)
Alice the Whaler (1927)
Alice the Beach Nut (1927)

After the Alice Series, Disney began a fully animated series called Oswald the Lucky Rabbit. Here we see the occult concept of luck (who hasn't heard of a lucky Rabbit's foot?) being subtly promoted. Disney cartoon may entertain, but they also indoctrinate while they entertain. In 1926, Walt Disney signed an agreement with Mintz and Film Booking Offices (EBO).

Film Booking Offices were Illuminati kingpin/mob boss Joseph Kennedy's company. For at least the next years, Disney worked under the control (auspices) of Illuminati kingpin Kennedy. All of the Disney pictures were registered by R-C Pictures Corp., one of the parent companies of Kennedy's FBO. Joseph Kennedy also controlled the RKO studio which worked together with the other big studios to insure that no small studio would develop as a competitor. By 1937, all the big studios--20th Cent., Paramount, MGM, Warner Bros., Cohn's Columbia Pictures and Kennedy's RKO were allowing the mob to skim money from them.

Kennedy's RKO gave Walt a guarantee in 1937 that they'd distribute Snow White sight unseen. Walt Disney had their films distributed by Kennedy's RKO from 1936 to 1956. Another little known detail is that in 1926, Leon Schlesinger (future producer at Warner Bros.) subcontracted animation jobs to Disney. One of these was Universal's The Silent Flyer. In 1928, Steamboat Willie debuted. This was an animated cartoon with a soundtrack starring a mouse later named Mickey Mouse. It had taken lots of hard work and determination on Walt's part, but it was the first cartoon with a sound track and it was successful.

In 1929, the cartoon The Haunted House came out. The story is, Mickey Mouse is forced by a storm into a house full of ghosts who force him to contribute to their spooky musicale. In 1930, Harry Cohn, one of the most ruthless and unsavory characters controlling a studio bailed Walt Disney out of Walt's trouble with con-artist Pat Powers who was stealing Disney's money. Harry Cohn was a former NY pool hustler and gambler who was brought in by Chicago investors to front their investments in Columbia Pictures, and run their studio. He wore a sapphire ring that the Chicago mafia man Johnny Roselli gave him. Roselli later became a rogue asset of the CIA, and testified before Congress (the Church Committee on Assassinations in '74) about a CIA contract which was handed him. Roselli worked for the Mafia Council of 9, which incl. Anthony Accardo and Sam Giancana. Harry Cohn was said by some to be the most hated man in Hollywood. His money gave him "the power of an emperor". His money got him the best female flesh available which he used for his pleasure. He always seemed to arrive from Las Vegas with rolls of new greenbacks, which had close associates wondering where all the money came from that he always got when he made trips to Las Vegas.

In 1931, Walt went into a long suicidal depression that lasted into 1932. In the summer of 1932, he took a vacation to try and recover from his nervous breakdown. By 1932, Ingersoll had marketed its first edition of Mickey Mouse watches. Disney products have served as a model of consumerism for the world. Disney watches have been made continuously since 1932 or '33. In 1932, eighty major U.S. corporations (such as General Foods, RCA & National Dairy) began to market Disney products. Ed Sullivan began regularly running stories that bragged about Disney's work. Freemason Dr. Rufus B. von Kleinsmid, pres. of the Univ. of So. Cal., gave Disney an award from Parents magazine for Walt's "work with children". In 1932, several artists who had worked for William Randolph Hearst came to work for Disney.

In 1932, Roy switched Disney from Columbia to United Artists. United Artists agreed to front Disney $15,000 for each cartoon. In the 1930's, the Illuminati' Bank of America financed Walt Disney. Years before, the Bank of America had been quietly created from Bank of Italy which was controlled by the same oligarchy that has run the Knights of Malta and renaissance Venice. The Bank of Italy was a powerful bank in Hollywood's first years. It's representatives A.P. and Atillo Giannini financed Walt during the 1920's with petty cash to keep him going, but not enough to get him out of financial bondage. Joe Rosenberg of Bank of America was sympathetic to Walt. Joe Rosenberg, a Jewish banker, came to all of Disney's board meetings, sat beside Walt, and would advise Walt on what direction Disney Studios should take. Joe wasn't a board member, but his advice got high priority.

Bank of America also bankrolled other Illuminati projects and organizations. Bank of America had one of their branch offices on Disneyland's Main St. from '55 until '93. They were open on holidays and Sundays for Disneyland. Bank of America is slated to be perhaps the only bank to survive the economic crash, when the Illuminati kingpins will allow their own banks to crash. Bank of America executive S. Clark Beise (who is a Scottish Rite Freemason) has been a member of Disney's board of directors from '65 to '75.

One of the biggest depositors in Bank of America is Roy E. Disney. Other Disney execs like Rich Frank have also used Bank of America as their bank of choice. The Bank of America bankrolled the Disney animation Snow White. Walt managed to sell Joseph Rosenberg on the idea, at a time when old time Hollywood people were advising Rosenberg that Snow White could only be a failure. When Snow White was successful, Walt announced a monster party for all Disney workers at Lake Norconian, near Palm Springs, southeast of San Bernandino, CA where the cost of everything the Disney workers wanted to order--food or drink or whatever, would be taken care of by the Disney's.

Under the full moon, the Disney male and female workers, finally free of the tight rules at the studios, had what amounted to a Roman orgy and a large nude skinny-dip at the lake. Almost all of the Disney workers participated in the orgy and Disney had only two options, 1. fire them all or 2. ignore that the party took place. Walt choose the later option, and after that no-one ever dared mention the party in his presence.

In 1937, Walt and Roy took a trip to Europe where Walt dined with the British Royal family, & met privately with H.G. Wells, the masonic prophet! planner of what Wells & other masons called "the New World Order". In Paris, the League of Nations (the forerunner to the U.N.) gave him an award.

After the success of Snow White, Disney chose Pinocchio to follow it. Many have asked why Pinocchio was chosen by Walt. If you look at the script, the puppet maker's wife is taken out of the original script, and there is an emphasis on the little wooden puppet visualizing becoming a flesh & blood son to the man who had created him. Here we have a boy with no soul, who is told if he works hard he will be given one. (Does this sound familiar to readers of VoL 2?) The script was definitely changed to have a storyline far more useful to mind-control programming.

For those who think Walt simply recreated fairy tales on the screen, if one examines the changes that are made from the original storylines, they are changed to make them more useful for mind-control. Both Snow White and Pinocchio have occult type "deaths and resurrections".

After W.W. II, Joseph Rosenberg persuaded A.P. Giannini, his boss, to bankroll Disney again. Although Walt was financed by the Mishpucka (Jewish Mafia), he didn't like the idea. Richard Rosenberg, a later Pres. of Bank of America, is also Mishpucka. Richard Rosenberg (his mother was a Cohen) was also in charge of Northrop Corp. and Marin Ecumenical Housing Assn. (Other examples of Mishpucka executives are R. Goldstein, v.p. of Procter & Gamble, and Marvin Koslow, v.p. of Bristol Meyers Co.)

In the 1930's, the elite promoted Disney's new cartoons. In 1935, Walt Disney received the French Legion of Honor for his Mickey Mouse cartoons. Also in 1935, the Queen of England (who readers of my previous articles will realize is Illuminati, involved in drug trade, and is involved with the leadership of Freemasonry) and the Duchess of York (also Illuminati) selected Mickey Mouse chinaware as gifts for 600 children. This was after Walt spent time with her in 1934.

The League of Nations (the pre-W.W. II equivalent of the U.N.) took the time to vote its approval of Mickey Mouse. (Finch, Christopher. The Art of Walt Disney from Mickey Mouse to the Magic Kingdom . NY: Harry N. Abrams, Inc., 1975, p. 53.) There is no doubt that Walt Disney had talent. There is also no doubt from the record that powerful people wanted to promote him. No doubt his 320 Masonic membership and his DeMolay activities helped boost his support, and also helped Walt's bent toward the occult.

Let's digress just to let people in on Freemasonry's involvement with acting and motion pictures. The famous 233 Club was a Masonic chapter for actors who were Freemasons. Examples of actors who were Freemasons include John Aasen, Gene Autry, Monte Blue and Humphrey Bogart, Douglas McClean, John Wayne.

Then there is T.V. DJ Dick Clark. Examples of Motion picture executives who were Freemasons incl. Ellis G. Arnall (Pres. of the Soc. of Ind. Motion Picture Producers), Will H. Hays (Czar of motion pictures 1922-45, and Pres. Motion Picture Produces & Distributors of Amer. Inc.), Benj. B. Kahane (v.p. & dir. Assoc. of Motion Picture Producers, Inc.), Carl Laemmle (Pres. Univ. Pictures Corp til '36), Frank E. Mullen (man. dept of info. RCA, VP NBC '39-'46, exec. VP NBC '46-'48), David Sarnoff (Chrm. of Bd. Radio Corp. of Amer. & „father" of American television), Jack M. Warner (v.p. of Warner Bros.) and the President & dir. of Universal Pictures since 1952. The Freemasons have made much of Walt Disney's membership in their membership sales pitches. Because the 2 Disney brothers' chief contributions to the production of Disney films were the finances and occasionally the ideas used in a film, it is rather misrepresentative of things that Walt Disney got all the credit for the success and quality of the Disney cartoons.

He was showered with 700 awards and honors from important people, including 30 oscars, and the Presidential Medal of Freedom (in '64). Walt Disney's great animators never got the credit they deserved, but no one should forget that Walt was the driving force that inspired and guided his workers.

In 1934, Walt Disney made a cartoon about a goddess of the Mystery Religions named Persephone. In the cartoon entitled The Goddess of Spring, the goddess Persephone is captured by Satan as his bride and sent to the underworld, with the agreement she could return to earth six months of each year. The Illuminati have rituals around Persephone. On Dec. 21, 1937, Disney premiered the first full-length color cartoon movie "Snow White and the Seven Dwarfs." This cartoon had taken $1.4 in depression-time money and three years to make. Over 750 artists worked on the film. Walt Disney had gotten the idea from a silent movie of Snow White which he saw as a boy in 1917. The movie has an important occult theme to it, and has been used for occult mind-control programming.

When the 1940's got started, Disney was in financial difficulties. At this point, Nelson Rockefeller hired his cartoon capabilities to make cartoons for South America, with the idea that South Americans would remain loyal to the American capitalist hegemony, rather than shift to rising ideologies of fascism/nazism, if they saw Walt Disney cartoons.

In Rio de Janeiro, Brazil on 8/24/42, Disney did its world premiere of Saludo Amigos, a 42 minute feature about Latin America. Goofy becomes a gaucho, a parrot teaches Donald Duck to dance the samba, as well as Disney art showing various landscapes of Brazil in the film.

However, the film The Three Caballeros, if it was meant to encourage South American loyalty to American capitalism, completely failed. The Three Caballeros showed a sexually lecherous Donald Duck who in bad taste tries to make it with Latin women. The mysticism was also seen as bogus. Although the Latin Americans hated the film, the establishment media's Look magazine praised it. Another reason that Rockefeller sent Walt to South America was to get him out of the way so that the government could settle the strike by Disney workers. Nelson Rockefeller was the government's Coordinator of Inter-American Affairs, a good position considering how much of South America the Rockefeller's controlled. Rockefeller told Disney that Disney couldn't beat the strikers, but that while Walt was in South America, FDR would see to it that the strike got settled.

When Disney returned he submitted to the powers that were, and accepted the unions and the mafia's control. Another change for Walt Disney was that in 1940, he and Roy turned Disney into a "public corporation" and initially sold 755,000 shares of common stock. The Illuminati Boston firm of Kidder, Peabody & Co. were the underwriters of the studio's public stock-offerings.

By 1940, the Disney Studio at Burbank had become a miniature city with 1,000 men & women employees and 20 buildings on a 51 acre tract of land. After the U.S. joined W.W. II, Disney Productions were made a part of the American military establishment. The very next day after Pearl Harbor, the military moved onto the Disney Studio, which leads this author to suspect that Disney was already part of the power establishment prior to the war breaking out. Disney made military movies/cartoons that taught the different branches of the military many things. They made propaganda movies for the allies.

One series of films was "Why we fight." Disney made movies for the IRS to get people to pay their taxes. Some of the Disney films were top, secret, and concerned secret military weapons or secret psychological tactics of the Americans. For instance, one military film was "Army Psycho Therapy" which taught army men how to instill fear, and about the basics of fear. Another army film was "Prostitution & the War". Another showed a carrier pigeon evading the Germans. In 1940, Disney came out with 2 full length animated cartoons, Pinocchio and Fantasia, both of which were soon used for Illuminati mind-control programming. Fantasia contains Schubert's sacred Catholic music Ave Maria, which was used in a concluding segment side to side with the profane Night on Bald Mountain song, as well as six other classical pieces of orchestra music.

As a feature cartoon it was a flop, but as a programming tool it was fantastic. Fantasia receives a comprehensive explanation of how it is used for mind-control programming at the end of this chapter. Because an explanation of the use of a Disney film for mind-control is complex, this explanation is placed at the end of the chapter so that it won't interrupt the flow of this chapter's information. The Pinocchio film has been redone and released 9 times over the years. Some of the next full length animated films to come out were: The Three Caballeros (1945) The Adventures of Ichabod & Mr. Toad ('49) Cinderella (1950) Treasure Island (1950) Alice In Wonderland (1951) The Story of Robin Hood & His Merrie Men (1952) Peter Pan (1953) 20,000 Leagues Under the Sea (1954) Sleeping Beauty (1959) Very soon after the production of all of these movies, the Illuminati and their intelligence agencies used them for Illuminati total mind-control programming.

To see their misuse as programming scripts one has to understand how the fantasy worlds of a programmed multiple are created and how the movie scripts are adapted to be programming scripts. Vol. 2 gave quite a few examples of how Alice In Wonderland and the Wizard of Oz scripts were used for programming scripts. When Disney had his animal-nature documentaries, he edited and used narration to give the animals human like characteristics--something he'd already been doing with animation. Disney played an important part in the Illuminati's plan to elevate animals and dehumanize humans.

One of the biggest Illuminati kingpins, and leader (Grand Master) of the Prieure de Sion was Frenchman Claude Debussy (bn.1862). Claude Debussy, a Merovingian, was Nautonnier (Navigator-helmsman) of the Prieure de Sion from 1885-1918. (See the document Dossiers secrets, planche no. 4, Ordre de Sion, written about in Holy Blood, Holy Grail.) In 1891, when some secret coded parchments (Merovingian documents) were found by a French clergyman Sauniere, he was directed by church officials to visit with Emile Hoffet, an occult acquaintance of Debussy.

Debussy was close friends with many of the top French occultists of his time. He is known to have been a close friend to both the notorious Satanists Jules Bois and MacGregor Mathers. Mathers started the Order of the Golden Dawn. Debussy was also a friend of the infamous Papus (aka Dr. Gerard Encausse) and W.B. Yeats.

Papus was one of the men who during his lifetime was part of the interlocking occult directorate of occult groups. Claude Debussy put some works of the previous P.d.S. Grand Master Victor Hugo to music. Debussy and his other powerful occult friends were influential with Monsieur Philippe, whose Russian occult circle influenced the Russian Czars and Czarinas before Rasputin came around. Debussy travelled to Russia and Rome. Some of Debussy's works became operas. Interestingly, Walt Disney was extremely anxious to make a cartoon using Debussy's Clair de Lane. The work was done, but it was never shown to the public. Disney never found a place to use it. It was originally done with animation with flying cranes for the occult extravaganza Fantasia, but when the Fantasia ended up too long, Clair de Lane was cut and shelved. It was again planned for the film Make Mine Music, but then Blue Bayou was substituted in. Walt used the Le Sacre du Printemps (the Rite of Spring) music for Fantasia. This piece of music was written AS a pagan ritual where a virgin sacrifices herself by dancing to death. Disney's mobster Gunther Lessing had threatened Stravinsky if permission weren't given for Disney to use the piece of music, it would be used anyway.

Dr. Julian Huxley got involved in the production of Fantasia. Aldous and Julian Huxley are well known by conspiracy researchers for their roles in the World Order. In the 1940's and 1950's, the Illuminati began using Disney's Alice In Wonderland and the Wizard of Oz films as programming bases for their total mind-controlled slaves. Alice in Wonderland had been done many years earlier by the Britisher William Cameron Menzies (who also did Freemason

H.G. Wells' Masonic forecast of the New World Order entitled "Things to Come" in 1936, and the film Invaders From Mars.). In 1944, Illuminati Kingpin William Randolph Hearst (with some minor help from others) funded the Motion Picture Alliance, and Walt Disney became a co-founder and its first Vice-President. In the early 1950's, Walt turned his attention from animated cartoons to other projects, such as True-Life-Adventures, television shows, and the creation of Disneyland. Seal Island was his first true life adventure which was released to the general public on May 4, 1949, and soon won Walt Disney an Oscar. Alfred and Elma Milotte had shot the film on some Alaskan Islands named Pribilof Islands. James Algar had put the movie together.

In 1952, Walter spelled his named backwards to create the name of another corporation "Retlaw". Roy and his family saw the move as an attempt to cut them out of the financial picture. In 1954, Walt Disney and ABC made a agreement. ABC would directly invest half a million US dollars as well as guarantee $4.5 million in loans for the construction of Disneyland. This made ABC 1/3 owner of Disneyland. In return, Walt Disney agreed to produce a regular television series for ABC. Remember too that ABC's president Leonard Goldenstein was a good friend of Ronald Reagan. On July 13, 1955, Walt and Lillian were attempting to celebrate their 30th wedding anniversary at a park and restaurant. Walt got too drunk to speak into the microphone, so he blew noisemakers into it, while Lillian rushed to pull him out of view. In 1961, Disney bought out the ABC investment (also labelled Paramount) for $7.5 million with cash and notes, and to bring this all up to date, later on July 31, 1995, Disney merged with Capital Cities/ABC, with Disney in nominal control. Actually Capital Cities has long been a CIA front company, so the merger placed Disney squarely within the CIA ranks, although it had been in bed with them for the CIA's entire history.

The Illuminati-controlled corporations of Coca-Cola and the drug firm Johnson and Johnson became sponsors for Disney's early TV shows. On 7/3/57, the Wall St. Journal announced that Atlas Corp. got 26% interest in Walt Disney Productions. Walt Disney worked quietly with some consultants on the concepts behind Disneyland. His brother and nephew tried to prevent the project from happening. Later they requested that Walt sign over Disneyland, Inc. to Walt Disney Productions, which Walt did. Walt kept 17.25 % of Disneyland holdings and Walt Disney Productions got the rest. Walt Disney Productions then shared their portion with others. The man who helped Walt finance Disneyland was the executive vice-pres. of ABC Kintner.

Walt Disney got the Illuminati's Stanford Research Institute to determine what would be the best site for Disneyland. A retired Navy admiral Joe Fowler was in charge of constructing both Disneyland and Walt Disney World. How do admirals fit into the power structure? Admirals are briefed each day, and are given information concerning the secret power structure. Most men who are at that military level are Illuminati or at least well controlled by the system. Within the last few years there has been an intense effort to weed out any admirals who are not loyal to the Illuminati. Morgan-Evans, who lives in Malibu, and who may be of the famous Morgan clan, was the one who created the spectacular landscapes for Disneyland, Walt Disney World, and EPCOT in FL. According to CIA informants opposed to the NWO, CIA contractors were brought in to build the underground tunnels under Disneyworld in 1977. These contractors were sworn to secrecy, but were only informed on a need to know basis why the CIA was involved with an amusement park. To work on the secret tunnel project took an "Above Top Secret" clearance. A major programming center was constructed under Lake Holden. (Many of the lakes in Florida are named Lake So-and-so, rather than So-and-so Lake.) The tunnel system was built for programming trauma-based total mind-controlled slaves. It was built of concrete with steel reinforcement. Lake Holden lies just to the northwest side of the Orlando International Airport and just south of Interstate 4. (It is close to Range 29E on quad maps.) It is only (as the crow flies) about 12 miles from Disneyworld.

In spite of Draconian measures of secrecy, numerous lawsuits (Fed. & State) were filed over the years by victims trying to expose the Disneyworld programming tunnels, so that finally the programming center was dismantled, cleaned up and a "maintenance" tunnel level and a "casting" tunnel level were opened to the public. During its heyday, the programmers (military & intelligence men) had exotic offices underground with unusual programming equipment. It doesn't take any imagination to realize that if Disney carried mind-control programming above and below ground, that they would need tight security forces to protect their secrets. Indeed, such is the case. Disney amusement parks have been granted draconian powers wherever they have been built! The Disney parks have also employed armies of spies dressed like tourists to spy on Disney's employees! If amusement park workers did anything slightly out of place, they were (and still are) reported by the spies in the camp, and they often have lost their jobs.

For instance, one ex-worker, who had 10 years with Disney, was caught discussing his divorce with another worker. Since divorce doesn't fit the wholesome image that Disney wants, when the spy dressed as a tourist reported his conversation, he lost his job. Many workers have tried to tell their personal horror stories of Disney's draconian rules and their draconian private police force, but most of the time Disney has had the power to suppress and intimidate away any bad publicity. An exception to that is the recent Nov. 4, '96 Napa Valley Register article on page 2D entitled, "Critics of Disneyland Say Security Abusive Inside Magic Kingdom." UCLA law professor David Sklansky commented about Disney's police, "One of the major problems we have is nobody really knows what they are doing- how often they stop, interrogate or search people. They are not subject to the same sort of regulatory controls."

It's almost superfluous to tell readers that Disney's amusement park with it's theme areas such as Fantasyland, Tomorrowland and Adventureland were a great success. Everyone worldwide was curious to visit this entertainment mecca to participate in something that had a clean, wholesome image to it. The entire world system pulled together to insure that Disneyland got the image and publicity that the top 13 Illuminati families and the various syndicates wanted it to have. For 40 years they've done this. When something that everyone thinks is clean and wholesome is not attacked by the world system, that should raise eyebrows among thinking people. Home schooling, learning to read phonetically and other wholesome activities for children have been viciously attacked and ridiculed by the established media. Why has Disney gone untouched?

Disney Studios for years strove to have a very clean image. Workers had dress codes, and any activity on the part of employees that wasn't morally conservative was grounds for instant dismissal. Of course, the exceptions were well covered up, such as an employee who used hypnosis to get quite a few of the females employees to undress until nude. John L. Hulteng, author of The Messenger's Motives (Englewood Cliff, NJ: Prentice-Hall, 1976, p. 213) informs us, "As communication researchers have emphasized, the greatest impact the media have on the formation or change of public opinion is in terms of impressions built up over a long period." [bold added] The wholesomeness of Disney is an image that has been built over a long period of time. Disney's occult themes of world citizenship, witchcraft, humanism and idolatry have also been long running impressions that have been craftively perpetrated upon this nation, so long that they began prior to this author's --& probably the reader's-- birth. People don't associate movie's like Consenting Adults with Disney, or The Corpse Had a Familiar Face with Disney. In fact as previously mentioned, when Disney wanted to put out more "adult" films, they did a slight of hand and created the label Touchstone films so that people wouldn't associate movies like Splash (which showed what looked like bared breasts) with Disney Productions.

Another label, Hollywood Pictures, was created by Disney to help distribute Touchstone films. At first the personnel of these companies was simply Disney's staff, but as time went on, they got their own production personnel. On Oct. 27, 1954, Walt Disney's Wonderful World of Color debuted on television. The TV show celebrated Disney's movie triumphs. The words Wonderful World of Color are not ill chosen. According to an Illuminati mind-control programmer, when Disney worked on his cartoons, and amusement parks, colors --special colors and color combinations--were specifically chosen for mind-control programming purposes. Wonderful World of Color under various names such as Disneyland aired for 22 years over the television networks.

In 1955, Walt Disney made his cartoon character Mickey Mouse real by creating a fan club--the Mickey Mouse Club, which aired five days a week usually just as children came home from school. Twenty-four children called mouseketeers would help Mickey, and they would dance and sing and do skits. The Mickey Mouse Club adored the unique, cute little beanie Mickey Mouse caps with their big ears mounted to each side of the beanie. In the 1950's, most kid viewers of the show wanted their own "Mouse Ears" and to become a Mouseketeer, especially children who were receiving Mickey Mouse scripts in their total mind-control programming. Disney used his Mouseketeers to play all the roles in an Oz movie Rainbow Road to Oz, which was never shown to the public.

Adults today (both men & women) who received Mickey Mouse programming during the 50's through 70's can still be seen with Mickey Mouse clocks, watches, lampshades, knick-knacks, tee shirts, etc. Years later the kids who watched can still remember "Spin and Marty" and the Mickey Mouse theme song. The image that everything was perfect including Mickey was portrayed by the Club's T.V. program. Still somehow the American people began to use the word "Mickey Mouse" as a synonym for a silly, pretend way of doing things. It became common for people to say, "He mickey-moused it together." to mean he did a poor job putting it together.

On Jan. 30, 1957, Walt Disney had a television show aired entitled "All About Magic" where a Magic Mirror explains about magic. The Magic Mirror also contains a "Bibbidi-bibbidi-Boo" sequence. In 1959, Disney bought 8 small submarines from Todd Shipyards for $2,150.000. When ABC wouldn't let Walt make a TV series out of a storyline where a magic ring changes a boy into a dog (a mind-control programming theme)--because ABC didn't think the public could swallow the story line--Walt quit ABC for NBC. Walt then made a scaled down version of this occult storyline entitled The Shaggy Dog.

Early in the 1960's, Walt and his brother Roy went secretly looking for an area on the east coast to build another Disney Park. Walt the younger of the two, died in 1966, and Roy finished the project. Beginning in 1964, 30,000 acres were secretly purchased at $200 an acre in the Orlando, FL area just west of NASA's Cape Kennedy. Using phoney names and paying cash, Disney buyers bought the land and swore the sellers to secrecy. The Magic Kingdom has been multiplying. In 1971, Walt Disney World was opened to the public. Bob Hope and others participated in a Disney special on Oct. 29, 1971 "Grand opening of Walt Disney World". From the time of its opening until Oct. 12, 1995, Disney World calculated 1/2 billion people visited DisneyWorld. This amusement park is in Orlando, FL on over 27,400 acres and includes the EPCOT Center (now also called simply Epcot). The EPCOT center was another dream of Walt Disney's (albeit more than slightly modified from Walt's original EPCOT ideas.)

EPCOT originally stood for Experimental Prototype Community of Tomorrow. It was to be an extension of the massive mind-control being carried out at Disney World. The original EPCOT city designed by Walt was to carry on its commerce (traffic) via underground roads and tunnels like the Disney Theme parks. After Walt Disney died, his successors changed the proposed experimental city into another theme park simply called Epcot. It is not unusual to see crowds of over 48,000 people descend on Walt Disney World and the EPCOT center in a single day. Some visitors arrive via a monorail. Visitors can buy 5-Day World Hopper passes which allow them to bounce around with admission to all the sites for a seven day period. In other words, some families stay for a week at Disneyworld. Hardcore visitors can get Annual Passports which provide unlimited use of Walt Disneyworld for an entire year.

In reality, many visitors to Disneyworld begin the day enthusiastic and after a day of hot sun and waiting in long lines with large crowds for imitations of reality, the tourists are zombie-like and looking forward to getting back to their hotels. Many people have felt the rides were not nearly what they expected. Some of the rides are better than others, and some typically get comments like, "It was stupid." Some of the spooky events like Snow White's Adventures, or the oversized heads of the Disney characters walking around can leave the little preschool children terrified and dazed for the rest of the day. In contrast, older children, who normally rarely show patience at home may show how much they want to go on a particular Disney ride, by waiting an hour and a half in the hot sun for a ride. Alien Encounter is a Walt Disneyland feature that invites tourists in for a "demonstration of interplanetary teleportation." When the "demonstration" as planned "breaks down" an "alien" with asocial traits appears among the audience and terrorizes the audience. A cute creature is hideously fried, deformed, and then vomited into space screaming. Here are some comments from visitors to this Walt Disneyland attraction:

· "Alien Encounter ...is one of those rides I can say I've seen and that I have no intention of ever doing again. In fact, parents who take children under the age of six should be brought up on child abuse." Woman, from MI

· "Alien Encounter was the WORST experience for my 10-year-old (and almost every child in there). It starts out cute enough during the preshow, but the actual show is a disaster for children. My daughter screamed and cried in terror throughout it. I thought the Disney warnings were vague and inaccurate. When we left, there wasn't one child with dry eyes (even sturdy looking 12-year-old boys were crying.). I think an age requirement of 13 or 14 is more appropriate. I talked to a few adults and we even agreed that the special effects were extremely unpleasant even for us. This show is not a Disney family experience--its ATROCIOUS!!" A mother from Phillipsburg, NJ.

· "We did go to Alien Encounter...The preshow is deceiving. It kind of lulls you into thinking "this isn't so bad." When the main part came up, I admit the experience gave me the absolute heebie-jeebies. . .I am never doing that presentation again--it was way too intense for me, and I'm now 27 years of age!--from a family in Laurel, MD

Michael Eisner, the President of Walt Disney Co., initially rejected Alien Encounter for not being scary enough when it was being considered as an addition to Disneyworld. One wonders what he would have liked! Snow White's Adventures, which was an attraction at Disneyland, was one of what the Disney people called "dark rides". After a while a sign appeared with a witch warning people that the attraction was scary. Later in 1983, they renamed it Snow White's Scary Adventures. It might be interesting to point out that when the original Snow White and Seven Dwaffs film came out, that England forbid the film to be seen by any child under 16 unless accompanied by an adult because of the scary content of the movie. How far we have come since then.

Schools in the Florida and California areas also make field trips to the Magic Kingdom that are arranged with Disney. EPCOT receives tens of thousands of children this way during March, September and October. High schools use the Magic Kingdom for proms or senior nights, and some couples use the facilities of the Magic Kingdom for weddings. Modem Bride ranked Orlando as the number-one honeymoon destination in the world. Group discussions of people who took honeymoons to DisneyWorld have had a consensus that the hype is not as great as the reality. Some weddings are done with cartoon characters. Disney offers "fairy-tale" wedding packages. A great deal for two mind-controlled slaves. They can reinforce their programming while getting married. The Disney fairy-tale wedding typically has its ceremony on a pavilion on an island in the Seven Seas Lagoon with the Cinderella Castle as a backdrop. The fairy-tale wedding can then be followed with a Fantasy reception with a choice of themes such as Beauty & the Beast or Aladdin. The fantasy programming can continue as the bride is delivered to a "Cinderella's Ball" by an actual glass carriage drawn by six white Disney ponies. A costumed fairy-godmother & stepsisters are also at the ball. Desert is served in a white chocolate slipper.

One of the after-dark shows is IllumiNations which consists of music, fireworks, erupting fountains, special lighting, and laser technology done at the World Showcase Lagoon. EPCOT has a show Cranium Command at the Wonders of Life in the Future World section where guests sit in a theater that functions as a command control room for a boy's brain. In 1980, Disney came out with the box office flop The Devil & Max Devlin. In 1984, Roy E. Disney brought in Michael Milken, of junk bond fame to help Disney out financially. In 1985, Disney bought MGM's rights to Leo the Lion logo and began using the MGM Wizard of Oz material. Later a remake of Alice In Wonderland came out in the modern motif of Honey I Shrank the Kids. In the 1990's, Illuminati controlled companies continued their promotion of Disney. For instance, the Nestle family's Nestle company promotes Disney movies on their chocolate bars. The Nestle family is exposed in this author's booklet Illuminati Control Over Foods and Grains, p. 4 as one of the elite Black Nobility families. In 1996, Walt Disney World created an actual residential town named Celebration on its property. This self-contained community has 20,000 and a school, a theater, a fiber optic information network linking business, as well as other features.

SOME DISNEY people of interest.

Over the years, the close associates of the Disneys' is very revealing. The public can get a feel for Disney's attitude toward Illuminati bloodlines in the Disney movie The Happiest Millionaire which is about Anthony J. Drexel Biddle and Angie Duke. Readers of this author's previous writings will recognize the Biddle and Duke names. In fact, the movie was based loosely on a book written by Cordelia Drexel Biddle about the Biddles.

X Atensio. His first name was Xavier, but was nicknamed and called X. He worked on the haunted mansion of Disneyland with WED enterprises. He joined Disney in 1938, and was an assistant animator of Fantasia.

Warren Beatty. (b. 1937 in VA) This actor is from the Illuminati Beatty family and starred in Disney's Dick Tracy. The Dick Tracy film uses color in a special way, and this ties in with the color programming of the mind-control. Some total mind-controlled slaves have programming based on Disney's Dick Tracy movie for them to track down and kill "targets" (people). Warren's sister is the famous (or infamous) Shirley Maclaine. Shirley "MacClaine" is not what she appears.

Her father was a professor who was a CIA asset. She was used by the CIA as a sex slave. She became popular with the studios because she went to bed with the correct people. Her talents were used to get her as an intelligence slave into places that an obvious intelligence agent couldn't go. She was married to a man in the NSA for nearly 20 years. Her adopted name Maclaine (reportedly her mother's maiden name) is a pun on McLain, VA where the CIA programmed her. She was used by the CIA in an operation in Australia, where the CIA used her as a sex slave to compromise Andrew Peacock, an Australian MP, so that they could establish the Nugen-Hand bank for their dirty money laundering etc.

She is friends with Satanist Stephen Nance who has provided her with some of her teachings. Lowell McGovern writes her material. The CIA has programmed many of their New Age slaves to adore Shirley MacLaine. An example of this is Christa Tilton, one of their mind-controlled slaves, who revealed in an interview how she considered herself a born-again Christian who had spent most of her life in Oklahoma, but had mysteriously been drawn to Shirley MacLaine. During her life she has gotten repeated "psychic urgings"--that is strong urges to do things and go places, which she doesn't understand where these urgings came from. After hypnosis, Christa drew pictures of the doctor who programmed her. Christa has had a federal agent monitor her constantly. Her husband has seen this agent, who has shown up on her door step and made calls to her. She names the agent John Wallis (most likely a cover name). This agent has a complete knowledge of her life, and government agents have taken photos of her during her supposedly "alien abduction" experiences. Christa is just one of hundreds of victims who have been programmed to adore Shirley MacLaine. (Christa is mentioned here because she is one case that this author is familiar with.) Warren Beatty, who peppers his speech with four-letter words was a student at the Stella Adler Theater Studio in NYC.

Black, Shirley Temple. Shirley Temple Black sat on the Disney board of directors (74-75). Her films were used for some of the early 40's and '50's programming and teaching slaves body movements/dance. She married someone in an elite Network family from San Francisco named Charles A. Black. Charles A. Black was a Lt. Col. in the Pentagon who lived at Bethesda, MD. Was Shirley an early example of brain-stem scarring to get geniuses? Shirley's brother appears to have developed "Multiple Sclerosis" from brain stem-scarring. It was Shirley Temple who co-founded the International Federation of Multiple Sclerosis Societies, and was a member of its exec. committee. Shirley represented the U.S. at the UN General Assembly in 1969, belongs to the Sierra Club, and has been decorated with the Cross of Malta. Shirley has shown clues that she may be an Illuminati mind-controlled child protege.

Stephen Bollenbach. Bollenbach was part of Walt Disney management, and was a key figure who helped engineer Disney's $19 billion buyout of the CIA's Capital Cities/ABC, as well as sell the idea to Eisner. He is the CEO of the Network's Hilton Hotels Corp. He recently has been involved with trying to buy ITT, in order to put together the world's largest hotel-casino combination. Bollenbach has an extensive background with the gaming-gambling industry. When the Justice Dept. began looking into the merger of Disney with Cap. Cities/ABC, Bollenbach resigned his Disney position. Some people feel his resignation was needed for Disney to get the Justice Dept. to approve the merger, because his past was vulnerable to be exposed.

Warren Buffett. A major stockholder in Walt Disney. He also owns 40% of Berkshire Hathaway Inc. which also owns lots of shares of Disney stock. According to S.F. Examiner, Buffett himself owns 24 million shares of Disney. Warren Buffett is part of the Ak-Sar-Ben fraternity and Monarch slave abusers who were exposed in the Nebraska Saving & Loan scandal. He is perhaps the second richest man in the nation, and too powerful for anyone to touch. In the kingpin vs. kingpin battles, some people close to the inside see Buffett as a good guy. Readers need to study the Lincoln Savings & Loan scandal and the scandals connection to programmed child slaves at Boy's Town to get more information on this Disney stockholder. Robert G. Hagstrom, Jr., who is the portfolio manager of the mutual fund Focus Trust, which has shares in Walt Disney, wrote the book The Warren Buffett Way. Hagstrom has a chapter on Disney in his The Warren Buffett Way. He quotes Buffett as extremely enthusiastic about Disney's merger with Capital Cities/ABC. Because of his enthusiasm Buffett says, "The odds are extremely high that we will have a very large amount of Disney stock."

Salvador Dali--This strange surrealist Spanish artist was a friend of Walt Disney. After Salvador was kicked out of Spain for Franco's belief that he was a communist, he came to America, and worked with Disney Studios in 1946. Salvador, an eccentric who had no particular work habits, described himself, "The only difference between me and a madman is that I'm not a madman."

The Tommy Dorsey Band--This band has had a number of men in it who are Mind-control slave abusers associated with the Network. Frank Sinatra, a sexual slave user, got his big break with this band. This band performed at Disneyland in 1984 at the Plaza Gardens. Tommy Dorsey was part of the Network's in-crowd. When he was on a USO Tour with Bob Hope, he stabbed actor Joe Hall and threw him out of a window. Joe had to have 32 stitches. But Joe didn't get justice, the judge dismissed his case against Tommy.

Michael Dammann Eisner, Chairman at Disney is a CIA asset and connected to the mob. Some insiders believe he is connected to elements of the CIA & mob that are anti-NWO. Even so, these anti-NWO factions also employ mind-control. Eisner ignored a threat by Red China to boycott Disney products if he made a movie about the nation Tibet that China controls with draconian force. The U.N., the Commerce Dept. and the State Dept. all tried unsuccessfully to get him to back down on the film. A paper trail connecting Michael Eisner and Walt Disney Co. to mind control is their support of the Boys & Girls Club of Napa Valley, which is used for a supply of children for pedophilia and mind-control. The Boy's & Girls Club is used to supply caddies for the Silverado Country Club, where these children are also used as mind-controlled slaves for the sexual perversions of the elite. Notice that Napa's Silverado Country Club invites in celebrities (such as CIA asset Pat Boone, Joe DiMaggio, ex-husband of sex slave Marilyn Monroe, Engelbert Humberdinck a slave handler, Digger Phelps, Notre Dame's coach who uses slaves, and Jack Vale nti CEO of Motion Picture Assoc. & Bohemian Grover) for a golf tournament which is billed as a "benefit for the Boys & Girls Club". The benefit for child slaves is they get to caddie & sexually service elite perverts.

Michael (bn. March 7, '42 in NY) came from old American money of a family that has been rich merchants and lawyers. Michael grew up in luxurious Park Ave. as well as his family's "country place" in Bedford Hills near Mt. Kisco, NY. He went to an elite private school Allen-Stevenson, which is famous for its children's orchestra. At the age of 14, he then went to Lawrenceville School, which is a prep-school for Princeton, whose tuition in '56 was $3,000. Eisner's class incl. NY's governor's son, and other sons of powerful men, such as the son of Saudi Prince Turqi al-Faisal. The school is a prep school for the establishment's entertainment industry. Students are only allowed to see their parents on major holidays. Eisner was in the Periweg Club, the school's drama society. His poor scholastic performance meant that he had to go to a small liberal arts college, rather than Princeton or Harvard such as was family tradition. For instance, his grandfather had attended Phillips Exerter Academy and Harvard. His grandfather has serve in many govt. commissions and belonged to the Harvard Club, the American Club in London as well as some yacht clubs. Between his junior & senior year in high school, Eisner was a page at NBC's HQ in the Rockefeller Center.

In 1966, he landed a job in the programming department of ABC. He had an influential position. Eisner had one good break for deciding TV programming. He was 21 when the target audience was 21 years old, and when he was 35, the target age of the film industry was then 35. He has been described as having "supernatural enthusiasm" coupled to a lifetime quest for untested ideas.

Rich H. Frank, was Executive Vice-President with Walt Disney until his sudden resignation about a year before this was written. He worked side by side with Katzenberg and left after Katzenberg resigned in a dispute with Disney's chairman Eisner. Rich Frank was President of Walt Disney's TV-Media Division. He acquired the estate of VanHoffenwiggen, when VanHoffenwiggen fled the country and vanished when Lendvest began to be exposed. VanHoffenwiggen was a major figure involved with Lendvest Mortgage Inc., a drug-laundering operation and drug smuggling operation operating out of Napa Valley. It was also the fastest growing real estate mortgage company in northern California until its drug smuggling began to be exposed. Lendvest did some tricks ala Nugen Hand Bank. Millions of dollars of investors and creditors have disappeared leaving lots of hurting people, and the mortgage company filed for protection from creditors in U.S. Bankruptcy court, and is still in operation.

International financier Edmond Safra's private bank, the Republic National Bank of NY, launders money from the Medellin drug cartel. Safra's bank sent Lendvest lots of crisp new $100 bills. The Safras are tied in with the Rothschilds. (The Safras are reportedly recent property owners in St. Helena near Napa (through Good Wine Co. which is the Spring Mountain Wineries), near where Lendvest was HQed. Edmond's nephew, Jacob Safra, has a partnership in Napa Valley's Good Wine Co.

The Rothschild's Citicorp gave Republic National Bank the transaction ability to issue international (world) bearer bonds ("bank notes") The Luxembourg/Belgium branch of Bank Nacional de Paris issued a bearer bond that was connected the Lendvest drug running operation. In Britain, a U.S. citizen Mike Spire ran the British operation of Lendvest and InVest. LandVest's parent was InVest which has operated in the U.K., Switz., Saudi Arabia & Paraguay. Long story made short, Lendvest has been an international CIA-Mafia drug running operation, with Illuminati overtones and connections to it.

With all this in mind, it is strange, that Walt Disney's President of its TV-Media Division, Rich Frank, bought the palatial mansion of John O. Van Hoffenwiggen after Van Hoffenwiggen disappeared from the country when indictments and arrests began to be made of people connected to Lendvest. According to insiders, Rich Frank is also one of a number of Napa Valley people involved in illegal labelling of wines. Rich Frank was a key figure in Disney's programming venture with three regional Bell Telephone companies (Ameritech, Bell South, & SBC Commun.) coming together. Bell Telephone wanted to get into cable TV. Michael Ovitz formed a rival group of 3 other Bell Telephone co.s. Calvin Robinson, who tied in with Land Vest, worked with Boyce, who in turn worked for TRW Co., in Redondo Beach, CA. Boyce was sentenced to 40 years for selling US surveillance secrets to the soviets.

Daniel Hillis, the co-founder of a supercomputer producer Thinking Machines from MIT, is in charge of the Walt Disney Imagineering unit. Hillis helped Disney develop a virtual-reality ride at Disneyland based on the Aladdin cartoon.

Jeffrey Katzenberg, has been the chairman of Disney's movie studio, is an aggressive worker, a model Type A person. "Ask 50 people to describe Jeffrey Katzenberg, and most will say tenacious. 'If Jeffrey were any more aggressive, he'd be in jail." says the producer Dan Melnick." (Harmetz, Aljean, "Who Makes Disney Run?", NY Times. Feb. 7, '88, p. 29.) Katzenberg is the father of twins, which people joke was typical of his efficiency. Katzenberg supervised the production of Star Trek. Most of his movies have been box office successes. In the '70's, Katzenberg worked for NY Mayor John Lindsay.

Sanford Martin Litvack. Sanford is the Executive Vice Pres. of Disney and in charge of "Human Resources" for the corporation. He is a Jewish lawyer who was educated at the Jesuits' Georgetown Univer. He is on the bd of dir, of Bet Tzedek.

Vincent Price. Price has been one of the major influential occultists who has provided the world with many occult horror books and scripts. He worked for Disney some, and was the voice for Ratigan in The Great Mouse Detective. Vincent Price's good friend John Hay Whitney is an Illuminati kingpin and vice-pres. of the Pilgrim Society and was raised into the Illuminati through the Yale Scroll & Key fraternity. His friend Whitney likes horror movies.

The Osmond Brothers. Merrill Osmond's boys were "discovered" at Disneyland when they were visiting the site in 1962. The Disney people on Main St. just "happened" to recognize the talent of the five boys and signed them up soon for their first professional singing contract. The Osmond Boys did some television appearances for Disneyland such as Meet Me at Disneyland, and Disneyland after Dark. (Considering the mind-control programming done to these Osmund children, these TV shows were a cruel joke.) Of the singing Osmond kids, Donny is the next to the youngest, and his sister Marie is the youngest. Both Donny and his sister Marie are programmed multiples who are slaves, who have been subjected to a lot of abuse. They have good front alters. Their father has made millions from drugs, porn and white slavery and is part of the Mormon Illuminati front. The Mormon front of the Illuminati has gotten a lot of good publicity off of the Osmonds. They sang for Andy Williams whose French wife was once arraigned on murder charges. Later they sang for the satanic Network's Lawrence Welk show. Swedish accented Lawrence Welk has been part of the Network. Marie Osmond has grown up, and she has adopted 3 of her 5 children in spite of her busy singing schedule which includes approx. 200 singing shows a year at places like Mafia controlled Atlantic City. In terms of occult families, adopted children are often programmed children, so this is a clue that her children have been programmed too.

Michael Ovitz. Ovitz was the no. 2 man at Walt Disney for a while until near the end of '96. Michael Ovitz was a high school classmate in VanNuys, CA with Michael Milken (later the junk-bond wizard), & there are many of the same people connected to both men. When Michael Ovitz's National Mercantile Bancorp (a saving & loan) began getting into the quicksand of several lawsuits & scandals, attorney Robert Strauss represented him. Illuminati member Robert Strauss has been a lawyer connected with drug running & the mafia. He was also an FBI agent from '41 to '45 with Hoover. He is admitted to the Wash. D.C. bar.

Pres. Bush appointed him U.S. Ambassador to Russia. He has been on the board of dir, of the Illuminati's PepsiCo, Archer-Daniels-Midland (ADM), and General Instruments (which have been exposed in other writings by this author.) He was also a board member of the Illuminati-mafia run MCA. Strauss is seen in Wash. D.C. as a behind the scenes power broker. Strauss represented Michael Milken associate Ronald O. Perelman, Chrmn. of Revlon, who made a $600 mil. killing off of the 1st Gibraltar S&L. Strauss represented MCA, which the Bronfmans took over in 1995. The book Knoedelsder, William. Stiffed-The True Story of MCA, The Music Business, and the Mafia. NY: HarperCollins Pub., 1993, does an good job of connecting MCA to the mob, the Network, and Iran Contra. See especially page 442. Time magazine 2/24/97 carried a page long story about Michael Ovitz being out of a job. In the article, they reported that he was spending time on his new yacht The Illusion, visiting Joe Silver's estate in So. Carolina, visiting his property in

Aspen, CO, and eating lunch with investment adviser Richard Salomon of Spears, Benzak, Salomon & Farrell. Gordon Crawford of the Capital Group is quoted in the article praising Ovitz, and saying he would invest in an Ovitz venture.

Ovitz is believed to be mafia by people in a place to know. He has also been known to threaten people using mafia terms, for instance, Vanity Fair (12/'96, p. 272) reports Ovitz threatening Bernie Brillstein, a producer, with his "foot solders". The San Francisco Chronicle (Fri., 1/26/'96, p. D20) quotes the latest issue of Columbia Journalism Review about an incident where a reporter Anita Busch who was investigating Ovitz got violently sick from the MSG in her food as she interviewed him. To top off it all off, Ovitz followed up her story which questioned his actions, by sending her a gift wrapped package of MSG with a one-word note: "Enjoy.". Michael Ovitz has had the clout to deal with Illuminati kingpin Edgar Bronfman head to head. He requested & got Bronfman to keep his dad employed, which was dutifully done. Edgar Bronfman Jr. had seriously considered having Ovitz head Seagram's MCA/Universal conglomerate.

Frank G. Wells. Frank was the President & the Chief Operating Officer of The Walt Disney Co. Wells was also on Disney's board of directors. He was a Rhodes Scholar, and a lawyer in 1955. Those who have read previous books (such as Vol. 1) by this author know how the Rhodes Scholars fit into things & are part of the Illuminati. He worked closely with Eisner & Katzenberg. Frank died in a helicopter crash in the spring of 1994 while heli-skiing in Nevada. His surviving sister is Molly Wells Chappelet who runs around in Illuminati circles. Molly Wells Chappellet has been featured several times in Betty Knight Scripp's magazine Appellation. Betty Knight Scripp was married to a Bohemian Grove member. Betty has been good friends with: the late Pamela Harriman (who was a recent U.S. ambassador to France & connected to the Rothschilds), as well as good friends with Her Imperial Highness the Grand Duchess of Vladmir of Russia, who owns the Chateau Margaux in Bordeaux. Betty Scripps personally monitors with care what is put into her incredible magazine Appellation. She has a column "Who's Who in the Wine Country" where the Chappellets have appeared in print numerous times.

Nearly all of Disney's 1920 movies had a black cat in them. Many had occult slants to the scripts. The occult slant never departed from Disney themes.

Some of DISNEY'S blatantly OCCULT MOVIES.

Aladdin. A wisecracking allpowerful genie is shown.

Bednobs & Broomsticks (1971) A witch finds a magic formula from a lion king. The magic formula raises a ghostly army of armor in a museum which stops a band of German commandos.

Beyond Witch Mountain (1982) A pair of twins leave Witch's Mountain and have to use their special occult powers to outwit a character named Deranian.

The Black Cauldron (1985), A Horned King uses his magic to fight a clairvoyant pig and the pig's keeper. This animation cost $25 million, but was a box office failure.

Bride of Boogedy (1987) An evil spirit visits the Davis family and puts the father under a spell. Directed by Oz Scott.

Child of Glass (1978) A glass doll must be found to set a ghost free in a haunted house.

The Gnome-Mobile (1967). A multimillionaire and his grandchildren encounter gnomes. In the end the multimillionaire deeds the forest to the gnomes for eternity.

Halloween Hall of Fame (1977). Jack-o-lanterns come to life.

Halloween Treat (1982). Cartoons about Halloween. This was followed the next year with a film Haunted Halloween which talked about the origins of Halloween.

Misadventures of Merlin Jones (1964) A genius tries to help other students. He tries to also use hypnotism & ESP which backfire on him.

Richest Cat in the World (1986) A wealthy man leaves his fortune to his cat, who the relatives later discover can talk.

H. DISNEY & its MOB connections

When this author spoke to the co-author's deeper Illuminati alters about Disney, their reaction was that Disney had been described to them when they were in the Illuminati as "a syndicate within a syndicate." They said that while in the Illuminati, they were aware that Disneyland had their own government, their own rules and their own police force. They were a crime syndicate within a syndicate. What these Illuminati alters casually mentioned, was verified by this author the hard way through research. One Disneyland Security Supervisor said, "There is no Constitution at Disneyland. We have our own laws." Once, when Walt Disney got miffed at a Hollywood policeman, Walt said, "I'll have your badge." If Disney guards decide to, they will get very rough physically with people, and assault them in any fashion they see fit. The people they detain are often thrown into tiny cells at Disneyland where they are kept without benefit of a phone call, without benefit of a toilet or water.

The judicial system turns a blind eye to whatever Disney police do. Many people pay Disney to get their children out of a Disney cell, and never get due process of any law. This type of treatment has gone on for decades, and is almost a daily occurrence at Disneyland. The Anaheim Police force is very chummy with the Disney private police force. Also at one point, the Burbank Chief of Police was the brother-in-law to Disney's Chief of Security. Recently, when a couple filed a wrongful death suit against the Magic Kingdom of Disney in Florida, the state of Florida surprisingly has appeared to have backed off from their traditional behavior of protecting Disney's sovereignty. An article on the suit said, ""there is evidence of some nervousness with Disney's relative autonomy."" (San Francisco Chronicle, article "Mickey's Dark Side" Oct. 1, '96, p. C6) An attorney in the case said, "Disney World's security people aren't just cops, they are bad ones. I don't think there is any corporation that has ever had the perceived power that Disney has."

Richard Foglesong, a professor of politics at Rollins College in Winter Park stated, "Because Disney World controls so much of its corporate and municipal universe, it can't help but act in a heavy-handed manner in order to ferociously protect its self-interest. They have immunity from state and local land use law. They can build a nuclear plant, distribute alcohol. They have powers local communities don't have. Do they abuse it? In my opinion, yes."

In line with Disney's previous dictatorial policies on their properties, Disney's new city called Celebration will not have any elected government. Since the city is unincorporated (a neat Disney trick) the mayor is appointed by Disney. Several Disney "quasi-government'" bodies control citizens of the city. For instance, the Celebration Residential Owners Association, which participates in binding all residents to a Declaration of Covenants, a legal binder of rules that residents must live by. Of course the Declaration of Covenants was written by Disney. These rules include such nit picky things as, no more than two people can sleep in the same bedroom, no pickup trucks can be parked in front of homes, and if Disney officials don't like your cat or dog they can forcibly remove the animal from your home. Disney Corp. has perpetrated numerous deceptions on the residents, incl. shoddy work on their homes, and operating their ""public"" school with Disney cronies. Still, the residents that have moved into Celebration are glowing with praise for the town in spite of the fact that the city is totally run by Big Brother Disney Corp. Of course those who don't love it, soon leave. So much for the American tradition of self-government.

Some MOB HISTORY.

Traditionally, the mob crime bosses have had a yearly summit. In 1928, they had their yearly conclave at Cleveland. In 1929, they had their secret yearly conclave at Atlantic City. In 1931, they held their secret annual conclave at Wappingers Falls, NY. At the Wappingers Falls meeting, attended by about 300 overlords and soldiers, the heads of the family clans discussed their crime family agendas. They decided where the first national Mafia convention was to be held. Once the Mafia was able to hold their yearly private national meetings, they were able to coordinate their activities, as well as decide such things as:

a. the direction of national & internal operations, and long range plans

b. the promotion of new bosses

c. decisions on turf & rank, commodities & cash

d. hashing out alliances or disputes with the Mishpucka, Triads, FBI, Illuminati, etc. and working with others in a concerted manner. The mafia clans would then leave the annual summit meetings and follow through in their area of operations, until they would meet the next year, review their successes & failures, get new assignments, and decide upon new short & long term goals. In 1927, the Mishpucka worked with Mafia to highjack a bootleg shipment of whiskey travelling from Ireland to Boston for the Kennedy Illuminati family. Most of Kennedy's guards were killed in the shootout, and J.P. Kennedy had the widows of the guards besieging him for financial assistance. Billy Graham's good friend Mafia Chief Joseph Bonanno was one of the chiefs who attended the yearly conclaves. He also met with J.F. Kennedy in the Winter of 1959. John Kennedy was known to have said that mobster Sam Giancana worked for his Kennedy family. The mob/Illuminati alliances and infighting are too complex to deal with in this book, but both groups had to put plans into action to deal with the repeal of Prohibition, which would end their lucrative bootlegging. The short term plan for the Mafia was to control the film industry in Hollywood, and to penetrate the unions better. The long term plans called for sending their next few generations of children off to the top schools and getting them into legitimate respectable corporate positions. By learning the ins and outs of honest, legal operations, they could then mix in the illegal operations with their legal ones & look legal.

They planned to extend their power base into politics, the Harvard-Stanford business schools, as well as the finest corporate board rooms. They intended (and have succeeded) in getting some of their offspring to produce/direct T.V./films. They would have an increasing presence within the Bohemian Grove membership, as well as some of the other great social & business clubs. Their plan to take over the film industry hinged on their union control over unions and theaters. The Chicago mob controlled the International Alliance of Theatrical Stage Employees Union. The mob controlled the projectionist's union, and if the film makers had the theaters where their movies were shown shut down, what good would it be to make movies? The film makers and the mafia both had power & money. Rather than fight a protracted war, they made a deal. The major studios would give about $50,000 a year to the mafia, and the small ones $25,000, to be allowed to function. Other agreements were also reached. Mob henchmen Willie Bioff and George E. Browne were mob lieutenants who orchestrated the mob's "Hollywood takeover".

Time Magazine, Nov. 1, 1943, wrote, "In the witness chair in Manhattan's Federal Court sat bland, wily Willie Bioft (pronounced Buy-off), blackmailer, panderer, labor leader, and now star witness against eight ex-pals, who are charged with shaking down $1 million from the movie industry...Question: Was it true that Bioft once had a five-year plan for taking over 20% of Hollywood's profits-and eventually 50% interest In the studios themselves? Bioff (wistfully): "If we'd lasted that long, we would have. Question: "Did you ever say you were boss of Hollywood and could make producers do whatever you wanted?" Bioff: "Yes-and I could make them dance to my tune."

Although Bioff rolled over on his pals and ended up getting car bombed, that didn't stop the mob/Mishpucka infiltration & control of Hollywood. (Bioff had tried to save his public image by helping Walt Disney settle his labor dispute with the mob-led unions, but Walt wisely rejected his offer of help, and made sure he didn't offend the Chicago mob leaders who were disgruntled with Bioff.) Hundreds of millions of dollars were poured by the Mafia & Mishpucka into real estate in southern California, by using legitimate local businessmen to launder the money. Hollywood was declared a "free zone" where all the Mafia/Mishpucka families could operate without a fear of a turf war."

Let us backtrack slightly to 1930. Columbia distributed Disney cartoons from 1930 until 1932, when Disney switched to United Artists, because Columbia wasn't bothering to pay Disney the money they owed. In 1930, Cohn, Pres. of Columbia Pictures, got Disney off the financial hook with Powers by intimidating Powers with some street toughs carrying a legal suit. If Disney wasn't indebted to the mafia before, he was at that point.

Biographers have been puzzled why Disney went into such a traumatic depression after Henry Cohn "helped" him. Tough guy Henry Cohn made sure Walt knew who was boss. His attitude was that Walt should be happy to be paid at all by him for the cartoons Walt supplied Columbia. After this, Walt would lock himself in his room and weep uncontrollably for hours. He was impossible for anyone to get along with. He was unable to focus on anything, and would stare for long periods out the window. Biographers blame Walt's behavior on the fact that his wife was pregnant. They also blame it on his friend Iwerks defection to another company. Frankly, Walt had treated Iwerk like a dog, and deep down must have known why Iwerk left such an abusive relationship. To claim that he wept for hours day after day because he realized he might become a father is too much to swallow. When Walt was asked years later about why he was so depressed he said it was the stress of the financial situation. Walt said, "I had a nervous breakdown ... Costs were going up; each new picture we finished cost more to make than we had figured it would earn when we first began to plan it...I cracked up."

This author submits to the reader that part of his breakdown may have indeed been the financial stress from having come under the heel of the mafia. They had all the means to make or break him, and he had no choice but to surrender to their overwhelming power to blackmail & destroy him OR to get out of the business. What this did was place Walt in a position where his two strongest traits had to clash--his overwhelming obsession to be his own boss, and his creative obsession to create animation which was wrapped up with his ego & his deep phobias and psychological needs. His mind couldn't give up its independence nor its creativity without great mental anguish, and therefore Walt was very saddened, knowing that he would have to admit defeat, and buckle under the heels of the big boys. Just when he needed emotional support his wife was going to have a child, and his best animator left. Walt had abandoned Iwerks years before, and Walt's wife had wanted a child for some time. Iwerk's departure and his arriving child do not in themselves account for the long intense nervous breakdown that Walt experienced. Biographers point out that Walt was very reluctant to have children, and that he was impotent with women including his wife much of the time. His impotency to carry out normal sex may help explain his secret sexual habits.

Walt's Masonic brother Carl Laemmle offered Walt a good deal to help him recover from Henry Cohn's abusive control of Walt, but Carl wanted the copyright to Mickey Mouse in return for the help, and Walt wouldn't part with Mickey Mouse. Instead, Walt signed a contract offered by Joseph Schenck of UA (United Artists), who was one of the Mafia's illegal drug kingpins. In 1935, the mob's illegal drug dealer Joseph Schenck went on to found 20th Century, Inc. which later merged with Fox in '38 to form Twentieth Century-Fox, whose board of directors would include two Illuminati kingpins William Randolph Hearst and Malcolm MacIntyre. Joseph Schenck's brother Nicholas Schenck and Marcus Loew merged Metro Pictures and Goldwyn Pictures and named Louis B. Mayer as its head.

Meanwhile over the years, MCA, headed up by Illuminati Kingpin Lew Wasserman gained a monopoly over the American film industry with the secret backroom deals that they made with Ronald Reagan's Screen Actor's Guild and Petrillo's American Fed. of Musicians. (By the way, Lew Wasserman would try to revive Reagan's acting career in the early '60's. Frank Sinatra and Walt Disney were both friends of Ronald Reagan, and all three believed in mind-control.)

Ronald Reagan and Petrillo in turn worked with the Mafia's NCS Council of 9 (which incl. Anthony Accardo and Sam Giancana), which at one point divided the U.S. into 24 mob territories. After J. Schenck went to jail (very briefly), he was replaced as Pres. of 20th-Cent. Fox by Spyros Skouras. Before his arrest, while Schenck was still in charge of 20th-Cent. Fox, he made numerous offers to Disney for Disney to incorporate his studio as a subdivision of 20th-Cent. Fox. Disney worked for a few years with them distributing his films, but he would not let go of trying to be independent. The FBI and American Intelligence turned to the mob to help them as the U.S. entered WW II. Perhaps Walt's mob connection added impetus for his recruitment. Walt went to a number of American Nazi meetings prior to Pearl Harbor. This author believes from knowing Walt's personality that Walt may have been on assignment, rather than a Nazi sympathizer. Still, why does one of Disney's pre-Pearl harbor cartoons display a swastika? Disney's Epcot Resorts is close to the mob's Atlantic City Board Walk with its nightclubs. The resort was designed by Robert A.M. Stern. (This author doesn't know about Robert Stern, but there are programmed multiples and Illuminati members within the Stern family.)

At Walt Disney World, the nightclub there was named "Cage", and then later '8 TRAX". Comedy Warehouse, which is a nightclub at Pleasure Island in Walt Disney World opened on May 1, 1989 and has used slave comedians as well having people who are mind-control abusers. On Feb. 11, 1987, Walt Disney Co. was reincorporated in Delaware. Delaware is the only state that allows total corporate secrecy. No one can find out who really is running a Delaware corporation, and many other secrets can be hidden under Delaware's corporation laws. Capital Group has considerable shares in Disney, as well as 29% of the shares of the Robert Mondavi winery at 7801 St. Helena Hwy, Oakville, CA. Wellington Group and Mellon bank also have shares. Behind Capital Group are mob controlled groups like Debartolo Reality Corp. and La Quinta Inns (a Bass bro. operation.) Sam Bronfman operates Sterling & Monterey Vineyards. There are countless people walking around that have felt the ruthless, impersonal, controlling, money-grabbing side of the Disney Corp. Also, there are a number of journalists who have experienced first hand the secrecy and paranoia that the Disney corporation has. Most journalists are not used to the secrecy that pervades Disney. Because Disney has shaped the myths of America for several generations, the public takes more concern over who is running Disney, than they would other institutions. Because most of America believe in the image that the Illuminati have built for Disney, they are rooting for it to succeed.

How the Disney Executives have figured out how to steal land all across the U.S.

Over the years Walt Disney has developed several very sneaky reliable techniques to acquire land. They acquire land through their executives and large stockholders and family members of the execs and stockholders. After all the deals are made in an area, and when everything is in place over a period of time, these people then turn their land over to Disney. Disney works with government officials and local bankers to line up special deals so they can succeed in their plans. After everything is lined up, the corporation announces their plans and goes forward. This methodology has been used repeatedly, for instance the American History Theme Park in the Manassas Civil War battlefield area of Virginia for which Disney has acquired 1,800 acres and has access to at least 1,200 more. In Nov. '94, after a new Virginia governor was elected, the Virginia "Disney's America" project was announced, and Virginia voted almost instantly for the money for transportation and infrastructure improvements to the area so that Disney's theme park would be viable. Disney set up 3 banks in Napa, CA. Their banks made loans to old families in the valley. The trusts and the wills for these families were made up by Stanford Univ. grads. These people set on the boards of these banks or connect with the boards of these banks. They charge large fees, and know every trick in the book to rob people of their estates and their living trusts. The Stanford grads, who connect in with intelligence agencies & the mob use certain code words when they set up their businesses, such as RESOURCE, EVERGREEN and PACIFIC. There are a number of scared landholders who are being intimidated to sell their land in the Napa Valley region.

DISNEY and the GOVERNMENT

Just prior to W.W. II, the FBI recruited Walt Disney. His job was to spy on Hollywood or anything else that looked suspicious. Documents obtained from the Freedom of Information Act, in spite of heavy censoring, clearly show that Walt Disney became a paid Special Correspondent asset of the FBI. He reported to FBI agent E.E. Conroy. In 1954, Walt was promoted to Special Agent in Charge (SAC) which means others reported to him.

After "leaving" the CIA, ex-DCI (ex-head) of the CIA William Hedgcock Webster became a lawyer for the Wash. D.C. based firm of Milbank, Tweed, Hadley and McCloy. In 1993, when news broke about Walt Disney's FBI membership, ex-CIA head Webster worked with the Disney family to cover up to the public that Walt Disney was an FBI agent. Webster went on TV and had interviews to spread the fabrication that Walt was not connected to the FBI. Why? One of the countless items that Disney was involved in was the investigation into the disappearance/rape of a six-year old child Rose Marie Riddle on 1/12/61.

According to documents gotten from the Freedom of Information Act, W.G. Simon was the FBI agent who met with SAC Walt Disney in L.A. about the case. W.G. Simon has been one of those people who has been publicly lying by claiming that Walt Disney never was an FBI agent. The paper trail proves otherwise. Why is it so important to the FBI and CIA to cover up that Walt was an FBI agent? Walt also worked for the CIA, even though documentation of that is not available. This author theorizes that the reason the FBI and CIA are so touchy about letting people know that Walt worked for the government is that the Network knows how the FBI and CIA worked together to procure children for mind-control programming purposes. Because Disney and Disneyland played such as enormous role in Mind-control, Disney's connection to them, although on the surface a seemingly minor fact, is in reality a minor fact setting on top of an enormous ghastly secret.

When W.W. II started, the government incorporated the Disney studios into the war machine. The military paid Disney $80,000 for 20 training cartoon, which cost Disney $72,000 to make. Disney studios also made some secret films for the military. Mickey Mouse and Goofy cartoons were slanted to have war themes, for instance, the Goofy cartoon of 1941 "The Art of Self Defense" and "How to be a Sailor" in 1944. Perhaps in honor of the contribution Disney had made to the war effort, "Mickey Mouse" was the password of the Allies for millions of men on the big D-Day invasion on June 6,1944.

Walt Disney produced a cartoon showing Donald Duck paying his taxes faithfully. The film was entitled The New Spirit. It was very successful in getting Americans to comply with the IRS. In 1946, Disney made a film for the public schools for sex education entitled The Story of Menstruation. For the United Nations, Walt Disney created "It's a Small World" attraction for UNICEF for the '64-65 World's Fair. This attraction was moved to the theme parks & has been a major feature for mind-control. After learning of the enormous amount of mind-control programming going on during after hours in secret tunnels at Disney as well as in the public facilities, it makes more sense why the Russian Premier Nikita Khrushchev would be denied a visit to Disneyland by the U.S. government "due to security considerations" when he was visiting the U.S. in Sept. 1959. Khrushchev obviously had his own security working in tandem with American security and the intelligence people for whatever reason(s) didn't want the complication of these Russians going to a major programming site.

Some powerful military men have been connected to Disney films. Two former commanding officers of the USS Alabama nuclear sub were technical advisors for the Disney film Crimson Tide. Walt Disney was tied to the U.S. government, and recent disclosures show that he was tied to the FBI. Walt used his FBI connection to destroy the life of Art Babbitt, who had led the strike against Disney in 1940. Babbitt found that everything he attempted in life after the strike was ruined by some hidden power. Was Walt part of naval intelligence attached to the FBI? Was he part of the FBI that is involved with child procurement and mind-control?

In the 1950's the Illuminati began organizing covens on the West coast and began solidifying their power. (This comes from several independent sources.) Likewise, it's clear that Disney didn't have the clout in 1953 with local governments, that it does today. Walt Disney was unsuccessful when he tried to get permission from the city of Los Angeles and the Burbank City Council for the construction of Disneyland (called Disneylandia at that time), in the Burbank area. One Burbank councilman told Walt, "We don't want the carny atmosphere in Burbank."" Inconsistently, within a few years they gave permission to Universal to build an amusement park in Burbank, which opened in 1964. Disney then ask the Stanford Research Institute to locate a spot for Disneylandia (Disneyland), which they found at Anaheim.

In recent years, Disney decided they wanted to build another amusement park (called California Adventure) across from Disneyland. In order to do so, the Interstate highway will have to have changes, and the Anaheim city council needed to approve the large 55 acre expansion. In contrast to the Burbank City Council in 1953, Anaheim's City Council was enthusiastic about the expansion in spite of lots of local opposition. The locals complained at council meetings to the City Council that the city had no business going hundreds of millions of dollars into debt to help a corporate giant. (Anaheim will issue $400 million in bonds.) Locals also raised concerns that the public school system in Anaheim is stressed to the breaking point where they are considering going to half days, and that Disney Corporation should give as much consideration for the school children of Anaheim as they do to their Amusement park. Disneyland's Pres.

Paul Pressler bragged about Disney's new California Adventure amusement park, "Disney's California Adventure is really a celebration of the fun, the beauty, the people and the accomplishments of this magical state. We really have set out to try to capture a bit of what the California dream is all about." (Sounds like the dream is to be wealthy and control people. The elite would rather give us BREAD & CIRCUS than an education.) The Dragnet films were done in part at the Disney studios. In an Office Memo from the 66-new LA SAC FBI agent to Hoover (12/16/54), which was obtained via the Freedom of Information Act, the typed memo states, "Mr. Disney has volunteered representatives of this office complete access to the facilities of Disneyland for use in connection with official matters..." Historically, we now know that Disney's use for "official matters" included mind-control.

J. DISNEY & MIND CONTROL

Once the reader is familiar with the programming scripts, the reader merely needs to watch the Disney "Adventures in Wonderland" that come on TV in the morning to see Disney mind-control at work. Within a few minutes one morning, this author had seen a white rabbit create "a world in your mind" (the quote is what the show said!) with a ring, watched Alice go through the mirrors, watched a White Rabbit [the programmer] read a book to a little girl, and the TV listener be told by the show "The White Rabbit is our only hope!" The deeper alters of Illuminati slaves who are programmed for espionage, for spying & blackmail, & seduction & assassination, are given programming to live in a fantasy world. They never touch base with reality.

Much of this type of programming has gone on at Disneyland. Disneyland visitors are taken in a boat where dolls sing an around-the-world theme song "It's a small small world". These doll world parts of the amusement parks are used for programming assassination & espionage alters. The song & dolls play important roles in these alter's mind-control programming. Some slaves at around age 19, have this type of programming tested to make sure it is solidly in place. The song "It's a Small World" was composed by the Sherman brothers for Disney originally as a theme song for a ride at the '63-'65 NY World's Fair.

The Sherman brothers were talent that Disney discovered. They were born in NYC, and both graduated from Beverly Hills High School. They wrote Disney songs for at least 29 films. Mind-controlled slaves, who repeatedly bump into each other, but don't know why, will be found saying, "It's a small, small world." Both rituals & programming go on at Disney amusement parks during both the day & night.

Steven Rockefeller and Walt Disney travelled and spent time together with Dr. Hadley Cantril, an establishment expert on human behavior. (See There Was Once A Time of Islands, Illusions & Rockefellers. NY: Harcourt Brace Jovanovich, 1975.) When Walt Disney began Walt Disney World he sent Card Walker to the Florida capital to request quid pro quo, and the governor gave it to Disney. What that meant is that Disney's property in Florida was totally controlled under Disney's jurisdiction, they had their own laws, their own police force, their own hospitals, and their own tax rate. No outside authority would interfere with Disney's jurisdiction. DisneyWorld's finances would be untouchable and out of sight by the state of Florida. Never had so much power been given away. DisneyWorld became its own crime syndicate within the syndicate. Disney amusement parks are like a city within a city. They have there own security forces, and the local police allow the Disney security forces to take care of their turf. Disney has their own policies (laws). Some of the security forces can be identified in plain clothes with clean-cut hair styles and have communication devices. The security forces have a headquarters room where TV monitors display-live the exit points at Disney as well as other locations.

America 's Most Wanted has a fairly large file on children who have been kidnapped at Disney Amusement Parks. One mother, who got separated from her child when getting off a train, frantically told a guard her child was missing. The guard took her to the monitor room, where they saw the kidnapper carrying the child out of the park with the boy slumped over his shoulder. In that short of a time, the kidnapper had drugged the child, cut his hair different, and put a different shirt on him. (This anecdote was mention in Inside the Mouse, pg. 52)

As written before, white slavery is part of what Disney is all about. This mother was one of the fortunate few who did manage to find their kidnapped children. An insider states that the Disney police are definitely part of those moving and abusing innocent children brought in for occult rituals. In addition, the Disney security forces spy on their own employees. Employees do not enter the theme parks like the visitors, nor do they move around like the visitors. They have underground tunnels and underground entrances and facilities for that. One victim of total mind-control mentioned that a tunnel entrance was at the Matterhorn mountain at Disneyland. (The Matterhorn was opened by Walt and his good-friend Richard Nixon, who rode in the first car down the mountain.)

The Disney productions has given the Illuminati the cover to bring together Illusionists, magicians, and special effects artists without anyone being suspicious. Some of these men were able to apply their talents toward programming children. As an example of their talents, Disney special effects artists were able to create 16 realistic-looking cadavers for the 1989 film Gross Anatomy. Walt Disney, Inc. has teamed up with Los Alamos and Sandia Labs, two other groups which are heavily involved in mind-control and people control to develop body scans, branding and access codes for the visitors to Disney's theme parks.

Each of the Disney Theme parks, such as Disneyland, DisneyWorld, EuroDisney etc. have vast underground facilities. These underground facilities allow many of the workers to get to the ride areas via underground passages. Each theme facility also has a vast infrastructure underground in order to maintain it. The underground areas contain wardrobe design and repair units, fitting rooms, restrooms, cafeterias, security units, computers, freight ramps, utility encasements, and large connecting tunnels. The underground areas also have programming rooms. They have their own power plants and water systems and their own police force. Disney company employs 71,000 people at several locations, tone recent TV show used the figure 40,000 Disney employees.] People are coming and going 24 hours at the Disney theme parks. Three shifts keep up the 24 hour business. The night crews maintain and repair the parks for the thousands of people that will soon arrive in the morning.

Disneyland makes a natural prop for carrying out mind-control. The items they sell are also natural props--such as the Goofy watch ($19.95) which has hands that move backward to confuse a slave as to what time it is. Was Walt Disney aware of how Disneyland was used for programming? There is no doubt. Disney lived much of nights at Disneyland, and had an apartment at the firehouse near the train station on Main St. At night, if he was not doing anything else, he'd roam the grounds of Disneyland scribbling notes on his own distinctive blue paper, which he'd leave for workers to follow the next day. The notes would say such things as "Replace these flowers," or "Move that bench". (Prince of the Magic Kingdom, p. 25) Walt Disney knew everything that went on in his Magic Kingdom.

The Epcot Center and the Disney amusement parks market all kinds of occult triggers, including crystals, rainbows, wizards etc. that reinforce the programming. The Epcot Center has two glass pyramids along with its "Journey into Imagination". Disneyworld has the Island of Atlantis on its sub tour. Fantasyland is one of the most used tours of Disneyland for mind-control purposes. It has carousels, merry music, an incredible castle, boat rides, story book characters etc. Sleeping Beauty Castle with its blue turrets and gold spires is the central visual object of Disneyland. You cross a drawbridge to get into it. Inside Fantasyland are Illuminati programming sites such as the Mad Hatter teacups, the King Arthur carousel horses, and Snow White's forest.

In the far corner of Disneyland's New Orlean's Square is the Haunted Mansion. This mansion is designed to frighten and scare, it has an ingenious design and many special effects and illusions. Realistic ghosts, a screeching raven, howling voices, and other scary things welcome the visitor. Life size holograms are created at the Haunted Mansion, and dance in sync with the music and then fade out at certain points. There is a hologram of a woman's head in a crystal ball who chatters non-stop. A real good laugh for the programmers of a little child. When you are toward the end, you will have a chance to look into a mirror where a hologram ghost will nestle up beside you.

Star Speeder is another great programming location at Disneyland. It was the creation of George Lucas and the Disney Imagineers. The technology is borrowed from Star Wars, and is similar to flight simulators used by the military to train pilots. Disneyland Hotel offers Character Breakfasts, where children eat breakfast with Disney characters, to people who make special arrangements. U.S. Special Forces, which carries out mind-control, owns two hotels near Disney World, and the Mormons have one also. Knott's Berry Farm with its Ghost Town, Amusement Park, & its Charlie Brown themes and characters is near Disneyland.

One of the Disney executives began one of the most horrible trauma-based mind-control programming centers in Los Angeles called Magic Castle a comedy warehouse. This trauma center had horrible torture chambers. Children were brought in from South and Central America to be programmed at the Magic Castle. A brave L.A. policeman exposed the place--for which he lost his job, and eventually was able to get the site closed.

One of Disney's recent ventures in their Disney Institute, which Newsweek labeled "the Disneyland of the Mind". (Newsweek, Mar. 4, 1996, p. 61) A private club called Club 33 at Disneyland located upstairs in the New Orleans Square is believed to be involved in mind-control. Cub's Den supervises children's activities at the Wilderness Lodge Resort at Walt Disney World. At Disney-MGM studios the major attraction is the Twilight Zone Tower of Terror. Guests take a strange scary trip through the hotel, where guests are finally sent into an elevator that drops out of control 13 stories. The ride has been advertized on TV. Disneyland now has a Temple to the Forbidden Eye--which is simply a Temple to the All Seeing Eye, the Illuminati symbol. Visitors, who have the patience to wait in line, can strap themselves in for a ride that is like a jack hammer that jars the rider through a temple filled with snakes, rats, and mummies. One aerobics teacher couldn't walk for three days after the jarring ride, which comes across as "hokey". The experience is more traumatizing than fun, but then maybe that is what was intended.

DISNEY VACATIONS FOR THE ELITE

Years ago this author's newsletters exposed Hilton Head Island, SC as a watering hole of the powerful elite incl. retired generals and admirals, and the site for the elite's Renaissance Weekend "meat market". Remember, that at one time Hilton Head Island was private, with imported alligators in the water around it. A person was only allowed on the island by going through security gates with a clearance. In a later newsletter, Disney's Hilton Head Island Resort was mentioned. This resort, built by Disney Vacation Development, Inc., is located on a 15-acre private island linked to Hilton Head island by a narrow bridge. Members to the Disney Vacation Club can exchange time for vacations at Disney and other resorts around the world. Memberships cost minimum $9,412.

(Chapter 5 Page 4)

MELODYLAND

Right smack across from the entrance to Disneyland is the Assembly of God's Melodyland Christian Center, the birthplace of TEN (Trinity Broadcasting Network). The Assembly of God denomination has been heavily infiltrated by the Illuminati, and has been heavily used as a front for programmed slaves.

Paul Crouch, president of Trinity Broadcasting Systems, Inc., was affiliated with Melodyland in 1973 when TBS was getting started. At that time, Melodyland was a rich heavily infiltrated charismatic church, with its share of programmed multiples. In 1973, closet homosexual minister Jim Bakker, and his wife Tammy Faye, a programmed multiple were with Paul Crouch in Anaheim at Melodyland. Paul Crouch had been the assistant pastor of Bakker's home church in Muskegon, MI. Crouch's right hand man was Alexander Valderrama, a charismatic Roman Catholic. TBS used an abandoned military base as their TV complex, using hangers as studios. In the early 70's, ABC put Bakker & Crouch's early shows on their affiliate stations on Sunday morning. Bakker had already gotten his career kicked off with Illuminatus Pat Robertson and his 700 Club. Jim Bakker split and went to the east coast. To help Bakker with his money, Bill Perkins, who had been a financial analyst for the World Order's mind-control research at Sandia National Labs in Livermore came to help Bakker run his ministry's finances. Later, televangelist Bakker began building Heritage USA, which was to be a big-money resort. Bakker hired people who had worked for Disney to construct Heritage USA. Bakker studied Disneyland, Disneyworld, and other Disney places as a model for Heritage USA.

After Disneyworld opened in Florida, Jim Bakker was a REGULAR visitor to it. Heritage USA's Ft. Heritage was modelled after Disney's Ft. Wilderness, Main St. was modelled after the Magic Kingdom's Main St., and Disney's wrought-iron fencing was also copied. Most people are aware of Jim Bakker's $265,000 payoff to Jessica Hahn to keep her sexual services to him a secret, his longtime homosexual relationship with his right hand man David Taggart, and his prison sentence.

James Orson (named after Orson Welles) Bakker was from Muskegon, the same place that Cathy O'Brien, a freed Mind-controlled slave came from. He was born pre-mature, and had some interesting family situations that make his family suspect. While Cathy O'Brien got programmed via the Catholics, Jim was part of another denomination which also was into programming, the charismatic Assemblies of God. His grandfather, who lived next door to Jim, and where Jim spent much childhood time with was popularly known in town as a "huckster", and nicknamed Kingfish after the manipulative character on Amos & Andy. Tammy his wife grew up in International Falls, MN in poverty in the home of her stepfather and mother. Besides having a "shopping demon," she has had her share of phobias and mental problems, as can be expected from someone who has had to suffer through programming.

It would be worth pointing out who has come to Jim Bakker's rescue when he was under attack. For instance, on Thursday, Oct. 4, 1984 when Jim was under attack, Jim Bakker's show had six people give endorsements and praise of Jim Bakker. Those were Ronald Reagan, Dale Evans, Robert Schuller, Oral Roberts, Billy Graham and Rex Hubbard. Of those, this author knows for sure that all are masons, except for Rex, who may or may not be. Robert Schuller, Billy Graham and Oral Roberts are "Christian ministers" who participate in using and handling mind-control slaves. These three ministers all participate in secret Satanic rituals. The last few paragraphs have given only a sketchy picture of the intimate relationship between Disney Mind-control and the charismatic movement and its use of trauma-based total mind-control.

DISNEYANA FOR THE PROGRAMMED & OBSESSED.

For people who have been programmed with Disney programming and who are obsessed with Mickey Mouse and everything else about Disney, and for other people who just have the collecting spirit for Disney memorabilia, there is a group called Disneyana.

Disneyana, was organized in the 1980's, and consists of people who are cult-like in their devotion to anything true Disney. Some of them to express their devotion outwardly tatoo their bodies with Disney characters. This group holds their annual convention at the Contemporary Resort in FL. One Disneyana at the annual convention said, "We collect to keep the good feeling inside." Another when interviewed said, "This is why it's all about love." The author knows as a fact some of the men who are obsessed with Mickey Mouse & Disney items are programmed multiples.

One of Kenneth Anger's occult friends has had the world's largest Mickey Mouse collection. Who is Kenneth Anger? Kenneth Anger, a member of LaVey's Magick Circle & later his Church of Satan, is an occultist and an underground film maker. Kenneth Anger (he choose the last name Anger) was raised on the Wizard of Oz books. His biographer Bill Landis writes that the Oz books "laid the groundwork for Ken's attraction to Crowley, the occultist who would rework Rosicrucian thought into his own magical system." Ken was obsessed with Crowley's life & magic. As a child, Ken had danced with Shirley Temple in competition after she became a child star. Ken Anger loved the OTO's solar phallic religion, and was also obsessed with Mickey Mouse. He spent part of his time studying his friend's Mickey Mouse collection. Ken Anger did his casting for his film "Lucifer Rising" by telling occult friends & acquaintances that they could live out their goddess or god power-trip fantasies by acting for him. The British government's National Film Finance Corp. fronted 15,000£ for Lucifer Rising's production. Famous occult musician Jimmy Page did the sound track gratis. Ken Anger acted as the film's Magus and made his Magus role resemble Mickey Mouse in the film Fantasia. (The role Fantasia plays in mind-control programming will follow as the last part of this chapter.) "Lucifer Rising" also starts with Fantasia-type volcanoes. Another of his well-known films was "Invocation of My Demon Brother."

Mind-control features in Disney movies.

The elements within Disney movies that are intentionally put in for mind-control would take volumes to describe. A detailed description of how just one Disney movie is used as a programming script soon follows. Fantasia was selected as the example. A random sampling of features in Disney movies for mind-control programming could include:

· Cogworth the enchanted mantle clock in Beauty and the Beast.

· The character Door Knob, which is a doorknob portrayed as a person in the Disney cartoon Alice In Wonderland, is useful for programming door knob alters.

· The Blue Yonder is a Disney movie on time travel of a young boy. Time travel movies are used for programming to mess up the victim's sense of time.

· Disney film "Animated Alphabet" has letters which come alive, which is useful for programming. And what about the '82 Disney movie "Computers are People, Too!" ?

· All the Illuminati members this author is aware of who have received trauma-based total mind-control were taught to astrally project and study on the astral plane what they needed to learn. A Disney movie that portrays this is Goofy over Dental Health. This is an educational film released by Disney in '91 and again in '93, where Goofy places a magical toothbrush under a child's pillow, so that the child astrally projects to a dentist office and while on the astral plane studies how to have healthy teeth.

· Illuminati alters believe that trees and flowers are alive. The 1932 Disney film Flowers and Trees is a story about two trees who fall in love. The film portrays the occult belief that trees can talk and sing. Internally, alter systems will be constructed with singing trees and flowers that represent people and which are alters. The singing trees give out internal codes to move alters internally where they need to go.

Return to Oz. (1985) This Disney film begins its story line about a girl who is thought to have psychological problems because of her tales of Oz. She is warned not to talk about Oz by her relatives. She is taken to a psychologist who wears a big ruby ring, who tells Dorothy that electroshocks won't hurt her, and that we are at the "dawn of a New Age." Dorothy is told that her memories are "just dreams" that stem from excess electrical current in the brain. She is sent to a mental institution to receive shock treatments for talking about Oz. A lightening storm allows her to escape the shock treatments and when she sleeps, she awakes in Oz.

In Oz she goes through many mind-control scenarios, ruby slippers, mirrors, etc., and toward the end visits with evil Mombi, Princess of Oz who keeps Ozma (Dorothy's twin) as a slave. Mombi eventually casts a spell and enchants Ozma into a mirror. Sci-Fi author J.D. Vinge in her Return to Oz based on the screen play writes on pg. 211-212, "Dorothy gazed at herself in the mirror, seeing her own reflection, and remembering the moment when she had looked at herself and seen someone else there, someone so like her that it could have been her sister." Parts of this film were filmed near Stonehenge, Eng. Disney has put out several films on the Wizard of Oz theme, all of which were used for programming.

The original series of Oz books were by Baum.

In '39, MGM did the famous Wizard of Oz film. In the Disney movie Tron (1982), a young computer genius goes into an altered state where he ends up becoming a computer program. After defeating the MCP, he returns to the real world. This is simply a programming script. A special effects team created a 3-D world, showing how talented Disney special effects people can be in making something seem real. This movie should show people their mind-control capabilities.

Mathematical Applications Group, Inc. (MAGI) were one of the groups that created the graphics. Disney came out with 3 videos of new adventures in Wonderland which are mind-control programming. In the mornings here 9-9:30, on channel 21, Disney has a Wonderland Show every morning which is mind-control programming for children. Within a few minutes, this author had seen a girl walk through a mirror, the 3 lives of Thomasina mentioned, and a little ditty "I'm a little tea-pot" where a person becomes a tea pot. They also had an "under the umbrella" scene. This was all pure programming, right on TV. Of course, they show the White Rabbit as a central figure.

ABC under the auspices of Disney produced a lengthy 140 min. film Wild Palms which depicts Illuminati mind-control and life. One reader of Vol. 2 stated that the Wild Palms movie would have made no sense except that having read the Vol. 2 book, the movie made lots of sense in the light of Vol. 2's revelations. The film depicts how children are kidnapped, switched at birth, programmed via TV cartoons, programmed to kill and use stun guns etc. The film depicts Illuminati bloodlines and arranged marriages. Although the name Illuminati" is not used, if viewers substitute in the name "the Fathers" for Illuminati fathers, they will get an insider's view of life at the top. The main controllers are addressed by their slaves as "Papa" or "Daddy" or "Mother". This is true to life.

A person opposed to the Fathers states, "One day we will wake up and discover we don't own this country and no one will care." The movie states that events are not happening randomly. The movie shows an underground tunnel system which has an entrance hidden by a swimming pool. Quite a few actual programming codes were said during the film, for instance, "down, down, down through the pool of tears..." and "we're going to go down the yellow brick road now." The movie was created by Bruce Wagner, who obviously is an insider concerning trauma-based total mind-control. The fact the movie was made shows the arrogance of the programmers' beliefs that their criminal acts in programming thousands of little children will not be exposed, and that people will be too stupid to realize that what is put out as fiction is actually mirroring what is happening. It's like they believe their own script that IF people did find out "no one will care." Because so much of the Illuminati programming involves the creation and programming of 3 alters linked into trinities, it is not surprising that Disney has helped such triad programming with a series of movies about threesomes, including:

3 Blind Mouseketeers

Three Caballeros

3 little pigs

Three Little Wolves

3 Lives of Thomasina

The Three Musketeers

3 Ninjas

Three Orphan Kittens

For Mickey Mouse programming they came out with Thru the Mirror, where Mickey Mouse steps through his bedroom mirror and ends up in another world (altered state). Not all of the Disney movies that have mind-control programming themes got released to the public. One unreleased cartoon had Penelope fleeing from a sinister looking Grandfather Clock which is carrying her to another world, and has another scene where Penelope tries to hold onto someone who personifies the Wind.

George Lucas, who directed the movie Star Wars, which was a movie planned by the Illuminati & used for Illuminati programming, also directed Disney's movie "Captain EO". Captain EO (who looks like a demonic entity) goes to rescue the Queen (who looks like the harlot describes as Mystery Babylon in the Bible). The Queen is in captivity simply because she and her people believe in black and white (which represent good and evil). When they renounce such a belief, they are saved by Michael Jackson (in actual life a mind-controlled slave) playing Captain EO. It's a New Age witchcraft film through & through.

By the way, Michael Jackson has gone to Disney amusement parks many times, sometimes in disguise. It is public knowledge that his Jehovah's Witness family has been very abusive mentally and physically to their children.

Disney has put out several movies on how the mind works, such as the educational film The Brain & Nervous System in 1990. Their film Runaway Brain is a cartoon where Dr. Frankenollie transplants Mickey's brain into a monster's body & vice-versa. A 1994 film, Puppet Masters shows the govt.'s secret Office of Scientific Intelligence trying to save the U.S. from aliens who live in human bodies.

In recent years, Bette Midler has been Disney's main actress. In the Vol. 2, it was exposed that she is possibly a Monarch Mind-controlled slave. She is famous for her "mood swings" (switches in personality), and she had a "mental breakdown" in 1985. Her eyes and body gestures are those of a programmed multiple. She has gone out on tour for Disney without making money, and she is best of friends with Jeffrey Katzenberg (second in command at Disney). Jeffrey Katzenberg by the way is extremely disliked by his counterpart Sid Sheinberg. Bette Midler plays Stella in the movie Stella. Stella is an occult name. In the movie, the script seems tailored for Bette Midler and for someone who is a programmed slave, rather than the actress fitting the role. At the movie's end, Stella (Bette Midler) attends her own daughter's marriage by peeking in a window and watching from the outside.

This is the script they give so many of the parts of a slave, so that they feel unworthy and feel like they are always on the outside looking in at life. Many parts (personalities) of slaves find it hard to connect with real life, because they feel they are on the outside looking in. And then in true Disney fashion, Disney had Bette Midler play the role of the lead witch in Hocus Pocus. The movie Hocus Pocus does some hocus pocus of its own. While pretending to make fun of witchcraft, they actually teach witchcraft. They do make the 3 witches look comical. By the way, the 3 witches stand for the maiden, mother, crone combo that the Illuminati reverence.

Disney subtly works in deep occult things, such as the all-seeing eye on the cover of the book, the little girl promising the cat (who is a familiar spirit) that her descendants would always care for it (true, because the cat was a generational spirit). The cat is killed in the movie but can't die. And Bette Midler as lead witch in her costume, which has some Mother-of-Darkness symbology on it, states as she gets ready to take the life force from an innocent girl, "We want to live forever, so we take children's lives." This is wholesome entertainment for children?

The Disney capacity for deception extends to its own workers. PR men recruit young people for its Disney College program. They tell the young people what a great stepping stone it will be for their careers. They have been known to make it sound like the greatest thing in your life. Kids come from all over the country due to the slick recruiting tactics to work for Disney. They are then housed in Disney housing, given menial jobs, and paid low wages. Most people in the College Program leave disillusioned. If the worker happens to think of a great idea, Disney officials have been known to steal the idea, and because the worker was working for Disney the worker will find that they are unable to get any credit or money for the idea that Disney steals and makes millions off of. One uncredited creator of a Disney sale item said, "literally, they're using everybody for everything." (Inside the Mouse, p. 239.)

>>> Next, will be the script for how the Disney film Fantasia has been used as a standard programming tool since the 1940's by the Illuminati.

K. DETAILED SCRIPT ON HOW THE DISNEY FILM FANTASIA IS USED FOR PROGRAMMING TRAUMA-BASED MIND-CONTROLLED SLAVES.

During the 1950's, '60's, and '70's at least 90% of the Illuminati's trauma-based mind-controlled slaves were subjected to watching Disney's Fantasia film in order for them to build the foundational imagery of the mind-control. Child mind-control victims had their eyes taped open, and then sat one-on-one with their primary programmers so that the programmers could give the scripts as the child watched Disney's Fantasia over and over. What made Fantasia unique as a programming tool is that it had almost everything the programmers needed to create the foundational imagery for their trauma-based mind-control. To build a dependable alter system means that the worlds need a solid foundation. Fantasia has provided the means to get a solid foundation for the internal worlds that the Illuminati slaves build in their mind. It is also a masterpiece in coordinating color and music.

The Disney film Fantasia which premiered on Nov. 13, 1940 (at Broadway Theater in NYC) was a financial disaster as a movie, but was an Illuminati programming masterpiece. The film was released to theaters in '40, '46, '56, '63, '69, '77, '82, '85, '90 in order to catch every generation of children. The video was released in 1991.

During programming much of the child slave's mind will watch the film. One particular part (alter) will be forced to memorize everything in the film. This small part (small alter) is well hidden in each victim's mind. This small alter, who has a vivid and total recall of the film Fantasia, is locked carefully away so that ONLY an access code will pull him/her up. Watching the videotape Fantasia is not going to pull this alter up. The programmers pull this alter up when they have a clean slate alter. When they are taking a clean slate of the mind, they will pull the clean part up and have the alter who has memorized Fantasia throw its memory onto an internal big screen.

The internal Outer space (aka Rubicon) is shaped like an amphitheater, and functions as a big vast screen for replay. There is an internal ball or sun created via the lighting effect of the movie Fantasia, so that the movie appears projected in the mind as on a globe. And the Fantasia film images hit this internal globe and go circular in the mind and spin through the system. The programmer will then say to the new part "THIS IS WHAT I WANT YOU TO CREATE. THIS IS WHAT WE NEED." In this fashion, Fantasia has provided the programmers with their primary tool for taking a dissociated clean slate part of the mind, and manipulating it to become a new workable part within the system. The young part that holds the entire Fantasia memory is strategically placed in the system so that it can be called up from anyplace in the system. No matter where the programmer is working in the system, he can access this small alter whose function is to remember the movie. Most of the system will go into a trance sleep if shown the movie. The front (as well as most of the system's alters) will be totally amnesic to having ever seen the movie. Since the programming put in with Fantasia is so fundamental it should come as no surprise that the programmers have done an excellent job in protecting this programming from everyone, including the slave. Abreacting the film for many alters could rip the system apart, because after the film is memorized severe trauma begins to be overlaid and attached to the film. There may be some small alters that still carry tiny bits and pieces of memory of the movie, but only one will really remember it.

The following script will be a running account of how Fantasia has been used as an important preparatory film for Illuminati trauma-based mind-control to train the mind-control victim's mind to be able to visualize the programming that will be layered in.

The time clock will begin when the feature film's action begins, and then will run its entire 116 minutes. This will give the researcher of mind-control a blow-by-blow description of how a Disney movie is used for programming. The film was often shown to child victims around 3 to 4 years of age with a wide screen while the child was under a guided LSD trip. (Prior to the use of LSD some other drugs were used.)

A Grande Dame or Mother-of-Darkness often worked with the Illuminati programmer as an Assistant Programmer. The scripts & the programming have already been discussed prior to showing the child the film, so the programmers know the direction they want to take the child, & will tailor some of what is said to the child victim to individualize the programming.

When a three or four year old is shown Fantasia on a hypnotically-prepared and controlled LSD trip, the colors & effects of Fantasia are increased about 1,000 times. The film is realer than real to the child. The movie will not be shown just once, but over and over so that the scripts are ingrained into the mind. The imagery for the child's internal world will be well established, because the big screen movie enhanced by both the drugs and the bright colors of the art work will seem more real that life itself. At this time, the child is a multiple, but the walls between the various parts of the mind are not solid, but similar to the walls between ego states in an adult non-multiple. A large part of the 3 or 4 year-old child's system will be allowed to view the system, including the Christian parts. Then the entire system (with the single exception of the alter carrying the entire memory of the film) will be hypnotically told to forget having seen the film.

Years later, the front alters will not remember having seen the movie, but they may have a strange dislike for the film.

They may find that they can't identify where their feelings of dislike of the film stem from. The child victim will watch the movie with its programmer and assistant programmer one-on-one, with no other children in the room. The child will watch the film repeatedly and be grilled about what is in the movie. The child will see the movie so many times in such a vivid form and will be tested to the point that the movie will be memorized. But it will be hypnotically locked up in the subconscious by the programmers, so that it forms a base for the mind to begin building programming, but will remain hidden from the conscious.

At the time the Fantasia film was made, the Illuminati had been creating trained multiples for years, but they knew they wanted to program the different personalities in accordance with the best mind-control techniques of the day. For this reason, the Fantasia film was planned ahead of time, so that it could possibly serve as a programming aid. The film is silent (almost no words) except for music so that it can be used for hypnotic visualization, so that the Mother of Darkness & the programmer can fill in the programming script with the child victim as they watch the movie. As it turned out, their plans were successful.

The New Age author David Tame states in his book The Secret Power of Music (Rochester, VT: Destiny Books, 1984, p. 292), that Fantasia is. . . "A superb marriage between the visual and musical arts. Most of the sequences.. .are what New Age cinema was intended to be!" The power of the movie to influence the mind stands out. In order to make the film, Disney used some strong arm tactics on a few people. The movie was a box office flop when first released in the 1940's, but then it was made for the occult world anyway. By the 1960's, the Illuminati had create a drug culture and had lots of undetectable mind-controlled slaves running around that had been programmed with Fantasia. In the 1960's, Fantasia became a hit with the drug culture which had its share of Illuminati slaves deeply involved in it. One more reminder, the sentences that are "ALL CAPS" in the script are things that the programmers are saying to the child victim as the child watches the film. (Bear in mind, that the child watches the film over & over, so not everything indicated in this script by caps that the programmer says will necessarily be said in one showing.)

00 minutes. Curtains open. Action begins with an orchestra. The Conductor upon a step pyramid is the center of the scene, and is shown to be the center of authority. Master Programmer Dr. Joseph Mengele liked Fantasia because he was a musician and a violinist. Mengele (Dr. Green) liked Bach, Beethoven, and Schubert and orchestra music. He enjoyed taking what he liked & using this music to make slaves. He would portray himself during programming as being the conductor, & all the orchestra were his children. The film will allow for a repetition of this theme.

00.5 minutes. The instruments begin playing. The musicians are silhouettes which cast shadows upon the wall. Alters will often see themselves in this fashion too, as merely a shadow or merely a silhouette.

01.5 minutes. The MC (named Taylor) begins talking. He begins grooming the viewer. He says that the film may suggest to your imagination "geometric figures floating in space."

02. minutes. The M.C. says there are 3 kinds of music. He says some music is to create definite stories, some to create definite pictures, and some music exists for its own sake.

02.5 minutes. The M.C. introduces us to the "Absolute music."

03. minutes. He states that „Abstract images that might pass through your mind...music will suggest other things to your imagination..." The Philadelphia Orchestra begins playing "Toccata and Fuge" by Bach in the background. As a cartoon for children (or adults) the film has already lost the normal audience at this point. (There is no way that Disney could have escaped realizing that the film starts out losing the normal audience.)

03.5 minutes. The conductor is standing out and everyone else is a silhouette with shadow mirror images (like so many of the alters become). Leopald Stokowski is now standing as the rising sun rises. This is an allusion to sun worship and the sun rising in the east. The music is going up and down, and this music at this point is used to train the child to go up and down the trance ladder (that is to go deeper or lighter in trance).

04. minutes. The conductor opens his hands and waves them in an Illuminati hand signal. The music begins.

06 minutes. A row of violinists play, they are merely silhouettes with shadows.

06.5 minutes. A harp scale is played in the background that is used in the programming. Triggers are attached to this harp scale, or the harp scale is used as a foundation identifier for a piano scale. More children can be taught the piano than the harp, so this scale is usually transferred to a piano scale.

07 minutes. A series of 3 musicians is shown.

07.5 minutes. The conductor (the programmer) becomes invisible. The Prog. Assistant will ask the child, "WHO IS GREEN? GREEN BECOMES INVISIBLE."

08 minutes. First lines representing bows are shown (the violinists are invisible), then the Golden Gate Bridge. "REMEMBER THE BOW, NOT THE VIOLINIST." The bow lines flashing on the screen represent energy. 08.5 minutes. Colored disks are flashed onto the screen. The lights are represented to the child victim 'THAT'S DR. GREEN'S ORCHESTRA." Geometric shapes and flashes of lines explode onto the screen. Concentric rings that will pattern the concentric worlds appear. (See Vol. 2 p. 196 for an illustration of this.)

10. minutes. Asst. Prog. will say, ,,YOU ARE HIS STAR." as stars flash on the screen. Many hidden alters (parts) are stars. Swirling lines arrive, and then colors and then more concentric lines.

11 minutes. Worlds within worlds are shown. Water is shown. Concentric circles that are the pattern for the worlds are presented. A varying number (5 or 7) of Castle-like structures materialize and then disappear. (These will form the pattern for some of the internal castles.) A quick flowing yellow line comes down the center of the screen, 'THAT'S THE YELLOW BRICK ROAD."

11.5 min. Lots of stars emerge.

12 minutes. Various worlds are shown, and an illusionary castle. Lots of stars are shown, which will be how the victim will model many of their alter parts after. Lots of purple stars appear, representing royal star alters.

12.5 minutes. Spiral splotches of cloud-like colors appear and disappear in dissociative colors. This is the Kingdom of the Gods during programming. The Asst. Programmer takes the opportunity to ask, "WHOSE ORCHESTRA?" This scene is used for the internal heaven where the kings are. Then the camera shows the conductor finishing.

13 minutes. The programmer has finished building his basic worlds.

13.5 minutes. The MC talks about Tchaikovsky's Nutcracker.

14 minutes. 13 circling lights come into view circling around and around. (The 13 lights are something like 4 yellow lights, 3 white lights, 4 orange, 2 blue-something like this. They don't have to be all the different programming colors at this point, because that programming will come in its own time.) Stars turn into fairies. A fairy with lots of fairy dust whirls around. ("Make a wish" the slave will be told later on, create what you want.) Flowers grow into butterflies. Hypnotic music plays as the fairy throws fairy dust. Soon, the Fairy spins a web.

15 minutes. The cabalistic tree of life is made with lights, and then the many colors of the ribbons are flashed up on the screen quickly. A compass image is very quickly flashed on the screen.

16 minutes. Lights multiply on the screen, and a spider web appears in the background. There are lots of stars which shine as lights in a spider web. (Stars will serve as alters in programming, the spider web serves as a system within the system, see Vol. 2.) There are several shots of multitudes of stars on a spider web. 16.5 minutes. There is an explosion of light which has a splintering effect (which will fit in well with an electroshock later on to create alters.) Around and around go 6 big mushrooms dancing, with a little one trying to participate. The programmer will point out that the mushrooms are "A FAMILY". When the splintering effect is done with real electricity in the future, the mind will splinter into a family.

17.6 minutes. Concentric circles appear in water. Flashing pedals emerge as if they were dissociation spreading through the water. The flowers are the top spinners (see the pages in Deeper Insights on spin tortures to create spinner families), they dance, & then they float away in the bubbles (of dissociation). "A FAMILY OF SPINNERS" the programmer will say. "SEE THEY SPIN YOU INTO BUBBLES INTO NOTHINGNESS." There is lots of dancing shown by the spinners. Everyone is dancing to the top. The child victim's head will be wobbling back and forth from the influence of the drugs and dissociation at this point.

19.5 minutes. When the family of fish make a star, the Asst. Programmer says, "SEE HOW SAD THEY ARE." The fish dance in circles and they also hide behind veils. "THE FISH MADE ITS OWN BUBBLES AND YOU CAN MAKE YOUR OWN BUBBLES TOO."

21.5 min. The child is trained to trance at the hypnotic 8's that appear in the water. This type of scene will put the deeper alters to sleep of a slave still actively being used. The movie here is being used to teach symbols, which will be important in the programming. Asst. Programmer, "LOOK YOU'RE JUST FLOATING.. ..FLOAT, FLOAT, FLOAT, SLEEP...SEE SHE WENT RIGHT INTO THE CENTER OF THE TRANCE STATE.. .YOU DANCE ROUND AND ROUND AND ROUND AND WHERE WE END UP YOU'LL NEVER KNOW."

22 minutes. Lots of bubbles begin appearing. They will be used in the programming to assist the child to protect its mind from the traumas. The asst. programmer may have a bubble toy to make bubbles in her hand as a game to play with the child. The child will be trained and programmed to put its memories into bubbles and let them disappear. ,,WHY WOULD YOU WANT TO GO INTO THE BUBBLE TO GET AWAY FROM THE DARKNESS? 1,2,3...NOW THERE ARE MANY BUBBLES, THIS IS WHAT WE WANT YOU TO DO." At this point the film is showing different colors of bubbles, for instance gold bubbles. This trains the child's mind to identify different colors of bubbles. The bubble-fish-flower scene is going on. "DON'T YOU FEEL LIKE THAT FISH, ROUND AND ROUND YOU GO" (dissociation encouraged). The fish continues going in a dissociative spin. The fish swim in graceful perfect figure 8's which have a subconscious hypnotic induction message to the victim. "SLEEPY LITTLE FISH" is said when the music gets hypnotic. "YOU'RE SLEEPY & YOU'RE TIRED, THIS IS NOTHING BUT A DREAM." "ALL THE DIAMONDS ARE ALL AROUND, NOT YOU" In other words, this is teaching the child that their entire internal world can be around them, but "you don't know that it's you." The child begins to lose the ability to realize that other parts of itself belong to itself, they are only stars, etc. The fish changes into anot her character. flowers are appearing in different colors of the color coding, red, green, orange, blue, white. . .All of a sudden it get's still. "SHH, LISTEN CLOSELY."

22.5 minutes. Eyes shine in the darkness. "EVERYTHING IS FINE, YOU JUST RELAX."

Silhouettes appear, which represent fish (alters, and people) who are there but you don't see them, they are behind the veil like the silhouettes. 'THEY AREN'T THERE, IF YOU SEE THEM THEY AREN'T REAL THEY LOOK LIKE A FLOWER, WHEN YOU SEE THEM, YOU WON'T SEE A CHILD- YOU WILL SEE A FLOWER." The silhouette veil gives the sense to the child that he can sense something but it's not there. 23 min. Different plants appear and dance. (This part of movie is very important in structuring.) The plants separate into many plants and flowers, and they multiply on the screen, but at the end they solidity into a solid plant. This is teaching the ,,you-are-one-but-you-are-many" concept. "FAMILIES ALWAYS WORK TOGETHER. WHETHER YOU ARE BLUE OR YELLOW OR GREEN, FAMILIES ALWAYS WORK TOGETHER IN HARMONY."

24 minutes. "BUBBLES ALL HAVE A LIFE SOURCE...THERE, LOOK, WHAT'S IN THAT BUBBLE?" 24.5 minutes. ,,YOU CAN HAVE YOUR OWN ORCHESTRA". Fruit that hangs on the tree is shown, which will be the basis for how they hang the programs (the fruit) in the internal world. Note the colors, orange, white, yellow, purple, blue, green,...

24.5 minutes. Fairyland appears on the screen. The Fairies awake and fly through leaves. 'THERE'S YOUR FAIRIES. SHE IS VERY MAGICAL. SHE CAN CREATE ANYTHING AND SO CAN YOU." "THE FAIRIES ARE SO MAGICAL."

When the core is being first split, the parts of the mind that are creative are taken and used to create the fairies. The programmers will only take these original creative splits, they will not try to get fairies from any more torture. The fairies are the creative parts of the child, how ever many creative parts that the child has splintered will be the number of fairies created. These parts of the mind receive very heavy programming. They are core splits. (If readers remember on page 87 of Vol. 2, it refers to a Core Protector coded "Creation". That alter was a fairy, a core split. Not only does this creative part make things "magically" for the system, it protects the core. Does that help people to understand how the Core can be so creatively protected?! (For more understanding about the Core see Cisco's very deep article on the Core.) Fairies are assigned to every part of an alter system. The child of 3 or 4, who watches Fantasia has had their core locked away at 2 1/2. The core's stars have not been locked away yet, & have access to her energy. When the system is built, the stars are locked away & become the core's guardians. They will act like the core to protect her. The real value of the fairies comes when the core's stars are locked away & the Programmers have to depend upon the creative power of the fairies.

24 minutes. A vine (which represents a system's double helix) lights up one leaf after another. The leaves are staggered (alternated) and they light up in sequence, which teaches the child the foundation of how they will create the DNA helix and its staggered exit permissions.

25.5 min. The leaves are now floating up and down, like the alters will learn to do. "SOME FALL TO THE GROUND AND DIE." This is the point where the story of the Oak Tree will be added in for programming. When the Illuminati programmers want "to destroy" an alter they can use the chandelier-MT 6:22-23 torture mentioned on page 310 of the Vol. 2 Formula book, and then have the splintered alters become leaves that fall to the ground and die. After this, these disobedient and now "dead" alters can be taken & be dissociated from their memories. The memories are locked up someplace permanent within the mind.

26. min. Out of a leaf like "box" come a series of fairies. The child is taught to put things (such as alters) in boxes of various shapes.

26.5 min. Leaves blow in the wind. Fairies cover things and keep them safe.

27. min. Fairies continue flying around. The seasons are passing in sequence. An internal green-skirted fairy will be connected to the internal hourglass during the programming.

27.5 min. The fairies quit flying and skate on ice. The season has turned to winter.

28 min. A winter scene. The four seasons have come to an end.

28.5 min. A sorcerer is introduced by the MC (emcee). The sorcerer is shown and then his assistant or trainee who is Mickey Mouse. Mickey Mouse wants to be creative and magical like the great wizard. Mickey Mouse sees the power that the sorcerer has, and wants that power. What is really being subtly portrayed here is the programmer (the wizard) and the core & the core's creative splits (Mickey Mouse). Showing the programmer as a great wizard is actually right on the money. The top programmers are all Grand Masters in the Illuminati and are very much into witchcraft.

29 min. The sorcerer (wizard) is shown again. This time the wizard,, with his skull beside him, creates from his witch's cauldron a big colorful butterfly which is forever changing. (Is this big yellow, purple, white, and blue butterfly meant to be a Monarch butterfly? The programmers will use it that way for this Monarch programming.) The great wizard magically creates the big colorful butterfly and then he shatters it into countless splinters!

Disney often portrays Mickey Mouse as a Sorcerer.

30 min. Mickey sneaks around and grabs the magic hat. (The magic hat is one of the few things in the film that doesn't mean anything for the programming. It merely has witchcraft symbols.) Then a magic broom appears.

30.5 min. The broomstick comes alive. The broomstick imagery will be used to help create the pancake people (ribbon alters who will haul the internal computer messages). The broomstick person in the film hauls buckets of water. The child is having story after story layered in over a period of time, which are being skillfully constructed toward a programming end. Parts of the child's mind that see the movie Fantasia will be dissociated clean slates. They will need to have some imagery given to them so that they have something to build mentally upon. In Cisco's section of the book, in the Truth article it is discussed how the mind looks at sensory inputs and tries to make sense of a pattern by comparing it to previous patterns that it has identified. Learning is a step-by-step building process, and so is programming.

31. min. Mickey as the apprentice sorcerer (in a sense the victim who the programmer is training) manipulates the broomstick person. "THE CHILD (Mickey) CAN DO WHAT THE GREAT MAGICIAN DID. YOU CAN TELL YOUR MIND WHAT TO DO. YOU GET POWER BY LEARNING TO BE CREATIVE." Mickey (and the victim) become mirror images of the Wizard over them.

32 min. Then the sorcerer sits on his throne, and while on the throne acts like the conductor. Here is a subtle mental tie-in that Mickey is playing the role of programmer (conductor) and is sitting on an Illuminati throne (like so many of the Illuminati Grand Master programmers have actually done.) Michael Aquino is just one of several mind-control programmers who have gone by the name of Mickey. Because Mickey Mouse is substituted for being the programmer at different points in programming, this scene will tie in well with other standard programming sessions.

32.5 min. Mickey in the film clearly is shown leaving his physical body and astrally projecting himself. This is such a vivid portrayal of occult astral projection, that it is mind-boggling that many Christians consider Walt Disney movies to be christian. (See Vol. 2, p. 319, for a discussion of the scientific methods to understand and induce astral projection.) This again is laying the mental foundation for the child to leave its body mentally and either hover over its body in dissociation or to travel somewhere via astral projection. Mickey Mouse then begins conducting lights.

p_starry-sky.gif

These lights represent the alters that the victim will make for the conductor. The lights (aka stars) are the conductor's orchestra. Lightning (such as flashes that come from electroshock) and stormy weather are being controlled by Mickey. Notice that the things Mickey is controlling are fear-based. After the child has viewed the film many times and memorized it, when the electro-shock is applied during this time of the film, the child will control it like Mickey by 'magically' creating splits.

33.5 min. Mickey begins conducting waves. Then, for those who understand the veiled scenes, Mickey begins going through the different magic spheres conquering the different spirits. This is Enochian Magic. 34 min. Mickey wakes up back in his body, and he is in trouble with rising water i.e. a water trauma. Mickey is thrown into the water. The child victim will identify this with the drowning tortures that are given to instill "no talk-no tell" messages. After Mickey (or in child himself) has done something, and returns to his body, then the "'no-talk'" message will kick in. Victims of mind-control often get the feeling of drowning when they trigger a no-talk message.

34.5 min. More water continues to flow.

35 min. All of a sudden without any continuity of action, Mickey gets an ax and kills the broom by splitting it. The broom dies and then multiplies when it comes back to life. This is such a clear picture of what the programmers want the child's mind to do. They will traumatize the child essentially unto death, and then they want the tortured alter to multiply itself into many more duplicate alters. Armies of brooms are formed from the broom. This scene here is a clear red flag that the Illuminati asked Walt Disney to produce this film. This scene with the trauma death of the broom, with it splitting in half, and then coming back to life in a multiplied form, is evidence that this film was meant to be used for training children in multiplicity. The assistant programmer will say "IT'S O.K. TO SPLINTER." "YOU ARE TIRED, YOU CAN ESCAPE THAT BY RESTING AND LET A PART OF YOURSELF COME OUT." At this point, it is necessary to explain what is going to be done when they begin to splinter the child's mind. After the splitting trauma, the programmer needs to be able to see what the child has created, so he wants the child to look at what's been made. "'CAN YOU LOOK AT WHAT YOU'VE CREATED?" However, the part of the child that looks back at the trauma will then see that the dissociated trauma was real and that will make the child angry. The programmers want the child to dissociate what he built, and when the child looks back at what he has created he goes into a vortex of dissociation. The child is told if he ever looks back at the memory he will go into the vortex.

35.5 min. Water is being thrown in by the brooms, while Mickey throws water out.

36 min. All of a sudden a hypnotic vortex sucks things in during the film.

36.5 min. The brooms all march in an army, while Mickey reads his magic book. Mickey then uses his magic book as a lifeboat when he gets whirled into a vortex. A vortex is often created from that part of the mind that is holding the high energy that accumulates in the mind just before the mind splits. It holds the highest energy of the mind. One way a vortex is created is to place the child on a traumatic Disney ride--like a rollar coaster. Special electrical boxes or electrical shoes are outfitted onto the child so that during the ride, at a particular timed moment when fear is increasing, that fear has pain of the electrical shock added to it. A cattle prod of course would be too dangerous to take up on some type of ride like that with all the motion. Also bear in mind, a small child doesn,,t take need the electrical power that an adult needs to take it down.

37 min. At the bottom of vortices in the Illuminati programming, the programmers place Guardian demons. In Fantasia, when Mickey gets to the bottom of the vortex, sure enough, there is a Guardian there to meet him. The Guardian spirit parts the water as if he were Moses with the Red Sea.

38. min. The Conductor and Mickey Mouse shake hands. The conductor does something very significant. Mickey congratulates the conductor and then the conductor (programmer) in turn says, "Mickey, you've done a good job." (Yes, the core/core splits have done a good job at this point, they have just created their inner world!) The MC tells us about the next song the occult Rite of Spring. Spring rituals are creation rituals and so this music is ritually connected to what the programmers are going to do in this segment. The MC states that instead of the viewer seeing tribal dances (which are by the way witchcraft dances), that instead Disney has decided to show us scenes of what went on billions of years ago. (This next part is also a subtle push for Darwin's theory of evolution. But because it is child's entertainment, people don't have their guard up. The theory of evolution is important, because it allows people including the victim to not take moral responsibility for their actions, and it is also the basis of some of the Hinduism and witchcraft teachings that will be given the deeper alters. This is a backdoor approach to destroy godliness that is carried out on children in general.)

39.5 min. The MC says, "Imagine a lonely tormented little planet spinning in a sea of nothingness." This is exactly what the programmer will say to the child as they work together at building an internal world. The "sea of nothingness" is what the reader will see described in our books as "Outer Space" or ,,the Rubicon." Also that "sea of nothingness" is used much later to reinforce the secrecy of the programmers. Much later as the programmer and torture has progressed the programmers will say to alters, "LOOK DOWN ON THE EMPTY SEA OF NOTHINGNESS. THERE IS NO DR. GREEN. THERE IS NO DADDY THERE."

40 minutes. A swirl of stars in a galaxy appears. Swirls of comet-like lights flash by. "MANY WORLDS THERE." This will set the base for the child to build galaxies and worlds within their mind. "BE LIKE GOD, CREATE YOUR WORLD. BE YOUR OWN GOD AND CREATE YOUR OWN WORLD" the child is told at this point.

42 minutes. The face of the planet emerges.

42.5 min. Lots of volcanoes erupt on the screen, setting the foundation to build realistic internal volcanoes.

45 min. Oceans, and water and fire are coming into being. The child victim needs to know how a world is created in order to create their own internal world. Lava begins flowing as the flute plays the background music. Lightening flashes. The violence of the fierce weather portrayed will be enhanced by the child on drugs to a thousand times its magnitude. This is important because it will take a great deal of mental energy and external torture to create the internal worlds. Having such super-vivid pictures will help when the victim goes to build their internal worlds. There will be special purpose fragments that will be made into the elements of fire and water. That's all these special purpose fragments will know. Breaking through the layers in the alter systems will trigger internal earthquakes. This and a later earthquake scene are used to build the foundation for the internal violent weather. If an internal earthquake shakes a slave's mind, it has the same effect as if a real earthquake were going off. Everything internally shakes and shifts. An alter system will also have fire children, who start internal fires, and will give internal alters the abreaction or sense that they are burning. The mind gets very survival minded when it thinks it is burning, and goes right back into the programming that is linked with the victim's compliance for survival during programming. 46 minutes. The oceans continue to form.

47 min. A calm occurs in the action.

47.5 min. The screen gets dark except for an amoeba, which becomes two amoebas. As the little amoebas multiply, the asst. programmer encourages the child, "IT'S O.K. TO MULTIPLY. GOD WANTED YOU TO MULTIPLY" Remember, the programmers are working with a pre-schooler with clean slate alters. The programmers must show images that the child can relate to. The concept of the broom being split in half and then multiplying and now the concept of the amoebas splitting are portrayed in a way that the child's mind can grasp the concept.

48.5 min. "IF GOD CAN MAKE A FISH, YOU CAN MAKE A FISH. YOU CAN DO ANYTHING, YOU CAN BE

ANYTHING."

49 minutes. Dinosaurs appear. The programmers will reframe the concept of dinosaurs into monsters and demons. The sea-going dinosaurs will be refrained as guardian demons which guard the internal rivers. These guardian demons tie in with Armageddon end-time programming. They also guard the various worlds.

50 min. Dinosaur-birds swoop down and grab prey. This imagery will be refrained to lay the basis for the winged-monkey watchers of the Oz stories. The winged-monkey watchers are the child alters who are assigned to watch and guard the system.

51.5 min. Fierce dinosaurs (later ref rained as Dragons) protect the swamps. Swamps are built into the internal worlds, so this is very helpful. Demons and alters like Dameon are set up as guards.

52 minutes- More swamps appear. The swamp scenes will form the base in the child's mind for the internal river Styx. (See more about this in this book's article "Programming, foundations, destruction of"). Some dinosaurs that have long necks that look like snakes begin appearing. The asst. programmer will reframe these to the child, "LOOK, THE SEED OF SATAN." "THAT IS A DEMON." While the child watches, they reframe the hugh dinosaurs as being demons. Pictures of reptilian looking demons will be shown to the child too. At that age, the child is not going to see the difference. (A note for therapists: Some ""demons'" may actually be important parts to an alter system, and are being used to protect unauthorized users from entering important areas of the system.)

54 min.- Fierce Tyrannosaurus Rex chases dinosaurs. This chase scene is especially frightening to a young child on a LSD trip. Long-necked snake-like dinosaurs appear. They may be refrained as a python snake. T Rex is also known as Leviathan, a demon that inhabits the kundalini spinal column and causes pain in the victim, he is written about on page 302 in our Vol. 2 book. In the film a long fierce struggle between T Rex and other dinosaurs ensues.

55 min. The dinosaurs begin dying and soon dies. "THE LORD DOESN'T LIKE THEM."' This will later be refrained that if parts integrate they are to die. If someone tries to get into the system, the alters are to bury themselves deep like these dinosaurs do on the film.

56 min. Dead bones appear

59 min. Mountains soar out of the ground into eminence.

59.5 min. It gets stormy on the screen, winds & floods appear.

60. min. Stillness comes as the sun rises.

61 min. The sun sets. (During the programming, this may be refrained as the moon setting. It can be both or either or. Remember, the programmer is working with the child's creativity.) Various scenes during the film show the moon in different phases which is important for bringing in programming concepts like Mr. Moon.

61.3 min. The orchestra is now playing. Music is an important part of mind-control programming. The affect of music on the mind and body has been studied. Music can double the heart beat, accelerate the respiratory rate, make that rate irregular, enhance perception, lower the threshold for various sensory stimuli, change blood pressure & circulation, and alter the muscles in the body. Dance music and "march" music done by orchestras change muscle response. Music is also a great way to cause dissociation.

62.5 min. The MC introduces the "'Sound Track' who he says is an important person for Fantasia who can be seen around the Disney studio. When Mr. Sound Track appears, he is simply a vertical line. The MC says he is "an important screen personality." The ground work is being laid for a person being anything, even a line. The MC states that each sound creates a picture.

63 minutes. The MC encourages the personified Sound Track ""don't be nervous."" Then a sound is made like an electrical shock and the line develops a splotch of color in it. During the programming at this point an electrical shock would be applied to the child.

63.5 minutes. The harp is ask to sound. The harp begins playing a scale and the line becomes double 8's and snake-like spirals. The child will be taught to dissociate when seeing such double 8's.

64 min. The violin begins going up and down. Each of these instruments is going up and down the scale, like do-ray-me-fa-so-la-tee-do. The music is used to teach the alters to go up and down the helix, which is figured in this part of the film. As the music goes down, an alter is taught to go down in trance, and as it climbs higher, the alter will trance higher. All these instruments (violin, flute, bass, bassoon) are being used to teach alters how to work in the system. The MC describes the flute as "very pretty".

64.3 min. A trumpet begins playing and the colors, yellow, orange, etc. begin showing.

64.5 min. When the bassoon plays, the MC says, "Go on. Drop the other shoe"-- "Go to the shoe" which translates "'go to the ground'" --the deepest trance level. The following is the double-pyramid, with a helix up the middle that appears when the bassoon plays: -(This configuration is very important to all these Illuminati alters systems.)-

p_rugbyball.gif

65 min. The drum plays and some other percussion instruments play. These are taught to the child as the cult's "HEARTBEAT". They will hear this sound internally for many years to come. Then some sounds that have a shattering effect (cymbals) like broken mirrors are made in the film.

65.5 min. As the sounds take place a line is made with a pyramid at the top. This is laying the groundwork for the system's structuring.

66 min. The MC laughs and talks about Beethoven's Pastoral Symphony (Beethoven's 6th) which is next.

66.5 minutes. The screen comes alive with magical Unicorns of different colors. Then Pan (a satan-like figure) appears playing his pipes, and soon lots of little Pans (little demons) are playing their pipes. The little Pans (demons) play and dance with the unicorns. The orchestra plays again. (This author, Fritz, remembers when I said that Pan was an evil demon, I was rebuked by a Christian minister. He then said Pan a benevolent cheery creature". A number of books which may be obtained from Satanic bookstores document that Pan is indeed considered a powerful demon by occultists.)

67 min. Pegasus (the mythical greek winged horse) flies in. As a Mother horse she takes care of little ones on the screen. She is a protector in the programming.

68 min. "FANTASY IS FUN. FANTASY IS A GAME YOU PLAY. MOTHER TEACHES YOU. SEE HOW MOTHER IS A TEACHER. SEE THE BLACK AND WHITE HORSE. THEY ALWAYS FLY TOGETHER, BUT ARE SEPARATE. THEY ARE FLYING OVER THE CLOUDS." "OVER THE CLOUDS, INTO THE BLUE YONDER." The child is rewarded for what it has to do with the game of fantasy. "THAT'S YOUR REWARD FOR DOING WHAT YOU ARE TO DO. YOU CAN LEARN TO FLY OVER THE CLOUDS." The child feels rewarded by the game of fantasy. The fantasy scenes in Walt Disney's Fantasia are like the Wizard of Oz scenes in Oz, fantasy-land is more colorful and fun than real life. Vivid colors will be splashed about during the fantasy-land scenes.

68.5 min. A castle appears as Pegasus flies around. This and other castle scenes will help the child develop the imagery for the spiritual castles that the child will build internally. Then they swim in the water. "SEE THE MIRROR IMAGES, WATER CAN BE GLASS." During the programming mirrors are put into the internal system. A mirror can be a piece of glass, the surface of a pond, or an asphalt runway. When the programming is complete, underneath the water &/or the runway lurk demons.

70 min. Waterfalls emerge and issue forth. The waterfalls are used by the programmers to erase all the slave's memory of what was done to them. The child will be told at the end of watching Fantasia (and this will be said at other programming events too), "JUST REMEMBER THE GOOD, JUST REMEMBER THE FANTASY". The fantasy is given so that the subconscious can rest in peace after the programming. The child is told "WASH YOURSELF CLEAN."

70.5 min. The little girls appear as girl centaurs (half girl-half horse). "SEE THE LITTLE GIRLS ARE HORSES."

71 minutes. Then a scene appears where one girl centaur braids another girl centaur's long hair. The Illuminati teach their slaves to braid their memories. They braid their memories up and then lock them in. All the Daddy memories will

be locked up & braided and then locked for good.

72 min. Male centaurs appear. They are near water and make mirror images in the water.

72.5 min. A crown is placed on a female centaur and 2 doves. During the Illuminati death, burial and resurrection ceremonies lilies are used for crowns, and doves are used. These are significant programming/ritual symbols. The female centaurs look at the male centaurs. This will be refrained as a system can have both male and female parts.

73 min. Starting with one female centaur, the females act seductive to the males, who then respond. For bras the females have bras of daisies. The Vol. 2 book explained how the daisy programming is a life-or-death type program. Vivid colors are used for each centaur. For instance, one may be purple and another one another color, which sets the groundwork for alters to have different access color codes. Alters do not usually see themselves as being in different colors, although it does happen on occasion.

73.8 min. A marriage takes place between the centaurs. The programmers catch these nuances of the film and use them. The marriage here teaches the child to be acquainted with the arm-and-arm marriage ceremonies. Remember, the programmers are dealing with clean slates that must be taught from the ground up. In the next few minutes, the cherub children will watch sexual body language, and the child victim is also picking up on enticing sexual body motions.

74.2 min. The centaurs go swimming. "I FEEL LIKE A LITTLE GIRL WITH A HORSE'S BODY."

75 min. Little cherubs are dancing and flying around. When pictured the artists at times single out 3 cherubs who blow flutes together. The female centaur appears, who is fair haired (blond) and blue-eyed, which is what the Illuminati like. When she hears the tone (of the flutes) she goes into a trance state and walks with her eyes closed. This imagery is used to teach alters that when they hear certain tones, they are to go into a trance state and do certain things. The little cherub turns into a heart, and when no one is watching goes into the tree. In programming, this part is the Keeper of the Tree. Notice how everything is veiled. The assistant programmer will point the cherub out to the child victim, "LOOK AT WHAT HE DID."

76.5 min. A curtain then shrouds the scene. The curtain appears to be tree-like. More bubbles appear, and more water. All the mythical creatures on the screen begin to dance and be merry and have a feast.

77 min. "SEE THE FEASTS, SEE THE BANQUETS, THE FEASTS ARE O.K. THE BANQUETS ARE O.K."

78 min. "THE LEAVES ARE FALLING." Blood-like wine is drank at the feast. "SEE THE BLOOD."

"SEE THE LITTLE DEVILS POP UP." The only human in this Disney scene is honored. This is done to teach the alters that humans and animals can mix. That they can be accepted for what they are, even if they think they are an animal or something else they will be accepted at the cult's feasts. These scenes are all for internal programming. By the way, one of the pretty female centaurs makes a sexual pass at the fat human, who then chases her. "MUST PLEASE THE MASTER."

80 min. A scary storm comes up, and Zeus, and the greek gods appear. ,,BETTER FEAR IT. HE'S A GOD YOU'D BETTER FEAR HIM. HE THROWS LIGHTNING." This demon who throws lightening is named Furfur. He also makes thunder & strong winds in the system (alter system's worlds). Readers can learn more about this demon, named Furfur, in Cisco's second part of Deeper Insights in the article on "Programming, foundations, destruction of".

81 minutes. Lightening bolts are thrown from heaven.

81.5 min. All the little cherubs run for cover in fear.

82 min. Pegasus the protector flies in to protect everyone, especially a new born Pegasus. The wind is personified as a two-headed blowing person. This two-headed Janus wind comes storming through the heavens. The programmer will often place his own voice "IN THE WIND." The greek god (internal demon) throws a lightening bolt.

83 min. "SEE THE GODS". The child is learning what to make internally. Zeus then relaxes & goes to sleep.

84 min. More vivid colors form. "FAMILIARIZE YOURSELF WITH ALL THE COLORS." The film at this point is

teaching the child to stay in the framework of the programming for safety. To go outside of the programming is terror. The child is learning to fear the godlike demonic guardians.

84.5 min. The fantasy world is coming alive. It is a happy fantasy world. A goddess in the sky makes a rainbow emerge. This is the rainbow goddess of the programming.

85 min. All the happy unicorns and cherubs fly '"over the rainbow." (Refer back to the Vol. 2 book p.94 to understand the significance of going over the rainbow.) The unicorn is derived from old British paganism where the lion represented sun worship, and the unicorn represented moon worship. This is why the Royal Arms of the British Royal Family have a unicorn on one side, & a lion on the other. Sexually the unicorn represents androgeny. During programming, the horses, pegasi, unicorns and centaurs shown in the Fantasia movie become the foundation upon which the Illuminati programmers build the Night Mare alters who are beasts of burden who carry an alter system's memories. These are logical no-emotion alters who are early splits & who are programmed after the child is verbal. See Cisco's article on Dream Work for more understanding about the horse alters, as well as chapter 7 on Structuring.

86 minutes. More rainbows and lots of bubbles come into view. The film has done an excellent lob of showing how the Furfur God of thunder protects the Rainbow. Once an alter has gone over the rainbow, they can not come back because a demon protects the Rainbow. The rainbow is also protected by alters who fear the gods. After seeing Fantasia, the therapist can understand why the little child protector alters have fear about these gods. The master (who represents Furfur) in the movie swallows the rainbow. If an alter looks internally for the rainbow, he or she will only find stars, because the protector will come up and say, "I swallowed the rainbow." The rainbow is kept well hidden internally. This scene is used to teach alters how to go over the rainbow. ""BEFORE YOU GO OVER THE RAINBOW, YOU HAVE TO PUT ALL YOUR MEMORIES IN THE BUBBLE. YOU CAN'T TAKE ANYTHING OVER THE RAINBOW INTO FANTASY LAND."

86.5 minutes. Apollo, the sun god comes out.

87 min. A big mother spirit who fills the whole sky is now shown by Disney. She hangs over the rainbow. When a system is built this is indeed what they put in. All go to sleep in the film.

87.5 minutes. Arrows shoot the stars into the heavens. This is more programming imagery. When you look for the rainbow, you see stars.

88 min. The conductor finishes again.

88.5 min. The next setting is a Venetian nobleman's (a duke's) palace. Curtains open. The use of curtains is spoken about in our previous books.

89 min. Curtains open. An Ostrich begins dancing, and gets others to ballet dance.

90 min. The Ostriches begin dancing in a circle, this is laying the groundwork for what the cult family does. The Assistant programmer may tell the child, "SEE IT'S O.K. TO DANCE TOGETHER. DANCING IS ACCEPTABLE." The programmers will not directly tell the child that this represents the cult family.

91.5 min. The Ostriches are eating grapes. They are playing, looking in the pool & they are seeing bubbles.

92 min. Hippos emerge out of the pool. "IT'S O.K. TO BE DIFFERENT. IT'S O.K. TO BE STRANGE. USE YOUR CREATIVITY." The hippos begin to dance and dance.

94 min. Elephants appear and are having fun and blowing bubbles out of their trunks. The programmers may be having fun blowing bubbles with the child. The programmers like to mix love and hate, kindness and sadistic behavior. That way the victim has a hard time separating love from hate. If you ask many slaves about "Daddy" they will tell you that they had fun with Daddy. They are right--they had fun intermixed with sadistic torture. Bubbles continue to lift off. One of the bubbles has a fish in it. This is imagery for the bubble programming. The child victim is trained to dump their bad memories into bubbles and let them float away. The therapist will notice that many victims feel like they are floating. They have an unreal feeling. The bubbles are floating their bad memories away.

98.5 minutes. A new setting and the hippos are hypnotically sleeping. 3 sinister alligators that remind one of the 3 primary programmers appear. The 3 alligators have robes that hide them, and shadow images of themselves lurking behind them. The alligators are trying to get the hippos. The 3 alligators are portrayed like the programmer is, he is someone to fear, love, & respect all at once. The hippo is running away and dancing. The alligator dances with the hippo, but makes menacing attempts to eat him. A flying hippo lands on an alligator. Elephants, hippos, alligators are shown. The elephants, ostriches, hippos and alligators all dance in fantasyland.

100 min. The orchestra is dancing. '"DO WHAT YOU'RE TOLD AND WE WILL HAVE FUN."

101 min. The MC announces the next part as ""the struggle between the profane and the sacred."' The conductor stands in a silhouette that suggests the same pose that the upcoming Satan takes.

102 min. A high dark mountain with a castle looms in front of the viewer. A winged fiercesome Satan figure raises his wings. His wings are sectioned like fingers with claws, and will form the imagery of the demon Malebrinche, whose satanic claws hang over the alters and terrorize them. In the Illustrated Guidebook, the reader will find lots of these claws in the pictures lurking in the background. A child victim will be taught to fear the hands of the programmer, Satan and Malebrinche. The wings (hands with claws) open. And Satan is portrayed as an awe-inspiring figure. (By the way,, the word maleficia means evil misfortune caused by witches. The witch in Disney's Sleeping Beauty has the demonic name of Maleficent.)

102.5 min. Satan begins raising the dead skeletons. This provides a foundation to layer in the Valley of the Dry bones coming alive with armies of skeletons.

104 min. The film also has some images at this point that will help with the foundation for the Armageddon programming. Satan calls everything to himself.

p_satan.gif

104.5 min. The hell pit is shown. This is laying a foundation for the hell pit with all its demons. All kinds of vivid colors are shown in hell, to make the scene more real than real for the child victim. Satan smiles as demons burn in hell. "NO MATTER WHAT COLOR YOU ARE, IF YOU ARE NOT GOOD YOU'LL END UP THERE.'"

Fantasia portrays Satan as a terrible powerful being.

105 min. "THAT'S WHAT HAPPENS IF YOU'RE BAD. YOUR THROWN INTO THE HELL PIT."

105.5 min. Three beautiful lady demons begin to dance in a circle, all of a sudden these demons take on their luciferian form, one becomes a goat.

106 min. The demons continue to dance with powerful Satan watching over them. The hell pit and the demons are portrayed in vivid scary graphic depictions. The hellish fire and the ghoulish dancing of its occupants continues for what seems a long time. "WHEN GOD FINDS OUT HOW BAD YOU ARE, LOOK AT WHAT HE'LL DO TO YOU."

107 min. Satan is portrayed by Disney in all his evil dark majesty.

107.5 min. Bells begin to ring, and the demons slink away, & the dead return to the earth to their graveyards.

108 min. Ghosts return to the graves. Soft music begins to play. Ave Maria by Schubert, which was written for the Catholic church, begins playing.

109 min. Satan folds himself into a mountain. '"DO YOU SEE LUCIFER ANYWHERE? NO. YOU ONLY SEE A MOUNTAIN."

110 min. Lights shine as if they are a column of moving people who are walking with lights, and then some walls appear.

110.5 min. An arched bridge appears with its mirror image. The column of silhouetted people who continue walking have mirror images in the river. The asst. programmer will be telling the system (which the front parts will hear) "TIME FOR ALL THE GOOD CHILDREN TO GO TO CHURCH. IT'S O.K. TO GO TO CHURCH. GO SERVE GOD."

113. min. An opening, a vertical sliver of light comes from what appears to be doors opening up. There is a mirror effect in the way the doors open, which will facilitate making mirror image front worlds. A whole new world opens up, which will be the front system's world. Both the front alters and the deeper ones will be told to forget the movie. Later when a system is better programmed, the programmers will pull up the front alters and have them walk through these doors into the light. When they are hypnotically taken through these doors into the light and away from the fear and darkness of the Kingdom of Satan, they are hypnotically told to close those doors and never look back. The Kingdom of Satan has been shown in detail and in great length. The Kingdom of Satan has been shown as powerful and fearful. Satan is shown as a mighty power that is to be feared. The Kingdom of Light is only shown as a peace, as a refuge from evil. It is not shown to be good. It is not shown to have power or intelligence. It is simply a place to go to escape the fear of Satan's power. This is all the programmers really want the church to be. It will be a stabilizing balance to let the mind recuperate from the hell of the programming, but it is not intended to be seen as greater than Satan and his Kingdom.

115 min. The film ends with a peaceful gaze at heaven. The child is being told in the last few minutes "THAT WORLD BELONGS TO YOU. IT'S A BEAUTIFUL WORLD. IT'S THE WORLD WE WANT YOU TO LIVE IN. IT'S BEAUTIFUL." After all the hell that is eventually dumped on the child, and the scare that Satan gives them in this Fantasia film, the child is only too happy to create a beautiful world to live in.

****

The effectiveness of Disney's Fantasia is that it is used to communicate to & build the unconscious structures within the child's mind. The unconscious mind is the seat of our creative abilities. Then the conscious mind makes adaptations upon this unconscious thinking.

SUMMARY

Now that the reader has covered so much, the following quotes (with bold emphasis's added) take on even deeper meaning: Joe Flower in Prince of the Magic Kingdom, "Walt Disney was obsessed with creation, driven to build magical worlds not, as many artists are, out of paint and canvas, or words, or even film, but physically, out of concrete, wires, smoke, electricity, and highly programmed employees." (p. 23) Julian Halevy in Nation decries Disney taking this nation into a "drift to fantasy." He adds, "...one feels our whole culture heading up the dark river to the source--that heart of darkness where Mr. Disney traffics in pastel trinketed evil for gold and ivory." For those who understand programming Aubrey Menen comments about Disney's success are profoundly appropriate, "the strongest desire an artist knows...to create a world of his own where everything is just as he imagines it." John Ciardi was not so nice, he termed Walt Disney as "the shyster in the backroom of illusion." Eliot said, "While his filmed fairy tales may have appeared at first glance to be light and dreamlike, upon closer examination they seemed more nightmares of deconstructed reality in league with the era's leading neo-Freudian Modernists."

· You have now finished reading a never-before-heard, unprecedented Warning about the Dark Reality of the Disney's Magic Kingdom, and how it fits in with Mind-Control. Most Americans when surveyed say they believe in God, most go to church, and many believe they are born-again.

Because of the Illuminati's deception campaign over several generations, the American public, and the world in general has been led to believe that Disney was good, and that Walt Disney was a good man. Because of his image, people suspended judgement about Disney and Disney movies. They entrusted their children to him. People had been manipulated into a frame of mind, a predisposition that whatever comes out of Disney is good. They entrusted their children to take in what Disney fed their children's little minds week after week. The public's predisposition of trust was used to introduce Illuminati beliefs and their political agenda, and to carry out a vast program of trauma-based mind-control on hundreds of thousands of tiny little children, whose minds and souls were stolen from them. Because many of the child slaves, who are programmed with Disney-themes, are programmed with roles in bringing in the Anti-Christ, Walt Disney and his family have played a major role for the Anti-Christ. And now you can see how accurate the Word of God is when it says, What is highly esteemed among men, is an abomination to God. First, there will be an Overview of the types of sources used, and then will follow a partial Bibliography on this Disney Section.

TYPES OF SOURCES

People who have worked for Disney and who are getting pensions and medical insurance have talked about Disney under the condition of anonymity. This is because the Disney hierarchy will not permit exposure without retaliation. Several non-Disney people who helped with discovering facts for this section were threatened that their children lives would be taken if they continued to investigate Disney. What I (Fritz Springmeier) finally have put in this, is solely my responsibility.

· One type of source for this was books on the Hollywood Film Industry and books on Disney Films. There were about 20 books of this category which were perused for a better understanding of who the Disney brothers were and what Disney Co. was about. One of the best in this type of source was The Art of Walt Disney from Mickey Mouse to the Magic Kingdom by Christopher Finch (NY: Harry N. Abrams, Inc., 1975.)

· Another type of source were the standard biographical reference books,, such as Who's Who, Who's Who in the West (1951), World Biography, Who Was Who,, Current Biography 1952, etc.

· Another type of source was critics of Disney's movies such as several articles exposing the Lion King, Media Spotlight's article Fantasia, Rush Limbaugh's comments and statements concerning how Disney had betrayed its viewers' trust, the Spotlight's Feb. 26, '96 p. 31 article "Disney Turns Back on Family Values."'

· Another type of source was magazine and newspaper articles about Disney such as the Oregonian's art. on a Disney director being a convicted child molester. NY Times, Newsweek and other magazine and newspaper sources. An important series of extremely good investigative reports which were written by Harry V. Martin for the Napa Sentinel in 1989 were very important in learning of some of the Illuminati/CIA/Contra/Drug Running activities in Napa Valley, CA that Roy Disney is associated with. Harry V. Martin went into all kinds of records and did an excellent job of investigative reporting. The magazine Monde 2000, no.12, had an article on non-lethal weapons that the NWO is developing. This article was reprinted in Encounter Chronicles Journal of Scientific Intelligence, and discussed how Disney has been working with Sandia Labs and Los Alamos.

· Another type of source were victims of Illuminati mind-control, who have recovered memories of being programmed at Disneyland and Disneyworld.

· Another type of source has been to watch Disney movies as an investigative tool to understand how Disney is programming, how they are skillfully indoctrinating the American people into witchcraft, etc. This author has also personally been to both Disneyland, near Anaheim, CA and Disneyworld, near Orlando, FL.

· Another source was the Walt Disney Co.'s Annual Reports, and also the reference book Directory of Corporate Affiliations (1986) published by the National Register Pub. Co.

· Another type of source were books which specialized in covering details about Disneyland such as Disneyland And Beyond the Ultimate Family Guidebook (edited by Ray Riegert, and printed by Ulysses Press of Berkeley, CA); and Walt Disney's Disneyland (by Martin A. Sklar and introduced by Walt Disney.) AAA had a 27 page booklet "Disneyland Park and Southern California", which came out in 1996, which provides information on what is being offered at Disneyland and vicinity. The book refers repeatedly to "Disney Magic". One has to wonder how Christians and non-occultic persons can't see how occult Disney is.

Partial BIBLIOGRAPHY

BOOKS.

AAA. Disneyland Park and Southern California. 1996.

The Walt Disney Co.'s Annual Reports. pub. by the Walt Disney Co. annually.

Auletta, Ken. Three Blind Mice. NY: Random House, 1991.

Cluran, Richard M. To the End of Time. Rockefeller Ctr, NY, NY: Simon & Schuster.

Commander M. The Controllers: A New Hypothesis of Alien Abductions. (subtitle Alien Abductions, or Government Secret Mind Control Black R&D Programs). 88 pages long. 1990.

Current Biography 1952

Directory of Corporate Affiliations (1986) published by the National Register Pub. Co.

Eliot, Marc. Walt Disney Hollywood's Dark Prince. NY, NY: Harper Paperbacks, 1993.

Finch, Christopher. The Art of Walt Disney from Mickey Mouse to the Magic Kingdom. NY: Harry N. Abrams, Inc., 1975.

Hagstrom, Robert G. Jr. The Warren Buffett Way. NY: John Wiley & Sons.

Hulteng, John L. The Messenger's Motives, Ethical Problems of the News Media. Englewood Cliffs, NJ: Prentice-Hall, Inc., 1976.

Jackson, Kathy Merlock. Walt Disney, A Bio-Bibliography. Westport, CN: Greenwood Press.

Landis, Bill. Anger, The Unauthorized Biography of Kenneth Anger. NY: HarperCollins Pub., 1995.

Moldea, Dan E. Dark Victory, Ronald Reagon, MCA and the Mob. NY, NY: Viking, 1986.

Mosley, Leonard. Disney's World. Stein & Day: NY, 1985.

Neelands, Barbara. About Ben Sharpsteen. Second Impressions, No. 1 A Sharpsteen Museum Reprints Project, Calistoga, CA: Sharpsteen Museum, July, 1990.

Riegert, Ray, ed. Disneyland And Beyond the Ultimate Family Guidebook. Berkeley, CA: Ulysses Press of Berkeley, CA.

Schickel, Richard. The Disney Version. NY: Simon & Schuster, 1968.

Siu, R.G.H. The Craft of Power. NY, NY: Quill, William Morrow & Co.

Sklar, Martin A. (with intro by Walt Disney) Walt Disney's Disneyland. Walt Disney Prod., 1969.

Smoodin, Eric. Disney Discourse Producing the Magic Kingdom. Routledge: NY, 1994.

Stein, Jeff, ed. The Basic Everyday Encyclopedia. NY, NY: Random House, 1954.

Sterling, Claire. Thieves World -The Threat of the New Global Network of Organized Crime. NY: Simon & Schuster, 1994.

Taylor, John. Storming the Magic Kingdom. NY: Alfred A. Knopf, 1987.

Thomas, Bob. Walt Disney An American Original. Hyperion (Disney): CA, 1994.

Wallechinsky, David and Irving Wallace and Amy Wallace. The Book of Lists. 666 5th Ave., NY, NY: Bantam Books, 1978.

Wallechinsky, David and Irving Wallace. The People's Almanac. Garden City, NY: Doubleday and Co., 1975.

Who's Who, Who's Who in the West (1951), Who Was Who World Biography

PERIODICAL SOURCES

Carson, L. Pierce, Who's Who in the Napa Valley, Appellation, Oct/Nov. '95

George Magazine, ""Here Comes the Son'", Dec. Vol. 1, No. 10.

House & Garden, "Sticks and Stones, Mickey for Mayor?", Oct. 1, 1996, pp. 61 -68ff.

Martin, Harry V. Napa Sentinel. A series of articles in 1989 were very important in learning of some of the Illuminati/CIA/Contra/Drug Running activities in Napa Valley, CA that Roy Disney is associated with. Harry V. Martin went into all kinds of records and did an excellent job of investigative reporting.

Monde 2000, no.12, had an article on non-lethal weapons that the NWO is developing. This article was reprinted in Encounter Chronicles Journal of Scientific Intelligence, and discussed how Disney has been working with Sandia Labs and Los Alamos.

Media Spotlight's article Fantasia,

Mother Jones, May-Ju', 97, p. 61.

NAPA VALLEY REGISTER, the following articles are samples of what was used:

"ABC Will Mount An Anti-Drug Campaign'" Friday, Jan. 10, 1997, p.1D

"Children's Books Get Red Carpet Treatment In Hollywood Films" May 16, 1996, p. SC

"Disney and McDonalds'" May 24, 1996

"Disney Buys ABC", Saturday, Aug. 19, 1995, D.

"Disney Earnings Up 28 Percent In Third Quarter", Friday, July 26, 1996, p. 8C

„Disneyland Expansion Given OK" Wednesday, Oct. 9, 1996, p.D

'"Disney Links to McDonald's May Be Back. Thursday, Apr. 11, 1996, 7A

"Disney World Makes Sure World, Remember the Magic"" (by L. Pierce Carson), Sun., Oct. 20, '96

"Federal Employees Get Disney Tour" Saturday, Dec. 9,1995, p. 5A

"It's Lights-Out For Main Street" May 14, 1996.

"An Overlooked, Different World Inside Theme Park" Sunday, Sept. 29, 1996, p. SC

"Mickey Going On The Road", Friday, 7/26/96, p. 8C '"Past and Future In Disney Community'", Friday, Oct. 4, 1996, p. iD

"Planned Parenthood Benefit On Sunday"--Events of Interest sect. on p. A2, Sept. 13, '96

"Pentagon Still Wastes Money", Mon., 4/15/96, p. 4B Newsweek

"Power Failure" 12/23/96, p. 34-36; '"Sending an SOS at ABC", 5/12/97, p. 54-55

NY TIMES (the following are samples of what was used: Articles during the "50's & '60's were looked at. „Disney Offers Faux Memories of Atlantic City Boardwalk" by Joe Sharkey, Tuesday, Dec. 10, 1996 "Baptists Censure Disney On Gay-Spouse Benefits" Thurs. June 13, 1996, p. A10 „Disney to acquire 2 radio stations", 4/15/97, p. C4.

The PRESS DEMOCRAT (the following are example of what was used:)

"Baptists, Disney Paths Diverge" Saturday, June 29, 1996, p. D4

"Disney To Buy Stake In Web Company" 2/15/97, p. E6

"Heavy Disney" Sunday, Oct. 20, 1996

"The Ins and Outs of Allen" by Frederic M. Biddle and Renee Graham, On Q,, Sept. 29, 1996, p. 27

SAN FRANCISCO CHRONICLE (the following are examples of what was used:)

"Disney, Miramax Bond", May 10, 1996

"Disney Signs Asian Animator"

"Miramax Plans To Make 'Thoughtful" Films", 4/11/96

SAN FRANCISCO EXAMINER (the following are examples of what was used:)

"Disney Institute Is A Short Course In Creativity" by Catherine Watson, Sunday, May 26, 1996, p. T9

"Mouse Matriculation Is A Great Experience" by Catherine Watson, Sunday, May 26, 1996, p. T9

"Tomorrowland Jumps Into The Future", Sunday, July 14, 1996, p. T3

The Spotlight's Feb. 26, '96 p. 31 article "Disney Turns Back on Family Values."

Time Magazine, "Job Hunting With Mike [Ovitz]" 2/24/97, p. 50; '"Hilton Has Room For ITT'" 2/10/97,

Wall St. Journal (many issues from several decades.)

SOME OF OTHER SOURCES (used & not used).

· Various Disney brochures.//· Rush Limbaugh's comments concerning how Disney had betrayed its viewers' trust.//· Interviews w/ Napa Valley residents.

· Interviews with disgruntled insiders to the NWO.

· Interviews with various types of Disney victims.

[Disney has used mafia-type tactics, i.e. death threats, to intimidate numerous people into selling their property. Roy E. Disney has been reported involved in these land thefts. Victims of this type of intimidation are in many states, but several prominent regions are Napa Valley, CA; Shenandoah Valley; Virginia, & FL Disney's land-grabbing operations could be a book in itself. This author has lots more research which I HAVE NO PLANS to reveal, which has been left w/ key others, such as the connections of VaVin, near Leon,VA, who produce Prince Michel de Virginia, whose chef & others connect to Belgium. The background of several key people, like Robert Podesta. Financial records, such as Fed. Judge Fern M. Smith (Burrows). ETC. This para. is not indexed.]

CHAPTER 6: SCIENCE NO. 6-THE USE OF ELECTRONICS & ELECTRICITY

Developments in fiber optics, computers, electronic communications, nano-technology, bio-chips & neuro-electrical research have combined to bring mankind to the point where mankind can be controlled by one centralized monolithic Beast computer. The ultimate mind-controlled slavery is now possible. We are in the first stages of its implementation.

The chapter will be organized in the following sections & subsections:

Section A. An Overview of the subject
  A1. Where this article is headed
    GLOSSARY OF TERMS FOR UNDERSTANDING ELECTRONIC MIND CONTROL
      Bio-medical telemetry
      EMF weapons
      Psychotronics
      Remote Viewing (RV for short)
      Syntel
  A2. Where the NWO is headed   Pyramider

Section B. An intro to implants
  B1. Three typical implant victims
  B2. Documentation of implants
  REFERENCE PAGE FOR UNDERSTANDING ELECTROMAGNETIC WAVES & MIND-CONTROL
  B3. GWEN Towers
  B4. Body suits
Section C. Specific Implants
  C1. Audio implants (a. public. b. secret)
    BACKGROUND INFORMATION

BRIEF CHRONOLOGY OF AUDIO IMPLANTS
BASICS OF HOW THE IMPLANTS CAN FUNCTION
USES OF THE IMPLANTS
TYPES OF AUDIO IMPLANTS:
  Part A. Publicly admitted audio implants
  Part. B. Secretly implanted audio implants   COCHLEAR   DENTAL AUDITORY   RIDGE
C2. Body manipulation implants
C3. Visual holographic implants
  HOW THEY WORK
  TYPES: FIBER OPTICS ARTIFICIAL LENSES BIO-CHIPS HOLOGRAPHIC OR H-INSERT
  HOLOGRAPHIC IMPLANTS VIA NANOTECHNOLOGY & NANOBOTS
C4. Memex/Brain Link implants
  INTERFACE DEVICES
ORGANIC BIOPROCESSORS LINKED TO VIRUSES
 PSYCHICS
C5. Torture/Nerve & Muscle Stimulation Implants
C6. Tracking & I.D. Implants

Section D. Direct monitoring & manipulation of the brain/mind
D1. Direct monitoring
TESLA WAVES USED TO READ MINDS & IMPLANT VOICES
D2. Direct manipulation
SUMMARY OF ELF WAVE MIND CONTROL CAPABILITIES

Section E. Auxiliary uses of electronics & electromagnetic waves
E1. hypnotic induction
E2. polygraphs
E3. attacks against people & objects
LIQUID CRYSTALS
"ALIEN" implants
BED COILS STANDARDIZED FOR MIND-CONTROL POTENTIAL
E4. virtual reality

Section A. An Overview of the subject.

A1. Where this article is headed

This chapter is designed to cover the complexities of hi-tech mind-control in simple-to-understand language. To accommodate those who are more technically literate and who want more, some clues to more technical sources are given, but time & space limitations mean that much has gone unsaid. My deep thanks to the many victims, who placed their trust in me to get their stories out to the world. I hope that I have vindicated their trust. There are a number of disinformation agents that appear to be putting out good information on implants, but are actually disinformation agents. We can error by undershooting or overshooting the truth. The principle topics that these pretend "whistle blowers" have been discussing are the tracking implants and remote viewing. (For RV info, see Theta Programming material in Vol. 2.) Neither topic is any revelation, nor are they the most dangerous items in the elite's electronic mind-control arsenal. If the reader has not skipped chapter 5 on disinformation, then he will be aware how factual information can be used in deception, such as in chicken feed & building bona fides. Why is it that the TV program "The Real X-Files" shown on channel 4 was created by a CIA operative, Jim Schnabel? And why are all the "private" Remote Viewing organizations run by what appear to be entirely all intelligence operatives (such as Ed Dames, et. al.)? And why do we see mind-control specialists, like "ex"-Intelligence officer C.B. Scott Jones who gets involved with several UFO research organizations & disseminating disinformation? One "researcher", who is publicly exposing" the NWO, tried to convince this author, "The government has no secrets." (A word-for-word quote by the way.) He needs to read a supplement to the National Industry Security Pro grain manual (Mar. 92 release) where the Air Force teaches their DoD contractors how to construct cover stories to lie about the nature of their work for the government. I will not take cheap shots at the World Order, & I will not intentionally mislead the reader. You will get the whole truth and nothing but the truth, as well a single chapter can present it. Vol. 2's chapter 6 which was on this same subject was not the final word and neither is this chapter. Before I start passing on lots of information, I should clarify one point. Human brain cells communicate by superconductivity, not electricity. Electricity travels near the speed of light, while superconductivity is in the range of the speed of sound. Government researchers have a device called a SQUID (Superconducting Quantum Interference Device) which actually monitors the light flowing from brain cell to brain cell. This is why over 5% of the brain's dry matter weight is iridium and rhodium. However, this does not subtract from the fact that electromagnetic waves have the ability to change what the brain experiences and thinks. I must also provide a small glossary for electronic mind-control terms that most people are not familiar with.

GLOSSARY OF TERMS FOR UNDERSTANDING ELECTRONIC MIND CONTROL

Bio-medical telemetry--Transmitter-receivers that are often located at the base of the skull which record body functions & brain wave activity. Their data is sent to remote computers for monitoring. A bio-medical telemetry implant may also function as the primary control implant on body suits of implants. Early versions were used on astronauts.

EMF weapons--Electromagnetic Frequency weapons. These basically are machines that can modulate and beam electromagnetic waves in such a fashion that they control biological/mental functions within the victim. Portals to the central nervous system can be manipulated to create visual images, project voices into the mind, and create pain, moods and emotions.

Psychotronics--This word was originated from Soviet research. The American public have mistakingly thought that the word is equivalent to psychic activity. A more precise translation of the Russian term would have been "applied psychoenergetics". American psychotronics research was initially done at Stanford Research Institute. This is the Theta Programming that Vol. 2 described.

Remote Viewing (RV for short)--This means psychic viewing of something.

Syntel--This is short for synthetic telepathy, which is the remote sending of voices and thoughts into a victim of electronic mind-control. The military and intelligence agencies have successfully achieved this capability and have carried out countless meetings over their possible uses of syntel.

A2. Where the NWO is headed

Since 1991, this author has been in contact with various victims of implants. The natural first reaction of many initial listeners would be skepticism to the subject. The psychological profession has had articles in their professional journals ridiculing these poor victims. If a fair-minded person will match the experiences of what one can witness happening to these implant victims (as well as their evidence) to the cutting edge of what science is researching and capable of doing, then there is no doubt that implants are being used on an ever increasing mass scale. The World Order is using amplifiers, generators, electronics, listening devices, non-ionizing electromagnetic radiation, a snapping type sound energy that hits and burns the body, closed-circuit videos to monitor implant victims, nanotechnology, and tracking devices that scanners (incl. mobile hand-held scanners) can pick up-- JUST to name a few. This chapter will provide an indepth overview of many of these electronic mind-control gadgets. Unfortunately, the twilight zone of Big Brother is upon us. People (such as limousine drivers) that have been around the movers and shakers report that they brag about these technological controls. The technology described in this chapter, such as nanobots, and holographic implants are in the "R&D stage" of use. What is meant by "R&D stage" means that the World Order is using a large variety of experimental items, but the reader should be forewarned that this does not mean that these items are any indication of where the World Order's actual secret R&D is at. This author has worked with enough mind-control victims to have established several facts:

· Society is getting only the crumbs of what is known by the World Order's hierarchy.

· The World Order is releasing technology at a control rate, much of it through mind-controlled slaves who are programmed to "discover" a particular "discovery". They are in reality only disclosing what has been known in secret, and their discoveries are actually helping cover up where the World Order's secret research is at. However, it's not difficult to see the direction the World Order is headed. They are working at making virtual reality (aka cyperspace) the "in" thing. They are fusing the human mind to computers. Computers/robots are taking over human jobs, and humans are becoming more like computers/robots. Sci-fi gurus, cyberpunks, and establishment scientists are selling and advertising this technological direction as "freedom", and the crowds of sheep are accepting things like brain implants as "survival equipment" and "freedom". The cool" technological pied pipers of our time are teaching our children that gadgets that remove their minds from reality are giving them new freedoms. But this chapter is written because there are still a few people with the neural-receptors and the computing capacity left in their craniums to comprehend the dangers that these mind-controlling devices have for humanity. Witnesses have told me that the creation of "robocop" type cybergs (the fusion of man & other equipment) has already been experimented on in secret. Indeed, the government gave out research contracts for cyberg research back in the 1960's. And the use of electro-magnetic waves (esp. Tesla waves), implants, and other electronic devices by the Illuminati for mind-control is on the increase. How much of a genuine threat do these things pose humanity? [I'll spell it out for the reader, but we must remain calm, a fear-based response only makes things worse.] Yes, it is true that the NSA can remotely track people if they know the specific EMF waves (evoked potentials from EEGs in the 30-50 Hz, 5 milliwatt range) of a person's bioelectric field. Each person's emissions are unique, just like their fingerprint, palmprint, and their voiceprint. This means that the NSA can remotely track anyone in public. And yes, it is true that the NSA's RNM system can remotely send EMF Brain stimulation signals which create visual images, subliminal audios, what appear to be audible sounds, and thoughts into people's minds. Yes, it is true that body suits of implants are used to control people's minds and bodies, as well as track them. Yes, it is true they have voice prints of hundreds of thousands of Americans and can identify & track via their computers all electronic communications in this nation. Most phone calls go through about 30 computers before they reach their destination. The phone companies computers, according to someone who worked for AT&T and witnessed it, record ALL phone calls using computers. However, to weed out the worthless from the worthwhile, the Illuminati's fronts use a list of key words, such as names or phrases called THE WATCH LIST which the computer uses to identify conversations worthwhile to listen to. Even though the NSA uses supercomputers, it is monitoring most communication on the entire planet so they have to squeeze the WATCH LIST as tight as possible. According to Bamford, James. The Puzzle Palace. NY: The Puzzle Palace, 1983, p. 459, "...according to Raven, programmers would simply reduce Malcolm X to the last two letters in his first name (lm) followed by a space and then the letter X. Then any time an intercepted data communications containing that particular combination of letters and spacing (lm X) streamed past the computer's reading head, it would automatically be kicked Out for further analysis. Part of the reason that the computers are swamped with Watch list submissions is that many items require numerous entries. When searching for derogatory references to President Richard M. Nixon, for example, technicians would have to program a variety of possible key words, such as "Tricky Dicky". This, according to the former G Group Chief would be converted to The new technology which is being implemented in stages includes computer imaging of a person which makes a "whole body map" of the person's body which is stored in the computer. Something that has been only developed for a narrow use by the NWO is the downloading of the holographic image of a person's thoughts so they can be transmitted to another. (See Appendix 3 on cloning for more on this.) The majority of the few people who know this is going on wouldn't waste time reporting it, because the public wouldn't believe it anyway. However, some prominent scientists are predicting that it is just around the corner. The three top research institutes in this field, Stanford Research Institute, MIT, and the Carnegie-Mellon Univ. all have people saying that this capability is "almost here". Austrian born Hans Moravec, dir, of the Robotics Inst. at Carnegie Mellon Univ., is quoted in The Indianapolis Star, 6/14/1987, in an article entitled "Immortality", "In an astonishingly short amount of time, scientists will be able to transfer the contents of a person's mind into a powerful computer, and in the process, make him--or at least his living essence--virtually immortal." MIT artificial intelligence researcher Gerald J. Sussman states, "I'm afraid, unfortunately that I'm the last generation to die. Some of my students may manage to survive a little longer.'' But as fantastic as all these powerful capabilities sound, there are gliches in their electronic control of humans.

As an outsider looking inside for a number of years, this author has been able to take note of some of the success and failures of the New World Order's electronic mind-control. First, the NSA picks up so much intelligence information, they are drowning in their own information. Only so many people can make decisions, and they can only digest so much information. They may try to manipulate people and events, but Christians (who are free of the mind-control) can step through those manipulations by having the mind of Christ. Next, if a person understands who they are & believes in following Christ, outside visions & outside or strange voices or thoughts do not alter the course that a person will take. Most of the people this author has met who have been subjected to remote electronic control over their mind--HAVE REJECTED the instructions & harassment of their electronic handlers. Not only is it clear that the voices are being transmitted from an external source to the victim, others can also detect that something is amiss. The element of secrecy is missing. One man spent an afternoon talking to this author about the World Order had tried to electronically control his mind, and turn him into a drug pusher. He had successfully foiled them for several years. Although he has had to flee & try to go into hiding to keep his own mind. The most powerful mind-control is still trauma-based mind control built on a foundation of multiple personalities (dissociated personalities and dissociated parts of the mind). It appears that electronic mind-control is being overlaid on top the mind-control based on dissociation. When this is done, the electronic mind-control is frightening, because the victim's consciousness is not able to think passed the electronic mind-control which catches their undivided attention. They are too distracted to deal with the deeper issues of trauma-based mind-control.

Imagine being a programmed multiple, and your handler doesn't have to even be near you to relay complicated codes and instructions. He can use your implant. But again, how serious is electronic mind-control? Let me relate to you about a guided tour that a civilian friend of mine took through a NWO's major beast computer center in Alaska back in the 1970's. The engineer, who was in charge of building and getting the center operational, gave him a tour of the site's capabilities. At that point, the NWO had built a massive computer center in Alaska, one in So. Africa (believed to be located at the U.S. embassy in Johannesburg), and one in Pine Gap, Australia. These three sites were very specific, because they formed a triangle on the globe, and couldn't be located anywhere else, due to the naturally occuring lines of force of the planet. These Beast Computer Centers consist of aisles and aisles of big state of the art computers. They each have several dozen people to run them. Even in the '70's, an operator could speak into the computer and it would answer. For instance, if you asked the computer about anyone on the planet, it could usually pull up all kinds of information about that person. If you asked the computer how could you get that person to kill someone? or how can I isolate this person? The computer would spill out a plan almost instantly, telling you all the people around that subject who could be manipulated and in what fashion those people need to be manipulated to cause the end result. This is the end result of years of "BLACK PSYCHIATRY--which means applying psychiatric techniques to manipulate people and nations. These computers electronically connect to some of those people who are electronically controlled, so that the controllers can actually control the world from a computer. These computers also store vast amounts of personal information about people's thought processes and thinking. It is possible that electronic surveillance is being done to read the thoughts of people and that the computers are actually able to store this information in some usable fashion. Because this is so secret, they can't give any hints of their vast ability to monitor thoughts, as well as organize and store those thoughts. This sounds like science fiction, but from people who invent & work at state of the art technology, this is actually said to be old technology. They are limited in how they use this technology because they want it to remain secret.

Meanwhile on the surface, the public system has automated fingerprint identification with the AFIS system, and has automated birth certificates electronically too. This all ties in with the intense desire of the World System to use the potential of their computers' memories. Large Neural computers that have artificial intelligence using neural processing which is a type of learning similar to learning done by the human brain are being used. Recently, the world champion chess player was beat by a computer. This author's friend, who toured the Alaskan computer center, was shown how a war could be created between any two nations. The operator merely asked the computer what it knew about a certain country and then ask it how could a war be created with a neighboring country. This is the end result of countless studies such as the U.S. military reference book Basic Psychological Operations Study (BPS) which outlines country by country, specifying where each country is vulnerable for PSYOP operations (psychological warfare).

This kind of thing has a long history. For instance in W.W. II, the Office of War Information and the 0SS cooperated in psychological warfare projects. What this author's friend saw was a network of Cray-type computers, perhaps similar to the EMASS system of Cray computers that E-Systems developed. Such a system can store 5 trillion pages of text and work with that data base with lightening speed.

The reason this author's friend was allowed to see this technology, was that he happened to be at the right place at the right time, and the Engineer operator of the Beast Computer said that this system was obsolete. Which is true, today's 9

Beast computers are much better at speech than the computers at these three control sites were in '73. The Beast computers can (according to another eye witness who used it) hear human voices and determine what language is being spoken and then can listen and answer in that language. These computers link directly to thousands of mind-controlled slaves and can-- via various methods-- almost instantly control the behavior of numerous people. This, along with good old fashioned phone calls, allows the elite to manipulate events very fast.

Anchorage is the site of a National Security Agency NSA listening post(LP). The Beast computer was located northeast of Anchorage, and so is the HAARP project. The HAARP facility is near Gakona, a hamlet about 140 miles north of Prince William Sound and its signals travel on a field line to Australia. The Beast Computer is also linked to Australia as well as satellite systems. The HAARP site took a 4-wheeled truck to reach, and the Beast Computer site in 1973 was even more remote. The University of Alaska Fairbanks (which has its own super computer) and the Alaskan Poker Flat Rocket Range also were involved with the HAARP project. 30% of the U of A's supercomputer's use was for DoD projects.

HAARP uses 3 powerful transmitter sites in Alaska. Somewhat on the flip side, the human brain which they control can, IF it has a memex implant, interface with the Beast computer which acts as a vast repository of human knowledge as well as answering questions to essentially all previously answered questions instantaneously. If the human brain has some type of virtual reality holodeck attachment, the computer can even walk the slave through a realistic setting indistinguishable from the real world. Robocop or robo-soldier has an incredible advantage with such extended memex/remote viewing capabilities.

The World Order has experimented in memex/remote viewing along several divergent paths. One method has been psychic (demonic) method, where the "natural" mental facilities of the human are trained. The other route has been high-tech. According to eye-witnesses both methods have yielded positive results, although it sounds like they are still refining their capabilities. The word telematics has come into use to denote the interconnection between computers and telecommunications. France has a National Telecommunications Research Center, which works with groups such as CII-Honeywell Bull (Jean-Pierre Brule, Pres., & Emmanuel de Robien, Sec.-Gen.). CII-Honeywell Bull did telematics and implant research, and so has IBM France. IBM's subsidiary SBS developed satellite-based communications. In Britain, their National Physical Laboratory NPL has been active in telecommunications research. Professional computer groups have umbrella groups such as the British Computer Society, which help determine policies.

In the U.S. the National Center for Supercomputer applications works on virtual reality interface with humans. Meanwhile SCAN (Swinburne Centre for Applied Neurosciences, Hawthorn, Australia 3122) has been working on how to monitor human thoughts. These are just a few of a vast network of research groups applying their efforts to the types of things you will read about in this chapter.

Around 1973, TRW began designing a satellite that would allow the CIA to communicate with its assets/agents in "denied areas". This was code-named Pyramider, and used frequency hopping. The signals can be hidden among random urban radio transmissions. (See Robert Lindsey, The Falcon and the Snowman. NY: Simon & Schuster, 1979, p. 218)

Some people who are related (in some fashion) to the CIA have been receiving Syntel implants that are communicating to them using signals that frequency-hop. So the proof is in the pudding, the CIA used Pyramider to contact implant victims. The World Order does not use every technological gadget they have in every situation. Use of secret weaponry is restricted so that the weaponry remains secret. This is one reason why victims of mind-control display such a wide variety of symptoms and control mechanisms. But what is scary is that any bozo can already purchase on the public market a frightening array of electronic mind-control devices.

Information Unlimited puts Out a catalog that any bozo on the street can order from which advertises 200,000 volt stun guns, laser ray gun, compressed air guns (Air Tasers) that knock people down with probes that attach instantly to the human target and jam their nervous system with T-waves, laser listening devices to listen at long range via their windows, implants along with the tracking system to keep track of people, animals or objects. They also sell other novel devices. While this author has that catalog that advertises for sale computer chips to implant people with, the psychiatric profession is helping cover-up Big Brother's implant technology.

For instance the Journal of Nervous and Mental Disease, Sept. 1995, Vol. 183 (9), pp. 603-604, has a story about two males (aged 33 and 53 years old) who were labeled delusional because they complained of implants hidden in their fillings in their teeth. The article is entitled, "Delusional electronic dental inplants: Case reports and literature review." The shrinks concluded the two men were obviously mentally ill and needed treatment with drugs because they are claiming that they have electronic dental implants. The psychiatrists wrote, "neither had any insight into the implausibility of the delusion." The doctors gave antipsychotic drugs, and physically intervened to "prevent an inappropriate dental extraction." According to the article, for some unknown reason, the two men "responded poorly" to anti-psychotic drugs. It never occurs to the psychiatrists that the reason the anti-psychotic drugs didn't work is possibly because the men's complaints were legitimate. The two shrinks were E. Sherwood Brown and Michael T. Lambert.

There are other cases too, where people complaining of implants have been labelled "delusional" by psychiatrists. The Amer. Psychiatric Assoc. is guilty of refusing to seriously review evidence that harassment & mind-control may be impacting people mentally. DSM-IV reflects this continuing refusal to accord victims of electronic mind-control any official recognition by the therapeutic community. Based on research by Drs. W. Fry & R. Meyers, the Network has learned how to make brain lesions of a minute controlled size with ultrasonics, rather than doing a lobotomy. In 1963, Dr. Peter Lindstrom at the Univ. of Pittsburgh was able to use a single unfocused sonic beam to destroy fiber tracts in the brain without damaging the nerve cells near them. Sonic beams (sound waves) can be used to control human thought. (We'll discuss sonic beams some more later, now let's delve into a key part of their electronic control--implants.)

SECTION B. AN INTRO TO IMPLANTS

B1. Three typical implant victims

Let's look at three victims who suffer from of mind-control implants & body-control implants, who are known by this author. We can refer to them as "Amy", Victim No. 1001..., "Betty", Victim No. 1002..., and "Cathy", Victim No. 1003... --"Amy" determined by using a spectrum analyzer that she had waves of 750 mhz targeted on her. "Betty" determined that she had the entire spectrum of radio-microwaves hitting her in a Morse code pattern. The transceiver (transmitter/receiver) for the signals was a fiber optic receiver made to look like a pubic hair that repeatedly burned holes in her underwear. Apparently, this side effect is a "bug" they haven't gotten out of the technology. "Cathy" has ELF & VLF waves of 435 & 1080 Mhz signals targeted on her. When she's active both types of waves come, and when she remains still the 1080 signal fades. (435 is in the 400-450 Mhz band which is the window to the human consciousness, and 1080 is in the 1000 to 1200 Mhz band.) They are also using a Nitrogen particle beam, which produces "nitrogen narcosis" (like the bends) in targeted victims. Xenon lamps can affect the mind and body, too. 435 Mhz is converted to 1080 by interaction with the high-atmosphere HAARP project. The 1100 (1000-1200) Mhz frequency can affect genetics. Implant RF frequencies have been damaging the eyes of implant victims. Although this gives us a starting point in our discussion, these are not the only frequencies that threaten mind-control victims. (See Section Dl for direct monitoring /manipulating frequencies.) Author W.H. Bowart in his Vol.1, No. 1, pg. 1 Freedom of Thought newsletter quotes Brian Bard of Glendale, CA who wrote, "I failed to discuss the utilization of power in modern mind control implants. Like Delgrado's stimoceiver, no internal power source is necessary. The same electro-magnetic energy which is collected through induction by such relays produces an internal electrical charge of equal energy. Utilizing a capacitance circuitry design, the charge is stored as a mechanical distortion of the crystalline lattice and discharged as a focused pulse of electro-magnetic energy at a lower frequency. Higher frequency E-M has a higher energy state than lower frequency. Thus, the effective output of photons may be twice or thrice the potential of the relays. "A more advanced design in use utilizes 50 or more distinct channels for various functions. Not only the encrypted primary input signal utilized for signal output, but several channels are reserved for supplementary energy induction. With integrated switching, both passive and active surveillance of brainwave activity may be enhanced. Contrawise, signal output may be boosted and focused on specific neural pathways. The devices remain active, programmable signal relays with multiple selectable channels so long as electro-magnetic induction continues to occur."

Modern microchip implants will have 250,000 components. Certain electrical freks will trigger certain neurochemicals. The frek 7.83, which is the elec. field resonating between the planet & its ionosphere, makes the subject feel in one with all creation. But it isn't quite that simple, because a 7.83 frek can be sent in numerous different wave shapes, such as the rolling sinusoidal pattern, jagged sawtooth waves, rectangular (flat on top, flat on bottom) waves, and they all have a different effect on the brain. (Mega brain, pp. 108-109) One can imagine the potential power an implant that could create the proper frequencies could have over an individual.

B2. Documentation of implants.

On the following pages, are the startling anechoic chamber results when two victims of syntel implants were examined. (Synthetic telepathy implants give thoughts & voices.) These two pages document that they were receiving signals, in fact, the anechoic chamber results helped to pin point what building those signals were coming from!

For pictures click here 2-14 jpg

REFERENCE PAGE FOR UNDERSTANDING ELECTROMAGNETIC WAVES & MIND-CONTROL

The best way for people to understand electromagnetic waves is to think of the ocean's waves. Some waves in the ocean are big, and some are small, size is amplitude.

Some beaches have waves that come quickly and some have waves that come slowly, this is called the frequency that the waves comes.

Researcher figured out how they could change the amplitude or the frequency of electromagnetic waves in a controlled way, and this is called amplitude modulation or frequency modulation.

Because all electromagnetic energy beams travel the same speed 3×10^{10} cm/sec, an energy beam with a short wave must have many more of those short waves pass in a given time such as a day than a long wave. The shorter the wave the greater the frequency that a wave will arrive. While our image of an ocean is that it moves up and down in relation to the surface.

In other words, the ocean wave moves (vibrates) up and down in relation to the surface (a mathematical plane). Electromagnetic waves vibrate in 3 dimensions (relative to 3 planes), generally they are only drawn as one-dimensional waves. Our brains operate on waves that are very low frequency (from one cycle per second) to about 50 cycles per second. A cycle per second is called a Hertz (Hz). Due to the wide range of different amplitudes and frequencies it has been more practical to induce various measuring units. It would be nice if all the measuring units could be done in feet or meters or whatever, but the range in size from the very tiny to the very large means that they use different measuring units. Just like you use different measuring units to get a quart of milk and 3 gallons of gas. The milk could be called a quarter-gallon but it isn't. In measuring frequency they use the following measuring terms:

1,000,000 cycles per second = Megahertz (MHz)
1,000 cycles per second = Kilohertz (KHz)
1 cycle per second = Hertz (Hz)

In measuring amplitude they measure the length of the waves with kilometers, meters, and centimeters. The very small waves are measured in angstroms, microns, and nanometers. What is an angstrom. A nanometer is one billionth of a meter. That is a very tiny fraction written as 1/1,000,000,000 of a meter or for short an nanometer. A micron is one millionth (1/1,000,000) of a meter. Ten nanometers are said to make up an angstrom. (In other words an angstrom is 1 ten-billionth of a meter.)

After they measure radio frequencies, the waves of different lengths are given other names. They could just say 'waves from 30,000 to 300,000 MHz", but instead they shorten things by having a special name for these waves EHF (Extremely High Frequency waves.)

This names are as follows:

Extremely High Frequency	EHF:	30,000 to 300,000 MHz
Superhigh Frequency	SHF:	3,000 to 30,000 MHz
Ultrahigh Frequency	UHF:	300 to 3,000 MHz
High Frequency	VHF:	30 to 300 MHz
Medium Frequency	MF:	300 to 3,000 KI-Iz

Low Frequency   LF: 30 to 300 KHz
Very Low Frequency   VLF: 3 to30KHz
Extremely Low Frequency ELF: Below 3 KHz to 1 Hz or less

BRAIN FREQUENCIES (FREKS) RELATE TO STATES OF ACTIVITY

The lower brain frequencies pertain to sleep and dream states. The middle brain frequencies pertain to normal wakeful activity. The higher brain frequencies pertain to aroused, or concerned or states of anxiety. No brain waves means a person is "brain dead", even though some body functions may continue. Naturally occurring phenomena, such as lightning in a thunderstorms, sunny days that soak a person with extra positive ions, can all affect the thinking of brain.

CHART GOING UP THE FREQUENCY SCALE

These frequency no's are in Hertz which is cycles per sec. (However the first part of the scale are non-linear, asymmetrical waves, which are mistakenly called Hertzian by many people.)

1 Approx. beginning of brain waves

6.66   Theta brain waves
7.85   Alpha brain waves
15.7   Beta brain waves
30-30.56 Government VLF stations
32-33   Government VLF stations
34-42   Government VLF stations
50   Approx. Upper limit of brain wave frequencies
60   Produces an audible sound

62-254.1 CTCSS (Continuous Tone Coded Squelch Systems). These tones CTCSS tones are broadcast continually interspersed on a frequency, which allows several different users to broadcast separately on the same frequency and only pick up the message that has their CTCSS tone.

Post Office Tones are 82.5, 91.5, 97.4. & 100.9. U.S.
Customs & border patrol is 100 Hz. U.S.
Secret service is 103.5 Hz. EPA is 114.8. IRS & BATF is 123.0.
Veterans Affairs, GSA, & Dept. of Energy is 127.3.
Fed. Aviation Admin. & U.S. Marshall service is 136.5.
Coast Guard Intell. is 141.3 Hz.
Dept. of State & Border Patrol is 151.4 Hz.
Drug Enforcement Agency, Fed. Aviation Admin., & Nat. Marine Fisheries is 156.7.
Justice Dept., FBI is 167.9.

10^2 (10 x 10) Ultrasonic

10^3 Lower range of true Hertzian waves, waves in cycles per sec lower than this such as the human heart beat or Brain alpha waves are not Hertzian.

104 (10,000)

16,000-32,000 Range of Frequencies used in European implants to signal the implant.

54,900,000 Hz (54.9 MHz) Cellular phones (Also 435 MHz, 750 MHz, & 1080 MHz have been discovered being targeted on victims of implant mind-control.)

10^{11} to 10^{12} Far infra-red

10^{13} "Raman" I.R.

10^14 Near Infra-red

10^{14} to 10^{15} Visible light spectrum

For picture #15 p_6-15.jpg

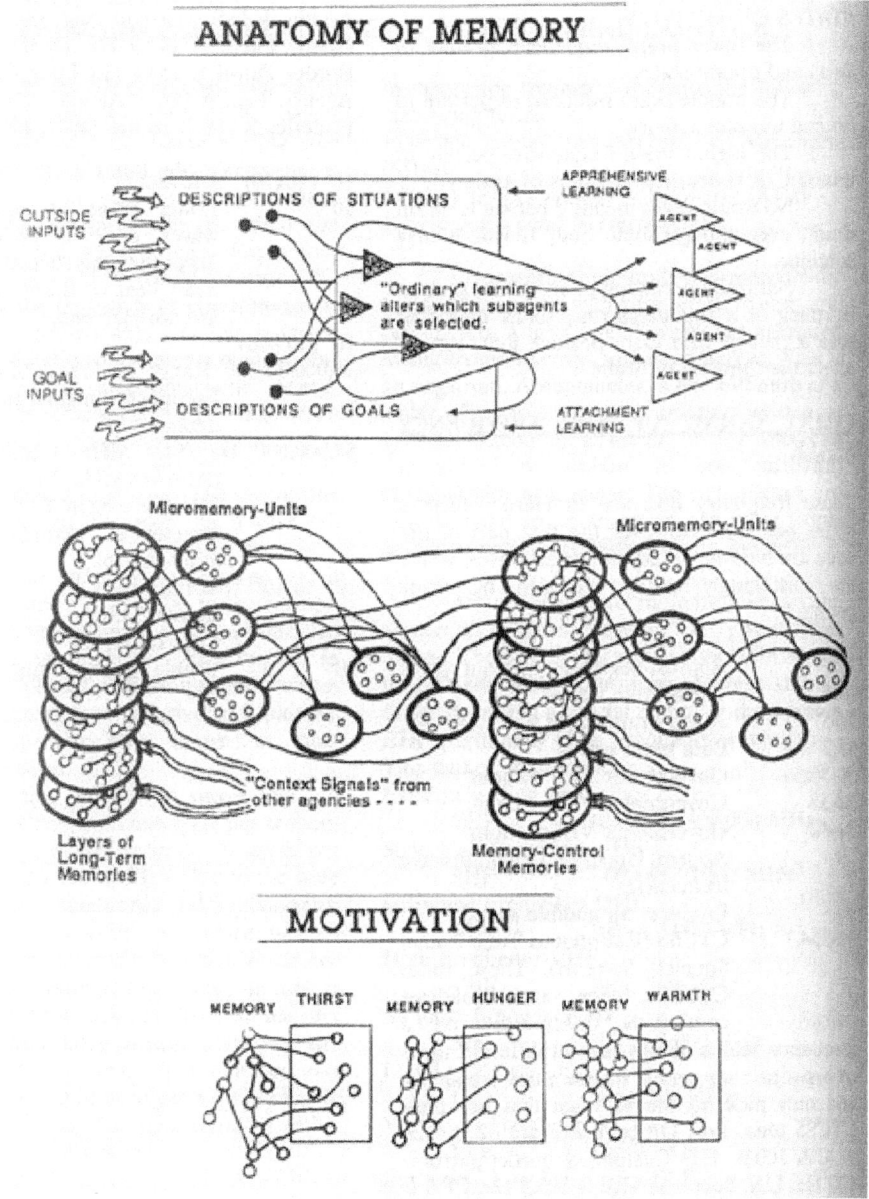

B3. GWEN Towers

The GWEN towers can be used for several purposes, including ELF waves used for direct mind control which will be covered toward the back of this chapter. Because they also are part of the implants system the are included before the chapter discusses implants. Unfortunately for us humans, ELF waves can penetrate almost anything. The U.S. Military has built a Ground-Wave Emergency Network (GWEN) all over the U.S. with several hundred 300-500' GWEN towers that broadcast a very-low-frequency wave (VLF) for mind-control of the American public. A single GWEN tower can broadcast up to 300 miles in a 3600 circle. Plus 8 secret powerful ELF transmitters have been established and 3 of them operate on the west coast. It also needs to be pointed out that many items that are receivers can also function in the role of transmitters. Televisions, cellular phones, even air conditioners can be used to bounce signals to somewhere. Many strange towers and transmitting devices have been installed all over the U.S. in recent years.

B4. Body suits

Victims of mind-control who receive implants often are given a body suit of implants. The location of these implant sites used on the human body have been mapped 10.00 out on the following charts. The mapped sites on these charts are verified by a. an insider, who learned from the inside what is going on, EM (H) & b. this author's experience in working with a sizable number of implant victims. Implants can be placed anywhere, but there are certain key sites that tend to be used. The location used also depends upon the type of implant. Implants over the body create the ability to trigger moods, pain, and other phenomena. Implants for auditory sounds are in the ear. Nasal implants are used for mind-control. Tracking implants are also placed into people.

Section C. Specific Implants

C1. Audio implants (a. public. b. secret)
C2. Body manipulation implants
C3. Visual holographic implants
C4. Memex/Brain Link implants
C5. Torture/Nerve & Muscle Stimulation Implants
C6. Tracking & I.D. Implants.

C1. AUDIO IMPLANTS

BACKGROUND INFORMATION

The concepts used in audio implants had been discovered in the first half of the 20th century, but the refinement of technology to take advantage of what had been discovered waited until the second half of the century. The development of audio implants ran on two tracks, one was the public medical research and the other was the secret Illuminati/Intelligence Agencies' research. Audio implants began to be publicly placed into people in the 1960s. The Illuminati was experimenting on some victims at this stage, and the military in the Vietnam war used auditory implant devices to aid communicating to their men who were sent into tunnels and who were placed into forest situations where audible noise would compromise their locations to the enemy. The Illuminati/Intelligence/& Military consortium was keeping the experimentation secret. It appears from looking at the worldwide research on audio implants that the Illuminati realized that the field was so ambiguous, and open to so many different approaches, that rather than straightjacket the research community by a specific strategy, they encouraged a wide variety of approaches in the research. Consequently, research by one group would overlap or duplicate research by another. Much to their credit, a few researchers rejected offers to get involved because they saw the sinister ramifications. By the 1970s, the intelligence agencies were willing to start using hundreds of people to experiment operationally with the implants. People in every state of the U.S. were selected as victims. Many of these implant victims had programmed multiple personalities already. The controllers were very heavy handed with the people they implanted, and they used the full force of the Illuminati/Intelligence agencies power to keep these people under their control at all times. These innocent victims have had their lives totally destroyed. Some tried to fight back, spending thousands of dollars to get out from underneath the incessant audio messages that the implants sent, but the system was too big and too powerful to fight. Police, congressmen, psychologists and many other people turned their backs on these victims. Some victims who initially fought back gave up resisting, some committed suicide, and some continued to fight. Meanwhile, on the public track during the 1970s & 1980s, medical researchers kept putting more and more audio implants into deaf and hard-to-hear persons. Hundreds of people in the U.S. and many hundreds in other nations such as the U.K., Germany, Austria, Israel, Australia, France and other countries began to receive the cochlear implants. Australia was so proud of their audio implant research/development they issued a postage stamp showing an implant device ("bionic ear") developed in Australia. The question begs asking, if thousands of people have publicly received audio implants, isn't obvious that the secret societies and secret intelligence agencies have done at least as much if not far more?

BRIEF CHRONOLOGY OF AUDIO IMPLANTS

1790--first known attempt by Volta to electrically stimulate the ears. He shot approximately 50 volts of electricity into his auditory system, and experienced the sensation of a blow to the head followed by a sound like the boiling of viscous liquid.

1850--Electro-otiatrics was begun by otologists who hoped electricity could help ear diseases in various ways.

1925--Sounds were created in people by radio engineers by placing electrodes near the ear with a modulated alternating current.

1930--Weaver & Bray discovered the principles used later in the cochlear microphonic implants.

1937--By passing an alternating electrical current in the audible frequency range from an electrode to the skin, Steven, Jones, Lurie and Flottorp found they could have people hear sounds. For a number of years these men studied this phenomena.

1957--Djourno and Eyries in France woke the world up concerning the ability to electrical stimulate the auditory nerves and produce sound with their reports. A patient from France reportedly gets William F. House, MD interested in developing an implant device.

1961--William House implants two patients with short-term audio implants. One patient receives a multiple electrode implant.

1960s--intense research for audio implants is conducted in California in places like Sanford, the Univ. of Calif., in L.A. etc. The military uses audio implants operationally to be able to talk to soldiers in situations where external noise would compromise the location of the American soldiers, such as exploring tunnel system.

1970s--Various researchers around the world begin publicly implanting audio implants into people. The Illuminati and intelligence agencies begin to secretly implant people, this is known because many of the early victims can pin point at time in the 1970s when they got their audio implants.

1980--The FDA establishes Federal regulations regarding cochlear audio implants.

1984--By this year, 369 people have publicly received the House Cochlear Audio Implants, which have been implanted by 36 different clinics. The 3M Cochlear Implant System! House Design for use in adults, which is already in hundreds of adults, receives FDA approval in Nov.

1990s--Audio implants along with other implants begin to be used more aggressively by the mind-control programmers. Successful intelligence operations are carried out with the aid of audio implants.

BASICS OF HOW THE IMPLANTS CAN FUNCTION

Thousands have publicly received audio implants, and thousands have received audio implants without their permission by the New World Order. The implants (whether secret or public) basically have to contain A. a receiver(s), B. a processor, C. a transmitter, D. electrodes or electrical stimulating device. When sound waves arrive to the human ear, the sound causes biological reactions all along the auditory pathway--from the cochlea, the auditory nerve, the brain stem nuclei and the primary cortical projection areas. Each of these areas are fair game for machinations of the mind-control researchers. There are brain stem potentials which originate in the auditory brain stem nuclei--primarily in the inferior colliculi. The public auditory implants produce a small electrical stimulus that bypasses damaged hair cells and directly stimulates the remaining auditory neural elements. This means that for the secret implants, the electrical impulse that is generated to stimulate the person to hear a sound or sentence is totally unnoticed by everyone but the victim. As mentioned before, psychologists are being used to shut victims up, by declaring that they are crazy for claiming to hear voices. How do these psychologists know that the person isn't hearing voices from an implant? Some psychologists are declaring the implant victims are "crazy", "delusional", & "insane", because audio implants supposedly don't exist--therefore it is useless to give any credence to the complaints of victims. In other words, psychologists are being used as the establishment's witch doctors to cover up the mind-control activities of the New World Order. What's new?

Establishment shrinks helped cover up the programmed multiplicity for decades by labelling the programmed-multiple slaves "paranoid schizophrenics". During experiments, it was discovered that the skin of a person can pick up auditory vibrations, so tests were run to see if implants in other parts of the human body could be used for auditory implants. The vibrotacticle system of the skin has an upper limit of sensitivity to 400 to 500 Hz. In contrast the auditory system had a frequency range between 20 to 20,000 Hz and an optimum range of 300 to 3,000 Hz. The auditory system had a dynamic range of 130 dB (decibels) which the vibrotactile had only a 30-35 dB range. In other words, using the skin like on the chest to send auditory vibrations to the brain was a very limited way to create sound. For most purposes it isn't a viable approach, even though some experimental auditory implants were placed in places like the chest. The ones that were tested only reconfirmed the suspicions that the best results are by using the inner cochlea and the auditory canal area. Dr. Begich's and later others showed that a nonlinear function will translate one frequency to another frequency, but although it does jump, this method is inadequate for the current mind control signals, and a linear function is used which operates simply on the energy that the implants have.

Originally single channel devises were used, but then multichannel devices were soon found superior. The processing units of a device, had to have an extraction method to determine the pitch of the signal and then would present a square wave at the rate of that frequency. Soon the miniature computers that made up part of the audio implant were made so that they were programmable. Some of the publicly implanted people (for instance some who got a 4 mm. cochlear auditory implant), who thought they were getting medical help, were later followed up a decade later by the intelligence agencies for their own agenda, and instead of just hearing the world, they got to hear mind-control drivel from some handler communicating via the implant. As sound waves come into the public implants, they are fast Fourier transformed into many channels lying between say 100 and 4000 Hz. Each channel may be assigned to a specific electrode located on an array of electrodes. The electrodes are stimulated for instance at 300 pulses per minute. The transmissions go to receiver/stimulators that then stimulate the subject to hear something. (Fourier transforms have also been identified being used by human brains to encode memory.)

In order to keep their signals to their implanted victims secret, the Network employs a tactic called piggybacking where they piggyback their own audio transmission onto standard FM frequencies.

CANAL is the acronym for an system that is used simultaneously for transmission and reception via the use of a double-frequency shift keying (DFS). Radio transmitters that send quick signals are variously called BURST, SQUIRT, SQUASH, or high-speed transmitters.

USES OF THE IMPLANTS

a. by themselves, b. with other implants, and c. in conjunction with other mind-control devices.

TYPES OF AUDIO IMPLANTS--

Part A. Publicly admitted audio implants
Part. B. Secretly implanted audio implants.

Part A. Publicly admitted audio implants.

The entire world has gotten involved in audio implant research. The British Cochlear Implant Group has been setting up "implanting centres" for the UK. Not all the publicly known implants will be listed here, for instance, some of those I chose not to list include some developed in Spain by Bosch & Colomina, the ones created in Thailand by upgrading american made implants, and several made in East and West Germany before the wall went down, and the Swiss implant which was simply the Austrian audio implant used with their own processor.

3M COCHLEAR IMPLANT SYSTEM/HOUSE DESIGN--MODEL 7700 (AKA ALPHA)

BANFAI, EMG --Several models developed by Banfai in Cologne-Dueren, West Germany. It is digital, with a pulsatile signal and a programmable memory. The implant can be communicated with using an interface device hooked to a computer. The patient has a keyboard. It was first implanted in 1977 and has 8/14 and 16 channels. It has been implanted into hundreds of people.

BRITISH, for instance UCH-- Developed by Douek, Fourcin and Moore in London and implanted with a single electrode in 1978 and multiple electrodes in 1990. The implant has bioglass, and promontory grooves for the electrode, and neural network programming in its computer memory.

CHEN AUDIO IMPLANT--developed in Guangzhoi, mainland China and first implanted in 1984. It was said by the chinese that 20 people received this implant.

CZECHOSLOVAKIAN--Implants were created by Volvoda and Tichy in Prague and implanted in the 1980s into a few people.

FRASER--Developed in London, and first implanted in 1983. It was notable because it had a round window in the implant. In the first few years it was implanted into 56 people. The encapsulated the implant in a high-grade Silastic rather than an epoxy, as some other European researchers had done

FRAYASE--Developed in Toulouse, France, this audio implant was implanted with its receiver in the chest. It was first implanted in

1981, and 22 people were said to have received it.

GOA--developed in Shanghai, China by Lee and Lin.

INERAID- (fka Symbion) produced by the Richards Company, USA. In the Journal of the Acoustical Society of America, Mar. 1994, vol. 95, pp. 1677-1678, they have an article about a woman who had an implant in one ear and not the other. She was asked to compare the pitch signals from natural sources versus the right ear audio implant. The most apical implanted electrode was not as accurate as the more basal located electrodes using an Ineraid implant.

IMPLEX COM 12--Comes with an interfacing computer and a Syncom patient self-tester

LAURA--Developed at Antwerp, Belgium. These were first implanted in 1986, and had an internal canal antenna, a microphone entirely internal in the auditory canal, a pre-amp, an antenna, and a data control circuit. Only a few subjects got this implant. It comes with a computer, and an interface unit. It does have a programmable memory.

MED-EL --Developed in Austria at Vienna and Innsbruck by Hochmair, and first implanted in 1977. Hundreds of people were implanted with this audio implant. Some were implanted externally with it and some internally inside the ear canal. It has one channel and a multitude of electrodes stimulating the audio channel. It is analogue, and sends an analogue signal. It does not have a programmable memory.

MXM- -Developed by Chouard in Paris and first implanted in 1974. It had been implanted by 1990 into 179 people.

NUCLEUS 22, NUCLEUS MINISYSTEM 22, and other NUCLEUS AUDIO IMPLANTS (aka CLARK's Implants)-- At least two models developed in Australia at Melbourne. This audio implant was first implanted in 1978. The implant is programmable from the outside. It has been implanted into many hundreds of people. It has a multitude of electrodes that stimulate the audio system. It is digital, sends a pulsatile signal, and has a programmable memory. The implant comes with a diagnostic and programming interface computer. The Australian government heavily subsidized with millions of dollars research into audio implants and got the Cochlear Corporation (Nucleus) going. Nucleus uses what is called MULTIPEAK which provides high-frequency information from 2000 to 7000 Hz. With this 4 electrodes are stimulated in rapid succession, and special algorithms are used which change the relationship between the pulse amplitude and the pulse duration in order to allow 4 pulses to occur within a single frame. The Nucleus Minisystem 22 was approved by the FDA for implantation in both adults and children.

Storz Instrument Co.'s Implant--developed at Univ. of Calif, San Francisco.

Part. B. Secretly implanted audio implants.

There were several profiles of people that were used in the World Order's selection of secret victims to implant. The following were criteria that they liked in the selection process, a. vulnerable, such as single women, b. people who were already programmed with trauma-based mind-control, c. psychics, who had already told people they heard or saw things ordinary people don't, d. people, not highly regarded by society such as minorities, criminals, street people, mentally insane, who would not be able to find a support system to help them fight the experimentation. They also did the audio implants into some of their own intelligence agents, apparently to some who were getting somewhat difficult to their superiors. Because of this type of profile, and some other things this author learned, it appears that the initial two decades were used more for experimentation and development than they were for actual operations. However, with more than 2 decades of experience, they are now fully operational. From watching their interaction (messages) with victims of audio implants, it is clear that they are not in the testing stage, but are fully operational, and have a full cadre of trained operatives (men & women) to staff the secret bases from which the monitor and broadcast signals to their slaves. The staff their bases with 3 shifts and the graveyard shift leaves approx. 6 a.m. In other words, from what we can tell they are using standard shift times for the audio implant control staffs.

COCHLEAR IMPLANTS--There are Cochlear implants for auditory control secretly implanted without permission. A rubber molding skin color covers the outer lining of the ear canal. There are tiny slits in this lining, which when pushed to the side would show the presence of coils and a plastic rod/wire embedded in the area. Sometimes burn marks occur on sides of face due to intense heat generated by implants, which is painful.

DENTAL AUDITORY IMPLANTS--At least a dozen victims have complained that after their teeth were capped they began hearing voices. Other sources indicate that during the filing process implants are being put into people. This is the type of implant placed into J. Z. Knight and left dormant for many years until they decided to activate her as New Age guru.

RIDGE IMPLANTS-- These implants can produce Theta waves and even voices. They are designed to suppress a particular type of thinking. The body may be sent into paralysis or given various stimulus-response stimuli in order to suppress certain thought patterns. If the slave begins to have certain thought patterns that threaten the programming and programming structures, these implants kick in to divert the person's mental activity to something else.

C2. BODY MANIPULATING IMPLANTS

The subject of body manipulating implants could have been placed in chapter 8, however the desire was to keep all the information on implants together. Mankind has placed objects into the human body for thousands of years in the hope that it would produce some type of change. So the history of this type of implants is volumous. Reader's Digest had an article about how to give to paraplegics the use of their arms and legs with implants. Implants are being placed into the human body to effect growth changes, to change hormone levels (such as to stop estrogen), to change DNA growth, to carry out behavior modification, etc. Several papers have recommended that sex offenders get implants. The Rambo chips that have been put into many men have been linked to some big crimes. In recent times, the following body manipulating implants have been written about:

CRYSTALLINE CORTICOSTERONE IMPLANTS-- These implants affect the hypothalamic-pituitary-adrenal (HPA) activity when there is stress or basal activity. It was placed into the medial prefrontal cortex (MpFC) to regulate the response to certain types of stress. Journal of Neuroscience, Sept. 1993, Vol. 13, pp. 3839-3847.

NORPLANT--a contraceptive implant placed into hispanic and black teenagers using the Mantel-Haenszel procedure. Written about in Journal of Adolescent Health, May 1995, Vol. 16(5), pp 389-395 by Nancy Campbell-Heider, John Glantz, Sandra Glantz, Eric Schaff, et al.

POLYMERIC BRAIN IMPLANT--These implants are ethylene-vinyl acetate copolymer matrix disks and are used to release into the brain dopamine for a period of a number of weeks. The testing of this has been done at Yale Univ. School of Medicine. Written about in the Annals of Neurology, Apr. 1989, Vol. 25, pp. 35 1-356. Written by Matthew During, Andrew Freese, and Bernhard Sabel, and Mark Saltzman, et. al.

PROTO-32 IMPLANT--Designed by Dr. McDaniels and a Dr. Paul Hod. This implant with a 32-bit microchip memory affects DNA growth within a person. The two doctors who developed the device are claimed to have died after they created the chip. The FDA has approved the use of the implant in the brain. It's believed that there is a patent on the chip.

SILASTICMELATONIN-FILLED IMPLANT- Used to alter the speed of resynchronization of the circadian rhythm in birds, and implanted by the Max-Plank Institute fur Verhaltensphysiologie, Andechs, Germany. Although this was for birds, mention of it is done here to point out the type of research done at the Max-Plank Institute. It was written about in the Physiology and Behavior magazine, July 1995, Vol. 58, p. 89-90 by Michaela Hau and Eberhard Gwinner.

TESTOSTERONE IMPLANT--used to release testosterone into the subject.

C3. VISUAL/HOLOGRAPHIC IMPLANTS

BACKGROUND.

Hollywood has given us movies where visual and holographic implants are shown, but what about the real world? Yes, it does happen in more than the movies. Publicly, the establishment has only experimentally placed visual implants into a few volunteers. On the real life side of the NWO, there have been a number of victims who have been subjected to visual implants without their consent. One victim in Massachusetts labels her visual implants "visual prosthetics', but mentions "I use this term loosely because they are more so attachments than replacements of my own vision.

Every now and then the public is made aware of where the World Order wants people to think research is at. In the Jan. 13, 1997 issue of U.S. News & World Report (p. 52), the unveiling by researchers of the retinal chip that could potentially give sight to the blind was reported. It was interesting the article's choice of words "retinal chip unveiled" (bold added).

After it was realized that sounds could be artificially made via electromagnetic waves in deaf people, researchers naturally thought of giving sight to the blind. In the 1960's and 1970's researchers struggled to produce implants that could restore sight to the blind. This research was hijacked by the NWO types and has been developed into another component for their mind-control.

In the 60's Giles Brindley and others at Cambridge Univ. and in the 70's William Dobelle and others at the Univ. of Utah, both were able to show that individual phosphenes could be evoked by electrical currents, thus showing the feasibility of visual implants. (See GS Brindley's paper "The sensations produced by electrical stimulation of the visual cortex" in J. Physiology, Vol. 196, 1968, pp. 479-493. and W.H. Dobelle's article in 1974 "Phosphenes produced by electrical stimulation of human occipital cortex, and their application to the development of a prosthesis for the blind." in J. Physiol, 243: 553-576.) The public development went forward with the blind. Since most blind people still have the neurons (which are like a natural computer) in the higher visual regions of the brain fully intact, the implants are designed to take advantage of this unused potential.

The body has sensory pathways, that were discovered to be maps. In creating a visual image, the brain actually takes an image through several maps before getting the final image. There is a map for motion, along with at least 5 others maps such as one for form. The photoreceptors of the retina react to the three primary colors and have 3 primary color maps created by the electrical image made from the photoreceptors of the retina. (One's genetics contribute to how each person perceives a primary color, we don't all see colors uniformly.) The retina's output (called optic nerves or retinal output) map the electrical image again onto the retinal ganglion cells. Then the optic nerves project the electrical image to a relay image (the lateral geniculate nucleus) where the brain begins combining the maps of the two eyes. Another network of neurons (called the optic radiations) then transfers the image back to the rear of the brain to the primary visual cortex. Then the brain takes the image through several higher level maps to its final finished product--the viewer's perceived picture. The microelectrode array that creates a map for the blind person may be hooked up to the primary visual cortex, or other points in the process. The microelectrode arrays that were initially tested were much cruder than the human eye. They pixelized (turned into pixels, that is points) what the video camera saw. The implant compared to the human eye's natural abilities something like what the old dot matrix printers created in comparison to a computer laser printer. The blind person's perception via the implants is somewhat cruder than actual sight. Experiments have found that the brain has a great deal of power in choosing how it interprets images, so that it is hoped that the plasticity of the visual system will allow blind people's brain to adapt to what they are being shown over a period of time to get the maximum visual advantage. This also implies that victims of visual implants--which are of a more sophisticated technology will also have a natural tendency to rewire their brains to accommodate the new sensory inputs.

One of several groups of public researchers into Visual Neuroprosthetics (visual implants) is Richard A. Normann, with the Dept. of Bioengineering, John Moran Lab for Applied Vision and Neural Sciences, at the Univ. of Utah. In 1990, he spoke to people at the IEEE International Conference on Systems, Man, and Cybernetics about visual implants. At that conference on cybernetics, there were already well thought out methods for creating silicon based electrode arrays. The John Hopkins University in Massachusetts is another research center into visual implants. MIT and Harvard have also been researching in the subject of visual implants. Advances in material available and micro-fabrication techniques has permitted the semiconductor manufacturer to create electrode arrays with 3-D architectures, which can then be implanted into the visual parts of a person.

HOW THEY WORK

In a true visual prosthetic, a video encoder (camera) transforms the visual world in front of a blind individual into electrical signals that are used to excite neurons at some point of the visual pathway. The video camera encoder will be a silicon retina that replaces some of the functions that the human retina performs, and then it makes what it sees into signal compatible with the neurons the encoder must stimulate. The signals from the encoder excite neurons either via a hard-wired percutaneous connection, or a telemetry link. "The stimulating electrodes must be implanted into visual pathway such that each electrode is able to excite only a small population of neurons in the vicinity of the electrode." (Normann, Richard. "Visual Neuroprosthetics Functional Vision for the Blind", in IEEE Engineering in Medicine and Biology, Jan-Feb. '95, pg. 77) To improve the picture sent by the implants to the brain, electrodes the size of the neurons they intend to stimulate in the eye were developed. Kensall Wise at the University of Michigan created small high density electrode arrays out of silicon. In one model, the electrodes are .08 mm at their base, and taper to a sharpened tip. An array of hundreds of such electrodes can be implanted into cortical tissue about 1.5-2.0 mm below the cortical surface. This is not all of the design considerations involved, but it gives an idea of the direction that public research has gone in. A special pneumatic inserter that can shoot the arrays at high velocities to insert them into the cortical tissue was created by Patrick Rousche. This method provided limited cortical-based-map images. To further improve the picture, implants are being created that create a retinal map, rather than a cortical map. This can take advantage of the image forming properties of the human eye, and may give satisfactory images. At the current pace of public development, visual implants that restore sight are only a few years away from mass production. Meanwhile, the Network continues to create and use visual implants that are more sophisticated than what the public sector has been allowed to create. Bear in mind that these researchers use either foundation grant money or government grant money to operate. The Network is very careful about what technology is developed. Some excessively ambitious implant researchers (not visual, but other) have seen their work have a national security gag order thrown over them, and the research ends up muzzled from getting out to the public.

TYPES

FIBER OPTICS-- Fiber optics permits the Network to use a fiber optic that looks like a hair as a television camera. In a body suit, several fiber optic cameras that look like hairs will be installed in key places to provide the handlers remote viewing. Fiber optics can also be mounted in the victim, to provide a means to receive remote pictures. Fiber optic implants can be placed by needle into any site on the body. One victim of electronic mind-control, who has repeatedly pulled out Fiber Optic hairs, had a tiny fiber optic hair shot into her chest above her tank top while she was in a restaurant. Some other implants that carry out the same function look like warts, moles, or blisters.

ARTIFICIAL LENSES -- One victim describes his eye implants: "They are oblong objects with a square opening in the middle of them. They appear to be located on my corneas or rapped around them to be more accurate. They are connected to rods or wires that are spread out over my facial area and under the skin like a mask. The implants also appear to be connected to cochlear implants which are the cause of the repeated voice transmissions that I hear." Via a camera, she was able to pick up the presence of a reddish orange smear or stain covering my eye lens. The color blends with her own eye coloring so it is extremely difficult to see anything in her eyes. The lenses of the implants are not lined up evenly with her cornea. The victim with the visual implants states, "Whenever I close my eyes, I see the presence of constant red orange haze centered with a tint of whitish blue. I also see a small area of fluorescent green color. When I sleep, I am subjected to virtual reality type pictures like programs being run through a computer with a 3-D effect. There is a constant whirring and clicking effect that comes from other implants such as the ears." In review. Visual implants are at time called visual prosthetus, but are actually attachments rather than replacements. They are oblong with a square opening in the middle of them. They are located on the cornea (rapped around them) and are connected to rods/wires that are spread out over the facial area and under the skin like a mask. The coloring of the implant is blended with natural eye colors to camouflage it. When the victim closes his or her eyes there is a constant presence of a red-orange haze centered around a small screen. There are also two orbs with a tint of whitish blue, and a small area of fluorescent green. Visual reality pictures are run like programs from a computer, that have a three-D effect. The left forehead scalp area has a whirring noise.

BIO-CHIPS that "talk" to nerve cells. Some of the readers will have already heard of the bio-chips that talk to nerve cells. Stanford Research Inst. has been working on such bio-chips. Bear in mind, public research is generally a cover for what has already been discovered.

HOLOGRAPHIC OR H-INSERT-- There is one type which has been called a Holographic Insert or H-Implant. A holographic memory is created by this implant. This may or may not be the Nanobots which are capable of creating holographic images in the mind. Let's discuss the nanobots.

HOLOGRAPHIC IMPLANTS VIA NANOTECHNOLOGY & NANOBOTS

Nanotechnology is technology pertaining to very tiny robots and tiny computers that are in the range of nanometer-size (10 to 1,000 billionth of a meter). Nano means "one-billioneth". In other words, extremely microscopic, we are talking about robots & machines one-billionth of a meter large. The Scanning Tunneling Microscope (STM) makes it possible to see something the size of a single atom. The STM will also pick up atoms and move them. People who are interested in nano-technology have regular meetings in the Silicon Valley. A Johannesburg, South African company Nanoteq (recently taken over by the Amer. company Microchip Technology) was the company that created nanotechnology encoders (based on a non-linear logarithm that mixes transmission lines and changes codes frequently). Microchip Technology is putting these encoders into their series of microcontrollers which are EEPROM-based.

The encoders are called Keeloq hopping-code technology. They are good in protecting micro-wave, ELF, infrared and radio-wave transmissions. Microchip Corp. is creating a sub-company group called Secure Data Products to work with this type of technology. In other words, the ALEX system reported on in Vol. 2 is being miniaturized. Another Nanotechnology company is Nanosystems, which is working with the Jansen Pharmaceutica N.y. unit of Illuminati-controlled Johnson and Johnson. We know numerous companies like the two mentioned above, who are working on Nanotechnology. We also know that they are not going to tell us their trade secrets and what they have really developed. For instance, this author had a hearty laugh when he read The New York Times (11/19/96 pg. Cl) article "Feat of the minuscule: scientists make abacus with carbon molecules: invention at Swiss research laboratory may be a step toward building faster computers", because the article is patently disinformation! According to the article a Dr. James M. Gimzewski and colleagues discovered how to make tiny balls of 60 carbon-atoms each. They call these balls "Buckyballs". They can move these balls via what they call a "scanning tunneling device". A picture of the teeny-tiny 60-atom balls was shown in the article. So what did they do with this ability? They built an abacus (yeah sure! Come on guys!). If the reader understands computers--a computer at the most basic level is simply a base 2 number system. Anything that can consistently move or switch can be the basis for a computer. A computer is simply an enormous amount of on-off switches, where 0 can stand for off and 1 for on, etc. The article states, "Scientists at Switzerland have invented an ultraminiature abacus in which spherical carbon molecules sliding along the microscopic copper groves act as the counting beads for performing arithmetic calculations." (So they are using it for arithmetic, yeah sure!) IBM reported that its scientists used the STM to move individual atoms so that they spelled "I-B-M" in atoms. If you believe that the ability to arrange individual atoms and tailor-build molecules was so that IBM scientists could spell IBM, then this book isn't for you. A more recent NY Times article (2/2/97, p. E6) discusses how Xerox Corporation has created sensors the thickness of peach fuzz. These are called MEMS (micro-electomechanical systems). The article states, "MEMS are all about doing more with less, about being lean, mean, and next to invisible." The article is lean on facts. It does give a hint of the incredible power these little gadgets have when the writer launches into his propaganda tirade at the end of the article, "Paradoxically the fear that accompanies the fantasy of nanotechnology is not that the culture will be as stratified and fragmented as Victorian England, but that the new culture will be one that is unrecognizable to everyone alive today." That is true, this nano technology is taking us to the place that society will not be recognizable. The age of the future is planned to be the age of robots--humans if they are to survive are to be robotic slaves for the illuminated elite. However, this is not paranoid fear as the NY Times writer implies, but it is the unfortunate reality humanity faces. Some people apparently are already experiencing it. One victim of mind-control, whose father is Military Intelligence and whose family is part of the Illuminati, claims that he has been subjected to tiny robots called nanobots. These nanobots have been featured on TV, where they have been billed as an asset for surgeons. Reportedly, these tiny robots can work off of 10-100 kilohertz of beamed power. They have coil-shaped antennas, 2 little six-pointed "wings" to attach and move themselves with. These tiny boron-carbon nanobots have all kinds of purposes. One use is for multitudes of these Nanobots to be placed into a single victim's head, where they are programmed to migrate to certain programmed positions where they can suppress the optical signals to the brain and replace these signals with their own holographic images that can be externally transmitted to the nanobots or preprogrammed in. They are trying or have succeeded, depending upon who is talking about nanobots, in making self-replicating assemblers. In other words, they have built miniature robots that build other robots. (Sounds like something the Japanese would do.)

Nanobot researchers talk about how great it will be to have tiny robots that are smaller than a red blood cell circulating in our blood removing fat, bacteria, and viruses.

SOME SOURCES. Recent articles on nanotechnolgy include: Electronic Times (12/7/95), Electronics Weekly (11/29/95), Electronic Engineering Times (11/27/95), the L.A. Times (11/11/94, 12/21/94, 2/7/96, 2/20/96), the NY Times (4/30/94, 11/19/96, 2/2/97), the Wall St. Journal (5/12/94, 1/9/96, 2/26/96). Eric Drexler wrote Engines of Creation (Anchor Press/Doubleday, 1986), a book about nanotechnology.

Books that will provide more information on nanotechnology:

Drexler, K. Eric and Peterson, Chris and Pergamit, Gayle. Unbounding the Future: The Nanotechnology Revolution. Morrow, 1991.

Hameroff, Stuart R. Ultimate Computing: Biomolecular Consciousness and Nanotechnology. Elsevier Science Pub., 1987.

Whitehouse, D.J. and Kawata, K., eds. Nanotechnology: Proceedings of the Joint Forum/ERATO Symposium held at Warwick Univ., 21-22 August 1990. Adam Hilger, 1991.

C4. MEMEX/BRAIN LINK IMPLANTS

The public doesn't understand that programs showing research are typically rmation to hide what's already in use. On "Cyberlife," 12/17/96, a TV story was done on Dr. Ted Berger, a biological engineer, at U.S.CA, who is working on a microchip that will be a substitute for the hippocampus' memory. The story stated that in two years a brain chip can be made that mimics the pattern of brain neurons so that it can be plugged in. The New World Order's computer-satellite system allows a. communication devices to be embedded within a victim, as well as b. memex devices that are linked to the natural brain to boast the brain's memory. In the Vol. 2 book, the ALEX (Amalgamated Logrythmic Encrypted Transmissions) system was described which allows the NWO to pulse codes on different frequencies in an erratic fashion that makes the transmissions hard to even spot. The ALEX system is one component of their ability to secretly transmit orders and information to their slaves. When a slave receives a body-suit of implants, one implant will be a central control implant that controls the body suit of implants and receives information from an external transmitting source. Some of the slaves have had their central controlling implant at the base of their skull. The concepts that Hollywood portrayed in the sci-fi movie "Johnny Mnemonic" where an oligarchy (in league with big business and the crime syndicates) controls the world, and uses a human who has an implant that stores tremendous amounts of information is-- sad to say-- not so far removed from what is already happening in secret.

INTERFACE DEVICES

The biocybernetic researchers for the New World Order have working on a number of interface devices to interface (link) the human brain with computers. A number of devices have been created. There is even a biochip the size of a large organic molecule that works as a memex implant. The idea of implants is difficult for some people to accept. I am in the possession of x-rays showing implants, of anechoic chamber readings showing that victims were receiving constant synthetic telemetry signals from outside transmitting sites, and a variety of other items showing evidence that this activity is going on. For instance, Professor Ingmar Wickbom, M.D. of the University Hospital, University of Calif. Medical Ctr., San Diego on 10/6/'83 wrote a letter "To Whom It May Concern" that skull x-rays of Robert Naslund indicated implants at the base of the skull that are "possibly some form of brain transmitters". Some of the victims I personally know have managed to extract fiber optic fibers from their bodies.

ORGANIC BIOPROCESSORS LINKED TO VIRUSES-- One direction that the New World Order took was to develop biochips and bioprocessors, that is three-dimensional organic circuitry that functions as computers. The conductive velocities of these miniature organic computers (protein lattices) are at least one million times faster than nerve cells. The circuit power of a given size of miniature organic computers is at least a million times greater than the same size of brain matter. Molecular computers made of living matter can be grown from DNA templates of genetically engineered bacteria. Synthetic proteins have been developed which match what they want to make into mini-computers. The end product is a bioprocessor (tiny computer) within a cell. These mini-computers are specifically linked with viruses which migrate to specific parts of the body. Viruses are primarily nucleoproteins, some of the small ones are not even alive, and they don't even have metabolism. They do not have a metabolism to kill with an antibiotic. The Neurotropic viruses migrate to the central nervous system (nerves), the Dermotropic viruses migrate to the skin, the Pneumotropic viruses go to the lungs, the Viscerotropic go to the abdomen, and other viruses go to other sites in the body. Because many viruses will select what area of the body they will reside in, the New World Order can tailor (in tissue-culture) their bio-implants (which consist of a virus plus a bioprocessor) so they can target where they will end up in the mind-controlled slave. Such an virus implant is also called a symbiote, because it lives off of the host, the mind-controlled slave's own body. These virus implants have life-expectancies that are a number of years long. A number of these implants within the victim serve as spies-in-the-camp, reporting detailed records of what the host's body is doing. Research into how to splice and dice genetic material and then recombine it has been going on for a number of decades, and is very sophisticated. There are a number of very technical books on how to do it, but only a reader familiar with the language of genetic research could decipher their techniques & abilities with miniature RNA and DNA pieces. Several genetic books/papers describe how viruses can get host genetic material or other genetic material, thus giving us a window on how they transfer the miniature computers made from DNA templates to the viruses. In the book Mechanics of DNA Replication & Recombination, Proceedings of a UCLA Symposium held in Keystone, CO April 3-9, 1983,(edited by Nicholas R. Cozzarelli, of the Dept. of Molecular Biology Univ. of CA, Berkeley, published in NY by Alan K. Liss, Inc.) one of the leaders in this field said on page 12, "I remain faithful to the conviction that anything a cell can do, a biochemist should be able to do." And yes they have been replicating strands of RNA & DNA, creating whatever they want. The Illuminati have been using these computers-in-viruses implants at least since the 1990s. The implants are easy to insert into the victim's body, and the specific virus transport themselves and attach themselves where they are to go. The Illuminati then build body suits of these implants. The size of these tiny implants vary from tens of millicrons to hundreds of millimicrons. Just their tiny size makes them difficult to destroy. From research on victims, it appears that a central computer is implanted to control or interact with the body suit of implants.

PSYCHICS-- One of the Illuminati's research projects was to discover the psi gene--the genetic gene that would permit them to breed a master race with psychic abilities. One of the groups that the Illuminati has controlled which did research in this area was Nazi Germany. Mengele, in fact, was interested in the co-relation of blood types to psychic abilities. Blood type B apparently has more psychics than other blood types. People who have true psychic abilities have a more complex molecular lattice structure than those who don't. They also have energy fields of 500 cps or higher. This is in contrast with most brain activity which lies in the 0 cps to 100 cps range. The heart operates at up to about 250 cps, and the resonant frequency for a nerve is 360 cps. In other words, the high cps. energy field is a tip off that the person is psychic. A secret program has been carried out by the Illuminati to identify every person on the planet who is capable of being psychic. They are identified and then assigned to people (a male and female) to monitor the person. Psychics are often recruited into intelligence agencies to bring them under the power of the Illuminati's establishment. In other cases, they are simply watched and monitored, some who are threats to them are killed, and others receive mind-control. They have been identifying people with psychic abilities and then trying to track and/or control them. They also will try to recruit or place these people under mind-control or both.

C5. TORTURE/NERVE & MUSCLE STIMULATION IMPLANTS

When a body suit is placed into a slave, implants are strategically placed in their body so that if they do not comply or if the Network wants to make the person dissociative they can direct the control implant to trigger these implants to activate. For instance two implants will be place on opposite side near the uterus and one in the lower back in order to give the handlers the ability to cause lots of lower back pain. Prior to electronically putting someone into an altered & controlled dissociative state, they will wear a person down with pain to make them dissociative. For instance, if an implant in the middle (square in the heel) of the foot goes off, a ball of electricity like a sparkler is activated causing pain, anxiety and discomfort. Some describe it as a hot pin prick in the foot. One victim and her mother both received these torture implants, and she was able to locate and remove some of them from her mother. I would like to paraphrase her description of finding these torture implants, "I discovered fiberoptic type implants on the lower back and also on the line where the leg and buttock join. The fiberoptic sites on the lower back was 1" to the left of the spine, and consisted of two holes where the implants had been inserted which were one above the other, and at a distance of 5/8' from each other. I was able to partially remove both of these fiber implants, but knots remained under the holes where tiny parts of the implants tenaciously remained. These two back implants seemed to connect signal-wise to the implant at the junction of the buttock and leg. This latter implant could create pain in the left leg and foot." Sometimes a crackling sound like crickets accompanies the signal to create pain. A vibrating electrical field is often used on victims of electronic control. (Unconfirmed but possible:) One victim described a device that could have a dial rotated to allow the sender to chose different types of signals to be sent. This would be pointed at a victim. As this sounds like a good possibility, it has been included here, although there is nothing to confirm such a piece of equipment which is probably if it exists

BELLDAME TORTURE IMPLANT--Nothing available to report.

SUICIDE IMPLANT--Some claim that an implanted chip has been created that will release a poison upon a signal which will kill its host. This author has seen absolutely no evidence that such an implant exists. It's use is likely disinformation.

C6. TRACKING & I.D. IMPLANTS

This type of implant has gotten most of the public's attention. For several years now the public has been aware that animals, military personnel as well as civilians have been given tracking implants. Objects also have received tracking implants. DCI of the CIA Bob Gates is reported to have said, "If you can't identify people, you can't control them." The Wall St. Journal, 3/30/1992 reported that the FDA proposed that tracking devices onto 35 classes of medical devices such as heart valves and breast implants. The excuse was that they needed to track life-sustaining medical devices better. The list of devices to be tracked includes cardiovascular filters, defibrillators, pacemaker electrodes, heart valves, tracheal protheses, breathing monitors, portable oxygen generators, ventilators, infusion oxygen generators, ventilators, infusion pumps and various silicone gel-filled devices such as testicular implants and breast implants, and spinal implants. The Hughs Identification Device has been placed onto such objects as breast implants. These tracking implants are reported to have a life of 250 years. Their tracking I.D. number consists of #, letter, #, letter, # etc. The U.S. Navy has employed RF/ID "waterproof bracelets" for tracking individuals underwater. The U.S. military has required its personnel to take tracking implants under the pretense of being able to find them if they get lost, and millions of men and women in the military have already gotten these tracking implants. A book published by the U.S. Army War College in 1994 (entitled The Revolution in Military Affairs and Conflict Short of War) shows the Army's interest in tracking implants. Many tracking implants were placed into military personnel during Desert Shield/Desert Storm operations. Some tracking implants are programmable and can record vital data about a person. They could also be used as a debit card for financial transactions, which is why they have gotten so much attention as the much feared Mark of the Beast. Texe Marr's popular book Project L.U.C.I.D. exposed the L.U.C.I.D. System which will be a central clearing house for keeping track of everyone. He reproduced a diagram from an issue of Narc Officer magazine showing how the system would connect an individual's universal biometrics card with the justice, data communications, and telecommunications systems of the World Order. Texe Marrs and others are fascinated at the choice of words & acronyms that the establishment keeps picking. Dr. Creusat, a medical doctor with Interpol is the official designer of L.U.C.I.D. He and his co-designer initially refused to reveal what the acronym L.U.C.I.D. stands for. Some speculate that it stands for the obvious: "Lucifer's I.D." system. It's also strange that AT&T called their new company derived from Bell Labs (which has been involved in mind-control for the Illuminati) "Lucent Technologies". Again some people speculate that Lucent means Lucifer's Enterprises. And what did Lucent come out with? They came out with a new computer network called "Inferno" (another name for Hell), written in a language called "Limbo" (a place in Hell) with computer protocols called "Styx" (a river in Hell). And then on the other side of the Atlantic, a world-wide net called Demon Internet is being offered to people in Europe. (To have Demon Internet installed for you by Demon Internet, Ltd. at 322 Regents Park Rd., Finchley, London N3 2QQ costs initially £1,762.50 for the first month according to recent company literature.) Again the obvious question, why are these companies using occult--even satanic terms for their products? Illuminati member and chairman of IBM Thomas Watson, Jr. set up a cryptology research group at IBM's research lab in Yorktown Heights in NY. This group was led by Horst Feistel, and it developed a cipher code called "Lucifer". Lucifer was then sold to Lloyd's of London. Lucifer was created under the auspices of the NSA. Lucifer worked off of an algorithm. The NSA had set things up via IBM so that it has had a back door to anything encrypted with Lucifer. (By the way NSA's partner in the U.K. is the brit's GCHQ.) The paper trail indicates that L.U.C.I.D. intends to keep track of people by using biometrics (iris scan, fingerprint, voiceprint, photos, and other bio identification features) that will be encoded on cards (or implants.) DNA databanks are already giving computers an enormous ability to identify millions of americans via their DNA. Texe Marrs also calls our attention in his book about L.U.C.I.D. to the important mandatory ISO 9000 program, which makes it mandatory for all products to have an ISO 9000 I.D. number and their approval and certification. Over 100 countries have adopted the ISO 9000 standards. In 1999, use of the system, which was voluntary, will become mandatory. The government is also setting up TPN (Trading Partner Numbers). While obtaining all these numbers to do business is not directly mind-control; if a person can't buy or sell without the approved numbers, it does tend to place a person or company under the World Order's control. The NACCB in England and the ASQC and the ANSI have been given power to accredit people with the ISO 9000 numbers. IOS is also in some type of overseeing role in the accreditation process. Here we go, more acronym monsters to control our lives! But while attention has been focused on this, many other implants have been implanted for mind-control. It all works together. The tracking implants certainly are an external means of controlling people that will work along side of the mind-control to lock people into their Established System. The tracking implants have broader application than just to keep track of an individual's location, or his financial records. Tracking implants can be used to send bio information on the heart beat, the BEG, EKG and other bio tracking methods. Researchers who are following the field of tracking implants will remember the article "An Eight Channel Micropowered PAM/FM Biomedical Telemetry System" in the NTC '71 Record, p. 309. The Air Force Office of Scientific Research, NASA financed that study which involved an 8-channel micropowered telemetry system designed to sense and transmit physiological data. The system was actually successfully used. They will also remember an earlier article in the IEEE Transactions on Bio-medical Engineering, Vol. BME-14, Oct. 1967 entitled, "The Design and Use of an FM/AM Radiotelemetry System for Multichannel Recording of Biological Data." And then they will remember an even earlier report from the Biophysics Lab, of the Aerospace Medical Labs of the Aerospace Medical Div. at Wright Patterson AFB, Ohio dated 1965 entitled, "Personal telemetry transmitter system." The point is that tracking implant research has been with us for several decades, and is being utilized to control slaves who have body suits of implants. They have been publicly monitoring animals with bio-telemetry for several decades, it doesn't take any stretch of the imagination to comprehend that they are also doing it with their slaves. While these articles were from the '60s, soon afterwards a book appeared Mackay, R.S.

Biomedical Telemetry, Sensing and Transmitting Biological Information from Animals and Man. John Wiley & Sons, Inc.: NY, 1970. Faceprints are a new method which uses a math algorithm that establishes distances between eye pupils, nasal base, lip center and other facial points. The algorithm produces a 50-bit number that is person-specific. The plans are to code this along with other unique I.D. features onto the magnetic strips of I.D. cards. The American CIA developed in conjunction with the Thai police a smart identity card for use in Thailand. The Computerworld Smithsonian Award was given to the Thai Ministry of Interior for this "innovative technology" in 1990. In other words, one part of Big Brother patted another on the back. Was the CIA protecting us, Mr. & Mrs. Citizens by doing this so-called "intelligence" work, or was it working on another agenda by developing this high tech ID card? Later the military adopted the MARC ID card based on similar ideas.

Bell Communications (in NJ) developed voice activated credit cards. Reports are that colds can throw one's voice off so that it's rejected by the flat microchip in the voice card. When this author calls the World Order's mind-control "total", he means just that--it is designed to control the body, mind and spirit of a person. By taking bio information via implants, DNA codes, blood types, retina scans, hand geometry and face prints, without our real consent the World Order has effectively stolen our Fifth Amendment rights. John Adams wrote, "Property must be secured or liberty cannot exist." (The Works of John Adams, Vol. 6:9, p. 280.) The purpose of the American government was to protect property. But they have stolen our privacy. They have put into law (contrary to the Constitution & Bill of -Rights) several laws that will force us to provide information to computer data banks that will be used to determine if we can buy or sell, if we can get employment or not, & if we are deemed politically correct or not. And those on the wrong side of the NWO may be incarcerated and programmed. While tracking implants are not mind-control per se, they will work hand in glove with actual mind-control to make sure no one under mind-control can effectively get away. Therefore all tracking devices must be seen in the broader context as being devices to assist in the implementation of total mind-control. One genius scientist who worked on the bio-chip and who still works as a civilian for the government personally told this author that he is excused for his help on the project because technology is neutral. Technology is neither good nor bad, so he claims. I disagree, and so did another scientist who did repent of helping with this infernal project, and apologized to this author. These bio-chips are going to be used for the enslavement of mankind, and for total mind-control. There is no justification, no excuse great enough to allow people to side-step their responsibility in the creation of such technology intended for evil. We have a responsibility to know how our inventions will be used before we create them. It doesn't take a rocket scientist to know what these inventions are going to be used for. Unfortunately, this man who assisted with the bio-chip is a rocket scientist.

Section D. Direct monitoring & manipulation of the brain/mind

D1. Direct monitoring of thought waves.

For many years, the basic waves have told us basic things about the mind. Rapid Beta waves come from normal mental activity like you are doing now, alpha waves indicate relaxation, theta waves mean meditation & memories, & ultraslow deltas mean deep sleep. Cognitive demands cause the gamma waves to synchronize. Alpha (as well as Theta) oscillations both encode and access cortical codes--what we describe as K-lines in this Deeper Insights book. The thalamus & the cortex are involved in memory. People with good memories have higher alpha freks than persons with poor memories. EEGs are used to watch these waves & their oscillations. PET scans are even more revealing. Thoughts can be analyzed in terms of the various parts of the mind that they require to produce them. In word-reading the mind activates specific posterior visual areas, and when the mind must identify a noun specific frontal & temporo-parietal areas are active. (See Posner, "Seeing the Mind", Science magazine, 10/29/93, p. 673). PET scans & BEGs are interesting, but evoked potentials tell it all. The National Security Agency has a monopoly on monitoring the evoked potentials emitted by people's brain's electrical flux which are electromagnetic emissions in the 30-50 Hz, 5 milliwatt range. When a person thinks, or moves their body, or sees something, the brain creates an evoked potential or set of evoked potentials. These emissions can be decoded to see what the person is thinking or doing. This is called RNM (Remote Neural Monitoring). It is reported that the Kinnecome group at the NSA is involved with this type of monitoring round-the-clock of victims of electronic mind-control using EMF equipment that is scattered across the nation. A Signals Intelligence EMF scanning network allows the NSA's computers to pinpoint and track any individual in the United States by watching for their specific bioelectrical field. In many ways, the tracking implants and the national I.D. cards are redundant, but the World Order wants to increase their control, while keeping their best technology secret. The NSA information is not randomly passed on to any individual, but they do have their ways to filter down information to mind-control handlers if they need to. They have exhibited an amazing ability to track the two co-authors, but that doesn't mean that they are all powerful, just because their computers can remotely detect and keep track of people. This book is evidence that there is still some elbow room for independent thought in this world. What's more frightening is the apathy in the world to stand up to the control. But the question may arise, how can they get any good reading on the brain's evoked potentials from a distance? The equipment is a combined use of ELF-modulated masers along with Doppler-shifted interrogative RMCT masers. This technique allows them to send syntel directly through walls. A Maser is a microwave equivalent to a laser.

TESLA WAVES USED TO READ MINDS & IMPLANT VOICES

According to reports, the Soviets were the first to discover in the 1960's that the human brain had 23 BEG band wave lengths, of which 11 of these were totally independent. By knowing those 11 band wave lengths, and then sending signals based upon those wave lengths, the human mind could be manipulated. The person's PRIME FREK, that is their biological frequency needs to be identified, and then it is possible to remotely implant thoughts and voices into their minds.

In the early 1970's, the U.S. Documentation Center as well as the White House's spokesman had both reported that electromagnetic waves could be used to communicate with "a target biosystem." (This was brought out in the U.S.

District Court of the State of Utah where inmates who had been subjected to mind-control in prison tried unsuccessfully to fight back in court.)

The University of Utah was just one of several dirty research facilities which researched on human guinea pigs how Tesla waves could be used to manipulate the mind into hearing voices. They discovered how simple it is to use these waves to override and implant thoughts into the mind, and to read the thoughts of the mind. Then they subjected hundreds of inmates at the Gunnison Facility of the Utah State Prison, the State Hospital and perhaps other Utah State Prison facilities to this brand of mind-control in order to test it.

It certainly works. Numerous inmates tried to fight the system, and the obvious mind-control that so many of them were being subjected to. Hundreds of the inmates were subjected to heavy drugs and other severe punishment when they protested. Still they continued to protest. This was in the 1970's, now the technology is being used over the entire United States.

The Tesla waves are sent to a victim in the following sequence of events.

Computers programmed with artificial intelligence handle most electronic controlled slaves. When the slave does something the computer can't handle then human handlers step in to help. Men and women staff consoles attached to CRAY computers where they monitor the victims that need special attention. The full fledged electronic monitoring involves an entire body suit of various implant devices in the victim's body. From the body suit, the controllers are able to track the victim, hear what the victim hears, and see via tiny fiberoptics some of what is going on around and with the victim. The staff have pre-recorded sound bites that they usually like to select, as well as occasion actual live messages. They transmit these messages, which are picked up by satellite and relayed to whatever large TV broadcasting antenna or GWEN tower or other antenna is near the victim. The signal is then relayed to some object near the victim, which serves as a relay antenna to pass the signal on to the victim. It's believed that some type of implant picks up the signal and broadcasts the correct Tesla wave pattern to create voices within the victim. Meanwhile, the tracking implant keeps the staff and the satellite system informed every few minutes as to exactly where to send the voice signals. The Master computer and central HQ for electronic mind control is reported to be Boulder, CO. Several places have been identified by this author as key points. One report came in that transponders are being made in Boulder, CO. The central cellular computer is in the Boulder, CO National Bureau of Standards building. AT & T is cooperating with electronic mind-control also. NORAD tracks both space and earthbound objects. They have a Cheyenne Mtn. Air Station. Although it is clear from reports from mind-control victims that NORAD is actively involved in mind-control, exactly how the different tracking responsibilities are delegated is not known to this author at this time. It appears that there is duplication of efforts, and several NWO branches maintain the same capability.

D2. VOICES / OR THOUGHTS SENT ELECTRONICALLY DIRECTLY INTO THE MIND

Brain waves are connected to thought. When thought occurs there is a great deal of brain wave activity. The brain carries out what some people call "parallel processors"--that is it breaks a thinking process down into components and works on all simultaneously. When the World Order's researchers have attempted to tamper with the mind they can place thoughts into the mind by tampering with the processes that create thoughts, without actually having to replicate the thought they want. In other words, they are deflecting the natural process into the synthetic process they want to get their desired result.

For group mind control, or isolated individuals, ELF waves can be sent that interact with the brain's natural waves. The human brain synchronizes with the incoming waves and the end result can be panic, sleep, or a hypnotic trance. The wrong kinds of ELF waves can even damage the brain. In 1961, Allen Frey, a free-lance biophysicist and engineering psychologist reported that humans can hear microwaves. This had been known by the military since W.W.II. To form complex words and sentences, Frey realized he'd have to approach the level of 10 -mW/(cm)^2, but the bottom line is microwave-created movement of cochlear hair cells can be done. In the late 1950's, Dr. Patrick Flanagan developed an electronic telepathy machine which was called the Neurophone. He writes about the Neurophone and its capabilities to transmit acoustic (sounds, voices) directly into the brain of an individual using the electromagnetic fields in his forward to the book Angels Don't Play This HAARP by Jeane Manning and Dr. Nick Begich. The patent office held up his patent on the machine for 12 years. Dr. Flanagan writes, "Certain types of electromagnetic signals can induce visual and auditory effects when the field around the head or body is at the right frequency, intensity and modulation levels. We are not accusing the developers of HAARP of amoral intentions for the use of this technology but the potential for abuse is there." (Angels Don't Play This HAARP, p. 6) First, this author highly recommends the book Angels Don't Play This HAARP; and second, this author is going to flat outright say that the developers of HAARP do not deserve the benefit of the doubt anymore--because some of them have a clear track record of developing and using mind-control techniques. HAARP is nothing less than a mind-control project. One of the persons that people trying to investigate HAARP kept running into was Col. John Alexander. Col. John Alexander was involved with the development of -HAARP. (Angels Don't Play This HAARP, p. 19) Trauma-based mind-control victims have identified Col. John Alexander as being one of the primary mind-control programmers. He has been a key player in a number of mind-control projects for the government. Wright-Patterson AFB, Dayton, OH also play-ed a role in research for HAARP. A number of trauma-based mind-control victims have identified Wright-Patterson as a mind-control programming center. Apparently, the Air Force used some of the brain-stem scarred whiz kids at the base to try and develop Tesla technology. ARCO (via their ARCO Power Technologies, Inc. subsidiary) was the Air Force's prime contractor on the first phase of HAARP's development. ARCO has company doctors who are helping program mind-control victims. One of ARCO's board members was Dr. Simon Ramo, who is a big player with the military and the secret government. The awarding of ARCO's subsidiary APTI for the contract smelled like a rat, because other companies were obviously better suited than this tiny subsidiary with a staff of 25 in Washington, D.C. Besides the mind-control aspect of things, the World Order set things up so that APTI has the patent (#4,686,605, Method & Apparatus for Altering a Region in the -Earth's Atmosphere, Ionosphere, and/or Magnetosphere) for the HAARP project, so they are a natural shoe-in for the project. There were other patents involved too, and about dozen of these patents assigned to APTI have now ended up with the large Raytheon Corp. (APTI was bought by B-Systems, and B-Systems was bought by Raytheon. All 3 are working fast and furiously developing technology for the NWO.) The NWO's Stanford Research Institute developed many of HAARP's high-frequency transmitting programs with money from the Defense Nuclear Agency. (This was from Angels Don't Play This HAARP, p.47, which cites an NTIA memo, "NTIA Preliminary Assessment of Air Force Ionospheric Research Instrument", 10/1/1993.) Mitre Corp. was also involved with HAARP. This author has exposed the Mitre Corp. in the past as being both Illuminati-run, & a co-partner with the NSA.

When a HAARP researcher pestered the Air Force for info, he was referred to Kirk-land AFB, NM another site deeply involved in mind-control and black projects. (Angels Don't Play This HAARP, p.63) Los Alamos Nat. Labs also is involved with both mind-control & I-IAARP. Their Blackbeard Team is connected to the Alexis Satellite, which may or may not be connected to the ALEX system which this author has been warning about. Supposedly this is a gamma ray re-search satellite, but this author doesn't know if this is the truth or a cover story. The Air Command & Staff College's Airpower Journal lets the "cat out of the bag" so to speak when they reveal that weapons like HAARP will be used against civilians. The military wants to use weapons like HAARP to disorient people's mental facilities. Newt Gingerich wrote the forward to an official US Air Force book entitled Low-Intensity Conflict and Modern Technology which described how electromagnetic weapons could be used to subjugate U.S. citizens who opposed their government. Cpt. Paul Tyler wrote the chapter on electromagnetic and psychotronic weapons. A paper trail does exist of the intentions to use HAARP for mind-control by our government. For the sake of completeness, and to provide the readers with a paper trail, I'll quote directly from this official Air Force book from the part written by Cpt. Tyler, 'The potential applications of artificial electromagnetic fields are wide-ranging and can be used in many military or quasi-military situations... Some of these potential uses include dealing with terrorist groups...crowd control,...and anti-personnel techniques in tactical warfare. In all cases, the electro-magnetic systems would be used to produce mild to severe physiological disruption or perceptual distortion or disorientation. In addition, the ability of individuals to function could be degraded to such a point that they would be combat ineffective. Another advantage of electromagnetic systems is that they provide coverage over large areas with a single system [this is an obvious reference to HAARP] . . . . Recently, pulsed electromagnetic fields have been reported to induce cellular transcription related to reproduction of DNA.... Knowledge of mechanisms of actions of Radio-Frequency Radiation (RFR) with living systems and the assessment of pulsed RFR effects, will demonstrate the vulnerability of humans to complex pulsed electromagnetic radiation fields... Experiments with electroshock, RFR experiments and the increasing understanding of the brain as an electrically-mediated-organ, suggest the serious probability that impressed electromagnetic fields can be disruptive of purposeful behavior and may be capable of directing and/or interrogating such behavior." THERE YOU HAVE IT, a PAPER TRAIL that the MILITARY WANTS

HAARP'S MIND-CONTROL capabilities. Dr. Abraham Liboff of Oakland Univ. has demonstrated how low-energy circularly polarized electromagnetic waves can change the brain's ability to keep out certain ions, minerals, and chemicals. HAARP can also be used with genetic manipulating ionized radiation and chemicals to specifically control the mind. (See Chapter 8, section 2 for a complete discussion of this.)

SUMMARY OF ELF WAVE MIND CONTROL CAPABILITIES

Naval Intelligence and other groups have conducted research into ELF waves upon the human body and mind. Some of the many things that can be done to the human body and mind with ELF waves include:

a. put a person to sleep
b. make a person tired or depressed c. create a feeling of fear in a person d. create a zombie state
e. create a violent state
f. create a state of being sexually aggressive g. change cellular chemistry
h. change hormone levels
i. inhibit or enhance M(RNA) synthe-sis/processes
j. control the DNA transaction process
k. control biological spin and proton coupling constants in DNA, RNA & RNA transferases.

But electronic control of the brain comes in many forms. Perhaps the controllers only want to carry out mood shifts. ELF waves which will penetrate walls, and even go through the earth will create mood shifts according to how many cycles per minute they are sent at. Studies have proven that the time for ELF waves to cause a shift in mood is between 6 to 10 seconds (not a long time).

ELF waves below 6 cycles per second cause subjects to become emotionally upset and this rate may also disrupt bodily functions. At 8.2 cycles/sec. the person gets an elevated high such as would be accomplished by a master of meditation. 11 to 11.3 cycles per second cause the brain to become agitated and to begin riotous behavior. ELF waves could be directed at a population to help incite riots. Research has been carried out to determine how the brain's sensory inputs are coded. It has been determined that visual input is relayed and built into a series of changing maps. The olfactory sense has thousands of specific codes to determine smells, and combinations of these are triggered by an object. One clue that gave researchers initially the idea that different individual human brains have a common internal electronic type coding for specific thoughts is that drugs will have such common effects on the human race--even -though one obtains individuals from widely different genetic pools. The best research is of course kept secret. We primarily have to report on what is released. E.R. John in Mecha-nisms of Memory (NY: Academic Press, 1967, pp. 348-349) announced his discovery that central neuro-electrical codes are indeed used by the human brain. Information transfers in the brain have been shown to be related to neuro-electrical frequency codes, and that a brain can be manipulated by beaming those codes from an external sources. For instance, Hippocampal neurons will have burst-firing frequencies between 100-200 Hz. Here are some of the resonance frequencies for manipulating these senses:

Visual centers of mind--25 Hz
Sense of touch center--9 Hz
Auditory (hearing) ctr-- 15 Hz
Motor control-- 10 Hz
Subconscious thoughts--20 Hz.

If the World Order wants to cause a person to make a gesture, they use ELF-modulated microwaves that are "KEYED" to distinctive brainwave patterns that are called "PREPARATION SETS." If the controllers want to create an emotion they use specific "EXCITATION POTENTIALS" by creating the correct resonance frek which in turn creates a specific emotional state. Victims of electronic mind-control often complain of electronic fields placed -around their bodies. Recently, when an electrical storm blew a major metro power grid, one victim of electronic mind-control lost the force field that had been encircling her body. The brain is also attenuated to the earth magnetic field. By manipulating the magnetic field around a person, the magnitude of the beamed codes needed to elicit a change in the brain can be reduced. For example J.I. Jacobson changed melatonin levels in subjects by manipulating the magnetic field in conjunction with beamed "signals". See Jacobson, J.I. "Pineal-hypothalamic tract meditation of pico Tesla magnetic fields in the treatment of neurological disorders." FASEB Journal, 1994, 8, p. A656. Sandyk also successfully used manipulation of the magnetic fields and reported this in Sandyk, R. Successful treatment of mul-tiple sclerosis with magnetic fields. International Journal of Neuroscience, 1992, pp. 237-250. It was discovered that if an alternating magnetic field at a distance (resonance) frequency is superimposed upon a steady-state magnetic field, calcium and other ions within the brain can be moved with little energy. When this was discovered, researchers began to watch to see if variations in the -earth's magnetic field during geomagnetic storms and in other situations, would affect the thinking of masses of people. They discovered that there were indeed changes to the human brain as a result of magnetic fluctuations. Cognitive thinking and conscious -thought occurs between the temperatures of 308° - 312° K (or 35° - 39° C) and the fundamental wave length associated with these thoughts are approximately 10 micrometers (which is an infrared wavelength.) Signals that blend with Background Radiation can be manipulated to control the brain. The temperature of the brain directly relates to how certain signals will affect it. It is believed that structures within the thalamus are involved with modulating the temperature sensitivity of biochemical oscillators. Heterodyne Principle Used. This principle is that multiple frequencies when applied to a nonlinear device produce new frequencies which are the sums and differences of the applied frequencies and their harmonics. In other words a local oscillator (also called a strong sinusoidal carrier wave) can multiply a weak signal. A microwave signal at a frequency A is mixed with a microwave local oscillator at frequency B in a nonlinear mixer. The mixer output signal which is A minus B is a faithful amplitude and phase reproduction of the original microwave signal but at a low, fixed frequency so that it can be measured simply with low-frek measuring devices. Heterodyne signals cost more to produce but cost is no problem for the government. Multiport network analysers, which use several simple power detectors and a computer analysis approach provide a less expensive way to measure both the relative voltage amplitude & the phase. Cell phone freks used. The controllers use the UHF cellular telephone frequencies, which are installed everywhere because the human cranium operates on the same frequencies that cellular phones operate on. This was not by accident.

PULSED AUDIOGRAMS--Pulsed audiograms use extremely low average power densities of electromagnetic energy acoustic amplifier driven by the rf transmitter's modulator, the peak power density is a critical factor which is approx. 275 mw/rf for carrier frequencies 125 mc and 1,310 mc. Acoustic noise is approx. 80 decibels. Another source, the electrical sine wave analogs of each word is processed so that each time a sine wave crosses zero reference in the negative direction, & a brief pulse of microwave energy is triggered. These voice modulated microwaves transmit words to the brain. Sounds are generated when pulsed microwaves are aimed at absorbers made of carbon-impregnated polyurethane. An Acoustical Energy Wavefront (AEW) is created by modified transducement of sound waves, which are in the ultrasound spec-trum (USS). In other words scalar energy is being employed. When people are asleep they are the most vulnerable. TV antenna can serve both as transmitters and well as receivers. It can be made to oscillate a suitable resonant frequency. By transmitting signals in the TV/FM range and then modulating them in the ELF/ULF range, they can send signals. The Nexus magazine of Oct.-Nov. '96 p. 16 reported on Dr. Ross Adley's research. Dr. Adley did some work for the CIA on their Pandora project (an electronic mind-control project). He recently worked at the Loma Linda Univ. Med. School, CA. His research showed that the brain will react to EM radiation. To get a reaction the frequency, amplitude, and dose of the microwave radiation has to meet certain criteria. In the 1980's, his experiments showed that microwave carrier-waves modulated with ELF waves will modify brain tissue. Weak EM fields will affect the binding of calcium ions to neuronal sites. This type of information is the type of information that pertains to the genetic mind-control covered in Chapter 8. Dr. Adley was able to prove that a 147 MHz (megahertz) field, which at a tissue level had an intensity of 0.8 milliwatts per square centimeters, caused an efflux or release of calcium ions from the irradiated brain tissue. "This response only occurred when the ELF modulation of the microwave carrier-wave had an amplitude modulated at 6-20 hertz (Hz). The maximum stimulation of the neurones took place at 16 Hz, but to either side of this frequency-range parameter there was no effect." (Nexus, 10-11/'96, p. 16 citing Adey, Ross W. "Neurophysiologic Effects of Radiofrequency and Microwave Radiation" Bulletin of the New York Academy of Medicine, vol. 55, no. 11, Dec., '79) Also microwaves as they enter the brain tissue, cause thermal expansion as -things heat up at the microscopic level, which produces strains in tissue. The strains produce acoustic stress waves that are conducted through the bone to the cochle-a, and the cochlea's stimulation by the wave gives the brain its perception of hearing a sound just as the cochlea's stimulation produces the normal sensation of hearing. For microwaves to do this they must be at 1310 MHz and 2982 MHz at the average power densities of .4 to 2 mW/cm². The peak power densities can be 200 to 300 mW/cm2 and the pulse repetition frequency was from 200 to 400 Hz. This makes an RF auditory sound. The sound appears to the victim as coming from within or near the back of the head. 2 criteria needed to hear microwaves are the ability to hear above 5 kHz, and good bone conduction.

Section E. Auxiliary uses of electronics & electromagnetic waves.

E1. hypnotic induction
E2. polygraphs
E3. attacks against people & objects
LIQUID CRYSTALS
"ALIEN" implants
BED COILS STANDARDIZED FOR MIND-CONTROL POTENTIAL
E4. virtual reality

E1. ELECTRONICS TO AID HYPNOSIS

In a normal resting state the alpha waves of a person are between 6 -12 per second, and their breathing rate is about 20-40 breaths per mm. and their heart beat about 70 to 90 per minute. External stimuli will affect these rates. If a person fixes their attention on flashes and tones, such as what happens at some concerts, the body functions will tend to synchronize around the external tones and pulsing lights. It takes about ten minutes for the human mind/body to reconfigure itself in line with the external stimuli, then that rate of the flashing lights and tones and be lowered with a resulting lowering of the body's alpha wave rate, their breathing, and their heart beat. Electronics can be an aid to hypnotizing people. If vibrations that vibrate at the rate of six to seven cycles per second are created in a room of people, the vibrations will induce alpha waves in the minds of the people. The increased alpha wave activity makes the listening subjects more susceptible to suggestion. This is similar to the effect Vibrato has on the mind. Vibrato is a tremulous pulsating effect produced by a minute and rapid variation in pitch either by a cappella or instrumental music. Years ago, public performances of vibrato music was outlawed in England because so many listeners went into altered states. A 6- to 7-cycle/sec vibration can be mask behind other sounds. Hypnosis with headphones repeating "You do not know this" are used simultaneously along with sonics as well as electrical patterns that scramble the brain.

E2. POLYGRAPHS FOR MONITORING PROGRAMMING AND MISSION ACCOMPLISHMENTS

Tyson II Corporate Offices, McLean, VA furnishes polygraph operators for the intelligence agencies, esp. Office of Security which is responsible for CIA polygraph examinations.

E3. ATTACKS on INDIVIDUALS and objects.

A victim of electronic mind-control in VA in a letter describing her torment writes, "I no longer have the stabbing pain in my back when I go in my back yard, as I did in Richmond; however, the pain from some type of directed energy weapon(s) is just as severe here as it was in Richmond. These electrical rays coming through the airways of my home cause me all kinds of physical pain and illnesses. They kill my house-plants; they kill my shrubs; they kill my vegetables and flowers in my garden; and most of all, they cause me tremendous amount of discomfort, as well as harassment. "Can you imagine having electrical rays directed at your bottom day and night, 365 days of the year. Can you imagine what it must be like to live around oversexed SCUM?...This technology is based on Scalar Technology and the Schumann Resonances or Frequencies. It is my understanding that the Schu-mann Frequencies from 0 to 30 hertz can affect every nerve, every gland, every muscle and every emotion of a human being. In other words, a person in my neighborhood can beam these rays into my home and control my body and I am having to suffer from their stupid appetites..." (letter in author's files) Oscilloscopes have confirmed that some Direct ELF/VLF attacks have come from only a few feet. Electromagnetic attacks sometimes hit the victims entire body, like defibrillator paddles. Masers (microwave equivalents to a laser are used for electromagnetic attacks that cause burns that look like "cigarette burns", favorite target areas are genitals, face and nose. The average power density can be at an rf such as $400\_u\_w/cm^2$. Let's quote another victim, whose letter is also in my files. At first years ago, they began using waves that were in the infrared spectrum that were barely discernable. The waves would target her and then latch on. Over the years they have gotten more sophisticated and more sadistic. She writes, "From time to time the field broadcast from my own head was in a 'field' about me, but, with the added feature of 'harrassment' voices also being broad-cast. These 'harrassment' voices had taken a downright filthy tone, being blasphemous words, and venally oriented.... Before I was hit with the full-blown sadistic torture program I was awakened one night by a feeling of my head being raped. A light went on in my brain and I heard voices discussing me and cruelly laughing saying, "There, got her."...The first added torture (accompanied by filty langauge, the language is all filth, obscenities, threats and intimidation) was a genital-urinary prod, pulsing about twice per second, and causing nearly incessant urination..., new added features ... are body bangs and head bangs...The arrogance with which they announce what torture will be next is unbelievable... .Other sleep deprivation techniques are loud noises, and the interposing of visual phenomena. They seem to have devised a computer imaging which taps the visual nerves--these are like bad dreams. I have had almost no normal dreaming since this system was locked onto me. Over the years she got to understand her harassers better. They have called themselves "social workers" and referred to her as "the package." They have enjoyed talking about her in front of her, and harassing her by talking to each other in public about the things she thought about the previous night. Finally, one more account of a victim who is constantly harassed. "I am being tortured with synthetic telepathy of emotive and voice bytes played over and over again in my brain to positively or negatively reinforce and ultimately con-trol my behavior. I get the sound on my left temporal lobe and in the right and left ear canals. I also get microwaved when I sleep and have vibratory pulsating fields on my lower spine, genitals, stomach, brain, feet or wherever. It is always in combination with the lower spine and something else. This seems to create an amnesiacal deep sleep with no feeling of pain. If I wake up suddenly (and this is the only chance I have of finding out what they are doing to me) I sometimes feel pain when the vibrations stop."

Other attacks/problems:

• Infra-sound attack

• magnets repelled from the cranium

• They use a "Gun" which sends an electromagnetic field which stops a car.

The Russians have been noted to have created a "wood-pecker" signal, the American version of this is the American Buzzsaw. These signals are designed to interface with the mind. And systems are designed to be carried in helicopters, or to be placed on the ground. These signals are broadcast by multiple carriers which hop from frequency to frequency anywhere from 4 MHz to 30 MHz. With the switching of these frequencies, they are creating what is know as a Levinson Transform, named after Norman Levinson. VLF (Very low frequency waves) will cause bizarre behavior in people. (They use 0 to 400 Khz for mind-control operations. The signals are apparently broken up into pieces and triangulated upon a target. Morse codes are used on some slaves to trigger them, which is sent via a number of methods. Victims often have the myelin sheathing of the brain disappearing, which is diagnosed as Multiple Sclerosis. MS has increased 100 fold over the past few years. Pre-conditioning is done by chemicals to the neuro-receptors in the brain and spine. When moving in a car or inside a store it is harder for a victim to be targeted. Also, as readers can imagine, signals being beamed from some tower or satellite will be blocked by large thicknesses of concrete, lead and -steel. In other words, there are some situations that provide limited shelter to the victims of implant body suits and syntel.

UNWANTED CHANGES

There is a complex symbiosis between mankind and the attributes of this planet. We are a life-form whose life is attuned to our environment. The human body at the cellular level has its physiological rhythms which are very attuned to the earth's electric and magnetic fields. When cosmic radiation cycles undergo unusual modifications, including cycle inversions, the metabolism in crabs and the oxygen consumption cycles in carrots, potatoes -shellfish and rats changes. The geomagnetic field helps protect us from cosmic rays. It has been shown that solar flares influence human behavior, and psych wards have an increase in problem behavior during solar flares. The human body is a complex set of rhythms. Permit me to recall some of these rhythms for the reader: Alpha rhythms, Blood Hormone rhythms, Body temperature rhythms (which fluctuate 3° on 24 hour cycle), Cell mitosis rhythms, Cellular DNA & RNA synthesizing rhythms, Cerebral-spinal fluid rhythms, Circadian rhythms, Enzyme rhythms, Food utilization rhythms, Menstrual & Sexual -rhythms, Pulse rates, Seasonal rhythms, and Urine Electrolyte Disposal rhythms. The 60-pulse-per-second power grids (of AC) that are spread over the earth, as well as numerous other man-made activities are disrupting the 7-8 hertz frequency of the earth. There are some side-effects to our tampering with the magnetic and electrical fields of this planet, and some of these side effects may be the disruption or change of the circadian -rhythms (as well as some of the other rhythms of the human body and mind.) In fact, two researchers have research that shows how human nerve cells are affected by ELF fields. (See Becker, Dr. Robert O. Cross-Currents: The Perils of Electropollution, The Promise of Electromedicene. LA: Jeremy Tarcher, 1990, p. 233.) It was discovered by CIT researchers that the human brain has magnetite. Salmon, homing pigeons, whales, and honeybees also have magnetite, a type crystalline iron, which allows them to sense the earth's magnetic field for finding their way around. The CIT researchers published their finding about mag-netite in human brains in the journal Proceedings of the National Academy of Sciences.

LIQUID CRYSTALS

For about 6 years this author has heard about liquid crystal implants. One military magazine should its use, and one person who was in military intelligence claims liquid crystals are used. Others claim that liquid crystals were tried and failed. It has also been reported that radio transmitting crystals, that fasten themselves to the brain have been the object of research.

Some ODDS & ENDS

• SERPENTINE SKIN

Another topic that for sure was tried by the NWO was serpentine skin. This is a type of specialized fungus that coats the skin and is used for some of its specialized features. Whether this concept actually flies outside of the lab, this author doesn't know.

• "ALIEN" implants

This author's take on the alien phenomena is that it is the Illuminati's Grand Deception for introducing the AntiChrist. The aliens are materialized demons, and manufactured "soul less" bodies. It's not the purpose here to put forth evidence concerning this Grand Deception, that would take another book, if not several books. (In fact, this author started to write it in 1993, but never got finished.) But no book discussing implants & mind-control could be complete without -touching on alien implants. There is a great overlap between "alien abductions" and mind-control. Whitley Strieber (UFO abductee and famous author) gave two workshops at the UFO Expo West LA. He was very interested in finding out about the implants that Dr. Lear and Derrell Sims had extracted and turned over to traditional medical institutions for study. While Whitley was talking about implants and our government's connection to them, his own implant in his ear turned on and the side of his face turned red like a bad sunburn. Other UFO buffs in attendance also had their implants burn them at this point, causing great excitement at the Wyndham Hotel that day. (This information came from the internet madsongroup@earthlink.net)

There are an increasing number of "alien abductees" who are remembering seeing U.S. military personnel during their so-called alien abductions. The abductees are being taken to U.S. Military bases. (An unusual place for aliens to work, but within the realm of possibility.) The reason that the number of people who are connecting the government with the aliens is increasing is a. more people are receiving mind-control programming, therefore there are more people for which the cover stories and electroshock fail to totally hide what has happened, b. better therapeutic methods are helping mind-control victims recover their memories better, c. there have been a rising number of people like this author exposing it. Karla Turner, who was a victim of mind-control and abductions, began catching on that the abductions were being done by our government. Vol. 2 quoted her on page 184. When she began to publicly expose what the government was doing, the government murdered her. (She joins a growing num-ber of people this author has seen die pre-maturely because they were publicly exposing the truth.) Alien abduction victims have been reporting human black-or dark helicopter activity and black-or dark helicopter harassment since the 1970's. (Perhaps as the Vietnam War wound down & ended, the U.S. government had a surplus of helicopters and delegated some to task forces that picked up mind-control victims in remote sites.) An example from this time period of an alien abduction also involving helicopters is the Betty Andreasson/Luca abduction. A number of victims have remembered the helicopters coming -around the time of their abduction. When bright lights are shined into their houses or into their cars these victims of trauma-based mind-control are programmed to see the helicopter's spotlight as a UFO. (Helicopters also carry spoofer transmitters.) Beth Collins of Oregon reports in her book Connections - Solving our Alien Abduction Mystery. Newberg, OR: Wild Flower Press, 1966, about how helicopters were involved with her abduction experiences. She lives in an area that is a hot-bed for covert CIA activities. In her book, she provides a transcript of memories of military personnel being the guilty party in an abduction. Some victims of these abduction experiences are implanted during their abduction. Researcher Helmut Lammer reports that "alien" abductees Debby Jordan and Leah Haley had implants removed from their ears. What is significant about this, is that the bio-chip implant designed for humans which is credited to Dr. Man, best works behind the ears. (Sources: The Kansas City Star, 7/19/87 carried an article about how Dr. Man's implants work best behind the ear. On Oct., '87, an article by Kathy Hart was run in several papers promoting Dr. Man's implants for protecting children. H. Lammer reported on implants & military involvement in abductions in his article "Preliminary Findings of Project MILAB: Evidence for military kidnappings of alleged UFO abductees." The Unopened Files, No. 2, '97, pp 64-67.) From this author's interviews with "alien abductees" it was clear that 100% of them were victims of U.S. government trauma-based mind-control and that many of them had been taken to underground pro-gramming facilities and made to believe they were at another planet. This is happening in foreign countries too. However, this doesn't mean that flying saucers craft do not exist, they do. And according to eye-witnesses some of the underground facilities in NM, AZ, and CO have personnel from all over the -world, Germans, Russians, British & Americans as well as aliens working side by side. (The American government denies this. Supposedly NORAD only has Canadians.) Some of these witnesses come across as credible. If their reports are true, then some implants may also have a true alien connection. Alien abductees are actually extracting implants from their noses and their feet. It is strange that -"alien" implants have gotten more technologically sophisticated over the years.

BED COILS STANDARDIZED FOR MIND-CONTROL POTENTIAL

Metal coil springs were standardized in size, are made of steel and are placed in a grid pattern in a common mattress. Standards were introduced that specify how many coils, and what tension were to be used in their manufacture. Their shape is an open ended hyperbolic which is the best suited to create a similar induced magnetic field. When one lays down the springs are compressed and have between 5 to 7 coils compressed. This makes a field of influence around the human body which is enfolded within the field of coils, which are natural antennas to incoming electromagnetic waves. Evidence suggests that the standardizing of bed springs was a carefully planned event designed to assist electronic mind-control.

E4. VIRTUAL REALITY.

Since 1989, Virtual Reality conferences-exhibitions have been held. On May 11-13, 1994, the largest conference-exhibition to date on virtual reality was held at the San Jose Civic Center and the Fairmont Hotel, San Jose, CA. Note some of the mind-control aspects of the different sessions:

Session C7--"Tactile Feedback" given by Paul Cutt. Xtensory Session C8--"The Immersion Probe" given by Louis Rosenberg, Pres. of Immersion Corporation.

Session D2--"Biomedical Technology and Biomedical Education" given by John Flynn

Session D9--"Biocybernetics and VR" given by Dave Warner, Medical Scientist at Loma Linda Univ. Med. Center During lunch Kenny Meyer discussed how simulated being in a virtual world are called various names incl. synthetic actors, situated agents, creatures and denizens. At another meal break Lt. Col. Martin Stytz, USAF, spoke on how the military was developing Virtual Reality to train men.

Session C17--AFIT Projects, that is Alr Force Institute of Technology at Wright Patterson AFB given by Elizabeth Block. (Wright Patterson happens to be a major hub for the mind-control and criminal activities of the secret government.)

Session C19--"ARPA/ASTO" given by Lt. Col. David Neyland.

The military is not the only group interested in virtual reality. A plethora of virtual reality companies has -sprung up, for instance Sense8 (which selling ready-to-use virtual reality systems), the Vivid Group which creates Mandala (which are virtual reality authoring systems), and Xtensory Inc., which creates virtual reality tactile feedback systems. The government also works through labs located on American universities working with government grant money, such as the state of the art Virtual Reality lab at the Univer. of Illinois Circle campus, which calls its virtual reality machine "the

Cave." Virtual touch has been created. This means that with a special machine for the person's hand (for shape perception) & special glove (for texture sensing) the computer users can feel the shape and texture of an object on the screen.

Hollywood has given us movies showing the mind-control potential of virtual reality in Lawnmower man & Brainstorm. For more information on virtual reality the reader might try consulting:

• Aukastakalnis, Steve and Blatner, David. Silicon Mirage: The Art and Science of Virtual Reality. Peachpit Press, 1992.

• Laurel, Brenda. The Art of Human-Computer Interface Design. Addison-Wesley, 1990.

This author has a catalog advertizing the EMCS-X-3000-Plus Electronic Mind Con-trol System, which was invented by Cabalistic Hermetic magician Karl Welz. The ad states, "If your intentions are to take control of others and to increase your own mental powers of direct action, then the EMCS-X-3000-Plus is your system of choice!" The article has an endorsement for the BMCS system on page 19 by a charismatic minister, "...I am a preacher of a charismatic church. for reasons you may understand, I was extremely skeptical initially [of the EMCS system]. However, I gave the new technology a chance to help me serve the Lord better, and I do not regret that decision! The membership of my church has more than doubled within one year ... Thank you very much." ---We live in some perilous times! Maranatha!

• List of other Books on this chpt's Subject

Bamford's The Puzzle Palace
Becker's The Body Electric
Becker's Cross Currents
Brodeur's Currents of Death
Brodeur's The Zapping of America
Burdock, Dorothy's Such Things Are Known (victim)
Calder's The Mind of Man
Chokroverty's Magnetic Stimulation in Clinical Neurophysiology
Clark's July 20, 2019
Dawes' Advances in...Quantum Neurodynamics
Eccles, Sir John C.'s Evolution of the Complexity of the Brain with Emergence of Consciousness
Galton's MedTech
Green's Beyond Biofeedback
Halacy's Cyborg
Halperin's Crimes of the Intell. Community
Heller's Of Mice, Men & Molecules
Hooper's The Three-Pound Universe
Hougan's Secret Agenda
Hutchison's Megabrain
Johnsons's In the Palaces of Memory
McKinnell's Cloning: A Biologist Reports
Mark's The Search for the Manchurian Candidate
McRae's Mind Wars
Pine's The Brain Changers
Stanford Research Inst., Journal of Scientific Exploration, vol. 10, no. 1, PP. 1-111
Regan's Evoked Potentials
Rein, Glen's Modulation of Neurotransmitter Function by Quantum Fields
Restak's The Mind
Rucker's Mind Tools
Valenstein's Brain Control

Weinstein's Psychiatry & the CIA: Victims of Mind Cntl The American military establishment lumped syntel and a number of other outrageous "weapons of torture and control" under the official heading of "non-lethal". Then the establishment media (TV & newspapers) such as the Wall St. Journal, Aug. 2, '94, had an article about non-lethal weapons where they wrote about the sticky-goo gun", which uses goo to stop people. Do you see how they create a cover? When the public hears of non-lethal weapons they think sticky-goo guns, not implants that are torturing and controlling people.

Herman Kahn of the Hudson Institute stated that total mind-control would be in place by 2000 and could be "imposed under the rubic of mental hygiene."

CHAPTER 7: THE SCIENCE OF STRUCTURING
A. STRUCTURING OF MPD WORLDS
WORKING WITH PARTS OF THE MIND
CONTROL ALTERS called PROCESSORS
BASIC DESIGNS of an ALTER SYSTEM
RINGS The Ferris-wheel subsystem MULTIPLEX
DATA ENTRY POINTS
TESTING ALTERS TO SEE IF THEY CAN BE USED.
THE SCRIPTS.
Assassination Models (Delta Models).
  AUTHORITY FACTORS ARE MAXIMIZED
  ACCOUNTABILITY & ANONYMITY
Monkey Alters.
Plant alters.
Presidential Models
Prostitute Models.
Psychic models.
Reporting Alters.
Repunzel alter.
Transformation alters.
Internal Wall alters
Structuring Internal Programmer Alters.
STRUCTURING WITH THE GRAND DRUID COUNCIL.
STRUCTURING THE SHADOW ALTERS
STRUCTURING IN THE MIRRORS
STRUCTURING THE TAPESTRY
STRUCTURING THE ALTER FAMILIES BY SPINNING

The programmers are experts in knowing how to mold the "clay" of blank dissociated parts of the mind into whatever piece they need. The following is a true account. The Chinese arrested a foreigner skilled in martial arts. They abused the man, but instead of becoming apathetic, he kept himself mentally & physically fit in spite of the horrible conditions of his solitary cell. The superstitious guards believed he was a magician. When the identity of the man was discovered, and the Chinese realized that he was one of the world's greatest martial arts experts, they decided to try everything possible to destroy him. He was tortured, starved, and humiliated. The man simply went into dissociative states of trance and endured the tortures without sign of pain or emotion. The hardened guards were awed. The Chinese decided to kill the man. They figured that they could place him in a cage with a starved tiger, he'd go into trance and the starved tiger would eat him, and then they could claim that the man had been a coward. They not only wanted the man's life but his reputation. When they threw the much-tortured prisoner into the hungry tiger's cage, the martial arts expert took on the appearance of a demonized man. With a demonic roar, he attacked the tiger, and instantly kicked the tiger's nose. The animal was stunned and disoriented. The man leaped upon the animal from behind, let out a terrifying scream and strangled the animal. In 20 seconds the whole affair was over.

The man looked like an incarnation of a tiger himself. In fact, the tiger had instantly feared the man the split second the master had landed in the cage. When the programmers ARE SUCCESSFUL with their STRUCTURING--they are able to create alters that match what you have just read about. Our Chinese prison story illustrates the type of end results the Illuminati want from hours of torture & training given to slaves, but HOW do they achieve such fantastic results? That is what this chapter is about.

Some of the programmed skills of the ninjitsu people (the ninja) are now being structured into Illuminati mind-controlled slaves. A disciple of the above prisoner in China wrote, [the Ninja]..."were the original practitioners of the 'art of [mind-control] programming'. They were taught from the cradle that nothing was impossible. Not knowing that a thing could not be done, they proceeded to do it." (The Karate Dojo, p. 101)

A. STRUCTURING OF MPD WORLDS

The purpose of the mind-control is to build a System within the mind that is a human robot. It would do no good to torture the slave and get thousands of pieces (fragments of the mind, alter personalities) if these were not structured. Very few Multiples have ever really gotten to see the deeper parts of their Systems.

WORKING WITH PARTS OF THE MIND

For many people who are unfamiliar with MPD, it can be expected that they would find it strange to watch how the programmers or the therapists work with parts of the mind. Most people mis-perceive the mind as a monolithic entity. In reality the normal mind is made up of hundreds of independent parts working in cooperation and competition with each other.

The top brain researchers (at least many of them) have come to realize that the brain is composed of many independent parts that at times work against each other. For the normal person, some of these parts can be called ego states and some small processes are called by Minsky "agents" of the mind. For the multiple personality they are called alters, splits, and purpose fragments. A normal person has a society of agents and ego states which are entities or parts of the mind which combine to make the whole thinking mind. A multiple personality does not have a society, but rather a system of parts. Whether a person has a society of agents or a system of alters, everyone experiences his or her mind as a combination of processes, conflicting motives, and internal tensions.

In order to bring some cohesion and unity to one's actions, so that a person didn't spend their life going in fifty different directions at once, the mind creates the illusion of self, the self image. The self-image by necessity must not change rapidly. One of the main reasons the mind creates a self-image is so it can have a single purpose to its actions. One of the functions of a self-image (of anyone) IS TO PREVENT RAPID CHANGES. Long range plans could not be pulled off if my personality were like Jane today and Tarzan tomorrow and Cheetah the next day. The mind refuses to change its self-image, even in the face of conflicting data, because self-preservation of a directed life demands continuity from day to day in our personality. Our self-image is a mental construct that stabilizes the mind's numerous processes. It is a global attitude registered in the mind that globally affects thinking in many of the mind's spheres. This is just one reason why the self-images constructed by the programmer for alters are so tenacious, and so difficult to change. Self-images do not want change, they are the restraints (the ball and chain) we subconsciously create so that we can't wreck all of our plans by skipping from one idealistic goal to another without continuity. (How convenient it is to be able to construct a single brain with many different alter personalities each having its own unchanging self-image!)

Pain and Pleasure are two agents which cause the mind to simplify its focus upon either the pleasure or the pain. The brain does not want to focus on anything that is not an immediate issue. This focus on the immediate pain or pleasure by the victim of mind-control diminishes the victim from focusing on more complex mental issues.

An example of one of world's top experts who realizes how the mind is naturally made up of parts is Marvin Minsky, co-founder of the Artificial Intelligence Lab at MIT, author of The Society of Mind, and who has been an advisor to NASA & the L-5 Society. Minsky's research was financed by the government (the Office of the Advanced Research Projects Agency). And he and other researchers in his field got their contracts by the Office of Naval Research. (See Society of the Mind, p. 324.) His incredible book The Society of Mind has an interesting format where the numerous parts (agents) of the mind are each given their own page in the book. Minsky shows in the book that the mind is a "society" that arises out of ever-smaller agents that are themselves mindless. He does an incredibly good job of explaining how the mind works. Minsky states, "In general, we're least aware of what our minds do best."

The Illuminati structuring of the MPD's fragmented mind is to create flawlessly working systems that can function without the conscious mind getting involved. In fact, Minsky describes how our conscious minds only get involved in simple mental processes that don't work well, the complex ones that work well usually work without the conscious mind being aware of them. "Some readers may be horrified at picturing a baby's mind as made up of nearly separate agencies. But we'll never understand how human natures grow without some theories of how they start.

One evidence for separateness is how suddenly infants switch from smiles of contentment to shrieks of hunger-rage. In contrast to the complex mixtures of expressions that adults show, young children seem usually to be in one or another well-defined state of activity..." (Society of the Mind, p. 171)

The Illuminati has long realized that they need to split the mind of the child before its various agencies connect and the ego-states form and develop their sense of self-hood and personal identity. Although adults can be programmed, the real Illuminati multiple systems are developed from the womb up.

How does the mind make decisions? The various parts of the mind compete with each other. All the parts are in a sense equal, none sits at the top of some hierarchy. The mind does not allow any natural part, such as ANGER, or SLOTH to be permanently enthroned and to direct the other parts. Too many chiefs and no Indians wouldn't work out. Natural parts can not order another part around. They must influence that part indirectly. That is why the following examples happen.

A young married man decides that he and his wife can not successfully work out their problems, because she is a programmed multiple in denial, who wants to manipulate his life and destroy it, while he on the other hand wants to be successful in life. One part of him is the LOYAL TO VOWS part, which refuses to quit the marriage because of the marriage vows. Another part is the GOAL SETTING part, which sees the marriage as an abusive dead end. How does the GOAL SETTING part convince the LOYAL TO VOWS part to give up (throw in the towel) and move on with life? It must indirectly trick LOYAL TO VOWS into feeling that its job has been done as well as possible, and that further concern over the vows are excused.

Another young man, a student, has his STUDY part of the mind really wanting to focus on some problems, but the BORED and SLEEPY part of him want to go to sleep. His STUDY part of the mind tricks his BORED part into allowing STUDY to go to work. He mentally creates a fictitious scare that another student will do better than he, and BORED and SLEEPY are tricked into thinking the problem is much more weighty than it really is.

A young woman bribes her eating processes of her mind, that if she follows through with her diet, she'll reward herself with a nice meal, and that other parts of her will be rewarded with other benefits. Rather than simply diet, she must bribe different parts of herself. Of course if parts of us, lie to other parts when they try to bribe ourselves into doing something, if we are not honest with ourselves in giving the reward, then it is harder next time to bribe the part that was lied to.

In order for the non-multiple's parts to trust each other, they subscribe to a single agreed upon character-an imaginary ideal self-image. Other wise we couldn't trust ourselves to carry out plans. If an ordinary person has amnesia, they could create a different self-image, which again would be an enduring character. By introducing MPD, the programmers create a hidden element of distrust within a person's mind. They no longer can trust themselves, now they must depend upon the stability of the programmer or owner. Now imagine that each of the "agents" or parts has been manipulated to think that it is a person with a personality and a history in its own little world. Because the mind is such a tremendous computer it can easily handle such mental processes.

The programmer and the de-programmer/therapist must work at "tricking" these parts into allowing the mind to do constructive things. I use the word tricking, because what is actually happening is that the therapist or programmer is using language that relates to the language of that part, but it is not language that has much external reality beyond that part. Structuring is the art of using special "languages" combined with other programming sciences to manipulate these internal worlds of the various parts. Our minds are instruments to solve practical problems. If an alter sees no practical use for a particular knowledge they will not want to learn it. This natural selecting process by the mind, helps isolate an MPD's system of alters, because many alters do not see a need to learn anything outside of their programming.

CONTROL ALTERS called PROCESSORS

Within the system of alters, certain alters are selected to be PROCESSORS. As a system is used certain alters are destroyed, disconnected, or regulated. Certain codes are used or changed. A SYSTEM PARAGUARD is what is used to decipher codes and to distinguish what is currently happening in a system.

BASIC DESIGNS of an ALTER SYSTEM

Most Illuminati systems are configured with a Universe or Star base system. In other words, the model for all that is put in uses clusters of stars, galaxies, etc. This is used in conjunction with grids that are shaped in various configurations. The ultimate master of the slave, some Illuminati kingpin who is a programmer or working closely with programmers, will design the system so that the entire structure of the system points to himself and Satan. The alters will be geographically set up in their internal world to worship the master to whom they must give their body, soul and spirit.

A cube or double-cube system is a closed system. The programmers who use cubes love to build boxes within boxes. The smallest middle box of the system may contain the Life force of the system. Those who love paper trails, will see the occult basis for the standard Illuminati cube shape of a system portrayed on page 83 of Clausen Commentaries on Morals & Dogma, which was put out by the Supreme Council of the World of 33° of Freemasonry in 1974. This Masonic book explains that the cube represent man and the pyramid is divinity. Divinity within a man would be constructed by placing a pyramid within a cube, which is shown in a picture on page 83. You will also notice in this Masonic book that the 2 Grand Masters on page 83 are wearing crowns that have 13 jewels. The crowns serve the same purpose that rings patterned on a similar pattern represent. Crowns and rings represent authority, and it is common within the mystery religions to place 12 or 13 gems within crowns and rings. The reason that this is important, is that some important Masonic/Illuminati secrets are here, and these secrets also pertain to how the Mystery Religions (the Illum. & Freemasonry) construct an alter system.

RINGS

Within the Illuminati (which is the continuation of the mystery religions of Babylon) the ring has for many centuries represented divinity. The mystery religions' higher understanding was that God had a ring with his name on it that showed His authority and exercised power over the earth, and that Satan imitated this many-fold in all the mystery religions that he created. For thousands of years, within the various mystery religions, hierophants have been wearing rings with particular secret symbols. The zodiac signs were assigned different stones, gems. For instance, the 12 gems of Rev. 21:18-20, which are the usual gems placed within an Illuminati alter system would correspond to the astrological signs as follows:

Jasper «»Pisces Sapphire «»Aquarius Chalcedony «» Cancer Emerald «» Taurus Sardonyx «» Scorpio Chrysolyte Saggittarius Beryl «» Leo Topaz «» Gemini Chrysoprasus «» Capricorn Jacinth «» Amethyst «» Aries

The creation of a Monarch system's gems is in imitation of the rings of Lucifer and God (as the Illuminati understand it). This ring of gems is able to control the fruit of the trees (programs) and change the internal weather. It is based upon the story that is told the alter system that is being made about how God had a ring. Until His hand swept the heaven of air (1st heaven) fruit could not fall and die, because nothing could die.

Satan and his followers like rings because they want to be godlike. (That doesn't mean all Satanists understand their own history.) When an alter is concerned about "Don't lose the ring", the alter may be referring to the ring of the gems that surrounds the pyramid at the base of the mind. This ring of gem alters may be referred to as the ETERNAL RING, and the RING OF FIRE. The achievement of divinity by a human was what constituted the hermetic marriage of the mysteries. This was the ultimate achievement by mankind. This was symbolized by a gold ring.

Within the Illuminati (which is a continuation of the Mystery Religions) rings are used for bonding (marriage commitments) and a sign of majesty or rank (such as your Masonic rings, and the ring Pharaoh gave Joseph, & King Saul's ring, & special papal rings allowed cardinals & abbots.) The Pope has 3 significant rings, one of which is for ceremonies, and another the important Fisherman's Ring, which is still used as the Pope's seal.

Within the Illuminati alter systems the 7 seals of Babylon are placed into a system. The cube with a pyramid was portrayed at the 14th Masonic Degree (the Perfect Elu degree). The 4 horsemen & the seals of Babylon are talked about at the 17th Masonic degree (Knight of the East & West). Also deep within a system may be the Ring of Fire.

Within the pyramid, which is within the ring of those 12 gems mentioned in Rev. 21, is the ETERNAL LIFE FORCE, a green light coming from Lucifer. In other words, the secret heart of the system is based upon the original lie, that man could become an eternal god. The Illuminati alter structure has at its heart the original lie. An example of how rings and demonology and authority intersect, can be seen in the Grimoire of the Testament of Solomon where a ring is said to have been given to Solomon which enabled him to learn the names of demons.

Rings and chains around the neck are also worn for the extremely secret reason that the wearer is identifying himself with Lucifer who was bound by God by a ring of fire and was chained in the abyss. This is what is really behind high ranking Illuminati Freemason & clergyman Robert Schuler's chain around his neck. The highest levels of the Illuminati have the understanding that Lucifer lost his power when Christ bound him, and that in identification with him, they wear gold chains around their neck, etc. Don't expect to read this in the material that occult world is permitted to read, these are high level secrets. Remember, there are many different levels of occultism, and Satanism. (In the early middle ages, Christians borrowed the idea of having marriage rings from the pagan Germans & Romans. The determination of what finger to wear it on (what has become known as the ring finger), was chosen by the ancient witches because that was considered the only healing finger. Christians of course, by and large, know nothing of the pagan origins and symbology of the rings they wear.) This author has noted that many of the handlers, programmers, & Illuminati adepts wear rings. Some of the rings are quite big.

The Ferris-wheel subsystem. A ferris-wheel configuration which creates compartments shaped like a piece of pie is often a small part of a larger system, and is used to house alters, or it may have some other internal purpose with its rotation. As was brought out in Vol. 2, the Illuminati like to use configurations that appear endless such as circles within circles, boxes within boxes, triangles within triangles. Star configurations are popular Illuminati power sources within their alter systems. The position of a star, the number of points it has, and the relationship it has to other objects in the sky such as a rainbow will be significant. Some stars are placed into the system to represent a point in time when the system is programmed to do something.

When a slave is programmed with multiple functioning sub-systems (aka "systems"), the Illuminati call it MULTIPLEX. In such as case, types and names of alters may be duplicated in systems that are mirror images of each other or of a similar design. Traver reports that one MULTIPLEX system had 55 Daves per sub-system with 7 subsystems, making a total of 385 Dave alters for the 7 subsystems in just one particular slave. (see Traver, Dan. Dissociative Disorders & Mind Control, p. 84)

The construction of an Illuminati system can not be divorced from the demonology and rituals that are performed throughout the life of the system. The Illuminati use mystical terms when programming, which reframes psychological processes in the language of magic. Programming and hypnosis are referred during programming as "SPELLS". The programmers will use fictional magical names for items, for instance, the subconscious mind may be referred to as the "HYPNOGOURD, A VINE THAT GROWS GOURDS." Creativity and imagination will be termed "MAGIC", and the programmer "A MAGICIAN". The programmer would instruct his assistant in language like this, "WOULD YOU PUT THIS GAP FORGET SPELL IN?"

The Generational Spirit (or Spirits from each occult bloodline) is laid into the child in the womb. It stays hidden deeply in the system, and plays a fundamental role in the system's creation empowering other demonic forces. In order to construct the trees that provide the structure for the internal worlds-programming, the Illuminati programmer will tell the victim the following hypnotic ritual:

"AS YOU BREATHE, REMEMBER TO SIT ERECT, AND AS YOUR SPINE STRAIGHTENS, FEEL THE ENERGY RISING [PAUSE] NOW IMAGINE YOUR SPINE IS THE TRUNK OF A TREE, AND FROM ITS BASE ROOTS REACH DOWN DEEP INTO THE EARTH. [PAUSE] INTO THE CENTER OF THE EARTH HERSELF [PAUSE] AND YOU CAN DRAW UP POWER FROM THE EARTH, WITH EACH BREATH [SHORT PAUSE] FEEL THE ENERGY RISING, LIKE SAP RISING THROUGH A TREE TRUNK, AND FEEL THE POWER RISE UP YOUR SPINE, FEEL YOURSELF BECOMING MORE ALIVE, WITH EACH BREATH, AND FROM THE

CROWN OF YOUR HEAD, YOU HAVE BRANCHES, THAT SWEEP UP AND BACK DOWN TO TOUCH THE EARTH [PAUSE] AND FEEL THE POWER BURST FROM THE CROWN OF YOUR HEAD, AND FEEL IT SWEEP THROUGH THE BRANCHES UNTIL IT TOUCHES THE EARTH AGAIN, MAKING A CIRCLE, MAKING A CIRCUIT, RETURNING TO ITS SOURCE."

The part of the system that will function within the Illuminati hierarchy will all be intimately part of either the SPIRIT TREE (that is the Caballistic Tree of Life) or the TREE OF EVIL (which is the evil mirror image of the Tree of Life). Both trees were discussed in the Vol. 2 Formula book. These trees are both totally connected to the Spirit of the AntiChrist and rooted in Lilith and Tubal-cain. The Moon child ritual is not only performed when the child is still a foetus, but also at age 3, 4, 5, 6, and 16.

When the Illuminati child is in their teens they do the Caballistic Tree of Life pathworking. The pathworking rituals are severe, and many splits of the mind will occur due to these rituals. All the alters created during this work will be arranged at the GATEWAYS that pertain to that particular ritual. Therapists who do not realize how the pathworking of the 22 paths develops entire sections of deeper alters, may incorrectly think they can simply toss out the caballistic Tree of Life from the victim. Countless deeper alters are part of this tree. It has been said in the Illuminati that in general an Illuminati system consists of "the father (core), the son (the programming), the holy spirit (the spirit Tree also called the Tree of Life)."

DATA ENTRY POINTS

The programmers have designed their systems so that one can only get into the Systems via a SEQUENCE. However, sometimes they themselves want to quickly down load information into the computer-like mind of their slaves, and they don't want to have to go through a sequencing procedure. For quick and sloppy downloading of information to their slave or quick deletions to the programming (there is only limited access to quick deletions), programmers put DATA ENTRY POINTS into most systems. This allows for an emergency entry and/or downloading. General codes most often open these points, rather than long specific codes. The trick is being able to know where those DATA ENTRY POINTS are on the person's alter grid or as the programmers say the slave's SCREEN. (With the advent of lap-top computers, what the master of the slave sees if he has to refer to his own reference notes is just that a screen with the system's layout. (Vol.2 pg. 88 gave a sample of how a page on the lap top computer or in a master's black or grey 3-ring binder would look like.) An example of a data-entry point would be a gatekeeper which has learned the entire system via trained LSD trips and then has been programmed to keep this understanding on a subconscious level.

TESTING ALTERS TO SEE IF THEY CAN BE USED.

When a trauma is carried out upon a child, the child is then debriefed and all the splits from the trauma identified. Generally only the first 10 splits will be used to create alters, and the rest of the splits will become special purpose fragments. The programmers begin with the first split and identify how strong the split is. The programmers test for four things:

a. how well can this split take a hypnotic suggestion?

b. how creative is this split?

c. Can this split hold memory?

d. Can this split hold the structuring that will given it?

If the split passes positive on these four criteria, then it will be used to make a full blown alter. The programmers move down the line, testing the splits in the sequence that they were created. If no. 4 split is unable to pass the 4 criteria, then they know that the rest of the top splits will also have to be "thrown away" and used as special purpose fragments. If they need 12 splits from an alter, and they only get 5 usable splits from the first torture, they will retorture the alter to get more first splits. They will continue the process until they get the splits they need. Usually they can use the first 10 splits. Seldom do they use anything beyond the first 10 splits for alters, they are just to weak mentally. If an alter shows extra promise the programmer may say, "This part was going to be a bit part, but we'll make her into a real character." If a special purpose fragment leans in a needed direction mentally, they may take what was to be a minor part, and develop it into an interesting alter. Alters that are waiting to be used are stored as gems that the dwarfs mine, and then the programmers program them. An Illuminati system has thousands of these clean slates. Diamonds are pre-programmed alters that are stored to be used in the end-times during the reign of the Anti-Christ.

THE SCRIPTS.

Each master programmer is responsible for the scripts that he uses. He will invoke the leading geographic spirits, and even Lucifer to gain up-to-date wisdom on what is best for that time at that location. A master programmer will get assistance from his Mother of Darkness or Grande Dame. The master programmer may use a written script of his own such as Michael Aquino uses his own version of Star Wars, or he may borrow from established sources, for instance, Dr. Star of Corpus Christi, TX, who uses the The Goetia The Lesser Key of Solomon the King (Clavicula Salomonis Regis). Dr. Star especially uses the Shemhamphorash, which is the first part of that ancient magical book.

Recently Avon books (which has been owned by Hearst Illuminati family, and which has published over 30 editions of the Satanic Bible) published a book by Piers Anthony entitled Visual Guide to Xanth. This amazing book Visual Guide to Xanth is based on Anthony's Xanth series. It contains so many programming scripts, that it is hard to imagine that Anthony is not a programmer. The scripts are too intact for it to be coincidence. The title page has a hoofed tailed Satan on his throne. It is popular among satanists to use X words, like Michael Aquino signs off his personal letters "Xeper", rather than "sincerely".

Anthony was born in Britian but now lives in Florida. He has had over 60 fiction books published, many of the early ones were very well promoted by the Illuminati, and became top best sellers. The back cover advertises this Visual Guide to Xanth this way, "Learn about the astonishing hierarchy--and lowerarchy--of sorcerers and shape-changers, of goblins, harpies and half-humans who inhabit this extraordinary universe! [internal worlds] Explore the perilous Ogre-fen-ogre-Fen and the inner chambers of the mysterious Castle Roogna! Revel in the history and culture of the most remarkable civilization this side of Ozz!"

The co-authors would have to agree that Piers Anthony's story telling ability rivals, if not surpasses Baum's Oz series. In fact Anthony has put out numerous series of books, not just one series like Baum. The Xanth series is the one that contains more of the programming scripts. For instance, a script would be used to get suicide alters to want to take drugs & champagne on an empty stomach, or to get into a bathtub of water & throw in an electric blow drier which is on.

Assassination Models (Delta Models).

A great deal was explained in the Vol. 2 book about Delta alters, Delta models, Delta teams, and Delta Forces. All of these are involved with killing humans. It is not the purpose of this section to cover what has already been written in the Vol. 2 Formula book on these various Deltas. Mind-controlled Amphibious men, (genetically altered Navy Seals--see Vol. 2 p. 26 1-262, the latter no. is a significant no. for these programmed men) are the Navy's attempt to get something similar to what is depicted on the film Universal Solders. These Navy Seals are not allowed to be touched by other sailors when they are on a ship.

There is still a number of deeper insights that can be provided to understand how assassin personalities are conditioned to be able to kill. Researchers in how the brain functions have found that our forebrains (the thinking part that makes us humans) shut down when we are angry or frightened and the midbrain (which resembles the brain of animals) takes over. The only programming that works for the midbrain is the same type of training that works for dogs, which is classical and operant conditioning. This type of conditioning is simply stimulus-response, such as IF fire bell--THEN walk the fire escape exit plan.

When it comes to killing, the forebrain will listen to many suggestions such as orders from a gang leaders, an officer, or the pressures of life when they demand that a person kill, but the midbrain has the instinct that is born into 98% of the population NOT to kill another human. This innate human resistance to killing is far stronger than has popularly been realized, and has historically stopped most people from killing. This may surprise most readers, because Hollywood movies would lead us to think otherwise. A number of top researchers, including Lt. Col. Dave Grossman, author of the excellent book On Killing, have uncovered irrefutable (albeit still controversial) proof that historically most soldiers have secretly refused to kill in battle.

Grossman was a Military Psychology professor at West Point, as well as having a long list of other military credentials. His superb book On Killing gives numerous reasons (proofs and evidences) that numerous soldiers have typically only pretended to try to kill the enemy. Many fired over the heads or only pretended to fire their weapons, if even that. During W.W. II, Brig. Gen. S.L.A. Marshall discovered that only 15 to 20 % of men on the front line would actually use their weapons against the Germans even during action over several days. 75% of the American soldiers would not even fire at the enemy to save their own lives. He made some suggestions on how to improve this dismal firing rate. By operant conditioning the U.S. military took those dismal firing rates to 55% in the Korean War and to a 95% firing rate in the Vietnam War.

What are behaviour modification techniques that turn teenagers into reliable killing machines? These conditioning and psychological tricks are the same methods that are used on the Delta alters and the Delta systems of Total Mind-controlled slaves, and we will discuss those next. The factors that are weighed as an equation in the human mind to determine whether a human will kill another human are as follows:

· What is the benefit of the kill?

· How do recent experiences relate to the victim?

· How much physical, cultural, moral, social and mechanical DISTANCE is between the killer and the target.? The more distance the easier it gets.

· How intense is the demand from some authority to kill, and legitimate is this authority? If the killer respects the authority that is asking for him to kill, and is in close proximity of that authority he will likely obey that authority.

· Are there a group dynamic working, and if so what is the power and legitimacy of this group to absolve the killer from guilt?

· Are there any stumbling blocks from unresolved guilt from previous killings?

· What is the temperament of the potential killer?

AUTHORITY FACTORS ARE MAXIMIZED

In the programming, the programmer can set himself up as God, or a god. The programmer may also be a satanic cult leader which further increases the victim's regard for his power and authority. The programmers of total mind-controlled slaves have tremendous potential to cause their assassin alters to overcome any resistance to kill.

ACCOUNTABILITY & ANONYMITY

A Delta Model with many multiple alters incorporates a built in ability to remove personal accountability. If need be, the person can split off a new personality to perform a particularly odious job. The alters form a peer group which works just like a military unit to inhibit the natural reluctance to kill. This is because the closer a group of persons is, and the closer bonded, the more powerful the enabling. When military units lose 50% or more, the men often lose the will to continue killing, because the group dynamic fizzles out.

The programmers who program in the programming, and then later the programmers who program in specific killing missions, have worked long hours insuring that the assassin alters feel morally distant (superior), and socially distant. The victim is made out to be an inferior being who deserves to be punished and killed. The killer will be doing a great service to his fellow man and country to kill the "target". It may be refrained as if it is a holy mission, almost a crusade. Often times the "target" is not even spoken about in human terms. Perhaps the target is hypnotically portrayed as an ant, a bug, or some wild beast, or simply a target.

Hitler helped his military to kill by labelling non-Germans as Untermensch (subhumans). The Americans called the communist Vietnamese "gooks", and they in turn called Americans "monkeys". Because the mind-controlled assassin will not see the face of their victim due to hypnotic programming, they are also limited in seeing the humanness of their victims. Most of the missions for Delta slaves allow them to kill without the threat of being killed. But the Programmer may put the fear of being killed into the slave. They may hypnotically see some object of victim as a threat. One killer (due to programming) saw the men she killed as having a big penis that would hurt her, so her instinct to survive would kick in to help her assassinate these men.

Practice is given to assassins with situations similar to actual hand-to-hand killings to desensitize them to close range killing. With mind-controlled slaves usually actual live victims are used to get the slaves totally desensitized to killing. Because assassin parts are stripped of conscious thinking and empathy they are handicapped to really think about what they are doing to another human when they kill.

Still the intelligence agencies and the Illuminati know that somehow the brain still can latch onto guilt--somehow the brain still can perceive in some dim way that it is guilty of killing another human, so they cover their tracks by warrior cleansing rituals. Warriors and soldiers have traditionally done cleansing rituals when they finish a war. An example of a cleansing ritual would be a parade at the end of the war, where the country turns out to tell the soldiers what a great job they did. A programmed assassin in many cases can not receive a parade, but he can be given lots of praise for having done a great job for humanity, or his country, or whatever ideal the Programmer uses as a rationale.

Clock-Time Programming. The victim may see their head as a clock and may be tortured in such a fashion. Twelve o'clock is straight up between the eyes. Six o'clock is straight below the chin.

Monkey Alters.

The creation of animal alters has been covered in previous locations in this book and Vol. 2. However, I felt Lynne Moss-Sharmon's description of Monkey programming was worth including here. Lynne is a victim of mind control living at Halifax, Nova Scotia. In her description of the memory that goes to her drawing no. 29 she quotes what was said during the cages, "You stupid monkey. Into your cage. Hit her and put her back in her cage. Lights on. Monkey time. Monkey business."

Plant alters.

In the older models, they used plants and fruit, but in some of the newer models it appears that they are using samphires (combination beast-plant creatures) and hamadryads (man-plant creatures). Magic from underground springs is the cover story for how these plant-animal hybreds are made.

Presidential Models.

Include both children and adults. They carry NWO messages to world leaders. They often have passports with accordion additions stapled in, because they do so much travelling overseas. Presidential models are kept in numerous locations. If high level individuals need to slip away for nefarious use of slaves, they employ look-alikes to stand in for them, while they do their dirty activities. This is why Presidents such as Clinton and Bush got away with sexually using far more slaves than their schedule seems to indicate. Bush was a pedophile, while his double (who has recently lived in France) was a womanizer.

Prostitute Models.

Slaves designed to function as prostitutes must receive training to protect themselves. One possible problem might be a female prostitute who is accosted by an aggressive male, when she is not to allow herself to be used by him. She can be trained to jump up slap the man on the face, warn him that she kick his testicles next time, and then kiss the man in a submissive makeup fashion to smooth his bruised ego. A prostitute slave will also receive code words to let people, say people in a casino, know who she is. Deeper prostitute parts which need to perform sex for long periods of time accomplish this for their masters by switching alters and by ingesting speed. The mechanical nature that sexual alters have is illustrated by the "I CAN WALK, I CAN TALK" phrases of alters with doll programming.

Psychic models.

Both men and women slaves were created to carry out various psychic functions. For instance, the AntiChrist needs to be able to look at people and totally understand them psychologically and their systems of mind-control (alter systems, programming etc.). The abilities to successfully perform psychic functions have been tested for years before they were created within the AntiChrist.

Reporting Alters.

The construction of reporting alters is very straightforward behavior modification. For programming reporting alters, they use purpose fragment splits. In other words, these reporting alters are not given the full range and exposure to life, but they experience life from the vantage of their single purpose. Some therapists are reporting that they are converting reporting alters over by giving them ice cream. They are most likely only dealing with fronts. Since most therapists only deal with front alters, and front systems, these front reporting alters may even be set up so that these therapists think they have converted the reporting alters. The truth is that most of these reporting alters are fragments that don't know what hunger is. All the ice cream in the world is going to mean anything to them. (Cisco will deal with these issues in her part of this book.) The point is simply, these are special purpose fragments who only see life from the vantage point of their little job.

Now we will explain what first and second stage reporting alters are, and then how they are created. Some of the first stage reporting alters are trained to respond to 3-taps, some to telephone calls, lights, and some to codes. The first stage alters are children from 6 to 10. In an Illuminati system there will be families of reporting alters. Every level ("section") will have at least one group (family) of reporting alters. The second stage reporting alters are also children from 6 to 10, and they are taught to want Daddy's or Mommy's love. Girl systems seek "Daddy" (the Master) and boy systems often seek "Mommy" (the Master). They are taught to talk about therapy issues, programming issues, and movements by the system. They are linked to the computers, and the eye of the computer. Just to hear "Daddy's voice" is gratification to them.

At stage 1 of the creation of reporting alters, they are the result of the sensory deprivation tank, and are taken from the dissociated part of the mind that feels like it doesn't have a body, or that it is nothing. Stage 1 Reporting-special-purpose fragments of the mind are painfully shocked in some sensory deprivation environment when the hear 3 taps. The pain ceases when they open the door. They continue to be locked in place in the mind and painfully shocked until they learn the lesson, which is that the pain stops when the door is opened. Over and over they are taught, THE PAIN STOPS WHEN THE DOOR IS OPENED. When they hear tapping they want the pain to stop (probably they abreact their previous tortures) and they open the door to stop the pain. They have only one job, stop the pain by opening the door when three taps (or whatever other trigger/code/signal they are programmed for.)

Stage 2 Reporting-special-purpose alters are given a fuller view of life. They are the watchers in the system. They were created under such horrible torture that they left the body and hover over the body. These are Out-of-Body alters. They are also placed in a fogged room, where they are taught to become one with the fog. They are also told ghost stories like Casper the Ghost. Through the combination of all these programming tactics and techniques, they learn to be invisible. They hover over their assigned position in the system, invisible to all the other alters of that section. These alters have excellent rapid recall. They have none of the Straw Man programming that Gatekeeper receive to make them think they are stupid.

To reinforce the programming, the reporting alters are always treated kindly when they obey. (If you get one that hasn't been, suspect a plant, a setup.) Internal protector alters are given the job to insure that reporting alters never miss a call, or never miss responding to a cue. They will go to work and punish lax Stage 1 alters. Again, several therapists claim to have gotten reporting alters to defect from their jobs, but haven't dealt with their protector alters who are taskmasters. If the taskmasters haven't been dealt with, then suspect a ruse to get the therapist to think all is well. The reason this subject is dealt with here, is that some of the top well known therapists have spread information contrary to what is actually happening. That doesn't mean that there may not be an exception to the rule, but the Illuminati is not so stupid as to make reporting alters that defect because someone offered them an ice-cream cone.

Reporting alters are very hard to convert, because during their lifetime they are treated nicely. They experience a nice life if they behave (its the other alters that suffer.) The Stage 1 reporting alter merely says HELLO and waits for the response HELLO PRINCESS. This is a standard format. If the HELLO PRINCESS occurs, the mind automatically in a flash switches to the Stage 2 reporting alter.

To reinforce the original programming, which would lose its effect over time, the programmer hypnotically command the reporting alters to think of their programming when they see certain objects, for instance, certain types of men's clothing, animals, certain cigarettes or lighters, certain trees etc. Everyday life is used then to reinforce their programming. The Stage 1 alters are also trained to have back-up amnesia, where they forget what they have done after they have responded to the cue. Once the job is done, the job is forgotten. Like the Vol. 2 book reported, reporting alters can perceive themselves in various shapes and figures, and they can be locked up in eggs or other containers also. The Stage 2 alters look forward to Daddy or Mommy coming.

Cisco's system, which helped at the programming level, verifies that during the 50's, 60's, 70's and 80's none of the slaves got free. The Illuminati was not the least bit concerned about losing a slave. They had not lost a mind-controlled slave in centuries, so the recent victories in a few slaves getting their freedom in recent years are a historical first. Many therapist who make great therapeutic claims are not freeing their slaves at all, but these slaves continue to be used by their masters. The masters just laugh at the deceptions they have pulled over legitimate but naive therapists. Their reporting alters are a key to their control and they have numerous reporting alters in families spread throughout a standard reporting system. If one realizes that the same mentality that created Stalin's USSR, or that created Big Brother is at work here, you will realize that they need a spy-in-the-camp on every block so to speak. Everybody watches everyone. They make many spies within a system of alters. The reporting alters are given some script such as "You can diffuse from supersolidity to insubstance, you can grow big or small, and can change shape to any for you wish." This makes it easier for them to go through the internal system.

Repunzel alter.

In the internal Mother's of Darkness castle there is often a Repunzel alter created by the Repunzel story, who has magical hair and can change her size at will. She is not an Illuminati alter, even though she resides at their castle.

Transformation alters.

In Chapter 5, in the section on how Fantasia was used as a programming script, the fairy alters (creative parts of the child's mind) were discussed. The Illuminati also create magical alters that can transform other alters into objects. The script for this is Alice In Wonderland, although some newer scripts are also being used (like Xanth's sorceress Vadne). When an alter is changed into an object, it does so without losing its character. This is where cartoons have been helpful to lay the foundation for visualizing this. When one enters particular internal rooms one needs to pick up certain objects in the room to get through portals to the next world. What makes the internal world difficult is that it is set up to change its appearance. An alter may think they see one thing internally and then the scene totally shifts. An alter may look into a mirror and turn into a leaf.

Internal Wall alters.

Some alters will be made into walls. This is why is can be difficult to go around internal walls. These alters shift so that no one can get around them.

Structuring Internal Programmer Alters.

The procedure for the creation of Internal Programmer Alters is several steps. After the child victim has been traumatized they are sorely in need of love. Using a drug that gives a sense of peace and ectasy, along with hypnosis, certain parts of the system are bonded to the programmer. The child alters are told to forget the trauma and merge with the programmer. It's instinct to want to be loved, touched and comforted. This is repeated so that they feel the "peace of God" with their three primary abusers. Scriptures about the peace of God are used to reinforce this programming. These alters who feel one with the master programmer will form a cover group which will pacify any front alters who think negatively about the external programmer. These alters are in turn used to build the actual programmers. The actual programmers will be programmed to take on the characteristics of the master programmers and the Grand Dame working with them. These alters will be formed via split brain programming so they have only logic, no emotion. They can interact for years with the rest of the system and will feel no emotion for the hell and abuse that they put hundreds of other alters through. These controllers will stand behind the Grand Druid Council to insure that they carry out their function correctly.

STRUCTURING WITH THE GRAND DRUID COUNCIL.

In Illuminati mind-controlled slaves it is typical to place at the bottom of the system a pyramid shaped table with a crystal prism life force within the pyramid's center. Around this pyramid table are the Grand Druid Council and Satan hovers over the entire thing. Mirrors on both sides surround the pyramid. The Grand Druid Council can astrally project and attend rituals. There are cover Councils to throw the unapproved seeker off. In fact, every section within the slave may have a Grand Druid Council. These are not the computers, but function closely with the computers. When the life force dies it becomes black. The slave will told that the life force of the system is within the pyramid which is inside the Grand Druid Council's table. The pyramid will spin constantly from the energy of Lucifer, and the Grand Druid Council may well spin on their table in the opposite direction. Each position on the Grand Druid Council (GDC) is significant, because if determines what that Council person is allowed to do. (This is a mirror of real life.)

The type of programming and commands that a particular council person can carry out are determined by their position around the table. The no. 3 position has access to the center pyramid. Within the spinning pyramid are 3 programmer positions, one for each corner of the triangle. If only one programmer occupies all three positions you are dealing with a master programmer. Very often a system is programmed by lesser programmers, and the inner pyramid has more than one programmer inside the pyramid. If a group/ series of cult programmers is used, one may see them represented somewhere in the system by their cult names.

Growing through the Grand Druid Council's table will be the generational demonic roots of a tree. Tied up at the base of the tree entwined in the roots is the life force of a foetus that has been sacrificed to empower the slave's mind-control system, as well as connect the slave to people that he or she is teamed with. During occult ritual the foetus is eaten as a seed. The dead child is connected to the roots. Another child, the child who is connected to the memory of these rituals will also be connected to the root of the tree. This child alter will not be able to talk or scream because it is locked in the horrible memories of some humiliating ritual. This child alter may have things in its penis or rectum, it may be covered with filth, it's skin is bruised and tender. This may be the "core"--the birth child.

In male slaves, sometimes the birth child or a first core split called "the core" is placed in the tree roots rather than the carousel. Egg shaped demonic power bases will also be set in at the root of the tree. The core of some slaves will be removed to the astral plane. The Grand Druid Council will astral project to different spheres and different ceremonies. This gets into black magic such as the 777 book of Aleister Crowley touches on, where there are colors for each planet for astral projection.

While we are discussing the deeper parts to a system, let's discuss the compass. Each system has a compass built into it, that is incredibly important. The 4-demons (goddesses) which control the 4 directions are called Quarter-Regents. The Eastern one controls Wind & Air. The Northern one controls the elemental Earth. The Western one controls water realms. And the Southern one controls fire.

STRUCTURING THE SHADOW ALTERS

Alters which are created in the sensory deprivation tanks which have no sense of being attached to a body are used in clusters on each level (section or world) of an Illuminati system of alters. These alters are the ones who no one else can see because they have no body, and yet they are the shadows that know what's going on in the outside world. Every level has access to what is going on in the outside world through the eyes of these shadow alters, but many alters do not care. Nor will the shadow alters tell everyone on the level. These clusters of shadows are also chained together, so that a link exists between them. They have no sense of self. They sometimes serve as directors to guide the child slave. They may protect the child by telling it to get home, to call home, or to not be frightened it will be OK. They are also willing to mislead therapists.

STRUCTURING IN THE MIRRORS

One of the movies which was developed to help program in the internal mirrors was the movie "The Hungry Glass" made in the early '50s. Let's review The Hungry Glass movie so that those who aren't familiar with it, can see the programming elements of the movie. The movie is about a fictitious haunted mansion that was built near the sea by a rich man named Bellman. The mansion lays dormant for decades until a couple buy the mansion. The mansion and its window is described as "a jewel box to pull the silver off the sea."

When they move in they experience many strange things connected with mirrors and glass. In the Monarch programming, glass and mirrors are similar. Many of the mirrors in a system are really one-way windows. The following are some quotes from the movie:

· "mirrors bring a house to life"

· "I'm great at turning nightmares into daydreams."

· "don't know if I saw it.. .it's imagination playing tricks...never get it out of your system."

· "we're both suggestible to suggestion...

· "...saw something and imagined the rest.. .just plain fear. ..did I see something supernatural?"

· "If you want anything just scream."

· "Miracles can be done with concentration."

· I got the house in order with "spell, book and candle" which is a phrase referring to witchcraft.

· you "never grow old in the mirrors". When alters of a slave look in a mirror it happens just like in the movie, they see themselves as young, which is a strong hypnotic image they have been programmed to see.

What the movie shows is that it is lethal to break mirrors. And if you go through mirrors you fall to your death. The one woman as well as a little girl are curious about the mirrors and they are pulled into the mirrors and die. In other words, the programming message is don't be curious about the mirrors nor go into the mirrors. There are demons in the mirrors.

In the movie they use the word "bogeyman". The room of mirrors is locked, and the message of the movie is, don't open locked doors in your internal system. In the movie, when Gil looks in the mirror, he sees a protector of the mirrors. This in the programming is called the KEEPER OF THE MIRROR, and is a demonic entity or demons placed to protect the mirror. Things are layered and hidden in a system behind mirrors. It also gives the idea that if you look into a mirror, even if you are physically old, the mirror can lie and give you a youthful appearance.

Young actor William Shatner, of later Star Trek fame plays the leading role in the movie. He tries to rationally explain things but gives up, when explanations fail. This is encouraging the small slave who would see the movie to think, if an adult can't figure these things out rationally, then the explanations for what I am seeing during programming are supernatural. William Shatner was raised in Catholic Montreal, Quebec and went to McGill Univ. when Dr. White (Ewen Cameroon) was carrying out programming there. He graduated in 1952 and married Gloria Rand. He has acted in a number of strange movies designed for programming, and it appears they have used him repeatedly over the years as a tie in to familiarize the slave to him. He also acted in The World of Suzie Wong (1958), The Brothers Karamazov (1958), The Devil's Rain (1978), Teklords (1991). The Hungry Glass was produced by William Freye, who also did some other movies for the Network. In some areas of a system, the script is that only the "dead"--alters who are so disconnected to their bodies they see themselves as spirits are allowed to cross between different internal worlds by using passwords such as "ELIADE". At other times, alters are given words to return to their "own time period" such as NICRO NECTRUM NECTO.

STRUCTURING THE TAPESTRY

A script is given for all standard Illuminati systems for an internal Sorceress to be assigned the making of tapestries. The tapestries enable alters to go into other worlds, in other words they are mirror gateways. For instance the sorceress may weave a door into the tapestry. Going into the mirror, going over the rainbow, going through walls or picture tapestries are ways that alters go from one world into another state.

STRUCTURING THE ALTER FAMILIES BY SPINNING

Spinning is used in a variety of programming purposes. We will review these together, so that a comparison can be made of the different purposes. Spinning tortures (which the victim endures while in drugged hypnotic states) are used extensively by the programmers as they construct alter systems. Programmed multiples will frequently complain of "spinning". All at once, whole sections of alters will begin spinning and getting dizzy. During such an abreaction, you will notice that the eyes change, the victim will appear disoriented and stare, or even grimace as if being rotated at a high speed. The head and/or body will rotate slightly during the abreaction.

During the programming of such a spin program, the programmer will lay in the experience for an entire section of alters, and attach the visual image of falling into an abyss, a cyclone, a tornado, a vortex, or a whirlwind to the memory of being spun. When a system goes into spinning the power of numerous memories, and the power of the dizzy spinning makes it difficult for much of anything. Certain alters trigger the spinning and certain alters maintain the spinning. In fact some spinning alters take pride in their spinning abilities. Obviously, their programmers commended them when they did their job correctly.

Another use of spin tortures is to create spin families. The spin torture creates spin alters which have been spun off a "parent" alter. The parent alter may later be age progressed hypnotically and given care over her children alters who she or he spun off during the torture. Spinning is a way of creating dissociation, and the spin memory dissociates the spin children alters from their original source alter. This creates alters which are close together internally, but dissociated. The spin training and memories are then used to teach these alters to spin away the pain. Spin alters are used for some of the worst abuse and the spinning sensation is used internally by these alters to dissociate the severe abuse they receive.

The actual mechanisms to do the spinning torture vary. Some are rotating tables, some are more upright like a Wheel of Fortune type wheel, or "Space trainer" type machine where the victim is inside the rotating mechanism. Flashing lights are used along with the spinning, so that flashing lights can be used in the future to cause the alter(s) to abreact the spinning sensation. Verbal triggers are also placed in. The spin kittens will actually physically go around when commanded. Certain alters will be trained to re-create mentally the sensations of spinning via enhance imagery and memory training. This is so that the system will be self-governing and self-propelled. The spin traumas may be used to help create the ring within ring, circle within a circle effect that is structured into so many systems.

Programs that are put in via Spin-based traumas or attached to spin-based traumas often affect wide areas of a system, rather than individual alters. For instance, if an area of the system is mis-behaving, a tornado program, or a tumbleweed program may be set off by the internal governing mechanisms and an entire world of alters will feel the program. Victims of mind-control often speak about walls full of different faces. The walls of faces are people who are in need of help. They are shown repeatedly to the victim, to solicit the emotion of wanting to run & rescue. This then is used as the cover program for alters for them to want to run back to the cult to "rescue" their "friends". Generally, all that will be experienced is the memory of walls of faces and the urge to run. Another element of programming, often seen in military programming, is where the victim is left in a totally dark room, and then for men, a hypnotic motherly voice is played repeatedly to them in the dark. For women, they may get their primary handler's hypnotic voice.

More structures used to build a system

p_7-2.jpg

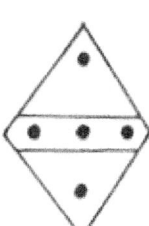 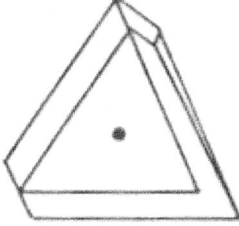 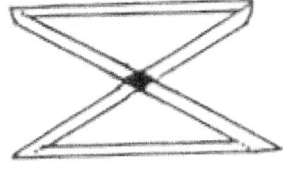

CHAPTER 8: THE SCIENCE OF BODY MANIPULATION & PROGRAMMING

Implants that manipulate the body and its functions have been discussed in Chapter 6. The body manipulating implants were placed there to keep all of the implant information intact in one chapter, even though some body manipulating implants are not electrically activated. When our previous book The Illuminati Formula Used to Create an Undetectable Total Mind Controlled Slave (1996) covered the 12 Sciences of mind-control, its chapter 8 on the manipulation of the human body did not cover the ancient secrets of cranial manipulation, nor the modern secrets of genetic mind manipulation via applications of radiation with chemicals.

A. CRANIAL MANIPULATION--Important Top Secrets of Illuminati Mind-control disguised as Muggings & other events.

INTRODUCTION

The information in this section exposes a previously unknown type of mind-control.

· The woman ran tripping through the woods, slipping on the wet leaves attacked by an unknown assailant for an unknown reason. The report of her mugging the next day never gets beyond the policeman who hears her story.

· A wife cries softly to herself as her husband beats her. The crime goes unnoticed in a busy world.

What do these acts of violence have in common with orthodontics, orthopedics, rolfing and other structural treatments? The shocking fact is that some of these kind of events happen for purposes of mind control. Any trauma to the head, be it an accidental fall, a fight, a bullet wound, or a motorcycle or car accident can cause permanent structural brain injury. But what passes for accidents are at times carefully designed & brilliantly executed cranial manipulations designed by the Illuminati to create specific mental and personality changes.

In order to get closer to the bottom of this type of mind-control, the author, Fritz, obtained the same books that cranial osteopaths study, and the same books that disclose the modern scientific studies of head shape/facial features in relation to personality, and then studied them. This author has tried to get as close as an outsider can get to understanding what a cranial-manipulating programmer has going on in his head. Until this chapter was published, the Illuminati's ability to perpetrate this mind control has been a complete secret. This is the first time that this secret has ever reached the public light of day. It is a secret known only to a handful of people in the world. It is a secret that various parts of Satan's realm have carefully guarded for centuries. How I got this secret is a long story. It is the confluence of many streams of research coming together. The people, who carry out this type of programming hate the God of the Holy Bible.

This art's academy's own literature speaks about "the Force". "The Mysterious Vital Force is a Universal Power of Intelligence present in all things." (Direct quote from the Cranial Academy's official newsletter). This is a Force similar to Jung's "Collective unconsciousness" and Star War's The Force. The God of the Universe, who loves each and every person in spite of their hatefulness & rejection, has also warned that all things will be revealed.

If I didn't write this, God would simply seek some other avenue to expose these hideous secrets. Who would have imagined that the Illuminati and a particular aspect of their mind control would end up to be connected to Transcendental Meditation, Kung Fu, modern Osteopathy, Theosophy and the Rosicrucians? None of us who research these groups are surprised that they are all tied together in the occult via the SPIN principle. However, you may be surprised by how they are also all affiliated to this form of mind control, which can be disguised as a typical mugging!

Even the Mafia are able to produce heartless criminal alters using cranial manipulation, and they don't have the best skills at doing it either. How do victims of cranial mind-control respond? Most victims follow the subtle guidance of their mind, completely ignorant of why their mind wants to go a particular direction. Some even attribute their mental drives to the metaphysical world. This author's hope is that the truth of this chapter will help restore free will to numerous victims of this secret mind-control technique. In spite of the extreme lack of information on this type of mind-control, it appears to have been more widely used than one might have guessed.

The benefit of this type of mind-control to the programmers is that a change in the body and head structure of a victim is permanent and undetectable, in contrast to hypnotic or drug induced states. A further benefit, is that a skilled person could be tampered with without their realization. Some of the procedures reduce the alertness of the subject, separate him from his memories and make the person more receptive to other forms of mind-control even if the subject has had no prior programming.

One example of a technique that causes a rapid adaption of the cranial bones with an accompanying neurological effect would be to flick the occiput posteriorly and inferiorly on exhalation (extension), then lift the vault (parietal) bones up from the temporal area on inhalation (flexion), then rapidly draw the vault posteriorly and inferiorly, then dislocate the sphenoid into a vertical or lateral strain position. These procedures will also speed up the appearance of aging. This is just one example of a quick procedure to control the mind of another. And as Cisco's section will bring out, power (including power over other humans) is the goal of the occult underworld.

A lot of research has gone into producing this finished report. At first glance, the polished nature of this chapter's report, which is replete with so many sources, may tend to mislead some people into thinking that this type of mind-control hasn't been secret. Quite to the contrary, the pieces of the puzzle were well hidden. This type of mind-control has been very secret and it is only the result of long hard research that the many divergent pieces of the puzzle have been assembled and placed into a coherent picture for the reader. Although the possibility exists that some may misapply the intent of this chapter and use this for evil, like so much of this book's material the really bad guys already have it. On the flip side, the potential for good, if medical science will use this secret knowledge for good is tremendous.

For instance, compare the improved appearance of Ivana Trump after her cranial work was done. This chapter has the potential positive by-product that others will be inspired to explore how cranial manipulation can be used to benefit humankind. God is in the business of turning evil into good. But perhaps in our fallen corrupted world, this secret knowledge which is being exposed in this chapter will no longer find good men worthy of this information who are also capable enough to put it to good practice. If so, then so be it. At the very least, some people will gain strength of heart to realize once again that when one know's how God's creation operates--it is easy to see how a paradise without problems could be created. Man's worst enemy is man. The Illuminati are sitting on technology and knowledge that could bring about almost a virtual paradise, but they are hoarding this technology and knowledge, and suppressing it. Further, rather than helping mankind, they are using this cranial knowledge to reward those who are friendly to their Luciferian hierarchy, and to abuse those who dare to seriously impede their agenda. After you read this chapter and are aware that the secrets of cranial manipulation could rescue children with cerebral palsy, and some of the children with Down syndrome, you too will cry with this author at the needless suffering that the Illuminati have perpetrated upon mankind in their quest for total domination of this globe.

CRANIAL BLOOD PRESSURE has been kept a SECRET

Recently, a Dr. Yoshiaki Omura in New York, discovered that the blood pressure in the brain is vastly different than the rest of the body. The blood pressure in the brain has major consequences on one's thinking (such as irritability, & insomnia) and also affects other things in the body, such as muscle tightness in the neck. High brain blood pressure is called cephalic hypotension syndrome. Yet, when this doctor went to see what the medical books/research institutions said about brain blood pressure, he found nothing. He has been making his discoveries known in speaking engagements. He recently addressed a large audience of Chinese doctors. When this author met Yoshiaki Omura, I unsuccessfully attempted to tell Yoshiaki the reason that this knowledge was suppressed was in the interest of mind-control; Dr. Omura has been treating various illnesses by working with patients' brain blood-pressure. The diagnosis of other problems, such as the early stages of cancer, has been done earlier by Omura by monitoring brain blood pressure levels than MRI tests results.

CEREBRAL SPINAL FLUID kept SECRET

Another important fluid in the brain, discovered by others is Cerebral spinal fluid. There are many technical details about this CS fluid that are extremely important to the way the mind-body functions. In this chapter, we will discuss a number of areas of medical science, acupuncture, personology etc. concerning the brain, which when known and used by skilled practitioners can give the practitioner control over another person.

The Mystery Schools and particular bloodlines have kept much of this knowledge to themselves and continue to keep the best secrets. Daniel Whiteside, a pioneer in behavior genetics and understanding the relationship of the shape of the skull to personality, provides some important confirmations of how the Mystery Schools transmitted this secret cranial knowledge.

In his important work "The Background of Structure/Function" (pp.2-3) he outlines that Structure/Function was studied and taught by the Greek Mystery Schools, and was the basis of the Roman Empire's psychology. The Catholic church suppressed this knowledge. This knowledge was kept alive by the Cabalistic philosophers and the Arabs, until the Knights Templars brought it back. If we build upon the information that Daniel has provided we discover that from the Knights Templars, this knowledge went to the leadership of the Prieure de Sion, who in turn disseminated low forms of it to the occult groups that they controlled. For instance, the Rosicrucian Order for North & South America in their Vol. 8 of their Rosicrucian Manual (San Jose, CA: Supreme Grand Lodge AMORC) pp. 91-108 deals with the spinal column, nerves, & the influence of color & music on the nervous system, etc. Grand Master Lewis writes on pg. 103, "The Rosicrucians were the first to have a complete outline of this system [nervous system] and to know exactly what part of the human body was connected with every other part."

One witness reported to this author that he watched an acupuncture specialist repeatedly work on clients' brains by inserting 3 long skinny needles through the skull. The acupuncture specialist bragged to this man that he could completely control a human via his skill with the needles. He showed this witness how he could kill pain, and how he could kill self-will by touching minute areas within the brain. He was also skilled in manipulating the mind of the client in other ways too with the needles.

There has been a great deal of research into determining what the different purposes of the different areas of the brain are. Several researchers have independently identified that the ability to make choices, that is what we call "free will", is located near the Broadman Area 24 in the Anterior Cingulate Sulcus. Tampering with this area can disturb a person's ability to have free will. (For more information on this one could begin with Crick, Francis. The Astonishing Hypothesis The Scientific Search for the Soul.)

Acupuncture was virtually unknown to mainstream Americans until a NY Times journalist in China reported that he was successfully treated with acupuncture in 1971. Pressure points can also be manipulated by Acupressure, which is similar to acupuncture except fingers rather than needles are used. This is just one example of a related technique which went unnoticed for decades (actually centuries by the Western World.)

The mugging-mind control information in this article has gone unnoticed by mainstream America too. Time Magazine, Nov. 4, 1991, reported that there are four types of alternative medicine, which they classified as Life-Style (such as Macrobiotics, Ayurvedic medicine, and holistic medicine), Botanical (such as Homeopathy, Herbalism, and Aromatherapy), Mental healings (such as with Crystals, Guided imagery, biofeedback and Hypnotherapy) and Manipulative/Hands-on (such as Reflexology, Rolfing, Shiatsu, Alexander tech., Chiropractic, and Acupressure & Acupuncture).

Reflexology dates back to at least 2330 B.C. in Egypt. Shiatsu is a Japanese finger pressure deep massage of pressure points is over 1,000 years old. The skull & head bone manipulations that are being exposed for the first time in this report, were used in ancient Egypt and other parts of the ancient world. That Nov., 91 Time Magazine article did not mention that acupressure/acupuncture has been knowledge that the secret societies in China studied and often kept hidden for centuries, as a part of Wushu (martial arts) in China.

For instance, in a recent Chinese book 72 Consummate Arts Secrets of the Shaolin Temple, (pub. by Fujian Science & Technology Pub. Co. Ltd., Fujian, China, 1990) by Wu Jiaming and translated by Rou Gang, diagrams and explanations are given of the important head/body points (for acupressure/ acupuncture/& kung fu.) What is important for our discussion on mind control are the Kung Fu (Wushu) points in the head. This book gives 4 points on the front of the head, seven on the side of the head, and four on the back side of the head. The Shaolin Buddhist monks have kept their martial arts (which is called "Kung-fu" in the U.S. and "Wushu" in China) a secret hidden within their temple on Song Mountain, Henan Province. This Buddhist monastery has a long history of teaching kung-fu and is exerting a big influence in the world as its type of kung fu spreads. The Japanese took kung-fu from the Chinese many years ago and then developed from it specialized forms of kung-fu, such as Karate, Judo, etc.

THE CHINESE SECRET OCCULT SOCIETY CONNECTION

The important item that this paragraph will emphasize is that the Chinese secret societies studied the pressure points on the skull completely. They learned how the skull could be manipulated and what it would do to a person. Of course this information was only revealed to the best Chinese kung-fu experts. It is sometimes referred to as the skill of bone setting. In China, bone-setters are a type of Chinese doctor which are popular to some Chinese. These bone-setters have kept their secrets within many generations of families who specialize in bone-setting and also within the secret Triad societies.

The Communist government admitted that it has failed to pry family bone-setting secrets from the families that have passed these secrets down generationally. This is due in part to the strong Chinese belief in ancestor worship and strong families. A family's secrets are considered one source of its strength. One communist Chinese tactic to pry the secrets loose was their "folkart barefoot doctor" system which they hoped the bone-setters would join.

Junxie Li wrote in 1990 that a Chinese Kung Fu document shows that bone manipulation was practiced as early as 2700 B.C. The secrets have been passed down for many years. An American writer stated in 1983, "Traditional Chinese medicine and chiropractic are remarkably alike in their underlying theories...Through deep massage at the occiput [head bone], for example, (contemporary) Chinese practitioners find that they can bring down high blood pressure, a practice analogous to that of chiropractors."

A Buddhist monk Bodhidharma is credited to having brought the martial arts and healing arts associated with martial arts to China. He must have been a very strong individual to have made the 2,500 miles journey which back before there were paths or maps must have been more like an 8,000 miles of perilous journey on foot from India over the Himalayas to the Chinese interior. Bodhidharma had studied big cats, dogs, bears, insects and other animals to learn how they defend and attack. His physical, mental and spiritual teachings became known later as Zen Buddhism. His monastery became the famous Shaolin Monastery. A master of the Shaolin Monastery would have two dragons deeply branded into his flesh. It is said that the Red Dragon represented knowledge in ancient China.

In the Tang Dynasty (6 18-907 A.D.) some of the Kung Fu experts at that time were Li Bai and Twelfth Sister Li of the Li family. Madame Gong Sun and Twelfth Sister Li composed a famous Xihe Sword Dance combining martial arts and choreographic arts. The Li family kept some of their secret martial arts skills (including bone setting) secret for hundreds of years, and as a top Illuminati family are secretly proud of their occult knowledge and history.

To illustrate how the head has been studied are some quotes from 72 Consummate Arts Secrets of the Shaolin Temple,

"TAJYANG ACUPOINT (Sun Acupoint)

Located on both sides of the forehead, the left being Tai Yang and the right Tai Yin. Nowadays it is generally called Taiyang Acupoint being a vital part of the head. It is 'Dead Acupoint' among the twenty-four Acupoints. One will be faint or even die if it is slightly seized.

TAINRONG ACUPOINT

Located on the back of ears and is in parallel with the ear. It lies on the outer-side of Fen Yi Acupoint, and is above the Tian Chuang acupoint. It is a vital acupoint of the back of one's head. It is also a 'Dead Acupoint' among the twenty-four acupoints.

FENGFU ACUPOINT

Located in the centre of the low part of one's back head and is below the Naohu Acupoint but above the Yamen Acupoint. It's in parallel with the left and right FenYi Acupoint. It is a single Acupoint. It is a vital part of one's back brain. It is a 'Dead Acupoint', too. If this acupoint is seized, one may faint or die immediately."

Washu (Chinese Martial Arts) went underground into the Chinese occult secret societies, because the rulers feared that it would make the common people too powerful, so they frequently banned the teaching of martial arts. The teachers of Kung fu teach their pupils that Kung-Fu has both an external work with the hands, feet and body and an internal work which refers to the occult spiritual work that provides the energy and spirit to do the martial arts that Kung fu masters do.

The Shaolin Temple masters have studied the human skeleton very closely for centuries. The books Shaolin Long Fist Kung-Fu by Yang Jwing-Ming & Jeff Bolt and The Way of the Sun Dragon Chinese Martial Art of Tai-Yang Lung Tao are other examples of books in English which also show points to hit on the head. The art of manipulating the skull and other bones has travelled from the secret societies to about 20% of China's doctors. As mentioned, this skill is called "bone setting."

Some Kung Fu experts and Chinese doctors learn bone setting, including how to work with the skull bones. In 1974, the U.S. Dept. of Health, Education and Welfare (which has been full of New Agers) along with the Fogarty International Center of the National Institutes of Health which works with WHO of the U.N. set up a conference in Seattle, WA which focused on Health Care in China. The U.S. Government Printing Office then printed up in 1975 edited versions of the papers presented at the conference. The resulting book on Medicine in Chinese Cultures has some very pertinent information to the ancient secret Chinese art of manipulating skull bones. After W.W. II, Chinese bone setters began to use X-rays. (p. 261)

· The Chinese bone setters had their own professional associations. (p. 261-262)

· Bone-setters' societies have been interwoven with secret societies, the link being Chinese kung-fu (martial arts) which the secret societies control. "Bone-setters get their knowledge of anatomy from practicing kung-fu, for part of the instruction is in how the bones and muscles work." (p. 262.)

· Bone-setters, in order to practice in Hong Kong, generally find it advantageous to get (buy) protection from the Triads (Chinese Secret Societies controlled by the Li Illuminati family, as well as other powerful Chinese families.) Doctors are licensed in Hong Kong according to British standards and bone-setters have not received much recognition from the British government. But someone connected with the CIA verbally let out that they have been very interested in studying Chinese bone setting.

T'ai Chi, is the philosophy associated in China with the yin-yang. It is incorporated into the name T'ai Chi Chuan (Great Origin Fist) which are the calisthenics which many chinese practice on a daily basis. The advanced student learns 128 movements. Practitioners of the exercises can be seen exercising at dusk, especially in Kuala Lumpur. "Instruction in Chinese medicine is considered a normal part of the training to become a T'ai Chi instructor, and many instructors are said to be skilled in bone setting and the treatment of sprains and strains.

One of the most famous T'ai Chi instructors in Kuala Lumpur, an elderly man who received his training in China many years ago, is indeed famous locally as a bone-setter. It is clear that it is difficult to draw a line between T'ai Chi Chuan and preventive or even curative medicine." (Medicine In Chinese Cultures..., p.310 Bruce Lee, who came from a very wealthy branch of the Li family, was half Chinese and half American by blood. He grew up in Hong Kong, and was taught Chinese martial arts beginning at the age of 14. Bruce Lee came to America, and was very American in his thinking. Due to his American thinking, he thought radically different from the traditional Chinese martial arts mentality, and there is strong evidence to suggest it cost him his life. He not only exposed to the western world secrets of Chinese martial arts, but he mixed various types of moves from the various oriental schools of martial arts. For doing this, he made many of the Zen martial arts masters furious.

When Bruce Lee died at 32 in 1972, his body was like a teenager's and it was in great shape. Bruce Lee had no equal in the martial arts. The Chinese/Hong Kong press felt that he was killed by the Zen martial arts masters of China. In fact, his student Abdul described Bruce Lee as a "renegade Taoist Priest." Whether or not Bruce and his son Brandon were killed by the Triads and/or the Secret Martial Arts Societies of China, doesn't change the fact that Bruce Lee angered them for exposing their martial arts to the western world.

From research in this area, it is clear that there are still secrets kept by Chinese martial arts which only a few carefully chosen members of secret societies know. Bruce Lee did not make it to this inner circle. The inner groups of the secret societies trade favors. This is a standard method of payoff. Well trained martial arts cults that know some of the secrets of cranial manipulation can be asked to assault a human target. What happens if the head injury is not fine-tuned?

Laurence Miller Ph.d. in the article "Unusual Head Injury Syndromes..." (The Journal of Cognitive Rehabilitation 11-12/'94, p. 13) states, "Memory disorders are virtually universal in head injury and typically top the list of symptoms reported by patients. The 'standard' pattern of posttraumatic memory disorder - and indeed, for organic memory disorders generally - consists of well-preserved old memories, patchy or impaired memory for events immediately preceding the injury (retrograde amnesia) and following the injury (anterograde amnesia), and subsequent difficulty learning and retaining new information."

This is exactly opposite of what the handlers want. They want the victim to forget the past abuse, but be able to remember a series of new commands for a new operation precisely. This underscores the reason WHY the person doing the assault needs to be skilled. There is no doubt that Chinese martial arts are being used to mug people in order to alter their thinking. The secret potential of Chinese Martial Arts to alter a person's skull bones and thinking has been one secret worth killing to preserve. Miller also points out that frontal lobe injuries can weaken the subject's hold over reality. Although Miller writes about accidental injuries, his article is extremely well researched about the wide variety of mental problems that develop from different injuries. The medical world have named many of these specific problems such as the Ganser Syndrome, the Capgras Syndrome, & Cotard's Syndrome. While this kind of research is helpful to establish that different specific injuries to the head can create specific symptoms, the written material is not specific about how to intentionally create a symptom.

The ancient EGYPTIAN CONNECTION

Skull manipulation was used by the ancient Egyptian priesthood, as well as trauma-based mind-control, astral projection, and hypnosis. At least some of these secrets got passed on to later secret societies.

THE TIBETAN CONNECTION

One religious black magic group are the Tibetan monks. Their man-god Dalai Lama, is coveted as a guest of many of the top Illuminati, Mishpucka, and other occult figures around the world. In 1966, the Dalai Lama wrote the book Opening of the Wisdom-Eye, which is typically referred to as the third-eye area which is slated by the NWO to be the initiation site for the mark of the Beast. Many leading European occultists have gone to Tibet to learn from the black magicians of Tibet. Hitler imported hundreds of Tibetan monks for his Third Reich. Nazi expeditions were sent to Tibet; and in 1942, Hitler, because of his occult ideas about Asia & Tibet, was excited to plant a Nazi flag on the highest peak of the Caucasian mountains, Mt. Elbrus, at the specific time of 11 a.m.

For those who didn't realize how dark were the secrets of the Tibetan monks, just a small sampling of books on their black magic secrets include: David-Neels' Magic & Mystery in Tibet (1958), Bromage's Tibetan Yoga, Beyer's The Cult of Tara- -Magic & Ritual in Tibet (1978), the Tibetan Book of the Dead (and commentaries about it), Suzuki's The Zen Doctrine of No Mind (1973), and Thomas' Out of This World to Forbidden Tibet (1954).

Qigong is the Chinese word for the healing arts taught within the secret schools of Martial Arts. Tibetans go to the S.W. National University in China to learn Qigong. Dapang Qigong is a derivative of Qigong where both martial arts and healing are taught together. One of the secrets of the Tibetan monks, is the physical manipulation of the third eye. T. Lobsang Rampa, a Tibetan from one of the 10 elite families of Tibet, at the age of seven entered the Chakpori Lamasery, the Temple of Tibetan Medicine, where the Tibetan masters taught healing arts including astral projection, clairvoyance and levitation.

Their mystic arts are similar to what the Illuminati believe in and practice. For instance, they learn about the silver cord that connects people. Upper-class boys such as Lobsang received extremely severe treatment from the time they were born to insure that they were tough enough to survive the harsh Tibetan life. Lobsang described the traumas of early boyhood as "brutal", but then adds on page 18 of his book The Third Eye, "Under this system weaklings did not survive, but those who did could survive almost anything." Children were kept awake eighteen hours a day, and worked hard during that time. Even very small babies are kept awake, so that according to Tibetan belief "they shall not become demon invested."

On Lobsang's eighteenth birthday, the Lama of his monastery opened his third eye. Lobsang records the brutal ceremony in his book The Third Eye (Ballantine Books, 1956). Ballantine Books advertises on the cover of this book, "Learn the secrets of the most controversial power of the new age...The Third Eye"." Before this author relates what Lobsang "reveals" about this great secret of new age power, let me interject an informed opinion--this story may be a cover memory to hide what this author has found out is the REAL THIRD EYE manipulation. But first, let's see what Lobsang describes, and then we'll discuss it.

On the evening of his 18th birthday, Lobsang went to a little room in the monastery. Three lamas of high degrees came and bound his head tightly with an herbal compress to produce some kind of drug effect upon him. They came back and removed the herbal compress, and wiped his forehead clean. Then Lobsang describes, 'A strong-looking lama sat behind me and took my head between his knees. The second lama opened a box and removed an instrument made of shining steel. It resembled a bradawi except that instead of having a round shaft this one was U-shaped, and in place of a point there were little teeth around the edge of the "U." For some moments the lama looked at the instrument, and then passed it through the flame of the lamp to sterilize it.

The Lama...took my hands and said, 'This is quite painful, Lobsang, and it can only be done while you are fully conscious. It will not take very long, so try to keep as still as you can." I could see various instruments laid out, and a collection of herbal lotions, and I thought to myself: "Well, Lobsang, my boy, they will finish you one way or the other and there is nothing you can do about it--except keep quiet!" The lama with the instrument looked around to the others, and said, "All ready? Let us start now, the sun has just set."

He pressed the instrument to the centre of my forehead and rotated the handle. For a moment there was a sensation as if someone was pricking me with thorns. To me it seemed that time stood still. There was no particular pain as it penetrated the skin and flesh, but there was a little jolt as the end hit the bone. The pain was not sharp at all, just a pressure and a dull ache. I did not move with the Lama Mingyar Dondup looking on; I would rather have died than make a move or outcry. He had faith in me, as I in him, and I knew that what he did or said was right. He was watching most closely, with a little pucker of muscles in tension at the corners of his mouth. Suddenly there was a little scrunch and the instrument penetrated the bone. Instantly its motion was arrested by the very alert operator. He held the handle of the instrument firmly while the Lama ...passed him a very hard, very clean sliver of wood which had been treated by tire and herbs to make it as hard as steel. This sliver was inserted in the "U' of the instrument and slid down so that it just entered the hole in my head. The lama operating moved slightly to one side so that the Lama Mingyar Dondup could also stand in front of me. Then, at a nod from the latter, the operator, with infinite caution, slid the sliver farther and farther. Suddenly I felt a stinging, tickling sensation apparently in the bridge of my nose. It subsided, and I became apparently aware of subtle scents which I could not identify. That, too, passed away and was replaced by a feeling as if I was pushing, or being pushed, against a resilient veil.

Suddenly there was a blinding flash, and at that instant the Lama Mingyar Dondup said "Stop!". For a moment the pain was intense, like a searing white flame. It diminished, died and was replaced by spirals of colour, and globules of incandescent smoke. The metal instrument was carefully removed. The sliver of wood remained, it would stay in place for two or three weeks and until it was removed I would have to stay in this little room almost in darkness. No one would see me except these three lamas, who would continue my instruction day by day. Until the sliver was removed I would have only the barest necessities to eat and drink." As the projecting sliver was being bound in place so that it could not move, the Lama Mingyar Dondup turned to me and said, "You are now one of us, Lobsang. For the rest of your life you will see people as they are and not as they pretend to be."

ANOTHER EXAMPLE

Bill Schnoebelen, who has publicly been exposing Satanism, writes about his experiences as a vampire and Satanist in several books. In his book, Lucifer Dethroned, he describes a third eye experience that he had during an "astral projection." "It seemed my eyeballs were turning to molten steel. My forehead was about to explode. I felt a claw tear into my brow, right between but slightly above my eyebrows and insert itself into my brain like a white-hot poker. I tried to scream, but could not. My entire body felt like it was going to burst from being filled with roaring, flaming hot light....I felt like a fish on the end of a hook being hauled out of the water by my very brain. I screamed in pain, but it came out: 'Glory and Love for Lucifer! Hatred! Hatred! Hatred! to God be accursed!...'

In order to interpret his third eye experience, it needs to be asked where is Bill Schnoebelen coming from? This author's best evidence to answer that comes from personal testimony. People familiar with this author (Fritz) have contacted Schnoebolen about Fritz for years. Why has Bill Schnoebelen taken a very cold attitude to this chapter's author (Fritz) and his work? Why has he opposed and slandered this author, and this author's work like the Vol. 2 book, and other information that this author has been putting out to expose Illuminati mind-control since 1991. One would expect a genuine ex-Satanist to be supportive of someone who risks his life to rescue Satanists from bondage. The reason I introduce personal testimony is that I know what side of things I am on, which is God's side, and when people like Bill Schnoebolen oppose me from the get-go, without even meeting me, it is solid evidence to me where they are coming from. From what Schnoebolen writes about his third eye experience, and from what this author has learned of third eye cranial manipulation, it appears that Bill is still under some cult deception and is very likely still under the mind-control that placed his cover memory of his third-eye experience into him.

It is very likely that both Lobsang and Bill were in a trance state induced by drugs, hypnosis and dissociation from pain, and that a screen memory was laid in on top of their sensory experience to hide the manipulation of certain midline bones such as the ethmoid, vomer, sphenoid, etc. The sensation produced by the "third eye" cranial manipulation is unforgettable, it feels like something is moving straight into your skull through the frontal bone of the forehead, and then penetrating deeply into the center of the head. In order to preserve their cranial secrets, the occult world has cleverly fabricated these kind of dramatic cover stories. What they are doing is improving the alignment of the ethmoid bone, which makes a person more sensitive to the environment, which will be perceived by some as improving one's psychic abilities. (As a final note, when this author met with Bill, Bill's view towards helping MPD was that it was demons that needed to be delivered. One of his supposed deliverance success stories, an Illuminati victim of mind-control, is still a multiple and still a double agent, and also actively working against this author's work. Bill personally told this author, that while he was a Satanist & vampire he was offered to have a mind-controlled slave, but that he turned the opportunity down. Bill is not the only person publicly exposing the occult/NWO who has over the years tried to prevent this author's information from getting to you.)

The third eye area, called the ethmoid, is physically manipulated by the monks for mind-control purposes. In the occult world, the third eye area actually extends to include the entire midline area, not just the ethmoid, but also the midline bones, and the related brain structures, especially the pineal gland. Midline bones are interesting to occultists, because the main endocrine and neurologic structures in the brain are placed around the central 3rd and 4th ventricular areas. (The first two ventricles, known as the lateral ventricles, repose on either side of the third.) The bones are one way to access these midline structures. the ethmoid is the front-most midline bone (behind the frontal, which is considered to be two bones; since in many people the metopic suture does not close). The ethmoid interfaces with other midline bones.

In the course of this book, the reader is introduced to the concept that the human brain is actually 7 brains. The 4th or mid brain that lies between the upper 3 brains and the lower three and functions as a crossroads, joins with the optic thalamus, which forms the floor of the 3rd ventricle. The ceiling of the 4th brain is the floor of the 3rd ventricle. The 3rd ventricle and the Cave of Brahma make up the 5th brain. The 5th brain is connected to the cerebral hemispheres of the Cerebrum and is critical to creating concepts and storing abstract concepts. It feeds on ideas, and reflects. (Marijuana activates this brain, and it is common knowledge among mind-control handlers that marijuana is forbidden to slaves.)

The roof the 5th brain is formed by the choroid plexus. At the front is the pituitary and at the rear the pineal gland, both exceptionally important to perception. The peptides (called enkephalins) that trigger intuitive awareness of what the 6th brain is perceiving, come from the pituitary into the Cave of Brahma. Can the reader now see why cranial manipulation that influences this area will affect our intuitive awareness?

Cranial Osteopath Ronald R. McCatty's book Craniosacral Osteopathy discusses the pineal body and pituitary gland from pp. 78 to 86. A discussion of the techniques to influence these bodies is beyond the scope of this chapter, but there are procedures. McCatty is very skilled, but he still has a ways to go to match the skills of the inner group that does mind-control. His page 25 also discusses a direct adjustment on the Pineal body via arm rotations and breathing. The occult world's physical manipulation of this third eye area can enhance a person's sensitivity. (It works off of straightforward body/brain mechanics, not the spirit world). It makes the subject feel that he is more telepathic. This is one of their big secrets. This secret was passed on the Gurdjieff, who went to Tibet to learn their secrets. Gurdjieffs communities, which this author has been investigating have a very good appearance to them, but there are lots of dark secrets within these communities, which indicate that drug use and mind-control are going on amongst them.

One of the mind-control techniques used is physical manipulation of the third-eye area of the skull. In fact, a number of cranial osteopaths (such as Cranial Osteopath and Rosicrucian Robert Fulford) have thanked Gurdjieff for enlightening them about how to do cranial manipulation. Some of what the occult says about the third eye is simply cover stories to hide some of the bigger secrets. It is not known to this author if Fulford can do a third eye manipulation. (In this exposure of cranial manipulation, R.C. Fulford is of interest to us due to his impact upon the course Cranial Osteopathy took, rather than his skill. W.G. Sutherland, the leader in Cranial Osteopathy had several Rosicrucians and other occultists as early students. After his death, three of these took Cranial Osteopathy in a more occult direction than Sutherland was going. Anne Wales, as Sutherland's editor & compiler, the person who took over his papers, also reviewed the papers of other cranial doctors, making sure she gave them all as much of a mystical twist as she could add to them. Olive Stretch was the second of the three and she and her husband ran the Cranial Academy from their living room. Upon Olive's death, her husband married Fulford's secretary of sixteen years, who in turn continued to run things when he died. Fulford, who is now in his '90s, did occult philosophizing, and some believe programming, but didn't develop the skill needed for entrance into the inner core of high level cranial knowledge.)

Rosicrucian Cranial Osteopath Robert Fulford also met Tibetans to learn what he could from the Tibetans. He became the President of the Osteopathy Cranial Association. He gives interesting talks, and writes about the Odic Force and the Vril (the light that the Nazis believed in), but it is not clear that Fulford, who is retired in Ohio, learned any deep secrets of manipulation.

However, Gurdjieff is not the only one who learned from the Orient. Cranial Osteopath Ronald Kurylowicz, of 754 Washington Blvd, Marina Del Rey, CA who is single and lives with his mother who serves as his secretary, made a special effort to learn what he could from the Chinese over a period of years, with what appears as a clear intent to use it for mind-control and malevolent purposes. The cranial group has long had an international effort to teach and proselytize worldwide. Much of this seems to be a sincere effort to spread the benefits of cranial knowledge allowed to the public. (This knowledge is often released only for substantial fees.)

When the inner core of cranial manipulation has travelled to learn from other cultures, China has been the primary focus. While in China, the inner core of cranial manipulation, who use it for mind-control, have met with their Chinese counterparts to negotiate occult relationships. Top level Theosophists have accompanied the inner core on their trips to China. In 1950, Gurdjieff came out with Beelzebub's Tales to His Grandson Vol. 1-3. IDHHB Inc. published in 1978 some of the secret talks that Gurdjieff had with a special group of disciples. The point is simply that Gurdjieff was willing to go to the occult world of black magicians to get some of his enlightenment, and one of the techniques he learned was the manipulation of the mind via physical manipulation of the "third eye area". One of Gurdjieff's big disciples in New England passed on to the cranial osteopaths manipulation secrets that Gurdjieff learned in Tibet. Gurdjieff is even more mysterious, when one realizes that he an asset of Russian and British intelligence.

This raises the obvious question, what were the Nazi's able to learn about skull manipulation from the Tibetans, the Japanese secret societies, and European occultism? It is known that the Nazi's carried out experimentation on skull manipulation. (Some of the records pertaining to Nazi human experiments are stored in the U.S. National Archives, incl. National Archives Record Group 238, the Collection of W.W.II War Crimes Records, the OSS's reports in Record Group 226, the Dept. of State records in National Archives Record Group 59, and Group 242. But it must be borne in mind that much of the records of Nazi experiments were confiscated and remained secret so that our government could continue the research. We see only glimpses of this research in such things as the SS skeleton collection, written about in SS letters used as Nuernberg Trial Doc. No.s 87, 88, 91. Prof. Hirt at the Strassburg Anatomical Institute received 150 Jewish skeletons for research according to a secret SS document, marked Exhibit no. 086. One thing is clear, there was no limitation for Nazi researchers as to what they could experiment on with human beings. Could the idea/chance to research in skull manipulation for purposes of mind-control have escaped those Nazi researchers who were steeped in phrenology and horse breeding?)

What did the Nazi's learn, and what did their mind-control experts such as Joseph Mengele pass on to American mind-control programmers, or is it possible the subtleties of cranial bone manipulation somehow escaped them? The practice of bone-setting in Germany had been known as Knochenartz, Knocheneinrichter, and Wundart. In recent history, Germany has a large number of cranial osteopaths who purchase lots of American books on the cranial osteopathy. It's this author's opinion, that the total mind-control of NWO slaves being implemented in the Black Forest castles,

Strasburg, Frankfurt, Berlin, and hundreds of other German sites includes cranial manipulation. However, in terms of Germany, this remains to be proven. In America, there is no doubt, for we have the victims (and photographic proof) to prove it.

Osteopathy is not "politically correct" within Germany's medical establishment. Most Germans, who purchase cranial books, are occultists (usually variations on Theosophy) and not people with medical or manipulative training. Europeans tend to be much more specialists in their professions than Americans. They don't tend to have as many people/per population practice a particular skill as America, but the ones who do are often very skilled. (This is an observation this author has heard frequently during his world-wide travels, and has also observed for himself.) For instance, in visiting Switzerland, this author learned that if a person wants to build a house he will have no option but to bring in specialists for the different tasks, while in America, it's not unusual for people to attempt building their own. This European approach of encouraging only very skilled specialists would also apply to cranial manipulation. We would expect a few very highly technical, skilled skull manipulators, and many curious entry-level folks.

THE JAPANESE CONNECTION

The ninjitsu people (popularly known as "the ninja" in America) were historically black magicians who hired out as assassins, and were feared and hated by all the Japanese people. They are now being held out as role models for our American children. The ninja learned how to dissociate pain. They learned martial arts and the art of stealth. According to the book The Karate Dojo by Peter Urban, "They were the original practitioners of the 'art of [mind-control] programming.' They were taught from the cradle that nothing was impossible. Not knowing that a thing could not be done, they proceeded to do it." It is possible that the Green Dragon Society of Japan passed on some of this mind-control training techniques to the German secret societies that were in cooperation with them prior to and during W.W. II. In other words, Dr. Mengele, the Nazi Angel of Death who carried out mind-control experiments for the Nazi's (& the Illuminati) during W.W. II may have attempted to incorporate Chinese, Tibetan, Japanese, Ancient Egyptian and Hindu mind-control techniques into their mind-control programming/research.

THE EARLY EUROPEAN OCCULT CONNECTION

Information pertaining to this has been floating around Europe in certain circles for years. We will touch on some of the various times and places that we know parts of cranial manipulation to alter the mind was being done. Over the centuries skilled horsemen learned that they could tell the temperament of a horse from the shape of its head. The best books on horse training would have sections on determining what your horse's temperament was based on skull shape.

The Celts were big on bone-setting. Wales has continued to preserve some of this Celtic enthusiasm. A rare book The Art of The Bone-Setter by George Matthews Bennett (London, Tho Murby publ., 1884) gives an excellent history of bone-setters in England, Wales and Scotland. It is likely that some of these men understood some things about how personality could be affected via bone manipulation in the skull.

George Matthews Bennett was a Freemason and a Druid. He was also a leading bone-setter in London, Stratford and other places. He was a descendent of the famous occult Matthews family, which had practiced bone-setting for two hundred years. His son, who also did bone-setting, was the last of that line to practice bone-setting. The skill (professional art) of bone-setting passed down in families for generations was not the equivalent of modern osteopathy.

Osteopathy had many different ideas and approaches, even though the two are similar. One of the early English books on bone-setting was The Compleat Bone-setter by Friar Moulton. In 1665, the book was enlarged by Robert Turner (an occultist/astrologer) and printed in England. In 1871, Dr. Wharton Hood wrote another publication on bone-setting in England entitled A Treatise on Bone Setting. But most of the skill of bone-setting in England was passed down as family secrets within a few bloodlines that practiced it for generations, such as the Thomases, the Taylors of Lancashire, the Maltby's of Nottingham, the Masons of Lincolnshire, the Huttons of Westmorland (& later of London), the Crowthers of Yorkshire, and the Matthews of the Midlands. (This list occurs in the book Medical Fringe & Medical Orthodoxy 1750-1850 edited by Bynum and Porter, pub. London: Croom Helm Ltd., 1987, p. 170, note 10.) Much about bone-setting in Europe, will remain secret, because so much was taught orally and shrouded in mystery. About a dozen British bloodlines passed their trade secrets down, a number of them were Welch. However, there were also many itinerant quacks who travelled around billing themselves as bone-setters.

NINETEENTH CENTURY OCCULT CONNECTION

Bone-setter Richard Hutton gained notoriety in London in the 1800's when he relieved the long-standing suffering of the Hon. Spencer Ponsonby. Hugh Owen Thomas, (1848-?) who was a qualified doctor, used what he knew from coming from a long traditional line of bone-setters to create modern fracture theory. His nephew, Sir Robert Jones (1857-1933) who was his apprentice, was the major ambassador for modern orthopaedic medical practices. In other words, some of the knowledge of the bone-setters contributed to modern established medical knowledge.

Charles Waterton, an English naturalist in old England, wrote in his Wanderings and Essays on Natural History that every nation in Europe had bone-setters, who were independent of the surgeons. Throughout Europe, the men and women who practiced bone-setting learned the skill from others and as a result of experience. The skill was not a text-book-learned skill, but an art that was taught via hands-on training. Many of the bone-setters never formally studied anatomy, pathology, or surgery. (See The Art of the Bone-Setter, p. 96.) Hand-in-hand with bone setting came ideas on the importance of the shape of the skull. In 1695, Balthazar Bekkar of London wrote, "Physiognomy, that is...the Observation of a Man's Shape, must be comprehended under this sort [occult arts], for this Art foretells things by the Looks, the Features and Lineaments of the Face, by which the Genius and Humour of Men are to be discovered." (This comes from book one of a four book series The World Bewitched; An Examination of the Common Opinions Concerning Spirits. London: R. Baldwin, 1695, vol. 1, p.30.)

THE WITCHCRAFT CONNECTION

Throughout the world, people have practiced bone manipulation. The names for folk bone-setting throughout the world of course vary from language to language. In Tahiti it was called "romy" or "rumi". In South America, it was called "abrazo del ranchero". In Bohemia it was called "napravit." In Mexico, it's been called "arreglador de huesos", and in France "reboutage." The Amish call it "Brauche", and some of their bone-setters practice folk witchcraft. (This is known from the author's own experience as an Amishman.) Bone-setting has often been associated with folk healing and the occult.

Contrary to what is politically correct today, witchcraft was not a group of poor innocent women chased by a malicious Christian society, but was a well-organized body which was a repository for the occult knowledge of Babylon, Egypt and Rome. Ex-Illuminati members have described (to this author) the ancient manuscripts of knowledge preserved in secrecy by the Illuminati down through the ages. The permission of the Grand Druid Council is needed for some Illuminati books. Illuminati members are only allowed to see certain manuscripts, if they are achieving a mastery in that field of secret knowledge.

In the middle ages, knowledge was dispensed through secret trade guilds, fraternities and bloodlines. The ancient healing/and harming secrets of the human body were secrets of the fraternal secret societies, i.e. what is known today as the Illuminati. Witches could accomplish either a healing or a harmful manipulation of the body without anyone knowing what had happened, because their arts were secret techniques that outsiders couldn't recognize.

Secret medical and psychological knowledge was hidden by lots of cover mystical claptrap, which made the real secrets elusive to outsiders. Witches were accused of witchcraft when the harmful results of what they did were noticed, but the people had little idea of the mechanics of what hit them. Some of the trials of witches during the late middle ages were legitimate grievances, even though the ancient trial records (by today's standards) contain no legitimate evidence of modus operandi. We are not in a position to judge their trials by our standards of evidence.

Throughout most history, the doctor-priest or the medicine man-shaman kept his health secrets to himself as occult/arcane /esoteric knowledge to pass to his chosen successors. Even today, our modern day equivalents for the medicine man & shaman --our doctors & priests are still popular careers for transgenerational pagans. And as this chapter is pointing out, there are still secrets.

The Mystery Religions of Europe studied the human head and body. One of Jacob Boehme's disciples portrayed the Hindu chakra points back in 1736 in his Theosophia Practica. The results of tortures during ancient and medieval times upon the bodies & skulls of people was also known to a few. A relationship appears to exist between bone-setting and witchcraft, in that wherever witchcraft was strongest in England, one also discovers an abundance of bonesetters. An advance knowledge of anatomy was needed to devise the tortures used in Europe by those who were in power. It was not uncommon historically for doctors & bonesetters to provide advice for torture devices. For instance, Dr. Guillotin, a French doctor & Freemason, invented the guillotine.

There are plenty of evidences of occult involvement in the torture of people over the centuries, (even though it is politically correct to blame it on Christians). At this point it is safe to say that there was some overlap between bone-setting, witchcraft, and those who made an occupation as torturers for the state, but the complete details are not available. Some families have traditionally been involved in torture, perhaps at some point those family secrets will surface. Hands of Glory of hanged men were used as health charms. Corpses & moss from skulls, were also thought to have healing powers.

Freemason/Druid/ Bone-setter George Matthews Bennett writes, "In the North of England, the origin of nearly all the men who are fairly good at Bone-setting can be traced to the Whitworth surgery, and while, so far as I know, the Taylors, in their various settlements at Whitworth, Todmorden, Stockwood, and Oldfield-lane, were the only qualified surgeons who practiced Bone-setting; amongst the hills and dales of Lancashire, Yorkshire, and the Lake district, there were many who did so without being qualified." (The Art of the Bone-setter, p. 106) Whether these Taylors were any relation to those Taylors today within the Illuminati, is not known.

Phrenology was very respected during the 19th century. Queen Victoria consulted the top phrenologist. Interest in Phrenology led Europeans to research what the functions of the brain are, & how the brain functions. Phrenologists Johann Gaspar Spurzheim and Scotsman George Combe "realized the potentiality to manipulate and control human behaviour" via their knowledge of the skull and brain. (Cooter, Cultural Meaning of Popular Science, p. 6) The writings of these men resulted in phrenological societies and publications springing up all over the U.S. and Great Britain.

Franz Joseph Gall, was an expert on the anatomy of the brain, having spent his life studying it. Encyclopedia Britannica says F.J. Gall was a "brain anatomist of considerable ability". (Ency. Brit., 15th ed., vol.26, p. 327) In 1800, Franz Joseph Gall, advocated to medical science that the shape of the skull was a guide to an individual's mental faculties and character traits. Based upon this, other researchers such as Pierre Flourens undertook experiments on animals to determine more exactly the functions of the various parts of the brain. Various men contributed ideas.

Leopold Auenbrugger discovered percussion to determine a fluid level. He applied his discovery of tapping his father's casks to gauge the level of fluid content to the body.

Fire In The Minds of Men, by James H. Billington a leading historian, is an excellent survey of how the French Revolution and subsequent revolutions were created by a small group of leading occultists. Utopian socialists, who embraced the occult ideal of a "revolving back to the Golden Age" helped promote the idea of phrenology at the important Paris Athenee, where debates were organized concerning the psychology of personality, physiognomy, and phrenology. (For those readers who haven't kept up with other written works of this author, the Illuminati when America was discovered believed that they historically had came from Atlantis, and that a new Atlantis could be constructed in the new world. The revolution of the United States was the first war in history called a "revolution", and it was called a revolution because it and subsequent revolutions were to revolve us back to the Golden Age of Atlantis. They named the ocean to reach their new Atlantis, the Atlantic Ocean.)

Charleston, S.C. was a major hub for the Scottish Rite and for Reformed Judaism, both which were interlocked and used the Cabala. The main goal of the Cabala is to create a mind-controlled slave called a golem. The main principle behind Freemasonry according to Albert Pike, who was the Supreme Commander of Freemasonry in Charleston, S.C. has been the cabala. This makes it easier to understand why Freemasonry has been involved in the creation of mind-controlled slaves.

It also makes it more understandable why hypnotism (called mesmerism) along with phrenology was introduced into Charleston, SC about 1830. After the occult world introduced phrenology coupled with hypnotism to Charleston, it was also introduced by the Frenchman Charles Poyen to Rhode Is. Brown University. The entire faculty was so astonished at the power of hypnotism, that they concluded that mesmerism was a more important science than phrenology.

Initially, the elite in Charleston were interested in hypnotism (called mesmerism) combined with phrenology. The craze spread to the common people, and hypnotism was the subject of a famous intellectual debate in Charleston in 1843. Phrenology, which was a science tied to Rosicrucianism, lost favor in the south, due to the large participation of phrenologists (Rosicrucians) in the abolition movement. The Abolitionist movement was created in the U.S. by the Illuminati via the Rosicrucian groups, as well as Unitarians and Socialists who were also tied to them. For instance, Rosicrucian/ Phrenologist William Lloyd Garrison started the Anti-slavery Society in 1832. Three other notable Rosicrucian abolitionists are John Brown, George Lippard, and Abraham Lincoln. John Brown, besides being a Rosicrucian, revolutionist and abolitionist, was a practicing phrenologist. He had been trained by Fowler and Wells, who promoted the Vegetarian City that A. Still visited.

Many of the Illuminati and leading European occultists, incl. men such as Charles Taze Russell (founder of the WT Society) and Joseph Smith, Jr. (founder of the LDS Mormon church) were students of phrenology. Interestingly, Joseph Smith, Jr. on Jan. 5, 1841 had a revelation that phrenology was an occult science from "the Devil". (Smith's words are recorded in The Words of Joseph Smith: The Contemporary Accounts of the Nauvoo discourses of the Prophet Joseph. Provo, UT: Brigham Young Univ. Religious Studies Center, 1980, p. 61.) And yet he continued studying phrenology, and endorsing phrenology to the "Latter-day Saints" (Mormons).

Quite a number of the Mormon prophets (the top leader) such as Brigham Young, Wilford Woodruff, and George A. Smith got phrenological readings done of their skulls. The Mormon church sold phrenology books and even printed a phrenology magazine in Salt Lake City for a while, which was entitled The Character Builder from the 1870's until into the 1940's. George Reynolds, First Presidency secretary and later President of the LDS Seventies (a group of men like the catholic cardinals) considered phrenological readings as valid as the patriarchal blessings that the LDS church gives to its members.

Since the Mormon church is one of the Illuminati fronts carrying out mind-control, it should come as no surprise that attempts to control the human mind by manipulation of the shape of the skull have been attempted. Interestingly, official church interest in phrenology by the Mormon hierarchy died out during the time period (1940's) that mind-control began to be scientifically carried out by the Illuminati in cooperation with different government front. Could it be that there was a grain of powerful truth in phrenology that these people wanted quietly buried?

Swendenborg, the founder of a mystical Masonic Rite, spent a great deal of time and some of his writing discussing the skull bones. This author has encountered victims of trauma-based total mind-control within the modern Swendenborg Church of New Jerusalem. Occult students of Swendenborg, including some of the Illuminati, such as some in the DuPont family, studied his ideas with fervour. (The DuPonts appear to be connected to at least one cranial osteopath.) (Because the Church of New Jerusalem does not tell the public nor its members about Swedenborg being a Freemason, etc. it would be advantageous to briefly identify to the reader who he was. Swedenborg wrote, "I live, besides, on terms of familiarity and friendship with all the bishops of my country, who are ten in number; as also with the sixteen senators, and the rest of nobility. The king and queen also, and the three princes, their sons, show me much favor." Swedenborg, born to a well-connected elite Swedish family, was a genius who wrote an incredible amount of spiritual writings that he believed came from alien encounters. His "alien" material in his Earths in the Universe is blatantly baloney, but at that time, people had no concept of what they'd find in outer space. The "aliens" even gave him the wrong number of planets in our solar system, 9. Swedenborg wrote that Saturn is "the farthest [planet] from the sun". He was certain of this and other ideas because of what the aliens had told him.

He also communicated with spirits. Masonic encyclopedias state that many of his ideas were Masonic. In Masonry Defined (publ. by National Masonic Press, a book based on 33° Freemason / Masonic historian Mackey's notes), their article on Emanuel Swedenborg states, "enlightened Masons will find many Masonic ideas in Swedenborg's writings." In the Be Wise As Serpents book, this author documents the interlocking directorates that control the top level secret societies. The Masonic Rite of Swedenborg with its 8 degrees and two "temples"-which means "sub-rites"- has had some of the worst Satanists as its leadership.)

In spite of the ridicule of the various ideas about determining personality from the shape of the body and head, Ency.

Brit. 15th ed. Vol. 25, p. 497 admits, "Nevertheless, structural differences in the body do seem to have some significance in pointing to such aspects of personality as intelligence and emotion." The 18th and 19th century researchers were onto something, they didn't manage to finish the job. The Nazi government, and other governments have secretly tried to finish that job. Unfortunately, it may be a long time before we learn exactly how they finished this line of research. So far, the only recipients of the 20th century research findings have been a few select people within the occult world.

An interesting story involving personality change due to changes in the skull and brain was the landmark patient Phineas Gage, who died in 1861, after an accident caused him to damage the brain's ability to make rational decisions and to process emotions. Recently, new research was performed on Phineas Gage's skull to understand better how his brain had been affected by an accident. (See Science, May 20, 1994, p. 1102)

Another example of how the shape of the skull and the movement of skull bones determines how the brain functions are the craniectomies that are now being carried out to relieve infants from mental imbecility due to premature skull sutural closure and microcephalus. (See The Journal of the American Medical Association JAMA, Jan. 8, 1992, p. 226.) Further, researchers into how the brain creates thoughts, who desire to remain confidential, have come to believe that the ionic crystalline structure within the cranium's 5 cranial bone plates: the occipital bone, the two Parietal bones and the two frontal skull bones which connect at fontanellas (fissures) called sutures play an important role in the creation of thoughts. They believe that the ionic crystalline structures of the skull bones interact with incoming theta waves from the brain, and a resonance is created that causes electrons to be generated, which are then translated via a Fourier-type translation into a thought.

You are probably aware that it is the grey matter that lies next to the skull that carries out the higher level thinking that distinguishes humans from animals. These researchers have stated that they believe that the fontanellas (connections between the skull plates) allow subtle lateral motions and non-linear complex vibrations to occur. These vibrations are part of the higher thinking process. If this is true, it could have far ranging ramifications.

These researchers believe the natural resonant vibrational frequency of the skull bones (the cranium) ranges from 840 to 890 MHz in non-herzian waves. This range was reserved for VHF television, but has now been reserved for the national cellular telephone network. When the 840 to 890 range was used for television, various neurologists noted that certain signals related to particular pitches and sounds would trigger reactions in people. For instance, the NY Times 7/11/91 reported that according to a neurologist an epileptic seizure was triggered via certain television signals. Cellular phones are now being used to transmit faxes, computer information such as modems transmit, and other signals. Illuminati connected companies of IBM, Motorola, and GE are some of the companies working with cellular phone technology. The creation of vibrations via cellular phone signals in the 840 to 890 MHz non-herzian wave range could conceivably implant thoughts into a victim near the cellular phone. This raises two questions. First, IS the establishment's big push to popularize cellular phone use, even to the point of giving out free cellular phones, part of Big Brother's mind-control? Second, since it appears the brains ability to creatively think is related to the vibrations that are subtly made in the skull, the question naturally poses itself--can cranial osteopathy disrupt or alter the natural abilities of the cranium's plates to vibrate?

THE MODERN AMERICAN OCCULT CONNECTION

In the United States, as in England, there were certain families who passed their bone-setting skills down as family trade secrets. The most famous bone-setting families were the Reece family (in west. Penn., and east. Ohio), the Sweet family (in Rhode Is., Mass., Conn., & NY), and the Tieszen and Orton families in South Dakota. The Sweets became orthopedists, the Tieszen and Orton families went into Chiropractic. The Irish Quain family were famous anatomists, surgeons, and physicians.

Osteopathy and chiropractic stemmed from the same occult philosophical roots, but went in different directions. Both shared the idea that the body has the ability to maintain good health if allowed to do so, and both emphasized the manipulation of bones and joints. Both were started about the same time period in America in about the same geographic area, by men who had Scottish ancestry.

A.T. Still (the founder of osteopathy) and D.D. Palmer both studied magic and metaphysics. Both attended many of the same spiritist meetings, for instance both attended the spiritualist meetings at Clinton, Iowa on a number of occasions. (Gibbons, 1980, p. 13)

The osteopath's goal was to move bones to improve circulation. The chiropractor's primary goal was to move bones to reduce pressure or the irritation of nerves, with the further goal of positively helping organs and tissue. A.T. Still & other osteopaths claimed Daniel D. Palmer visited Still at his house, but Palmer's descendants say it's not true.

Early on Still's two best assistants were two doctors from Scotland, William Smith & James Littlejohn. Daniel David Palmer (1845-1913), founder of chiropractic, was a Freemason & an occultist. His original practice was to heal people with what he called "magnetic healing" which was a combination of laying on of hands, hypnotism and white magic. Of course it was not called white magic, it was called "magnetic healing" by Palmer.

Part of the magnetism was his own magnetic (hypnotic) personality. Palmer also knew phrenology and had a keen sense of touch concerning a person's head. D.D. Palmer taught phrenology. D.D. Palmer was a mixture of good and bad traits. He was an excellent scholar and had good organizational skills for what he learned. One of his difficult traits was his megalomania. In 1905, at a coroner's inquiry, Palmer refused to take an oath to swear the truth "so help me God", because he said that "I don't want any help from God." It must have been hard on his pride, when his own son B.J. Palmer, who had been cruelly raised by cruel step-mothers, turned Judas and stole from his father both the honor & money that was due his father.

His son Bartlett Joshua Palmer (1882-1961) worked in a circus as an assistant to professional circus hypnotists known as Professor Hunt, and later Professor Herbert L. Flint. Later, with mysterious connections to the right people, B.J. Palmer, got the money and the political clout to get started in building a school for chiropractic. His powerful Davenport radio station, WOC, said to be the second largest in the U.S., had Ronald Reagan (our future president) as one of its sports announcers.

B.J. Palmer was connected to the occult world. He liked to encourage the idea that he was a Christ figure. New Ager Napoleon Hill, author of Think and Grow Rich (1937) considered Palmer his mentor. B.J. had prominent Masons and other elite as his personal guests. Elbert Hubbard, a friend of B.J.'s, was the person who persuaded John D. Rockefeller's personal physician, to get Rockefeller to use chiropractic care. Later in 1963, Nelson Rockefeller would be the important person to get chiropractic accepted as legal in NY, and then appointed chiropractor Albert Cera to his Medical Advisory Committee.

Illuminati kingpin California Gov. Edmund Brown appointed 12 chiropractors to regional committees associated with the California Board of Medical Assurance. Hollywood got into the promotion of chiropractic, with the 1990 film Jacob's Ladder which was a film exposing the U.S. military's use of BZ (a derivative of LSD) in Vietnam to experimentally try to create aggression via drugs in American soldiers.

It appears that chiropractic occult ties have been beneficial in its fight for acceptance. The occult world has worked hard to keep chiropractic within its domain. This is why you will find Christians exposing the occult connections to chiropractic such as T.M. Clement's book A Warning to Christians About the Origins of Chiropractic. (Moses Lake:WA, date of printing not known).

As the reader will discover other sciences involving the relationship of the mind, brain, the body and personality have also been kept in the domain of the secret societies. Like Palmer, Dr. Andrew Taylor Still, who founded osteopathy, was interested in phrenology, hypnotism, spiritism, magic. The reference book 10,000 Famous Freemasons (Vol. 4) outlines his Masonic career in Freemasonry. His writings include such Masonic phrases as "Great architect of the Universe." His grandfather had been Scotch-Irish. His father was a Methodist Episcopal minister, who was an abolitionist who fought with John Brown and the free-state forces in Kansas.

Andrew Taylor Still ran for the legislature of Kansas Territory as a free-state candidate and won in the Oct. 1857 elections. Later, he married Mary Elvira Turner, who was from the "burned-over" district in New York. She had been exposed to abolitionist ideas, phrenology, and hypnotism (called mesmerism) which were all popular in the area she grew. Her area of NY was where Spiritism began in 1848. Horace Greeley of the NY Tribune then made these seances with spirits famous. In 1867, after his children died, Andrew Taylor Still embraced spiritistism. Still's beliefs in spiritism included ideas from Freemason Swendenborg's writings. (For details of Andrew Taylor Still's life refer to the book Trowbridge, Carol. Andrew Taylor Still. Kirksville, MO: The Thomas Jefferson Press, 1990.)

A.T. Still built osteopathy on the foundation of teachings of men such as phrenologist/hypnotists such as Joseph Rodes Buchanan. Buchanan used hypnosis and manipulation of the head to radiate the cerebral fluid from the brain to the body, which was coming close to the basics of cranial osteopathy. How did A.T. Still come up with these new ideas? A.T. Still was able to study and conduct experiments on bodies by raiding Indian graves for bodies, which he says in his "Circumstances and Personal Experiences" he did thousands of experiments on.

Certainly, he was unusual in having had a boyhood interest in digging up skeletons. He also read every book on anatomy he could find. In spite of his preoccupation with digging up skulls of people, Still seems to have been a decent person. Today, the occult world dislikes him. Why? In view of the historical facts, and the historical occult campaign to denigrate who Still was, it appears Still revealed secrets. Still was interested in scientific investigation. He proved things as he went along. He was a true researcher, and contrary to many researchers he was willing to openly share his knowledge with mankind.

Andrew's two brothers, Ed and James, were M.D.s. They may well have been loyal to the occult world, and it is speculated that this may account for part of their attempts to destroy the work of Andrew Still. It appears that in spite of Andrew's own occult connections, Andrew Still wanted to give the world cranial osteopathic knowledge that the occult world deemed to be secrets.

Andrew Still joined Freemasonry in Baldwin, KS's Palmyra Lodge No. 23. (10,000 Famous Freemasons, Vol. 4, p. 194). He came from a transgeneration occult background. He did speak and write with the type of terminology that the occult world uses, although today some of his "occult" writings only appear so because they are taken out of context. Recently, the Internet has a website with the "Sage Sayings of Still" with excerpts from a "spiritual diary" he kept. On the other side of the coin, the supposed sage occult sayings of Still were renounced by Still himself after he wrote them. He not only exposed occult secrets that the bonesetters had kept in the occult families for centuries, he made a point of tossing occultists out of his school.

I believe Andrew Still was one of those people that the generational occultists could say, "He grew up and dwellt among us, but he wasn't one of us." No wonder the occult world has had a campaign against him after he died. After Andrew died, his son Charles an excellent compassionate skillful doctor was to have taken over A.T. Still's Kirksville Osteopathic College. Instead, a rich financial backer, Warren Hamilton, who owned pivotal shares of stock placed James Still's grandson into the Osteopathic College's president's chair. The knowledge that Still tried to get to the world was now stifled. As an example of where things have progressed the Cranial Academy (the American Academy of Osteopathy) is now situated in three buildings in Indianapolis that are identical copies of the Great Pyramid, & use pyramids for their logo. (By the way one of Dr. A.T. Still's great-grandnephews is William Still who wrote the book New World Order. William Still is descended from the doctor's brother Thomas, who was an M.D. William's father was a U.S. general who was part of World Order, and although William's book was great, when one considers how the NWO order creates their own opposition and how double-agents are created, this author has some personal reservations on what is happening with William. For those who haven't obtained a copy of the book, this author recommends it.)

Back to discussing Still's ideas. Eventually, A.T. Still developed his own ideas for healing the body without using drugs, or the dangerous medical practices of his day. In 1874, Dr. Andrew Taylor Still, devised osteopathy, a medical practice that seeks to help the body via manipulated of the bones. 16 Osteopathic Schools have successfully sprung up in the U.S. over the years to serve the need for osteopath doctors. A few others failed. A small specialty within the Osteopathic medicine is Cranial Osteopathy which has the Cranial Academy (formed in 1946), which is a component of the American Academy of Osteopathy. The Cranial Academy is headquartered at 1020 Market Tower, Ten West Market St., Indianapolis, IN 46204 in a building that looks like 3 Egyptian pyramids.

Osteopathic students who have taken a Basic Cranial Course approved by the Academy are eligible to apply to the Cranial Academy to learn about osteopathy as it applies to the skull. Just recently, in June 20-23, 1996, they had their annual conference at Walt Disney World Village, Lake Buena Vista, FL. Walt Disney World happens to be a major mind-control programming center and the significance of this was brought out in Chapter 5.

The Cranial Academy, founded by occultist Sutherland in 1946, is affiliated with the Applied Academy of Osteopathy (this AAO is a group that is concerned with manipulative work, & also based in IN). WG Sutherland developed Cranial Osteopathic concepts. It appears that the occult world were upset enough with Andrew Still's revelations, that they planted WG Sutherland into the new science to bring the science back into the realm of the occult world. Sutherland (and those that followed him) was not above spewing out disinformation. Another leader following Sutherland in the field was another occultist Fulford, who helped insure that the Theosophists and Rosicrucians took over the science that A.T. Still had tried to give the world in a scientific form. Fulford, almost a god to some of the doctors interested in cranial osteopathy, functions as a bulwark to prevent most doctors from learning the deeper arts of manipulation.

Only a small inner group are taught the most advanced manipulative methods and anatomical details. The crucial cranial research work is being done privately by doctors affiliated with the Rosicrucians and this research is reported only in their literature for Rosicrucians only. The American Osteopathy Association helps to keep things low key by making no reference to the Cranial Academy in their materials, and only referring to the AAO once.

In 1953, one of the leading Cranial Osteopaths, William G. Sutherland, an American of Scottish descent, formed a foundation called the Sutherland Cranial Teaching Foundation in Denver, CO to promote the teaching of Cranial (head or skull) Osteopathy as developed by Sutherland. The cranial osteopathic work is taught by the Cranial Academy, but the inner knowledge, the inner secrets that are needed to successfully use cranial manipulation for mind-control are not taught by the Cranial Academy. This is taught privately by doctors who keep their relationships to each other secret. The inner core leaders (the top 3) of this small highly proficient group were all based in the south, and have all died since 1990. They have been replaced by carefully recruited handpicked successors.

There are occasion groups in other places that do cranial work. Some research on bioenergy and bone motion was done at the Univ. of Michigan School of Osteopathy and the Upledger Institute based in Florida has taught a very mechanical and rudimentary version of cranial work. These are just side activities. The U.S. Air Force and Navy provide scholarships which cover full tuition, books and living expenses for certain applicants to go to osteopathic college for four years. This has been carried out via the Director, Washington Office, American Osteopathic Association, Cafritz Building Suite 1009, 1625 Eye Street, N.W., Washington, DC 20006.

One of the military Cranial Osteopaths is a Maj. Beverly I. Maliner, and another is David R. Lemme at the Naples, It. Naval Hospital. There are reports that this hospital along with other American military sites in Europe are being used for mind-control. However, that does not necessarily connect Lemme or Maj. Maliner with government mind-control. This author knows of no evidence that would connect them. The military has used civilians to carry out some of the mind-control on their bases for decades, so they wouldn't have to use their own people if they didn't want to. The military has conducted secret research into the effects of skull bone movement, and traumatic skull injuries which are still classified.

One example of many of the type of modern research done is Susan Ann Bloomfield's Ph.d. dissertation "Site-specific changes in bone mass and Alterations in Calciotrophic Hormones with Electrical Stimulation Exercise in Individuals with Chronic Spinal Cord Injury." Her research showed that electrical stimulation of the muscles around spinal injuries helped the bones grow.

The casual researcher will soon find out that Cranial Osteopathy is a hidden subject. One of the better books discussing the potential of Cranial Osteopathy and how it works is a hard-to-get out-of-print book Craniosacral Osteopathy by Ronald R. McCatty. As this subject is so important to mind-control, this author availed himself to find a copy of the book and to study it. Some of the techniques described in the book will be hard for regular doctors to verify. If the curious were to use standard medical tests such as X-rays or MRI (which are too big), they will not get anywhere in discovering the details of how to manipulate the skull. The science is much more minute than these tests. An M.D. who asked the Cranial Academy about cranial literature was told that their literature is copyrighted to the writers and not available to other professions. This is an example of how protective the Cranial Academy is of their knowledge and they aren't even teaching the hard core inner secrets!

The secret cults continue their iron grip over the deep secrets of cranial manipulation. They continue their monopoly over who gets benefited by cranial work, as well as who is destroyed by cranial work.

In review, a number of sincere men have tried to develop Cranial Osteopathy including Dr. Andrew Still in 1874. Interestingly, as soon as each one of these men began discovering new techniques informed members of the occult world would take over their work, and insure that the work was kept within the confines of the occult world. For instance, Dr. Sutherland's experiments revealed to him that Cranial Osteopathy could influence the way a person thought and their personality. In the book, With Thinking Fingers The Story of William Gamer Sutherland by his wife Adah Strand Sutherland, she writes, "It was Dr. Sutherland's cherished dream that a day would come when the benefits to the mentally ill through the cranial component in osteopathy would be investigated to the satisfaction of scientific insistence; that it would be approved and made available institutionally, in the curriculum's of osteopathic colleges as well as in the majority of private practices." (Sutherland, Adah S. With Thinking Fingers. The Cranial Academy: Indianapolis, IN., p. 62).

However, clever people in the occult world saw that Cranial Osteopathy could not only be used to help the mentally ill, but to control the minds of people. They realized that this valuable information could not be shared with the world but should confined to the occult world where its full evil potential could be exploited.

Part of why it was so easy to hi-jack Sutherland's research is that he wrote very little. He wrote only two short articles. He didn't like to write, he liked to do research and work with people. Strangely, his wife divorced him, and a Rosicrucian lady married him. The details of it all have the feel of the occult world moving in and micromanaging Sutherland's life in order to control his research. Two years after Sutherland died in '54, his Osteopathy Cranial Association was already starting to praise a new age type of "Christ" in its literature. Anne L. Wales, a Rosicrucian, archived his work, and it is through her that we have received some of his work. She makes sure that when Sutherland's ideas see the light of day, they are steeped in occult Rosicrucian ideas. This helps insure that sincere non-occult scientists disregard what appears to be Rosicrucianism, rather than the research of a doctor.

Anne L. Wales has been more than a Rosicrucian. She was a member of the Church of Scientology, which is practicing trauma-based mind-control and which is a recruiting organization for the OTO and the Process Church which are also both practicing total mind-control in coordination with the Illuminati. This author is aware of two separate victims of trauma-based total mind-control who came out of different Rosicrucian groups. As their are several groups claiming Rosicrucian philosophy, this author hasn't sorted out if there are any Rosicrucian groups which AREN'T being used as repositories for mind-controlled slaves. In other words, it appears that all Rosicrucian groups contain mind-controlled slaves.

Rosicrucianism (its various forms) has long attracted membership from the medical community, and there is evidence that it even recruits in the medical, chiropractic and osteopathic schools. The Rosicrucians, who like to track their history back to the alchemists, brag about their large numbers of medical members. AMORC indicates that at least 11% of its members are doctors. The Rosicrucians also hint about their secret medical experiments and secret medical knowledge. One Rosicrucian claim to fame is their mystical theories about the connections between the mind and the body (particularly the skull & nervous system).

The luxurious Clymer Health Clinic near Philadelphia offers cranial treatments at very modest prices by their staff of Rosicrucian chiropractors. Rosicrucian (& high ranking Mason) Swinbourne Clymer, MD, donated the land and funds for that clinic early this century. Clymer was a millionaire with eccentric health ideas. He financed the entire Rosicrucian Philadelphia-based group, too. His writings have tidbits that show he was an insider. Their headquarters has pyramids with capstones. Their books mention the Illuminati with great frequency. It is beyond the scope of this chapter, but there are connections between theosophy and Rosicrucianism and the Illuminati.

Theosophical groups tie in to the Nazi's religious beliefs, and today theosophical-minded young people are showing an interest in cranial manipulation. In other words, the interconnections between the occult world begin popping up when one investigates cranial work. One outspoken Doctor of Cranial Osteopathy (DO) Donald E. Woods, recently spoke out in the journal of Cranial Osteopathy entitled The Cranial Letter against the occultism that clearly controlled his specialty. He wrote in protest, "Yet, in the past we [cranial osteopaths] have bordered both on being a cult and on being occult. We must be neither to be effectively acceptable in health care, and it can be done since osteopathy, including Cranial Osteopathy, is based on valid human physiological and anatomical truths. Where do cult and occult fit in?"....Occultism says you do not have to pay attention to any of the old rules. Everything goes. Kick the walls out. Be tolerant of everyone's behaviour....Both the cult and the occult have the tendency to think that things outside their sphere of influence are unreasonable. They might say, "It is necessary that you belong to our group." (The Cranial Letter, Aug., '94, Vol. 47, No. 3, p.9)

While this letter printed in The Cranial Letter helps establish to the reader the occult world's influence in cranial osteopathy, the Cranial Academy may have printed this because the doctor in question is a multiple and they are possibly helping him separate himself publicly from the occult. And while the secrecy of cranial manipulation has been well kept, the Cranial Academy is considering disbanding itself, and letting the 16 osteopathic schools teach a more basic form or cranial work, which would further isolate the secrets for occult's elect.

Osteopathy itself has been accepted into mainstream medicine and one medical reference book states, "It is important to note that the osteopathic system of diagnosis and therapy is used in conjunction with the standard medical procedures of drug and surgical therapy." The curriculum at an osteopathic college or school is almost identical with that offered at the standard schools. The most popular school is the Chicago College of Osteopathic Medicine. There are approx. 150 osteopathic hospitals in the U.S. Most osteopaths are general practitioners and only 20% of the osteopaths specialize. Of these only a tiny percentage do Cranial Osteopathy full time. Of the small clique of DOs (Dr.s of Osteopathy) who do Cranial Osteopathy full time (Note: there are about 150 DOs nationwide that spend approx. 100% of their time doing Cranial Osteopathy--which no. was determined by this author using info provided in the Member Information Directory of the Cranial Academy.), and then based upon observations at programming sites and other criteria there is an inner circle of about 9 doctors who understand Cranial Osteopathy well enough to use their skills for the Illuminati in mind control.

Recently, there have been a number of magazine articles, for instance, American Medical News, June 26, 1995, p. 3 which discusses how osteopathic medical techniques of manipulation are becoming more acceptable to mainstream physicians and to the public. The article mentions that the American Osteopathic Assn. is getting $6 million for research. Obviously, the American Osteopathic Assn. is politically correct and moving with the stream of today's general trend toward new age ideas, and a global government.

Many osteopath doctors specialize. A Canadian government survey of chiropractors, osteopaths, and naturopaths in Canada revealed that 66% of the Canadian osteopaths specialized (See Royal Commission on Health Services Study of Chiropractors, Osteopaths and Naturopaths in Canada. Ottawa, Can: The Queen's Printer, 1966, p. 166), a figure much higher than revealed in a study of American Osteopaths in A Statistical Study of the Osteopathic Profession, Dec. 31, 1960, Dept. of Information and Statistics, American Osteopathic Association, May 1961, p. 2 Table 7.

In the Canadian study, osteopaths reported specializing in headaches, neurology, cranial work and cranial osteopathy. Their naturopaths reported specializing in fields including psycho-therapy, radio wave, electrotherapy, and cranial correction in mongoloids, spastics and body reconstruction. In exploring mind-control, it must be born in mind, that the American CIA was quick to recruit Canadians to help. Some of the cranial osteopaths themselves appear to be in controlled trance states, so they may well be under total mind-control themselves. These people are obviously of Celtic (probably Illuminati) bloodlines.

BONE & SKULL STRUCTURE

Bones are alive and changing. It might be helpful to review what bones are made of, and how they change and grow, just in case the reader had some misconceptions such as that bones are fixed solids that don't change. Bones within the human body, esp. the skull give support and protection. Bone is comprised of "an organic matrix synthesized and deposited by osteoblastic activity, calcium-phosphate precipitates, and a mineralized phase of hydroxyapatite, which is primarily composed of calcium and inorganic phosphate (Robey, 1989). The primary ingredient of the organic matrix is a collagen in the form of fibers that are extensively cross-linked. applies to 90% of the matrix. There several types of collagen, Type 1 predominant. This are is Numerous noncollagenous proteins have also been discovered in bone, including some which have been identified as growth factors. Bone development and turnover is regulated by various bone cells (see Teltelbaum, 1990)

The exact method the body uses to recreate new bone is too complex to describe here, but let it suffice that researchers are studying all the minute complexities of the abilities of the body to produce bone. Old bone is constantly being absorbed and reproduced new. BMUs are important to development of new bone. (see studies like Frost, 1965, & Parfit, 1987). According to the Wall Street Journal, Feb. 23, 1996, p. A1 (in both Eastern & Western editions) some physicians are remolding lopsided skulls of infants with unnecessary surgery when the only problem is the child's sleep position, and the lopsided skull can be corrected with a head band rather than surgery.

In terms of head shapes, which can be created by skilled manipulation of the skull bones, a Vertical Strain Superior is associated with passiveness and dissociation. This is why some of the cults are either manipulating people's heads or recruiting people that have long faces in their cults. The vertical Strain Inferior is said to be connected to criminals. The programmers for the NWO have been intentionally manipulating people's skull to get passiveness and dissociativeness.

Daniel Whiteside and John Wesley Grossman did extremely valuable work in statistically validating the clear connections between 60 behavior traits and physical structures. The physical shape of the brain is related to how the brain's cells are proportioned. This science is called Structure/ Function.

Daniel's father Robert L. Whiteside was one of the founders of 3-In-One. Robert wrote an amazing book Face Language. The Air Force academy used it in three of their courses. Prior to encountering Robert's book, this author has noticed that the Japanese and Chinese have done a great deal of research and writing in this area. Our own language has come to reflect some of our intuitive ideas about Structure/ Function such as: "He is level-headed." "She is nosey." "He's a real high-brow." and "He leads with his chin." (cf. Face Language, p. xi-xii)

Whiteside takes 40 pages to identify traits that are shown by the eyes. Then he explains traits that are shown by the mouth area. Then he deals with overall facial traits and finally profile traits. For instance, a large difference between one side of the face and the other indicates how much the individual changes with their mood change. If the head steadily gets wider as it runs from the mouth to the ears, then the person has the trait of acquisitiveness. A person who loves to be precise with words will develop little lines that fan out from the inner corner of the eye toward the cheekbone. The 3-In-1 college doesn't teach that the face reveals all behavior, but they teach their students what to expect from people, so that they can communicate better.

Another 3-In-1 publication Advanced ONE BRAIN by Gordon Stokes and Daniel Whiteside reveals eye modes. NLP has also been teaching some of these eye modes to detect what a person is thinking. Another publication provides charts (designed by William Mariboe) which explain different traits and how they exhibit themselves physically. For instance if the eyes are extremely wide apart, the person will either see an open viewpoint as valuable or feel inadequate. The chart then charts out how the trait (of emotional tolerance) will exhibit itself under different circumstances. For instance, in doing a job they tend to loose track of time. Perhaps the value of all this in not clear in the reader's mind. In terms of mind-control, if you know what physical structures will give you a particular trait, you can enhance what you want by skilful manipulation of the skull bones.

The key to manipulating the skull lies in the fact that the skull bones actually float on the Cerebrospinal fluid, while the brain floats in the fluid. In the booklet The Cranial Bowl by William G. Sutherland (1984), he writes about what he calls "the moulding technic". The moulding technic is the reshaping of the skull. He writes on page 28, "The moulding technic is especially adaptable to children, and even to the adult well along in the later period of life." In the booklet, he goes into details about the cerebrospinal fluid.

CEREBROSPINAL FLUID

The Cerebrum (brain) and the spine float in a fluid that surrounds them. This fluid is called cerebrospinal fluid and is referred to on page 1050 of the massive anatomical reference book Gray's Anatomy 36th Brit. ed. (edited by Williams & Warwick, printed by W.B. Saunder Co., for Churchill Livingstone). In 1920 and 1938, Weed published research on the circulation of the cerebrospinal fluid. As just one example of many of the roles that the CS Fluid plays within the brain, that has been discovered is that the carotid artery has a branch that passes upward through a water bed of cerebro-spinal fluid. The CS Fluid follows that internal carotid artery to the choroid plexus, so that it can perform the function of interchange with the arterial blood. The CS Fluid is "in command" of this exchange. (I mention this because see how this ties in with the 5th brain?)

In fact, a Fourth Ventricle Compression is the most valuable and powerful CSF technique for helping people. (It is mentioned simply to show people the effect that CSF has on some very important brain areas.) Because the brain and spinal cord float in a fluid, a brain weighing 1,500 grams in the air, only weighs 50 gr. in cerebrospinal fluid which distributes the brain weight more evenly. The fluid itself is clear, slightly alkaline with a specific gravity of 1007. About l00 mls of CS Fluid will exist to float the brain and spinal cord. The spine rests in this cerebrospinal fluid, which has waves that approximate the breathing rhythm of the body. 50% of the cerebrospinal fluid is manufactured in one part of the head (choroid plexuses), and spends its time fluxuating. It is absorbed and replenished, as other body elements are. The plexuses which are located in the lateral recesses of the fourth ventricle also put cerebrospinal fluid into the subarachnoid space, and this supplies the cerebello-medullary cistern and the pontine cistern with fluid. The cerebrospinal fluid makes up a single fluxuating system of fluid within which the central nervous system/brain operate. As the brain coils and uncoils, waves of motion (energy) fluctuate in a spiral pattern through the cerebrospinal fluid in the skull, down the spinal column and up again, so that there is motion from front to back in the head and also laterally.

As the human brain develops the CSF seems to appear at the earliest stages. The brain goes through stages of development as the brain-spinal cord divide. The forebrain develops into several items, the midbrain into two parts, and the hindbrain into the first three brains. The cerebrospinal fluid is manufactured by the body, fluctuates in a single Head-spinal cord system and then is absorbed and replenished by the body. The fluid does not circulate like blood. The fluid and the skull bones continue to fluctuate even if a person holds his breath. As long as the CSF oscillates like it should, things are fine, but if something occurs to pervert the rhythms, the health of the person goes down. Loss of sleep can influence the rhythms adversely. If the occipital motion is restricted schizophrenia can result. When severe spheno-basilar symphysis locking occurs, there is frequently manic-depression. Most people are totally unaware that these mental problems may be resulting from a CSF problem.

Very little information is let out about the cerebrospinal fluid. Very little is released to the public about how over a period of time Cranial Osteopaths can develop the manipulative skill to control and change the fluctuations of these fluids. Only a few top people are allowed in on the secrets, and those people are handpicked members of the occult world. Some of the top Cranial Doctors are under Monarch-type mind control themselves. The osteopathic libraries are staffed with people loyal to keeping cranial osteopathic secrets within the occult world. Could other doctors teach themselves? The ability to manipulate the cerebral-spinal fluid is an art that has taken years to develop, and for practitioners to learn. As stated, the tests that doctors rely on such as x-rays and MRIs are too big and clumsy to be of any value in this area. The doctors would have to ''reinvent the wheel and then the automobile'' if they wanted to self-teach themselves. It often takes two to three years of study in this area, before a doctor is able to feel the movement of the fluid.

The cranial bones have sutures between them, that allow a skilled person to move them. The sutures have been proven to move as much as 1/20 of an inch. The trained finger can perceive the natural motion of these sutures even if the natural motions are only 1/40 of an inch. In McCatty's excellent book Essentials of Cranio-Sacral Osteopathy, (Bath, Eng.: Ashgrove Press) p. 3 he states, "Contrary to some schools of thought, all circumstances being normal, the cranial sutures (or joints of the head) do not fuse--regardless of age, race, sex, or geographic location. They are perpetually motile, influencing the dynamics of fluid exchange and mebraneous tension within the cramo-sacral mechanism."

When early cranial osteopaths like Sutherland looked at the skull and its membranes and cartilage they realized that the 18 human bones that make up the head were actually designed to articulate (move slightly). In fact, researchers have discovered the cranium has 3 distinct oscillations. (Magoun, Harold Ives, D.O. Osteopathy in the Cranial Field, p.322).

Maud Nerman, D.O. presented the outline of an interesting lecture and lab class that she gave in 1992, entitled "Visualizing the brain under our hands" in which she taught the techniques for feeling the bones of the brain move with CS Fluid fluxuations, as well as sensing what it was doing internally. Coordinating the movement of the skull bones with the movement of the CS Fluid was called "directing the tide" by W.G. Sutherland. His Journal of the Osteopathic Cranial Assoc. reported successes doing this. Ronald McCatty teaches that "some heads are less pliant than other". The practitioner will rest his trained hands on the head, wait, and allow the cranial motion to teach the cranial osteopath what is happening or needs to happen. The client will usually be laying down, and the doctor will be relaxed and focused. The motion of the CS Fluid is called the Cranial Rhythmic Impulse (CR1). It will pulse about 10-14 times/mm. in normal adults and 12-16 times/mm. in children. When a person is frightened the CR1 can stop for up to 20 seconds. (The mind is literally frozen.) Tranquilizers will slow the CR1 rate down, as well as poor health.

For someone who has been traumatized, such as with electroshock, the very mention of the traumatic event, will cause the CR1 to temporarily stop. The cranial osteopath does not really force any bones, but rather gently encourages a skull bone in the direction it should go. Lightness of touch is a necessity. An example of the health benefits of the trained osteopath is given by McCatty, "That kink in the straight sinus can be, and often is, one of the primary causes of epilepsy and internal hydrocephalus..." By treating the kink the osteopath takes care of the problem, where the standard method is often to give the subject strong drugs.

To give an example of how the CS Fluid (CSF) can relate to our state of mind, consider the following by McCatty, "And again, change of direction of C.S.F. from anterior-posterior to lateral is of paramount importance in the sleep-wake phenomenon. When you are standing there is parallel action of C.S.F. flow. When you lie down with your head on a pillow this alters, you impinge on one or other temporal bone, you decelerate C.S.F. activity. You, as it were, slow down the pendulum. You inhibit parallel action. By inhibiting this pendulum you automatically produce an anteroposterior swing which is parasympathetic; that is to say, the parts of the automatic nervous system that slow down the action of the heart when the body is not under stress, in order to conserve bodily energy." This author thought it was exciting to understand better how the mind/body relaxes and slows down when we lay our heads down.

TRANSCENDENTAL MEDITATION (TM) & the HINDU CONNECTION

Years ago, back in 1974, this author was a West Point cadet who was watching the U.S. Army introduce TM into the academy. It was presented as a scientific technique, and many officers, some friends and other cadets availed themselves of the chance to train themselves in TM's mystical method of training. A fellow cadet who was already trained in martial arts quickly learned the techniques. After initially maintaining a safe distance, this author decided to investigate TM after I got out of the military. The U.S. government gave substantial grants to get TM introduced into this country. Fortunately, Christians didn't sleep long, and exposed that TM is Hinduism. Everyone that is taught TM is initiated into it by the TM instructor singing a puja (worship) song in Sanskrit which is a Hindu devotional song while incense and candles burn.

Until the Christians exposed this, our national government went blithely along in promoting Hinduism into our public schools. For instance, the Dept. of Health, Education, & Welfare gave a $21,540 grant for 150 high school teachers to learn TM. TM has grown to be a powerful organization, with many organizations set up attached to it. It has its international headquarters at Hotel Sonnenberg in the Swiss village of Seelisberg.

When I investigated TM back in 1975, this TM instructor who was friends of mine, talked about her experience at Seelisberg. From the conversation with her it was obvious that people had had to surrender their will to the organization to go to Seelisberg, and some mind altering experiences had taken place there. She participated in the Siddhi program to be able to dematerialize, walk through walls and levitate. But the program clearly had emotionally disturbed her and others who had been in it. Once a person is involved in the higher levels of TM, you don't just walk away from this cult. From my personal observations, I discovered that TM is involved in some types of mind-manipulation, and that the organization is not above using deceit on unsuspecting people.

What then becomes doubly interesting is that after observing these things, I learned that TM have a large interest in the cranial osteopathic techniques which can alter the mind and personality of a person. For instance, this author has obtained a list of TM instructors in Santa Monica, CA area who are also Doctors of Cranial Osteopathy. (But bear in mind, this whole thing is bigger than labels, when people are interested in the occult they study eclectically.) These TM Cranial Osteopaths are concentrated where TM has a secret MUM Mountain, CA training site. There are cranial doctors in the nearby towns of Aptos, Capitola, Cupertino, Hollister, Los Gatos, Salinas, Santa Cruz, Saratoga and Watsonville. It's boggles the mind that 12 cranial doctors are needed for the rural area near MUM Mountain, while L.A. only has 10. Concentrations of cranial doctors occur in close proximity to TM centers, particularly around the Maharishi University in Fairfield, 10 as well as the secret MUM Mountain training center. Other cranial DOs who are part of TM are scattered about the United States.

Another observation which I made, was that some of the people that got really big into TM are still searching for something to fill the voids and needs of their life. TM didn't turn out to be as big of an answer as they expected. TM is not the final answer. However, the Maharishi who brought TM to America has a college in Fairfield, Iowa (the Maharishi International University) and 20 North American "heavenly communities" operating in the quest to create a heaven on earth. The Maharishi International University has been used for medical experimentation on people. The close connections between the leadership of TM and the Illuminati leadership suggests that TM is being used as another haven for the NWO's mind-control to be perpetrated on unsuspecting victims. There are bone-setters in India also. Perhaps the Maharishi got his original interest in the potential for mind-control via skull manipulation in India. Wherever the interest came from, it is evident that TM in America is involved in skull manipulation for its mind-control results.

The 3-in-One school Connection.

If one wants to surrender oneself to a cult, and allow one's mind to be control, in order to learn, the 3-in-1 school will be happy to teach you about what others would call phrenology and manipulation of the skull to control thinking. The school has a number of courses. They do not call their principles phrenology. Nor do they call their instruction mind-control. They identify to the student areas of the head and what type of thinking that area of the head is involved with. They also provide information so that their students can evaluate how people will act based on the shape of their heads and how that shape will interact with other shapes. The school is located at 2001 West Magnolia Blvd., Burbank, CA 91506, ph. no. 818-841-4786. They teach Ericksonian Hypnosis (good for programmers to know), Bodywork (incl. cranial osteopathy, which is good for programmers to know), and they teach NLP, Mind-controlled relationships (along with scripts), Mind-controlled adolescent problems, and a pantheistic religious philosophy/religion.

When the 3-in-1 school got started they were teaching muscle-testing and other important skills to their students (who can become "facilitators" in teaching others). The muscle-manipulation they have taught is extremely gentle and way beyond what the chiropractors knew. The school in California began about 10 years ago and then a few years later they began to tighten their hold on all their graduates and their students. The school has been drawing students from Europe, Japan, China, Russia, and South America (incl. Brazil). They have moved more and more toward being an occult cult or perhaps an Illuminati front.

When given information that their muscle techniques could be used to help multiples, they have made it clear (according to one school administrator) that they are not interested in helping multiple personalities. One school administrator named Gordon Stokes said, "We're off in another direction." In fact, Gordon Stokes is the founder of 3-In-1. (Technically, a co-founder, Daniel Whiteside and Candace Callaway helped. Some speculate that the Three-in-One name refers to this triumvirate, and perhaps to their relationship together.)

Gordon Stokes has been reported to be a member of the BOTA which is an international Mystery School of the Hierarchy. BOTA stands for Builders of the Adytum. It is a Qabalistic-Hermetic Order of adepts founded in the 1920s by Dr. Paul Foster Case reportedly on direction by the hierarchy. The BOTA teaches higher states of consciousness to its adepts. It is located at 5105 No. Figueroa St., Los Angeles, CA 90042. Daniel Whiteside's parents are deeply involved in personology. And Candace Calloway's mother, their book keeper, has also been a major figure at the 3-in-1 school. This 3-in-1 school in Burbank seems to be a finishing school for Illuminati programmers. The school ridicules people who want to examine their life or have a conscience. Christianity is considered to be an obnoxious tyrannical religion by the school. The information that they teach would be very helpful for mind-control programmers, and their occult philosophy would scare off moral people from participating.

The 3-In-1 research has been geared into how the brain works. Their research shows that if a person has more brain cells in a particular region of the brain, they are more developed in that intellectual area. For instance, if the Action-based-on-feeling area (the parietal lobe) has lots of cells, the person will be more active than thoughtful. If the person has more cells in the brain's Conscious-associational thinking area (frontal lobes) they will think more than act. They call their system based upon this research comparative cell proportion. There were many ancient works that noticed personality traits in relationship to head shapes.

Three-In-One article "The Background of Structure/Function" states, "You can read about the basis of Structure/Function in the Hebrew CABALA'S book of ZOHAR (which is literally Aristotle's PHYSIOGNOMONICA) as well as in the writings of Maimonides and those of almost every famous Arabian philosopher during Medieval times." (Stokes, Daniel. The Background of Structure/Function, 1991, p. 2) The Cranial Academy's The Cranial Letter also picked up on the connection between the Cabala and cranial manipulation.

A class on the "Cabala and Osteopathy" is advertized in the May '95 issue, p. 9. Until Freud captured the interest of students of the mind, phrenology was psychology. Phrenology studied what could be measured, Freud got people looking for the hidden. In 1938, Dr. Edward Vincent Jones improved upon Phrenology and classic Physiognomy and developed Personology. His system was an instant hit and he was given the go ahead and conduct research on inmates at San Quentin Prison, and what is now LA's giant USC County Hospital.

Interestingly, it was not long after Jones' research there, that Cisco Wheeler's father (trained as a programmer) was assigned by the Illuminati to organize covens in the San Quentin Prison. The Whitesides became disciples of Jones research and went on to statistically validate his system. One of their best students then was Gordon Stokes of Sacramento, who then moved to San Francisco to be better trained by the Whitesides. As mentioned, sixty traits have been validated statistically. By looking at the skull and head, the skin, the body tone, the eyes, and other areas, the practitioners of Structure/Function can accurately tell a person's personality. Because this type of information has been in the possession of caballists, it is not surprising that the average person is ignorant of all this. However, the potential for good or evil with this knowledge is tremendous.

They also used Applied Kinesiology to defuse emotional stress. For this work they divide the brain into the dominant side (the left), and the alternate side (the right). Then each of these hemispheres is again divided between the fore and back brains for defusion. Applied Kinesiology is used to gain information about a trauma, and the defusion is used to release any negative emotional stress around an incident. (This also possibly could be used to dilute the emotional impact of some assignment done by a slave.)

In the first 3-In-1 newsletter of 1995, pg. 1, they write, "Self-image is the key to good learning performance. What 'magic' do we use to help slow learners and people labeled as 'learning disabled' change for the better so dramatically." This is just one minor example, of how these groups like to reframe what they do in occult terms. The mind-control programmers need only have someone skilled in the manipulation of the cranial bones and the skull bones and they can with repeated delicate precision reshape a person's skull and also his brain's shape, thus manipulating the personality & looks. Photos of Marilyn Monroe (Erma Jean) during her life strongly suggest that type of cranial manipulation was done to her for mind-control purposes.

The occult world has maintained a dogged resolve to keep the deeper cranial knowledge and skills secret. Dr. Sutherland's wife wrote his story With Thinking Fingers. She states on pg. 62, "It was Dr. Sutherland's cherished dream that a day would come when the benefits to the mentally ill through the cranial component in osteopathy would be investigated..." If that was his dream, it is being hijacked today by those who see it as a tool for power over their fellow men.

B. GENETIC ENGINEERING

A great deal of secret experimentation has gone on in underground installations with genetics. This author has had the privilege of debriefing someone who worked at the Area 51 underground installation. He was murdered after having had several long interviews with this author. Truth is stranger than fiction. It goes without saying that the Illuminati has gathered up every hair-brained idea for controlling and manipulating the human race. That doesn't mean everyone of them has been attempted, but they have the means to carry out very bizarre experiments in their underground facilities, such as the ones at Area 51.

There is no question that they have tried to augment natural human features and replace natural human parts. Who knows what weird transgenetic or cybernetic beings have been created? This author knows that they have been successful in some of their work at reshaping humans. This author has accumulated a great deal of information on the underground installations from eyewitnesses, but there is no way of knowing what is accurate and what is disinformation. However, a few details are definite. These underground installations are massive and they involve genetic manipulation to create new species or breed special types of people. In the Vol. 2 book, we discussed the Aquaman subspecies that the NWO has created with gills and special skin. These people look like normal people unless observed closely. They had extra genetic material inserted in the genetic material that created them. They are called Transgenic humans because they still closely resemble other people.

In order for transgenetic humans to pass their new added features to the next generation they need to mate with other similar transgenetic humans. However, the NWO has been secretly creating Chimeras. Chimeras is the widely used name for beast-men. This research is generally not for the public to see but is done in some of the underground facilities listed in Appendix 2. An example would be a creature that was half human and half some other beast.

On a BBC TV show on Oct. and Nov. 1988, the British showed the result of a gorilla being artificially inseminated with a human sperm. The experiment was done by British researchers working for the government and the result ended in a child looking remarkably like a normal person. However, the common people who viewed it were outraged. Most people are not really excited about scientists playing God and destroying the human race by genetic tampering. Of course the scientists who do these genetic games have lots of excuses and rationales, many of which have been put into print, to justify their research.

People are being bred for specific purposes by the Illuminati, just like this author bred dairy cows. Parents with certain desired features are obtained. (In fact, the Nazi's secret superdog Lowenhertz Dogo Argentino - which looks like a race of weight-lifting dogs, and the secret 100 yr. old Paraguayan Nueva Germania colony of special bred Aryans are still in existence.)

The NY Times had an article on 9/17/92 where a Washington psychiatrist Dr. Peter Breggin accused the federal government of a genetic "violence initiative" in which the government was involved with genetic research as it relates to crime and violence. Dr. Susan Solomon, is one of the government's leaders involved in researching violence. However, from what this author can gather, the government's research is far more reaching that the NY Times' article even begins to imply. By genetic breeding and manipulation, the Illuminati are trying to strengthen certain mental features. Considering that this has already been done for centuries by mankind to other species, for instance, when mankind domesticated the horse, the dog, the cat, the lama, the chicken, then it is no secret that a docile servile slave class of humans can be created. The primary goal of this Illuminati breeding is to create a class of people who can work together with others (herd instinct), and who will take orders willingly. Independent thinking and intelligence are not wanted. Educational goals and a world-wide educational system that can accommodate these types of workers is being created world-wide to deal with the eventual working-class-drones that the Illuminati want to create. The creation of this educational system at this present time has four goals, 1. to develop a group mindset, 2. to have education carried out by the multinational corporations, 3. to have students educated on the premise that truth is relative, 4. to teach compliance.

Already the public schools in America are gearing up for the government to dictate what occupations young students can study for. In other words, our educational system is being set up for mind-control, and this is to eventually work hand-in-hand with worker slaves that have the genetics needed to be good compliant stupid slaves.

There have also been studies of intelligence such as the five volume Genetic Studies of Genius started by L.M. Terman in 1925, (pub. by Univ. of Stanford Press). The World Order has specific and successful methods to create a class of technical people. At this point, people whose thinking abilities have been created by the monitoring/ manipulating of their genetics is a small but increasing number. Genetic control of breeding is unfortunately where the programmers are headed. This is not happening for the genetic betterment of the human species, this is for the perverted lusts of these demon-possessed megalomaniacs who think they deserve to rule with a sadistic iron fist. Those who mistakenly think the mind-control programmers are trying to improve the human race, need to get to know the programmers better. (See Appendix A for biographical information on some of the programmers.) Those poor gullible naive people who think that when the global masters visibly introduce the New World Order that the NWO will be tolerable if they can simply keep their noses clean, not fight back, and do their jobs, are sadly mistaken. They do not know the dark - sinister side to these global masters. As one man very close to the center of power said to a common man about the men who rule the world, "If you stepped on an ant, you would have more conscience than the global elite have in manufacturing wars and killing millions of people. They want power and they intend to amass total power no matter what the cost."

• Another area of ILLUMINATI DECEPTION & CONTROL--

Ionizing radiation used in conjunction with chemicals to manipulate the genetics of the mind; or say this another way: USING RADIATION & CHEMICALS TO CHANGE GENETICS associated WITH THINKING.

When a retired high-ranking military man first told this author that radiation research had to do with mind-control, my reaction was probably like most people's, puzzlement. I thought that radiation was quite lethal and that genetic research with radiation was to protect us from some kind of atomic attack. Wrong. That is a nice cover story.

Since that retired colonel (who may not have long to live) talked to me, others have said similar things. Like many things that the World Order does, if we don't have a frame of reference of what is going on, we can live around what they are doing day in and day out and never see all the clues as to what is going on under our noses.

One trauma-based mind-controlled slave (Chris DeNicola) spied on the files of the doctor who did radiation experiments on her. She saw the following radiation file headings, & their codes: Canker Sore (D-7040), Laser Documentation (D-7000), Nautical Science (D-1015), Pediatric Radionthology (L-6542) [One idea is that this file might pertain to child alters.], Penetrating Wave Activity, Radiation Experimentation (L-6540), Radioactive Distortions, Radioactive Material Contamination, Radioactive verification, Radioactive Waves, Radionthology, Electrolite Prodigies Experiments (654-011), Laser Light Distortions experiments (654-012), & Laserlight Technology experiments (101-015). One reason, that this author is providing the code numbers of these files, is that memories of slaves who are involved in these experiments or projects often are internally coded with these file codes. The date the experiment was done will also be added as part of the code.

When this author researched their genetic research, I was utterly amazed at how many institutions world-wide are carrying out deep research into genetics--much of which will contribute to the enslavement and mind-control of the human race.

Just a sampling of countless labs working hard on this mind- control related genetic research include Brookhaven National Labs. Upton, NY; John Hopkins Univ., Baltimore, MD; Institut fur Genetik, the Free University of Berlin, Germany; Institute of Hygiene & Epidemiology, Czech.; Radiation Genetic Lab & Chemical Mutagenesis, State Univ. Of Leiden, Sylvius Labs, Leiden, The Netherlands; MIT, Cambridge, MA; Gesellschaft für Strahlen und Umweltforschung, Munich, Germany; National Inst. of Environmental Health Sciences Research Triangle Park, NC; Sandoz Labs in Basle, Switzerland; Biology Division, Oak Ridge National Lab, Oak Ridge, TN; Roswell Underground Labs, NM; Stanford Research Institute, Menlo Park, CA; Shell Labs, Kent, England; University of Michigan, Ann Arbor, MI; the Zentrallabor für Mutagenitätsprüfung der Deutschen Forschungsgemeinshaft, Freiburg, Germany.

This is just a tiny sampling of the enormous world wide research devoted to genetics that pertain to mind-control. While there are numerous surnames among the genetic researchers, because this author knows as a fact that some of these researchers are Illuminati, it doesn't quiet one's curiosity to see the better known Illuminati surnames such as Dupont, Hersey, Fox, Frey, Jung, Li, Paterson, Stuart, Sinclair, Sutherland, and Russell appearing among the genetic researchers doing research that pertains to mind-control.

Obviously, this author can't give all the ways they have figured out to use radiation, along with chemicals and genetics to control the human race. I will try to give you a peek in the window. The real deep & dangerous information is of course highly classified material and protected by their mind-control of those scientists who work for them.

When I say mind-control, that includes such methods as blackmail and threats of assassination.

There is a type of radiation called ionizing radiation-that means it is radiation that gives off electrons (thus producing ions). There are many different types of ionizing radiation. Some go right through the body, some damage the cells, but the body repairs itself, some causes genetic changes, and some simply hits your cells like a sledge hammer & kills them.

The ionizing radiation that changes genetics has been the focus of an incredibly enormous amount of (mostly secret) research. Genes are instructions that tell non-life material how to organize itself into something living. A gene consists of genetic material called DNA and RNA. Genes also provide instructions for how something is to develop. As a person or animal develops, the genes interact with the environment to create what the person or animal is like. For instance, different breeds of dogs when born are more similar, than after they grow up. Different breeds of dogs have been bred for different genetic traits, and as different breeds grow up, their genes continually interact with the environment to create the adult dog.

So full genetic expression can take a life-time. The link between genetics and behaviour can be seen in this quote from the Quarterly Review of Biology (art. by T.C. Schneirla, 1966, p. 283), "Behavioural ontogenesis is the backbone of comparative psychology. Shortcomings in its study inevitably handicap other lines of investigation from behavioural evolution and psychogenetics to the study of individual and group behavior."

Genetic psychology has revealed that the genes program in methods for an organism to adjust to their environment. So genetic instruction is, for instance, more than just the instruction "be smart, be aggressive, be tall" but it is tailoring the way a person's develops to deal with its environment. In other words, behaviours are programmed into a person via their genes (genetic instructions) to provide mechanisms for quick, dynamic adaptions to changing circumstances. These mechanisms (created by genetic codes) may even have the person (or animal) reverse their behaviour for purposes of survival.

p_

8-1

Within the human brain (also all mammal brains) all the neurons are believed to be generated before birth with the exception of the following cells: granule cells of the olfactory bulb, fascia dentala granule cells in the hippocampus, the granule cells of the cerebellar cortex, and the granule cells of rhombic lip in the brainstem.

Its the brainstem cells that the Illuminati manipulate through brain stem scarring to produce photographic memories for their scientists and computer programmers. The germinal cells create neurons in the germinal zone. Brain cells with a common function develop from a common lineage although from different sites. After a new neuron develops in the germinal zone, they migrate to whatever location they are to live in. The complicated process of how a neuron discovers where to go (migrate to in the brain) has been not been discovered according to what this author has read. When neurons establish themselves they deal with certain neurotransmitters, that establish communication between them and other neurons.

Researchers have discovered that neurons can change their own make up to take different neurotransmitters if they decide their "environment" in the brain needs it. They also grow their dentrite connections depending on what type of connections are needed for that particular brain to function. For instance, a piano player will develop dentrite connections to be able to play well.

These discoveries show once again that even on the cellular level, genetic instructions are complex and designed to give flexibility and adaptability of the cell to the situation for the cell. Genetic programming begins at the cellular level. There is a cellular consciousness besides the consciousness that we think about. DNA structures which are inherited affect the cellular consciousness. Body memories are contained within the physiological structure. The first brain and the body work off a stimulus-response recording mechanism. Body memory and programming are stored at this level. This is an area of the brain that is always on. However, its view or perception of events is not an exact copy of what other higher brains are thinking. Your conscious mind doesn't remember how the stairs and the room are arranged, but in the dark, you primal part of your mind helps guide your steps.

Various drugs and chemicals have been identified that influence particular learning sequences in the mind, such as imprinting. For instance, hexamethonium chloride antagomzes the nicotinic actions of acetylcholine on the ganglia, or in other words, acetylcholine will depolarize the ganglia but is prevented by the hexamethonium. The overall result is that impulses that the sympathetic ganglia would transmit are blocked. This is just one example of countless examples of how a specific chemical can affect a specific brain action.

There is a branch of genetic research called "developmental social behaviour genetics" which deals with how genetics program in social behaviours of animals and people. For instance, these geneticists study how genes create aggression, courtship, territorial behaviours, behaviours involving mothers and fathers, dominance (peeking order) behaviors, sexual behaviors, attraction behaviors, recognition behaviors, etc.

Men are very much controlled by the sexual lusts, power lusts, and aggressive behaviors. Can the reader see how genetic manipulation of these genetic based behaviors could radically change the potential behavior of a person. A fox's genes cause him to react differently than a rabbit's genes. Having a rabbit grow up in a fox home is not going to change the genetic instructions. (The Bible even says, Can a leopard change it's spots?) But the World Order has figured out how to change those instructions.

Genetic researchers had to begin sorting out behaviours, and sorting out genes that affected them. For instance, genes create a person's (or animal) reproductive "instincts". These instructions include instructions on fighting, nest building, mating, and care of their offspring. These genetic instructions are different for different people and different animals. Researchers into imprinting have discovered that IF a set of animals (or people) is prevented from learning a particular imprint, and IF that set of animals breed, THEN they pass on a lack of ability to receive that imprint. In other words, genetically we learn from generation to generation.

Let's say that we prevent men from naturally imprinting a sexual desire for women as they grow up. If we mate those men to women, the offspring will show a reduced ability to be heterosexual. Males seem to develop their sexuality, but females seem to react more on the basis of genetically present "releasers". Genetic researchers have gone in and identified what people's behavioural instructions specifically are, and how to change them. The instructions are written in DNA, and manipulation of DNA can change those instructions.

When I researched their genetic research, I found that they have developed maps for how to change genetic material to change those instructions concerning behaviour. The maps for changing human genes related to behaviour are classified, but an example of one that isn't is found in the book The Genetics of Behaviour (ed. Ehrman & Parsons. Sinauer Assoc., Inc. publ.: Sunderland, Mass, 1976, chapter 8 figure 4.). This map shows 3 sites in a HK gene that are intentionally mutated by the scientists in order to change the way a particular fly sings its mating call. The specific changes in how the fly sings its new mating call (after the genetic code is changed by geneticists) are even graphed out in a recording graph in another book Developmental Behavior Genetics: Neural, Biometrical, and Evolutionary Approaches (ed. by Hahn et. al., Oxford, Eng.: Oxford Univ. Press, 1990, Fig. 6-1.)

Again bear in mind that we only get the crumbs of what they know. We get a map of how they can change the way a fly sings a song--while they secretly keep the genetic maps to change human behaviour! An easy example of how genetics play a role in human behaviour can be seen in how infants behave toward their mothers and toward strangers. By using twins and adopted children, etc. it could be clearly demonstrated that the behaviour of a child in how it touches its mother was genetically inherited. But remember that the genetic instructions as a child grow older are designed to give it flexibility in relationship to its environment, so the environment is going to interact with the genetics to form the final behaviours. The study of these reactions of genes to the environment is called the study of epigenesis.

Another easy example of the genetic role in human behaviour is that intelligence has been linked to brain to body size. Genes ultimately determine that ratio of brain to body size. The factors involved are largely prenatal maternal influences. A great deal has been learned in this area. Brain size relates less to body size than it is a function of body metabolism. (See Research by Lande & Martin) To give a tiny sample of the types of genetic studies done in this area:

- Hahn, M.E., & Haber, S.B. "Dominance for large brains in laboratory mice..." Behavior Genetics, 1979, 9, pp. 243-244.

- Fuller, J.L. & Geils, H. "Brain growth in mice selected for high and low brain weight." Developmental Psychobiology, 1972, 5, pp. 307-318.

- Riska, B., & Atchley, W.R. "Genetics of growth predict patterns of brain-size evolution." Science, 1985, 229, pp. 668-671.

Research into how to control humans genetically proceeded in several directions. First, scientists realized that radiation was the key to changing genetics. Radiation causes breaks and changes in the DNA instructions. If only one little bit of genetic DNA instruction is changed in 1 million bits of information, that change could radically change the life of the person or animal. We see that everyday cleft lips... But how does radiation affect genetics? DNA has been studied from every angle. DNA has been looked at, probed, tested with all kinds of chemicals and countless other manipulations. The scientists figured exactly how the different DNA is constructed, what makes it tick, how it joins, holds together, reproduces, etc. They can disassemble and rebuild DNA however they want. DNA is the genetic instructions.

Since radiation will affect DNA they tested a long list of ionizing radiation substances on DNA. Different radiations will break the DNA in different ways. Chemicals will join to DNA in certain ways. Long story short, there are millions of ways to manipulate genetic material, and the World Order set out to discover how to precisely manipulate certain kinds of genetic material in certain ways.

An example of how skilled they are in understanding most everything about to construct and take apart the molecules of genetic material, at Cold Spring Harbor Labs one of the 1997 courses offered students is Molecular Cloning of Neural Genes. They understand what makes a nerve cell and how to create one. This science is called molecular neurobiology. (This course at Cold Springs H.L. happens to be taught by instructors from Rockefeller Univ., Harvard, John Hopkins, and UC of Berkeley.)

One area of intense study for many years was a long-term scramble to find chemicals that would cause different types of mutations in DNA. This research was called Comparative Chemical Mutagenesis. In fact one of the books this author studied was entitled just that Comparative Chemical Mutagenesis (ed. by DeSerres & Shelby). This book's Chapters 16-18, 22-25 are about chemical-genetic research concerning how to create genetic changes in mammals using chemicals!

When it comes to genetics, much of what is learned from studying one mammal will apply to humans. The chemical principles are the same, the DNA is written in the same code, only the genetic instructions written in that code is different. To make an analogy, this book is written in English. Once someone understands how English works, they can take apart a sentence and rewrite it. Top level Genetic scientists know how to take apart genetic instructions and rewrite them. Radiation used in conjunction with chemicals presents them a tool for the mass editing of human genetic instructions. No wonder the Chernobyl nuclear accident happened. (Insiders in the know say that it was caused on purpose.) What a great way to carry out more mind-control research.

According to public research, genetic mutations were created by scientists in mammal cells first in 1968. It is likely that this had already been accomplished in secrecy before this. Labs all over the world went about testing genetic material with specialized chemicals to see what would happen to various genetic material when it came in contact with specific chemicals. Some of the commonly- tested mutagent chemicals that were widely tested to discover their "mutagenicity" (mutagenicity is the word geneticists use to describe the power of a chemical to cause a mutation) include:

Aflatoxin B1 (AFT)(This is a mold metabolite and is not always effective without another agent.)
Cadmium chloride
Cadmium salts
Cyclophosphamide (CP)
Dimethylnitrosamine (DMN)
Epichlorohydrin
Ethylenimine
Ethyl Methanesulfonate (EMS)
Methyl methanesulfonate (MMS)
Mitomycin C (a strong mutagenic at low doses)
Myleran (aka Busulfan)
N.Methyl-N,-Nitro - N - Nitrosoguanidine (MNNG)

Natulan (aka procarbazine, this chemical was strongly mutagenic in the lab with the presence of S-9, but weak without the presence of S-9)

Tepa
Theo-Tepa
Trenimon
Triethylenemelamine
Vinyl chloride

When these chemicals (and others) were tested on genetic material, the mutations they caused in the genetic material were observed, and then the specific type of mutation each caused was charted. Some caused chromosome-type changes, others caused chromatid-type changes, and some caused sub- or half- chromatid changes (these sub-changes usually were in the mitotic portion of the cell cycle.) When the chemicals broke chromosomes they were called clastogens. Others cause chromosomes to lose genetic material by damaging the mitotic apparatus. Many of the chemicals that were first tested only produced chemical changes in the chromatid-type of change. They discovered that the protective mechanisms of animals, plants and humans were protecting against many of their induced mutations, but they also learned what mutations they could create that the body would not fix or recover from.

Along with finding out what certain chemicals would do, the World Order wanted to find out what would happen at the molecular level of DNA when subjected to different types of radiation. The key to using radiative material is that there are many different types of radiative substances, not just uranium. For instance, cadmium is radioactive and can be used in genetic manipulation. In researching radiation, the first stage is when free radicals are created. This takes only a very small fraction of a second. The next is the chemical transformation of those radicals into stable radiation substances, and finally the last stage are the effects of these substances when the body incorporates them. The effects of the radiation substances on a person may last several years. The effects of radiation take place on the molecular level of DNA.

When you and I went to school we were taught that DNA occurs as a double-helix around an invisible common axis. The core of the helix is a series of purine and pyrimidine bases stacked in a parallel array and are arranged almost perpendicular to the invisible axis of the helix. However, the reality is that DNA can also exist in three (triple) double-stranded helix structures which are called the A-DNA, the B-DNA, and the C-DNA. At high humidities the A-DNA will transform into a B- DNA if excess salt is in the area. In A-DNA the normal of the base pairs is tilted by 200 to the helix axis. In contrast, in the B-DNA the base pairs are perpendicular. In some viruses and bacteria single stranded DNA is found. DNA also comes in supercoiled in some situations.

The point is simply that DNA occurs in ways other than we learned in school. They discovered that the energy of the sugar-phosphate backbone of the DNA allows for the DNA bases to be stacked, and is the key to the stability of the DNA. The verticle stacking of the bases gives stability of the DNA helix. They discovered that the helical structure of DNA is strongly influenced by its base composition and molecular weight. I mention these only to point out, that they know all about what DNA is and how it is built and holds itself together.

The genetic-radiation researchers had to learn how the bases of the DNA held together electronically. They needed to learn how well these molecules of these different bases would accept electrons or donate electrons, because ionized radiation is substances that give off electrons or other ionizing particles. Directly ionizing particles are atomic particles that are charged such as electrons, protons, alpha (a) particles, "heavy" ions, etc.).

An example of something the researchers found is that the cytosine base was the best acceptor of all the DNA bases. They began the process of testing different radioactive substances on DNA to see how they would cause mutations. To study this type of research, this author read several books such as Effects of Ionizing Radiation on DNA (Springer-Verlag Publ.: Berlin, Germany, 1978). An example of a chapter in this book is "Radiation-Induced Degradation of the Base Component in DNA and Related Substances". This chapter shows charts of what happens to DNA components (such as thymine, cytosine, & uracil) when they are exposed to radiation. This author wants to cover some details of the type of discoveries these researchers made to make a point that specific chemicals and specific types of ionizing radiation will produce different effects upon DNA. Although these are very specific minute details, the reason they are mentioned here, is that the bottom line is that SOME CHEMICALS WORK WITH SOME TYPES OF RADIATION TO PRODUCE SPECIFIC MUTATIONS.

They discovered that if a mutagenic such as aminoacridine dye is absorbed by cells, this dye which binds to the nucleic acids, absorbs light to such a degree that the cells are destroyed. Different variations of dyes bind to the DNA in different strong and weak binding processes. Lambda radiation was tested on DNA. They observed that positive and negative ions were randomly produced throughout the DNA and that these are chemically unstable and undergo free radical reactions to form stable radiation products. They discovered that there was a consistent "oxygen effect" which was made into a radiobiological law which described how the presence of oxygen enhances radiation damage in all forms of cell life.

Another interesting discovery was that 5-bromouracil (BU) enhanced the rate of radiation-induced free radicals forming within gamma-irradiated DNA. Researchers discovered that an naturally occurring substance in cells, the sulthydryls, would bind with iodoacetic acid and N-ethylmaleimide, which made them radiosensitive, and would result in certain mutations. Still one more example of a compound that works with radiation to cause changes in the DNA is triacetoneamine-N-oxyl (or TAN for short). This is a stable free radical that combines with DNA. TAN comes from a group of nitroxide free radicals which all have the same influence on DNA. Metronidazole (aka Flagyl) was also found to be another of the nitroimidazoles and nitrofuranes that are oxygen mimics that worked in the lab as radiosensitizers of DNA.

Chemical-Biological Weapons are referred to as CB Weapons. In a transcript attached to the Dept. of Defense appropriations for 1970 (part 6) that I have of CB Weapons researchers talking, they indicate that the United States has BZ which "brings about complete mental disorientation as well as sedation which induces sleep. First of all the individual is completely confused as to what he is doing or what he is supposed to do and in addition he has hallucinations. He cannot carry out his assigned duties nor can he remember what his assigned duties were." The affect of BZ lasts for about 3 days and then the person will begin to recover. It can be given via the air or the water. If it is drank or inhaled it will work. It takes affect about 1 to 1 ½ hours after it is ingested. There are a number of corporations that can produce BZ in the U.S. At the time of the transcript, it was stated that BZ is $20/lb. and a lead time of six months for production.

Chemical incapacitants have been developed that affect the mental functions of the mind in various ways. Today, research and deployment continues of chemical and radioactive substances that can control people. One of the methods that chemical and radioactive materials work is to change genetic structures. Some of the genetic changes that can be created chemically, are chemical changes that affect the way the mind thinks. In a nutshell, we are looking at a situation where the thinking of an entire race could be altered via chemicals dropped into their air and water. How long would these genetic changes last? It is conceivable that some of the changes might have long range consequences. Again, the bottom line is that the World Order has at its disposal radioactive substances that can distributed in conjunction with chemicals to mind-control large geographic regions by genetic manipulation. These radioactive substances and chemicals can be distributed over vast areas by the air and water of a geographic region. It is conceivable that within a short time, the United States will experience chemicals administered via the air, or the drinking water used in conjunction with specific external stimuli to reinforce certain types of mind-control programming on a mass of people. A chemical that makes people susceptible to suggestion could be used over a geographic area while hypnotic television messages and ELF waves, etc. contribute to the mind-control operation.

Therapists are going to begin encountering victims of mind-control born in the 1960's or later that have been subjected to chemical-radiation changes to the genetics that control human behaviour. There are already dozens of very vocal victims of both radiation experiments & mind-control that are speaking up. Unfortunately, the ones that this author knows do not have a long life-expectancy, and speaking up usually has the effect of shortening a whistle-blower's life.

In this Deeper Insights book, the movie Jacob's Ladder was mentioned. This movie shows a unit in Vietnam which was given a drug to make them aggressive, but the drug backfired because they killed each other. However, the reason the movie was allowed to be produced is that it was a good cover for the fact that the military did not give up, but that they actually succeeded in producing their "magic chemical potion" to turn soldiers into killing machines. The biology of aggression has been figured out. Military studies on the relationship between drugs and the ability to kill have been numerous, one example is Gabriel, R.A. Military Psychiatry: A Comparative Perspective. NY: Greenport Press, 1986. The World Order has the ability to create the warrior spirit, actually its worse than that, they have the ability to turn men into killing machines.

WHAT WE'VE COVERED

As horrible as the physical manipulation of the brain and its fluids is, and as monstrous as the genetic manipulation of the growth of the brain as outlined in this chapter are, they are only a few methods of mind-control of many that the Illuminati have at their disposal. These techniques seriously raise the question how much longer will humanity as we know it survive? The next generation of children will have to face mind-control in the form of genetic tampering and the use of chemicals already stockpiled by the NWO.

left. This Las Vegas casino photo booth could greatly assist in confusing a mind-controlled slave. The photo machine can be set with different backgrounds so the person can be made to appear in another country, and will also blend the person's face with various animals, and will distort it in other ways in the Gene machine setting. Using a machine like this along with hypnosis and drugs, could assist a handler in genuinely mixing reality with fantasy to totally confuse a slave. They would have the photographic evidence to some cover story.

below. Oregon Museum of Science and Industry OMSI, which has Illuminati members on its board of directors, has been used as a programming site for the Network and the Illuminati. Recently, the theme of the Museum was Star Trek. The OMSI museum advertized its Star Trek theme on metro buses, and benches throughout the entire Portland area. The author's photo shows one of the museum's Star Trek bench ads. Vol. 2 covers Star Trek programming.

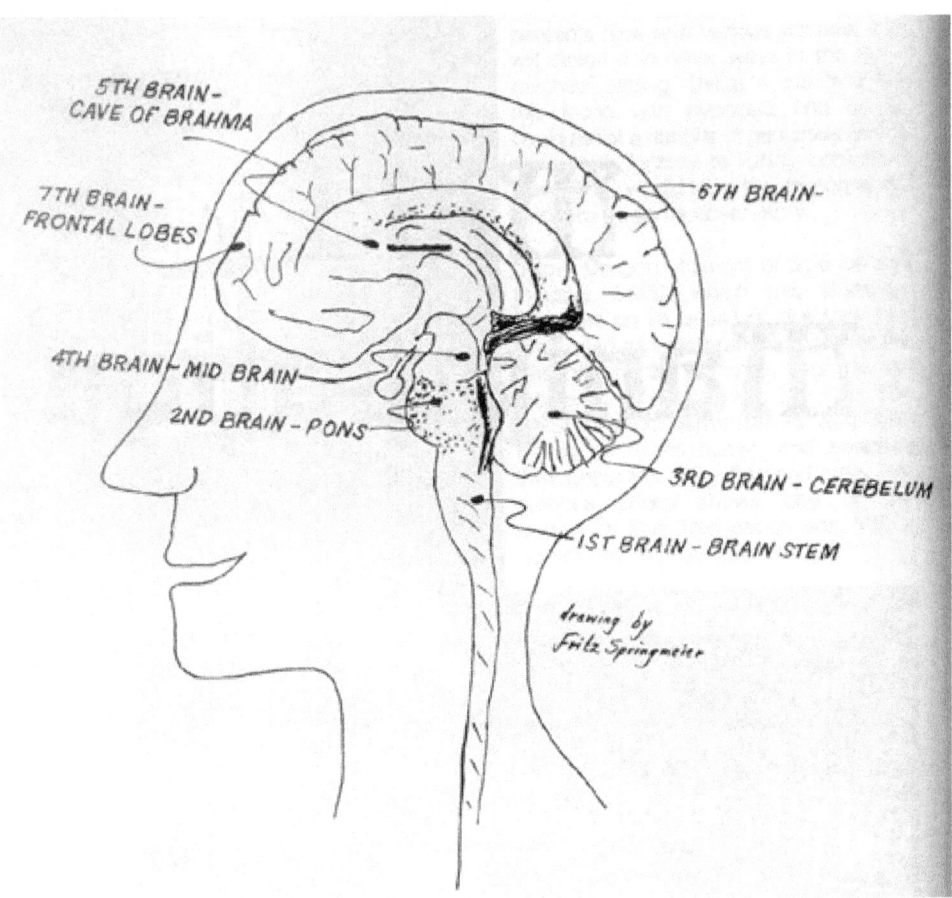

CHAPTER 9: THE SCIENCE OF MIND MANIPULATION BY PSYCHOLOGICAL PROGRAMMING METHODS: BEHAVIOR MODIFICATION, PSYCHOLOGICAL MOTIVATION & NLP

"STRIPPED" OF FEELINGS
PROGRAMMING TO HIDE REVEALING DREAMS
PROGRAMMING LANGUAGE
EFFECTS OF PROGRAMMING
FALSE IMPLANTED MEMORIES
PERCEPTION CLOUDS MEMORY

A person's "selfhood" is hard to define, but one could view it as the central important center of consciousness to which the person has placed both trust and purpose. A professor of Pastoral Counselling defined the self as "the purposive core I have learned to trust in myself and others." Although this author prefers his own wording as written above, the definition of "selfhood" by this professor of pastors is in agreement with this author's. A mature person is a person who has developed a "selfhood", a sense of self, that is able to make creative choices in line with values and plans for his or her life. By the destruction of the "selfhood" of many of the alters, the programmers derail the ability of the slave to make creative choices in line with values and plans. Not only do they destroy the sense of identity but they also destroy the development of values.

When a normal person grows up, the values, that an individual adopts, will enable that person to integrate his or her many actions into a cohesive unified agenda for living their life. What happens when a person is not able to adopt their own values, but is force fed values? What happens when the person does not even adopt any values, except to acquiesce to the brutal demands of a mind-control handler? The natural process for developing a unified agenda for life is cut short. The thinking of mankind is predicated on socialization with other humans. It is natural for people to want to work and be around other humans. The family, neighbourhood, city and nation all give an individual nurturing that fosters a sense of identity and values. What happens if an individual is cut off from society and most of humanity, in fact is even cut off from most of their own mind and will?

What typically happens in this situation is that the individual becomes demoralized, feels dehumanized, and as a person is enfeebled to deal with life. What happens when a person is not allowed to chose values freely, and allowed to give consideration to various alternatives and the consequences for these choices? It means that the person is not going to be happy with the choices they make, but will go through the motions of life in a rather dissociated manner. What happens when a person feels powerless? Feelings of powerlessness, can lead to feelings of meaningless. And meaningless makes an individual feel trapped by life. The meaninglessness imprisons a person. The person no longer has the freedom to make choices, and without choices has no real values, and without values life becomes meaningless.

The above situations are standard results of the total mind-control programming agenda. The person's natural built-in abilities to plan their life is short circuited. The person is demoralized and feels incomplete as a human because of his or her's lack of connectedness to their fellow humans, and as a result allows his or herself to be dependent upon the master. Because they are forced to do actions without any values, they dissociate their actions from feelings. Finally, they feel trapped because they have no values to give life meaning. A sexual slave will be forced to have sex. They are not allowed to have a value system, or else they would pick and choose who they wanted to have sex with. The result is that they feel dehumanized and they dissociate feelings from their actions. Without values, life feels like one big trap, with no purpose and no goals. The only purpose the slave has is to survive the brutality of its master, that is to stay alive.

Some slaves give up along the way, and are discarded as unsuccessful attempts by the Illuminati. The programming agenda prevents the natural God-given gift for mankind to make their own choices. As explained above, this in itself reinforces several items that the programmers have been intentionally creating such as dehumanization, isolation, dependence, and dissociation. It is built into human thinking to enjoy a sense of accomplishment. This happens when a person perceives his or her life as meaningful. The perception that his or her life is meaningful results in the person feeling power. Powerlessness and meaninglessness are two items that are related to each other when we understand human thinking. A normal child in a normal environment will naturally learn when to trust itself and when to trust others. This is important to the development of values. This is important for a person to become mature. The programmers short circuit this natural learning process.

The front alters continue learning who to trust and who not to trust, and when to trust oneself, because they hold the body from day to day. However, a special purpose child alter doesn't experience this. Without learning how to trust, it becomes hard to make decisions by one's self, and so the victim of mind-control transfers the right to make his or her choices to the programmer. By arresting the natural process of learning trust, the programmers detour the mind, so that it travels right where they want the mind to be.

Normally, a child would grow up, and as it grew up would realize that not everyone can be trusted. He would also come to realize that even his own self at times can not be trusted. Yet, the child would also learn that there are times that people can be trusted. This maturation of awareness moves a person from being dependent toward being independent. The programmed slave is afraid of seeking true love, and to find authentic relationships with people. Without these things, they remain incomplete and more pliable to the control of the master, who then attempts to provide in some substitute manner some of the things the slave should have developed for himself.

Many of the slave's deeper alters do not have the capacity to creatively look forward to the future, with the understanding that they can create their own life, their own future. The process of maturation that would have given that ability to them has been prevented from taking place. If these deeper alters do not experience life outside of their programmed trance states, they will have no chance to mature and to realize that they are capable to design and create their own future. Rather, the slave endures life with anxiety and dissociation, and limits his mental horizons to the present. The big reference point the slave has is to their master and his commands.

Many of the slave's alters are limited in their freedom to really have consciousness. Their thinking is below the definitions of conscious behavior--it is simply programmed behavior. Our consciousness has a big role in how we perceive the world. How we perceive the world in turn determines our values. The programmers can disrupt the process of a slave obtaining values in life, by disrupting the consciousness. Values in life are important in determining how we build our world-view, our frames of reference. The programmer constructs various worlds for most of the alters (except for the front alters). These alters are never given the chance for what psychologists would label "conscious behavior". Reality is not part of the package. Choice is not part of the package.

In normal life, conscious behavior is developed by interaction between a person and his environment and the freedom to make real choices. The bare necessities are grudgingly provided in a haphazard way to the alters of a total mind-controlled slave, so that IF they are aware of their needs, it is at a very basic level, such as survival, and security and warmth. A fully conscious individual has gone way beyond that to realizing his or her's needs for creativity, intimacy, community, justice, integrity, and spiritual fulfilment.

The challenge for the slave master will be to balance the freedom of activity and maturity of the front part of the slave's alters, with the control that the slave master needs to accomplish his nefarious goals. It is safer to bring a slave up to have a world view dependent on others that lends itself to the owner's agenda such as witchcraft values & a witchcraft world-view, or a Mormon/ or Jehovah's Witness/or Catholic world-view of obedience to the church, THAN to have the slave's front alters becoming independent self-directed mature thinkers.

It doesn't matter whether the person's front alters are Jehovah's Witnesses, Mormon or Catholic, they have surrendered their personal sense of power and control to institutional control. The victim ceases to do things because of personal choice, but accepts institutional values as a cog in a machine; and the person, whether they realize it or not, loses meaning in their life. Personal choice, value and meaning in life are all related. Because man is made in the image of God, he has an inherent desire to have meaning to his life. Mankind also has a desire to be in unity with his environment. This is also a God-given desire. To make himself feel at home in this world, man spends much of his activity taming and domesticating the wild world to conform to what feels comfortable. What happens when this is stripped from a person?

In order to provide substitute answers to these desires of the slave, the Illuminati's covens provide rituals. Rituals make the slave feel that some order is being brought out of the chaos and nonsense of life. But true meaning in life can only come from realizing the goals of our actual Creator, Almighty God. Substitutes for this, leave people unfulfilled and weak. Of course, the unfulfilled weak sense of meaning in life of the Illuminati members, can weaken some in their ability to realize their true spiritual potential. It becomes a vicious cycle of low base evil goals. Who will provide the safety for the deeper alters to move out independently in life? and then further, who will teach the deeper alters the social skills, and the other skills to step out and grow? Even if the complex programming should break its death-grip on an alter, (which seldom happens) an alter can not find freedom without some outside support system providing safety and instruction. The bondage that most deeper alters remain fixed in, is a very complex bondage of body, mind, and spirit. This complex bondage calls for group package answers, that address the type of issues that have been raised on these last two pages. The lack of this type of answer insures that few slaves will find full freedom. Partial freedom is still slavery.

On the flip side, because deeper alters have not had a chance to develop their own values, make their own choices, and experience reality, the power of the programs will be diluted simply by real life. This occurs even in the absence of intense deprogramming. One of the weaknesses of the programming is that the handlers often fail to allow alters to ever establish real personal values. Hand-me-down values that are accepted under duress or torture, are quickly discarded if the alters ever do get free.

Illuminati slaves who accept the values of the Illuminati, and progress to positions of power can be resistant to freedom, because they have internalized for themselves a value system, have some feelings of self-worth and self-competence. The Illuminati have long understood the value in having their members progress through the levels of initiation, and to pass through tests that bestow a sense of achievement upon the slave. When the Illuminati in Bavaria had their safe houses raided, their paperwork showed extensive disciple and training programs. At first glance, raising an initiate through an initiate degree system of training may not smack of mind-control, but it is like an anchor that ties in the mind-control. It is important for the Illuminati to attach an occult value system to the mind-control so that the slave is more resistant to wanting freedom, because their self-worth and identity are tied up with the Illuminati.

"STRIPPED" OF FEELINGS

Another side-effect of the total mind-control is that the deeper alters of a victim, and indeed often even the front alters are unsuccessful in morally meaningful relationships such as love and friendship. The reader may be wondering, what does Fritz mean by "morally meaningful"? Allow me to take several paragraphs to explain ... Has the reader ever tried to recall a name which you knew, but your mind seems blocked? And yet, when someone offers this name or that name, you realize that it doesn't have the correct feel, the correct rhythm, the correct beginning. Your mind can recognize what it is looking for on a subconscious level, but you are not pulling the name up to the conscious. Your mind can look for things on a subconscious level and identify what it is looking for, without consciously telling you.

Has the reader ever loved someone for many years? If you have, you know that you didn't consciously think of them and your love for them every second of the day. Grief or love or another strong emotion can lay in our subconscious mind and yet still influence our thinking. It is not a matter of us turning this love on. It simply is there quietly in the background exerting its influence on our mind.

Grief, love, anger, and other strong emotions are similar to when our mind is seeking for a name subconsciously. These emotions seek out the appropriate scenes, and items in the surrounding area, and colors and sounds that go with the emotion that the subconscious mind feels. A blue person will notice "blue, sad" type things around them. Other things just don't fit the subconscious fill in the blank. In other words, our emotions determine our perspective on what we see in life. Our emotional perspective guides what items our mind focuses on. This is why it is absolutely imperative for balanced human growth that a person feel compassion, love and sympathy directed toward oneself.

Feeling loved in turn opens the mind to focus its emotional-perception-guidance system on compassion, love and sympathy. In contrast with most people, many parts of total mind-controlled slaves are never meant to have feelings, or if the parts do, they repressed, suppress, and dissociate their feelings. Our emotions play a fundamental role in a person's moral life. They transform values into actions. This is what is called strength of will, courage of convictions, etc. Emotions play a critical role in strength of will and courage of convictions.

To be stripped of feeling emotions, strips the victim of one of the ingredients to make and carry out moral choices. This helps explain why emotions are harnessed so completely by the programmers. When researchers have studied unemotional people, they find that their dealings with others are shallow, lifeless, and mechanical. The programmers want their programmed assassins, espionage agents, prostitutes, etc. to be mechanical. People rarely want to form friendships with unemotional persons. Of course, the parts that are created to interface with the public are programmed to be effacious, gracious, and to sparkle. But the deeper parts which influence the victim's own internal thoughts, which the victim wisely keeps to himself, fail to connect with the outside world emotionally.

Having been stripped of emotions, the slave is consequently stripped of one of the most important ingredients involved in morality. An unemotional or emotionally deficient person or alter may suffer from a particular kind of a "morally-weak will". This is because failure to do what a person believes is good and failure to restrain from doing what one believes is bad is a natural consequence of lacking emotions such as care, concern, compassion, courage, love and sympathy. Certain emotions are critical for doing and being moved to do what is right and in not doing what one knows is bad.

Friendships are one of the most valuable commodities a person can have. The victim is stripped of external friendships. They may substitute interactions within their own internal world as a way to substitute for this loss. In normal human activity, two people in love intertwine the activities of their lives into the complex whole of their love relationship. A walk together is not seen as a walk, but as a joint expression of their relationship.

Humans emotionally value what is good for their friends and lovers. Without emotional attachments, the relationship is only a facade. The victims of mind-control are taught how to create great facades. Unfortunately, they fool many of their therapists, and therefore don't step out of the make-believe roles they play out.

Human love and friendship is one of the most vital, powerful, fundamentally good items of human behaviour. They provide the foundation for many other things. Without love and friendship, the victim's alters live in isolation, alienation, abandonment, discontinuity, and purposelessness. Cisco's half of the book will discuss some specific programming tactics that are used to hide the "shadow" alters that are used to take any emotions that the principally used alters might develop. What we have been covering is that one of the side effects of "stripping" the victims from feeling emotions is to cripple them from taking moral stands, from seeing love & concern in the world around them, and from reaching out & forming ties to the outside world.

PROGRAMMING TO HIDE REVEALING DREAMS

The programmers realize that the mind is able to reveal secrets via dreams. During the programming a Mother-of-darkness will be assigned to a child and she will have to wake that child up when it is in its deepest sleep to ask the child what's happening and if the child is dreaming. If dreams are surfacing, the programmers know their programming is not holding.

When the child's mind which is being programmed no longer releases revealing dreams, the programmers know that their programming is holding. The front alters receive repeated programming (hypnotic commands, etc.) not to dream or to know their dreams. When the programming begins to collapse, the deeper alters will begin to dream and flood with memories. The slave must have their dream sealing programs reinstated approx. every three years. If this is not done, dreams (which are actually memories) will begin to surface. A therapist can also help the victim train their mind to remember their dreams (dream state of mind).

PROGRAMMING LANGUAGE

A skilful programmer can use language to communicate at several levels. The programmer can use derogatory tones, big words that the child doesn't understand and obscure language that confuses the child in order to humiliate, dominate and confuse the child. He can also pronounce the words with a twist in order to protect the programming. Have you ever met someone in the occult world who pronounces many of his words strange? The programmers are also big on play on words which are done intentionally to protect the programming. The victims of the occult programming must deal with symbology. Those who attempt to understand programming must also deal with the world of symbology.

The programmer must learn to think like a child and to step into the child's world. Likewise, the deprogrammer must learn to step into the victim's world. Certainly, the deprogrammer wants to stay grounded in reality, but he also wants to be able to understand the world that the victim must live in. The deeper parts of the victim lives in a magical world, full of demons and powers from other dimensions. When the Illuminati carry out programming, they often frame what they are doing in magical and satanic terms.

Most therapists do not want to step into the victim's world to communicate with them. Just as the psychologists want this author to step into the psychologists' world to communicate with them, the psychologist should realize that the victim would like the same. It is irrelevant whether the therapist believes that objects can be demonized or not. The deeper alters have spent their life-time learning how demons attach themselves to objects, and how to gain power to cause demons to attach themselves to objects. A deeper alter may have the occult wisdom to place demons into a fluid so that that fluid can be drank by a child. From their understanding of demonology, these demons are so powerful that the only non-lethal entry for them into the child is by the child drinking a particular fluid. These images are the images that deeper alters experience during the programming rituals. The language & images of the programming will be very magical, mystical and satanic.

EFFECTS OF PROGRAMMING

The mind is a holographic type of memory. The psyche of the multiple personality is a multiple image hologram. The body is set up to match the mind. When one alter switches to another, another hologram seems to take control over the mind. This is like the instructions for the body are written on a card, and when the switch occurs, the holographic cards are shuffled like a deck of cards. In fact, the programming have used this analogy as part of their programming codes.

FALSE IMPLANTED MEMORIES

Once the truth about trauma-based mind-control began coming out, a massive counterattack by the controlled establishment occurred. This counter attack was that you can not trust the memories of the victims. Numerous establishment articles call attention to memory research, especially memory research into how to implant an illusory memory.

Two examples of this massive counterattack are Bruce Bower's article in Science News, 8/24/96, pp. 126-127 entitled "Remembrance of Things False Scientists incite illusory memories and explore their implications".& Harvard psychologist Daniel L. Schacter's book Searching for Memory (1996).

First, these countless articles prove that the controlled psychiatric research community is working hard at developing techniques to implant false memories. This is indeed a big part of the mind-control, producing cover memories and false identities and false histories for alters. However, these articles always ignore the enormous evidence of severe abuse and government/cult involvement in the lives of countless victims of mind-control. This author has seen first hand the Illuminati-satanic cult-CIA involvement in the lives of a number of these people. The events of these people's lives, which this author has often witnessed, can't be explained away by poor memory. Further, traumas that are so severe as to cause amnesia walls, are locked up by the mind and preserved. They are like a mummy in a tomb in Egypt, that is still locked up in its preserved state. Memories that aren't locked up can deteriate and be contaminated, just like a dead body that is left to rot, but programming traumas are not in that category of memory. Remember, the mind protect itself. Research shows that the mind does not want to latch onto false memories that hurt it. For instance, when researchers try to get subjects to remember a kind parent hurting them, the mind will resist the false memory.

PERCEPTION CLOUDS MEMORY

The brain in order to be efficient uses its framework of knowledge--its world view--in which to hang new incoming knowledge. This author's Be Wise As Serpents book considered this to be the biggest barrier to people coming to the truth. Because education, television and society in general control how people's framework of knowledge is built, and these frameworks are built skilfully to exclude major truths that would expose how the World Order is controlling mankind, it is really difficult to speak to people about mind-control, and the control of the world in general.

The victim of mind-control has frameworks built into his subconscious that make it difficult to drive the truth into their thinking. Memories are stored as they relate to these frameworks. An efficient way around that is to speak and teach in way that the subconscious mind is spoken to, and the conscious barriers are by-passed. The mind puts up a grid to prevent non-approved information from coming in that doesn't fit it's accepted concept of truth. Much of this grid is fear based. The problem for the victim is that once their mind is bent a certain way by the programmers, it will naturally create a grid to protect the programmed world-view.

This is why the external philosophies-news broadcasts-disinformation from establishment magazines, etc. that are layered in on top of programming, (see Chapter 12) are like a protective coat sprayed on to make sure the foundation doesn't weather over time. For instance, the front alters of some of the most severely tortured victims have latched onto the idea that Satanic Ritual Abuse doesn't exist, and are actually some of the greatest public crusaders against people believing that SRA exists. The external politically-correct view is in this case protecting the deeper programming.

FALSE FEELINGS. Using drugs & hypnosis, and the creation story about God breathing things into existence, the "love" & "kindness" of the programmer is placed into Moriah the Wind. When this is done, should a gatekeeper alter hear something negative about their master, they instantly go into the melting (drug memory) where drugs made them feel one with their programmer. This is refrained during programming as "the peace of God."

ELDETIC IMAGERY. There is a type of visual imagery called eidetic imagery. 5 to 10 % of children have it, but it is very rare in adults. Eidetic imagery is similar to a photographic memory. People with eidetic imagery can look at any object or page of numbers and when they look away the image of what they have seen is as clear as a photograph. They can focus on any detail of the image, enlarge it, make out more details than what they had originally seen, and then they can carry this image with them for several days, just like the rest of us carry a photograph. This author has not seen much info on this, & believes that further research into this topic might reveal some more methods that the mind-control programmers are utilizing. Child-hood impressions & memories can have a far greater impact and retention than adult memories. This paragraph has only introduced this subject of eidetic imagery & childhood vs adult memory ability.

FINAL SUMMATION. The programming regimen destroys the victims sense of self, so that the person has only an identity within the cult. The victim can not express rage over their own victimization, but is encouraged by the Illuminati's satanic beliefs to express violence & rage toward others, thereby creating a mechanism to help perpetuate the mind-control. The rage also seeps out as self-punishment. A deep loneliness sets into victims, & they despair of hope. They see no place to turn to except to whatever cult is controlling them. This chapter has focused on the type of skills & knowledge psychologists study, & how this knowledge can be applied to insuring compliance by the slave.

p_9-2.jpg

CHAPTER 10: THE 10th SCIENCE — USING SPIRITUAL THINGS TO CONTROL A PERSON.

What makes a programmed multiple tick? This chapter will provide some of the most important answers to that question. In this chapter, you will be provided with important brand-new information.

CONTENTS
PART A. Intro on the importance of spiritual programming tactics.
PART B. The history of Programmed Golem
  KABBALISTIC BLACK MAGIC
PART C. The 3 foundations: Loss of identity, Fear, and Demons
  UNDERSTANDING THE RELATIONSHIP BETWEEN FEAR & DEMONS
  DEMON POSSESSION & SPIRIT GUARDS
  The Use of Giving Demonic Assistance to entrap.
  The Use of Occult Focal Points.
  DOES IT GLORIFY DEMONS TO CAST THEM OUT?
PART D. A complete Chronology of how the victim experiences the early spiritual programming. Steps a through o. (by Cisco)
  FINE-TUNED
  HIDING THE INTERNAL SELF-HELPER
  INTERJECT DISKS
PART E. Specific spiritual programming maneuvers
  WHITE GOLD, other information

PART A. INTRO on the IMPORTANCE of SPIRITUAL PROGRAMMING TACTICS

It is important for therapists and ministers to understand the spiritual ramifications of what has been done. The witchcraft, spells, and demonology is a way of life for the deeper alters. The programming and the hypnotic trances are deeply embedded into the ritual life of the deeper alters of a mind-controlled slave. An enormous amount of suffering has transpired because therapists have dealt with obvious spiritual problems with psychological techniques that aren't even remotely related to the real problem. Secular therapists can be quick to offer glib criticism of the subject of demonology, a subject they often know nothing about. (While Christians generally acknowledge that mankind is in a spiritual war (cf. 2 COR 10:3-5), they too are generally ignorant of Satan's devices, and are not skilled in dealing with spiritual attacks from the world, flesh and the demons.)

An analogy for demonology is microbiology. Many people never see a virus, and many people never see demons. Some people still debate whether the germ theory of disease is correct. There will certainly be differences of opinion about demonology--anything said about it is bound to find someone who disagrees. But just like it has been useful for many sick people's health to deal with viruses, victims of Illuminati mind-control have found it helpful to deal with demons. Demonology can be a useful subject for understanding programming from both a programmer's point of view and a deprogrammer's point of view. If this information is useful, then it will have served a purpose.

Men of God, who have found themselves in remote places (where trauma-based mind-control is not practiced), have found themselves confronted by obvious cases of demon possession that have been successfully handled by deliverance prayer. This author has personally witnessed many people who have had wonderful healings due to deliverances. I rejoice in their freedom. I pray that others who portray themselves as therapists would come to the same place that they could appreciate healings even though they do not recognize the spiritual dimension of human life, or even better yet, that they would recognize the spiritual side of humankind. In Asia, it was common for this author to see flies swarm over people and food. Demons swarm around people in that type of abundance. This is why the title Lord of the Flies (Beelzebub) is the name of a chief demon, and is sometimes used as another name for Satan himself.

Part B. The History of the Programmed Golem

KABBALISTIC BLACK MAGIC

A number of the Illuminati bloodlines (and sects) that are involved in trauma-based total mind-control are Askenazi hasidic bloodlines. Legends abound from the 15th century onward about how the Askenazi hasidic leaders created golem to serve them. These golem have been called "benevolent robots". For those readers who are unaware of where the word golem came from, it is used once in the Word of God in Ps 139:16, "Your eyes [God's eyes] saw my substance, being yet unformed. And in Your book they were written, the days fashioned for me." This is believed by the Kaballists to refer to Adam when he was only a body without a soul.

Golem are believed to be soulless bodies. One can almost hear the rationalization in medieval times when torture, and black magic or a trance state ended up creating an alter personality that this magical part was viewed as soulless, because it was only created via magic. This personality (alter) didn't exist like real people, it was merely a golem in the magicians' eyes--therefore it could be abused or used as a robot, because it was soulless.

The use of Cabalistic black magic in mainline Illuminati programming in the deeper aspects has led this author to believe that during the torture of jews in the concentration camps--Dr. Mengele was assisted by some Askenazi hasidic black magic adepts who gave him some of the secret names of God. The Cabalistic magic viewpoint is that there are creative powers intrinsic in God's names. God's names are used by the Illuminati for such alters as the gems (jewels) from which other alters are created. For instance the gems will be tortured while Cabalistic black magic is employed to create more parts.

In such deeper aspects of programming, what occurs? Have the Illuminati programmers created new parts via psychologic torture techniques, have they created them with black magic or both? One thing is sure, if the "golem's mind"--that is that if parts of the victim subjected to trauma-based mind-control remember what occurred, then it will be associated with a Cabalistic black magic ritual.

There are several other features of Cabalistic black magic that are important features of Illuminati programming. Many things pertaining to the mind-control have slipped out into public view at one time or another but are not recognized as having anything to do with programming. The European Jew Joseph Achron wrote the musical Golem Suite (1932) for an orchestra. The first piece of music introduces the golem and the last piece of music is the exact reverse mirror image of the first piece and it represents the disintegration of the golem.

In programming, the deeper alters may have a musical cord to call them up, and the reverse of that cord will "disintegrate" them back into the mind. The following excerpts are taken from Gershom Scholem's book Kabbalah. (NY: Keter Pub. House Jerusalem, 1974.) "General summaries of Kabbalistic doctrine rarely referred to its 'practical' side [which Scholem go on to explain is black magic dealing with demons and blood]..." Of course not, the practical side of the Kabbala is occult--secret knowledge. It is the secrets of black magic. "Various ideas and practices connected with the concept of the golem [mind-controlled slave] also took their place in practical Kabbalah through a combination of features drawn from the Sefer Yezirah and a number of magical traditions." (Kabbala, p. 183) The practical side of the Kabbala which was concerned with creating golem employed trances, magic and visualization. Scholem writes, "In this circle the Sefer Yezirah was nearly always interpreted in the manner of Saadiah and Shabbetai Donnolo [who was into what is known as Satanism], with an added tendency to see the book as a guide for both mystics and adepts of magic.

The study of the book was considered successful when the mystic attained the vision of the golem, which was connected with a specific ritual of a remarkable ecstatic [altered state] character." (ibid., p.40) Two other points should be made showing the connection between medieval ashkenzim black magic practices and the programming going on today. The medieval jewish magicians would use the secret Kabbalistic names of God in accordance with detailed sets of instructions to try and create a golem. The golem in turn would say the combination of hebrew letters in reverse order. This has been done in modern programming.

Further, the "Seal of the Holy One" in medieval times was written on the forehead of the golem. This is the word "emet". At some point the word's first letter (an aleph) is erased and this leaves the word "met" which in Hebrew means "dead". Such types of sealings have also been done in modern times with deeper parts of slaves.

PART C. The 3 foundations: Loss of identity, Fear, and Demons

The programming has three basic foundations, fear, rejection of God (which entails the rejection of who they are), and the entrapment by demonic possession. If the person is paralyzed in fear, unable to seek God's help, unable to know who they are in Christ & to see God's plan for their life, and lives in bondage to demons, then the Illuminati programming will hold.

The Word of God states that each person is intricately designed by God and developed according to His plan (Ps. 139:14-16). A person's self-image of who they are profoundly affects everything else about them. The Illuminati want to insure that the potential for good that the person is born with is destroyed or controlled. They want the victim to feel rejected and cheated by God. This is what Colossians 2:8 warns about, & then the next Bible verse states, "...for in Him dwelleth all the fullness of the Godhead bodily. And you are complete in Him..."

If the slave could ever be complete through their devotion to God, they would have no use for their Illuminati masters. The Scriptures in several Psalms teach that God made us in accordance with His plans for our lives. Even today He is not finished with us. "We are (present continuous action verb) His workmanship..." Eph. 2:10 A 124 pg. secret CIA book Manual on Human Resources, 1983, (recently declassified via the Freedom of Information Act) states, "When a threat is used, it should always be implied that the subject himself is to blame by using words such as, "You leave me no other choice but to..." He should never be told to comply "or else!"... The threat of coercion usually weakens or destroys resistance more effectively than coercion itself. For example, the threat to inflict pain can trigger fears more damaging than the immediate sensation of pain."

UNDERSTANDING THE RELATIONSHIP BETWEEN FEAR & DEMONS

Dr. W. Grey Walter, of the British Burden Neurological Institute at Bristol, England did a lot of research involving drugs, electroshock and demonology. Walter would drill from 50 to 100 holes in his patients heads and then insert electrodes into their heads. The patients would walk around with a beret-like covering over their electrode implanted heads. The suborbital area of the brain was determined by Walter as being the seat of demonic fears. Walter would cause a small lesion in the paracingulate region to calm patients who saw demons. This in effect is like a miniature lobotomy. The electricity causes a selective lesion. What his work showed was that there is a connection between the area of the brain that creates fear, and images of demons that people see.

The Word of God in 2 TIM 1:7 states categorically that "God hath not given us the spirit of fear; but of power, and of love, and of a sound mind." This means that the Spirit of fear comes from the Satan and his world system. The Spirit of fear is demonic, and it has the power to paralyze its victim. This Spirit of Fear is nothing less than a demonic anointing. That demonic anointing drives away positive angelic spirits. Christ asked, "Why are ye so fearful? How is it that ye have no faith?" The demonic anointing of fear meant that faith was lacking. If we listen to the Word of God, we get faith. (ROM 10:17). This is why it is important to the programmers that their deeper alters are programmed not to be able to read or hear the Word of God (Holy Bible). If the victim could hear the Word of God, they would receive faith, which would tamper with the demonic anointing of fear.

On a spiritual level, our fears are open doors for Satan to carry out an act. It is a vicious bondage loop, because then the victim says, "I knew it was going to happen, I knew from the beginning." Little does the victim realize that the Spirit of Fear within them, opened the door for Satan to carry out his will in that area. In fact, it is standard procedure within the secret societies and intelligence agencies to identify what fears their opposition have, and then build upon those fears. It does no good to spread disinformation about things that the enemy is not fearful of. But if a fear is identified, they will play upon that as much as possible.

In Howard, Michael, Strategic Deception in the Second World War. Vol. 5 of British Intelligence in the Second World War. W.W. Norton & Co.: NY, 1995, p.33-34, "One of the first rules of deception is to play on the real fears,..." On page 4 1-42 Howard quotes a British intelligence directive, "It may be taken as a principle of strategic deception that it is neither economical in time nor productive in results to attempt to produce in the enemy anxiety over an area concerned with which the enemy himself has had no previous fear...Knowledge of the trend of enemy anxiety was therefore of very great value...On the foundation of fear, and having regard both to inherent plausibility and to contact identifications which the enemy was likely to have made, it was possible to build up a fictitious and misleading structure and to represent Allied capabilities and intentions as very different from what they really were."

In this author's previous writings, the connection between demonology and military tactics in general and specifically British intelligence have been closely documented. Military structures are based upon demon structures. It is no surprise then, that demons and intelligence groups study to determine what a person's fears are. And it is no wonder that they attempt to instil as many fears as possible into the victim.

DEMON POSSESSION & SPIRIT GUARDS

Christians are called upon to guard what was spiritually entrusted to them by the using the Holy Spirit (2 TIM 1:14). The Illuminati do a mirror image of this, by layering in spirits (evil ones) to guard things in the system. For instance, in the VoL 2 book, the programming parallels to the movie Labyrinth were discussed in chapter 5. It was mentioned how the dogs portrayed guardians. Demons named Toto are layered in to protect the spinner kittens. If one were to try to activate the spinner kittens without going through the proper chain of command & codes, the guardian demons known as Totos, or after Dorothy's Toto will be activated. The spinner's in fact are often called "Dorothys".

Some other examples of guardians spirits that are placed into a system are Bes, the spirit that rules the dwarfs; Geb, the voice behind the earth God in a system; Pan, who has various roles, including being a protector of the green wood; and Shu, which is the voice "behind the wind" which controls the internal weather within a alter system's world. The foundations of a system are the demons layered in at the beginning. Spirits of Confusion, Despair, Torment are called down by the programmers and laid in. Lying and Perverse Spirits are brought in too.

At first this may seem like very subjective sci-fi to the reader. Hopefully, after the programming rituals are described in detail, and a basic foundation concerning what demons are is laid, the reader will have received a more systematic understanding of the topic. The goal is teach the reader programming as a programmer would understand it. The victim should not be made ashamed of demonic attachments. That serves no spiritual benefit for the victim, and only contributes more guilt and shame, and adds to the problem of giving them hope. The victim has been a helpless victim.

"Mystery" demons (which is not their actual name) are placed into the child when they are innocent babies. Part of the power of the mystery demons, is that they are able to remain anonymous within their host's body. They remain in the host secretly generally for the person's lifetime. These mystery demons have to answer to their chain of command. Within a victim's alter parts, are demons which have their own ranks and commanders. Christians who carry out deliverances will deal those commanders.

The Catholic Church, which has been so active in trauma-based mind-control and in placing in the Spirits of Legion into a victim, had one of their clergy write, "Evil is Someone, Someone who is multiple and who name is legion..." (Mauriac, Francois. Life of St. Margaret of Cortona.) The Catholic Church's official public stance is that Demon possession is rare. On Aug. 15, 1972, Pope Paul VI put out a motu proprio which abolished the order of exorcist. This office had already become rather rare, and besides included men who were mind-control programmers. Cases of "demonic possession" of Catholics are occasionally taken to places like Georgetown Hospital in Wash. D.C. which is run by Jesuits working in tandem with the CIA. Accounts of exorcisms of Catholics are filled with clues that the victims of "demonic possession" are victims also of trauma-based occult-based mindcontrol.

This writer, trying to explain a difficult subject (demonology), feels fortunate to be able to recommend a book which does a good job of explaining it, this is Howard O. Pittman's book Demons. (Foxworth, MS: Philadelphian Pub. House,

c. 1988). I originally read the book in 1992, and have had it recommended by those who work in the area of demonology. The book is written by a devout Christian who worked 28 years in the field of law enforcement during his life. The book explains such things as: how man is made in the image of God (and as such is a clone, so to speak of God;) How demon possession has come about due to man's sovereign will allowing it; & How demons can interact with the physical world.

He explains how Satan despatches orders from his throne which go through a chain of command, and how special emphasis is placed on Christians. He explains the forms of demons, their expertise, how they can read minds, and how they have no love for their master, and no love for themselves. Nor does their master have any love for them. (I, Fritz Springmeier, your author have discovered in talking to people for years, that it is essential for people to grasp that the mind of Satan is devoid of love, and that where love doesn't seek its own, Satan's mind always has his own interest in both mind & action. Everything in his world system is functioning for a goal of his, they are not random events, because he is a control-freak.)

Pittman describes warring demons--which look like giant humans and are the cream of Satan's crop.' These warring demons are assigned to formulate wars upon the earth. While Pittman is a spirit-led Christian, it is interesting that a non-Christian historian/author William Bramley, (of the Gods of Eden), who believes that the "aliens" were viewed as angels, has found traces of proof that the aliens (angels) were involved in the creation of wars down through the history of mankind. "Now the Spirit speaketh expressly, that in the latter times some shall depart from the faith, giving heed to seducing spirits and doctrines of devils; Speaking lies in hypocrisy; having their conscience seared with a hot iron;" 1 TIM 4:1-2.

Pittman writes about 1 TIM 4:1-2, "In this passage of scripture, we are told that in the last days the devils would have their own doctrine. We know that if the Bible tells us that devils would have their own doctrines, then, most assuredly the Bible would tell us what these doctrines would be. Evidence of what the devils will be teaching is found in the following passage of scripture: 'But he knowing their thoughts, said unto them, Every kingdom divided against itself is brought to desolation; and a house divided against a house falleth. If Satan also be divided against himself, how shall his kingdom stand? Because ye say that I cast out devils through Beelzebub.' (Luke 11:17-18)

From this very scripture, it is clear what the devils will be teaching as doctrine. They will be teaching that THERE ARE NO SUCH BEINGS AS DEMONS! Where are these demons teaching their doctrine? They are teaching it in the churches to the Christians! They are teaching their doctrine to the very ones who have the potential to believe that these demons are real and can expose these beings. If Satan did try to reveal himself and his helpers, then his house would be divided." Pittman warns, "From congregation to congregation, from one church to another church throughout all this land, we find preacher after preacher playing down the existence of demons and even the existence of Satan! Then, there are others who, when they admit that Satan and his demons are real, deemphasize their importance and capability. Not only are local ministers doing this, but many Christian authors are doing this through their books...The false doctrines of devils are intended to enhance the anonymity of Satan and his angels. Much of this misteaching is spread through good Christians who have been sold a lie and really believe what they say.'' The Word of God is clear that not one sin entered into this world without Satan. Every sin committed by mankind is (according to the Word of God) the result and influence of Satan. However, because Satan and his demons are masters at deception and at staying behind the scenes, and remaining anonymous they are not discovered. They are better at such deception than the intelligence agencies that are Illuminati fronts, and to give credit where due, the NSA, CIA, and MI-6 are good at what they do.

The programmer will be looking for methods to open up a person to demons, and he will be setting up scenarios so that the victim will reject the Spirit of God in their life. 1 JN 5:18 teaches that a person's identity in Christ protects against the wicked one, so the victim's identity in Christ will be stolen very soon by the programmers. According to the Word of God, submission and humility before God are also said to be protections against evil spirits.(cf. JS 4:7, & 1 PTR 5:6,8,9). Resistance to catching demons, involves a person "not giving place" to the demons, (Eph. 4:27) and to be strengthened by Christ (Phil. 4:13). How does this happen? The Word of God teaches us that the Spirit of God in our life repels demons naturally. A close walk of fellowship with the Spirit of God is one spiritually natural immune-builder. We need to get Christ deeper and deeper into our lives. However, the programmer will deflect this, and say that submission and humility before God means to submit to some church authority, and of course this church authority will be part of the mind-control abuse system.

The Use of Giving Demonic Assistance to entrap.

One of the principles (giving tactics) of the spirit world is that if you go to get help from demons, they have a spiritual opportunity to enter into your life in other ways. This involves spiritual laws. People, who have been healed by occult healers, have discovered that it set them up for demonic activity in their life. Of course, it is easy to write this, but often only the victims of occult help, who have already learned the lesson the hard way, believe it.

The ultimate that Lucifer can pretend to give is divinity. Divinity is sometimes symbolized by the Illuminati as an 8 on its side or the infinity symbol. The divine within a hierarchy member is called the High Self. It also goes by the name Dian Y Glas or Blue God in the hierarchy's parlance. The given names of Joan, Janicot, Jean, and Jonet are popular in generational witchcraft families because they mean the High Self. The cabalistic name for the High Self (internal divinity) is NESHAMAH. According to Illuminati hierarchy beliefs, the High Self can only be communicated to via symbols, music and myth that go through the unconscious mind. In other words, don't talk to it, show it. This is part of the reason Illuminati witch covens make noise in ceremonies, dance and use objects, they believe these are essential to communicate to their High Self.

The Use of Occult Focal Points.

Another principle (giving tactic) of the spirit world is that focal points (occult objects) are used to bring demonic entities into a person's life. I can not write a technical manual on the mechanics of how or why the presence of evil spirits is aided by amulets, rings, occult jewelry, rock & roll albums, etc., but the fact is, that demonic entities ARE AIDED. It is common for mind-controlled Illuminati slaves to keep demonized nick-nacks given by their programmers, handlers or other contact people. Generally, the mind-controlled slave's front system is unaware of the spiritual ramifications of the occult objects.

The ancient grimoires are used in rituals & programming. Even if it is seldom that therapists work that deep in a system, it still might be useful to provide a list (for reference sake) of the ancient grimoires which are used to invoke demons:

Almadel, the

Arbatel of Magic, the

Black Pullet, the

Book of Albertus Magnus, the

Enchiridion of Pope Leo

Fourth Book of Cornelius Agrippa

Grand Grimoire, the

Grimoire of Pope Honorius

Grimorium Verum, the

Heptameron, the

Lesser Key of Solomon (aka Goetia)

Key of Solomon (aka Legemeton)

Pauline Art, the

Sword of Moses, the

Theosophia Pneumatica

The Use of giving occult power for SOMETHING IN RETURN. One of the tactics of controlling a person is to give them occult power. Generally, people who have psychic abilities and other occult powers, are reluctant to seek a true Christian faith. Because they enjoy the power they have, they will not trade leaving the occult world and their power behind for freedom.

In the case of many mind-controlled slaves, the programmer will create a legitimate spirit-filled Christian front. He knows that the spiritual principle, "A double-minded man is unstable in all his ways" will work in his favor. Even though he creates a religious front that is opposed to what the programmer wants, a thousand-minded person has no choice but to rely on the programmer. The programmer is the only one who can bring order out of chaos. The victim is so unstable with all his or her programmed and hurting parts, that these parts need their programmer to function. Evil spirits are like unwelcome visitors to our home. They can even be compared to an unwelcome mouse running and hiding in our house. That a visitor or mouse troubles us does not mean that he possesses us. Christians have problems with unwelcome mice as well as unwelcome demons. Mice corrupt our homes, likewise demons come to corrupt the House of God.

The programmer knows what encourages demonic activity. This is why certain occultic structures are built into the mind, and why the systems are set up to carry out occult rituals regularly. Some victims of mind-control are unfortunately going to witches for their therapy. A therapist who is a pagan witch, and who encourages further occult activity, is preventing the victim from gaining freedom. This is because there is a spiritual foundation to much of the control. (Readers would be surprised at how many psychologists are part of the occult world.)

How much of our life has been turned over to Christ? Many Christians have what could be termed "hidden rooms" and hidden compartments in their life & their thinking which they have not given to Christ. In fact, many Christians compartmentalize their life into their secular job and their Sunday of Christianity. In this sense, their lives are like a house with many rooms, many of which are not given to Christ, but are available for other spirits. Even the non-multiple Christian will have problems with compartmentalization in life opening a door to demons. But Christ asked his disciples to go farther than just stay in fellowship, he commanded them to heal and cast out demons. MT 10:7,8. He also commanded his disciples to evangelize. The strongest deliverance have been seen on the cutting edge of evangelism, as a testimony to God's power.

DOES IT GLORIFY DEMONS TO CAST THEM OUT?

The threat of deliverance has the Satanic leaders of the Illuminati scared enough that they have actively disseminated a doctrine among the Christian churches that it gives power to Satan to believe in demons. There is a kernel of truth here, but it doesn't give glory to Satan to defeat demons and to expel them. If you were fired from your job, would that glorify you? No. Defeating demons is actually showing how weak they are, not glorifying them. Healing and deliverance are part of the ministry of freedom that Christ demonstrated to his disciples, and they are to accompany the preaching of freedom (evangelism).

PART D. A complete Chronology of how the victim experiences the early spiritual programming. (by Cisco)

Steps of Programming:

a. The mother-fetus trauma
b. The Apple-Woodsman ritual
c. The 1st Ritual Theft of Birthright
d. The 2nd Ritual Theft of Birthright
e. The Satanic Wedding Prog. Ritual
f. The Lockup of the Guardian Angel
g. The Revelation of Demons
h. Providing Satanic Toys
i. The Participation Ritual
j. The layering in of witches/monsters
k. The prog. base-Fairy Tales told
l. The Ritual to Test Loyalty to Oaths
m. Prog. building blocks- Nursery Rhymes

n. The Hell Fire Ceremony
o. The Cutting the Penis Ritual
p. The Traitors Death Ritual

It is important to understand the nature and the sequence of these standard programming rituals. I, Cisco, have decided to reveal them so that the therapists will comprehend better what the programming is really all about. We have touched on a few of these rituals in our two previous books, but we haven't spelled them out. These programming rituals in real life are extremely traumatizing, even to the hardened cult parents who often must offer their children up to abuse that even they don't want to happen to their children. When these programming rituals happen to a child, they are so severe that they split the child's mind. We don't want therapists and readers falling apart by reading about these programming rituals, so you will find the descriptions of these rituals are clinical, and are written without a great deal of emotional content.

a. The mother-fetus trauma

We have written about the traumas given to the mother and fetus in chapter 1 of this book and chapter 1 of the Vol. 2 book. Between these two books, there are approximately 9 pages concerning the traumas at this pre-birth stage. It could also be explained that the intensity and nature of the pre-birth traumas relate to whether the mother is Illuminati or not.

During the 1940's-'50s the Illuminati made it a high priority to marry members of the Illuminati to Christians for the purposes of infiltrating the churches. After a 20 year period of intense infiltration to such groups as the Southern Baptists, the Mennonites, the Pentecostal Holiness, the Four-Square, and the Assemblies of God, then they could rely upon their members within those groups to generationally continue their presence within these groups. Initially, they wanted the infiltration to be covered by marriage into these denominations. If a mother were not of the Illuminati, she was typically prepared for an overwhelming trauma to be administered during her pregnancy. If she drank coffee or tea, she could be given potent herbs daily to set the stage for later drugs administered during the torture. The herbs set the stage for drugs which would make the mind more pliable to hypnosis, because many Christians are resistent to hypnosis. When the Illuminati would finally by force grab and traumatize the mother, their goal would be to see if they could get the mother to renounce (blaspheme) Christ. They hoped to use this to blackmail the person into future submission and shame. They also were gaining experience into what kind of resistance they would face in the final takeover. An hypnotic trigger would be attached to this torture memory, and then the mother would be hypnotically made to forget the

b. The Apple-Woodsman ritual.

The powerful Tin Man Ritual is described on page 103 of the Vol. 2 Formula book. It is where the parent(s) presents the child to Lucifer, "the god of light". The Tin Man appeared in the first picture (page 4) of our illustrated Guide to Monarch Programming. It was positioned there because it is often the first ritual memory. The child eats an apple that is poisoned and dies, and then is brought back to life because the coven has the antidote on hand. Next, the parent dedicates the child to Lucifer; if not, then the child will have its head severed by the Tin Man's ax. This dedication mocks the Pentecostal dedication. Bear in mind, that some parents and programmers can only justify what they do, because they feel they are following "Lucifer's orders." They will say, "We do it to please Lucifer." They feel Lucifer wants the child in its purest state, so they will do the moon child ceremony in the womb to allow Lucifer to plant his spirits in the fetus (which is a mockery of God's spirit in the Christ-Child.)

c. The 1st Ritual Theft of Birthright

When the child victim is four, this ritual typically is done to them during the 10 days to 2 weeks of rituals done around Easter. The ritual is not always done at this time. If both parents are Illuminati, then their primary job is to see their children get programmed; but if only one parent is Illuminati, then the group may have to work with the child whenever they can manipulate some time to do so. Also the Illuminati have so many children to put through programming, that many simply do not start this ritual at Easter. But if they are not done at Easter, they may be told when it is done that it is the time around Easter. The programmers have certain windows of time for certain programs and schedules to follow for each child. They can be untrue to the real calendar date, and still set the internal clock/calendars of the slave correctly later.

This first ritual is to make sure the child victim experiences a staged rejection of God where they are found unworthy to be in "His' Book of Life. This ritual like all the others that we will describe in this series are sealed with rape and the implantation of demons.

d. The 2nd Ritual Theft of Birthright

This second ritual is done shortly after the first ritual, generally a few days after. It consists of a death, burial and resurrection ritual. To die means death towards God, burial means to bury all that makes up a person's worth, and resurrection means to be resurrected with a new name and birthed to Satan. This and the 1st theft ritual are designed to remove any bonds the deeper alters might ever conceive of having with Almighty God.

e. The Satanic Wedding Prog. Ritual

Within days of the 2nd theft ritual, the Illuminati will follow with a mock satanic wedding. Usually the father will marry his daughter, but there is a chain of responsibility and if the father can't sexually abuse his child, then the grandfather is next in line, and then the uncle, and then the programmer. They will serve as the satanic covering for the child. At this point the rejection by God is still fresh on the child's mind, and they want the child to at least remember the rejection, whether they remember the incident or not depends. The child may already have dissociated the previous week or two, so the programmer may simply tell it "REMEMBER THE FEAR WHEN GOD DIDN'T LOVE YOU."

The child may really be looking forward to this wedding. They may have been dressed up nicely, and may be excited about marrying their father, even though he looks like a giant to the little infant. When their dress is pulled up and they are abused, then the fun stops.

f. The Lockup of the Guardian Angel.

The Internal Self Helper, also called the Guardian Angel of the mind, is magically locked up by the demonic power of the programmers, and a shrewd lying demon substituted in its place. The evil spirits that will be laid in will be the totems of the victim's bloodline--the spirits of the person's bloodlines who are to help guide the person.

Many people in the New Age movement who are under total mind-control speak about their guardian angel or their totem guiding them. An example of a total mind-controlled slave doing this are the Indian spirit guides that help Loretta Lynn. Hillary Clinton consults the spirit Eleanor Roosevelt. In order to familiarize the child with the proper demons they will be dressed up in a costume that resembles the bloodline spirit they are to become acquainted with. They will participate in a ritual in this costume.

g. The Revelation of Demons.

At this point, both the front (the light side) and the deeper occult dark side alters will be allowed to see the demons that are layered in. The front side sees them in their Luciferian form, and are scared out of their wits. They may respond to this by having an ongoing fear of monsters under their bed. The front's fear will keep the front away from trying to go deeper into the system. Later on in adult life, the Illuminati may want the front part of the system to go through a "deliverance", so they will think they have dealt with everything, and they don't need to look further. (For instance, this trick was done to a programmed multiple this author has worked with, the result being, the victim gave up any type of therapy or helpful work, because they were sure they'd received the answer to their problems, which would be nice if it were true, but isn't.) On the flip side, even though the dark side alters are also scared of the demons, who are quite terrorizing when seen by humans, the inherent need of humans to look for supernatural help pulls them toward the demonic. It is an inborn survival trait in most humans to look to supernatural help. By seeing the spiritual (even though these are dark spiritual forces), it becomes a normal function for the deeper alters to commune with the dark spiritual realm.

h. Providing Satanic Toys

The deeper alters will be given candles, knives and other ritual paraphernalia to play with. The establishment department stores with all their demonic toys are helpful, for the parent only needs to go to the local department store to buy his children occult toys.

i. The Participation Ritual

Soon after the wedding ceremony, another ceremony takes place where the child dresses up in the cult's red and black ceremonial robes. This is meant to integrate them into the cult family. It is an opportunity for the child to feel like it is part of the group and its rituals.

j. The layering in of witches/monster scripts

The normal American fairy tales, which are filled with stories of monsters and witches, are read to the child. The goblins, warlocks, vampires, and witches they hear about will help lay a mental foundation for what will happen later.

k. Cult Fairy Tales are told.

Next, the people in the child's life who are guiding the programming will tell the child programming stories, such as the Wizard of Oz stories and Alice In Wonderland. In the 50's and 60's, the Tall Book of Make Believe was popular. For instance the character Mr. Moon became a foundational part of the programming. Over the years the Wizard of Oz, Alice In Wonderland, and Mother Goose seem to have been overall favorites. The child will most often be in a trance state when these story lines are told. The children will have the stories repeated and they are expected to memorize these scripts. Because the programmers will build upon the child's awareness of these stories, the stories are modified to better fit the future programming.

For instance, if a programming team is going to use the Goldilocks and the 3 Bears story, they might modify the story like this: The 3 bears and Goldilocks went for a walk. Goldilocks was somewhere she shouldn't have been, so she was eaten up by the bears. Bears will eat you up. Policemen are like bears. A Policeman found her? Do you know what happened to her? Goldilocks got locked up and put in a cage. Or maybe they might say, Goldilocks was sitting where she wasn't supposed to.-- At that moment the chair is pulled out from underneath the child and the child is probed with a stun gun.

In the last 20 years, tens of thousands of children are getting "Pleiadian" programming, and it is not known what base fairy-tales are being used for this type of programming, or if they are using sci-fi stories as the base. There are tens of thousands of children with programming that can be activated to make them think they were raised on Alcyone in the Pleiades. This is to part of the Grand Deception of the End Times.

l. The Ritual to Test Loyalty to Oaths

The next step is to test the loyalty of the child slave to the oaths that were extracted from it. To prove the child's loyalty, the coven demands that the child sacrifice another child. From what we witnessed, even after all the abuse and hypnotic tampering of the child up to this point, not one single child was "loyal" to the oath. The inborn aversion to taking a human's life is strong, and the child will still refuse to do it. Therefore, the cult will have a member guide the child by taking the child's hand and forcing it to sacrifice the innocent little life before them. In spite of their reluctance, the forced act begins to rip the fabric of the child slave's mind and to sear its conscience. The cult will be sure to insure that the child is made to feel responsible, and that they are given guilt and shame for the deed.

Once the innocent victim is sacrificed, the child slave is required to cut the bloody heart out and eat it. The child has already been groomed for this, because the cult has been feeding blood in their milk as a pablum. The child has been allowed to get very hungry and then given blood so that in the end hunger is associated with death, and blood is associated with satisfying that hunger.

m. Prog. building blocks- Nursery Rhymes

The Nursery rhymes are now layered in. There is something mentally powerful about rhymes. Mother Goose nursery rhymes have been popular for over a half century for programming little children. The child's mind will refuse some things (such as it distaste for killing an innocent child in the previous ritual), but the child's mind doesn't realize anything devious about the adorable nursery rhymes. The child's mind will not put up any barriers to learning them. The child has no idea that by hearing these rhymes they are helping lay the foundation for their own mind-control.

n. The Hell Fire Ceremony.

This ceremony is basically the burning up of a child to instil in the child victim fear of disobedience and to show them what hell is all about. The reason this is done will be explained soon. This ceremony is done with one of four possibilities, a. a real baby, b. a dead miscarriage, c. a stage pretend child, d. movies.

For sure, the Illuminati will have a real bonfire, and there will be the stench of death. They will play tapes of screaming, terrified children to amplify how bad it will be in hell. Why do the Illuminati want the children to fear hell? First, if they ever do learn about the Bible, they will "know for sure" that this is the punishment that the God who rejected them wants for them. Next, the Illuminati tell the children that IF they are bad, they will suffer in hell, but if they are good in the cult, Satan their father will protect them and let them rule with him in hell. They want the child to be terrified of Hellfire and Brimstone. This ceremony is often done where there is a crematorium. The Presideo in CA was popular because a underground crematorium was there. Bear in mind, that the child by this time has lost its true self, and is simply in terror at watching a child like themselves turned to ashes. In certain types of hot fires, the child is turned to ashes so quick that the child's figure becomes a silhouette of ashes. The Illuminati will then begin teaching the child an important item, they will teach it to take on the spirit of the child through guilt manipulation. They'll say, "Don't you feel really bad that this happened to her, but you can fix it by internalizing her to yourself. Take the spirit of the child into you."

o. The Cutting the Penis Ritual.

This ritual is just as it sounds. The child is forced to emasculate another male. This ritual is intended to be severe. It again forces the child to choose between following their oaths or following what their heart tells them is a right. Because they will again refuse to carry out their oath of obedience, and will again be helped to obey, they will be an easy preplanned target of lots of shaming and guilt. This is one of the primary foundations for the shame and guilt that is built into the dark side alters. The child will be hit with sticks by the cult, while the Illuminati coven snarl, "Shame on you, you didn't obey as you promised." It is at this ritual, that the Illuminati coven will first begin to double-bind the victim by threatening them, "It's you or them [the person the child slave is to hurt], you choose." The little child sees two kinds of people in life, victimizers and victims. He or she will generally choose to be a victimizer. There will other times when the slave will not be given a choice and will have to suffer pain during the rituals.

p. The Traitor's Death Ritual.

The child victim will be left relatively drug free so they can have full awareness of the Traitor's Death which they witness. A person will receive the horrible traitors death during a ritual. The strong satanic alters will be built off the dissociated pieces caused by this ritual. And as is standard practice the ritual is sealed by a rape of the child to layer in more demons.

**This ends Cisco's very informative chronology. Let's sort out some of the specific programming maneuvers.

Part E. Specific Programming maneuvers. The MANIPULATION OF NEAR-DEATH-EXPERIENCES (NDEs)

People, who undergo Illuminati programming, will be candidates for near-death experiences. In several of the programming scripts, the victim is brought to the point of clinical death and then revived. In hospital settings, resuscitation of heart failure and other deathly events like surgery has produced tens of thousands of cases of Near-death experiences (NDE's). According to Raymond Moody, who worked with or experienced people experiencing NDEs, the typical NDE involves the person hearing himself announced dead. Then a loud ringing or buzzing noise occurs and a long, dark tunnel appears with a light at the end. The person will meet others and a being of light, and this light-being will play back events in the person's life, and evaluate his life, and then the person reaches a point where he must go back.

People, who experience a NDE are profoundly changed. Any profound change that follows patterns can be manipulated and the Illuminati have discovered this is simply just another way to manipulate people. The NDE experiences follow patterns. We will not go into the details of why most of the NDE explanations can't be the actual explanations, but the bottom like is that most explanations fall short and do not explain the phenomena. The frequency and consistency of a tunnel being seen with a light at the end rules out hallucinations in terms of symbology. The mind could just as well see a gate, or keyhole, or a door as an entrance to a new world but doesn't. Some researchers believe that the answer lies in the structure of the visual cortex, and that the dying person's center of the visual field receives an ever increasing electrical noise while dying which produces an ever increasing circle of light being seen.

On the flip side, for those who have a biblical perspective, there are explanations that also seem to explain the phenomena. At any rate, it's been known after Heinrich Kiuver published his research in the 1930's that the brain has four constants in its Near-Death hallucinations: the cobweb, the grating (or lattice), the spiral and the tunnel. Drugs have been found to produce an experience similar to NDE at times too. Whatever spiritually and physically happens to cause a NDE--and there is lots of debate as to the mechanics of the cause--the common experiences that people have during NDE's provides a pattern for the programmers to manipulate. Various people, the Illuminati, some Christians, and others believe that Eccl. 12:6-7, --which is talking about when a man dies ("dust return to the earth as it was") and his spirit returning to God who gave it,--these various people believe that the silver cord spoken about in verse 6 is a cord that links a person to his god. This verse makes a good verse for the Illuminati who do program in wheels and silver cords into their slaves linking them to their pretending-to-be-god masters.

FINE-TUNED

One of the side "benefits" of the brain-stem scarring, the repeated tortures, the attention that is expected if the slave is to survive, etc. is that they may develop extremely sensitive perception. This extremely sensitive perception may come across as ESP, but it is really subconscious understanding of things such as body language.

HIDING THE INTERNAL SELF-HELPER

Psychologists have discovered that deep in the mind is an area of thinking they refer to as the Internal Self-helper. Psychologists who attempt to help programmed multiples have been told to find the ISH (internal self-helper) of the victim. Sometimes the "ISH" have surfaced as ''angels'' and ''spirit guides'' in a system. They may regulate which alters come out and hold the body. The therapist may point out to a person that angels and spirit guides are never internal, unless they are demonic. The Christian is permitted scripturally to only be led by one internal spirit guide, and that's is the Holy Spirit. In some systems, the slave's "Holy Spirit" may turn out to be a cult ISH.

The programmers were many steps ahead of the psychologists. Even years before the psychologists began looking for the ISH to help them, the programmers had foreseen this and had their bases covered. In everyday life, for normal people, the internal self-helper serves as a type of guardian angel over each person. The programmers during the early LSD trips watch for the ISH. When it surfaces, they lock it up in the person's mind, and replace it with a demonic generational spirit, which is commanded to report any work done in the system to the master. When psychologists find the ISH and ask for its help, the ISH does cooperate with them, but this demonic ISH is also one of the principal reporting agents that reports back to the master in photographic detail everything that the therapist does. This is one big reason the programmers have always been several steps ahead of the therapeutic community.

INTERJECT DISKS

Splintered souls captured on Interject disks is a subject that is beyond verification but is mentioned here because therapists and "UFO abductees", and SRA victims of mind-control may run into it. Readers must draw their own conclusions as to what soul interjects are--whether merely a deception, a new technology, or magical demonic manifestation.

Hermetic magic is a nasty form of magic from ancient Egypt. There are a few of the top Illuminati Grand Masters who believe they are capable of carrying out rituals to raise the dead and create interjects onto interject disks. Specialized magic is performed on the dead to raise zombies in order to splinter the zombie's soul. The Grand Master then believes he can place the splinters of the soul on interject disks, and place these interjects into live slaves.

Interestingly, humans claiming contact with "aliens" have claimed that the aliens can separate a human soul from its body, keep it captured, recondition that soul, and finally implant the soul into another body. Some researchers are claiming that they have evidence of a holographic energy template that is associated with a physical body. Is this the soul? They believe that this template works with cellular genetic mechanisms. There is certainly more to learn about what humans are, perhaps some day these claims about zombie souls will have some scientific merit, but for now they lay in the realm of Illuminati Grand Master high magic.

I have reported upon Illuminati beliefs and practices. Likewise, an anthropologist will report on the practices & customs of a people, whether or not the anthropologist personally practices or believes like the people he observes. Of course, these Luciferian (or should one say satanic practices) are abhorrent and the author has never practiced them, so the author can't speak from the viewpoint of a witness, but he can describe as a reporter the views of Illuminati witnesses.

One Illuminati belief is that they have managed to design equipment that can catch the soul of a dying person. This capability will play a role in the reign of the anti-Christ. When the Anti-Christ dies, his soul will be captured and he will be resurrected with demons animating the body. When a very high ranking Illuminati adept goes berserk, the Illuminati will insure that they preserve the soul of the man by killing him with equipment that is portrayed in the recent movie Lord of Illusion. This is a mask-brace that fits over the portals of the head and then is screwed into the head to capture the soul as it tries to escape the dying body. Then demons are called in to live off the soul matter.

Normally, according to Illuminati occult knowledge, the demons can only live a short time within a body, but by the mask-brace capture of a body's soul, the demons can inhabit a body for a longer length of time and create the walking dead. This is that "line between heaven and hell" that the movie refers to. The Illuminati believe that the highest gift they can give Lucifer are captured souls. They will place souls into jars. This is the highest most secret magic of the Illuminati. Notice, that during the Lord of Illusion movie, jars are smashed during the ritual where a soul is captured.

Interviews with alien abductees reveals that some of them believe that the aliens are stealing the souls of mankind. The similarity of the Illuminati beliefs about demons, and the perceived actions of the aliens by abductees are remarkably similar. Also the Illuminati have secretly used special tubing during millions of abortions performed by their abortion clinics to capture the souls of the aborted children. (This is author is not making any claims that they do or don't succeed, but they believe they are succeeding.)

The movie Lord of Illusion is full of Illuminati/high level Masonic symbology. The movie begins with programming concepts, first the galaxies & stars, then the yellow brick road, then a dust storm... An Illuminati phrase "Flesh is a trap, magic sets you free" is mentioned in the movie. In contrast with the movie, these things are not written to entertain the reader, but with the good-natured intent that therapists and victims may gain something by knowing better what is going on to these Illuminati mind-control victims.

The Illuminati believe that they can suck the life spirit out of a person through intercourse with what they call the Eye of Horus (the anus). This is why the leaders of this World Order (such as George Bush, Bill Clinton, and tens of thousands of others) are into sodomy, they are trying to vampirize all the years of life out of the victim to gain a longer life. Some of the sad child victims, who have been kept exclusively for this purpose do look like the life force has been sucked out of them. Sodomy has its own secret chamber on the cabalistic tree of life.

A metaphysical UFO type magazine entitled WE Walk-Ins for Evolution puts out articles on how souls walk-into a body and how souls braid themselves to other souls. For instance, there was an article "Soul Braiding" in the April-June, '96 issue of WE. This appears to be a reframing of various practices that the Illuminati carry out to demonize and control the minds of their people. Rather than speak of a demonization or an interject, front alters of slaves who are not Christians can use metaphysical terms like "soul braiding". The words soul and spirit, and concepts attached to those words are important in programming. Programmed Mormon children will think they have the "Spirit of Elijah" in them, and will robotically sing their programming, "Follow the Prophet, follow the prophet."

WHITE GOLD, other information

Since writing about powdered white gold's ability to make a person clairvoyant, in Vol. 2, it's come to my attention that Nexus magazine has had a recent article on this. For those who are interested in crystal travel, crystal travel is an OBE also known as astral projection and is covered in the Vol. 2 book as astral projection. Besides the silver cord, some victims have mentioned a supernatural dark red violet umbilical that connects them to the AntiChrist.

```
picture 1 p_10-1.jpg
information about the picture
This is a Masonic drawing called "The Second Portal". it shows nude boys facing a throne undergoing some type of
```

magical ritual. The drawing appears In The Hidden Life in Freemasonry after pg. 198. in 1926, Charles W. Leadbeater, a 33° Freemason, printed his book The Hidden Life in Freemasonry. This book was written for people involved in Luciferian rituals In the higher more occult rites of Freemasonry. In the preface, Leadbeater talks of butterflies (pp viii-ix), which has the double meaning in the occult of souls (spirits). in the last chapter, chapter 10, he gives Masonic rituals to Invoke angels (demons) through Egyptian magic. In these Masonic temples, the checkerboard square is used in a similar fashion as a magic circle for a coven. This picture is given as a paper trail to show the sex-magic rituals that take place within various Masonic groups.

The Illuminati Sisters of Light alters rarely appear in therapy because they are used in horrendous Masonic rituals, and must be buried very deep in the system. Typically, a Sister of Light would be blindfolded and taken down many flights of steps and through tunnels and would end up in an elaborate underground Masonic temple. She would be used as a nymph. In one ritual, for example, she'd be given a golden circle band for her forehead, a cloak with a red lining, and a tunic of black silk with golden rays. The hall would have important masons of society who would be sitting in a semi-circle. The Sisters of Light are given to Beelzebub in an excruciating marriage ceremony. There is a veil which fails into 4 equal parts, which mean the 4 corners of the world. The sisters take oaths around the compass, so that the victim feels locked in no matter what corner of the world they go to.

picture 2 p_10-2.jpg

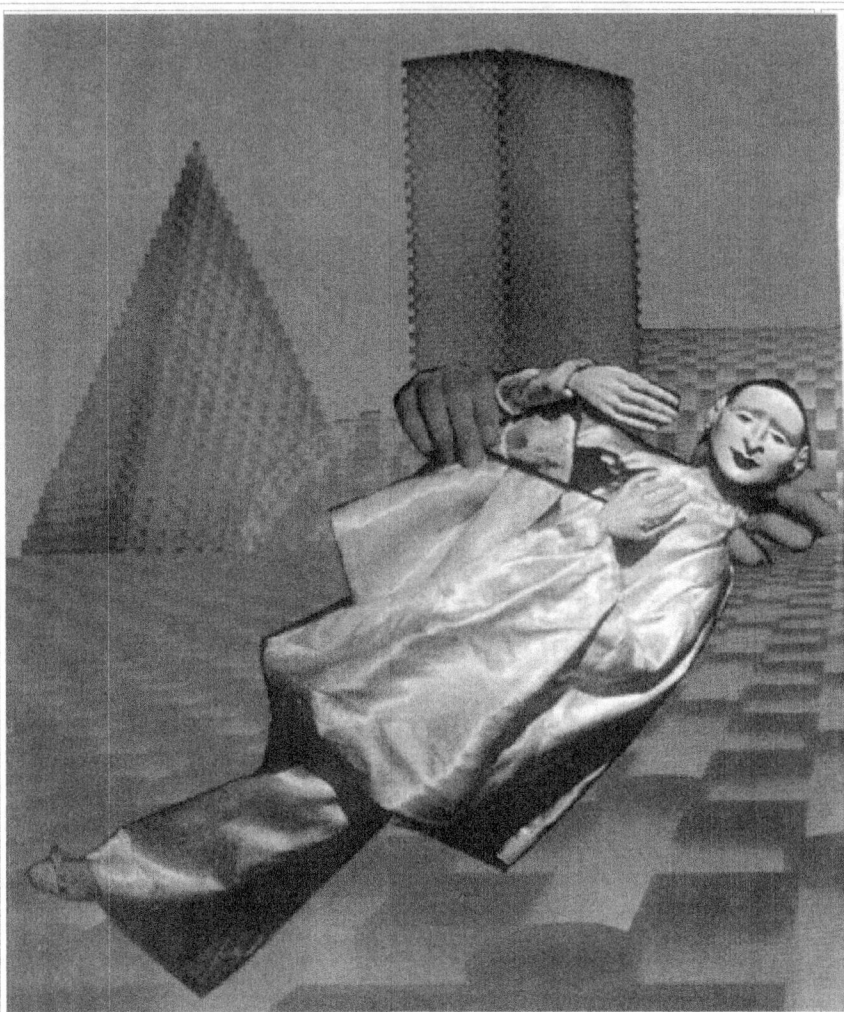

11-1.jpg

[ab]out the picture

[Th]is was some early art work by Cisco to [co]nvey what her mind felt as a mind-[co]ntrolled slave. What the picture shows [is] the hand of the puppet master [co]ntrolling his puppet. The puppet is [flo]ating--not grounded in reality, but [dis]sociated from the external world in [or]der to survive. All the cities and [int]ernal worlds are grids. Everything [att]aches to grids. The color programming [ca]n be seen in the Green, Blue, Silver, [G]old, Red, and Yellow colors of the [gr]ids. The puppet is totally in the hands [of] the puppet master and its hands are in [a s]ubmissive hold, while the puppet [m]aster has his fingers covertly wrapped [ar]ound the left side of the puppet's head.

CHAPTER 11: SCIENCE No. 11- INTERNAL CONTROLS

A. TEACHING OCCULT PHILOSOPHIES
B. INTERNAL COMPUTERS
   Installation of the Standard Programming
   Front Programs of Front Computer.
   Misinformation Computers.
   Beast Computer.
   Programmer Access to the Computer Areas.
C. INTERNAL HIERARCHIES
   THE INTERNAL HIERARCHIES form RATIONALES

A. TEACHING OCCULT PHILOSOPHIES

This is an important ongoing aspect of the mind-control. Vol. 2, introduced this subject:

"Learning plays an important part in perception. The Programmers try to get their victims to subscribe to philosophies and ideas that will make it hard for them to rebel against their controllers. This is what is termed indoctrination. The same methods of teaching that others [any other educator would] find useful are employed. Ways of thinking are incorporated by the slave via handlers, programmers, and the cult they belong to. "Everyone tries in their own way to make sense of life. This is a natural brain function, so that the human mind can understand how to deal with the future. The mind takes raw data, and then applies some type of logic, and comes to conclusions. Once accepted these conclusions can be as hard as nails, and they will defy any attempt to change them, even in the light of new evidence. If the Programmer is smart enough, he can get an alter to logically believe anything. Once the belief is embedded, it will remain there tenaciously."

In the previously book, it was discussed how indoctrination is done. I will provide more of the details on how indoctrination is accomplished, because it is not being done via rational logical thinking. Rather, the programmer or cult leaders want to access a person's non-logical imaginative right brain. In order to do that he must distract the left brain.

Bill Clinton, an Illuminati handler of slaves, and a good liar, has his speeches prepared in such a way that they take advantage of the brain's natural functioning to manipulate it. Bill Clinton, when he gives a speech will initiate it by pushing everybody's green buttons. He will say a number of things that everyone wants to hear and will agree with. This is called "generating a YES SET'. There will be a number of these, the number of these often desired is 3. Then the second stage is to bring in TRUISMS that are facts that after the audience has already been mentally saying yes, the audience will probably accept these facts without any disagreement. Finally, after the approx. three YES SETs, the approx. three TRUISMS, Bill will plant the suggestion, such as "support me in such and such."

On important points, Bill will move his left hand, to help imbed certain commands to his viewers. He will also use some subtle hand signals/codes to trigger mind-controlled slaves too. He will ask during his talks for people to imagine or visualize what he wants for them. Again this is manipulation directed at the right brain.

One of the most crucial things that protects the mind-control of the Illuminati is the frame-of-reference and world-view they build into people from the cradle to the grave. Our previous experience and the information we have available directly influences how we assign meaning to information we receive. The Illuminati's control over so much of society allows them to create people's frames-of-references. Fragments of information that people receive which do not relate to the person's frame-of-reference will be discarded. A person needs a place in his frame-of-reference to hang information on. The person may puzzle over the tidbits of incongruent fragments, but being unable to relate them to his world view, he finds himself unable to file the fragments away in a meaningful manner.

Some of the front alters of very well controlled slaves have had world views (frames-of-references) that believe, a. there is no such thing as Satanic Ritual Abuse, b. there is no such thing as a conspiracy, c. there is no such thing as absolute truth, d. there is no such thing as sin. e. There is no connection between God, living a moral life, and finding Truth. f. there is no such thing as Multiple Personality Disorder. g. My religious organization can do no wrong.

Making a fundamental change in our frame of reference is a frightening task. This is why victims of total mind-control who have been A. programmed not to believe that a New World Order conspiracy exists, and not to believe Satanism and SRA exist, and then they are B. placed in a culture that reinforces this programming, end up being extremely hard to break free of their mind-control.

Conferences where mind-control victims can begin to see the significance of all the fragments of clues that they discarded are very valuable. This author has met a number of mind-controlled victims who didn't know what their problem was, but had countless clues in their life. But these clues were useless fragments of information until they were given a framework to use them.

For instance, one victim of Illuminati total mind-control knew nothing about the significance of the Illuminati bloodlines, nor who the bloodlines were. She stated that her relatives were so and so, and it was then pointed out to her that she was from Illuminati bloodlines on both sides, and the significance of the bloodlines was gone over. Now a meaningless piece of information (her genealogy) had been given a framework of meaning. But this was just one area of many which the establishment has carefully controlled us to have misunderstandings about. Understanding her heritage, allowed her to understand why she was selected for mind-control, when it seemed to her that others might have been better candidates.

Occult philosophies by their very nature create frames of references that make it hard to see reality and to see the Truth in Jesus Christ of Nazareth. The New Age, Witchcraft, and Hindu idea that all paths lead to God, is utter nonsense. The idea that Christians are narrow minded is nonsense, but is a common idea taught by many people. It is narrow minded to insist that Christians must go to the same place Hindu's end up, if Christians seek truth. The New Agers see only one track for truth seekers, since they hold all paths lead to God. The concept is even illustrated by the wheel in India's flag. All spokes on the wheel lead to the same center point of the circle.

The Biblical Christians see two tracks for truth seekers--some don't find God and Truth, but rather find an imitation of the truth and end up eternally lost, while some do find God and Truth. Perhaps at this point the reader is getting slightly upset because he or she is thinking, "Fritz is preaching what he believes," and is also thinking "there is no absolute truth." That is exactly my point. By accepting the lie--the programming lie--the frame of reference--the paradigm that there is no absolute truth, then every time a fragment of absolute truth comes to you, you will reject it.

When I showed evidence to two followers of J.Z. Knight (J.Z. Knight was/is a mind-controlled slave, who has set up an Illuminati front religion in Washington State where converts are subjected to mind-control techniques) that children were being sacrificed by Satanic covens and that this was evidence of Satanic ritual abuse, their world view could not accept the concept of absolute wrongs and sin. They responded, "These satanists may well be killing their babies, but that is not abuse, that is only your idea. It's just your idea that it is abuse. It's not abuse to these people."

In review, one of the hardest shells protecting the programming of a total mind-controlled slave is when the front part of their system, which holds the body regularly, has been indoctrinated into a frame-of-reference that will not allow them to see the reality of what is being done to make and keep them in slavery. A final example of this, are the zealots of the False Memory Syndrome Foundation who are mind-controlled zealots. These zealots, who are launching a counterattack against books like this, have had their world-views carefully constructed by a combination of several techniques of persuasion, a. mass indoctrination, b. subliminal messages via the T.V. and other places in their lives, c. controlled education, and Neuro-Linguistic Programming, in addition to all their regular trauma-based programming. It's like their world-view is the hard varnish that is first seen & heard, protecting people (even themselves) from realizing that the underlying motivation of these zealots is not their world-view, but Total Mind Control Programming.

Within witchcraft, the cosmology that is taught is that a person was originally swirls or vortexes of energy. This coupled with a belief in reincarnation, allows the mind-controlled victim's witchcraft alters to believe that they began with some molecules of energy forming, and that death is nothing, because everything continues on a vast wheel of reincarnation. The beliefs that are inserted into people via witchcraft are conducive to locking the person into their servitude. European culture, which has been based on Christianity, has had a respect and value on life way beyond the oriental view. For centuries Europeans have marvelled about how little value human life has in the oriental view. This is because these Oriental views are identical with what is now called New Age beliefs, which are also about the same thing as witchcraft. Gnostism/ witchcraft philosophy justifies seeking and having power. Persons, who are power hungry, gravitate to this philosophy. Persons who are inculcated with the desire for power rationalize their behavior with the witchcraft philosophy which they are raised in, or programmed to believe, or "discover" to set their minds at ease.

B. INTERNAL COMPUTERS

Internal computers are elaborate arrangements of dissociated parts and memories built into the slave's mind to cause the victim's mind to have mechanical computer-like responses.

For years, the internal computers escaped the detection of the therapeutic community. The illustrated Guidebook introduced the subject to readers and the Vol. 2 gave the first major & so far to date the only comprehensive expose of these computers. This Deeper Insights book will provide a number of pages to deepen the readers understanding of this important subject. This is all fresh (never been exposed) material so don't write and ask what book it came from. You may have to refer back to our previous books for a complete understanding.

Installation of the Standard Programming.

The Illuminati take a screen about 6' by 6'. On the screen is a grid with a Greek or English letter. In front of the screen are colored flashing lights. The flashing colored lights prevent the conscious mind from seeing the screen, but the subconscious mind sees the grid. An Alpha symbol or capital A with tails at the base will be shown on the grid screen for Alpha programming. A Beta or B will be shown for the Beta Programming screen. The programming that is placed in using the different programming associated with various Greek and English alphabets can be read about in Chapter 4 of the Volume 2 Formula book and Chapter 4 in this book. The victim is strapped into a chair with their head locked in place and their eyes forced open. They must endure the flashing lights and the subliminal grid and letter on the screen.

There is a paper trail that they are using flashing lights for hypnotic control of a subject in order to place in messages at the subconscious. One of the pieces of the paper trail was an article "New Device To Induce Hypnosis Developed" in the Chicago Tribune (June 7, 1959). The article was about a Dr. William Kroger, who had tested the use of flashing lights on 200 obstetric patients at the Edgewater hospital in Chicago. Interestingly, this Dr. Kroger lived in Beverly Hills, CA and worked with a Sidney Schneider of Skokie, IL.

Schneider was skilled in electronics and Kroger was an obstetrician. The article said, "The pulsing pattern in reality an electronic brain wave 'achieves control' of the brain's alpha rhythm, thus inducing a drowsy state, according to Dr. Kroger." "The apparatus...operates on the principal of subliminal and photic stimulation of brain waves...about 30 per cent of the subjects who had received no explanation or had no knowledge of what the brain wave synchronizer would do were hypnotized to various degrees." Now these type of machines are available to any bozo who knows where they are sold.

Another piece of the paper trail is a government study by the Defense Intelligence Agency of July 1972, entitled Biological Effects of Electromagnetic Radiation (Radiowaves and Microwaves) --Eurasian and Communist Countries, ST-CS-01-169-72. DIA,, July, 1972, pp. 77-86. This study, of which this author has a copy, in part VI is written about "Light and Color as a Means of Altering Human Behavior." Although the report claims the communists are the ones who are using flashing light and color to alter human behavior, the real inventors were the Illuminati, and both the Americans and Russians are using flashing colored lights for programming.

This DIA study also reports on an American symposium held in the at Tulane Univ., Covington, LA in 1957 concerning the effects of flickering light on the brain. The participants of the 1957 American symposium drew up a paper with 11 conclusions, which included a. flickering light interferes with the human nervous system, b. flickering light can put a person to sleep or into a trance, c. flickering light can interfere with the brains s alpha waves, and d. "photo driving of the EEG by periodic flicker is a well known phenomenon although many subjects do not show the effect..."

During the '50's through at least the '70's, the Illuminati used flickering lights to place into the subconscious the grids used for the various computers. Each block on the grid would have codes, programs, memory and alters attached to it. In other words, dissociated parts of the mind become parts which are built into computers. The mind of victim is hijacked by the programmer.

To fully understand what the computers are, we must understand the mind-set of the programmers. The programmers are looking to Lucifer for their inspiration. An imitation of God's Book of Life for people, is for Lucifer to construct an internal computer that will contain all the history of all the alters. It might be helpful if some items that were in the illustrated Guidebook and in the Vol. 2 book were briefly touched upon again, as we discuss how the internal computers are made. Remember, that a computer is placed one per layer (section) and that they also build in back up computers, and that the computers have coded memories stored in them, as well as coded programs.

The deepest computer is called the Beast computer, and it has an eye (the all-seeing-eye) that opens and shuts like a camera lens. It can go behind the veil, and this is in mockery of the rent veil of the Holy of Holies. When the internal computers are built, the Illuminati use a doll house with different colored rooms for the child to visualize what is being done. Each room in the dollhouse has a different color. Each family of alters (a group of alters that are on the grid together) has the exact same color code. In the Vol. 2 book, we showed the color coding differently--we showed the color coding running diagonally across the grid, it can be done in any fashion, but generally the color code for a single family (alters a-through-in on the chart) is the same, and the cover program to hide it is that the colors run diagonally. What that means is that an entire family of alters, say alters Mary 1 through Mary 13 will all be connected by a color ribbon alter (who works just for them) back to that same color of computer room. All the family get the same programming, although they hold separate memories.

This will help therapists understand the behavior & programming patterns of various alters. The Beta and Delta alters, who as the readers realizes live in entirely a deep trance imaginary life, have entirely negative programming in their computer section. The Betas and Deltas have two ribbons per alter, which is an exception to the rule. This is so they can function together--espionage, seduction, and assassination all go together. Another type of alter who gets two ribbons are the 13th alters which connect two levels. These poor alters have so much programming going off, and mixed signals, that they are real basket cases.

When a system is seen in its entirety, the more powerful system hierarchy and Illuminati hierarchy alters will be coded with Platinum, Gold, White, Purple, Bronze & Silver. Front alters who will be helpful will be coded pink and yellow. Orange alters will be perceived as helping alters, but they are actually guards, protectors, and they protect sections of the system below them, which they usually can't see, and often don't know that they guard. Alters coded brown, tan, grey, or clear will give the therapist & support team fits, because they are full of deceptions & cover programs, and illusions. Host alters or key front alters may have a clear or white diamond as their gemstone. Alters who cover things up may have obsidian as their gemstone. Other alters who play along with the programming may have such gemstones as Fire Opal, Topaz, and Turquoise. (Also see Vol. 2 , p. 328-29.)

Front Programs of Front Computer.

The front computer that is linked to the front section will be different than the deeper computers. It's big difference is that its programs (which are linked to all the front alters) are logical. The logical programs of this level provide the alters with logical reasons and excuses to believe the lies, and to reason their life out. Of course they draw false conclusions from good logic using faulty information.

Misinformation Computers.

Misinformation computers are laid in on the 3, 6, 9 and 12 levels. Thousands of demons are placed into the Misinformation computers to not only run them, but to dispense misinformation. Since the demons are not under drugs or hypnosis, they are under full awareness and are very crafty in their deceptions. When memories are too clean and too complete, the therapist should suspect that they are getting a demonic false memory. Bear in mind the child is in a drugged state during much of the programming and has blurry eyes and may have their eyes rolling in the back of their head. They have their short term memories splintered by electro-shock, and are fed lies about their memories via hypnosis. Real memories are in bad shape when retrieved. (This is why some persons apply "hypnotic correction programs" to restore the memories back closer to the original event, such as reversing the hypnotic air-brushing/blurring of faces that was programmed into deeper alters. The mind put in the distortion program and seems in some cases to be able to reverse the distortion program.)

Beast Computer.

End time names such as Gog, etc. are believed to be given to some of the computers within recent years, to represent the names of the 10 countries that will make up the global government of the New World Order. For years the computers have been called "Beast" computers with the big important Beast computer laid in at the bottom of the mind in the hell pit. Remember that the core is at the bottom of the mind below the hell pit--but she is almost always never connected to the Beast computer. This is because the core receives very little programming. The core is told she is sleeping beauty and that her father Lucifer, who she is married to, will someday return for her and wake her up. Lucifer wanted the purest virgin bride he could get, so he marries as his top bride within the system the innocent core. The core is told she belongs to Lucifer. The core is protected by the false trinity in the pyramid and the Grand Druid Council. The core is linked to the Grand Druid Council, but not the carousel. In the VoL 2 book, we reported the cover program, which is that the core is in the carousel. If therapists want to take out computers they need to take them out from the first computer that was laid in, the Beast computer (at the bottom of the mind), and take them out in the sequence they were put in.

Programmer Access to the Computer Areas.

When the external programmer wants to put information into the computer he opens up the various "rooms" (areas or programs so to speak) and then the internal programmers take over. The story line used to build in access to the computer is the King's Chamber story in Alice In Wonderland. The king comes to the chamber and he has the right to make 3 wishes (the 3-part access code). If he doesn't make 3 wishes, everything disappears like in the Alice In Wonderland story. 3-part access codes are usually DATE, COLOR, ALPHA-NUMERIC CODE. But they could be three objects within the room, or they could be a sound, a touch, and a third-sight signal. Generally, the Illuminati have used the actual date that an alter (a part) or a family of alters was created as the actual code for that chamber of the computer. That chamber will then be linked to all the alters of that family. So lets say a family of alters was created on 4-30-64. This would normally be written on the charts as 43064 or because the Illuminati often work with things backward, some programmers will write it 46034. Which ever method, forward or backwards, will then be used consistently as the first part of the access to that family's computer chamber.

There are 26 rooms in the dollhouse, or in other words, 13 families of alters on a grid with 13 mirror images to mirror those 13. This was very standard for years. When the programmer places the information in it is put on a mental imaginary "computer disk" or in the older models "spools". The reader needs to remember back to the hypnotic surgery that we discussed in the Illustrated Guidebook and the Vol. 2 book, to remember that the victim has their insides hypnotically removed and the spools or computer disks placed inside of them.

Let's say a therapist touches one of the misinformation computers, which are the most assessable. These computers will then activate mirror images and lots of demonic activity. The therapist may end up integrating demons, and working with constructs and mirror images, and the proper excitement by the real alters is even programmed in. These are what may be termed "FALSE HOPE PROGRAMS". The system will rest and relax and the therapist will declare everything finished. (For years, the two authors have tried to explain this, but it seems to be a hard subject for therapists to understand.)

Finally, a very important warning, tampering with the computers is serious business, from the co-authors experience in working with therapists, we strongly advise them not to tamper with the computers, because the self-destruct programs are so strong. The self-destruct programs will turn the person into a vegetable, or into pure insanity if the victim survives the suicide programs. The skill level among the therapeutic community is not yet at the level needed to tamper with the computers, but we hope with the publication of this book and with more experience that that will someday become a reality. This author, Fritz, is aware of therapists that have tried to tamper with the computers, but the programming has beaten both them and this author. For instance, it took lots of work to discover that this author's week of work with a front computer actually was only playing with a misinformation computer and its FALSE HOPE PROGRAMS.

C. INTERNAL HIERARCHIES

OVERVIEW.

The internal structuring of alter systems are built with alters being arranged in hierarchies. Often the hierarchal arrangement is a mirror of the group carrying out the programming. The CIA and other intelligence groups use SECTIONS. You will find the grids of alters arranged in SECTIONS. The Illuminati have a Grand Druid Council and other councils, which will be mirrored within the system. Alter families will be set up as mini-covens within the system, often with 13 to an alter families. HUBS will be created in reflection of how Satanic groups are organized into hubs.

THE INTERNAL HIERARCHIES form RATIONALES

Some of the structures within the programmed alters reflect the philosophies of the ancient occult world. The structures are buttressed by the occult beliefs that are connected to them. Cisco, who has helped me co-author two books on mind-control, pointed out how the ancient world had a god which could only be adored by one family. Each city had its own gods, and religion was tied to the family and the city units. This was the Religion of the Hearth, as some have called it.

The Roman Gens was an extension of this, the Gens were political associations of several families who collected into a religious union, as the Illuminati families have done. When we see how the ancient religious customs were, we see how the internal Illuminati structuring parallels this thinking. Each internal city or world is assigned a god (demon) during the programming. The Illuminati families have collected themselves into a Gen. This is an example of how the internal structuring is buttressed by some occult philosophy which will in turn buttress itself by its claim to antiquity, as if length of practice makes a mistaken superstition valid. The myths of the occult world and their symbology are very extensive. The programmers have many items to choose from as they construct the deeper internal worlds of an Illuminati slave. There is a twisted logic to many of the names they give.

The Magna Mater is the sybil, the symbol of truth, a goddess who can take the form of a city in the occult world. To apply the name MAGNA MATER to a part of the mind then creates a triple or quadruple pun--we have something that can be truth, a city, a goddess, and a sybil. The programmers thrive on puns. The personification of the stages of spiritual life which are called fairies are named White Ladies, Green Ladies, and Black Ladies. Dissociated parts of the mind can be given the name Green Ladies, and then the secret meaning attached that they are fairies that connect to the system's spiritual development. The possibilities seem endless. Since cabalism is behind much of the Illuminati programming, and double images are so important--some systems may incorporate the dual being known as Metatron on top, and Samael on the bottom. This is the occult concept that all phenomena has an essential ambivalence. This is the Gemini concept.

Another Cabalistic concept that appears in programming is the silver palace also known as the silver thread that connects man to his origin and to his end. The palace in the occult world was to have secret chambers (dissociated areas in the subconscious) which hold treasure (programming truths). In the occult world's beliefs, it has been said that the palace of glass represents the magically appearing ancestral memories of mankind from the Golden Age. In Druidism, the horse was linked to the solar wheel, which had more wheels within itself.

During programming: Concepts are linked in series, Concepts are mirrored, and Concepts are related to the whole. The function of occult symbols lends itself to such applications.

p_11-2.jpg

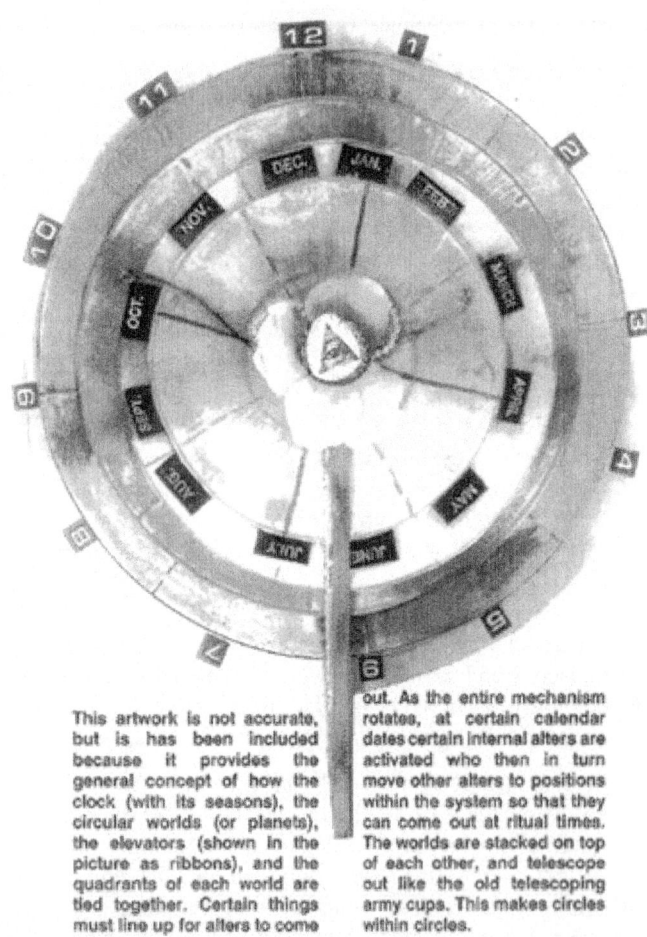

This artwork is not accurate, but is has been included because it provides the general concept of how the clock (with its seasons), the circular worlds (or planets), the elevators (shown in the picture as ribbons), and the quadrants of each world are tied together. Certain things must line up for alters to come out. As the entire mechanism rotates, at certain calendar dates certain internal alters are activated who then in turn move other alters to positions within the system so that they can come out at ritual times. The worlds are stacked on top of each other, and telescope out like the old telescoping army cups. This makes circles within circles.

p_12_1.jpg

about the pic

Barbie Dolls are used for the mind-control programming. Interestingly in 1995, while fighting over Barbie dolls a 6-yr. old girl in Modesto, CA stabbed a 7-year-old playmate with a knife while telling her she was going to kill her. Police did nothing with the girl who had used the knife except to have the parents take her. One wonders what was this all about. Meanwhile Barbie Dolls have drastically changed and are now very occultic.

CHAPTER 12 SCIENCE No. 12-EXTERNAL CONTROLS

Advertising & Trauma-based programming.
ASSET CONTROL
SURVEILLANCE.

HARASSMENT
CAR COLORS
TELEVISION
BUILDING FAMILIES AND COMMUNITIES THAT HAVE INTERWOVEN PROGRAMMING
ISOLATION
BOARDING SCHOOLS & BODY PROGRAMMING.
When controls fail, THE FINAL SOLUTION.
The Programmers

Advertizing & Trauma-based programming.

The Oregonian newspaper, Sat. Mar. 9, 1996, (p. E1) ran a story about women entitled, "She sells, She purrs, she percolates, she's a power player: Ads reflect society's view of women." At the top right is an ad with a Marilyn Monroe type of model with puckered lips selling cigarettes. Below her is a picture of a girl with the caption, "You were born a daughter. You looked up to your mother. You looked up to your father. You looked up to everyone. You wanted to be a princess. You thought you were a princess."

The themes in this article match the thinking within Monarch type programming scripts. Is this coincidence, or just a sign of the times, that so much in our lives echoes programming scripts? Some of the ads in today's magazines are obvious manipulations of the Monarch trauma-based mind-control. For instance, Royal & Sun Alliance Insurance Group controlled by the Rothschilds had an add in a recent popular magazine which has nothing but an entire page of violet-blue haze with an eye [an allusion to the All-seeing eye] staring out of the haze along with the big caption "YOU HAVE OUR ATTENTION." This would reinforce many of the mind-control programs. Ostensibly, the ad was for insurance.

Another ad that is an obvious manipulation of mind-control programming is an Aveda ad placed in Vogue & Vanity Fair magazines, where a woman's face is broken up into 4 pieces and put into a glass bottle along with a white daisy type flower & a yellow flower. The caption reads 'You, bottled." the subcaption reads "what would you be if you came back as a pure-fume?" Notice the play on words that the programmers love.

Another more subtle example is a Virginia Slims ad which is designed to hit the subconscious of the Monarch slave. This ad has three thrones across the top of the page. In front of the three thrones is the Virginia Slims lady. The first two thrones have a chubby queen sitting on them & the third on the far right is vacant. The 3 queens are an allusion to the 3 hierarchy queens and the maiden-mother-hidden crone sequence in programming. The queen holds a scepter which adds some more power to this as a subconscious trigger. The caption reads, "Virginia Slims remembers the shortest reign of a female monarch. Queen Katrina of Valenski was crowned at 10 past the hour, lit a cigarette at 12 past the hour and was dethroned at 13 past the hour."

The hidden meaning behind this is that the front woman, remembers on a subconscious level the threat that if you don't remember the authority & power (thrones), and the power structure (the triad), then you shall remember the programming threat. This ad subtly reinforces the programming threats to slaves.

Other ads that manipulate programming use Wizard of Oz, Alice In Wonderland and Star Wars themes. They use allusions to the programming scripts and show subtle occult symbols. The hypnotic eye is very popular in ads. Some ads simply seem to be a reflection of how our culture has become part of the programming, for instance a Sportsman device that is sold by an add with a big caption "Split personality", or a Merit cigarette ad that sells its product with the caption "Split personality." A watch ad for Bulova has an empty chair with a banner over it "Personality of the year' and the caption "Is your watch making you a missing person?"

During the programming, shifts in time certainly do make certain alters disappear, so although this ad is may not be a direct attempt to manipulate programming, it certainly is a product of today's mind-controlled society.

>>>On the next pg. is an ad appealing directly to the thinking of a programmed multiple.>>

p_12_eve1.jpg

p_12_eve2.jpg

ASSET CONTROL

SURVEILLANCE.

Over the years of watching the Illuminati manage their slaves, it is clear that they like to have their slaves under constant surveillance. Often times they use friends of the slave to keep tabs. For instance, the teams that they put together are great for using to monitor other team members. If they find that the acquaintances and friends of the slave are not contributing enough, they will send out people to keep tabs on the slave.

Surveillance of a slave is done either to let the slave know that he or she is being watched (obviously as an intimidation device), or is done in line with common intelligence/police type tactics. Many times the Illuminati surveillance is so obvious, that this author has to conclude that it is intentionally so. For understanding undetectable surveillance, Hollywood movies are not teaching manuals. To watch someone's house the people working for the Illuminati will often try to maintain about 2 blocks distance. If they have to they can use battery operated bugs or bugs installed using the wiring in the house. If they want to get high-tech they can use fiber optics or even go to satellite-ground antenna monitoring of what a person is doing. If you are looking for a bug, get a counter that will go up into the higher ranges, & expect them to stick bugs away from equipment like refrigerators and air conditioners which make a lot of noise.

They also have directional microphones called bionic ears which can be used to pick up outside sounds from a distance. Sophisticated filters can be placed on their listening devices to screen out background noise. Lasers beamed onto windows can be used to listen to conversations within a building, but these have the drawbacks of picking up building noises, & noises from the street. Laser listening devices are going to function better at night. Telephone taps are commonly done by the Network to control and monitor their slaves. There are low-tech and high-tech ways to do this. The bottom line is that all telephone conversations in this nation (U.S.), all CB-radio traffic, all radio traffic has been totally monitored since before the 1970's. It is a given that anything you say on the telephone will be fed into a large computer which has words to watch for. Unless you believe you are a high-profile person, who is monitored 24-hours a day, it is best to stay away from mentioning trigger words in your conversation.

Often times, the people monitoring slaves team trail the slave. Teams of people can track a person on foot or in a car. Using a team is the best method in many situations. Often they tag team follow a person. They also have team formations that are used to keep track of a person, such as one person on the opposite side of the street, and one immediately behind and one far behind. Having a distant tracker allows the close one to avoid being caught if the slave tries to take evasive action or to ambush the stalker.

If the person watching the slave gets really concerned they may end up using special headlights called "blackout lights" to shadow the slave at night, which are shielded to keep the beams of light from showing in front or to the side of the car. These special lights light up the road in front of the car only, so the car remains unseen by the stalked mind-controlled victim.

There are a number of secret devices to aid the abusers in their control over environment that the slave must live in. The intelligence groups often use a radio device called AGENT ALERT which looks like a ballpoint pen which sends out a continual beeping when it is activated.

Besides their Global Positioning Satellites, intelligence has Pegasus, a ship that can monitor & record electronic transmissions while sailing offshore. After reading the mind-control significance of Pegasi, it clearer the Navy picked an appropriate horse to record electronic transmissions. Even though all slaves have Reporting Alters, & are tracked in other ways, the Illuminati often has redundant safety features to monitor their "human assets".

Because the slave is monitored from so many different unseen methods, it does begin to seem hopeless to some to ever be free of Big Brother. If you add to all this, that the slave has been programmed repeatedly that there is no escaping their All-seeing eyes, then it is easy to see why so many slaves acquiesce & just comply.

A Vol. 2 reader, who caught onto to what the book is about, pointed out how the new film The Juror reflects their approach to control. The movie shows a controller who is obsessed with who he is controlling. This holds true in real life for the programmers too. Even though Dr. Mengele programmed thousands of people in his lifetime, he had his "pets" (Lieblings), pet slaves that he was obsessed with. In the movie, the controller says, "Do what I say." and "If I can keep you scared, I can save your life." These could have come straight out of a programmer's mouth. He picks out a juror who is creative & intelligent to control, which are the criteria for selecting victims in real life. The movie illustrates some of the concepts which actually happen that this chapter 12 is trying to describe.

HARASSMENT

One of the things that the Network does to any slave that tries to break free, and the Illuminati does to any of their hierarchy slaves (like this book's co-author Cisco) who tries to get free is to harass them constantly.

Stephen Knight who researched the Freemasons wrote a chapter in his book The Brotherhood, The Secret World of the Freemasons about how they harass any opposition. (See chapter 16, pp. 140-149). When Knight interviewed ex-Masons they were in abject fear of the Masonic system. They didn't even want to talk about how much power the Freemasons have to ruin careers, spy, and harass people. Since Knight's book is available for the reader, and since there are a number of books (like those from Loompanics) that are very detailed on harassment techniques, this book will only briefly touch on the subject. However, just because it is only briefly mentioned please don't mistakenly think this is a minor topic.

The Illuminati and their co-workers the Freemasons, the Mishpucka, and CIA put outrageously great amounts of efforts into harassment. It is not unusual for a recovering victim of mind-control to find their favourite pet killed, or human faeces in their oven, and other bizarre harassments that show the warped character of the controllers. The CIA, the Masonic leaders, and the Mishpucka keep extensive files on everyone for purposes of blackmail, and coercion. The Masonic leadership of Freemasonry in a given area will have thousands of "blackmail" files on essentially everyone of importance in their area. Upper echelon people such as judges, lawyers, and politicians are generally controlled via IRS infringements, and many of the lower echelon people are controlled through weird sexual items. This is where the Delta and Beta Monarch slaves are so helpful to the Illuminati. The Freemasons can have a sexual alter seduce a man, contrive a scene, and then an alter that is in a death trance takes the body so that the target of blackmail thinks he has killed the woman. It works great for blackmail. (This information comes from several witnesses who are informed about the blackmail files & their methods for blackmailing.)

CAR COLORS

The Vol. 2 book apparently neglected to relate how the colors of cars are used to access victims. Some victims around the U.S. are programmed to red & white cars. Autos with both colors will arrive. Red & White are the great mystical colors assoc. with the 2 headed eagle & Janus. White cars are for high ranking slaves. Very specific sexual slaves are picked up in red and black cars. In N.Y. brown Volkswagens were frequently used for accessing slaves. Two tone cars will be used to trigger particular alters to come out. Another common practice that is occurring across the U.S. is for the draconian enforcers to borrow cars from dealerships so that they can't be traced. The license plates of cars are also used as access triggers for some slaves.

TELEVISION

The all pervasive television, which has been so common place in the lives of Americans, is used a great deal to manipulate trauma-based mind-controlled slaves. Tests by researcher Herbert Krugman have shown that TV watchers used their right brain twice as much as their left brain and released Beta-endorphin into their brains. In other words, TV watching trains the mind to go into an altered state. If a blank black frame is interjected every 32 frames on a show, a 45 beat/minute pulsation is created that puts a person into a hypnotic trance. In Vol. 2, it was brought out how the Lawnmower Man movie, displayed the symbols used to program many of the slaves. The movie was advertised with the slogan "God made him simple...Science made him a god." This is a slogan fitting for an Illuminati member who has been programmed to think he is a god, and yet he must serve his superiors.

BUILDING FAMILIES AND COMMUNITIES THAT HAVE INTERWOVEN PROGRAMMING

The Illuminati has increasingly wanted to keep their members within Illuminati family settings. They have had more problems with placing their members into families which are not part of their mind-control than they have had with children which are raised within Illum. or cult type settings. If one or both of the parents have programming, the Illuminati often weaves the programming together so that the entire family becomes one programmed dissociative mechanism.

For instance, on a ritual night the child as it is being tucked in bed will say to the mother, "MAY I HAVE A DRINK OF WATER." This is the code trigger for the mother to give a drug in a drink. The child is to say another trigger to the parent when they get the drink, then is programmed to drink the drug. The second trigger causes the parent to switch to a personality that feels compelled to get the family into the car and drive. The family all mechanically click into a series of alter switches and end up at a ritual. They mechanically trigger and reinforce each others programming as they return from the ritual, and end up at home with everyone's front alters not knowing what the family has been involved with. Here we have an entire family whose testimony could reinforce each other that they did nothing but sleep at home that night!

There are some locations, for instance, two entire towns in southern Utah that are a strict offbeat shoot of Mormonism, which are entirely programmed multiples. There have been some television shows about entire towns being caught up in secret satanic rituals. It is true, but they also have occult mind-control programming along with those rituals. Here we see how an entire city can trigger each other's programming and all be involved in the insanity of all this without full awareness. This is in fact, where the entire world is headed very rapidly.

ISOLATION

While control mechanisms are put into place world-wide, the Illuminati still must keep their children isolated from the world. To successfully raise a child slave, the mind-control's success depends upon isolation. Children involved in cult rituals do not talk to other children. If they are caught talking, the standard punishment is to tie the child to a dead child. They want their children to shut down, and only do what they are told. They want the child to respond only to the Programmer and its Mother of Darkness. They heap lots of guilt upon any child that breaks the rules of no communication. Children still manage to learn to speak with their eyes and fingers. They become skilled at this even though they know the punishment will be severe if caught.

BOARDING SCHOOLS & BODY PROGRAMMING.

Most people would naturally think that this topic would belong to this chapter. Actually, this topic DOES NOT belong here. But it was placed here on purpose, because its placement here will emphasize its point, while not detracting from the Cranial Manipulation and Genetic Manipulations sections of Chpt. 8.

Boarding schools not only give the elite a chance to isolate, educate, and indoctrinate their children, but it is also a great way to layer in body memories that instil a subconscious ethic of elitism. It is an attitude of elitism that allowed the Pharisees to crucify Christ, the Nazis to kill Jews, and Moslems to kill Hindus, etc.

How does this layering of body memories happen? The memories of our bodies are buried within the cells of our bodies. Therapists have known about body memories for some time now. Cellular level body memories are way beyond the grasp of the consciousness. Buried into a deep unconscious repression are the body memories of the social values (elitism) that are contained in how the social elite walk, hold a spoon and knife, how a person must stand up straight with good posture, and how the person holds and uses their facial muscles. The boarding schools teach an entire world of elite mannerisms such as "keep a stiff upper lip" to "don't hold your knife in your left hand."

West Point performs the same programming of body memories, to insure that their West Pointers develop an elitist attitude. The effect of these body memories is to subconsciously encourage the mind into thinking that it is elite. The erect posture and military gait that this author was taught carry with them the implication of superiority. While the conscious awareness of this elitist indoctrination can be gotten in touch with and defused, there are none-the-less buried elements of body memory that resist tampering. This author would ask his fellow West Pointers, how do they feel if they walk like a general around civilians?

This type of body programming contributes to an ethic of elitism. How it is created and how it works has not escaped the detection of the elite bloodlines. This is why the British boarding schools are so strict about "good manners." Through a plebe year of bracing, the mind develops body memories of how to stand in a military brace. Some cadets are so traumatized by their first year, they never return to a normal posture. A military brace has been proven to not be the healthiest posture. It's this author's contention that the military brace is insisted upon for mind-control, and not for health reasons.

Victims of mind-control have been placed in many humiliating body positions, as well as many painful body positions. It takes years of slow subconscious work as well as deep massage to pull these up and work with these body memories. For instance, during the tortures to create cat/kitten alters, the children often crouch like cats. Kitten alters will retain their body memories of crouching (hunching the shoulders) like a cat. Sometimes when their masters begin to beat on kitten alters, they will reflexively crouch like a scared kitten. And what's with the woman called Queen Sheri who has been managing the two professional wrestlers Macho King and Randy Savage? Both of these professional wrestlers are part of a "family" called the New World Order. Queen Sheri walks around in a cat costume and facial makeup that makes her look like a real wild cat. Is this wildcat a Monarch wildcat?

When controls fail, THE FINAL SOLUTION.

The World Order can send out teams of professional killers. (What's new?) These killers often emotionally distance themselves from their victims by thinking of their "targets" as inferior forms of life that they are "liquidating", "terminating", "cleansing from this planet", etc. In 1996, a 4-member hit team took out the entire Bill Mueller family

(Bill, Nancy, and 8 yr. old Sarah). Bill was a member of the Special Ops Group SOG of the Navy Seals. He had become a Patriot and a big gun dealer living in Arkansas. Someone decided he was too much of a threat and sent a team in to take not just him but his entire family out. Booz-Allen & Hamilton, Inc has been hired by the NWO to infiltrate the militias. This author has known in this area several disobedient slaves, and one therapist who lost their lives to assassins, as well as another one who committed suicide according to programming. But anymore what isn't dangerous? Crossing the street and eating at a restaurant can kill you too. The reader knows this. This author also knows of several who were going to be killed but escaped. One troublemaker was to have been sacrfficed but broke free and hid, another was ritually tortured, buried alive, and left for dead, but managed to survive.

The Programmers

p_lewis.jpg

APPENDIX 1 - PROGRAMMERS/RESEARCHERS

DIRTY PSYCHIATRISTS involved with MIND CONTROL
DIRTY RESEARCHERS
DIRTY TAVISTOCK CONTROLLERS
SOME OF FREEMASONRY'S MIND-CONTROL PEOPLE
REMOTE VIEWING MIND-RESEARCH
ODDS & ENDS
LIST of PROGRAMMERS (continuation from the list given in Vol. 2)
A FEW random CIA/INTELLIGENCE MEN involved WITH MIND-CONTROL
Anton LaVey--Profile of a trauma-based mind-control programmer
WHAT TO LOOK FOR.
MICHAEL AQUINO, a military/cult mind-control programmer
  HIS CAREER
  PERSONAL HISTORY.
  UNDERSTANDING The CHURCH OF SET
  UNDERSTANDING SOME OF AQUINO'S PROGRAMMING.
  BACKGROUND
  SEQUELAE OF ABUSE

The Illuminati set up the Josiah Macy, Jr. Foundation to direct some of the mind-control its research, and its financial affairs. Harold Abramson became one of its leaders. One of the Macy Foundation's directors has been military intelligence chief and relative to Winston Churchill, Gen. Marlborough Churchill. Both Winston and Marlborough are of the corrupt Illuminati Marlborough family.

DIRTY PSYCHIATRISTS involved with MIND CONTROL

Dr. Van O. Austin, Utah
Dr. George Brock Chisholm, Tavistock
Dr. Lawrence D. Ginsberg
Dr. Robert G. Heath
Dr. Paul Hoch, Scot. Rite Mason
Dr. Robert Howell, Utah
Dr. Nathan Kline, Columbia Univ.
Dr. Nolan D.C. Lewis, dir NY State Psyc Inst. & Scottish Rite Mason
Dr. Amedeo S. Marrazzi, Missouri Inst. of Psychology
Dr. Sudha Tayi

DIRTY RESEARCHERS

Dr. Ross Adley, formerly of the Brain Research Center at Univ. of So. CA, now at Loma Linda Univ. Med. School, CIA, worked on ELF waves and the brain, and EM radiation.

Dr. Emmanuel Donchin, head of Psyc. Dept. at Urbana-Champaign's Univ. of IL, worked on thought-controlled machines.

Dr. Wayne O. Evans--U.S. Mil. Stress Lab, Natick, Mass

Dr. Dave Morgan, Lockheed-Sanders, worked on the syntel

Dr. Arthur Upton, head National Cancer Inst.

DIRTY TAVISTOCK CONTROLLERS

W. R. Byon

Richard Crossman

H. V. Dicks

Ronald Lippert

Brig. Gen. Dr. John Rawlings Rees

SOME OF FREEMASONRY'S MIND-CONTROL PEOPLE

Dr. Robert Hanna Felix--33°, dir of psyc. research for Scott. Rite, oversaw the Lexington KT programming facility

Dr. Franz J. Kailman-jewish Nazi who did research at NY State Psyc. Inst. while at Columbia Univ.

Seymour Solomon Kety- exec. of Scot. Rites psychiatry experiments, & nat. dir. of American Eugenics Soc.

Winfred Overholser- overall leader of Masonic research into mind-control, sup. of St. 'Elizabeth's Hosp. a mental hospital in Wash. D.C.

REMOTE VIEWING MIND-RESEARCH

Private organizations doing research into RV in the U.S. are run by "retired" intelligence people.

Joe McMoneagle -- "retired Intelligence officer" left govt.'s Stargate to set up "private" RV research.

ODDS & ENDS

· Hillary Clinton, who is a Grand Dame in the Illuminati, started in the early 1960s a group of mind-controlled slaves which is called Royal Project. She reportedly exercises power in the White House via 16 staffers who have been given authority over the different departments of government. One mind-control victim claims that one of Clinton's talks gave triggers for him to kill. One of Clinton's never mentioned cronies, who works closely with him, and travels to meet him at various locations is Charles Whitmore of Arkansas.

· One of the big areas where a great number of mind-controlled slaves congregate are MUFON meetings. An example of a slave handler, who is also a programmed slave is Dea Martin, who tells people she has worked for the government and who does aura readings. She controls her sidekick Jim Courant, a commercial airline pilot. An example of a programmed multiple with "alien" programming was serial murderer Robert Moody. Film taken of Moody in jail shows his MPD (DID).

· Kleinknecht was National Director of NASA during the Moon Flights when lots of mind-control programming was being done by both the Masonic lodges and NASA. C. Fred Kleinknecht was not only director of NASA but the Sec. General of the Scottish Rite 33°.

· The Doors Singer Jim Morrison used the occult code name Lizard King and The Exterminating Angel. He was involved with mind control.

· Col. John Alexander, (also called Doctor) who has been living in Arizona, and who has been in charge of making psychic warriors for the U.S. Army, has the inside reputation of being the Illuminati's top mind-control programmer.

· James Monroe. It turns out that there have been two James Monroes involved in programming. The first one was bn. perhaps in the 1920's, was 6' tall, and he was the CIA man who set up the Society for the Investigation of Human Ecology, a CIA front for mind-control, He had a very polite front in spite of being a sadistic programmer. The second one was James Monroe Martinez, bn in 1938, 6' tall, who was busy setting up underground bases such as the one at Los Alamos under the cover of working for GE. One report said he died in 1965. His mother owned a Catholic half-way house in Albuquerque, NM.

· There are all kinds of events happening around us that show evidence of mind-control. One example, is the case of a Catholic man quitting the monastery and becoming a NASA physicist.

· Part of the success of the mind-control lays within their child procurement abilities. The' corrupt Finders group, which consisted of FBI/CIA men who helped procure children, were led by Marion Pettie, who was called "the Stroller" and "the Game Caller" by Finder members.

* The establishment allowed CIA programmer Dr. Louis Joyon "Jolly" West to examine Jack Ruby in his jail cell. When Ruby refused to admit to insanity, West labelled him "paranoid and mentally ill" and Ruby was placed on pills, which were called "happy pills". Ruby believed he was being poisoned by the establishment.

· Part of the success of the mind-control lays in the fact that there is such a widespread network of pedophiles. On Channel 5, May 6, 1996, during a show "Priestly Sins," it was stated that "at least 3000 [catholic] priests are sexual abusers of children." The program stated that 600 priests have been reported to law enforcement within the last few years for complaints of sexual abuse of children. The show stated that catholics are silenced and punished if they speak up. Priests who speak out are penalized. For instance in 1985, a senior official at the Vatican's embassy in Wash. D.C. discovered rampant sexual abuse and wrote a report on how it should be dealt with responsibly. The church promptly buried the report.

LIST of PROGRAMMERS (continuation from the list given in Vol. 2)

Stephen Aldrich

Morse Allen

Dr. Charles L. Brown

Col. Campbell

Dr. Cleghon

Hillary Clinton

Jack F. (Uncle Jack) & Jill Coogan

Sen. Alan Cranston

"Gen." Earman

Don Ebner

Dr. Charles Evans

Dr. Tom Fox

Floyd & Mildred Frost & dau. Carol Frost Buls

Dr. George S. Glass

Dr. Goldshe

L. Wilson Greene

Dr. James Hamilton

Dr. Robert G. Heath

Richard Helms

Dr. Paul Hoch

Dr. Hyde

Dr. Korim (sp. not known)

Dr. Lowenstein

Mateland

Dr. Gary E. Miller

Dr. Moore

Dr. Martin Orne

Dr. Rosenberg

Dr. Woolsworth Russell

Cpt. George White (nickname/cover name Stormy)

Dr. Robert E. White

A FEW random CIA/INTELLIGENCE MEN involved WITH MIND-CONTROL

John Bacon
Tennant (Pete) Bagley
Col. Matt Baird
Bill Brown
Richard L. Conolly, Jr.
Burt Courage
Cong. Bud Cramer
Jerry Droller
Robert Feldman
Jim Ferguson
J. Peter Grace
Cynthia Hausman
Richard Helms
William J. Hood
Jack Kindschi
John McCone
Charles McKay
Cord Meyer
Comm. John R. Miller
Herbert Quinde
Wade Thomas

Anton LaVey--Profile of a trauma-based mind-control programmer

When someone coined the phrase "dynamite comes in small packages" the phrase was an apt description of Anton LaVey. (Released photographs of LaVey prevent people from realizing how short his is.) In a personal letter which

Anton LaVey wrote, "With my swastika, I'm strong. My Satanic amulets give me power. I'm not a misfit anymore, with pimples and a heart murmur and flat feet."

Anton LaVey is famous for having started the Church of Satan. He chose Walpurgisnacht, April 30, 1966 to start the Church of Satan in San Francisco. Previously he had began holding midnight magic seminars in 1960. He and his occult friends held Magic Circle meetings until he founded the Church. His Church of Satan is officially recognized by the U.S. government and the military.

He turned an old Victorian House, at 6114 California St., San Francisco into what has been called "the Black Castle". It was for years indeed black on the outside, and LaVey would drive a hearse. Anton LaVey kept a full grown 400 lb. Nubian lion named Togare from Ethiopia at his house (which was allowed both inside & outside) that scared the neighbours when it roared. He also has kept a black leopard.

LaVey loves to play his Hammond organ music in his black castle as if his house were a stereotypical horror house. Inside the house are rooms used for rituals, occult books including books on cannibalism, coffins, a maze of secret passageways, and LaVey's private saloon called the Den of Iniquity. He called his satanic covens "Grottos."

This author is aware that the Church of Satan got Grottos going in the following cities: Amsterdam (Magistralis Grotto, Neth.), Boston, Chicago, Dayton, Denver, Detroit, Edmonton (Can), Indianapolis, Kansas City, Las Vegas, London (Eng.), Los Angeles, Louisville, New York, Paris (Fr.), Phoenix, Portland (OR), St. Petersburg, Seattle, Silverton (OR), and Vancouver (Can).

Undoubtedly, there are other groups, as well as a scattered following of individuals. The Church of Satan has had many Ph.D.'s. The church has had a high percentage of professionals such as: doctors, lawyers, teachers, former FBI agents, IBM executives. Cult underground film maker Kenneth Anger was a member of the Church of Satan. An ex-high priest of the Church of Satan told this author how he was recruited for the position of high priest. He was promised anything he wanted in life, any woman, any money etc.--and they made good on much of that promise. As high priest, he micromanaged everyone's lives in his grotto. His people came to him for permission and advice and orders for everything. It wasn't just mind-control, it was total control of their lives. But giving orders and micromanaging the lives of many people became a drag.

One of Cathy O'Brien's abusers was LaVey's High Priest Merle Kilgore, father of Steve Kilgore. LaVey (bn. April 11, 1930) comes from a Rumanian bloodline from Translyvania. As he grew up he love the story of Frankenstein. As a teenager he loved the occult. He dropped out of high school to be part of the Clyde Beatty circus.

LaVey likes to work from dusk to dawn. Like his ex-right hand man Michael Aquino, another mind-control programmer, both LaVey and Aquino are fascinated with the Nazis. (Michael Aquino's wife Lillith Sinclair was formerly the head of the Church of Satan's NY Lillith Grotto.) LaVey sports a Van Dyke beard, and a head shaved in the same fashion of executioners during the middle ages. Most of his followers never see him. Although LaVey has gotten wide press coverage, thanks to William Randolph Hearst's newspapers and his publishing companies like Avon, LaVey is a very secretive person and very rarely shows himself to even his high priests, or even talks to them.

His Church is a collection of self-sustaining dictators. He exaggerates the numbers of his church, apparently by claiming people who come in contact with his church. Before we discuss more about his organization and their rituals, let's touch on his role as a trauma-based mind-control programmer. Anton LaVey has openly advocated the creation of android humans. Even more startling is a music video shown on TV in which Anton LaVey personally gives a graphic description of how Anton LaVey intends to make the listener into his "mind-controlled sex slave". The audacity of this is mind-boggling. But then LaVey has tended to be more frank than other occult figures. The approach seems to be "I'll shock you so boldly, that you will not believe what I am saying, but will think its an act."

Taking inspiration from Orwell's 1984 LaVey wrote, "Up is down, pleasure is pain, darkness is light, slavery is freedom, madness is sanity..." This is actually the language that is used at times in the mind-control programming! Anton LaVey has been the mind-control handler/programmer of a number of Hollywood actors & actresses, including Jayne Mansfield and Marilyn Monroe, who both serviced him as sexual slaves. Jayne Mansfield, who was a High Priestess in the Church of Satan, shocked people when on a USO tour in Vietnam she asked for a satanic religious service. Sam Brody, one of

Mansfield's handlers, had a bitter struggle over who would control Jayne, and one of LaVey's followers claimed to have tampered with Brody's car. Anton LaVey has also been the programmer of his daughters such as Karla and Zeena and his son. An ex-member of a satanic cult in the Ozarks said, "If LaVey says jump, you jump." Some of his followers call him ''Uncle Anton'' as if they were programmed by him. LaVey's cover is that he is simply a showman, a buffoon. His cover has fooled many people, the truth is the man is not to be trusted and has a lot more evil power than people have realized.

LaVey has always had what some describe as a "warm relationship" with police. In fact, he was on the police force in the 1950's as a photographer. The police were reluctant to question LaVey about the death of Jayne Mansfield (4/19/33-6/28/67) who was one of LaVey's high priestesses and slaves in his Church of Satan. Her color was pink. Anton LaVey has been seen going onto military programming bases, and was at the NORAD area in Colorado for a while.

Dick Russell interviewed Anton LaVey with his approval. Russell wrote up the interview in "The Satanist Who Wants To Rule The World", (Argosy, June 1975, p. 41) that the Anton LaVey believes that he and an elite force of Satanists will rule the world. LaVey took an obscure occult tract from the 30's and some thoughts from HG. Well's book The Island of Dr. Moreau for a ritual. From this, he came up with a ritual which includes these stanzas:

"Man is God. We are men. We are gods. God is man."

When the reader is done reading this book, he will see how this ritual can fit in perfectly with trauma-based total mind-control. In fact, when people attend the Church of Satan's secret rituals, once people enter the ritual room two hooded guards prevent people from exiting prematurely through the closed doors. The rituals have been reported as being very disgusting. It well publicized that LaVey uses naked human altars for rituals, after photos were published of his satanic baptism of his 3 year old-daughter Zeena in May 1967. Does the Church of Satan involve summoning demons and worshipping Satan. Yes, most definitively. For instance, here are the some of the words of an important invocation used by his satanic rituals:

In nomine Dei nostri Satanas Luciferi excelsi! In the name of Satan, the Ruler of the earth, the King of the world, I command the forces of darkness to bestow their Infernal power upon me!...By all the Gods of the Pit, I command that these things of which I speak shall come to pass! Come forth and answer your names by manifesting my desires! Hail Satan!"

LaVey's book The Compleat Witch (NY Dodd, Mead, 1971) p. 266 advocates that one achieve self-understanding and "embrace and cherish the demon within him." In LaVey's book The Satanic Witch (LA: Feral House, 1969) he states that a witch to be successful must make a pact with the devil. His church loves to chant "Hail Satan". They like Crowley's law, Do What thou Wilt. LaVey & some of his members teach that at the core of each person is a demon waiting to be released.

LaVey loves Black Masses and desecrating anything sacred to Christians. LaVey urges people in his books and talks to bring out their "darkest" urging. He hints at human sacrifice in his Satanic Bible, by having a section on it, but is careful not to go too far out on a limb publicly. He always publicly denies that Satanists should do human sacrifices. One of the doctors of the San Francisco Church of Satan is said to have brought LaVey's church a severed human leg from the hospital he worked at, which was basted in Triple Sec and eaten by LaVey and his group. Most of the rituals are done in secret, there are no way to confirm rumours that they eat human flesh, but knowing the mentality of some of his church members, they would do it just to check it out as a new experience.

Illuminatus William Randolph Hearst gave Anton LaVey some big help. His Avon Publishing published his Satanic Bible in 1969 (it was first released in Dec. '69). Since then it has reportedly gone through over 30 printings. LaVey's next book The Satanic Rituals also was published by Hearst Avon in 1972. It talks about the power that blood sacrifices give the magician. Hearst's papers also gave him publicity.

LaVey is always thinking of ways of promoting his theology. Years ago, he had a topless witches Sabbath on San Francisco's North Beach. In 1990, the Church of Satan went into the Heavy Metal music business. The Church of Satan puts out a monthly magazine The Cloven Hoof which for most members is their main indirect communication from Magus LaVey.

WHAT TO LOOK FOR.

One of the most asked questions is, "Fritz, what does one look for?" One of the best covers for Illuminati kingpins is religion. Another is philanthropy. Philanthropy ties in with Illuminati beliefs that your good deeds must balance your evil deeds to gain power--it's a Gnostic cabalistic view point. The Illuminati kingpins are great philanthropists even though much of their philanthropy is self-serving.

Perhaps giving an example of a family that is suspect due to their circumstances would help illustrate this point. There is such a family which has gone almost undetected for years, and although some people fear them, they have not been reported on. Just because the police place a person on the suspect list, does not mean that the person is guilty. Everyone deserves the right to treated as innocent, until proven guilty.

One of the groups that concern this author are the rich ultra-secretive ultraconservative Talmudic Jewish groups. This exclusive group keep their children away from contact with the outside world and send them to exclusive, semi-secret schools. An example of this would be the Reichmanns of Canada, who are billionaires, and have had some connections to the Rothschilds of England. It's not that this author has problems with people observing their religious beliefs strictly (or in the ultra-conservative Talmudic groups, "ultra-strictly" better describes their extreme strictness). It's great that people have standards of belief and conduct. However, the author sees the same patterns of legalism and secrecy that pervade Old Order Amish groups, -- except in the case of families like the Reichmanns, the potential for mischief is great, because they are not involved with milking cows, but international banking.

While most people are simply ignorant about the Amish but are not fearful of them, people who know rich billionaires like the Reichmanns scared to death of them and a heavy cloak of secrecy envelopes them. Renée Reichmann was the great matriarch of the Reichmanns of Canada who are Talmidim Chakham, followers of the Talmud. They are not Hasidic. She is a descendent from King David, and King Solomon. She lives in Toronto. Her great-grandfather, a Gestetner, was one of the wealthiest men in Hungary. Most of her family lives in Montreal, two of her sons live in Toronto. Her children are Eva, Edward, Louis, Albert, Paul & Ralph. Samuel Reichmann is the father of the dynasty in Canada.

In 1929, his egg business made him rich. He learned how to work finances and currency exchanges between different countries to make money by tricks to circumvent legalities. Their family has also gotten Rothschild financial help, and during W.W. II they worked with Koppel, who ran the Rothschild's City Bank in Gibraltar. Their family did a great many things during W.W. II from the trading center Tangier in North Africa. Tangier was located in a position to trade between the Axis and the Allies. Also during W.W. II, under the direction of the Bank of Spain the Reichmanns and others kept the Spanish currency artificially high, by creating an artificial demand for the currency. The Reichmanns made perhaps millions of dollars on currency exchanges during the war years.

Don Eduardo Reichman was the administrator of del Real Estate & Commercial Bank of Tangier. Eva Reichmann married a British merchant banker. Albert Reichmann is President of Olympia & York Developments Ltd. Paul sits on the board of the Canadian Imperial Bank of Commerce (CIBC) & on the board of Rockefeller Center Properties, Inc. (a real estate investment trust for some of the Rockefeller properties in Manhattan.) Albert sits on the board of the Mt. Sinai Hospital in Toronto, and on the board of Landmark Lands Co., Inc. which owns some of the great golf courses in Palm Springs, CA. The Ontario Ministry of Consumer & Commercial Relations has offices in buildings owned by them. They tried to buy banks in Israel. Their sect of Judaism has a Yesodeh Hatorah school for ultra-orthodox boys. Their children have very little exposure to outside world. Their children do not have access to newspapers, television, or radios. Ralph and Paul were privately educated in England at Gateshead. It's a perfect setup for trauma-based mind-control.

Samuel Reichmann is known among his kind of Jewish sect as a philanthropist who supports Torah institutions. These Talmudic families consider pedigrees and genealogies very important, which is very much in line with the Illuminati's mind-set. The reason that this family is mentioned is that the Reichmanns haven't been mentioned in my previous books, and the circumstances that pervade the family have the earmarks for what this book is about. It may be that this family of billionaires consists of only wonderful people, but it is a given that most of the readers would be considered animals by these strict Talmudists, who would never allow any of us of the wrong bloodlines to be accepted into their "in" group. Obviously the Rothschilds are of the right bloodline.

Likewise, international bankers tend to be a Machiavellian clique, (that is not this author's opinion, but the opinion of honest hearted person who have ran in those circles.) Why has this clique accepted a family like the Reichmann's from such a narrow-minded judgemental sect into their fold? This paragraph is not written toward anyone specifically, it simply calling our attention a family of billionaires that no one knows about, which lives in veil of secrecy, and a religious setting that would make mind-control as easy as imaginable. (The Reichmanns would deny what's been written here.)

There are victims of mind-control coming in to therapists from conservative Jewish groups, and at least some of these are Illuminati. The religious front could just as easily be Christian. Some of the readers of Vol. 2 reported back that the book helped them unveil the religious fronts that had helped derail their suspicions of puzzling situations that don't add up. The next programmer to be written about uses the front of being a leader of a Satanic Cult. I say front, because Michael Aquino has created a public image for his satanic cult, and hides behind that public image. Anytime someone wants to reveal the ugly truth about him, he hollers to the effect that he is being persecuted by a wild witch-hunt. He hollers that people are just having a knee-jerk reaction to his satanic occultism, and that he is really safe.

MICHAEL AQUINO, a military/cult mind-control programmer

An OVERVIEW. Michael Aquino has been a trauma-based total mind-control (Monarch) programmer for the DIA Psychological Warfare Division. He is also a prominent public satanist. A photo of Aquino in his military uniform is in the center picture section of Carl A. Raschke's Painted Black (San Francisco: Harper & Row, 1990.) Other books contain various pictures of him in satanic garb with ritual items. Most of the programmers have chosen to remain in the background, Aquino with his enormous ego, has chosen otherwise.

Senator Byrd (KKK leader & Freemason) and Aquino have done a great deal together over the years, and have been like a team. With the legal expertise of U.S. Sen. Robert C. Byrd, Aquino established the Temple of Set, a satanic cult as a legal religion recognized by the U.S. government and the U.S. military. This exclusive cult was designed to give these unchallenged criminals of the Network:

A. a legal organization whose membership consists of a mixed group of slaves and handlers, B. a market outlet for their illegal drugs and porn, C. a good public, legal, openly satanic front with which to attack all media coverage of ritual abuse.

The controlled media could now excuse itself from covering ritual abuse, by saying that they had been threatened to be sued by the Church of Set. Although the Church of Set has had the entire power of the establishment protecting it from investigation and criminal prosecution, the climate of control over the United States is still not complete enough for Satanists to openly get away with their mind-control. By identifying itself so intimately with the Church of Set, U.S. military intelligence has given the world an open trail of clues to help whistle-blowers expose the mind-control that has been going on throughout most of this century. Michael Aquino openly associated with men like President Ronald Reagan at the White House, again giving us the leverage to expose the secret satanic philosophies of America's leadership. Most of these men lead double lives, and due to the mind-control it has been hard to establish (except for eye-witnesses) that they are secret Satanists.

HIS CAREER

The army has known about Michael Aquino's Satanism from the beginning, clear back in 1968. Aquino (and some of his satanic lieutenants) received a High security clearance (reportedly level 6), and he served with the World Affairs Council.

A dozen leaders within the Temple of Set were Military Intelligence officers (for instance, Capt. Willie Browning and Intelligence Officer Dennis Mann). Aquino wrote "From PSYOP to Mind War: The Psychology of Victory" published in the establishment's prestigious Military Review magazine. Aquino writes in this "From PSYOP to MindWar..." article, "...we shall create MindWar. The term is harsh and fear-inspiring, and so it should be: It is a term of attack and victory..." Aquino is a sadistic programmer, who loves to inflict pain on others.

Aquino has a doctorate in political science. He has two masters degrees (one is in political science, Univ. of CA, Santa

Barbara, where he also got his doctorate). Aquino is Airborne qualified. He studied at the U.S. National Defense University. He was in Military Intelligence in Vietnam & Germany, and the Presideo. He was a Defense Intelligence Agency attache, and taught political science on the university level. He reported directly to the Joint Chiefs of Staff and worked one on one with the Secretary of Defense Cheney. He is a pseudo-intellectual whose ego and astronomically-large pride gets in the way of real learning.

He was the former national commander of the Eagle Scouts Honor Society. (The Boys Scout system is heavily influenced by Freemasons and contains unfortunately some perverts that try to take advantage of the system for their own perversions.) There was a massive coverup in the Presideo Day Care scandal in which Aquino was involved in. There were hundreds of witnesses of the abuse. The military and intelligence put strong pressure on the San Francisco police to get them to back down from doing anything to Aquino. During that time period, the Pentagon transferred Aquino from the Presideo back to the National Defense University, Wash., D.C. (And later he wound up in the St. Louis area.) During the investigation of the Temple of Set, the FBI claimed they had no record of such an organization. The military at the Presideo, had a spokesperson tell the press that Aquino was a good soldier who did his job. Aquino hides behind his religion. In his Scroll of Set Aquino accuses the father of the girl who pointed him out as her abuser as persecuting him because he is a Satanist. Aquino writes, "Also relevant is his profession as a Christian clergyman; I certainly doubt that he would have made such an outrageous accusation against any Lieutenant Colonel who was not known to be a prominent Satanist." (p. 4 Oct. XXII)

The truth that everyone will realize on their own is that any loving, caring father when he discovers some pervert has severely sexually molested and tortured his daughter is going to go to the police no matter what religion the villain belongs to. In 1985, U.S. Army major Grady McMurtry of Berkeley, CA and Kenneth Grant's OTO got into a legal battle over who was the actual chartered OTO lodge in the U.S.

Col. Michael Aquino of U.S. Military Intelligence watched the legal battle, and wrote these comments in the Scroll of Set Vol. XII no. 5, Oct. '86, "While sitting in the courtroom watching Judge Legge preside sternly over the slug-out, I couldn't help wondering if he had any idea he was ruling on which group had legal claim to anal sex as the supreme religious sacrament in the United States." Witnesses report that one of Aquino's favorite types of sex is necrophilia, which of course can also be carried out with alters that are in a death state.

PERSONAL HISTORY.

Michael's father was an Italian Catholic. A Canadian police document that this author has indicates that Michael's mother was Betty Ford. Michael's wife is Lillith Sinclair. Besides being a Satanic High Priest & Ipsissimus, and an Military Intelligence Officer in Psychological warfare, Michael was a stockbroker for a while. In 1970, he joined the Church of Satan, and led a grotto in Kentucky. Michael gave lectures on Satanism at the University of Louisville, and used his house in Louisville for rituals. Aquino claimed to be anointed as the Second Beast, the one that Aleister Crowley prophesied in The Book of the Law. (See Aquino's The Book of Coming Forth by Night.) While LaVey shaved his head and wore horns to look the part, Aquino cut his hair in a widow's peak, plucked his eyebrows, and had a 666 tattooed under his scalp.

UNDERSTANDING The CHURCH OF SET

His Temple of Set was set up using ranks borrowed straight from the secret Illuminati--Priests or Priestesses, Adepts, Masters (Magus or Maga), and Ipsissimus or Ipsissima. (The Order of the Golden Dawn also uses the rank of ipsissimus. His cult uses new terminology such as Setian for Satanist. It's a common tactic of cults to use new terms to separate the cult followers from the external world.

In Aquino's bi-monthly periodical The Scroll of Set (Vol. XIII, No. 5, Oct. XXII, 1987, pg. 2 Aquino states, "Christianity is finished as a serious contender for the minds of intelligent humans." Aquino's brand of Satanism attempts to pre-date Christian ideas and goes make to Egyptian Hermetic magic and mythology for its symbolism.

Aquino also studied the Black Order and the SS in Germany and attempts to incorporate Nazi occultism and symbology into his satanic orders. The Temple of Set advertised in occult magazines, computer bulletin boards, and ads in the San Francisco Yellow pages. When the Temple of Set expanded to Britain, David Austen from Kent, England, became

Aquino's High Priest in Britain.

To let the reader see just one more example of collaboration behinds the scenes of the Network, a Jesuit member of the Temple of Set continued teaching at a Catholic School after he joined the Temple. Aquino coined the word Xeper (pronounced keffer) to mean the process of evolving a higher consciousness. Scientifically conducted research by Graphoanalysts has determined that a preoccupation with x's means a preoccupation with death. Aquino and some other Satanists show their preoccupation with death by their fascination for words that begin with the letter "x". Aquino's girlfriend Linda Blood has supposedly left the Church of Set and was at a conference that this author attended. She was very antagonistic toward the victims of mind control at the conference, and acted in every way like a cult plant. She was very disruptive of what the victims of mind-control were trying to gain at the conference.

He has written in favour of black magic and left hand path, but since most people don't know what black magic & left hand path is, buzz words. Aquino stated on Ophray's show that Satanists work "for the good of humankind." How? By exploring the "freedom of the will." The undercurrents of his writings in his publication The Crystal Tablet of Set is that he and his followers have power while the rest of us are basically wimps. Witnesses report how actual human sacrifices have been alternated with faked sacrifices in the Temple of Set so that it is difficult for witnesses to tell the real from the fantasy. The Temple of Set, like the Illuminati have strict rules that members are not allowed to keep incriminating items. Their precautions to go undetected resemble the Illuminati's precautions.

UNDERSTANDING SOME OF AQUINO'S PROGRAMMING.

Like so many programmers, Aquino flies all over the country, and has victimized people in numerous states and military bases. Michael Aquino's programming is standard military-type programming. Aquino puts in his own spirit guide into people. He likes to use his own version of Star Wars, with himself as Darth Vader, for his programming scripts. He programs in sexual and death (suicide) programs--such as the Rivers of Blood suicide protection program, and all the rest of the various types of programs.

His Temple of Set functions as a programming vehicle. The rituals are designed to break the practitioners grip on reality and logic and take them into the world of visualization, and creativity. Members of Set take on a magical name, they attempt in rituals to become another persona, which is a magical double of the person called "KA". And this ka work is done on the astral plane. Aquino is friends with Paul Kantner who is part of the mind-control scene and who put out an obvious programming song entitled White Rabbit.

In the Vol. 2 book, the significance of Leviathan was covered. The Church of Set has an Order of Leviathan headed by James Lewis VI° of Baxley, GA. Michael Aquino is familiar with all the standard programming, the Wizard of Oz and the other fairy tale themes. He is very proficient at programming, having many years of experience. In 1981, he used Cathy O'Brien to make two HOW TO films for training military officers in the skills needed to program slaves. These two training films were entitled "How to Divide a Personality" and "How to Create a Sex Slave." (See Cathy O'Brien's monograph "Dick Cheney and Reagan's 'Hands-On' Mind Control Demonstrations" written/released 6/92.) President Reagan respected Aquino and encouraged the military to learn his programming techniques.

Aquino likes to work with Catholic mind-control victims. He is proficient at manipulating the concept of hell and of doing satanic reversals like the Black Mass.

On the following pages are a little of the paper trail on Mind-control Programmer Michael Aquino:

· Some favorite photos of Michael Aquino in satanic garb.

· A two page letter of Aquino showing his fascination with Darth Vader. He rewrote his own version of Star Wars to use as a programming script. Programmers are given the freedom to decide what scripts they want to use.

· last page of a letter by Michael Aquino showing his preoccupation for Hitler and Nazi things.

· two pages showing the trauma that therapists discovered in children that Aquino had sexually traumatized at the Presideo Day Care Center. As readers are aware the Judicial system never pursued the case against Aquino.

· A page from the police report where the girl who claimed she had been sexually molested by Aquino was interviewed.

Michael A. Aquino at age 32 — Damien Thorn at age 32

Not bad casting ... and the Final Conflict is dated from 1975

> I am pleased to report that it more or less does, save that Martin Bormann's tunnel into the Kehlstein mountain begins with copper/bronze doors and is 130m long. The brass elevator takes only a couple of minutes to reach the Eagle's Nest, and there is no flagstone in front of its upper door. On the other hand there is a very conspicuous flagstone right in front of the big fireplace, so I expect that the 10 commandments are entombed there [or were until Indiana Jones & party went off with them].
>
> Adolf Hitler's own house - the Berghof - is now so completely overgrown with forest that it's impossible to find it unless you know where to look. [It took me a half-hour's plunging around in the underbrush]. On Walpurgis 1952 the ruins of the Berghof were dynamited by the German government; only one partially underground room remains.
>
> Back in San Francisco I am now recovering from jet-lag, reading mail, and pondering many things.
>
> Xeper.

p_aquino.jpg

p_xeper-2.jpg

.... of women, is as much an act of violence as it is a sexual violation, it is argued here that the abuse reverberates in a chain reaction of violence-related responses in the child victim, in his or her family, and in the mental health system that is meant to serve the child. The Presidio case was made particularly poignant by the setting (the U.S. Army) and by the necessity for the victims' families to face simultaneously the abuse of their children and the failure of goodness of the government that serves them.

BACKGROUND

At the Presidio Child Development Center. in 1986-87. a single incident of suspected child sexual abuse led to a full-scale investigation during which all the parents were informed that their children may have been victims of sexual abuse at the Center and were invited to come to the army's Letterman Medical Center if they observed any unusual physical or emotional symptoms in their children. Here the children received medical and psychological evaluations by U.S. Army representatives.

Over time, the army, the FBI, and the San Francisco Police Department became involved in the investigations. Accusations of ritualistic abuse were made against a teacher (G) and a lieutenant colonel ("Shamby") and his wife (Mikey'): Shamby was also a high priest of a satanic sect. It was attested that children had reported group sexual activities with other children and with a doll: playing 'games" in Mr. G's bed: and being brought to a house with a black room, where sexual activities of an occult nature ensued with Shamby and Mikey. Both boys and girls reported acts of fondling and penetration by Mr. G. their teacher. Clearly, this was a newsworthy event and it was quickly picked up by the media across the country.

Three years later, the army had made out-of-court financial settlements with the families of the alleged victims and the teacher was reported dead of AIDS. This case-study analysis is based on the author's participation as an evaluator of and psychotherapist for the girls (boys were assigned to male therapists) who were alleged victims. The author's involvement began two years after the occurrence of the alleged events when a team of lawyers was filing suits against the army on behalf of alleged victims and their families. Using process notes and evaluation records from the assessment and treatment of two of the girls (aged 3-4 when they were allegedly abused) and their families, along with anecdotal evidence from other cases, this ar-tide addresses the consequences and sequelae of institutional molestation for the child, the father, the mother, and the family system (consultation with therapists of the male victims revealed similar overall findings). More specifically, it underscores the unique features of sex and violence in the nursery when the perpetrator of the abuse is that historic symbol of patriarchal protection, the military establishment.

SEQUELAE OF ABUSE

· All the victimized children who received a medical evaluation tested negative for the HIV virus at the time of their initial evaluation. Recent research, however, indicates a possible incubation period during which negative test results can be found.

Finkelhor and Browne (1985) proposed that the experience of sexual abuse should be analyzed in relation to four trauma-causing factors: traumatic sexualization. betrayal, powerlessness, and stigmatization. In addition, they recommended assessing both the preabuse and postabuse situations in determining the psychological effects on the child victims. In the case of extrafamilial abuse, this model is applicable to the victims' families, as well as to the victims themselves. According to Finkelhor and Browne's model, the preschool child who is a victim of sexual abuse is at risk of severe levels of trauma, of which, in addition to the obvious sexual traumatization. betrayal and powerlessness are particularly salient factors.

Often, when a child enters a day care center, it is his or her first contact with the institutional world outside the family. At a young age, the child is asked to trust a stranger for care, succor, and daily guidance. The child relies on the parents' assurance that this unfamiliar situation is safe and healthy. Given such assurance, the child typically allows an attachment to develop with the day care provider or teacher and literally puts him- or herself in that person's hands.

At the Presidio, it was that very person who victimized the children, first by violating them sexually and then by warning them that, if they ever told their parents great harm would come to them and their families, and that they would probably never see their parents again. The majority of the children did not tell their parents, who did not find out about the situation until the Center sent a letter warning them that their children may have been abused.

As with incest, the preabuse situation in which the child has trusted an adult who then accosts that child creates great emotional and cognitive confusion ("If this person is caring for me and I am totally dependent on him, he couldn't possibly be doing anything bad"). In addition, it engenders strong feelings of betrayal when the child comes to recognize that this person did do something bad to him or her and that mother and father did nothing to stop it. The severity of the trauma for children at the Presidio was immediately manifested in clear-cut symptoms. Before the abuse was exposed, parents had already noticed the following changes in their children: vaginal discharge, genital soreness, rashes, fear of the dark, sleep disturbances, nightmares, sexually provocative language ("Go down on the doll-69." "Get it up the butt," "Lick the doll's twat," "Hump on the doll"), and sexually inappropriate behavior (a four-year-old girl grabbing her older male cousins genitals).

In addition, the children were exhibiting other radical changes in behavior. including temper outbursts, sudden mood shifts, and poor impulse control. All these behavioral symptoms are to be expected in preschool children who have been molested (Haugaard & Reppucci. 1988: Mac Vicar. 1987: Sink. 1988). Of particular note were the children's responses when they were first asked by their parents if something bad had happened to them at the day care center. One child screamed and ran out of the room. Another whimpered, "They're going to hurt you if I tell," and still another said, "I can't tell, or they'll kill you."

Only later, after they were reassured that they would be protected, were the children able to report that "Mr. G touched my private parts," "Mr. G had me touch his penis," "We passed around a doll and were told to touch the doll in certain parts," "Mr. G took me to his house to see his beds," "I had to do something embarrassing in front of all the kids."

Deeper Insight Into the Illuminati Formula

These responses highlight the second salient feature of the children's trauma: their sense of powerlessness. The children had felt powerless to tell their parents because of the grave harm they believed would coma to their families if they did. This was not paranoid or fabricated fear a trusted adult, a representative of the U.S. Army, had actually told them so. But, left to the devices of their own fantasy lives at the age of magical thinking, the children elaborated on these rears, sometimes to a bizarre degree. Their only choice was to channel the anxiety and trauma into formation of symptoms, until their parents, on the basis of the warning letter, began to question them on the matter. Only later, once the children entered the mental health system, did the full cycle of trauma, terror, and rage unfold. This phenomenon can best be understood by tracking the children and their families through the postabuse process, from discovery to treatment.

p_presidio.jpg

Deeper Insight Into the Illuminati Formula

INCIDENT REPORT FORM CONTINUATION — SAN FRANCISCO POLICE DEPARTMENT

CASE #	REPORTING OFFICER	STAR	DATE(S) & TIME(S) OF OCCURRENCE
870 910 025	INSP. G. PAMFILOFF	228	Mon. 09/01/86 - 0730 To Fri. 10/31/86

NARR: ON THU. 08/13/87, 1530 HRS, R/O WAS TOLD BY (R2) THAT HE HAD INTERVIEWED (R/P1), (P2) AND (V) AND HAD GOTTEN INFORMATION THAT (V) HAD BEEN MOLESTED IN THE CITY AND COUNTY OF SAN FRANCISCO. R/O PHONED (R/P1) AND AN APPT. WAS MADE WITH HE AND (V), FRI. 08/14/87 - 0900 AT JUVENILE DIVISION.

(R/P1) STATED THAT BETWEEN THE ABOVE DATES AND TIMES, (V) WAS DROPPED OFF AT SAN FRANCISCO PRESIDIO DAY CARE CENTER APPROXIMATELY FOUR OR FIVE TIMES. (R/P1) STATES THAT ON TWO OCCASIONS WHEN HE PICKED UP (V) AT THE END OF THE DAY, HE WAS INFORMED BY (S3) THAT (V) HAD WET HER PANTS AND (R/P1) WAS PROVIDED WITH THE SOILED PANTIES, AND ON ONE OCCASION WITH SOILED OUTER PANTS. THIS WAS UNUSUAL AS (V) HAD NOT WET HERSELF IN APPROXIMATELY A YEAR. AT THIS TIME (V) STARTED HAVING NIGHTMARES, AND WOULD WET HERSELF WHEN FRIGHTENED.

(R/P1) STATES THAT IN JAN. OF 1987 HE BECAME AWARE A CHILD MOLEST INVESTIGATION INVOLVING (S3) AT THE PRESIDIO DAY CARE CENTER. (V) WAS QUESTIONED ON 01/14/87 BY AN FBI AGENT BUT MADE NO DEFINITIVE STATEMENTS. (V) WAS SUBSEQUENTLY ENTERED INTO CHILD THERAPY IN FEB. 1987 AND AFTER FOUR VISITS, THE THERAPIST INFORMED (R/P1) THAT (V) HAD DISCLOSED BEING MOLESTED. DURING THE NEXT FEW VISITS (V) TOLD (R/P1) THAT SHE HAD BEEN MOLESTED BY (S3) AND A 'MIKEY' AND A 'SHAMBY', WHOSE IDENTITIES WERE UNKNOWN.

ON WED. 08/12/87 (R/P1), (P2) AND (V) WERE AT THE PRESIDIO PX WHEN (V) RAN TO (R/P1) AND IN A FRIGHTENED WAY CLUTCHED HIS LEG. (R/P1) AT THIS TIME LOOKED UP AND SAW (S1) WHOM HE KNEW TO BE MICHAEL AQUINO. (S1) WAS WEARING A WHITE SHIRT, AND (R/P1) ASKED (V) IF SHE KNEW THE MAN IN THE WHITE SHIRT. (V) LOOKED UP BUT DIDN'T RESPOND. (R/P1) CALLED OVER (P2) AND AGAIN (V) WAS ASKED IF SHE KNEW (S1). AT THIS TIME (V) SAID "YES, THAT'S MIKEY." (R/P1) THEN TOO

Deeper Insight Into the Illuminati Formula

APPENDIX B. THE PROGRAMMING SITES

Some MAJOR MIND-CONTROL PROGRAMMING SITES with explanations of their programming. (Fritz Springmeier originally exposed many of these sites in 1993, so it is possible they have made some changes since they were originally exposed. Most of these operated for years, and may still be operating. We are aware of that some of their programming bases have been moved after exposure.) Besides these major programming sites, there are countless minor ones. For instance, some of the programming sites for water-beach tortures have been visited by the co-authors, but are not listed. The massive Boeing Plant in the Seatle, WA area with its large amount underground tunnels has been used for programming, as well as the ARCO Beaver Valley Plant in Pennslyvannia. So has the chapel at the Coast Guard Academy at New London, Conn. which was built by A.W. Mellon of the Mellon Illuminati family via their Mellon Foundation. This list is not put forth as comprehensive. Without question, this list is only the tip of the iceberg.

29 Palms, CA-

Area 51 (Dreamland, Groom Lake), NV--Area 51 is also known as Dreamland. There are a number of extensive underground facilities in the area. This was one of the first genetic research facilities in the U.S. and perhaps the first major genetic research facility. The people/workers & victims are brought in by airplane and tube shuttle. The worst cases of UFO/alien type of Monarch programming is coming out of Area 51. The eggs from slaves are being harvested and weird genetic creatures are being developed from human eggs which have been genetically mixed with other things.

Bethseda, MD--The Bethesada Naval Hospital

Bingham, UT--A red brick house, which was a closed House of Prostitution. The building was used for KKK programming. Child porn was produced in the basement, and upstairs programmed child slaves serviced KKK members. The KKK activity in the area connects in with the Illuminati controlled Kennecott Copper Co. (aka Utah Copper Co.) Russell G. Frazer, head of Bingham's Klavern & doctor for Kennecott Copper Co. did the electro-shock to split personalities.

Black Forest, Germany--Because the U.S-U.K. and Germany do so much programming, and some of the people in the U.S. were programmed in the U.K., Germany or Russia, it is worthwhile to mention some of the German programming sites. A number of witnesses report about castles in the Black Forest which are used for programming & ritual. Basal, Sw. on the border with Germany is a important Illuminati center. Frankfurt, Berlin and Zurich are all important programming/ritual sites. The Jesuits and the Catholic churches are very active in programming in Germany.

Boulder, CO--The headquarters for EMC, a type of electra-magnetic mind control that is being broadcast to modify the thinking of Americans, and to control slaves.

Butner, N.C.--Center of Correctional Research, all types of mind control are carried out and experimented with on the inmates.

Camp Peary, VA--The CIA's The Farm is located on a narrow strip of land between the York & James Rivers near Williamsburg, VA, used for programming CIA slaves. It has red brick buildings, and looks similar to a small college. The official crytonym was ISOLATION. People who are brought in who don't know where they are for training are called Black Trainees.

China Lake Naval Research Base (Inyokern), CA--

This facility had a country store, and hangers, and a hospital (address for the hospital is the code- 232 Naval Air Weapons Station) which all provided sites for programming. This site has been operational since the early 1950s. Large numbers of children (batches of 1000 or 2,000 or 3,000 children were run through this facility at a time. This facility did much of the original traumas and mind-splitting tortures that created the MPD. Other facilities then specialized in further programming that was then layered in on top of the original China Lake programming. A great deal of dehumanization in cages was done to large numbers of tiny children at China Lake Naval Facility. Nimitz Hospital did drug testing of the children prior to their programming.

Colorado Springs, CO--The ALEX system programming and end-times Military programming is coming out of Colorado Springs and is connected to NORAD. One of the Colorado sites is doing alien programming with mock UFOs.

Dillsboro Nike Base--Monarch programming of many kinds

Disneyland, CA--Disneyland has been an off hour site for Illuminati and satanic rituals for years.

Programming has gone on using Disneyland as one big prop for programming. Many of the Disney movies are used for programming, and some Disney scripts are especially tailored for Monarch slave programming. The Peter Pan programming can use the ship. The space programming can use the space props. The satanic programming can use the castles. Lots of mirror programming is done at Disneyland, and Disneyworld. There is also Magic Mountain programming, and programming using the Around the World Dolls, and its theme song. Some of Wizard of Oz and the Cinderella programming was also done at Disneyland using costumes. Preverbal children are taken to Disneyland to get them ready for the scripts.

Disneyworld, FL--Disneyworld was created as the eastern counterpart to the Disneyland programming site. One of the rides in Disneyworld plays "It's a small, small world" which is Disneyland developed programming theme.

Ft. Campbell, KT--Base programs are placed in here.

Ft. Detrick, MD--involved with medical/biological experimentation

Ft. Holabird, MD--This site is no longer in existence, but was the Army Intelligence School. CIC used the school. The place was known as "the Bird."

Ft. Hood, TX--programming involving military uses of Delta Monarch slaves was done here.

Ft. Huahuachua, AZ--HQ for Army Intelligence.

Ft. Knox, KT --The 1st Earth Batt. was developed here.

Ft. Lewis, WA--involved with the Psychic warfare part of the Monarch Programming.

Ft. McClellen--Ft. Meade, MD--The National Security Agency was created on 4 Nov 1952. Its headquarters were Fort Meade, VA. The National Security Agency (NSA) employs tens of thousands of employees and has a budget larger than the CIA. It has also been kept far more secret, while the CIA has been used as the fall guy to protect the National Security Agency's reputation. In the late 1960's, under Operation Minaret and Program Shamrock, the NSA and its British counterpart GCHQ began monitoring much of the communication within the USA and UK. The NSA monitors all American calls via computers using trip words, specific names, specific addresses, specific telephone numbers, etc. NSA has several computer to record all the millions of conversations which the computers have examined and deemed worthy of recording. How the NSA can get any use out of millions of recorded telephone conversations is beyond me? What intelligence agency could adequately process so much information?

These organizations now monitor all communications within both countries. At least one congressman got upset that his phone was bugged by the NSA. (see David Corn's article, "The case of the bugged senator" in Nation, Feb. 6, '89, p. 152.)

The NSA has developed a fiberoptics network called Internet computer network. An orange book is used to specify some of the NSA's security levels.

An informant in the National Security Agency states that establishment newspapers like the Wall Street Journal and the New York Times are used to communicate secret messages which are placed within want ads, buzz words in editorials, and via other methods. Because of some of what this person told me, I have given some possible examples in this newsletter of how people might be using the papers for secret messages. For instance using Michael Jackson with his hands making some type of sign might be a signal. Manfried Adler and the US Senate Committee investigating the CIA found that 90% of the CIA's secret messages are transmitted via the media, with the aid of coded texts and pictures.

A raised forefinger or two raised forefingers while a speaker is talking means that the message is a masonic message coming from a masonic speaker.

The Illuminati uses code words within the large establishment papers to warn their people what they are going to do with the economy. In this way, people in the Illuminati can take appropriate responses.

Goddard Space Flight Center--NASA mirror-theme programming

Grissom AFB, IND--

Hollywood, CA--One of the programmers/handlers in the Hollywood area is surprisingly Anton LaVey. This is one reason Anton LaVey has followers who will carry out his very wishes. LaVey's children of course were programmed too. His own girls have been participating in the nude in satanic rituals since little children.

Homestead AFB, FL--

Kirkland AFB, NM--Lampe, MO--This has been the site of a CIA near-death trauma center where slaves are programmed. It is an R&R center for the CIA where they can have any sexual perversion or drug they want. This has been a large cocaine supply depot also. Hal Meadows was director of this center which is deep in the woods surrounded by cabin chalets overlooking a small deep lake. A gravel road leads to the site which is fenced and well-guarded. Hal Meadows address was Box 27, Lampe, MO 65681.

Langley, VA-- Slaves for the wants of intelligence.

Las Vegas (sites in and around Las Vegas), NV--MGM's Grand Hotel and Theme park were built for programming, but there are also some sites outside of the city used. In the general area of Las Vegas in remote sites, the elite gather for slave auctions once a year where Monarch slaves are sold and traded. One of the favorite slave auction sites was 20 miles out of Las Vegas and 10 miles off the main road into the site. The Mob is involved with Monarch slaves in Las Vegas. A blue-eyed 11 year old girl will go for $50,000. Toronto, Canada is another regular site for Monarch slave auctions.

McClellan AFB, CA - Very bad Child and adult porn using Monarch victims is distributed through this base as well as the other bases listed in this list. A T.W. Sanderson worked with Monarchs at this base.

MacDill AFB, FL --Near Tampa, FL

Maxwell AFB, AL --

Montreal, Que., Canada -McGill Univ., McGill Psychiatric Training Network, Allan Memorial Inst., St. Mary's Hosp.- The Zombie Room (Sleep Room) in the basement, the Isolation chamber and the Grid Room at St. Mary's Hospital were used for programming.

Mt. Shasta, CA--Underground facilities around this huge mountain in the Lake Shasta area are putting out Monarch programming that makes the people think they are in communication with aliens. This facility is for torturing & reprogramming captured runaway Monarch slaves. People are brought into the area via helicopter, plane, or flying saucer. This site is probably the largest mind-control programming center. It is in a remote wooded area. It is heavily guarded, has fences, and a large contingent of black helicopters. Mt. Shasta is equipped with state of the art high tech programming equipment. Mind-controlled slaves who are soldiers are programmed and trained at the Mt. Shasta facility.

Nashville, TN--These sites work with the Country Western Music Industry which is actually a CIA front for moving drugs to finance their dirty black activities. Fiddler's Inn, Nashville fits in with the Monarch Programming.

Papillion, NE--

Patrick AFB,--Portland (Old OMSI, New OMSI, Bldg. Near Monarch Hotel at 8800 SE Sunnyside Rd., Mormon Temple, etc.), OR. The Old OMSI building had a back door on the west side in which slaves were taken in to the bottom floor and reprogrammed. Although security guards aren't visible, they are there with electronic surveillance. The people running OMSI are tied in the Illuminati. The DC-3 airplane outside of the building was used in the programming as a hypnotic trigger. The submarine docked outside of the new OMSI building is also used as a programming hypnotic tool.

The new Mormon Temple has an extremely high tech underground tunnel facility for programming built underneath it. Witnesses have collaborated their testimony on this high tech programming site under the Portland Mormon Temple. Although building plans are to be public information, the city of Lake Oswego makes it very difficult to view the temple's building plans. The plans show that the foundation walls are far thicker than any conceivable earthquake would ever call for. The reason is that the foundation helps house an underground arena for the Illuminati & and their guests to watch perverse shows.

Presideo, CA (incl. Alcatraz, San Francisco)-- The Illuminati and various Satanic cults used the Presideo for their programming. Split-brain & other programming was done at Letterman hospital. Fort Point was used for Illuminati ritual & programming, as well as a number of churches, underground gun emplacements and the large circular Greek column art building at the Presideo. Alcatraz, abandoned as a prison, was used for water tortures and other programming. Tunnels connected buildings, and the Mule/Horse buildings and the cemetery also were used. This is one of the older programming sites. Psychic warfare activity also was experimented on in this area. Letterman Hospital has been used for the initial drug testing of the infants before programming. Lots of isolation programming in damp cold places was done at the Presideo. Lots of porn and military programming have also been done here. Redstone Arsenal, AL-- San Antonio, TX-- Salt Lake City (Mormon Temple)--This underground facility works in conjunction with the Mormon hierarchy who are allowed to create slaves. The Illuminati put in base programming that still gives them ultimate control beyond the control that the Mormon programming has.

Scotty's Castle, Death Valley, CA-Mengele (Dr.Green) programmed in some of his "internal boxes" as well as other Illuminati programming was done at this site. Mengele had a large circular red bed in the castle which he stocked with his little girl slaves, who already had kitten sexual alters. Scotty's Castle is a castle located in Death Valley CA. It has a very interesting history. To reach the castle one is required to drive through many miles of desert. If one drives to Inyo County, CA, the same county that has China Lake Naval Testing Grounds, and Inyokern, and then you drive on Hwy. 190 into Death Valley National Monument (it is not a park or forest, dead valleys are called monuments), next you go north on a road after Stove Pipe for 35 miles.

The man who built Scotty's Castle was Walter Perry Scott (1872-1954). Walter P. Scott was the son of an alcohol distiller and horse breeder in Kentucky. Walter did not get any formal education. He left home and went west where he worked as a mule driver, and a water boy. From there he became a horse wrangler. Because of his talent with horses Buffalo Bill made him the feature rider along with Annie Oakley in Buffalo Bill's family show. The show travelled and Scotty was with it eleven years. During this time, Scotty made many important friendships with men of power and wealth. In 1900, Walter married and left the show. He got a loan from Julian Gerard, a NY banker, to go prospecting for gold which he failed to pay back. Julian Gerard was repeatedly sending people to hassle Scotty to get his money back. In 1905, Walter Scott ("Scotty") scattered gold nuggets and $100 bills from N.Y. to L.A. Where he got all this gold and $100 bills is a mystery, but it wasn't from prospecting. The idea of finding a secret mine was very obviously a cover for however Scotty managed to get his money. Scotty is well-known for his penchant to throw away $20 gold pieces as if they were candy wherever he went. Nobody believed he had a mine, strangely the IRS never got interested in Scotty. Why? The IRS went after Charles Caughlin who was exposing the elite, the bankers, the Freemasons, etc. in the early 1930's on his radio show. There was no reason to suspect Caughlin of any cheating on his Income Tax, and the audits found the IRS actually owed Caughlin money.

However the national papers printed front page stories of the IRS investigation, and practically ignored that the man was exonerated. Yet, the IRS left Scotty alone. Hmmm. Although Scotty was married, he became intimate friends with Albert Mussey Johnson (1872-1948), a Chicago millionaire, who was v.p. from 1906 to 1926 of the National Life Insurance Co. Albert M. Johnson was born in Ohio, and lived in Arkansas and Missouri before moving to Chicago. Johnson came out and stayed in Death Valley. The stay helped his health, and he and Scotty remained close friends. In 1924, construction secretly began on a castle in Death Valley. The best of materials were used and the materials had to be hauled clear out in the desert by truck to Grapevine Canyon where the castle sits. Hundreds of workers were hired. The castle got its kitchen tiles from Spain. Special rugs were made on the European island of Majorca for the castle. Tiles for the incompleted pool came from the Mediterranean. Many of the furnishing of the castle came from cathedrals and palaces in Spain and Morocco. Draperies made for the castle were hand-tooled in selected sheepskin leather. Sixty hand-carved panels, each of a different design, were installed in the music-room ceiling. A Welte Mignon organ reported to have cost $160,000 --the finest of its kind in Western United States was placed in the music room, even though Scotty could not play the organ. Twelve bathrooms were installed. Several kitchens were installed. Tunnels and secret rooms were built under the buildings. Around $2 million (dollars of that time period) were spent on building the castle, supposedly from Scotty's "gold mine." The castle became known as Scotty's Castle. It is ideal as a Satanic ritual site. It can accommodate numerous people. It is remote. It has hidden rooms and areas and tunnels.

Tavistock, England--This has been the primary programming center for England. The Rothschild programmers work out of Tavistock. A large number of slaves in America have been programmed there.

Tavistock has been doing mind-control since before W.W.ll. Under the supervision of London's W Board & 20 Committee MI6 and MIS's Section BIA ran double agents and mind-controlled spies/couriers during W.W. II. MI6 has had an office at Century House, No. 100, Westminster Bridge Road. MI5 offices have been in part on Curzon St. MI5 has operated behind a number of fronts, incl. their fake travel agency Casuro Holidays. MI-5's address for mail is Room 055, The War Office, London. Special Intelligence Service (SIS) dealt with all types of mind control. Tavistock was under SIS. The British government has had their own telephone exchange with a 222 prefix, which was later linked to another secret exchange YTAN. Outsiders could dial 222 8080 to get into the secret govt. exchange. Men like mind-control expert/hypnotist Eric Trist worked for Tavistock. A six-man team which wore black berets also helped w/ mind control at Tavistock.

Two people who became terrorists after their visits to Tavistock are Angela Davis and Stockley Carmichael who went to a conference at Tavistock entitled Dialectics of Liberation in 1967. It's main building is a bland 6-story building. The address is The Training Office, The Tavistock Clinic, 120 Belsize Lane, London, UK NWs SBA. Tel. no. 071-435 7111. The chief exec. is Anton Obholzer. The Chair of Prof. Comm. is Nicholas Temple. Both are skilled in psychology. The Tavistock Clinic was founded in 1920, and in 1946 the Tavistock Institute was created as an independent body to assist the Tavistock Clinic. The Institute does more of the research. The Royal Free Hospital at the University of London works with Tavistock Clinic, as well as the Science Policy Research Unit (SPRU) of Sussex University. A large number of Britian's psychologist, social workers and police get their training at Tavistock. Tavistock has set themselves up as the authority on ritual abuse and MPD (DID). In other words, the primary programming site, is pretending to be the leading institution trying to solve the problem! That's a good cover.

Tinker, AFB, OK--Tinkerbell programming is carried out here. This programming makes alters think they are like Tinkerbell in that they will never grow up or age.

Titusville, FL--At the Kennedy Space Center. Mind control testing is done, and base programming such as the Wizard of Oz programming is done here. Also NASA high tech programming is done here.

Tulsa, OK—Believed to have an Alice In Wonderland theme to their programming. Oral Roberts University is used for programming. The programming to infiltrate and capture the Christian church via the healing/charismatic movement has centered around Tulsa and Oral Roberts University.

Utah State Prison--The prison has carried out mind control for over 30 years on their inmates for the intelligence agencies with the help of the U.S. government's power to cover it up.

Versailles, IL—Brain implants are put into Monarchs here.

Washington, D.C. area--The basement of the Pentagon and other facilities around Washington D.C. such as the Jesuit Georgetown Univ. Hosp. are involved with Mind-Control. Presidential Models are moving in and out of Washington, D.C. carrying messages and performing their sexual acts for the lusts of politicians. There is also a NASA Mind-control Programming Center in Washington D.C. Secret tunnels connect the White House to other buildings. These tunnels are used to bring in slaves. Some secret rooms in the lower White House are set aside for rituals.

Wright-Patterson AFB--Near Dayton, OH, Virtual reality programming is carried out here.

Youngstown, OH--The Youngstown Charm School has been run by Illuminatus Prosser Seward Mellon along with a U.S. Congressman named Jim Trafficant. The old stone building originally belonged to one of the railroad elite. This school is for Beta models and gives them advance sexual charm training. This school produces about 6 new Monarch slaves every three days. Mafia deals are carried out on the second floor of the charm school. A slave who is being trained/programmed at the Charm school will take a course that last a few days. The first day may be spent hanging in a dungeon which was once a basement wine celler. The torture dungeon has all the traditional torture devices, a stretching rack, whips, hanging chains, etc. In the dungeon rooms were a black Nubian goat "Satan", a small donkey "Nester', and a small white pony "Trigger", as well as dogs and snakes. The slave is taught silence in the dungeon as they are subjected to bestiality.

Click here for picture 1

Click here for picture 2

Click here for picture 3

Click here for picture 4

Click here for picture 5

Click here for picture 6

Click here for picture 7

Click here for picture 8

Click here for picture 9

Click here for picture 10

Click here for picture 11

Click here for picture 12

Click here for picture 13

· We have just touched the surface of the vest network of programming sites. Two examples of an entire series of programming sites--1. the Coast to Coast campground resorts & 2. the Jesuit-run institutions, which are often programming sites incl. Jesuit College, WV. An example of the former is the Park City Diamond Caverns. KT Coast to Coast resort, which has had a sensory deprivation tank, headphones for state of the art harmonic programming. etc. These membership camp sites are used to program children. Nor have we touched upon the large numbers of programmed Russians & Eastern Europeans that are coming Into this nation. When this book was written more people immigrated to the U.S. from Russia than anywhere else. Europe is teeming with prgmg sites. incl. the Vatican. Sebulun Zuflucht in Marienheide, Ger. is about the only european attempt at deprogramming.

p_cloning.jpg

Deeper Insight Into the Illuminati Formula

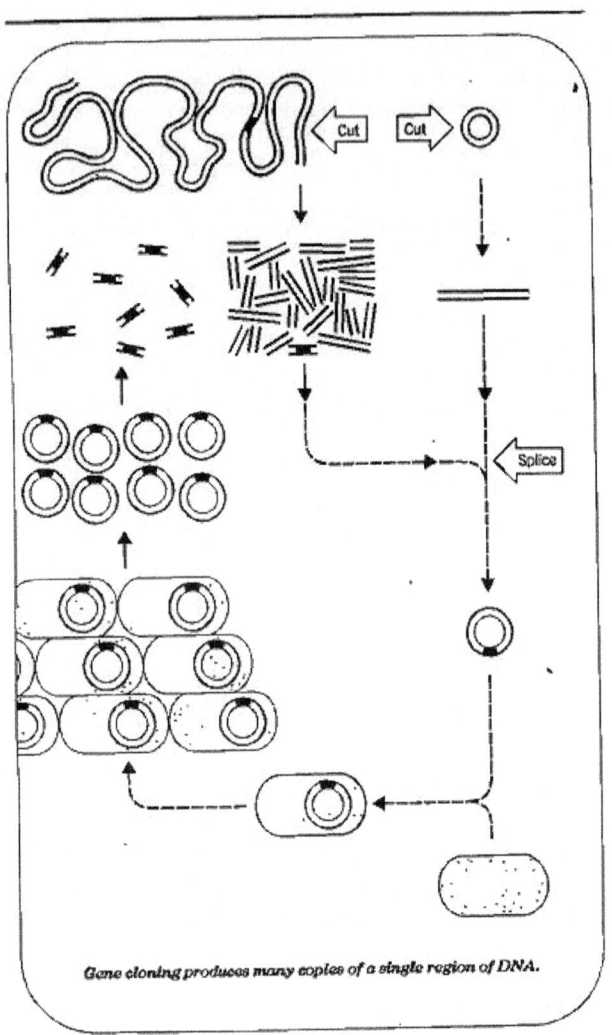

Gene cloning produces many copies of a single region of DNA.

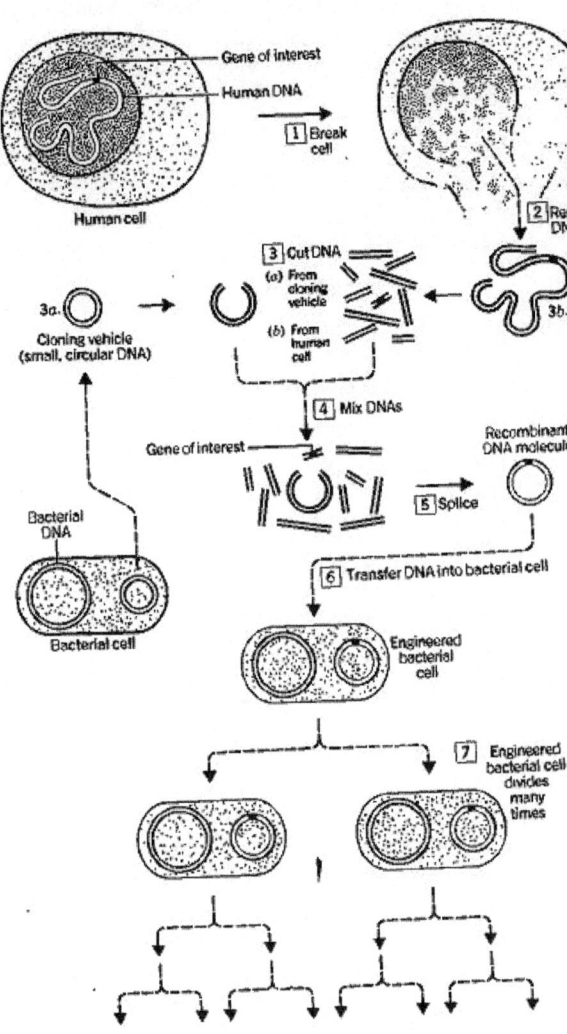

Major Steps Involved in Gene Cloning.

APPENDIX 3. CLONES, SYNTHETICS, ORGANIC ROBOTOIDS AND DOUBLES

PUBLICLY ANNOUNCED GENETIC EVENTS

Section A. The "Future Shock" that this topic subjects the common person to
Section B. Instructions on how to clone a person
 A TECHNIQUE--INSTRUCTIONS HOW TO CLONE A HUMAN
Section C. The four types of "clones" that are used by the Illuminati,
  1. actual clones,
  2. synthetic people,
  3. organic robotoids,
  4. doubles (look alikes)   How the memory of a person is transferred for the organic robotoids

Section D. Secret cloning sites (See also Appendix B, where D.U.M. bases are listed.)   Simon Wiesenthal
   OREGON'S UNDERGROUND SECRET CLONING FACILITY
   FURTHER INVESTIGATIONS AT DULCE'S UNDERGROUND CLONING FACILITY
SUMMARY OF THE FOUR METHODS.
FINAL NOTES.   Clintons

PUBLICLY ANNOUNCED GENETIC EVENTS

1890-- A rabbit embryo was successfully transplanted to a foster mother rabbit's uterus.

1944-- A human ova was fertilized in vitro, that is in layman's terms an egg was artificially inseminated in a test tube.

1952-- Briggs & King in Indiana University clone a frog.

1970s-- Rand Corporation predicts that "para-humans" will be genetically created to do menial tasks in the future. In a totally different affair, Lord Rothschild, who is a physiologist who has studied genetics, warned that self-centered fanatics might set up cloning shops privately. Lord Rothschild suggested to genetic scientists that a clone controlling organization with world wide jurisdiction to license cloning be set up to protect the world from evil men who might want to clone people for evil purposes. He called his suggestion 'Commission for Genetical Control."

1977-- Announcement of the first successful cloning of a person, which was done for someone very wealthy. This whole affair came under strong attack by the establishment. The book giving the shrouded details came out in 1978. The author went into hiding, and our Congress had a parade of establishment research doctors testify at a hearing to debunk the book and to reassure the public that medical researchers were too concerned about ethics to clone people. The author was convinced of the veracity of the cloning event, although the media/establishment doctors claimed the author wrote the book merely as fiction.

1980-- Twinning (bisection of an embryo), which is a form of cloning was successfully done with horse foals, sheep and cattle had -already been cloned in this fashion in the previous years.

1981-- Mice are cloned. And embryo transfer for cattle becomes a thriving business.

1983-- A water buffalo embryo was successfully transplanted to a foster mother buffalo.

1984-- A human embryo was successfully transplanted and born with a human foster mother.

1997--A successful human clone is publicly announced.

Scientists working in secret got serious about cloning in the early 1960's. Abortions began to be performed wholesale at this time to provide fetal tissue for their cloning work. The young generation of Americans are asking, 'When will cloning of people take place?" The answer is that it already has long ago. An article recently written by Andrew Kimbrell that was placed in many leading daily papers across the U.S. is quite revealing. He comes right up to almost telling people what has been going on. The article was entitle, "Science is about to Deliver." (June 22, 1993) "...most Americans are unaware of the real-life exploits of current genetic engineers, science facts which in many cases are as chilling as any science fiction....Pigs have been genetically designed to contain human-growth genes in the hopes of creating "super pigs" that would have more meat. "...U.S. government and private researchers have expended billions of taxpayer dollars in the creation of tens of thousands of genetically engineered animals never before seen....One prominent scientist predicts that we may soon see "five-ton cows and pigs 12 feet long and 5 feet tall. "Genetic engineers.. .have cloned higher mammals, including cattle....One writer notes that "genetic engineering has the potential to create a vast army of identical clones, each produced to some preset specification. Canon fodder, scientists, opera singers, all could be manufactured to order..." "The New York Times has editorialized, 'Life is special, and humans even more so, but biological machines are still machines that now can be altered, cloned, and patented.' " --(WOW! Readers do YOU REALIZE THAT BETWEEN THE LINES THEY ARE TALKING ABOUT BIONIC ROBOTOIDS--the robots that are now being created to take the place of people in high places. And the chilling idea that human-like machines will be produced that will not be treated as anything but machines--that is a chilling idea too.

In this author's September, 1993 newsletter there were two article by this author on cloning, one entitled "Clones,

Synthetics, Organic Robotoids, and Doubles" and the other article "Dulce Genetic Research/Cloning Facility." In the month following my September '93 newsletter's release, the establishment came out with stories about humans being cloned. [I felt that this was confirmation that God's had directed me to publish the information I had on cloning 1/2 months before the secular media came out with their stories about the "first" laboratory duplication of a human embryo.]

This '93 cloning was the first publicly revealed & publicly accepted human cloning, but the truth is that it had already been done for about 30 years secretly. In December, 1993's newsletter I had a followup article on cloning where I reviewed what the media was telling people about cloning after the 'first" human cloning had been announced. My article also discussed the novel Multiple Man which is about how exact copies of the President are made. The book has some surprising similarities with what they actually did with President Carter!

Finally in September of '96, this author's newsletter came out with its fourth article on cloning. This appendix is not the final word on the topic. The whole topic about clones, synthetics, robotoids and doubles could have a great deal more said. This appendix is merely a review of what those four articles contained. Cloning also relates in a big way to the cranial/body manipulation that was introduced in this book. It also relates to the group mind/proxying that is being done. Perhaps at some point this author can go into the deeper intricacies of cloning, but for now this appendix will provide its information in the following format:

Section A. The "Future Shock" that this topic subjects the common person to.

What happens when a technologically backward people are suddenly confronted with a technologically advanced people? What happens is that people are called on to change, in many cases the stress is what Alvin Toffler described and called "Future Shock". The overstimulation of new ideas, new decisions, new ways of looking at things can cause great distress to the mind and body. Radical changes to adapt to the new situation are demanded. In the case of the Navajo, one can see pickups parked beside hogans. In Nepal where I lived, the Nepalese had never gone through a horse and buggy era, so they had no word for drive in their language. When cars suddenly appeared--the first was carried into Katmandu on the backs of porters, they had no word for "drive", so they used the words they had "sit and go." So where we say "Let's drive to town." They would say literally, "Let's sit and go to town."

The American people have in general been kept in the dark about the limits of scientific developments. The known reasons people have not learned are varied. The Cold War was one reason. Capitalist corporate advantage is another reason. They call it trade secrets. Scientific pride and the ability to outstrip other researchers is another, and for the public just their technical jargon is enough to prevent people from closely watching the level of research going on.

But underlying most of the coverup is this: that the overall satanic plan is to keep people ignorant of these scientific advances BECAUSE they are being used quite often to control and manipulate the world. What has developed is a situation where the American people are no longer in touch with where the elite's secret technology is. It is clear that the elite know this and are aware that some of the "Future Shock" needs to reduced if they don't want to self-destruct society. You need to be aware (mentally prepared) that most of the readers of this will experience future shock when they read that cloning of humans is possible & has gone on for decades. The elite had a dilemma. If society isn't moved forward to match their secret scientific advances, it will soon be like cave-men meeting modern-day men. Society won't be capable of adjusting--only self-destructing. On the other hand they certainly can't tell us what they are already doing, because they are using this technology against us to control us. For this reason they are giving us movies that show us things that they have already invented--but these are put forth as fiction in these Hollywood films. They hope to lesson the Future Shock, which their own secrecy has greatly contributed toward creating, while maintaining control over the general population.

SOME OF THE FILMS THAT SHOW EXISTING TECHNOLOGY:

Clone--cloning; Jurassic Park--cloning

Genesis II--underground genetics laboratories that are connected by tube shuttles.

Terminal Man--brain stem implants

Star Trek--various items. In addition to some of today's secret technology being shown, the attitudes and beliefs shown on the two series, especially Star Trek the Next Generation are the attitudes the Satanic elite want people to have.

READERS PREPARE FOR FUTURE SHOCK

The Scriptures give strong indications that genetic monsters, the half-breed Nephalim will exist in the end times. God's Word also forecasts that the mark of beast will be needed for buying & selling.

One item conveyed by the Bible's book of Revelation is that totally unexpected sudden change will characterize the end times. Christians need to be prepared for unusual big changes. So great will these changes be that the nations will be distressed, and men's hearts will fail them for fear (LK 21:25-27). The Bible predicted that knowledge shall increase in the last days before Christ returns. (DN 12:4) But that knowledge will be used for evil, because the Bible also says that the world will be totally corrupt as in Noah's time (MT 24:37)--which was a time of the genetic monsters, the half-bred Nephalim. It also says men and horses will be out of work. (ZEC 8:10) And it is believed that Nahum 2:3-4 must be describing automobiles, and that Isaiah 31:5, and 60:8 are describing and prophesying airships in the last day. The description of the "mark of the beast" is startlingly accurate in describing the microchip which is being inserted into people's hands and foreheads.

The information that is allowed out for the public to access has been heavily censored. Still in spite of all the intense secrecy, if a person takes the time to dig and to find key items written by scientists, enough of a shadow picture develops to allow a person to realize that they already can produce several things the public is unaware of. Many times the articles will discuss only a tiny aspect of a larger process, or will say we have the knowledge to do such and such but the actual doing is years away. And somehow people swallow that we could have the capability to do it, but aren't. For instance, in a book that was published in 1979, Robert Gilmore McKinnel, Professor of Genetics and Cell Biology, College of Biological Sciences, University of Minnesota, wrote "It has been reported that mice and some large domestic animals have been cloned. Humans have not. Because the reproductive biology of humans...is similar to that of mice and other mammals, it is likely that humans could be cloned." Some of the men who know what is actually being done, are afraid to tell what they know. However, I do not have neither a professional reputation nor a job to guard. I have never taken any oath of secrecy to any of these organizations of the establishment. I can simply tell you the truth without fear.

Section B. Instructions on how to clone a person.

For those who want the medical description of just one way that cloning of people can be done (and this capability has been around for at least a decade--and much longer secretly.) The idea that we don't have the knowledge to do it is simply a myth for public consumption. Any microbiologist worth anything knows that we have the knowledge and the means--they can only claim that cloning of humans hasn't happened because supposedly no one wants to do it.

A TECHNIQUE--INSTRUCTIONS HOW TO CLONE A HUMAN:

The ovulation and ovaries of the woman can be monitored. Just before natural ovulation, there is an increase of luteinizing hormone which is called the luteinizing hormone surge. This can be detected by either blood or urine samples. The growth of the follicle can be monitored by visualization with ovarian ultrasonography. Ultrasound diagnosis will reveal on which side of the woman's ovaries the ripening follicle is found. This procedure will allow people to know when the follicle is ripe for the retrieval of the oocyte.

When the time is appropriate a hollow aspiration needle is inserted into one or several ripe follicles under visual guidance of the laparoscope. The oocyte is removed with some follicular fluid. Experienced laparoscopists have a success rate over 90% in recovering the oocyte. Prior to this, it is likely that the woman will have been given Clomiphene citrate, or this drug used in combination with another drug so that there will be several eggs that can be retrieved at one time.

The oocytes obtained from the ripe ovarian follicles are not fertilized when retrieved, although another process would be to fertilize first, before extracting. If they don't fertilize first, then they can take the harvested oocytes and incubate them in a culture medium for several hours to get maturation. They need maturation because they have been taken from the ovary before ovulation, and are not as mature as spontaneously ovulated ova.

Thawed or fresh semen is washed and certifuged so that it will be diluted to the proper concentration to fertilize in vitro.

The in vitro fertilization is carried out. After some amount of hours, (about 12) both pronuclei are identifiable for enucleation. The enucleation is accomplished with either one of two well-established methods. One method is to surgically enucleate it with a micropipette, another is with a bleb of cytoplasm containing both the male and female pronuclei. Either method has worked fine. These nuclei by the way have been obtained from the inner-cell mass of an early human embryo. This again is a well established practice.

Let us digress slightly and explain the method to obtain the nuclei. The zona pellucida must be removed from a cultured embryo, the trophectoderm separated from the inner cell mass, and then, the cells dissociated with an appropriate enzyme in a calcium-and magnesium-free salt solution. Going back to the cloning process, there are several methods for doing a donor nucleus (obtained from its source using the just mentioned method) with enucleated cytoplasm (obtained from the woman's in vitro fertilized ovum). One might be to surgically implant it with a micropipette, another is fusion with an inactivated Sendai virus. Whichever way is considered most viable by those performing this will be used. And then the human nuclear transplant will be cultured until it can be placed into a human foster mother.

When the clone has reached the 8 - to 16 cell stage it will be transferred into the foster mother. If needed, the transfer can be done later, and the clone is simply frozen. When the transfer takes place, the clone is drawn into a fine plastic tube (a catheter) which, then in turn, would be introduced through the cervical canal into the interior of the uterus. --- This is just one process for successfully cloning humans. Other more refined techniques may well be in use.

Section C. The four types of 'clones' that are used by the Illuminati:

C1. Actual Clones. This is a person who has been grown from a test tube (called "in vitro") or implanted womb, which has the identical genetic makeup to another person--an identical twin so to speak in terms of genetic makeup. The genetic coding has reproduced, and a new person who is an identical twin is now in existence.

C2. Synthetic People. These are "persons" who look everybit as real as a real person, but simulate human beings. Certain tissues extracted from cattle are the starting point. (This is part of the reason for cattle mutilations.) The process is an advancement of a process discovered in the late 1950's. This 1959 experiment was reported in a book in 1968 called The Biological Time Bomb by Gordon Rettray Taylor. Taylor describes the experiment done in France, "They had extracted DNA from the cells of the khaki Cam phells and had injected it into the white Pekins, thinking that just possibly the offspring of the latter might show some character derived from khaki Campbells. To their astonishment the actual ducks they injected began to change. Their white feathers darkened, and their necks began to take on the peculiar curve which is a mark of the khaki Campbell." The scientists working under the auspices of the Rothschilds, (who are directed by Satan himself) developed this process by working at secret breakneck speed. They developed an advanced development of the process they discovered with the DNA chicken experiment. By the late 1970's, synthetic people could be produced by the Illuminati.

C3. Organic Robotoids. This is an "artificial life" form that is created through processes that are totally different than cloning or synthetics. Organic robotoid technology is being made to make exact as possible copies of important people such as Presidents and some of their staff. For instance, the Jimmy Carter who came to Portland a few years ago who I stood two feet away from and examined visually was not the Jimmy Carter that had run for President.

On Easter, 1979 the first robotoid model of Jimmy Carter replaced the man Jimmy Carter. By the time "Carter" was seen by me, they must have been on at least robotoid no. 100. This is why a friend of mine who was recently in Washington D.C. almost bumped into President Clinton jogging. My friend was surprised by the lack of security.

Kaiser Aluminum News which is put out by Kaiser Aluminum & Chemical Corporation put out a series of articles to a specialized audience in the 1960's. This material was also published under the book title The Dynamics of Change (Prentice-Hall: Englewood Cliffs, N.J., 1967).

Under the title heading "GENETIC MANIPULATION" we read, "The ability to control the formation of new beings may be one of the most basic developments of the future. Recent discoveries about the nucleonic acids, the basic building blocks of life, have led to the belief that man may some day be able to treat genes in such a way that desired characteristics can be realized..."

Under the heading "MAN-MACHINE SYMBIOSIS" we read, "...Computers exist which can learn, remember, see, seek goals, reason, walk, sing on key, talk, be irritable, play games, grasp, adapt to an environment and even design improvements in themselves...man-like computers may one day contain plasma circulating through a viscera-like envelope, allowing them to be self-healing."

Under the heading "HUMAN ROBOTS" we read, "...An electronic circuit that imitates two neurons, the cells of the human brain, has been built, and has enabled a robot to deal with some unexpected situations, but the neuron structure was bulky. The brain has billions of neurons, meaning an incredible miniaturization job will be necessary before truly 'human' robots are developed." As the reader knows since the 1960's when this was written an incredible miniaturation job has been done in computers. What the public knows of that miniturization is incredible and that is only part of what has actually occurred. In fact, scientists are now able to manipulate DNA to create computers.

A basic thing that is needed to create a computer is material that will consistently change given some type of "signal". This is because the computer works off of base two--or what is simply an on--off switch system, or a 0 or 1 system of numbers. Living biological material is superior to other material for making computers because the heat created by the methods in conventional computers slows the speed. For super-computers to work at great speeds they need to use biological material that will not heat up. This type of miituration has already been done. It creates computers far beyond what we are familiar with. Organic robotoids are amazingly humanlike, so humanlike that it is hard for the scientists who have created them to get used to the idea that they are not humans.

Biological computer brains for the robotiods came as a result of research into holograms. If you tear up a conventional photograph you ruin it, but if you tear up the film that produces a hologram, each piece still contains almost all the same image. This is why part of the brain of people can be removed and the brain regain what it had lost. A holographic image of a person's brain is made, and then when the brain of a robotoid is made, the biological computer in its head is caused to form according to the holographic record of a person being copied. Some deviations from the holographic record are needed, because the "person" is a robotoid and not a person. The brain of the robotoid has almost all of the correct memory of the person reproduced, but the robotoid brain is really a computer made from biological material which is programmed, it is not a human brain.

First, "Clinton" has the energy to jog because it may well be a robotoid, and second thing, an assassination of a robotoid is not so serious. These robotoids have a biological computer-brain that is programmed. They can think in the sense a computer thinks, but secret advances in understanding the human brain, have allowed the makers of organic robotoids to have the memory of a person at a given point in time transferred to an organic robotoid. The key then for making what appears to be a clone--but they are not a real clone--is to capture the person to be copied and make a holographic copy of the brain memory and transfer that to the robotoid.

How the memory of a person is transferred for the organic robotoids. In order to successfully make human organic robotoids--in a sense to make bionic robots--the ability to simulate the personality of the person being copied was necessary. The only viable solution was to learn how the brain coded memory and duplicate that process. The brain is entering into its memory about 10 million bits of information a second. The incredible storage capability of the human brain which weighs on the average 3.25 lbs in human males and 2.9 lbs in human females is incredible. The brain can easily store 100 million billion bits of information. It's no wonder we don't use it all.

All the computers in the world put together do not compare with one intelligent person's brain. Numerous tests and experiments from many different angles all showed investigators that the brain stored information as a hologram. The place in the brain where a memory is stored isn't in just one location. Memories are stored in synapses in sequence, but they are stored in a holographic method. From what I understand, rhythmic pulses radiate from a small area of the brain like a stone creates ripples in a pond. Waves go through the cerebrum, in the way that laser light is used to create a hologram. Different frequencies are used by the brain and different neuron impulses are used to reference (tag) the different details. These tags are the brain's own codes or reference standards for cataloging information. The brain has to be able to access the encoder/decoder (holographic code standards) for a particular piece of information to be retrieve for the conscious.

Brain injuries can destroy one decoder, and leave other decoders for a memory intact. When a multiple (a person with

MPD/DID) is created layers and layers of amnesia walls (actual walls) are built into the brain, and then specific codes are created which cause the mind to bring these compartments of memory to the surface. Each compartment is built into an alter (personality) or a functioning part of the System (built somewhat like a series of computers). Where a normal person may be aware of a conscious and a somewhat subconscious track running simultaneously, the mind of a multiple runs several tracks at once.

On a local level within the brain, researchers have called a memories storage unit an engram. Polypeptidenucleic acid holds a piece of information, such as a trauma memory. Proteins and other substances are involved in the memory process. How a person eats can influence their mental abilities. But it must be born in mind that a memory is retained holographically in countless locations in the memory storage area of the brain, just as the ripples of a stone dropped into water flow throughout an entire pond. The mind will have a number of reference points from which a particular memory can be decoded. The information that is stored in the brain is both dynamic and holographic. It is not stored like a book. If the dynamic impulses of the brain cease, so do the memories. Freezing and reviving a human brain will serve to erase its memory.

I will try to explain things in clear terms if the reader will bear with me. The reason that we recogmze objects so quickly is that the brain performs what is similar to what researchers call a Fourier transfer. Messages are transmitted through Fourier-transform messages. What is a Fourier-transform message? A Fourier transform is a mathematical method where a complex wave, or a complex pattern is broken down and converted into a basically longer, but precise signal of simpler frequencies. In other words a squiggly line is hard to communicate, but via the Fourier transform it becomes a string of numbers which is quite easy to transmit. In other words, a complex squiggly line and a straight line after the conversion are both just as easy to record. The brain stores information in a form similar to a Fourier transform, so that when it must look for similar patterns, it can quickly overlook everything but another identical Fourier transform pattern. A mental comparison is done so quick that it gives the ability to the brain to "instantly" recognize people who one hasn't seen for years. The Holograms of memory that the brain makes are transmitted through Fourier-transform messages. Holograms are hard to destroy, for each piece contains the whole. Rip a holograph in half and you still have the same picture. Rip it in half again and the same picture remains. After a great many cuts in half the holograph begins to get a little fuzzy, as it loses some of its detail, but the entire picture is still there. That is why memories begin to get somewhat fuzzy, because we are only puffing up a small piece of brain that recorded the memory. However, if we can pull up more of the holographic image of the memory we get a more distinct detailed picture.

It was secret research into holograms that gave Illuminati scientists the ability to copy the memory of an entire brain. A holographic image is made of the host's brain and that is transferred into the biological matter functioning as a brain of the robotoid. Since the body and brain of the robotoid are not identical to the original person being copied, adjustments have to be taught and programmed into the mind of the robotoid. The entire process is sophisticated, but then so are many manufacturing processes today.

C4. Doubles (look alikes). There is an ongoing program to find look alikes for prominent people, as well as a program to create secret identical twins (which are separated at birth and never see each other).

George Bush's double was promiscuous, while George Bush is a pedophile. His double was living in France after Bush was no longer President. By the use of doubles, (or one of the synthetics or organic robotoids) the elite are able to sneak away and perform satanic rituals. On certain occasions, if Clinton or Bush only needed to do low level tasks in front of the public, they could have their double substitute for them. The Illuminati working with several organizations has had a look alike operation where doubles of certain key people are found and then used.

In the book Desert Shield and The New World Order pub. by Northpoint Tactical Teams, Topton, NC, if you look on page 32 you will see a picture of the original FDR who had a mole over his eyes and then you will a see a picture of the double of Roosevelt who they used, who had no mole and had different ear lobes. Roosevelt may have died prior to when it was actually announced.

Over the years I have seen numerous photos exposing either the Robotoids or the doubles that they use. This author's previous S' '93 article had some pictures about the dead Pope Paul VI, who my Be Wise As Serpents book said was murdered. This recent Pope was replaced with a double who had had plastic surgery. As a double gets older the plastic surgery will not look as convincing, because time changes people differently. One ex-Catholic said the whole thing sounded like science fiction. It does sound far out at first, but the evidence is there for people to see. For myself, the ex-Illuminati have told me about the double's program. From what I understand the double or look-alike program has been more successful than the robotoids and synthetics. The reason is that people live longer and are more dependable in some ways. The project to find look alikes for prominent people has been very successful. Plastic surgery has also been done to help touch up the doubles.

Section D. Secret cloning sites (See also Appendix B, where D.U.M. bases are listed.)

Ada, Oklahoma's underground facility is being used to clone humans. The other cloning facilities are turning out weird creatures. Due to the processes involved they give off lots of gamma radiation (Gamma is at the far end of the electromagnetic wave spectrum--it is even a longer wave than ultraviolet). Because they give off Gamma radiation, these facilities must be deep underground. The cloning is done at level 7. The average depth (according to one of the men who built these Deep Underground Facilities - D.U.M.) is 5,600'.

The secret government has been building them no stop since W.W. II. I personally have only been in an underground city in Oahu, HA, but I have spoken to others who are wanting to save humanity and stop the NWO, and these witnesses know a lot about the underground facilities.

One of the men who betrayed the human race and helped with the cloning was Austrian born Simon Wiesenthal. Simon Wiesenthal, was a US intelligence agent with a photographic memory (perhaps a scarred brain stem). Wiesenthal seriously hunted Nazis that were not on the CIA's payroll or CIA associated groups. Simon Wiesenthal, under the disguise of being a great Nazi hunter, actually assisted protecting the FBI's and the CIA's agents who were Nazi criminals. Wiesenthal tried to stop CBS from doing a show exposing the FBI-Nazi connection.

Jewish Intelligence (the Moussad) knew all about the hundreds if not thousands of Nazi War criminals that worked for American Intelligence and the FBI, but never went public about it. Instead they occasionally used the information as leverage against American intelligence. One of the code no.s for Simon Wiesenthal given by a Monarch slave was something like 063 097. If someone else knows the full and correct code for him, go ahead and share it.

Unholy Trinity is a book written about how the Vatican, the US State Department, and MI-6 smuggled Nazis out of Germany at the end of WW II. An entire book could be written about the thousands of die hard Nazis who have been working for American intelligence, however Simon Wiesenthal's name is mentioned here because he helped start the cloning for the worst elements of the NWO.

OREGON'S UNDERGROUND SECRET CLONING FACILITY

In at least one of my newsletters, the secret cloning facility at Bull Run near Mt. Hood, OR was discussed. Bull Run is a large tract of forested land with some water reservoirs/lakes that is set up to help provide water for the Portland Metro area. My house on Lincoln St. was also near 8 reservoirs that were built at nearby Mt. Tabor. These reservoirs at Mt. Tabor were for Portland drinking water too. The Mt. Tabor reservoirs have simple single fences on their perimeter, and people are able to throw garbage into these reservoirs if they want to be nasty. However, the Bull Run water supply which is very isolated is extremely well protected. It is rare that people would stray up into the area anyway. People are told that this large tract of land is simply for Portland's water supply, and yet several years ago a Patriot military unit reconned the area after getting info from me. They were able to identify 3 strongly guarded rings of defense at the Bull Run reservoir. The area has lots of electronic surveillance, etc. It is either the most valuable water on God's green earth, or there is something else in the vicinity of Larch Mountain (south of the famous Multnomah Falls which sit on I-84)-- something besides a water reservoir. Of course, those in the know, know that it's an underground facility which the CIA use. It's not an accident Tektronics here in the Portland area does work/research with holograms.

FURTHER INVESTIGATIONS AT DULCE'S UNDERGROUND CLONING FACILITY

My article about Dulce [which I investigated in person on foot] also sparked a small group of dedicated Christians to try to retrace my steps and find the Duke facility. They reported back to me that they found nothing and that the reservation police and the local people claimed they'd never even heard of any underground facility. All I can say is that, doesn't that strike you as fishy that all kinds of people have been up in that area looking for the site, interviewing the Jicarilla Apaches that live in the area for years, talking about Dulce over Art Bell's Radio show, etc. and locals have never heard anything about it?? At the very least they should know that other people looked for the site. The reservation and town of Dulce, NM have a small population. There is little that everyone doesn't know about what goes on in the area, and yet they are surprised by the topic of an underground facility? The whole thing smells like the key people in the area have been convinced to keep their mouths shut & pretend they know nothing.

My comments: sometimes when you're looking for a rat, you'll smell it before you see it. According to someone who has worked in the Dulce Underground Facility the openings on the north and SW face (Aztec Cliffs) are still in use. Actually the cliff that has a face that looks like an Aztec on Mt. Archeleta has been cemented shut because hikers kept straying into the area. A deep needle detector which could detect metal or magnetism deep down could reveal the Dulce Underground Facility--but people who get this close often disappear.

SUMMARY OF THE FOUR METHODS.

This Appendix covers 4 different methods that have been used to make copies of people, these were cloning, creating synthetic duplicates, creating organic robotoids, and finding look alike doubles. [Programs for all four of these methods have had almost unlimited funding by the intelligence/Illuminati elite.]

Next, the basic principles for creating a synthetic human were covered. Synthetic humans were in some ways found to be superior to the robotoids that were created. The first few years of robotoids were fraught with problems. [Since my inside information is somewhat dated, I cannot give readers the status of current robotoid abilities, however, I believe from what I've seen that the program continues.]

The synthetics were people who had their genes altered to look more like the person they were to copy. The robotoids were the formation of new beings that look human but are actually bionic robots. Their memories were created by using living "brain tissue" which is some type of programmable living biological matter, and programming this material as a sophisticated computer. In order to get the memory of the person being copied, a holographic image of the person's brain is made and transferred to the robotoid. Because the robotoid "brain" is not functioning like a human (although the end result is nearly identical so that viewers have to know what differences to look for), there are of course some adjustments that have to be made after the holographic image of the host is transferred to the living biological matter that will function as the brain of the robotoid. Lord Willing, this author may write some more on this topic later. The ability of the Illuminati to copy people using the 4 methods listed above, are not going to be the deciding factor in their moves to control the world, but it does give them a great deal of flexibility in their operations. This author frequently reflects on the words of the Illuminati Grand Master who told Cisco, who was then a child, while touring a cloning facility, "Never, never think you are seeing who you think you are seeing.'

FINAL NOTES.

As this author's reflects back on what's gone into this first part, he can't help thinking about how God will reveal all things that are secret. (See Dan, 2:22 and other verses). The prophet Daniel called him the revealer of secrets." The secrets which are revealed in this book are minuscule compared to what God Almighty will reveal in His day. And as this author reflects back he realizes that there is so much more that could be said.

This author has neglected to get my information about the Clintons into this. For instance, this author interviewed a woman who went to school with Hillary, and two of Hillary's mind-control victims. Our establishment media have neglected to tell the American people about Bill Clinton's roots & ties in Hot Springs, Ark.

Hot Springs is a city that has forty-seven thermal springs which have brought the jet set from all over the world. The mafia syndicate & their nightclubs made Hot Springs a hot bed of vice, gambling, prostitution. During the 1920's the territory so popular with organized crime, that they classified the territory "neutral ground" like they did Hollywood. In the early 1960's, Hot Springs had the largest illegal gambling operations in the entire U.S. Billy's uncle Roy was a politician in Arkansas's legislature connected to all this mess. And Bill Clinton's uncle Raymond Clinton, who had a Buick dealership, was tied to all this corruption.

Bill & his brother Roger's cocaine habits are well known by those familiar with them, as well as their wild parties at the Coachman's Inn, Little Rock, Ark. What are not known are Hillary & Bill's membership in the secret Illuminati.

And for some reason some of their more intimate associates are also not known, such as Charles "Chip" Whitmore, a Satanist & programmer. Chip & Bill have met often on a weekly basis over the years. This continues, for instance when Bill was in England so was Chip, when Bill went to Florida so did Chip. Chip played drums with mind-control programmer Jerry Lee Lewis. He was also a friend of Jack Ruby. (It's a small world at the top of corruption.) Chip owns Cash McCool's Tavern. He is 5'6, glasses for his poor eyesight, has good hearing, and has a filthy mouth. He changes the car he owns & drives every 3-5 months. Chip had a programmed girl murder a man, and then the Network got him off of his murder charges. Chip's family's Villa Mare in Little Rock was pictured in the opening shots of Designing Women.

Chip Whitm ore has been in charge of assassinations in his area, and controls the local law enforcement in Arkansas. Jack Stevens, said to be the largest investment banker in Little Rock, is CIA/part of the Network. He exchanged information with Chip via their mutual black cleaning lady. Further, Whitmore & Stevens tie in with a string of corruption that extends into the Assembly of God churches & other parts of Churchianity.

Over Chip is a Dr. Paul Palmer. The media just gives us glimpses of the depth of occult corruption. For instance, Insight magazine Feb. 26, '96, page 48, in an article by Suzanne Fields had a photo of Hillary's backside wearing what appeared to be a golden dragon on her black coat when she went to court to talk about the Rose Law Firm billing records. She has sometimes been called the Dragon lady for good reasons. Will today's modern equivalents to shamans, our psychiatric community help protect us from murderers like Chip Whitmore? Not likely.

The Biographical Directory of Fellows and Members of the American Psychiatric Association reveals that in 1957 there were 7,104 American members in the American Psychiatric Association. Of those 7,104, a total of 1,253 had moved to America from Germany and Eastern Europe. This helps us understand the enormous influence Operation Paperclip had on America. Operation Paperclip was the CIA's project to smuggle Nazi criminals into our nation, some of which have now made Penn's campus infamous. No wonder the False Memory Spindrome got started at Pennsylvania University. We were warned by a psychiatrist in a Weekly World News story of Jan. 9, 1996 about a strange new sleeping disorder where people die after seeing a hooded robe figure chase them. This new "Deadly Dream Syndrome" sounds strongly like mind-control. Perhaps there is no way to have given the readers anything but a drop in the bucket.

Some of the details that got left out on the way include:

the Seventh-Day Adventist church's secret cooperation with the government to supply young men (1,500) for government experiments called Operation Whitecoat;

how the Dept. of Energy set up hotlines for victims of radiation experiments, in other words the fox is in control of where the victim goes for help;

Peter A. Petito, "Mr. Intelligence" in Italy, and his connections to the Network;

William Randolph Hearst's costume parties and his half dozen homes like San Simeon;

Torrance, CA's Penthouses and Disney's mind-control;

the Masonic peace sign of uplifted hands with wrists crossed in the film 1984;

the movie Army of Darkness with its mirror image programming, "London Bridges falling down" programming ditty, etc.;

how FEMA works with the 6th Army that Aquino was part of, how Voodooism uses Waterfalls for healing such as at Sardo, Haiti;

how Mothers of Darkness alters are trained to love a marble, fed the marble, care for it, and then to shatter it with a hammer until its fine like salt and then to repeat the process and only split the marble but not crush it as part of their training to program;

how a certain torture is done to make the victim think they have a butterfly as a head with the head of the butterfly in their third eye area;

how scribbling is used to anchor programming in child victims;

programmed soul-ties to aliens;

Mr. Greenjean's (of Capt. Kangaroo) talk of Mr. Moon & how it was used for programming;

the blood sacrifices under the Temple Mount on March 13th this year;

the Masonic corruption in Arcadia, FL and the G. Pierce Wood Memorial Hospital;

how secret meetings of the CIA have studied how UFOs could be used as "clever hostile propaganda" trick to take advantage of the populace's gullibility; how Mengele's family never claimed his bones--they knew they weren't the real ones, and how the International Red Cross gave him an I.D.S. to travel with; South Africa's occult Shu Shung Palace... maybe someone else will pick up where this author has left off, the mind-control is all around us!

Printed in Great Britain
by Amazon